MASTERING WEB Design

MASTERING™ WEB Design

John McCoy

San Francisco • Düsseldorf • Soest • Paris

Associate Publisher: Amy Romanoff

Acquisitions Manager: Kristine Plachy

Developmental Editor: John Read

Editors: Valerie Potter and Michelle Nance

Project Editor: Shelby Zimmerman

Technical Editors: Constantine D. Mengason and John Dale Wright

Book Designers: Dan Ziegler and Catalin Dulfu

Graphic Illustrators: Catalin Dulfu, Patrick Dintino, and Inbar Berman

Desktop Publisher: Franz Baumhackl

Production Coordinator: Robin Kibby

Indexer: Ted Laux

Cover Designer: Design Site
Images © 1996 PhotoDisc, Inc.

Cover Illustrator: Jack D. Myers

Library of Congress Card Number: 96-68704
ISBN: 0-7821-1911-5

Manufactured in the United States of America

10 9 8 7 6 5 4 3 2 1

Warranty

SYBEX warrants the enclosed CD-ROM to be free of physical defects for a period of ninety (90) days after purchase. If you discover a defect in the CD during this warranty period, you can obtain a replacement CD at no charge by sending the defective CD, postage prepaid, with proof of purchase to:

SYBEX Inc.
Customer Service Department
1151 Marina Village Parkway
Alameda, CA 94501
(800) 227-2346
Fax: (510) 523-2373

After the 90-day period, you can obtain a replacement CD by sending us the defective CD, proof of purchase, and a check or money order for $10, payable to SYBEX

Disclaimer

SYBEX makes no warranty or representation, either express or implied, with respect to this medium or its contents, its quality, performance, merchantability, or fitness for a particular purpose. In no event will SYBEX, its distributors, or dealers be liable for direct, indirect, special, incidental, or consequential damages arising out of the use of or inability to use the software even if advised of the possibility of such damage.

The exclusion of implied warranties is not permitted by some states. Therefore, the above exclusion may not apply to you. This warranty provides you with specific legal rights; there may be other rights that you may have that vary from state to state.

Shareware Distribution

This CD contains various programs that are distributed as shareware. Shareware is a distribution method, not a type of software. The chief advantage is that it gives you, the user, a chance to try a program before you buy it.

Software Support

The software on this disk and any offers associated with it are supported by the individual manufacturers. Should the manufacturer cease to offer support or decline to honor the offer, SYBEX bears no responsibility.

Copyright laws apply to both shareware and commercial software, and the copyright holder retains all rights. If you try a shareware program and continue using it, you are expected to register it. Individual programs differ on details—some request registration while others require it. Some request a payment, while others don't, and some specify a maximum trial period. With registration, you get anything from the simple right to continue using the software to program updates.

Copy Protection

None of the files on the CD is copy-protected. However, in all cases, reselling or redistributing these files, except as specifically provided for by the copyright owners, is prohibited.

For Mom and Dad,

who helped me believe I could do ANYTHING

Acknowledgements

HIS BOOK WOULD STILL BE a figment of my imagination if not for the tireless and dedicated work of many people and sources of inspiration:

To John Read, for giving me this opportunity and being coach, Chief Diplomat, and friend; Valerie Potter for her diligence, patience, and understanding of my crazy schedule during this project; Laura and Richard Norris for connecting me with this whole project in the first place; and Jeff Neugebauer of SpiralWest Interactive (**http://www.spiralwest.com**) for brainstorms and the very generous use of his space, computer, and resources—I owe you big time!

To all of the contributors, especially Peter Bray at CyberSight for his boundless enthusiasm and support; Tom Lakeman at Digital Planet for writing a great piece in only two days; Joe Speaks, Dale Horstman, and Joe Lachoff at Process 39 for their dedication and perseverance; Dave Carlick, Craig Marr, and Kay Seidel at Poppe Tyson for rising to the occasion and being such great team players;

Tim Smith at Red Sky Interactive for his humor and insightful work, plus April Minnich for her competence and faith in me; Dave Kleinberg and Moneka Dean at NetObjects for their overtime effort while in the midst of their startup launch; Aaron Marcus for being the first and a believer; David Shen at Yahoo! for supporting the effort while managing tremendous growth; and to Carl, Patrick, and the whole gang at Dimension X, Shel at *The Net*, Jennifer and Sharon at Dow Jones, David and Nate at Rare Medium, Jonathan and the folks at Organic Online, John Holland at CKS, and everyone else that made a contribution to the completion of this book—thank you!

To Amy Romanoff for patience and cracking the whip when I needed it; Michelle Nance and Shelby Zimmerman for cranking this puppy out in record time; Catalin Dulfu for the courage to design boldly where no one had gone before—the rent is in the mail!; Patrick Dintino for help when I was in HTML Hell; Dan Ziegler for creating a lush design to fit the concept in an incredible three days' time; Tracy Dean at Design Site for building a great cover; Kristine Plachy for diligence and persistence in the face of nearly endless delays; Robin Kibby for hours and hours of careful proofreading and production work; and Franz Baumhackl for placing every figure, building every page, and generally going above and beyond the call of desktop publisher.

To Fran Zone for perpetual inspiration, motivation, courage, and friendship; Frank Gardiner for reminding me that The Word Is Cousin to the Deed; Howard Rheingold for helping to envision our future—What Is >>> Is Up to Us!; Randy Haykin for consistent support and new opportunities to build great ideas; Judy Tarabini for her encouragement and valuable feedback; Linda Preble at Seed Communications for her prompt work and ever-cheerful attitude; Jodi Pliskin and Carol Kammen—the Work works!; Rick from Federal Express—you guys are the best in the World On Time!; Larry McCullough for his support and enthusiasm; and Jesse and the whole gang at Kinko's—what a team!

To Aphex Twin, deep space network, David Hykes, Mychael Danna, Cabaret Voltaire, Lee Ellen Shoemaker, Robert Rich, Leo Kottke, The Gypsy Kings, Pat Metheny Group, MJQ, Gerry Mulligan, Stan Getz, Tori Amos, The Sundays, Bob Seger, The Freddy Jones Band, Robert Plant, Pale Divine, Steely Dan, Dire Straights, and The Indigo Girls for their collective spirit and artistry.

Thank You All!!

Contents at a Glance

Table of Contents

Part 1 - Design

The New Web Publishing Paradigm and NetObjects

***The Net* Magazine - Balancing Fun and Function**

Yahoo! Corporation - Achieving Good Web Design

Poppe Tyson -
Building Brand Applications for a Global Audience

The Wall Street Journal Interactive Edition

Part 2 - Tools

GNN and GNNpress - User's Guide to GNNpress 1.1

Introduction

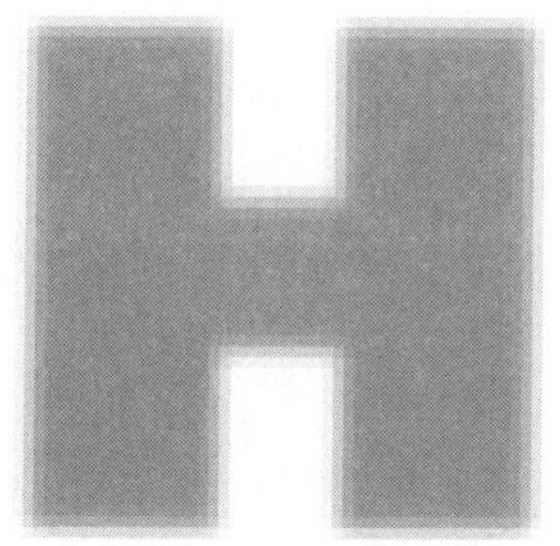

HISTORY HAS FUNNY WAYS of repeating itself. Writers often search for metaphors to explain the growth of the World Wide Web: the Gold Rush, movable type, television. I think the best comparison is the U.S. railroad system in the late 1800s. The metaphor fits not just because railroads grew quickly, but also because of the way they grew and the relationships they built. Ultimately, this book reflects this same historic shift.

Between 1860 and 1870, America's burgeoning rail system grew by over 5,000 miles of track. This growth came at a significant cost of human and natural resources, despite the constructive effect it ultimately had on America's economy. Among its important achievements, the railroad created interdependent economies between the small towns and major cities across the country. The railroad system's greatest power was not its ability to move passengers and freight, but to create new methods for people to interact, build enterprise, and change their lives.

I believe the Web has this same power, but it will only become reality if the people creating the medium are mindful to build it with care, foresight, and integrity. Inside this book you will find opinions, tips, knowledge, and skills from some of the world's leading Web developers, reviewers, thinkers, and technology providers. These people fundamentally shape the medium with their work. This book is for all Web developers as they take the responsibility of making their own mark upon the Web.

As of August, 1996, multiple conservative sources estimate over 200,000 Web sites operating on the Internet, with about 250 new ones coming online each day worldwide—a growth of about 30% annually. Yet many Web users believe the bulk of these sites are unattractive, uninteresting, or unreliable. As a member of the development community, I ask myself, "If the Web is a revolution in communications, is it a shift in quality or just quantity?" Consumers and Internet professionals must use good examples of design and implementation as the Web incorporates multimedia and broader bandwidth. If ignored, the problem will become worse very quickly.

Dig into this material: ponder it, disagree with it, let it inspire you to make great work. The Web has succeeded so far primarily because of its freedom from "top-down" management. Many of the design contributors, though leaders in the field, readily acknowledge they do not know where our business is going. These elements mean you have an opportunity to make a valuable change in what is known and useful. My goal with this book is to give you the concepts and basic skills to make those changes possible.

I take great ironic pleasure in knowing that a large portion of a vital component of the Internet, the fiber-optic communications network, lies in gravel railbeds across the U.S. Many of these iron and fiber "roads" are the exact same routes used since the creation of the rail industry. History *is* repeating itself, but this time we can form it into a revolution that never stops evolving. This train is fast, but it is not too late to catch it and make a difference.

All Aboard!
John McCoy
Tiburon, CA
1996

Using This Book

This book exists for designers who want to refine their skills to match a new medium. To be successful, you must have a spectrum of information about design practices and theory, followed by the tools to implement them, and that is how this book is organized. This way, you will have many concepts and philosophies to consider prior to actually building your ideas.

Parts 1 and 2 are organized into chapters, and each chapter forms a self-contained contribution from a designer or a technology provider. Each design chapter in Part 1 functions both independently, addressing its own specific issues, and interdependently, answering questions that have been asked of all the contributors. Each technology chapter in Part 2 is a tutorial that works in conjunction with the book's CD-ROM or the Web, yet as a group the chapters demonstrate different ways to solve similar problems.

This book is useful for both Macintosh and Windows developers. The design issues are the same for all platforms, as Web browsers work on several operating systems. Most of the technology tutorials are designed for Windows, unless otherwise specified. Though most designers are Macintosh-based, the reality is that nearly all the most relevant and freshest technology comes out for Windows. In many cases, technology developers don't even bother to create Mac versions of their Web software, as the pace of innovation makes the traditional Win/Mac product release rhythm irrelevant. Many of today's best designers have skills on both platforms—so should you.

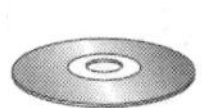

Some passages of the book have the icons you see in the left margin signifying a CD-ROM or the Web. In each case, the icon indicates optional use of relevant material complementing the printed text. The CD-ROM icon corresponds to the disc bound into the back of this book. The Web icon represents a site on the Web referred to in the adjacent text. Type in the URL from the book while you are logged on to get a live experience of the work while you read about its creation and significance in the book. In either case, go to the area of the CD-ROM or the Web address listed in the text for ideas and examples.

Designing with Part 1

Part 1, Design, includes chapters that vary from the general and theoretical to the specific and pragmatic. As a designer, you cannot just use Photoshop or write HTML: you must also have a good set of principles in mind for conceiving your Web site. With solid thinking skills, you will become adept at creating a personal design vision complemented by a variety of specific practices. For this reason, the design chapters, become more specific and task-oriented with each page.

The contributors in Part 1 come from many different backgrounds. They include writers, industrial designers, graphic designers, marketing professionals, music producers, academics, and videographers. Many are self-taught about the Web, and all are visionaries in their own way. Each contributor made a transition in their skills to accommodate the Web's idiosyncrasies and to push the boundaries of what could be done with the medium. Each contributor has been asked the following questions:

- How do you define good Web design from the perspectives of look, feel, and function?
- What are the design processes you use?
- What are your best design inspirations?
- What do you think current and emerging designers should keep in mind when they are creating sites for now and the future?
- What are some examples of good design and why?
- What do you think Web design will look like in a few years?

As you will see, the responses are varied in form, tone, scope, and structure. Please make sure to look on the CD-ROM bound into the back of the book for digital samples of work from many of the contributors. A good way to use this book is to read it while you are looking at the images on the disc or exploring the site referred to in a given chapter.

This way, you get the benefit of a deep explanation from the text with the supporting visuals and behavior of the ideas being discussed.

There is a Profile for each design contributor, so you will know their differences in focus and major points. Further, the Chapter Profiles address relevant issues of the Web design process. The contributors at the beginning of Part 1 concentrate on rhetorical concerns: international design, branding for commercial sites, conceptual models, and design philosophy. The contributors at the end of Part 1 focus mostly on the pragmatic issues of Web design: technical challenges, project management skills, and design processes. I encourage you to become well-rounded by understanding the entire spectrum of design thought, as the technical specifics of this industry change daily. Developing your ability to conceive design ideas from trends will last years and serve you well.

Working with Tools in Part 2

Part 2, Tools, has valuable tutorials for applications that deliver your ideas to the world. As with the design chapters I discussed above, the tools are briefly compared between chapters to give you perspective. The tools in this book are primarily for designers, not just programmers. All of the tools have a graphical interface, not just a confusing array of complex commands. Each is easy to use and extensible for the future. Many tools work seamlessly with powerful programming languages, scripting languages, or databases. Each of these extensions gives you room to grow your skills and ideas.

Assumptions about You

The purpose of this book is to provide designers and technologists with the essential tools and inspiration for superior Web design. One skill set that will help you use this book successfully is basic fluency in Photoshop or a similar image editing tool. Further, it is quite helpful if

you have a good Web browser, such as Netscape or Internet Explorer, and a reliable Internet connection. If you need a browser, either contact Netscape at (415) 254-1900 (**http://www.netscape.com**) or Microsoft at (206) 882-8080 (**http://www.microsoft.com**). You can also use the GNNpress application included on the CD-ROM in the back of this book. Yet *the* single most important criterion for success on your part is *curiosity*. That is how nearly all of the people in this book got where they are, and it will guide you on your own path of discovery and growth!

A Final Word

As an emerging designer, you must anticipate the direction of technology and develop appropriate skills before they become widely needed. The tools presented in this book focus on multimedia on the Web, which will be one of the most important innovations for the next few years. Multimedia is vital to the future success of the Web, as static text and graphics are not compelling for most consumers. Faster computers and increasing bandwidth will make multimedia on the Web much easier. These trends are moving very quickly, so the skills you gain from Part 2 will make you more valuable as a designer. Keep in mind that these tutorials are designed to get you up and running—becoming an expert will take some time. Most important, you must get moving right away.

About the Author

John McCoy is a cofounder and the director of marketing and business development for Electric Minds, a large-scale virtual community devoted to technology and the future, which publishes the collective intelligence of its members on the Web, in print, and on cable. Prior to Electric Minds, John was the president of KiNetica Systems, a Web consulting firm, where he performed strategic management and Web-site development for America Online, Oracle Corporation, AnyRiver Entertainment, and many others. John was also manager of business development at Ikonic Interactive, a corporate multimedia production house, where he was responsible for such clients as Time Warner, Dow Jones, Pacific Telesis, NEC, and others.

John can be reached at **kinetica@sirius.com**

http://www.minds.com

Desig

Part 1

This section will give you an array of opinions, practices, and guidelines to build great Web sites. Each contributor has been asked the following questions:

- How do you define good Web design from the perspectives of look, feel, and function?
- What are the design processes you use?
- What are your best design inspirations?
- What do you think current and emerging designers should keep in mind when they are creating sites for now and the future?
- What are some examples of good design and why?
- What do you think Web design will look like in five years?

Some contributors have taken this list literally and have answered it point by point. Others have used it merely as a starting place to take off from. Still others have developed their own versions of the questions to ask themselves.

Please make sure to look on the CD-ROM bound into the back of the book or at the Web sites themselves for digital samples of work that correspond to each chapter. A good way to use this book is to read it while you are looking at the files on the CD or exploring the site referred to in a given chapter. This way, you get the benefit of a deep explanation from the text with the supporting visuals and behavior of the actual work discussed.

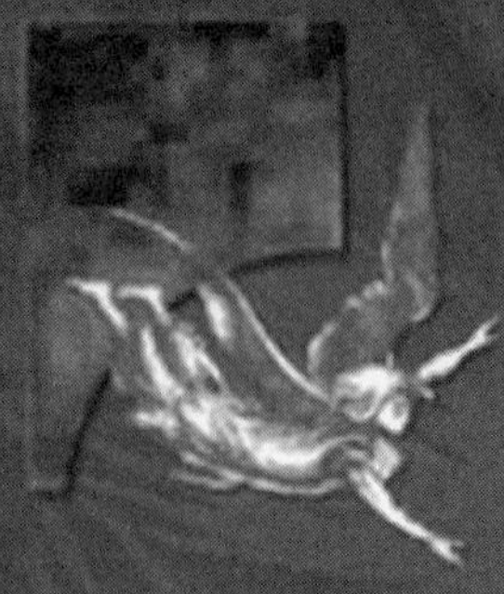

identity

creativity

process

technology

community

digital planet

portfolio

shockwave

Check out Digital Planet's first original entertainment Web adventure, *MADELEINE'S MIND*.

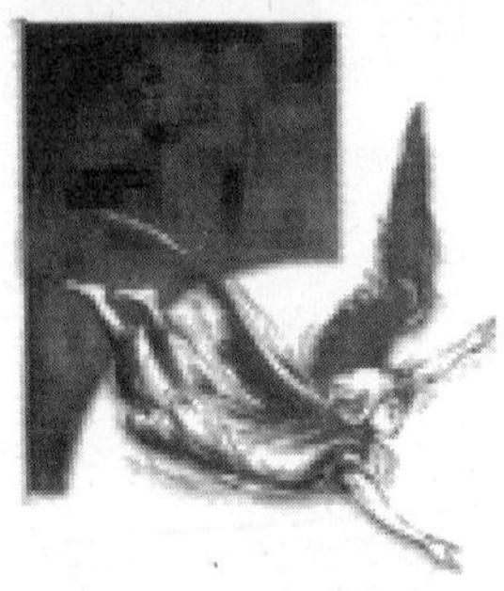

Digital Planet, Inc.

Company Profile

Digital Planet was founded in 1994 by Joshua Greer and Paul Grand with $8,000 and a dream. Despite the early days of being laughed off Hollywood studio lots with comments such as "What's the Internet?" Digital Planet is now a leading Web studio and marketing agency, having produced over one hundred prominent Web sites. They concentrate on developing sites promoting new films from major studios and original interactive entertainment. Their Web credits include sites for Universal Pictures' *12 Monkeys*, *Casper*, and *Apollo 13* and Philips' CD-ROM game Burn:Cycle.

Thomas Lakeman is senior vice president of creative affairs for Digital Planet. Having participated in developing the company's creative direction for consumer marketing and advertising, Lakeman is now concentrating on building Digital Planet's original entertainment division. He is very tired.

Chapter Profile

The ideas of social computing and building virtual communities have gained lots of momentum in the last several months. Many Web developers are adding to their skill sets and even forming entirely new companies around community building. Of the many contributors to this book, Digital Planet shows itself as a studio that is highly aware of the need to blend human sensitivity with cold technology. This knowledge has three primary forms: vicarious experience, social cues, and problem-solving.

I once commented to a friend who was developing a series of car titles, that more posters, clothing, toys, videos, books, and memorabilia about Ferraris are sold than actual cars. Products providing a high-intensity vicarious experience frequently sell well. If you doubt this premise, look at the money spent on computer games, pornography, and movies—over $15 billion a year combined. Future Web success belongs to developers who create intelligent, deep, insightful real-time interaction between people sick of banal, trashy dialog. Such a synthesis will combine a vicarious experience with the thrill of immediacy.

The importance of social cues and initiation cannot be underestimated. In the last two years, a chasm developed between those already inside the Net and those just in the door. People unaware that the Caps Lock key MAKES IT SEEM AS THOUGH THEY ARE SHOUTING are ignored or flamed by others. Ostracized, they may log off and not return. For the Web to succeed as a participatory medium, situations such as these must have a buffer.

To adapt a well-known phrase, "A Web community that clicks together sticks together." In other words, the digital tribes most valuable to its members are those based on sharing and sincere interest in helping each other. Most new members of the Web have never experienced gardening tips online or connecting with an extended network-based family. Weave your Webs with the intent of inclusion and they will grow on their own.

Essay

Inside a Two-Way Mirror: Creative Design for the Online Medium

by Thomas Lakeman

I AM ONE OF THE PRINCIPAL EMPLOYEES of a company whose business is the development of content for the World Wide Web. Less than two years old (as of mid-1996), Digital Planet is practically venerable in terms of the Web industry itself, which did not even exist prior to 1993. Our business is a moving target, evolving too quickly even to fix with a name. At various times, we've been labeled an online service provider, a Web developer, an interactive marketing agency, and a digital entertainment studio. We've watched our audience, our client base, our competitors, and the very nature of our product change radically in less time than it takes for most CD-ROM publishers to issue a single title. And all of this is typical of many start-up companies within this start-up industry.

In such a climate, continuous evolution is the only certain means of survival. We and our colleagues at other companies often find ourselves having to define the form even as we attempt to create for it. The state of the art reveals influences ranging from mainstream broadcast media (radio, television, and film) to comic books, CD-ROMs, and animated cartoons. Multimedia is able to embrace these influences while remaining unique.

Design for the online medium is both like and unlike design for any other medium. It combines the functionality of software interface, the real-time interaction of live TV, the symbolic vocabulary of graphic design, and the representational vocabulary of photography. So far, however, it has lacked the bandwidth, technical reliability, tactility, and clarity these other media are able to take for granted. Under current conditions, developing good content for the Web is often like trying to print Picasso's *Guernica* on the back of a Bazooka Joe comic.

All of this is changing, and needs to change, as new technology and consumer expectations combine to drive the medium forward. By the time these words appear in print, several technical limitations are bound to have been erased. Yet the lessons we've learned in the medium's infancy are still valuable, as I hope to show in the following pages.

In an attempt to answer the question "What makes good Web design?" I've chosen five key concepts that I believe are fundamental to the success of any Web image: spontaneity, identity, closure, transparency, and simplicity. None of these is exclusively dependent on aesthetics—pretty pages can fail miserably on all counts—although many people do feel more comfortable talking about the outer wrappings of design rather than its inner workings. "I want this one to pop!" is something we hear quite a lot; other people want pages that are "simple and elegant." By themselves, however, these terms are meaningless; only with an understanding of what the design is supposed to communicate can they provide any useful direction.

The Web is a medium designed to connect people, and Web design succeeds to the extent that it is able to fulfill this purpose. Marvin Minsky once spoke of mirrors as the perfect medium of representation—they create moving images in real time, with little distortion, full clarity, and richness of hue. In its ideal form, Web design embodies the qualities of a mirror—or, given the medium's interactive nature, a two-way mirror, where both messenger and audience are able to reflect on each other, and on themselves, with as few distractions as possible.

Spontaneity: Before We Learned to Smile

On April 17, 1927, in Washington, D.C., Herbert Hoover (then U.S. Secretary of Commerce) achieved the distinction of becoming the first politician to speak to the American people via what was then known as Radio Vision—what we today call television. In New York, a breathless audience of VIPs gathered around a crude monitor, only to be treated to a fuzzy, glaring mass of white: the future president's bald forehead, filling the screen.

Hoover's broadcast illustrates the awkward formality with which we tend to approach any new medium. Look at any pre-1860 photograph (or pre-1950 television broadcast, for that matter) and you're bound to see a lot of discomfort: the stiffly arched back, the forced expression of calm, the eyes just slightly averted from the probing lens. The subjects seem not to be engaging the camera but enduring it, like swimmers wading chest-high through heavy surf.

And yet, paradoxically, it's the early, formative years of a medium that give us the most revealing glimpses of its all-too-human avatars. Before we learned to smile for the camera, 19th-century families posed with their dead relatives for official mourning portraits that somehow convey to the modern viewer a feeling of having intruded on a deeply private moment. Such quiet familiarity would be difficult to achieve nowadays, even if it were considered socially acceptable.

The same is true for poor old Hoover, who showed his sweating forehead mainly because he had no way of knowing how the angle would made him look to viewers; it was an unrehearsed, uncomposed image, the kind that makes television producers cringe in horror. Hoover more or less knew what the camera did, but he hadn't learned how to behave for it—that is, shield his vulnerable, mortal self from the observer.

The World Wide Web began along similar lines. It grew out of the Internet, itself a bottom-up medium like CB radio, in which thousands of individuals groped for kindred spirits. There was an affable, frontier mentality at work among its devotees. This remained true even as the Web provided new opportunities for visual expression. With notable exceptions, noncommercial content even now tends to reflect a garish, unself-conscious design aesthetic—crude, hand-painted, but oddly energetic.

These days, people with serious ambitions for the Web are frequently embarrassed by tens of thousands of pages featuring their authors' favorite *Dilbert* cartoons or sexy pictures of their significant others—and yet this is a large part of what makes the Web tick. It's an arena by, for, and about voyeurs in a generation that feeds on vicarious experience. The same dirty-laundry spirit that gave us *Jenny Jones* and *America's Most Wanted* feeds the vulpine appetites of Internet newsgroups and Web sites with names like **alt.sex.adultbabies** and **www.ojguilty.com**. The Internet may have started as an arena for scientists and defense strategists, but it quickly evolved into a global backyard fence.

By now it's clear that commerce has crashed the party and has, to a large extent, dulled its schoolyard exuberance. Over the last two years, thousands of companies (mine included) have formed to serve the demand for advertising content on the Web. I would argue that this was something that needed to happen: commercial content is a recognition of the Web's viability and has helped to introduce uniform standards of quality. Companies like Digital Planet would be hard-pressed to support these standards without someone to pay the bills. As the medium continues to evolve, advertising will inevitably provide a critical source of revenue.

What we risk losing (have already lost, some say) is that first breath of spontaneity. We have learned to smile for the Web, just as our great-grandparents learned to smile for the camera, just as our children will undoubtedly learn to smile for some kind of real-time, immersive Virtual Reality. In the nightmare scenario, the online medium becomes clean, hard-edged, inhuman. In a very real sense, Web design needs to counter that trend—to raise the standards while continuing to remind users that they are taking part in a live, communal experience with other human beings.

In the site promoting the CD-ROM game Burn:Cycle (**http://www.burncycle.com**), Digital Planet experimented with animated graphics, using them to create action sequences that illustrated the game's kinetic pace (see Figure 1). During the summer of 1995, most Web users were connected to the Internet by 14.4 Kbps modems (many still are)—and graphics are notoriously slow to download. Using various techniques, we were able to reduce the overall size of the images, animating selected parts of the screen to create the illusion of fluid movement. Since then, Shockwave and Java have permitted ever more flexible expressions of coordinated sound and motion.

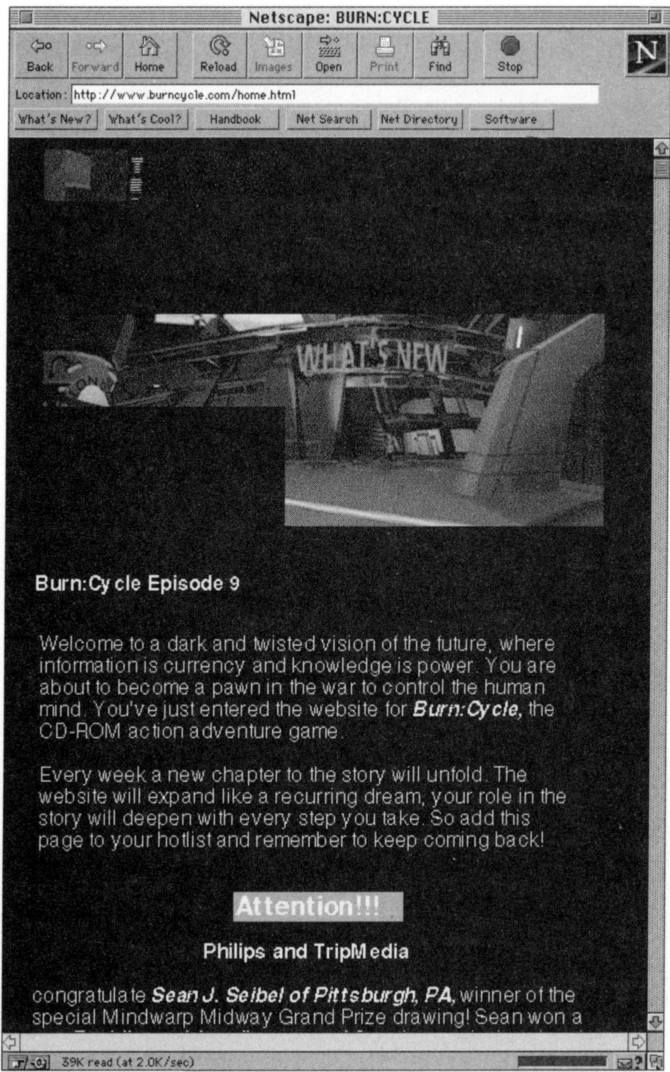

Figure 1:
Animating only part of the screen speeds up the action at Burn:Cycle.

Spontaneity does not depend exclusively on movement, however, but on surprise and implied action. In our site for the movie *Casper* (**http://mca.com/universal_pictures/casper/**), we use static images to dramatize the haphazard, slurring lines of a haunted house, based on the art deco designs of the architect Gaudi (see Figure 2). Various images show ghosts peering out of shadowed walls, or play on dramatic perspectives that convey a sense of wayward movement from one screen to the next.

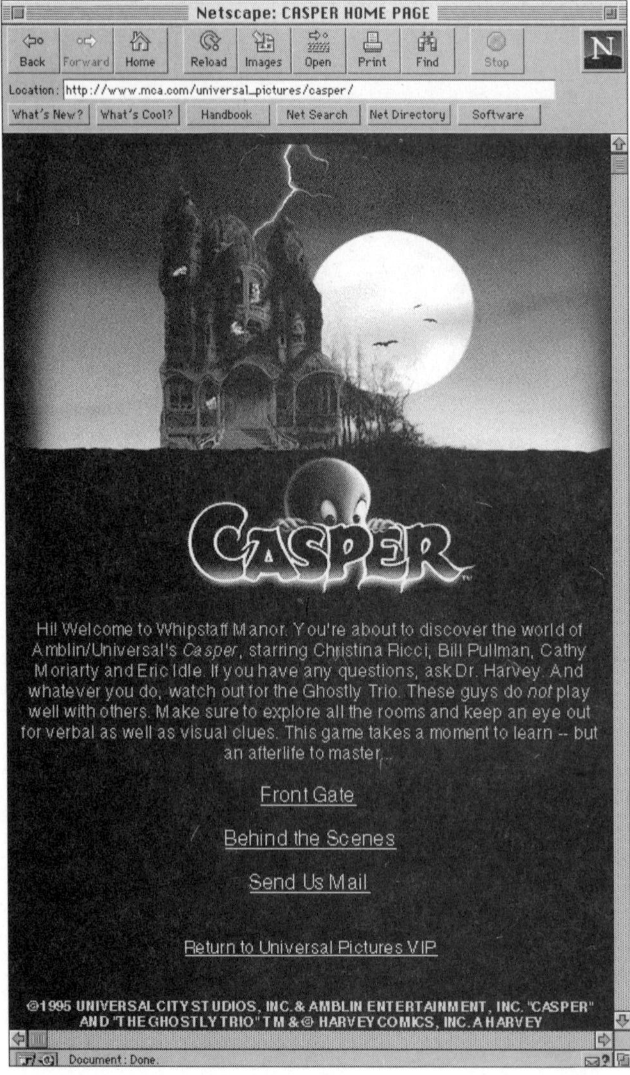

Figure 2:
Casper's world

In both cases, the goal was not so much to create (or imply) movement for its own sake as to convey a sense of the unexpected—keeping the player guessing as to what would happen next. In the absence of human actors, a sense of spontaneity conveys the feeling of a live performance within the computer—a ghost in the machine.

For the storyteller, spontaneity is more often in the details than the big picture. In our site for Terry Gilliam's *12 Monkeys* (see Figure 3) **http://www.mca.com/universal_pictures/12/**, a picture of a teddy bear adorns a prisoner's iron cot—weird, but there it is. Real life is full of such examples. Witness Neil Armstrong's radio broadcast from the surface of the moon. After saying his canned lines ("One small step for man..."), he began more or less to talk to himself, remarking that walking on the moon was a lot like stepping on a "dirty beach"—a distinctly unpoetic and yet surprisingly vivid image. It's rarely quoted, but statements like Neil's are what convinces us that life is really happening.

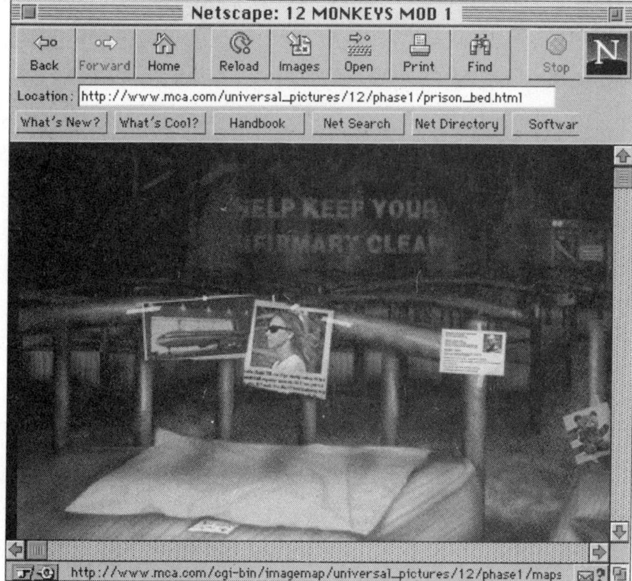

Figure 3:
Exploring the details in the film 12 Monkeys

Identity: Cry Like a Baby

Because you are reading this, there is an implied relationship between us. For convenience's sake, it may help you to imagine my voice, or my face, or the room I'm sitting in, just as I know it helps me to imagine you, the reader. What the online medium does is make that active relationship an acknowledged fact: we do not inhabit the same time or space, yet the medium enables us to proceed as if we did.

From the moment I get up in the morning, I am defined by my material body and the lifestyle that surrounds it. For the record, I'm male, 32 years old, about five feet eight inches tall, somewhat nearsighted, fair-haired, and fair-complected. I was born in the southern United States and have since lived in various places around the country. I am college-educated, vote Democrat, enjoy spicy foods, subscribe to several magazines, and watch an average of five hours of TV each week. To you, these may or may not be relevant facts. To anyone whose livelihood depends on market research, these facts are highly relevant—but only to the extent that they can be correlated with similar information about other people. My attributes are not unique to me; they are, in the grand scheme, only statistics.

The moment I enter the online universe, however, everything you just read about me disappears. Unless I choose to tell you about myself—as I just did—you have no reliable way of gleaning any information about me. The medium's inability to convey an individual's physical presence is thought of by some as a technical limitation, but in my opinion it is actually one of the Web's greatest strengths. It is not the identity I possess, but the identity I choose to express, that is relevant. People who gravitate toward certain online forums or role-play in multiuser dimensions do so out of an active desire to express or reinvent their identity.

With traditional broadcast media, we have a vicarious, one-way relationship with the content of the medium. The power of that relationship can be immense: if you've ever cried like a baby during a really bad movie, you recognize that certain experiences (for example, a crying baby) can manipulate your emotions, even against your will. Most of the time, however, we're willing participants. We lean towards certain TV shows because they embody a lifestyle—an identity—we want to have for our own. *Seinfeld* and *Friends* are about the pals we wish we had; *Cheers* is a bar where everybody knows your name.

In the interactive medium, the principle is the same, but the dialog is two-way. The messenger exists for you as an individual or group of individuals, just as you exist for the messenger. The medium—the Web site—becomes a level-ground meeting place, erasing time, space, and social distinctions. Because the Web site is essentially the messenger's territory (a home page), it must necessarily embody the messenger's personality. This is an important function for which design is largely responsible.

Most artists with any degree of technique can be identified by their individual style. In creating a Web site, however, that style often has to be subordinated to the unique demands of the message. If the design aggressively calls attention to itself or in some way conflicts with the personality of the messenger, it has to a certain degree lost its function. If it fails to specify the terms of the relationship between messenger and audience, it has likewise failed to create identity.

In the early days of television, performers tended to avoid looking at the camera (as noted in the previous section) or, at best, treated it as a passive member of the audience. An important evolutionary step took place when television host Ernie Kovacs began to use the camera not simply as a stand-in for the observer, but as an active participant in the drama. To him, and his followers, the camera was a fellow performer—it played tricks, moved around the room, even followed the performers backstage. For the first time on television, the image was used to imply an active relationship.

In Web site design, the medium likewise has to encourage an active relationship. When a user arrives on the doorstep of the home page, the relationship starts at zero. The first question the user asks is, generally, "Where am I?" The one that follows is even more significant: "Who are you?" The user wants to know if there really is a man hiding behind the curtain. Implied in this is a more fundamental question: "Who are we to each other?"

Web sites that create a graphic environment lend themselves well to the task of answering that question. In our design for Universal Pictures' home page (**http://www.mca.com/universal_pictures/**), we depicted what most people at the studio consider its strongest asset: Universal, home of the famous back lot tour, is where you go behind the scenes and see how movies are made (see Figure 4). The use of soundstage doors at the Web site implies that the user—the privileged outsider—is being brought in for a rare look at the way movies are made, from an insider's perspective.

Once inside the virtual gates, the focus is placed on the stars and filmmakers themselves, their faces and voices; they are, after all, the living personalities that animate the movies. Witness the site for *Apollo 13* (**http://www.mca.com/univeral_pictures/apollo13/**), an interactive documentary in which director Ron Howard takes the user on a guided tour of his film (see Figure 5). Users are able to feel as if they are closer to the talent as a result of having visited the

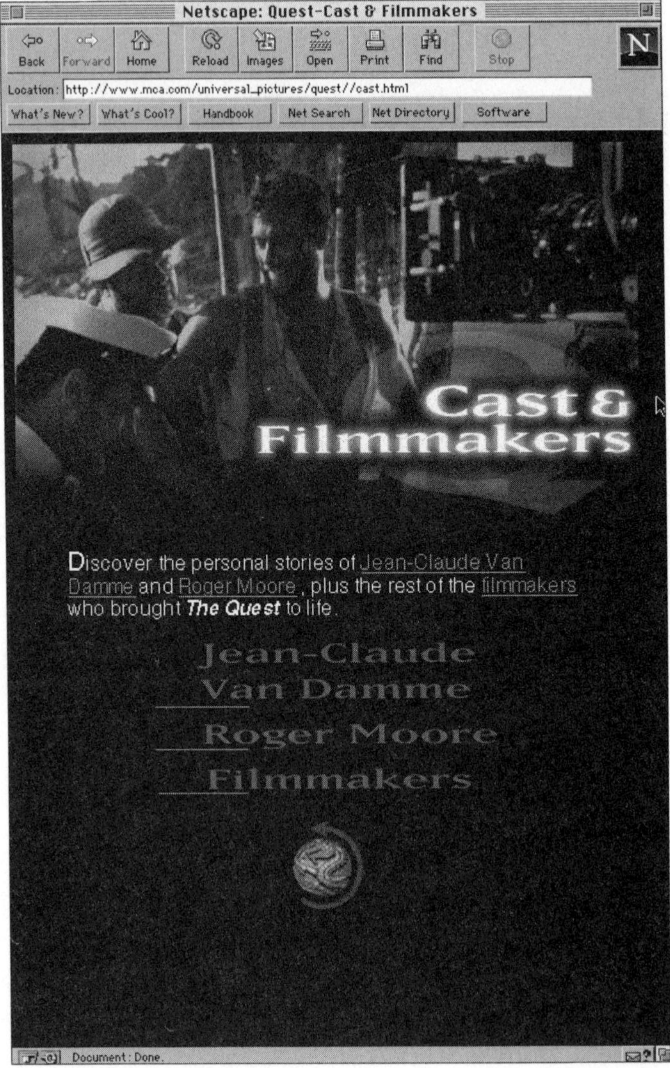

Figure 4:
Universal Pictures takes you behind the scenes of their new movies.

site—hearing their passions, their likes and dislikes, and their ideas firsthand. The next evolutionary step forward is already being explored by developers of Virtual Reality environments: creating a visual stand-in for the user that is capable of existing within the same virtual space as the messenger.

If this trend takes off, as it most probably will, the need to create identity through agreement will become more important than ever. Suppose two children find a

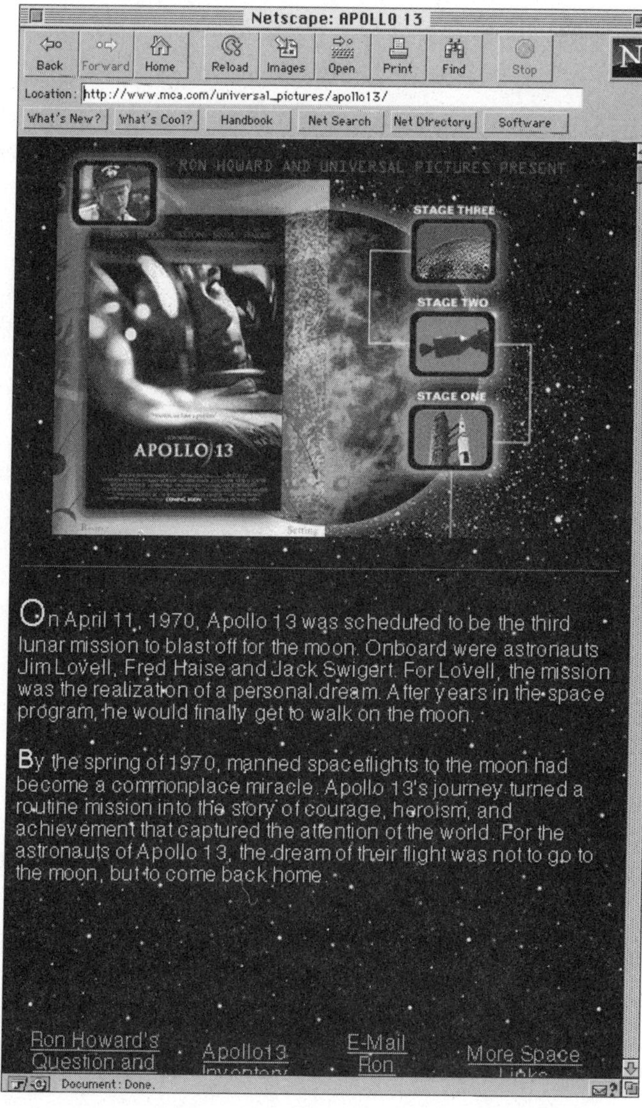

Figure 5:
The start of Director Ron Howard's tour of the making of Apollo 13

cardboard box: one says it's a spaceship; the other says it's a house. If they can't arrive at some agreement, who's at fault? The box—that is, the meeting place between them—if it doesn't provide sufficient common ground. Interface design on the Web must answer to the same responsibility by providing a sense of place that is identifiable, but empathetic to the needs of messenger and audience alike.

Closure: Fleas in a Barnyard

Ever wonder why you never see commercials for color TV sets any more? As recently as the early 1980s, they were everywhere. One ad featured a woman telling us, "My eyes are green. My hair is red. My skirt is vivid blue. If these colors don't look right to you..." and so on. Writing copy for those ads must have been a tough assignment: how do you get a person who doesn't have a color TV set to appreciate what you're showing them? And even if they do have one, how can you convince them that your color TV is better than the one they're watching?

And therein lies the reason why those ads are no more: first, virtually everybody who wants a color TV owns one; and second, color quality is practically the same for every brand. There just isn't a competitive advantage to be had in color these days.

The PC-based, telephone-wired client network we call the Web has yet to reach a comparable level of technical maturity. Connection speeds are variable, from 9600 bps modems (a good many of these are still in use) to ISDN (the fastest available to most consumers) to the T1 and T3 lines that make up the backbone of the Internet. The amount of data flowing through those lines is likewise variable and can radically affect the speed of transmission through the network. There's no guarantee that your computer's processor will be fast enough to handle the demands being made on it or that your monitor will be capable of displaying the right colors—or, for that matter, that you'll have installed the proper Web browser, or the right plug-ins, or the correct helper applications...

Putting it bluntly, the Web is a crapshoot. To paraphrase Abraham Lincoln, transmitting information online is like shoveling fleas across a barnyard: not half of them get there.

And yet the World Wide Web is supposed to be the ultimate expression of communication: millions of people communicating directly with one another, unfettered and unfiltered by the structures of conventional broadcast media. How does it manage to accomplish this function in such an unreliable, low-bandwidth environment?

A lot of people are working on solutions, mostly technical ones: increasing the pipeline or finding a way to get more information through it, shifting the responsibility of generating data from the server to the client's own PC, and so on. All of these will solve the reliability problem, but they won't enhance the Web's function as a communications network if no one knows what it's supposed to communicate.

From a design perspective, the best solution to the bandwidth problem is to pack the most information into the smallest container. To accomplish this, the messenger needs a willing partner: the end user has to provide some of that meaning by him- or herself. The conceptual term for this is *closure*—the leap of intuition that enables the viewer to see more than is actually on the page. Closure is a dynamic act of cooperation between the storyteller and the audience, using images more or less as a set of hand props.

Take the example of the color TV commercial. Imagine that you're watching the commercial at home on a really old black-and-white TV with tinfoil on the antenna. The spokesmodel is telling you that her hair is red, her eyes are green, and her skirt is vivid blue. Are you seeing it? Good. That's closure. The black-and-white TV gave you a few clues, but you provided the rest of the information in your mind.

Incidentally, what just happened in the previous paragraph was also an act of closure: in reality, there was no black-and-white TV, no spokesmodel, no skirt, no tinfoil. You created all of that yourself. The tinfoil was just for effect, but didn't it help you visualize that TV set?

You can read more about closure in Scott McCloud's *Understanding Comics*, one of the best books on media to emerge in recent years. McCloud, a leading comic artist, talks about the reader's creative participation in the act of experiencing a comic book. In the first panel, a man aims a pistol; in the second, another man lies on the ground; between them is an empty space. Note that the comic is incapable of conveying sound or motion, and yet, in that white gutter, the reader's mind creates a connection, causing an action to complete itself. Reading the last few sentences, your imagination witnessed a murder—in a very real sense, caused it to happen. Don't bother denying it.

From a design perspective, closure is great because it reduces the amount of actual information the image has to contain. Take a look at the space below:

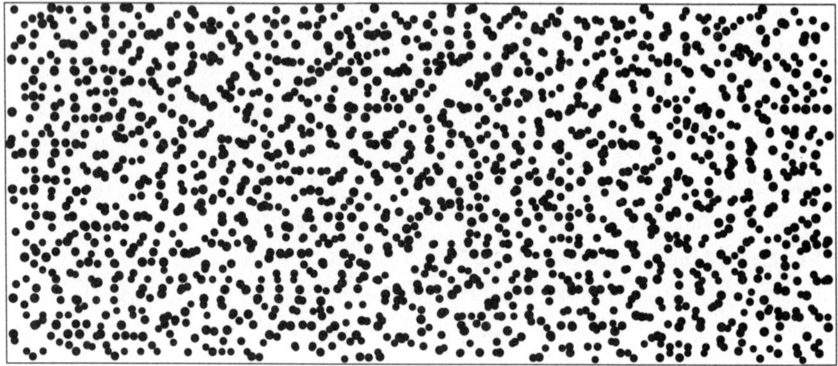

The human mind is very good at discerning patterns, even when they don't actually exist. In the absence of any given direction, your mind is apt to play connect-the-dots any number of ways. If, however, I title the drawing *Fleas in a Barnyard*, I've committed you to a very specific direction—it now takes some concentration *not* to see fleas jumping around. Closure is to design what misdirection is to stage magic—the observer's implicit agreement to join in creating the effect.

Because the Web's protocol divides each site into discrete documents, or pages—and because there's a time lag every time the user links to a new page—closure is not simply a choice, but an absolute necessity. You cannot take user's commitment for granted: they are never more than one click away from another site. Design has to imply a continuity, a sense of place, and an intuitive understanding of what options are available. In our site for *12 Monkeys* (**http://www.mca.com/universal_pictures/12/**), we created a virtual tour through the world of Terry Gilliam's film (see Figure 6). Within each image are various visual cues that add information as to where the user is, where they came from, and where it's possible to go next. The trick is to convey this effect with as few "in-betweens" as possible—which the user, given the minimum information necessary, is generally happy to supply.

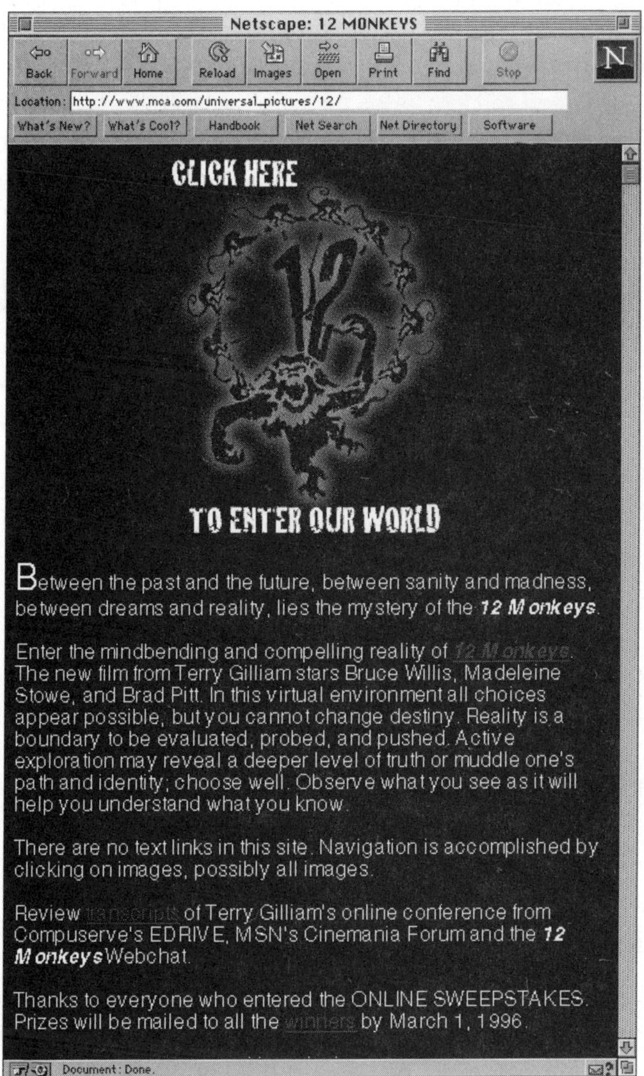

Figure 6:
The home page for Terry Gilliam's film 12 Monkeys

Transparency: Body Language

In his books *The Psychology of Everyday Things* and *Turn Signals Are the Facial Expressions of Automobiles*, design theorist Donald A. Norman speaks of the need for human-centered design. An object follows this principle, says Norman, to the extent that we are able to think of it as an extension of ourselves.

The idea of extensions is one of the fundamental, unspoken laws of human tool manufacture. It's why repairmen do work on the body of a car and why Victorians modestly covered the legs of chairs with skirts. It's also why we kick recalcitrant vending machines—to show them who's boss. Very often, we design objects not to serve a practical function, but to enable us to empathize with them better. Preston Tucker proved that three car headlights are better than two, so why don't all cars have three? Because it's useful for us to think of headlights as the eyes of the car, an extension of our own eyes—and a third eye is just not something most people are prepared to deal with.

On a functional level, such everyday machines as automobiles, telephones, and handguns have changed very little since they were first introduced. Those basic functions have simply been optimized. From a design perspective, however, these machines have changed radically. To some degree, the change is meant to embody something about ourselves—why the big road cruisers of the 1950s gave way to small economy cars in the 1970s; why the clean, simple lines of Western Colt .45s were replaced by the urban frontier's coldly efficient automatics.

To a much greater extent, the changes in design are meant to promote bonding between ourselves and our machines. Modern plastic telephones are lighter and fit more neatly to the hand than the old, heavy ones made of Bakelite. The touch-tone keypad is better adapted to the index finger than the rotary dial, and visual display (now standard in many telephones) makes it possible to see the number you just dialed—as well as the number of the person calling. Consequently, you don't concentrate on the act of dialing as much as your parents did, so you're not as conscious of the telephone as a foreign object.

I call this function *transparency*—the ability of good design to eliminate cognitive barriers between messenger and audience. Another term, *ergonomics*, implies the human-friendly aspect of design. By transparency, however, I mean something more—that design can erase perceived barriers between individuals. The more intuitive the design, the better it serves as a medium of communication.

This is true even when communication is not a machine's principal function: as Norman has noted, certain functional elements of cars—turn signals, for example—allow you to announce your intentions to other drivers. In reality, however, the language of driving is much more complex. The vibration of the road through the soles of your feet, a slight acceleration, the size and model of your car relative to others, can all combine to speak volumes. Ever drive over a pothole and say "Ouch"? Or get in a fender bender and say, "He hit me"? It's because design is functioning so well, it's ceased to announce its existence, as if the car isn't even there at all to shield you from the elements.

These days, the trend on the Web—set by HotWired (**http://www.hotwired.com**) and others of its ilk—is to create highly obvious, intrusive design that aggressively announces its presence. Whole sites are literally about design. Marshall McLuhan's warning that "the medium is the message" is being taken by many as an imperative; I would argue that the time is right to reverse the balance. The function of design—in my opinion, its highest function—is to connect people by putting content first. It seems now that, in many Web sites, the clothes have no Emperor.

Simplicity: An Empty Box

For my final point, I'll return to a favorite analogy, mentioned earlier. Two children are playing with a large cardboard box. One says it's a spaceship; the other says it's a house. Which is it?

The question has no answer. Or, more pointedly, it has no answer until you provide one.

Some people feel that a home page is the embodiment of a destination, and expect most of the designer's efforts to go into creating that sense of place, of having arrived home. For others, the home page is simply a navigational tool, a vehicle for getting from one place to another as quickly as possible. In other words, it's either a house or a ship. In my opinion, this is not a decision that can be made without the conscious participation of the observer, and it is the role of the designer to provide the observer and the messenger with equal opportunities to arrive at that decision together.

To Zen Buddhists, the highest embodiment of order is an empty vessel. In earlier sections, I've spoken of a Web image's *spontaneity*, the extent to which it creates *identity* or *closure*, and its inherent *transparency*. All of these are really aspects of a single idea: good Web design is immediate, personal, open to view. Its power lies in *simplicity*.

The empty vessel, like a theater stage or blank canvas, contains any number of potential meanings. Only human beings are capable of filling that space, with themselves. In its essence, the Web is nothing more than a series of human interactions happening on a massive scale. Web sites, whether created by studios, corporations, or college students, are nothing more than individual attempts to fill part of that empty space—as Jung put it, to "kindle a light of meaning in the darkness of mere being."

Interactive design, much more than conventional media, enables the active and conscious participation of the observer in filling that space. Interactivity is agreement. I provide an image, but I can't tell you what to do with it or how to interpret it. For this among other reasons, interactive design has been likened to architecture, wherein the goal is to create an open space where any number of activities are possible.

Many people who are involved with the medium have expressed concern that, as it gains in popularity, it will revert to the conventional—the passive experience of television. I believe the opposite to be likely. As it grows, the interactive medium must certainly remain connected to its root force—the direct, unconfined act of agreement among individuals on a person-to-person basis.

In this regard, simplicity of design certainly does not mean ordinariness or lack of detail. It means that, regardless of the scale of the design or the depth of its information, its essential meaning can be grasped instantly—because its meaning is as immediate, personal, and open to view as my saying "hello" to you. Take a look at an online chat: the most common words spoken by any newcomer are generally, "Who's out there?" In a sense, these are words spoken in darkness: in a simple and direct fashion, visual design is able to provide a measure of light.

Red Sky
Technologies

Red Sky Technologies' Complete Web Authoring and Serving Solution

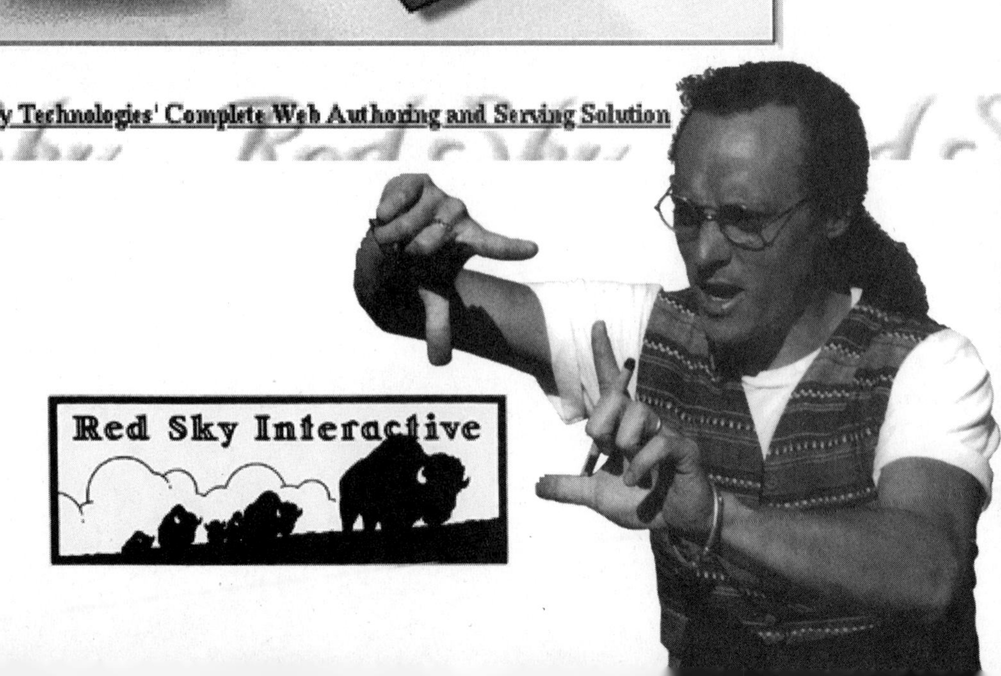

Red Sky Interactive

Company Profile

In January of 1990, Red Sky Films was formed in San Francisco by Doug Humphreys, April Minnich, and Doug Werby, all industry veterans from a well-known post-production firm. In 1994, Red Sky spun off their interactive division under the leadership of president and CEO Tim Smith. The group had one basic premise: combine emerging technology with the aesthetics of films to creatively serve a broad range of business communications applications. Smith has focused the efforts of his talented staff on a variety of digital products and WWW sites for clients such as US West, Lands' End, Wells Fargo, Hewlett-Packard, and Intuit. Tim Smith's first computer was an IBM 360 mainframe, on which he played Adventure for the first time in 1977. He has been a hopeless early-adopter of new technologies ever since and takes great pride in the fact that his Osborne can still boot CP/M and run Visicalc. Tim is a graduate of UC Berkeley and began his career in the Silicon Valley working in the Advanced Technologies Group at Ernst and Young. Tim's mantra "we've been here before" comes from his belief that we have much to learn from the past: there is absolutely a place for art and storytelling in even the most mundane business application.

Chapter Profile

Esther Dyson, editor of the newsletter Release 1.0, recently wrote that the nature of media was shifting from *chunks* to *streams*. Instead of buying information as separate components, such as books or CDs, the future of media production and consumption will migrate to ongoing, participatory flows of content. Her observation demonstrates great wisdom and foreshadows some of Tim's brilliant ideas on the following pages.

The shift from chunks to streams means media designers must consider three primary changes:

- The connection between content producer and content consumer is more of a relationship than ever before. Creators cannot build, ship, and forget a product, such as a CD-ROM. Many developers in the past have correctly assumed that once the title hit gold master, it was the marketing department's problem. The Web, however, is unforgiving of people who seldom "tend their garden." There must be constant attentiveness to visitor demands and interests, or a site will die. As Paul Winter, CEO of The New Century Network said, "Web users are like locusts: they land, they consume everything in sight, and they leave." To succeed on the Web, you must keep feeding the locusts. The notion of *product* must include *community*. The nature of Web design changes not only the relationship between creators and consumers, but also the relationship between the consumers themselves. Someone visiting a site for Specialized Bicycles (**http://www.specialized.com**) may want information about cycling groups in her area, not just the latest scoop on tires, fitness, or frame geometry. Sites that last for years keep pace with both the content focus and the natural human urge to share ideas and stories. If you build it, they will communicate.
- Many developers hope or assume the transition from chunks to streams will occur immediately. But very few Web sites serving the consumer public succeed in the long run without a partnership with traditional media. Hotwired has *Wired*; clnet has its cable program; Pathfinder has the support of Time Warner magazines representing huge circulation. At best, a healthy exchange of power exists between the media types that builds both interests. This transition reaches far beyond the Web—it reflects fundamental changes in global society and economies. Such changes don't always occur in days or even months. Commercial media designers must create products—chunk-streams—that straddle change with a profit margin.

Sadly, many site designer/developers will fail to make use of these ideas. Their ideas and microcommunities will dissolve in rushing currents of new ideas. Treat your brainchildren with the respect of good design *and* good functional conception. They will live long and prosper for it.

Essay

Printing on Water

by Tim Smith, President

Approaching the River

I AM NOT A LUDDITE. Let's start with that. I work in the interactive new media industry, but I have both a healthy respect for and a healthy suspicion of technology. I look for the reasons why we design things the way we do, for reasons why some things inexplicably work and why others don't.

In trying to explain design, sometimes stepping back to look for context—historical, cognitive, technological—and then reapproaching the project, is helpful. Communication has an immensely complex history, one that has been examined on many levels by people in a myriad of fields. There is a lot we don't know yet, a lot more we know but have not articulated well, and, related to this, a lot we know but have forgotten we know.

Tibetan monks used to sit on the banks of streams "printing pages of charms and formulas on the surface of the water with woodcut blocks" (Ong, p. 93). While the religious significance of this act must not be trivialized, I would like to borrow the image to serve here as a reference point.

The beauty of the scene, allegorically, is in the combination of the discrete (the woodcut blocks) and the continuous (the stream). Much of what we are wrestling with as Web designers is wrapped up in this simple idea.

We begin, then, by stepping back to gain perspective.

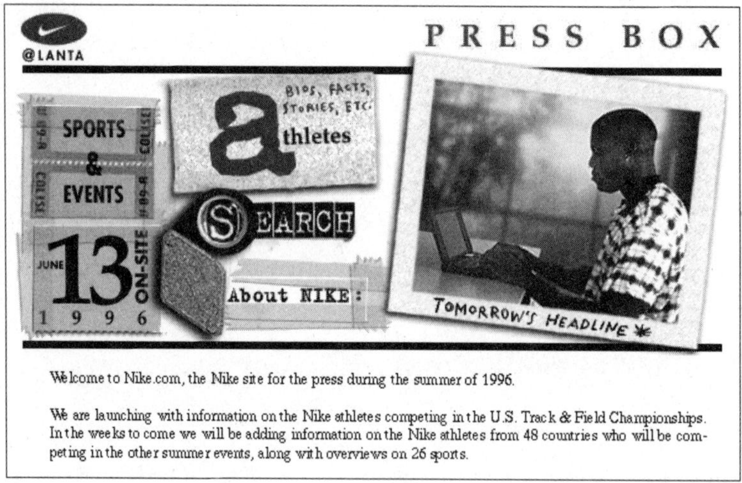

Gaining Perspective

When Red Sky begins new projects—especially with new clients—we work hard on finding a different perspective, a different angle on the opportunity at hand. Clients are typically very close to tactical objectives, their particular "brandedness," how they market to others right now, etc. At the beginning we attempt to pull back from the tactical, forget about limitations, and speculate about what we'd love to do if we were unfettered by the realities of production or technology.

The word *perspective* has great application here because it has meaning in both physical and temporal senses. While a lot of new media design mirrors notable events in the development of art (including perspective, realism, dimensionality, impressionism, etc.) that's not the point I want to focus on here (although it would make a great discussion). Instead, I'm more interested in the temporal sense of perspective; in looking at the macroeconomics of new media design in order to better explain some of the microeconomics.

Here are the points I would like to establish in this essay:

- New media does not afford us the luxury of ignoring traditional media and communication, but rather relies on our ability as designers and information engineers to leverage what we have learned in the recent and distant past, to do things we have not been able to do before.
- There are two aspects of media—the discrete and the continuous—and two aspects of communication—broadcast and interactive—that can help us better understand the implications of designing for the combination of both as represented by online media.
- While technology changes, many principles of communication remain the same. While renaissance designers will need both creative and technical experience, the emphasis is on the creative, grounded firmly in a deep understanding of storytelling, metaphor, and symbol.

Four States, Three Transitions, and a Full Circle

My point is difficult to make without grossly oversimplifying a few things. With all due respect for the cultural anthropologists, who will flinch at much of this concept, I'd like to describe four states of communication into which we can begin to group all communication methods, and three significant transitions in the history of communication. This is all in an attempt to say that in some ways we have come full circle, as others besides me have pointed out, with technology ironically affording us the ability to communicate with a richness and interactivity that has not been a regular part of life for centuries.

Let's set up a few ideas before we get started.

Four States of Communication

I'd like to suggest that almost any form of communication can be logically grouped into four categories with certain characteristics:

CATEGORY	EXAMPLE
Discrete/broadcast communication	Book
Continuous/broadcast communication	Television
Discrete/interactive communication	CD-ROM
Continuous/interactive communication	World Wide Web, ITV

Three Important Transitions in Communication

Three great transitions in communications history are of particular relevence here:

- The transition from speech to writing
- The transition from writing to printing
- The transition from printing to new media

Coming Full Circle

In *Orality and Literacy: The Technologizing of the Word*, Father Walter Ong argues that computers have brought us into what he terms an age of "secondary orality" that "has striking resemblances to the old [oral, preliterate culture] in its participatory mystique, its fostering of communal sense, its concentration on the present moment, and even its use of formulas" (Ong, p. 12). Designing for this secondary orality is another transition on the scale of the three I've selected from history. But let's go back to examine why.

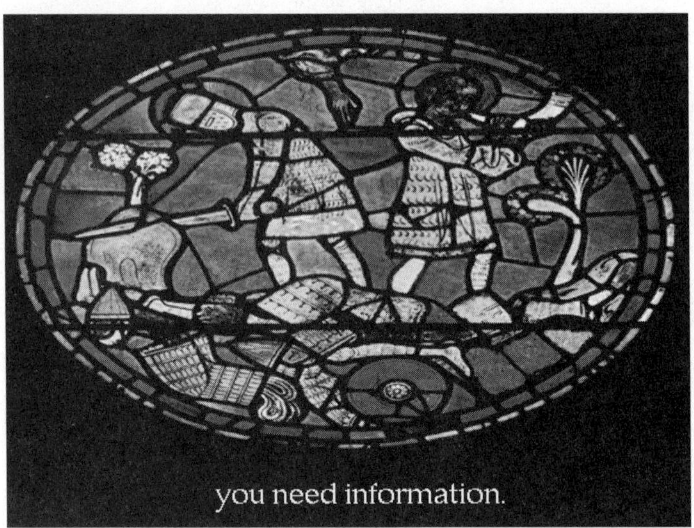

Remembrance of Songs Sung: The Transition from Speech to Writing

Preliterate communication was far richer than today's. Plenty of people would argue with me, but I'll stand by this assertion. Without the means to physically record ideas, people relied on mnemonic, iconic, anthropomorphic, and—most importantly—poetic and rhythmic techniques to store information. Storytelling was an intensely interactive and rich endeavor; the "technology" of the medium—voice, facial expression, body language, instrument—in many respects greatly exceeded what we consider the richest electronic media of today—film, television, the computer.

Good design for ancient Greek storytellers and performers involved the use of mnemonic cues, allegorical references (which evolved into myth and the anthropomorphism of nature), signs, symbols, and icons. Communication was very personal and highly interactive. Close proximity to the audience allowed virtual control of the performance through human response—facial expressions, sounds, the throwing of fruit.

Theater, opera, and other public forums still retain vestigial characteristics of our preliterate culture, but they have evolved to meet the needs and expectations of a postliterate audience. The transition from spoken to written communication resulted in a pervasive cognitive change (over a long period of time, granted) in society.

"Oral communication unites people in groups. Writing and reading are solitary activities that throw the psyche back on itself" (Ong, p. 69). The transition from an oral culture to a written one introduced formal introspection and the concept of the privacy of a dialog between author and reader, performer and audience. This is also the first example of a transition that in a sense disabled certain ways of communication that we may never discover again.

As Father Ong eloquently puts it, "Learning to read and write disables the oral poet...it introduces into his mind the concept of a text as controlling the narrative and thereby interferes with the oral composing processes, which have nothing to do with texts but are 'the remembrance of songs sung'" (Ong, p. 59).

Because there was no mass literate public, this transition tended to result in archives and libraries for the elite class—strangely similar to a period in recent history of document management and technical communication: the Internet before it was discovered by the masses. In this case, the elite class was academia and government.

Most people are surprised, and many distressed, to learn that essentially the same objections commonly used against computers today were used against writing by Plato in the *Phaedrus* (pp. 274–7) and in the *Seventh Letter*. These included: writing is inhuman, a manufactured product; writing destroys memory; a written text is basically unresponsive; writing cannot defend itself as with the give and take of oral tradition. Print created similar misgivings when introduced (Ong, p. 79), which we'll see in a moment.

Table 1 compares the basic characteristics of spoken and written communication.

Table 1: The characteristics of spoken and written communication

	SPOKEN COMMUNICATION	WRITTEN COMMUNICATION
Category	Continuous/interactive communication	Discrete/broadcast communication
Characterized by	Emotional, nonsequential thought	Sequential development and self-containment
Type of experience	Public, collective	Private, individual
Single- or Multichannel	Multichannel	Single-channel
Benefits from	Performance mnemonics, allegory, mythology	Elaborate, formal verbiage and ornamentation
Strongly influenced the development of	Sign, symbol, icon,	Logical, sequential thought
Other	Lack of a permanent record made accumulating knowledge difficult	Brought a legitimacy, sometimes false, to points of view
Examples	Storytelling, theater, opera	Medieval manuscripts, letters

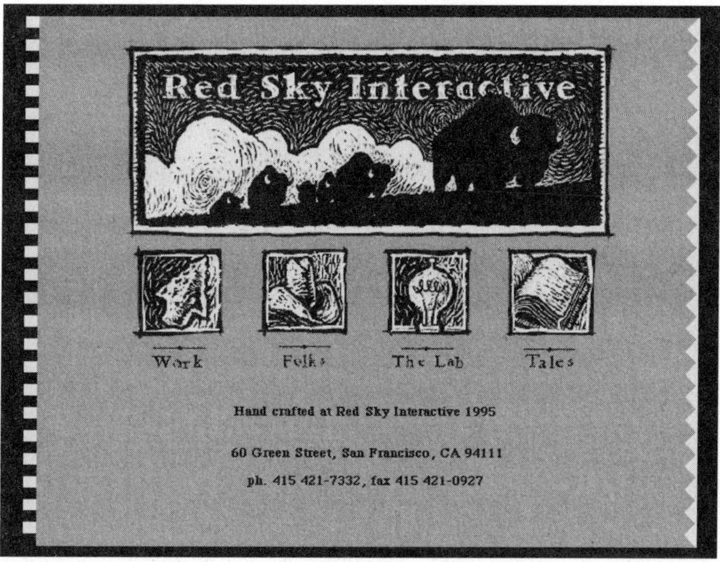

The "Splendid Isolation" of the Book: The Transition from Writing to Print

The transition from writing to print is a subtle one, but of extreme importance to thought and social development. The fifty years after the popularization of the Gutenberg press—roughly the first half of the 16th century—is popularly known as the *incunabula* (from the Latin "in cradle"). Because books were previously copied by hand in very limited numbers, their use was primarily limited to royalty or the wealthy literate, who were few. The incunabula represented what many have called the first true democratization of the word. The cultural impact, however, was not immediate (a point we will return to later) because there was not a literate public.

Alphabet letterpress printing, in which each letter was cast on a separate piece of metal, or type, marked a psychological breakthrough of the first order. It embedded the word itself deeply in the manufacturing process and made it into a kind of commodity (Ong, p. 118). It was also a major factor in the development of the sense of personal privacy that marks modern society, setting the stage psychologically for solo reading in a quiet corner and eventually for completely silent reading (Ong, pp. 130–131).

So long as text is married to physical media, readers and writers have taken for granted three crucial attributes: the text is *linear*, *bounded*, and *fixed* (Landow and Delany, p. 3). The book marks the primary and best example of *discrete* media.

Table 2 compares printed communication to spoken and written.

Table 2: The characteristics of printed communication compared to previous types of communication

	SPOKEN COMMUNICATION	WRITTEN COMMUNICATION	PRINTED COMMUNICATION
Category	Continuous/ interactive communication	Discrete/ broadcast communication	Discrete/ broadcast communication
Characterized by	Emotional, nonsequential thought	Sequential development and self-containment	Emotional or logical sequential thought and self-containment
Type of experience	Public, collective	Private individual	Mass individual
Single- or Multichannel	Multichannel	Single-channel	Single-channel
Benefits from	Performance	Elaborate, formal verbiage and ornamentation	Wide distribution, high production values
Strongly influenced the development of	Sign, symbol, icon, mnemonics, allegory, mythology	Logical, sequential thought	The "ideal" audience and first principles of mass communication
Other	Lack of a permanent record made accumulating knowledge difficult	Brought a legitimacy, sometimes false, to points of view	Frequently associated with the democratization of the word
Examples	Storytelling, theater, opera	Medieval manuscripts, letters	Books, magazines

The New Orality: The Transition from Print to New Media

The term *new media*, like *multimedia*, has been used so promiscuously that it has almost lost real meaning. The "digital incunabula" of the past fifty years has nonetheless required us to coin new terms to describe the impact of electronics, communication, the computer, and binary/digital information processing. I loosely refer here to new media as representing most of what has happened since the development of print. On the historical timeline, even the telephone and film are new media.

The transition from print to new media marked the modern (20th-century) rush to build what Marshall McLuhan called the *global village*. To oversimplify, the most important of the subtransitions of the period included:

- The transition from text-based to graphical/aural communication (film, television, radio)
- The transition from linear to nonlinear communication (hypertext/online media)
- The transition from discrete to continuous content (from books/film to television/multi-user dungeons)

We are moving, inexorably, back toward forms of communication that are richer visually, aurally, and experientially—a new orality—that we as audiences and designers are not necessarily prepared for. At present we seem to take visual literacy as a given, despite the fact that our entire educational process aims at verbal literacy at the expense of the visual (Rubens, p. 7). We've now come full circle, in a sense. Technology has reintroduced a macrocommunity through networking, increased bandwidth, and hence richness, that will allow a new oral discourse. Sven Birkerts writes in *The Gutenberg Elegies: The Fate of Reading in an Electronic Age* (p. 173):

> *The earlier historical transition from orality to script—a transition greeted with considerable alarm by Socrates and his followers—changed the rules of intellectual procedure completely. Written texts could be transmitted, studied, and annotated; knowledge could rear itself upon a stable base. And the shift from script to mechanical type and the consequent spread of literacy among the laity is said by many to have made the Enlightenment possible. Yet now it is computers, in one sense the very apotheosis of applied rationality, that are de-stabilizing the authority of the printed word and returning us, although at a different part of the spiral, to the process orientation that characterized oral cultures.*

In terms of advertising (an inescapable reality), we are back to talking to individuals again, but one-to-one marketing, which is all the rage right now, is something of a myth. If you are talking about one company out there, and many consumers, sure, that company can tailor messages to each of those consumers. Easy. The reality, however, is that there are thousands of companies (or will be) vying for each consumer's time now. It's really many-to-one marketing (a complete flip from many-to-many marketing, the traditional mass marketing of the past). Jerry Mander, in his book *Five Arguments for the Elimination of Television*, relates traditional mass media advertising to a standard gauge railway, with marketers marketing to an "ideal" public that did not originally exist, yet began to, over time, as advertising had its Darwinian effect on the public. One-to-one advertising will require an "infinite-gauge" railway (yes, one-to-one marketing), but only the best content, the best storytellers, and the best creativity will get the patronage of the public.

With telephone, radio, television, and various kinds of sound tape, electronic technology has brought us into the age of what Walter Ong terms *secondary orality*. This new orality has striking resemblances to the old in its participatory mystique, its fostering of a communal sense, its concentration on the present moment, and even its use of formulas (Ong, p. 136). The World Wide Web has brought us even further on this circular path, as Table 3 shows us. Compare the last column, future new media, to the first, spoken communication; the similarities are not coincidental.

> *Alone, alone,—all, all alone;*
> *Alone on a wide, wide sea.*
> —*Coleridge,* The Rime of the Ancient Mariner

The combination of extremely powerful computers and increasingly extensive and friendly communications have combined to create a medium that is actually the amalgam (I refuse to use the word *convergence* anymore) of many. Along with that has come the need for designers with new skills and perspectives, and an audience that is able to play a role it has never played before. Are we alone as we surf the Net? Or is this a massively participatory and collaborative environment that is simply waiting for the right stage to be set?

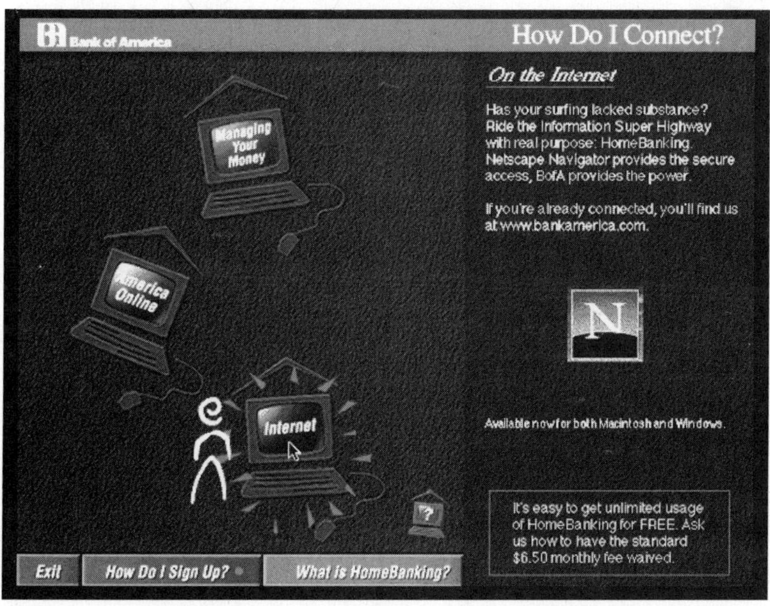

Table 3: The characteristics of conventional and future new media compared to previous types of communication

	SPOKEN COMMUNICATION	WRITTEN COMMUNICATION	PRINTED COMMUNICATION	CONVENTIONAL NEW MEDIA (TO DATE)	FUTURE NEW MEDIA
Category	Continuous/ interactive	Discrete/ broadcast communication	Discrete/ broadcast communication	Continuous/ broadcast communication (with a few exceptions)	Continuous/ interactive communication*
Characterized by	Emotional, nonsequential thought	Sequential development and self-containment	Emotional or logical sequential thought and self-containment	Passive consumption, minimal participation, manipulative content	Active consumption, high participation (physical, cognitive), self-exploratory, collaborative and/or unpredictable content, high volatility
Type of experience	Collective	Private, individual	Mass individual	Mass individual	Individual as well as collective
Single- or Multichannel	Multichannel	Single-channel	Single-channel	Multichannel	Multichannel

*Future new media *should* (a very important point of this essay) fall in the category of continuous/interactive communication, which, by definition, includes some form of online media (including wireless); however, designers should understand those aspects of discrete media that are still important and use them as competitive advantage in the pursuit of audience/participants.

Table 3: The characteristics of conventional and future new media compared to previous types of communication (continued)

	SPOKEN COMMUNICATION	WRITTEN COMMUNICATION	PRINTED COMMUNICATION	CONVENTIONAL NEW MEDIA (TO DATE)	FUTURE NEW MEDIA
Benefits from	Performance	Elaborate, formal verbiage and ornamentation	Wide distribution, high production values	Visual richness and consumption by a wide audience	Immersion and high degree of participation
Strongly influenced the development of	Sign, symbol, icon, mnemonics, allegory, mythology	Logical, sequential thought	The "ideal" audience and first principles of mass communication	More global reach and vivid depiction of events and stories	Alternative content and communication channels for those unsatisfied with mass communication
Other	Lack of a permanent record made accumulating knowledge difficult	Brought a legitimacy, sometimes false, to points of view	Frequently associated with the democratization of the world	Shows a large audience high-impact messages but breeds passivity	
Examples	Storytelling, theater, opera	Medieval manuscripts, letters	Books, magazines	Radio, television, film	Online interactivemedia, e.g., the Web

The New Democratization of the Word

The shock St. Augustine reports he felt the first time he saw someone reading silently to himself beneath a tree (Barrett, p. xvi) is hauntingly similar to the consideration of the individual logged onto the Web, silently (figuratively speaking) participating in the most massive communication environment we have ever known.

While the book spread knowledge at an astounding rate and began to level the playing field of privilege, the creation of the content was still largely autocratic. The printed word was not quite the true democratization of the word: getting published has always been difficult. On the Web getting published is easy; the problem is getting an audience.

Ironically, we have in some respects seen a swing from the autocracy of the word (the publishing and broadcast industries) all the way to something that looks a bit like anarchy. The Web frequently reminds me of the Mel Gibson *Road Warrior* films: suddenly the nature of order and chaos, right and wrong are questioned because the forces at work are so different from those of the past. While Ted Nelson and others have taken a swing at bringing some suggested order to the anarchy of the Web, what it really will boil down to is good old-fashioned supply and demand. The new democratization of the word is really the democratization of publishing. The barriers to entry are, right now, pretty low. But as demand drives the provision of content to the richer and more responsive end of the spectrum—toward a new orality of communication—which requires deep creativity and high interactivity, the barriers to entry will raise. We will approach the need to craft and distribute *experience*.

The Democratization of Experience

Intel's Andy Grove states:

> *Infinite processing power will only get you so far with limited bandwidth. But the coming era of nearly free bandwidth will liberate the computer to fulfill its powers. Just as the 1980s saw the demolition of the vertical structure of the computer industry, so the 1990s will see the demolition of the vertical structure of the communications industry. (Gilder, p. 210)*

A literate public is required before the impact of a new technology is really felt. In a sense, online marketers are increasingly seeing the consumer as "apprentice... learning by discipleship, by participating in the message, practicing, helping to craft" (Ong, p. 14). The WWW and browsers have in effect become the Gutenberg press of the digital incunabula, but we have not yet seen the true realization of the potential. "In 1997, multimedia as we know it dies. Interactive telemedia takes its place." (GISTICS, p. 10) We are seeing now the collapse of the boundaries between author and reader, between filmmaker and audience.

The Transparency of the Delivery Mechanism: Immersion

With the introduction of a new communication technology, the focus is usually first on the mechanism itself, the wondrous box. Technology is always invasive, but never more than at its introduction. Early theaters prominently displayed the technology (as the "new" IMAX theaters still do). Magic lanterns smoldered in the same room as the audience. Early televisions were all box and knobs with a tiny screen. Today's televisions are an expanse of glass seemingly floating in space, with controls hidden behind panels.

The important comparison here is with today's browsers. They're all box and knobs surrounding a screen. I'm sure we will see them recede to the edge of the screen soon, once the novelty of their function has waned, and allow the content to take over. Jerry Mander refers to "the illusion of neutral technology." Marshall McLuhan's "the medium is the message" speaks also to the invasiveness of the delivery mechanism. But its receding to the edge of the screen, then off, underlines the point that we are moving back into a space where the content, the story, the image, the sound, the natural interactivity, is everything.

Printing on Water

Where is the Life we have lost in living?
Where is the wisdom we have lost in knowledge?
Where is the knowledge we have lost in information?
—T.S. Eliot, The Rock

In a sense, we are reliving the early days of television when filming radio shows was novel, but did not represent tremendous added value. When cameras were taken out into the world and to the scene of events and stories, television came into its own. Interactive new media is still a horseless carriage; we have not made the transition into realizing the automobile yet. In other words, the industry is largely viewing interactive new media as an incremental improvement to traditional media—which is evident in tentative, lackluster design—and not as a combination of molecules that make up an entirely new element. We can now build things we have not built before.

> *The page is flat, opaque. The screen is of indeterminate depth—the word floats on the surface like a leaf on a river. Phenomenologically, that word is less absolute. The leaf on the river is not the leaf plucked out and held in the hand. The words that appear and disappear on the screen are naturally perceived less as isolated counters and more as the constituent elements of some larger, more fluid process. This is not a matter of one being better or worse, but different. (Birkerts, p. 156)*

Historical analysis is just a lot of rhetoric unless some practical application is derived. I hope the discussion to this point has induced a different perspective on new media. But just in case, a couple of very specific ideas are worth exploring in a little more detail. Try applying these to current projects and see if anything happens.

Ask Why First

If certain content can be better served in an alternative medium, do so. Don't put it online unless you can instill clear value in the user. At Red Sky we refer to the violation of this rule as *gratuitous digitization* or *gratuitous conversion*.

Posting your corporate brochure to the Web is succumbing to novelty. It is neither good design nor good communication. It will probably not help you much. Most of what I see on the Web today I would be happier to have received in the form of a brochure (saving the earth aside).

Depth works alone for now, breadth does not. Providing comprehensive information about a particular concept is far more acceptable online than providing very general information about a range of concepts. One of my favorite ironies is that the specific is always easier than the general.

Tell Stories, Make Connections

Almost anything can be improved by a story. If you buy the idea that we are living the new orality, then you buy this.

We are human. Where the medium will support it (as is increasingly the case online) we respond well to visual and audible cues, to allegory and myth, to emotion and music, to storytelling. In fact, the online world has the potential to overcome the disconnectedness of television and to discourage the passivity that characterizes television audiences.

This has a big implication for advertising, of course. It has been said that television's highest potential is advertising (Mander, p. 305), that the bias is inherent in the technology. Whether this is true also for interactive online media, where the audience may participate much more, is up in the air.

Stories require concepts. Even where there is no real "story," developing a concept when designing for new media is still important. A concept serves somewhat as *axis mundi*—the center of the world—from which everything springs; everything is somehow related. This can be as simple as a particular use of color, or as elaborate as an interactive 3D environment. Design without a concept is frequently unguided, axisless, and, because of a low design common denominator now, easily recognized on the Web.

Just as in the preliterate society we discussed, you have to know your audience and speak to them in the vernacular. Increasingly, as interactivity evolves, the audience will in fact influence what is presented to them in very literal ways—similar to the way an audience reacts to a real live storyteller, and the storyteller subtly changes pace, action, and tone to better work the crowd.

Balance High-Tech and High-Touch

It's tempting to lean, conceptually, on the high-tech rather than the natural when designing for new media, because that is the aesthetic of almost everything involved in its production: computers, software, programmers, engineers. Red Sky was founded in part on the concept of balancing high-tech and "high-touch." We have, in fact, become known for our ability to soften the edges of digital interactive experience.

Our basic rules are these:

- Do not let technology overinfluence design
- Do not let design overinfluence technology

What this means is once you have a "shoot for the moon, land on the roof" concept, do not let the technologists reduce it too far with their patent comments like "It can't be done." I can say this because I am a programmer first and foremost. Similarly, do not let the aesthetes (the creative department) constrain the functionality of the product with *their* patent comments like "I really don't think we should animate that." I can say this because I also have done plenty of animation and know how hard it really is.

What we're really trying to do is avoid what Mander calls "the bias toward technique as replacement of content," and, I would add as corollary, the bias toward content as replacement of technique. We see the former in the current twitch games on the market. We see the latter in most of the current CD-ROM offerings.

Try Soft Metaphors Instead of Hard

Red Sky frequently applies a technique we call *soft metaphor*. Something we have never quite understood from a cognitive perspective is the much-overused technique of creating literal physical space on the computer screen. Why put a bank lobby on-screen as a navigational aid? Really? When you think about it does it help, or does it get in the way?

What we mean by *soft metaphor* is the creation of environments that break some of the rules of physics, interface design, and high-technology. These environments break the rules and yet are still hauntingly familiar to the user. One that is familiar enough that, while the environment is not something users recognize from the physical world (e.g., a modeled bank lobby), it is something they very much recognize from their own aesthetics (e.g., wood, brass, green felt, engraved paper).

This is all well and good, but, as designers who work frequently with large corporations, we never lose sight of the "brandedness" of the product where that is important (which is usually every job we work on). It's OK to stretch the brand a little bit—there are new things to do in a new medium—but do as we do and compare your designs with those of the company's in their other advertising channels: outdoor, broadcast, print, even radio.

Balance Continuousness and Discreteness

In his essay "Online Information, Hypermedia, and the Idea of Literacy," Philip Rubens writes:

> *The volume of information presented by a seamless information data pool implies that more information is better or more inclusive. In reality, more information simply requires the user to consider and process more information that may be indiscriminable. (p. 8)*

What we also think is dangerous and violates the balance between what you can do and what you should do, is invoking a feeling of "choice shock" in the user. This happens through providing so many options, typically without concept or metaphor, that the user comes nearly to a stop—much like the tale of the donkey stuck midway between two hanging carrots. "Enter and explore" is a condemnation, not a solution (Jaynes, p. 159). We are balancing here the absolute narrative control of the book with the total anarchy of hyperspace. And there are all kinds of balances that work. Consider for a moment the regulation that must be behind the signage on a typical American superhighway. Crack the Yellow Pages. Think about flying all the way across the virtual country in Microsoft Flight Simulator.

Quantity is easier than quality.

Shoot for the Moon, Land on the Roof

This is another favorite Red Sky motto. What we mean by "shoot for the moon, land on the roof" is to throw out reality for a while when designing new content. Imagine what would be the most effective way to communicate a message in a world with no technological, logistical, financial, or political constraints. Got it? OK, now work back from there. Usually we find that on the way we have developed a strong concept that, even after paring back to what *can* be done, retains enough magic to be exceptional against the field.

When you take this approach, a few things happen. You irreverently throw out traditional interface design, which, as studied and safe as it is, was still developed for pre-multimedia communication. You begin to see the automobile instead of the horseless carriage, the paradigm shifts instead of the incremental improvements.

The Web is not a quaint extension of books, radio, or TV. Why treat it as such? Just as in the early days of television, we are still, figuratively speaking, standing in the radio station pointing cameras at radio personalities doing monologues. Time to take the cameras out of the studio.

A Theorem of Truth in Design

I'd like to end with a developing theorem, one that binds much of this together but is, by definition in its relation to new media, never complete.

The combination of new media and online media has created a vast new territory to explore. Design, on technical and creative axes, will range more widely than at any time in history. Innovation will be tremendous. Public response to design will shift like big weather patterns across the surface, and be subject to about the same extent of predictability we have now. We can look about a week ahead; that's all.

We're printing on water here. Some aspects of human communication will always stay the same; our love of story, of music, of symbol, of myth. Some aspects of communication without a doubt are ever-changing. Technology is moving at such a pace that it constantly distracts us with its novelty, which we frequently misinterpret as improvement. The key is to let go of technology. It is the stream that will always run. You won't be able to stop it. You can print on it, however, at any moment. Use whatever technology is in front of you at the time.

Ultimately, the real power is in the wood block, the content. The best designers will find truth in design not from technology, but by a clear focus on what has always made people communicate; information that is compelling, well-crafted, and well-performed—and that responds well to applause.

Bibliography

Barrett, Edward. *The Society of Text*. MIT Press: Cambridge, 1989.

Birkerts, Sven. *The Gutenberg Elegies: The Fate of Reading in an Electronic Age*. Fawcett Columbine: New York, 1994.

Gilder, George. *Life After Television*. W.W. Norton & Company: New York, 1994.

GISTICS, Inc. *1996 Survival Guide for the Interactive Telemedia & Multimedia Developer*: Larkspur, CA, 1995.

Jaynes, Joseph T. "Limited Freedom: Linear Reflections on Nonlinear Texts." *The Society of Text*. Ed. Edward Barrett. MIT Press: Cambridge, 1989.

Landow, George P., and Paul Delany. "Hypertext, Hypermedia and Literary Studies: The State of the Art." *Hypermedia and Literary Studies*. MIT Press: Cambridge, 1990.

Mander, Jerry. *Four Arguments for the Elimination of Television*. Quill: New York, 1978.

Ong, Walter. *Orality and Literacy: The Technologizing of the Word*. Routledge: New York, 1990.

Rubens, Philip. "Online Information, Hypermedia, and the Idea of Literacy." *The Society of Text*. Ed. Edward Barrett. MIT Press: Cambridge, 1989.

cyberSIGHT

info@cybersight.com
corporate: 503.228.4008 | 514 sw 6th avenue, **portland, or**
sales: 310.449.8660 | 2444 wilshire blvd., suite 503, **santa monica, ca**

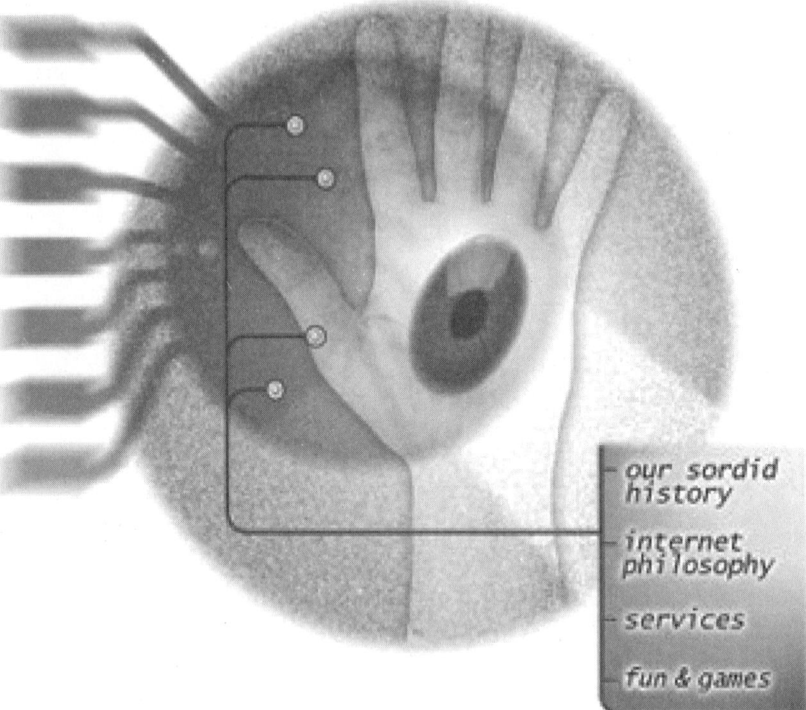

CyberSight

Company Profile

Founded in April, 1994, CyberSight initially used direct response marketing with traditional Internet protocols to pinpoint effective online strategy. With the advent of the World Wide Web, CyberSight focused on this medium as an ideal tool for "relationship" advertising and marketing. The combination of creative talent, technical innovation, and a close knowledge of Internet culture has established CyberSight as a leading interactive design and marketing firm. CyberSight has created sites for Molson Breweries, K2 Sports, Visa, and Mexicana Airlines, and has contributed to many others including Sony Music, Sun Microsystems, Intel, and Stoli Central. The company specializes in Internet community building, highly-customized programming of Internet technologies, and elegant interface design. CyberSight is currently developing a series of entertainment-oriented sites. CyberSight maintains offices in Portland, Oregon, and Santa Monica and can be found on the Web at **http://www.cybersight.com**.

As a regular Internet user for the past 12 years, Peter Bray gets in trouble on BBSs, initiates flame wars, and has other *de rigueur* Internet stunts under his belt. As a founder of CyberSight (and now Chairman, CEO, and Creative Director), Peter leads the creative team, where his close understanding of Internet culture with his traditional marketing background contributes to the development of elegant online promotions. He is a regular speaker at Internet events, from Comdex to bank marketing seminars. He studied psychology at Reed College.

Chapter Profile

In the Red Sky Interactive chapter, Tim Smith discussed the full circle media has traveled: from oral tradition to the written word and back. The revival of the oral tradition fascinates me, and the discussion is perpetuated in this chapter by Peter Bray. Peter's four principles (community, relevance, entertainment value, and interconnectedness) represent much of the role of the storyteller in ancient cultures. Great Web sites, regardless of their function, work in much the same way: they unite people as a community, they are relevant to the members' lives, they are entertaining or insightful, and they connect to other communities with similar interests and values.

I was quite struck a few years back to hear that the last human who could sing Homer's *Odyssey* had died. Though many people know the *Odyssey* as a printed epic, it has always existed as a song—a mnemonic used to keep an incredible amount of information in one's head. Since the origins of painting and writing, humanity has been on an epic quest to store information outside our heads: books, tapes, CDs, databases. Now that we are uniting so many media onto the Web, we are running even further from the memory power used years ago. Yet Peter's essay reflects the opportunity the Web poses to reinvigorate storytelling in novel ways.

I was invited a over a year ago to cofound a Web venture based on storytelling for children. At the time, I recall telling people the value of storytelling was apparent in intimate settings—small groups looking for good, clean fun. Clearly, traditional storytelling can't rival rock and roll in a stadium for audience draw. Despite the commercial shortcomings, the notion of intimate group entertainment carries on and is proved by Peter's laws, his development experience, and the success of chat rooms as a moneymaker for AOL and other online firms. As developers and designers, I encourage you to dig into your creativity for ways to generate community through storytelling. Now that we have multimedia, the oral tradition may become the visual tradition—not movies, not music, but narrative communities where the world tells its tales.

Essay

The World Wide Web, My Dad, and Creativity

by Peter Bray

Y DAD CALLS LATE one Saturday night. This must be trouble.

After all, this is gadget day. Shut into the guest room, now wall-to-wall with high-tech flotsam, my father ponders the techno-wonders *Newsweek* lauds as the latest and greatest. As the "technical son," I'm the pro bono, long-distance consultant for these adventures. I plot obscene combinations for VCRs, TVs, and stereos. I try to get sourdough out of a bread machine. I talk shop with put-your-Dad-back-on salesmen. I do lots of things I know nothing about.

On the last visit, I thought I stopped these conversations dead in their tracks. I sat down in my Dad's dungeon for a good five hours. I showed him the basics of DOS, plied him with Apple OS, and assured him that phone lines do not readily electrocute. After a while, I was satisfied that he was thoroughly initiated with Doom, Marathon, and Myst. More important, I'd hooked up an account and supporting devices (rice cooker, mini-fridge, etc.) for his latest fad—the Internet.

"Hey, Peter," my Dad begins, "no questions for you. Just a URL...check it out," he says.

"Why didn't you just e-mail this to me?" I ask.

"I forgot how to use e-mail," he says.

I type in the URL. I half expect some obscure site about the lower intestine (my father, the expert on the subject—he's a gastrointestinal radiologist who loves to point out "wonderful" resources to help me learn "the trade").

My Dad's mug loads up, then a little biography and some words of wisdom from the newly self-appointed King of the Web. I sit back, shocked. I teach my Dad e-mail; he forgets that it exists. I teach him DOS; he confuses it with the Christmas light regulator. He's a wanna-be technoid, but not quite there (no offense, Dad). After all, he even hates "those illogical, pull-down menus on that Mac," and you can't get worse than that! Yet he somehow set up his own Web page. On a Unix system, no less.

I'm in the right business.

First, if my thoroughly Web-addicted Dad, who was surely born sometime during the Industrial Revolution, can figure out the Web, millions and billions of other people will get it too. Despite the hype, it's so easy, addictive, and wonderful that it stands to compete with television, that media granddaddy. Who wouldn't want to be part of Web-beats-television patricide?

Second, I know more about the Internet than my father. I know what makes Internet protocols work. I could chat with the original Unix developers if they weren't so nerdy. My Dad knows intestines. I know Internet.

But this personal history is self-aggrandizement. I got into the business because I love the Internet. I almost failed out of college because I was online eight hours a day. I was a member of the "elite nocturnals"—those Reed College students who reversed their schedules, waking up at 5 p.m. and going to sleep at 10 a.m. to play online when it was least busy.

Unlike my vampire-like siblings, I did not become an accountant, a lawyer, or a doctor. I stayed online, year after year. As a senior, I started a business on the Internet. This was the best cure.

I got to play online all the time. We soon upgraded from my apartment basement to a dirty office facing a bridge. From there we moved to a 20-office complex in Portland and offices in Los Angeles. This growth continues because my compatriots and I don't care if we spend 18 hours a day "working." In the early days, some of us even slept in the office.

This essay discusses our creative principles—beliefs that wake us at night to write hurried e-mail to each other.

Good Sites Are Good Communities

I don't share Bill Gates' vision of a computer on every desk with Microsoft software.

Computers are lonely devices. You can't experience them with family, like television. Nor can you discuss shared experiences around the water cooler at work, as you can sports events.

"A computer on everyone's desk" is not specific enough. While Microsoft Word is great, you only need word processing programs so often. To avoid gathering dust, a computer needs to bring people together. As a tool for active communication, it'll always have a use. I'd modify Gates' statement to read "networking on everyone's desk!"

Communication, not software, is the power of the Internet. E-mail, not word processing, is the most widely used application. On private services such as America Online, the most popular areas are chat rooms. What addicted me was Multi-User Sensory Hallucinations (MUSHs) where I virtually engage other guests. To date, a MUSH has been a text-based "world" in which users can explore various strange experiences together. With the advent of Virtual Reality Modeling Language (VRML), 3D graphic MUSHs are beginning to flourish. Imagine millions of people in their attics playing with computers. Social flagellation? Not really. Frequently, it's to meet new people in new ways.

Unfortunately, the Web is easily static. You can look at my Dad's picture, but you can't talk to him. HTML gives people layout tools. But currently, there are thousands of inappropriate magazine-type pages online. Communication tools such as Perl, C, and Java are a lot more difficult to use than HTML.

Effective Web sites build communities. Layout is important, as is allegiance to the Internet's history as a communications tool. CyberSight learned these lessons the hard way.

Way back in early 1994, we were considered cutting-edge with The Phlogistician's Corner (**http://www.cybersight.com/cgi-bin/cs/newsic/news**), which is a pretentious reference to flaming. This newsgroup-type program put us on the map creatively. Although we've moved on to other things, you can still see this behemoth on the Web (see Figure 1).

The Phlogistician's Corner allows *chaining* of messages: a person posts something with a subject such as "I like frogs," someone else tacks a response onto this post entitled "Toads are better," and so on. As a guest, I initially see the topmost subject ("I like frogs"). Ten levels down, this banal topic might evolve into a thousand responses about the psychedelic medicinal uses of toads. However, I don't know the posts are there until I descend the hierarchy of messages. Creatively, we like having this type of discovery and mystery on a site. It provides an endless variety of hidden messages and surprises at every bend.

We built The Phlogistician's Corner to be self-maintaining. It is complete with automatic filters, parsers, and utilities to ensure that everything is clean, concise, and regularly updated. Unfortunately, they can't do everything.

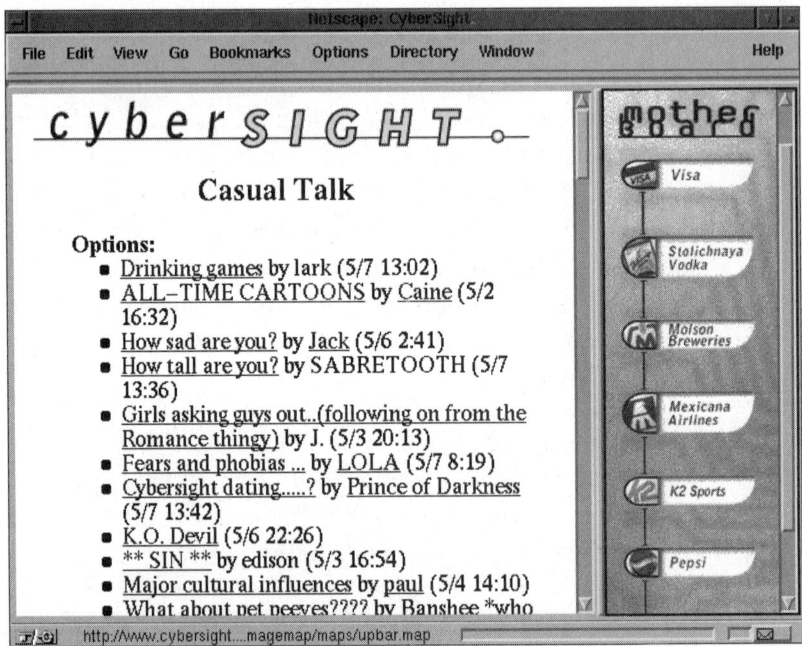

Figure 1: *The Phlogistician's Corner provides a friendly (at times) community for guests to talk to one another.*

A week after we launched the site we discovered that we were suspiciously low on disk space. A few Unix commands later, we found that the posts to The Phlogistician's Corner used over 500 megabytes of space.

Hundreds of guests had used (and abused) the program in every conceivable way. We had provided no content, only an extensive suite of tools for people to talk to one another; guests had grown the content themselves. They had talked and talked beyond anything we had anticipated. For the next few months, this was my petri dish. Every major creative principle I have stems from what I learned with this program.

People seek out direct, immediate dialog with others. We had lost a great deal of disk space because we had hundreds of posts asking "Is anybody on right now?" Eventually, these posts evolved into a complex system, formally documented in a FAQ by one guest. An area called LIVE CHAT prompted people to post the current time to try and catch the eye of someone browsing at the same time. When two guests find each other, an odd procession of "How's it going?" "Fine, what's up?" "Nothing" begins, requiring guests to repeatedly hit Reload until another post processes.

We learned three important things from these attempts to live chat in a not-so-live-program. First, people say a lot of really uninteresting things. Avoid applications that allow people to use their vocabulary. Instead, offer focused programs where dialog occurs through limited yet constructive means between guests. For instance, at Stoli Central, the Stolichnaya Vodka site (**http://www.stoli.com**), guests can montage Stoli-related graphics to create greeting cards. A secret URL is mailed to recipients, who then visit the artwork (and hopefully drink more vodka). This allows communication with graphically rich and textually sparse virtual products, a marketing plus (see Figure 2).

Second, when people do say something interesting, it is usually offensive. Provide parameters. When guests were allowed to input text at the Stoli site, they wrote in all sorts of lewd drink names, there for all the world to see. Stoli solved this problem by imbedding dirty entries in a series of pull-down menus that users can open or not at their own discretion. Limit how much freedom people have. Not only does this focus guests around a product or central theme, but it also prevents obscene language.

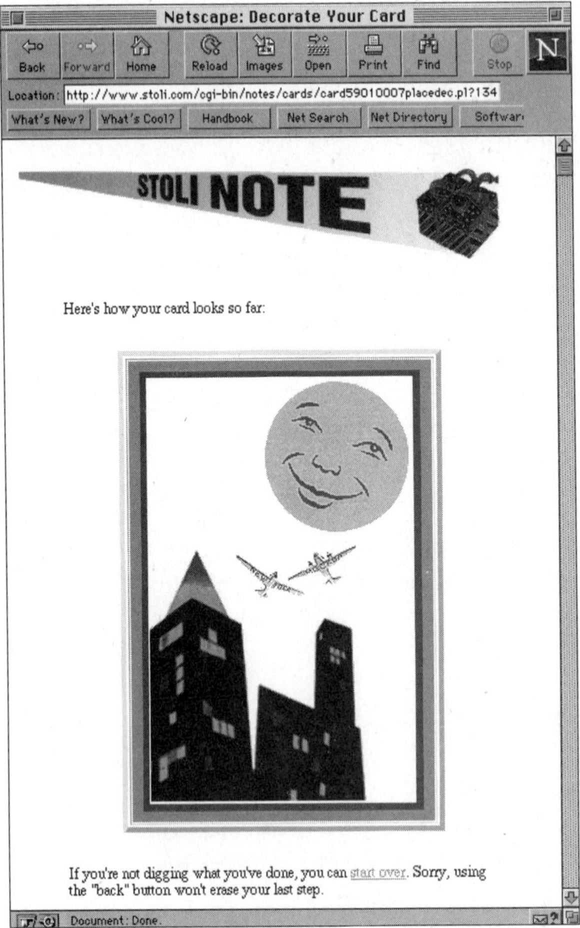

Figure 2:
At Stolichnaya Vodka's Stoli Note, guests communicate with each other, but only through the product, by creating and sending Stoli-laced notes. This focused dialog provides excellent brand-building and a unique way to engage other people. It's a successful refinement of the oft-boring, oft-ribald chat.

Third, people are drawn to one-on-one communication. This is the medium of e-mail, newsgroups, and other personal protocols. It isn't mass media, but thousands of intimate microcommunities. An effective site does not present a corporate facade. With copy that talks personally to each guest, it presents the faces behind the company. Ragu's Mama's Cucina (**http://www.eat.com**) does an excellent job of making a corporate site personal (see Figure 3).

People want to build something that lasts. In The Phlogistician's Corner, people do not leave anonymous posts. They want a legacy of interconnected comments. They build palpable, online personalities. At first, people signed with their e-mail addresses. This was insufficient, as evil posters forged messages, causing all sorts of havoc. To counter, people created their own "home pages."

There, they zealously kept track of all conversation within their domain. Forgery was quickly met with "This is not me!!!" responses. We learned, incidentally, that authentication is important in more than just credit card transactions!

The home pages give people their own turf. Any offending post in these turfs is flamed into oblivion. A guest developed a standard home page template that prompts users to tell the most important details for any online discussion—namely, gender, age, and whether they're single. Often, this home-away-from-home became users' first stop for any online activity.

People want to belong to a community. Those sites that make guests realize that they are vital members are popular. The Internet is about everyone contributing a little, as seen in Usenet. Sites should harbor this feeling and give guests tools to shape the site.

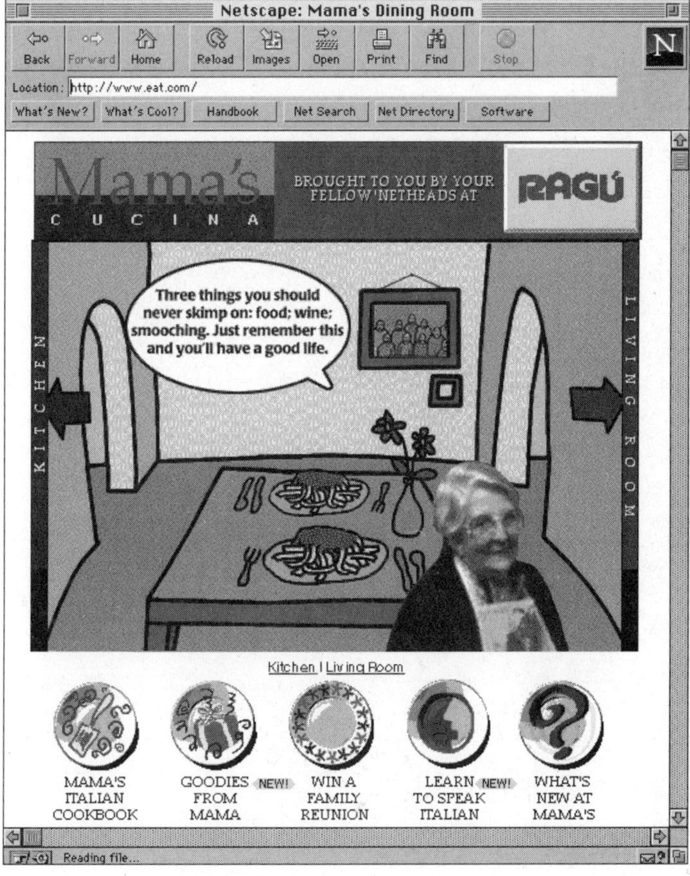

Figure 3:
With friendly copy, Ragu's Mama's Cucina keeps in tune with the Internet's history of close, personal dialog, rather than impersonal broadcasting. This site narrowcasts.

Community building can happen in a few ways. Polls allow guests to vote on the coolness of hot lists. The hot list sorts itself by popularity, with the most accessed link atop the page. Polls provide outlets for guests who are tired of being told what is cool and hot in static lists. Polls show what their peers think is neat, and they allow people to voice their opinions. Incidentally, the urge to vote serves as a potent reason to bring guests back to the site, which is always an important consideration.

An extensive online community offers a variety of tools to build and communicate. The Molson Canadian site (**http://www.molson.com**) allows guests to create their own profile pages (similar to home pages) and to make facts about themselves available to others (see Figure 4). Users can search these profiles, looking for male guests aged 21–25 who live in Toronto and like to play chess, for instance, then visit these guests' profile pages to find other facts such as name, last login, number of logins, and interests.

Figure 4: *Molson's I Am Online offers guests a variety of interweaving applications for guests to talk to others. The guests' personal profile pages are the hub of this activity.*

Supporting programs allow guests to "Webmail" each other. People have their own mailbox on the Molson system, where they send and receive mail from other Molson users. Guests can also post public messages that link to their profiles.

This web of communications devices has paid off for Molson; their site has a high rate of repeat visitors. Focus groups tell us that people feel a strong community on Molson's site—and they appreciate the site's innovative and unique channels of communication. For instance, the Hockey Net In Canada area of the site lets guests barter for various NHL players, assign them to teams, and compete against other "general managers" (see Figure 5). It's an idea we at CyberSight return to again and again: provide a kernel of content and let the guests use our tools to massage it into all sorts of fun things.

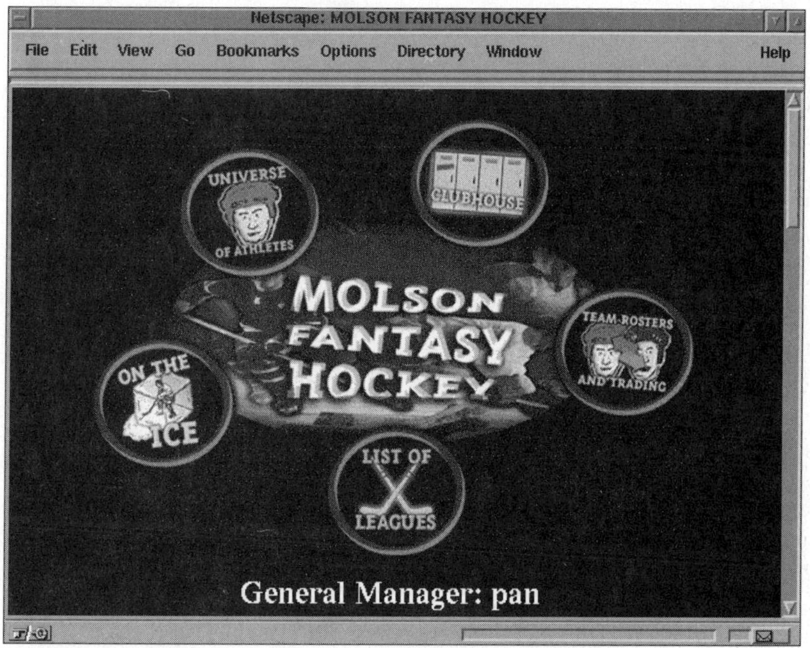

Figure 5: *In Molson's hockey pool, guests rant and rave rinkside. As general managers, guests join leagues, trade players, and otherwise try to beat the socks off other hand-picked hockey teams.*

Perhaps one of the only problems in the Molson site is the use of usernames and passwords. While visitors to the site do not have to use this feature, it is necessary for advanced functionality. Unfortunately, this process discourages some people from registering. When CyberSight created a site for Visa (**http://www.visa.com**), we learned to build a better system. We let people create their own personal entryways to the site—private URLs that preclude usernames and passwords. These private URLs are very similar to Netscape's "cookies," incidentally.

People crave fresh, diverse content. The Phlogistician's Corner is stuffed with posts because good interactive content self-replicates. Java is a perfect language for fresh content, since it is designed to allow guests to engage one another. I look forward Macromedia's Shockwave having more networking capabilities. This advance will be significant, as it will not limit guests to playing a one-person CD-ROM.

HotWired is great (**http://www.hotwired.com**). After a while, though, it gets a tad boring reading the opinions of those cats in San Francisco. Even in *HotWired*, apparently, the most popular area is the newsgroup program, where people can contribute freely.

A chief complaint from users is that sites do not change content frequently or that content is too narrow. How many times have you been to a site that has not changed for several weeks? Offer guests tools to provide new content, or to structure and grow provided "content modules" in novel ways. With tools for guest-generated content, fresh information and a diversity of opinions are ensured.

My first principle suggests focused user involvement. It gives the guest a level of commitment to the site. It makes the guest feel at home and strengthens the affinity between guest and site. A diversity of opinions are presented, and content is always new and fresh. Finally, it is in tune with the culture and history of the Internet, which is about many people contributing a little bit.

Good Sites Are Relevant

At dinner tonight, my business partner said, "Peter, I don't think selling people on personalization is going to work anymore."

I bit my tongue.

Despite its possibly limited sales ability, personalization is the greatest thing about the Internet. It allows sites to receive data about guests and use this data to *narrowcast* rather than broadcast to them.

I did my senior thesis for United Way. I designed a 2 x 2 x 2 x 2 factorial design direct mail campaign (i.e., it consisted of 16 experimental groups and 4 controls). Each group received 250 mailings, each deviating slightly. I was tickled pink. This was the largest sample size for any psychology study done at Reed College. Surely I would go down in the history books. Of course, the typical response for a direct mail campaign is 2%. My 4% return did not generate enough data to do any statistical tests.

At the same time, I was playing with the World Wide Web. With log files, I found that I could keep track of where a person was going in a site. I knew everything they were doing. The one Web page I created had hundreds of visitors daily. My eyes gleamed. This was robust data in the making!

I could create a site with two pages. On one day, the first page would have certain graphics and copy. I'd keep track of how many people went to the second page from this first page. On another day, the first page would have different graphics and copy. I'd again measure how many people went to the second page. With the hundreds of responses, I could readily see which graphics and copy were more effective at motivating people to visit the next page.

A number of applications can automatically change content based on what people do in random situations. No need for drawn-out correlations or other hand-done statistics. One program randomly throws up a different graphic every time a person loads the home page. Another program makes a different graphic load up depending on whether the guest leaves the site or looks at another page. Intertwining programs can change everything about the site.

There is limited need for hands-on content changes. Rather, a series of "content modules" dynamically mix and match information and graphics based on user interaction. There is no need for random graphics, as we can design them to load in a way that matches user behavior.

For instance, in the site we created for Visa (**http://www.visa.com**), we offer programs that interact globally and personally. The Global Top 10 List displays the most popular sites for all guests. The Personal Top 10 List highlights the top visits of that particular guest (see Figure 6).

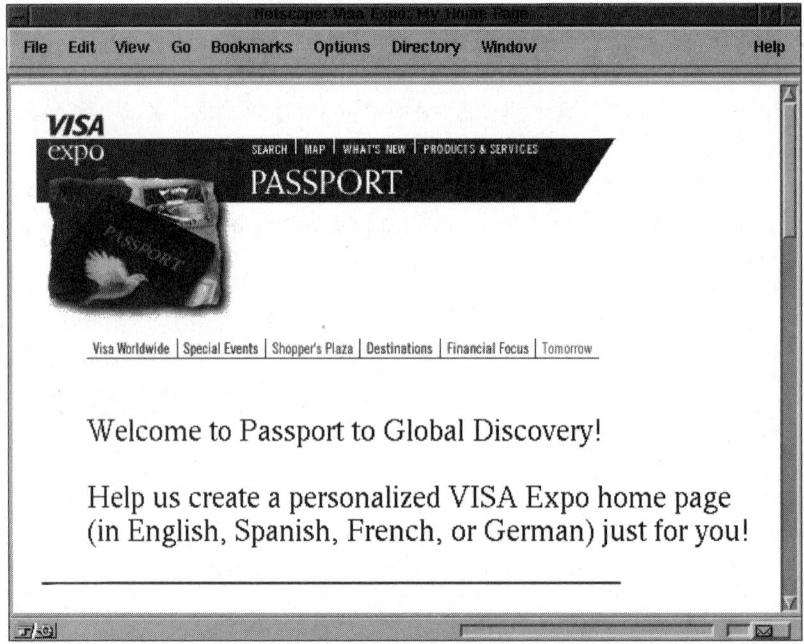

Figure 6: *At Visa's Passport to Global Discovery, guests have their own back-door to the site. By answering a variety of questions, they are assigned private URLs (which precludes the need for a username and password) that allow them to reaccess their customized sites.*

There's so much information online, and personalization is only one way to keep guests at your site. Last night I looked for information on tropical fish. I sidetracked to sites about great white sharks; then to a fascinating site about the Great Barrier Reef; and then to one about Australia in general. I ended up at a home page for a neat graphic artist at the University of Auckland. Nothing in any of these sites kept me there, and I'll probably never see them again.

The Web is like a conversation with a friend. You start to talk on one subject, and half an hour later, you're talking about something completely different. Conversations jump from tangent to tangent. The Web does too, and the goal is to keep guests focused on your site and give them incentive to return.

First, create a site with outgoing links that offer motivation to come back to the site, such as polls. Sites that provide navigation to other sites are in tune with the "you-scratch-my-back-I'll-scratch-yours" Internet mentality. As long as people come back, sending them elsewhere first is fine.

Second, create a site that is ostensibly flexible but really quite linear. In other words, while you may offer a number of forks in the road, they all lead in roughly the same direction. They provide a purpose and overarching structure that guides guests from page to page. For example, Karakas VanSickle Ouellette Advertising & Public Relations (**http://www.kvo.com**) uses a detective story to lead guests through the content of their site (see Figure 7).

Third, laser-target content. Information should speak directly to what each guest wants. Unlike magazines or television, the Web allows precision targeting. We know an awful lot of information about each guest. Imagine structuring the site totally around these facts. Males from Vancouver who drink 5 beers weekly and watch *Friends* might get a different interface than Toronto males who drink 20 beers weekly and enjoy *60 Minutes*.

What a nightmare personalized content must be for the programmer, you might think. Not necessarily. Programs do not need every possibility hand-coded. Fuzzy logic can look for correlations, such as recognizing that most *60 Minutes* fans make certain choices at the site, and exploit these matching behaviors.

For instance, there are several wonderful programs that use fuzzy logic. In one, you answer a few questions about your favorite and least favorite movies. Your answers are compared to what other people have entered. Perhaps you indicate *Jaws* and *Hard Bodies* as your favorite movies. Other people who have these interests might also show an 80% tendency to like *E.T.* The program looks for correlations like this and spits out data that conforms to people similar to you—in this case, that you will probably like *E.T.* This paradigm, called *automatic similarity conformation*, has great potential on the Web.

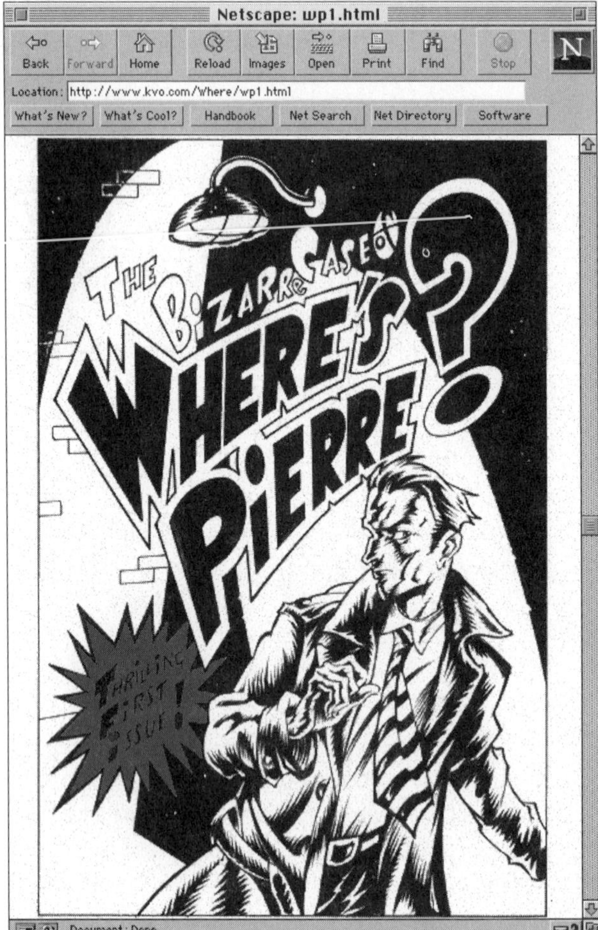

Figure 7:
KVO uses a detective story—"Where's Pierre?"—to entice guests through their content. If you help find the company's partner, you may win a T-shirt.

Finally, relevance also means a connection between the amorphous cyberworld and the real world. More and more people online are new to the Internet. It's difficult for these people to find a connection between this odd frontier and their everyday lives. Sites should ground people to the real world. They should create virtual communities that mimic real-world communities. After all, talking to someone in France is lovely…for a while. After a bit, I'd prefer to talk to people in my local community about real issues that affect us daily, rather than sexual/philosophical chit-chat. Build sites that plant people in a firm geography (**http://www.interportland.com**) and that make them feel at home with approachable imagery and human faces (see Figure 8).

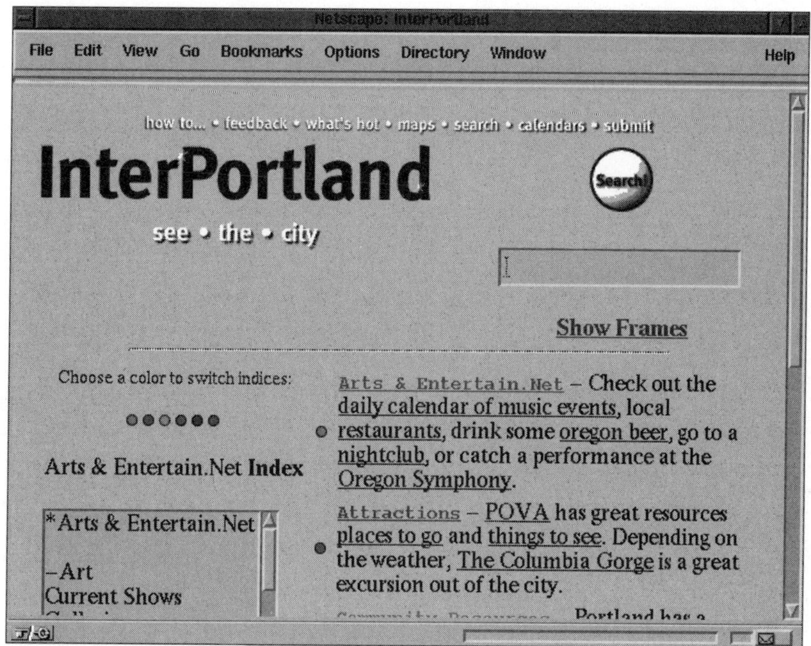

Figure 8: *InterPortland provides a strong "sense of place" through maps and Portland-esque visual cues.*

With these concepts of community in mind, I believe that VRML is somewhat over-hyped. The idea of wandering around a 3D space may be attractive to adolescent, video-game-addicted males, but it is generally unapproachable for others. Not only does VRML fail to help people navigate through information effectively, but it uses interfaces that are clunky and unappealing. At its base, an interface should effectively give people the information that they want. It should offer them a metaphor that is approachable, rather than overly-wired.

The basics of my second law are personalization and relevance. A site should provide a structure—an hidden agenda—to this potentially formless and loose medium. To provide a sort of linearity allows guests to fit into a process, rather than abjectly wander. With so much information online, sites should deliver targeted information by analyzing both personal and global trends. Finally, the Internet needs to connect to the real world and not remain an interesting oddity.

Good Sites Entertain

Every night I race home to watch *Seinfeld*.

Web sites do not make me this excited. They should. With an increasing number of average Americans (such as my Dad) flooding the Internet from AOL, MSN, and other services, this is no longer just a medium for college kids, researchers, and government types to swap technical facts. To keep this new audience, the Internet has to be more appealing than a rerun of *Seinfeld*.

Unfortunately, interactivity is often ignored. *The Spot* (**http://www.thespot.com**) is a wonderful, *Melrose Place*-type environment (see Figure 9). But is it suited for the Web? While it has a clear cast of characters, it still lacks focus. Its home page, which allows the guest to go in several different directions, does not offer a directed story, but a loose, detached experience with limited motivation.

Figure 9:
The Spot *is the original online soap opera. Perhaps because of this, it's more suited to television than an interactive medium, since we're not dynamically involved in the plot.*

The Spot nicely provides a sense of a scene, but how connected are we? It does not personalize the site or allow guests to communicate (apart from e-mail) with one another, the characters, or the story itself.

Imagine instead a site that allows the guest to direct how the story develops. It uses data about the guest to create characters and scenarios that are personally relevant, and it offers guests new ways to talk to one another. Let's learn from the popularity of AOL's chat rooms and create narratives that bring people together.

Of course, part of entertainment's appeal is the ability to access other people's imaginations. As my partner, someone quite steeped in Hollywood culture, notes, "There are a lot of bad scripts out there." Do we really wish to be caught in a bad script of our own creation? No, a structured program allows guests to interactively explore someone else's ideas in-depth; at the same time, it provides enough room for guests to use their own imaginations.

The site we created for Pepsi (**http://www.pepsi.com**), for instance, offers both micro and macro interactivity. The guest enters a Java-animated screen with five flipping panels of Japanese *anime*. The guest stops and starts these different panels with mouse clicks (see Figure 10). This application is similar to those books where combinations of different torsos, heads, and feet result in humorous configurations. For our Pepsi story, there is one correct choice, but incorrect combinations of plot elements offer funny results. In terms of plot, we exploited formula scriptwriting elements, where each panel is a classic plot twist from sitcoms and dramas.

Figure 10: *Pepsi's* Adventures of the Three Dragon Eaters *presents a basic plot-line with a twist. Japanese* anime *offers different scenarios that guests interactively weave together; rather than disconnected viewers, we're active participants in the story development.*

There are three different pages of these flipping stories. Each story presents a different approach—inane sitcom meets purposely bad '70s sci-fi and quasi-gothic fantasy. Each story ends with a different cliff-hanger, and guests vote on which story they want continued next month.

This application mixes storytelling with interactivity. The narrative is precise, but we allow guests to plug and play with the plot elements for a number of predicted outcomes. We allow enough freedom to make the story engaging and dynamic, and to connect guests with what happens. They control the story to some degree, but the writer's imagination is still largely in control of the experience.

My third law suggests that successful online entertainment creates community around narrative. Plots are structured for each guest. The narrative offers enough interactivity to provide fresh content and new possibilities on each visit, and, most important, to give the guest an active voice in the story.

Good Sites Do Not Stand Alone

Every so often in *HotWired*, a banner for Toyota's *alt.terrain* site appears. How odd.

The *HotWired* site is content-rich. It offers advertisement banners—like the *alt.terrain* banner—which link to sponsors' sites (see Figure 11). What motivates people to go to these advertisements? After all, no one wants to browse a sales pitch.

alt.terrain is Toyota's own online magazine; its purpose is obviously to keep people on Toyota's site. It's not by any means a direct sales pitch. In fact, there is little information about cars. Instead, you read about horseback riding, Teri Garr's opinions on men's fashion, and other articles geared to Toyota's target audience. To get people to this magazine, Toyota advertises in another magazine—*HotWired*. How different is this from *Time* advertising in *Newsweek*?

The online banner paradigm is shaky. Paradoxically, it requires the advertiser to create content that competes with the *HotWired* content for readers. Otherwise, why would anyone leave entertaining *HotWired* to visit an advertisement?

In television, advertising *temporally* interrupts content. You cannot easily avoid the advertisements, but must sit through them to find out what Kramer does with Jerry's hairbrush in the next scene. In magazines, advertising *spatially* interrupts content. To get to the latest article in *Rolling Stone* magazine, you flip past several print advertisements.

We see both temporal and spatial advertising on the Web. In *HotWired*, (see Figure 11) guests are subjected to a promotional banner either below or above articles (**http://www.hotwired.com**). In *Word* (**http://www.word.com**), another online magazine, you must sit through a sponsor's three-second logo before an article loads.

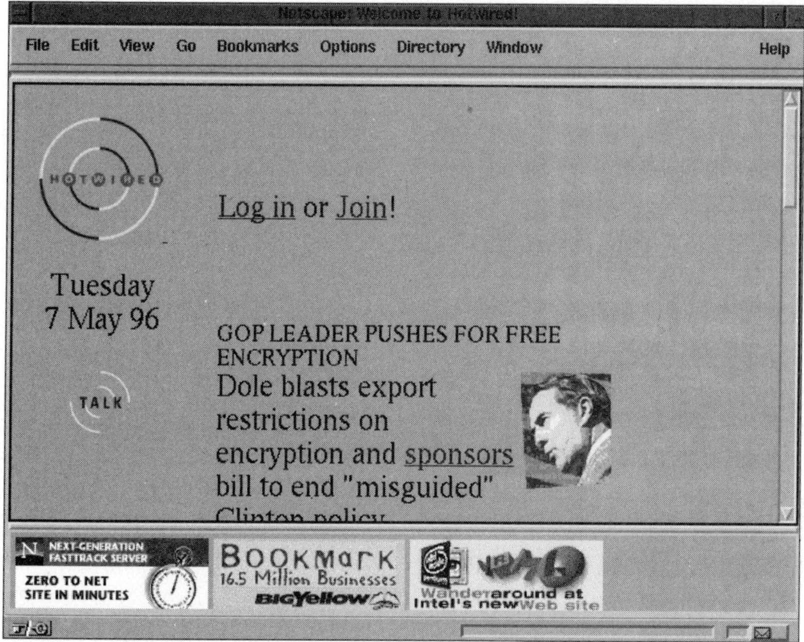

Figure 11: HotWired*, a content-rich publication, contains expensive links to content-rich advertisers. Traditionally, advertisers rely on well-placed advertisements for their audience. Not so at* HotWired*, where advertisers have to build their own competing content to pull people away from that site and to theirs.*

Both of these examples are fine. However, they are passive, not active, ways to promote products. The guest sits and watches, rather than experiencing and responding to promotions. These protocols are geared to a television or magazine environment. Neither of them really prompts the guest to visit the sponsor's site.

The Web is a wonderful marketing medium because it allows guests to actively engage products. This cannot happen with brief glances at logos and banners, but occurs with in-depth "virtual use" of an advertiser's product and information.

Attractive content like Toyota's *alt.terrain* draws visitors. It might work for a little while, but companies like NBC, Time Warner, and so on offer superior content. After all, they dedicate themselves to content development, not to making cars.

What can an advertiser do to successfully promote their product? No Web site is an island. They require each other, and rely on each other. They share content, cross-link, reference one another, and otherwise powerfully exploit one another.

Proper promotion support takes a form similar to product placement in television and movies. Content and promotion should fuse. The advertiser should only worry about the sell and assume that online media-buying will guarantee an audience to their entire site, not just the banner.

Sponsored games propel guests to actively use product to explore content. The Riddler (**http://www.riddler.com**), a brilliant site, uses commercial sites to hide scavenger-hunt-type items (see Figure 12). Eventually, promotion online will evolve, and we'll soon collect widgets to compete with other guests, explore advertisers' sites looking for lost princes/princesses, and so on. When guests play the game, they actively explore the whole of an advertiser's site. The advertiser is guaranteed an audience, and they don't have to create competing content as they currently do in *HotWired*.

My fourth law suggests that the Web is an environment where the user is in complete control. They can avoid advertisements easily. One unsustainable solution is for the advertiser to create their own content. A better alternative is a fusion of content with multiple sponsors. This fusion will shift content away from basic information and toward games and interactive experiences that better support engaging promotions.

Figure 12: *The Riddler offers a game that drives guests to explore advertisers' sites for puzzle pieces. Advertisers do not need to create their own entertaining content, but can rely on the media-buy to supply an audience.*

Summary

Popular Web sites carefully design with their users in mind. They develop one-on-one, relevant relationships with guests. They make guests comfortable and provide a strong set of tools for guests to talk to one another and manipulate content. They provide an overarching motivation—often in the form of a personalized story—that prompts guests to explore the site (and promotion) repeatedly.

Simply stated, good sites are communication devices: relevant and entertaining. They exploit relationships with other sites to build steady traffic.

Even my father is learning this idea. He has plans for "The Interactive Intestine" on his Web page.

NETObjects™

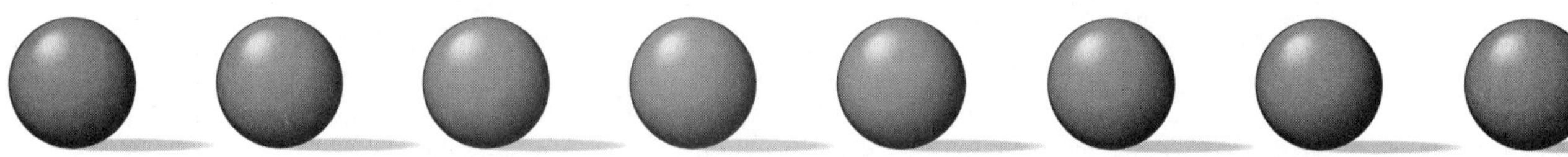

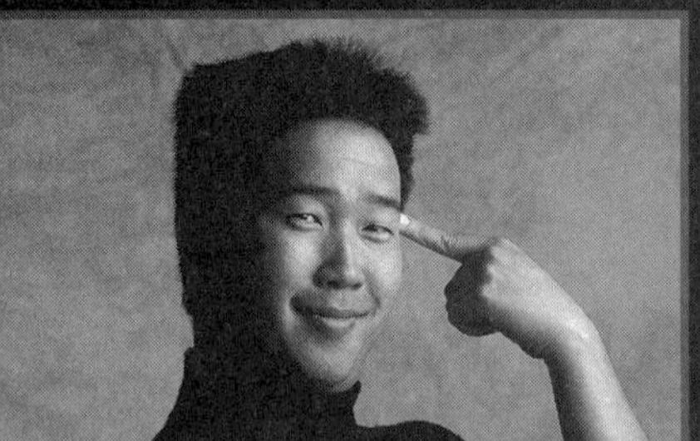

(Formerly Clement Mok designs)

Studio Archetype

Company Profile

You can see the work of Studio Archetype, formerly Clement Mok Designs, every time you launch Microsoft Network, watch CBS Sports, or visit the Mirage Hotel and Casino in Las Vegas. Clement Mok founded Studio Archetype, a 50+ person identity and information design firm, in 1987. Their design work has included CD-ROM, online, and Web site design for companies such as Adobe, QVC, Microsoft, NBC, and Sony. In 1993, Clement founded a digital publishing company, CMCD, whose Visual Symbol Library received the Silver award from the 1995 Business Week/IDSA Design Review. Clement is a founding partner of NetObjects, Inc., the unique Web authoring technology used to construct the templates and the immense Web site for the *24 Hours in Cyberspace* project.

Prior to 1988, Clement served for five years as Creative Director for Apple Computer, where he led corporate communication, packaging systems, event marketing, and product introduction projects. He also defined and evolved many of the graphic standards that were closely associated with Apple's corporate image. He began his design career in New York, where he developed print, broadcast graphics, and exhibition projects for clients such as Rockefeller Center, Republic National Bank, and CBS.

Chapter Profile

One of the Web's greatest democratic strengths comes from individuals telling stories to a global audience. Despite the downside of this ability—endless pages of pet photos and boring monologues—well-edited personal narratives form a part of who we are as a species. Yet the most powerful narratives focus our attention with immediacy, not just personalization. Combining these two traits continues as a critical challenge to Web innovators. A recent success of this convergence is the *24 Hours in Cyberspace* project, created by Against All Odds Productions, and whose sponsors included Studio Archetype, NetObjects, and hundreds of volunteers around the world. *24 Hours*, which took place on February 8, 1996, was a complete day of extraordinary real-life stories, told by ordinary people, sent as words and images from around the world to a single production center.

Author Howard Rheingold recently wrote that his new Web/print publishing venture, Electric Minds, will work as a "worldwide jam session of articulate futurists, technologists, artists, journalists, community builders, and multimedia communicators." A jam session is a great metaphor to describe the combination of personalization and immediacy that the Web embodies. A site has a responsibility to connect stories in real time, which is the core of the *24 Hours* project. In the future, many more sites will form ongoing "jam sessions."

Upholding this responsibility for a global audience was perhaps the greatest achievement of the *24 Hours* project. The infrastructure, design, and production challenges were significant. Developing infrastructure for the project included mirrored sites around the world and dozens of donated components. Creating a design for the site compelled Studio Archetype to consider a global audience, rapid content changes, and simple presentation of a wide array of reports. Site production required a rapid, simple authoring tool, SitePublisher by NetObjects, which is profiled after Clement's piece in this essay. Sadly, many present and future developers will fail to integrate these principles adequately. Those who do learn the lessons of *24 Hours* are much more likely to see their ideas succeed, driven by the power of community, not just individual interests.

Essay

About Design—and About Web Design

by Clement Mok

ALKING ABOUT "WEB DESIGN" seems to imply that designing for the Web is a different, somehow unique discipline from designing for print materials such as newspapers, magazines, or advertisements. It isn't. Design—whether for the Web, for print, or for any other media—is about creating order and structure from the world's inherent chaos.

On the other hand, the Web really is a new medium. While my print background provides a certain bias to my own designs for the Web, a lot of the aesthetics—you might even say constraints—of print no longer apply. Of course, new ones arise to take their place.

For example, take illustrations, which in the world of traditional print design are static. What the designer prepares—a one-dimensional image on a page—is what the viewer sees. In the digital world, however, we can create illustrations that the viewer can rotate and examine from different angles. The viewer's ability to "participate" in the design is just the beginning of this new medium's unlimited possibilities for growth and change.

For in all other media, design reaches a finished state. To stay with print as an example, once the presses roll, the product is complete, the design is fixed. With film, video, audio, even with software, once the project has wrapped, the designer's work is over. With the Web, once a page is sent over the Internet, the designer can add new pictures, change text, slip in an audio interview, and, in fact, redesign and update a page endlessly. What one viewer sees on one day may be completely different from what another viewer sees the next day.

In print, the reader sees exactly what the designer planned. On the Web, what the designer creates is just the beginning of what the viewer sees. As designers, we might select the world's most legible font, but that means nothing if a viewer has set a condensed font like Helvetica Narrow as a default. Because the viewer can select any font they choose—as well as its size—the type on a designer's screen may not look anything like the type on the viewer's. Currently, we rely on the fonts on a viewer's hard drive, without even knowing what they are. This user-determined aspect of the Web introduces yet another new design aesthetic.

Additionally, a viewer's Web experience is determined by such things as modem speed, bandwidth, monitor size, and color capabilities. We can design an attractive page that looks terrific on a large and expensive 21-inch monitor, but what good is it if it can't be appreciated on the viewer's constricted 14-inch screen?

And great color images or graphics, while wonderfully effective on paper, are frustrating to someone with a painstakingly slow modem, waiting for what seems like hours to see a picture build on the screen. Even worse, the color picture or graphic that appears in lovely hues on the designer's screen may instead be viewed by someone with a black-and-white monitor who will never see the image except in shades of flat gray.

Which brings us back, in a way, to the one constant in designing for all media: the audience. We can't lose the audience with the design, regardless of the medium for which a design is created.

When designing for the Web, we're concerned not only with how the audience perceives the message being delivered, but also with how they physically and mentally interact with the message. We have to go beyond the purely visual aspects of design and also focus on viewers' behavior. We can no longer evaluate our designs exclusively by what is visually beautiful.

We must re-examine traditional conventions. We must go beyond the table of contents typical layout of a magazine or book, for example, and also consider how easy is it for the viewer to navigate a Web site and find a way "home" again. There's no more flipping to the front of the book to look for a new topic! On a printed page, the viewer merely runs their eyes over the type and pictures. On a Web page, the designer must consider how easy is it for the viewer to see the underlined text and find the interactive buttons that shuttle visitors around the site and even off to pages located elsewhere on the Internet. This is a new way of thinking for most graphic designers.

Nobody, least of all the consumers of our well-designed information, wants to wait. With print, readers open a publication and immediately see a completed page containing type and four-color photographs. Visitors to a Web site click on a page and, depending on their own equipment, the page can zip into place or grow slower than grass. I call this aspect of Web design the *performance* aesthetic. Designers must consider not only the eye-catching value of a large color photo, but also how long that photo will take to travel and then appear on the viewer's screen.

Technology aside, what we design for the Web has to be bolder, shorter, and/or simpler just to get people's attention. Using pastel colors and subtle type is not going to work. Subtlety, however, can be incorporated into the written text or can be designed by linking to pages that add something new to the overall experience. With Web design, subtlety has more to do with anticipating the viewer's behavior—with playing off the viewer's enjoyment of clicking off to someplace new.

Finally, designing for the Web is the logical progression of what we've come to know as desktop publishing—the use of computer technology to merge typesetting, design, and production to streamline the publishing process. Desktop publishing as we have come to know it still produces a product, which moves from film to plates to a printing press that still spits out a piece of paper. This paper still has to be packaged, mailed and distributed. Web publishing, the next step in desktop publishing, not only eliminates the plates, the press, and the paper, but also integrates more intricately than ever before the entire editorial process, from gathering information to, ultimately, handing it directly to the reader.

The *24 Hours in Cyberspace* project, which took place on Feb. 8, 1996, was an electronic publishing first. Our role in designing not only the site but also the system within which it took shape has given us an intimate knowledge of the brave new world of real-time electronic publishing.

In the true ever-changing spirit of the World Wide Web, references to this project can easily shift tense from past to present. The *24 Hours* Web "project" was organized prior to and climaxed on Feb. 8, 1996. However, the site continues to exist today at **http://www.cyber24.com**, and is evolving, even as this is being written, with additional material and new links added daily. So for the purposes of this discussion, we'll refer to the project itself in the past, and to the site in the present.

24 Hours in Cyberspace: A Case Study

The *24 Hours in Cyberspace* project would have been an ambitious undertaking had it stopped at being a photo documentary. Rick Smolan, who over the past 15 years has been able to harness the time and talents of dozens of top photojournalists to produce such popular photo books as *A Day in the Life of The Soviet Union*, *A Day in the Life of Australia*, and the best-selling *A Day in the Life of America*, had again enticed 150 professional photographers to participate in one of his massive documentary projects. This time, their assignment was to photograph, over a 24-hour period, the global online revolution. Their goal: through photography, to put a human face on the new ways in which we work, play, learn, conduct business, and interact thanks to the Internet.

However, in addition to producing a book and a CD-ROM this time, Rick wanted to use the graphic capabilities of the World Wide Web to aid in its own documentation. He wanted to use the Internet's speed and reach to publish and distribute the work on the day it was created. And, in the true spirit of the Net, he invited the online community not only to visit the site, but also to contribute to it from afar with stories of their own. For 24 hours, the project became a living example of a famous journalistic adage: "a deadline every minute."

Either using digital cameras or shooting with traditional cameras and scanning negatives, more than 1,000 photographers (including nonprofessional contributors) from 27 countries transmitted digitized images to a site in San Francisco called "Mission Control." There, 80 editors, designers, and technicians sorted through incoming pictures and audio clips, selected material, rewrote stories, composed pages, and built a World Wide Web site during the course of a single day.

Periodically in that 24-hour time period, the Web site was rebuilt and updated with the new stories pouring in. The continuous updating meant that the shape and the bulk of the site also changed all day long.

The current Web site's feature attraction is an editorial section focusing on six themes. Each of the thematic areas is introduced with an essay written by a personality and followed by written stories, pictures, and captions laid out like pages in a photo magazine or picture book. In some cases, audio interviews accompany the text. Additionally, the site contains background material about the *24 Hours* project, how it worked, the technology behind it, and information about its sponsors.

The site received more than four million hits in the 24-hour slot from 9 PM Feb. 7, 1996, through 9 PM on the 8th. Nearly 55,000 people signed the guest book that day.

Never before had so much material been generated for publication at one site. Never before had it arrived from so many sources. Never before had so many professionals gathered to edit, compose pages, and publish information. And never before had a project of this scale been streamlined into a single 24-hour period.

In fact, participation was so great among students and amateurs in the online community that fewer than 10 percent of the stories that were generated on Feb. 8 were uploaded that day. The site continued to grow after Feb. 8, with the permanent *24 Hours in Cyberspace* site launched a month later with the best images, not only from the professional team, but also from students and amateurs around the world.

The Assignment

The assignment for *24 Hours in Cyberspace* evolved at various points in our discussions with Rick Smolan. Initially, the idea was to design a Web site that would be organized both by theme and by hour of the day. Using the 24-hour model, the stories would be organized by what hour they had been delivered or by what theme they supported. Viewers would select stories according to themes or by any one hour of the twenty-four covered by the event.

But a deeper examination of the site's purpose showed that we were really dealing with editorial content. The stories were the point, not the time in which they were taken or delivered over the course of a day. Our decision to focus only on the stories drove a very different structure and approach to how to build the site (see Figure 1).

Earthwatch TABLE OF CONTENTS

Figure 1: *Eventually, we decided to focus on the stories rather than the time-frame to organize the site.*

We decided against using presubmitted stories and adding new submissions in real time as a basis for building the site. We decided instead to have all of the stories filed on the day of the event, creating pages on the fly. This approach generated a different set of design decisions.

We wound up constructing a prelaunch Web site featuring pages with how-to-participate information, sponsor links, and project background. We incorporated all of this into the larger site that appeared on Feb. 8. On that date, the site became dynamic—a real-time Web magazine with newly generated and edited stories, pictures, and audio clips being added every 30 minutes. Much of what a visitor saw at 6 PM on Feb. 8 had not even been transmitted to Mission Control at noon, let alone assembled into a completed Web page.

Consequently, this was not a case where all the elements were handed to us in advance and we could study them, manipulate them, and package and launch a completed, controlled site on the Web. Beyond designing attractive pages the viewer would see on Feb. 8, we had to go further and design a system to be used by photo editors and text editors who knew nothing about HTML coding. Before ever seeing the content, we had to accommodate unknown images and stories in a flexible and attractive way.

You might say we were planning an electronic potluck dinner. We didn't know what food was coming, but we had to set the table so that whatever did arrive would look beautiful and taste great. Our technology choices allowed us to implement the design and the process for carrying it out, as you can see in Figure 2.

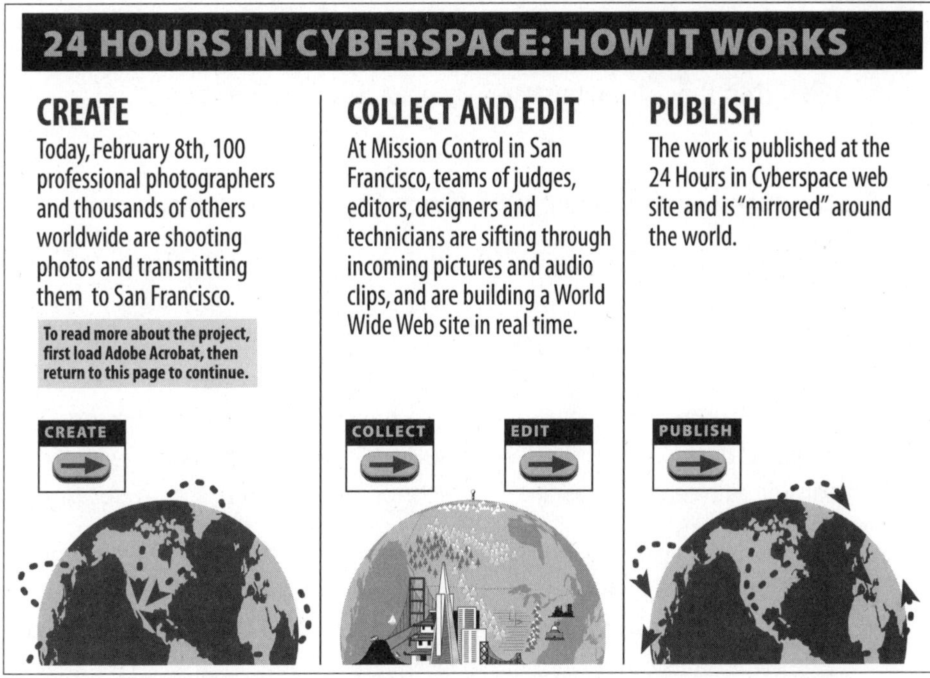

24 HOURS IN CYBERSPACE: HOW IT WORKS
CREATE
Today, February 8th, 100 professional photographers and thousands of others worldwide are shooting photos and transmitting them to San Francisco.
To read more about the project, first load Adobe Acrobat, then return to this page to continue.
COLLECT AND EDIT
At Mission Control in San Francisco, teams of judges, editors, designers and technicians are sifting through incoming pictures and audio clips, and are building a World Wide Web site in real time.
PUBLISH
The work is published at the 24 Hours in Cyberspace web site and is "mirrored" around the world.
CREATE
COLLECT
EDIT
PUBLISH

Figure 2: *We used technology to set the table for our "electronic potluck dinner." (Infographics by Nigel Holmes.)*

The Process: Approaching the Problem

Design is always a very messy process. When we start any project, we gather as much information as we can possibly put our arms around, everything from verbal descriptions to visual references. We do the same thing when we approach a corporate identity or packaging problem. So we began this project the same way.

Because *24 Hours* was based on the traditional publishing model, we spent many hours with the project's director, Rick Smolan, and with his editorial team discussing not just the design conventions of the publishing business, but also the professional editorial team's working environment and the newsgathering and production process. After the shoots for Rick's previous 24-hour projects, he and his editorial team would spend months editing pictures, determining themes, and considering designs.

But *24 Hours in Cyberspace* would be compiled and published in hours, not months. The volume and the speed at which the site would be built would outpace even that of the busiest daily newspaper or wire service.

Collecting and Organizing the Information

Understanding the actual work process was crucial, because we were faced with a unique situation: the need to bring in all the information electronically—everything from images to words to sound—and then to organize those diverse elements and store them for easy access by editors. Those editors, untrained in HTML markup and Web publishing, were to implement our designs for the Web pages and then distribute the pages every 30 minutes over the Internet. These combined needs influenced first technology and then design decisions.

The intensely compressed publication schedule—from months to hours—was what finally drove the decision to design a series of layout templates into which editors could drop images and stories. But the templates were only one part of a three-part design/technology solution. The other two sides to the triangle were a database (Illustra) that would receive, catalog and distribute diverse pieces of electronic material and an "authoring" tool (SitePublisher, by NetObjects) that allowed not only the construction of the 30 preformatted layouts we designed, but also the automation of the navigational links that connected the stories throughout the site. Everything had to be integrated (see Figure 3).

NOTE

More details about NetObjects' SitePublisher immediately follow this essay.

With the content changing all day long, this integration and automation were critical to maintaining a steady work flow and a coherent site (see Figure 4). For example, each Table of Contents showcased a different story every time the site was republished. With each change, the Table of Contents automatically updated itself in SiteBuilder and rearranged new links so that the new story seamlessly fit into the constantly growing "erector set".

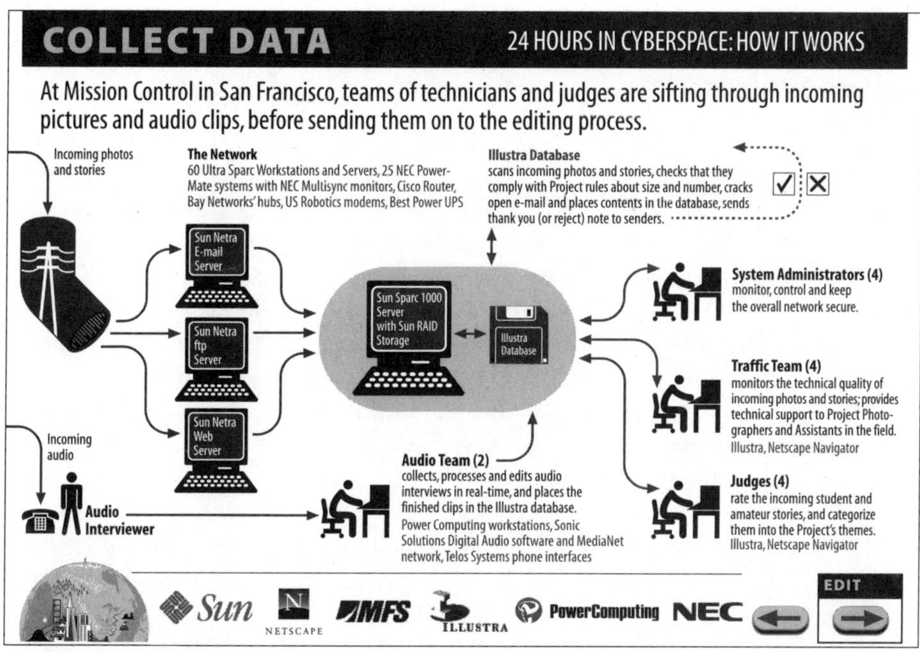

Figure 3: *To keep the site up and running, everything about the publishing process had to be integrated.*

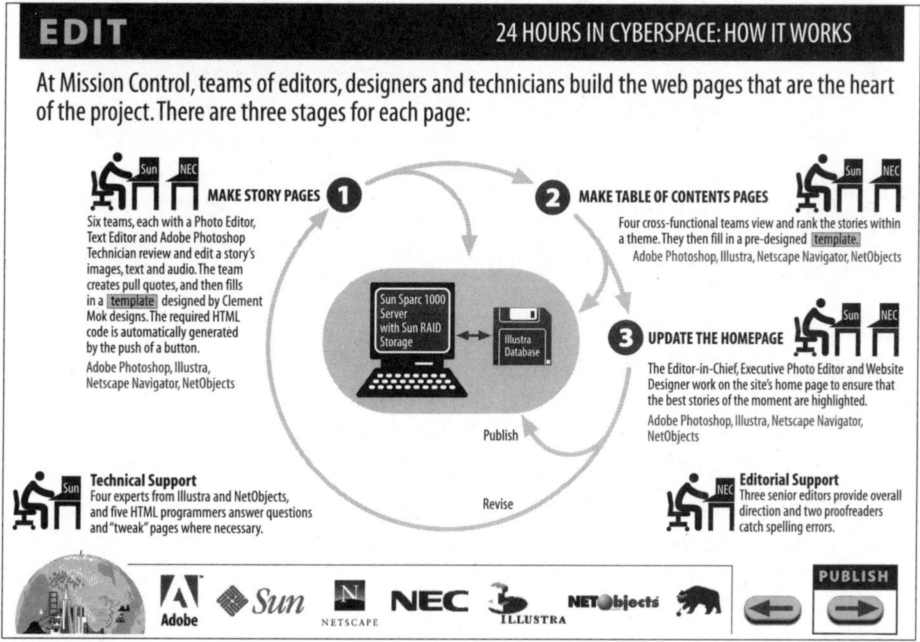

Figure 4: *Integration and automation were crucial to maintaining a steady work flow.*

How It Worked

From their locations around the world, photographers submitted digital photos as attachments to e-mail messages that contained captions for the pictures. The Illustra database opened the e-mail at Mission Control and then stored the images. A traffic team categorized the incoming photos before making them available for the editing teams.

Complementing many of the images were audio clips based on extensive telephone debriefings of the professional photographers, as well as interviews of celebrity visitors to Mission Control. An audio team collected and edited the digitized interviews, which also were slotted into the Illustra database, assigned to appropriate stories, and attached to pages that made the final cut.

Each of the site's six themes had its own editorial team waiting for photos and captions to arrive. The NetObjects publishing tool allowed photo editors to retrieve the images and text stored in the Illustra database, and to lay out the stories using the templates we had designed. A Photoshop expert prepared the images, and an editor wrote stories to fit the template. The tool and the templates allowed editors to use a copy-and-paste approach to build each page and to toggle quickly between different story designs. Once they had selected a template, the tool automatically generated all the HTML code, the links for each page, and updated all of the site's story listings and indices. The NetObjects tool automatically tracked all the pages and allowed editors to republish the Web site with new stories and updated story listings every half hour.

To avoid gridlock during what we all knew would be a day of heavy hits, the site was copied every 30 minutes to MAE West, the world's largest Internet hub, operated by MFS Communications. MFS then passed the sites on to Internet World Expo, MCI, BBN Planet, and Sun Microsystems. Though using one URL, the 4 million far-flung hits were routed to the server nearest them.

Designing Templates

Using templates wasn't a foreign idea to the professional editorial team. On magazines, they often write to fit within a page, and they often work within the parameters of a grid, if not a predesigned template. The template designs addressed editorial concerns like the integrity of the photos, headline placement for stories, pullquotes to draw people into the stories, and size and readability of type.

We worked closely with both Rick and photo director Karen Mullarkey to determine whether the photographers would be shooting 35mm or 4x5 film; whether photos usually ran cropped or full frame; and how the corresponding ratio would translate in pixels and file size—which, in turn, would affect the speed at which the pictures would appear on the screen.

Pullquotes (a sentence or phrase set apart from a story in large type) are a design device used in the publishing business to draw readers into stories. Since we were unable to control the size and selection of type on each viewer's screen, we developed specifications for creating the pullquotes in Photoshop and treating them as graphics the viewer would see exactly as we intended. Whether photographs or graphics, though, each graphic element on a page delays the time it takes for a visitor to see the completed page. But the pullquote was an essential editorial device the publishing pros didn't want to sacrifice.

In addition to creating a solution for the pullquotes, we worked with Rick and Karen to anticipate and accommodate various picture/text combinations: text-heavy pages with only one photo; multiple-image pages; pages with large photos; pages with just one pullquote; etc. In all, we provided the editors with 30 different layouts from which to choose. What the viewer saw as the stories were uploaded on Feb. 8 were electronic pages that looked very much like pages from a photo magazine. You can see some of the templates and the pages that were created from them in Figures 5–8.

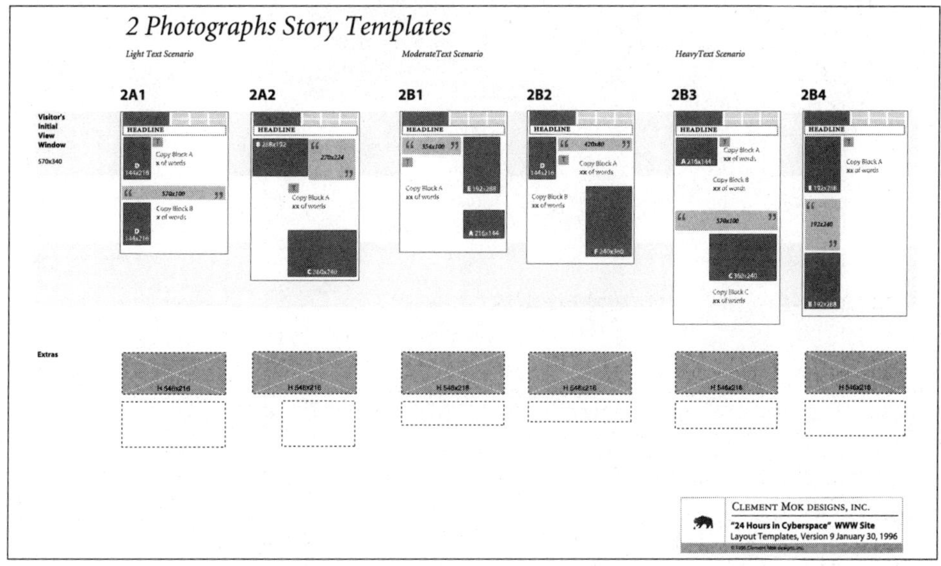

Figure 5: *A set of two-photo templates*

Netscape: Rockin' the Net

Back | Forward | Home | Reload | Images | Open | Print | Find | Stop

Netsite: http://www2.cyber24.com/html/1_154.html

What's New? | What's Cool? | Handbook | Net Search | Net Directory | Newsgroups

24 HOURS IN CYBERSPACE

Faster, Cheaper, Better

Sponsors | How It Works | Site Map | Guest Book | Submit Story | Themes

Rockin' the Net

Digitally savvy band wins fans in cyberspace

San Francisco
California, USA

PREVIOUS | NEXT

The Housejacks, an a capella group from San Francisco, perform at The Paradise Lounge. (Photograph by E. Kashi.)

It's a rocky road to the top of the charts, but the House Jacks, an a capella rock band from San Francisco, are using the Internet to smooth a path. With a mailing list of 10,000 fans around the country, this digitally savvy group is playing to an audience most bands on the rise can only dream about.

The Jacks -- Bert Bacco, Tristan Bishop, Andrew Chaikin, Rob Penn, Deke Sharon and Austin Willacy -- met while singing in various a capella groups in college. They joined forces after graduation and soon moved beyond doo-wop to forge their own style out of a combination of funk, rock, hip-hop and pop.

The group started making a name for itself in the Bay Area, but a rock band can only reach so many people in local clubs. That's where Art on the Net, a not-for-profit virtual-art gallery that also features musicians and poets, comes in. When it offered the band space on its Web server, the Jacks jumped at the chance. AUDIO

"We get all sorts of new fans from our web site."

The Housejacks, an a capella group from San Francisco, bring an unsuspecting fan onstage during their performance at The Paradise Lounge. They use the internet to keep up with fans and release bits of their music from their own wedsite. (Photograph by E. Kashi.)

The House Jacks' home page includes "fun facts" about the band, a datebook with upcoming shows, sound clips, photos and a gift shop, where fans can buy CDs, T-shirts and related paraphernalia.

"The object of this is to get the word out to as many people as possible," said Chaikin, the band's vocal percussionist. "We get all sorts of new fans from the Web site. People just wandering around download our songs and e-mail me to say, 'Wow, I've never heard of you before. Send me stuff.' "

It's paying off. The House Jacks recently signed with Warner Brothers label Tommy Boy Records, and have an album due out by the end of the year.

On a recent Northeast tour, the Jacks added daily, blow-by-blow accounts of life on the road. They even included a song recorded into their laptop while traveling in a Winnebago on the Massachusetts turnpike. "It's a great way to communicate with our fans," said Chaikin.

Site Map | Themes
Sponsors | How It Works | Guest Book | Submit Stories

Figure 6:
A real page set from a two-photo template

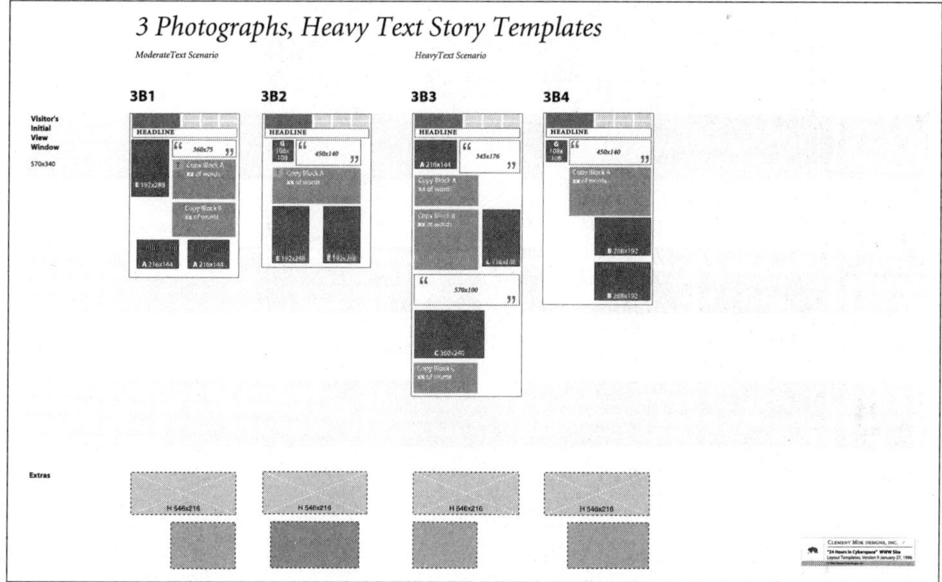

Figure 7: *A set of three-photo templates*

While the traditional publishing model overwhelmingly influenced both the technology supporting the editorial process and the overall look of the actual *24 Hours* pages, the idea of navigating the vast amount of information that would be generated in one day was a concept unknown in traditional publishing and, at the time, untested on this scale on the Web.

Think of a Site as a Subway

When we're designing for the Web, we actually are using a signage system—like a subway map—as a way to organize the structure and navigation. We spend a lot of time doing organizational mapping for all our Web projects. I find myself doing a lot of it in my head and then putting it down on paper and moving it around until things begin to make sense.

With *24 Hours*, we were to publish a large and complex site with multiple themes and sections. The six thematic areas containing the stories, though the primary attraction, were only one part of a much larger site.

Figure 8:
A page designed using a three-photo template

Aside from the stories and the tables of contents introducing them, we wanted pages to perform several functions:

- Invite students and amateurs to participate
- Tell the background of the project to show how the whole process worked

- Document who had visited the site and let visitors know who else had joined them
- Allow visitors to download software they might need to enjoy the site and contribute to it

In all, there were more than 15 major sections in the site, most with additional pages layered behind them.

Neighborhoods Served by the Subway

With the need to organize all these diverse content elements, we started by dividing the overall Web site into four general areas:

1. An editorial area divided into six themes containing the stories, photos, essays, and interviews. The most important section, this was the most challenging to construct because of its dynamism. With content arriving all day long, where the stories fell among the pages within each thematic area would change. The Table of Contents for each area would change all day long, as well.
2. Another area listed participating schools with links to their home pages, displayed an assignment map with the shooting locations of the professional photographers, and, for those with Netscape 2.0, provided a real-time look at who was actually at the site at any given time during the course of the 24-hour period. This area was also dynamic, in that the information in it was changing, but it didn't contain editorial content.
3. A third section included the invitations, instructions, and forms for participants to complete, as well as a guest book for visitors to the site on Feb. 8. We grouped these pages together because of their interactive components: sign-in sheets, submission forms, etc., that visitors could actually complete and return to us.
4. The final section included all the behind-the-scenes information: pages with graphics showing how the whole process worked, pages about sponsors (with links to their home pages), pages about contributors, pages with links to downloading software that would make experiencing the site more fun. Most of these pages linked to outside sites.

Stops Along the Subway Line

We wanted the look of the site to be like that for a magazine. The pages in the editorial section would have a distinct design like that of the main feature stories in a magazine. Like the departments of a magazine, which feature other kinds of diverse content, the other areas in the Web site would share a common look, as well. Originally, we planned to use different background colors to signal the change from one noneditorial area to another. In one of several design/performance compromises, we decided to forgo the color shifts in the noneditorial areas. That way, once a noneditorial background had downloaded, going to another noneditorial area wouldn't slow down the visitor's computer waiting for a new color graphic to appear. Functionally, mapping the three groups as we had originally planned made sense, but graphic distinctions among them were not essential to how a visitor moved around the site. However, the primary consideration—that the editorial section look completely different from everything else—was preserved. You can see a noneditorial page in Figure 9. Compare the look with the editorial page shown in Figure 10.

Getting Around the Site

As far as navigational issues, we decided that certain elements had to be ubiquitous —that visitors had to have access to certain pages at all times. We wanted visitors to always have access to these pages:

- Site Map
- Themes
- Sponsors
- How It Works
- Guest Book
- Submit Stories
- 24 Hours in Cyberspace Home Page

There could be additional cues on some pages, but these were found on all.

The navigational breakthrough was using NetObjects to preformat these links—with no additional coding—on all the pages, even those being updated all day long in the editorial section. Each of the 30 templates we designed already had in place the navigational buttons that would automatically link to the key navigational pages above (Figure 11). The editors composing the new editorial pages

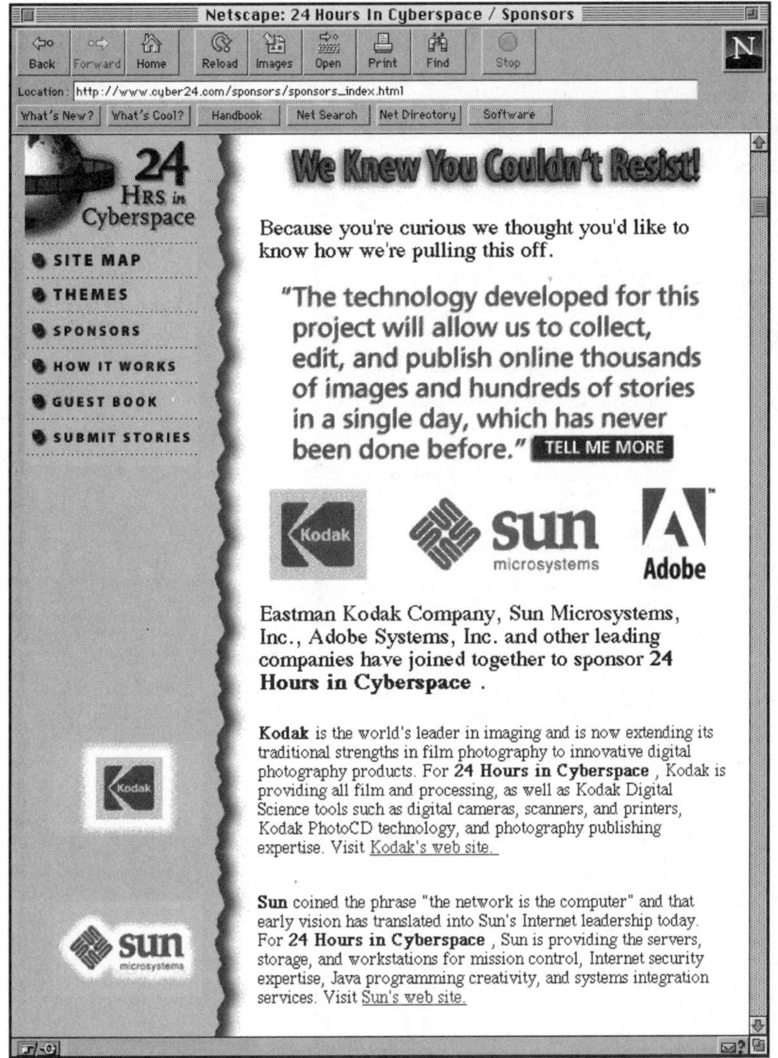

Figure 9: *Noneditorial pages had a distinctive look, as you can see in this sponsor's page.*

dropped in pictures and wrote headlines and copy to fit. They did no coding to link their pages to others in the site. We also wanted visitors to the editorial section to be able to effortlessly move to previous and next pages and built those links into the preformatted templates. Both the design elements and their links throughout the complex site were generated automatically each time the site was rebuilt.

Let's take a look at some of the noneditorial pages that visitors used to navigate the site.

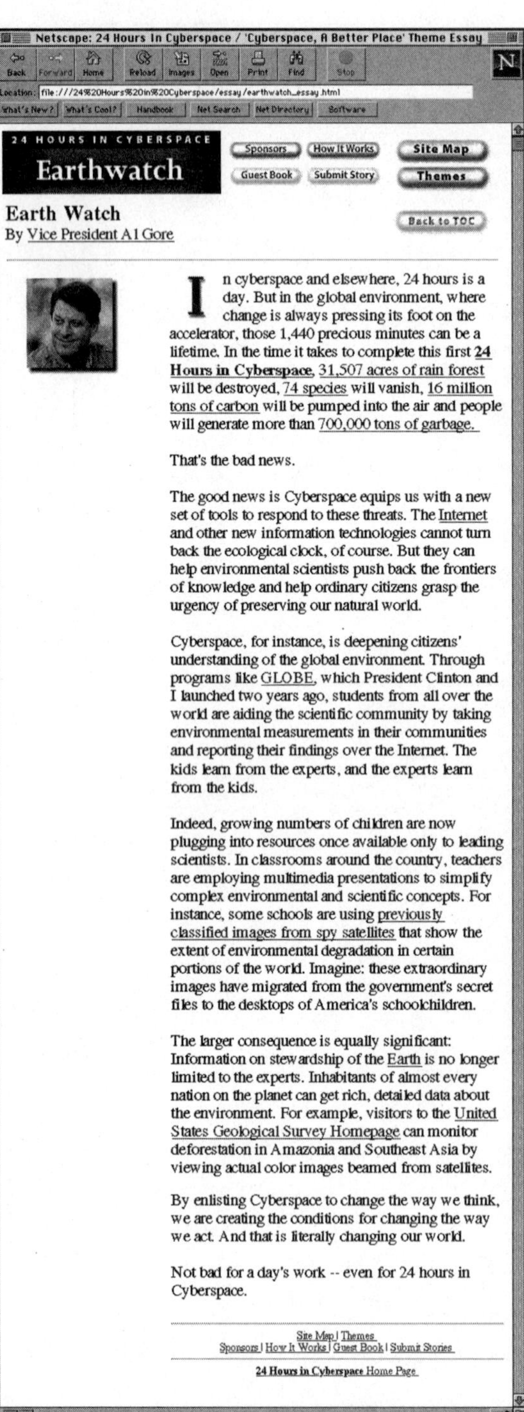

Netscape: 24 Hours In Cyberspace / 'Cyberspace, A Better Place' Theme Essay

24 HOURS IN CYBERSPACE

Earthwatch

Sponsors | How It Works | Site Map | Guest Book | Submit Story | Themes

Back to TOC

Earth Watch

By Vice President Al Gore

In cyberspace and elsewhere, 24 hours is a day. But in the global environment, where change is always pressing its foot on the accelerator, those 1,440 precious minutes can be a lifetime. In the time it takes to complete this first **24 Hours in Cyberspace**, 31,507 acres of rain forest will be destroyed, 74 species will vanish, 16 million tons of carbon will be pumped into the air and people will generate more than 700,000 tons of garbage.

That's the bad news.

The good news is Cyberspace equips us with a new set of tools to respond to these threats. The Internet and other new information technologies cannot turn back the ecological clock, of course. But they can help environmental scientists push back the frontiers of knowledge and help ordinary citizens grasp the urgency of preserving our natural world.

Cyberspace, for instance, is deepening citizens' understanding of the global environment. Through programs like GLOBE, which President Clinton and I launched two years ago, students from all over the world are aiding the scientific community by taking environmental measurements in their communities and reporting their findings over the Internet. The kids learn from the experts, and the experts learn from the kids.

Indeed, growing numbers of children are now plugging into resources once available only to leading scientists. In classrooms around the country, teachers are employing multimedia presentations to simplify complex environmental and scientific concepts. For instance, some schools are using previously classified images from spy satellites that show the extent of environmental degradation in certain portions of the world. Imagine: these extraordinary images have migrated from the government's secret files to the desktops of America's schoolchildren.

The larger consequence is equally significant: Information on stewardship of the Earth is no longer limited to the experts. Inhabitants of almost every nation on the planet can get rich, detailed data about the environment. For example, visitors to the United States Geological Survey Homepage can monitor deforestation in Amazonia and Southeast Asia by viewing actual color images beamed from satellites.

By enlisting Cyberspace to change the way we think, we are creating the conditions for changing the way we act. And that is literally changing our world.

Not bad for a day's work -- even for 24 hours in Cyberspace.

Site Map | Themes
Sponsors | How It Works | Guest Book | Submit Stories

24 Hours in Cyberspace Home Page

Figure 10: *Editorial pages looked much different than noneditorial pages.*

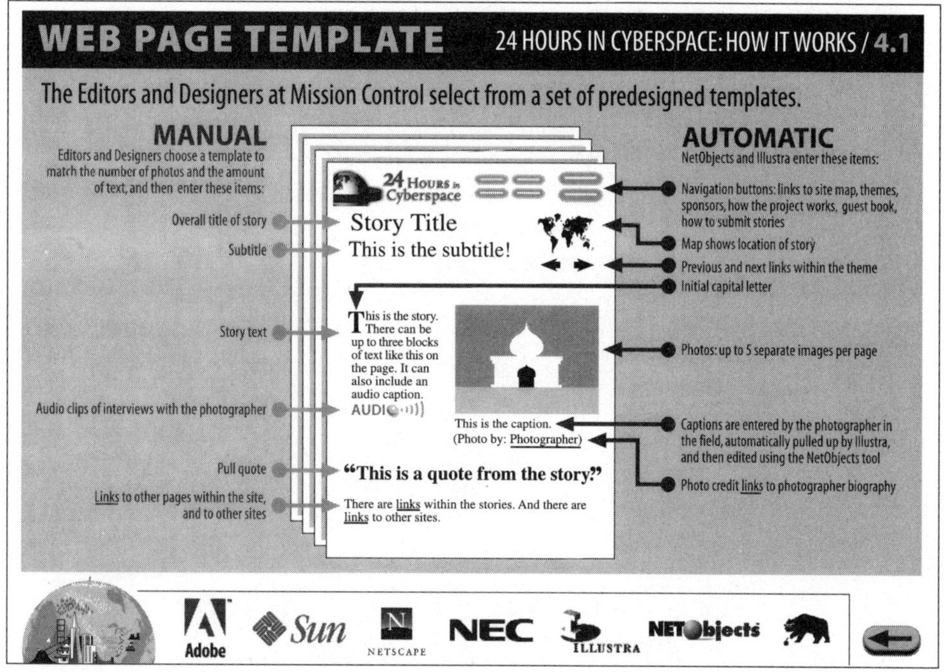

Figure 11: *The templates we designed had all the navigational features built right in.*

The Mission Page Normally, a visitor arrives at a Web site on its home page. Under most circumstances, this is the welcome page and an index. Many sites open with flashy but slow-to-load pictures and graphics. We approached entry to the *24 Hours* site differently for two reasons.

First, the mission page contained a brief project description and acted as a sign-post informing visitors we were using Netscape 1.*x*. We wanted to warn those not using this browser that they would not be seeing what we had planned. We even provided a link so that they could download the software if they chose.

The page also served as a form of traffic control on the day of the event, warning people on Feb. 8 that if they were faced with slow performance, they could try entering from one of our mirror sites around the world, all of which contained exactly the same information. We provided specific links to Tokyo; Washington, D.C.; London; or one of 14 other U.S. sites.

Finally, this mission page provided a means to enter the *24 Hours in Cyberspace* site.

The Home Page

This is the site's point of entry from the mission page (see Figure 12). Instead of treating it as a traditional (if you can call anything *traditional* in such a new medium) home page with an index, we designed it more like an editorial "teaser" page, with links to three showcased stories as well as to other specific areas within the site.

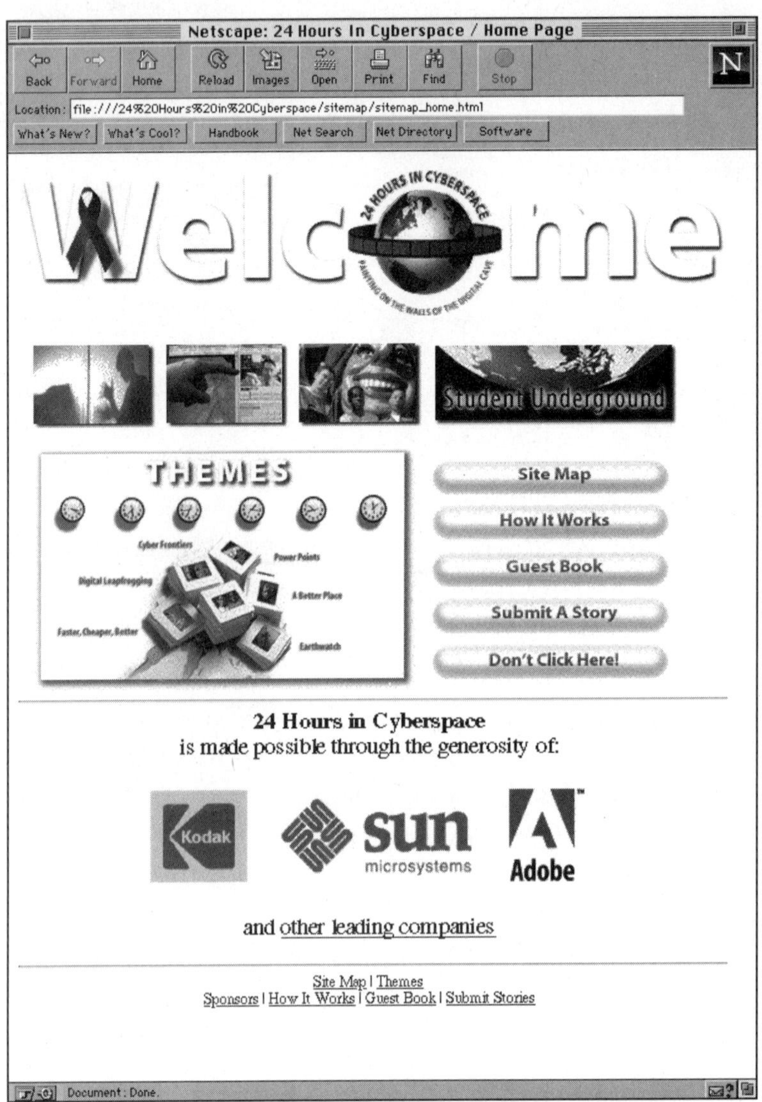

Figure 12: *The home page was a "teaser" page with some links to showcased stories.*

The Site Map This page provides links to all the site's primary areas, both graphically and with text (see Figure 13). It served more like a traditional home page, and we assumed that most people would use this page as their chief navigational tool. There are links to this page from every page within the site.

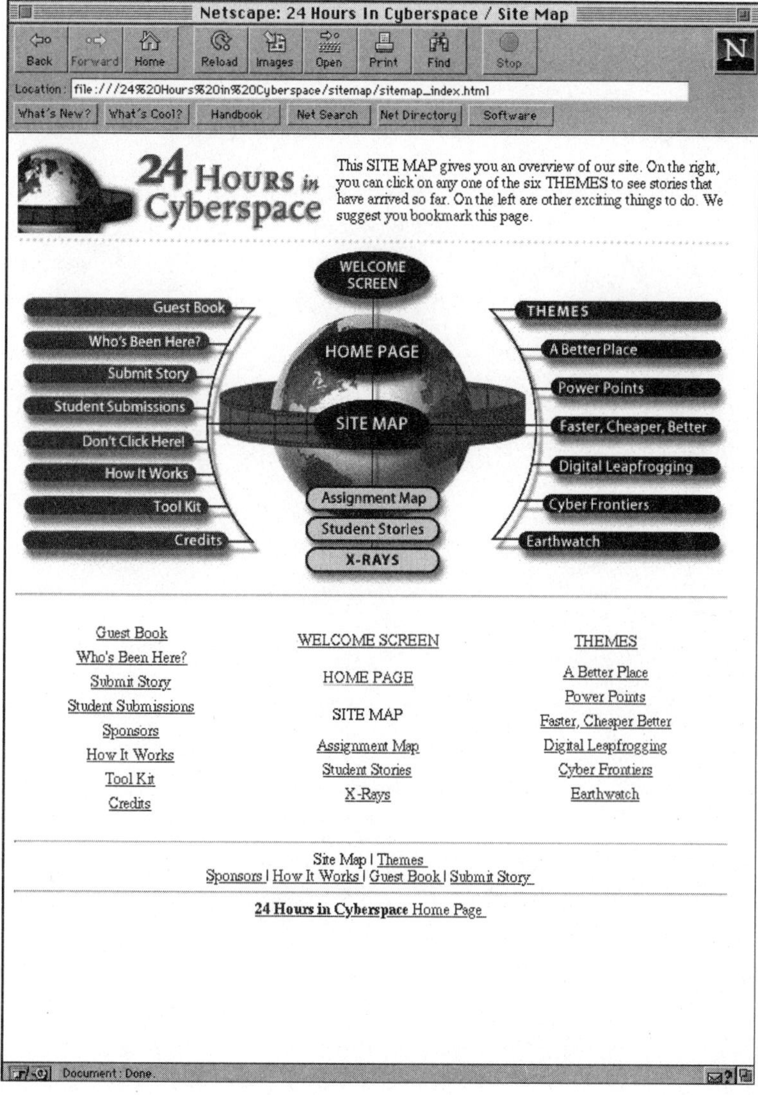

Figure 13: *The Site Map page provides links to all the site's primary areas.*

The Themes Page This page is not unlike a magazine's table of contents, in that it displays the six editorial themes (see Figure 14). Each thematic area accessed from this page contains related stories, pictures, and sometimes audio. Individual table of contents pages (see Figure 15), with introductory essays linking to a continuation page, follow the Themes page. There are links to this page from every page within the site.

D-Day Arrives

After months of preparation and weeks of testing, Feb. 8 arrived. There was no turning back. The world, literally, was watching. Mission Control was crowded with almost as many reporters and photographers covering the event as there were editorial participants making it happen. Tension and excitement hung heavy in the air.

But those of us on the front lines were as exhilarated as we were tense. Our work had paid off. Stories and pictures were pouring in, were being routed appropriately, and being formatted and broadcast over the Internet as planned. Occasional bottlenecks were the kind to be expected when previously untrained editors set about using new tools in a new medium. The preformatted templates and the NetObjects software were succeeding beyond our highest expectations.

The March, 1996 Seybold *Report on Desktop Publishing* had this to say about the project:

> *Everyone talks about repurposing and automating; few are able to do it for magazine-style illustrated stories. This site looked good...editors did not have to fiddle around fixing work they had already done, just because a page was being updated. The system took care of building all the generated navigational links (next page, previous page, etc.), freeing the writers to focus on their stories instead of on repetitive navigation buttons....The final look and feel of the site was first rate, well above what's usually found on the Net....From every angle, [the site] was certainly a project everyone could be proud of having produced....The only thing better than watching the project unfold on Feb. 8 will be to visit the final site next month.*

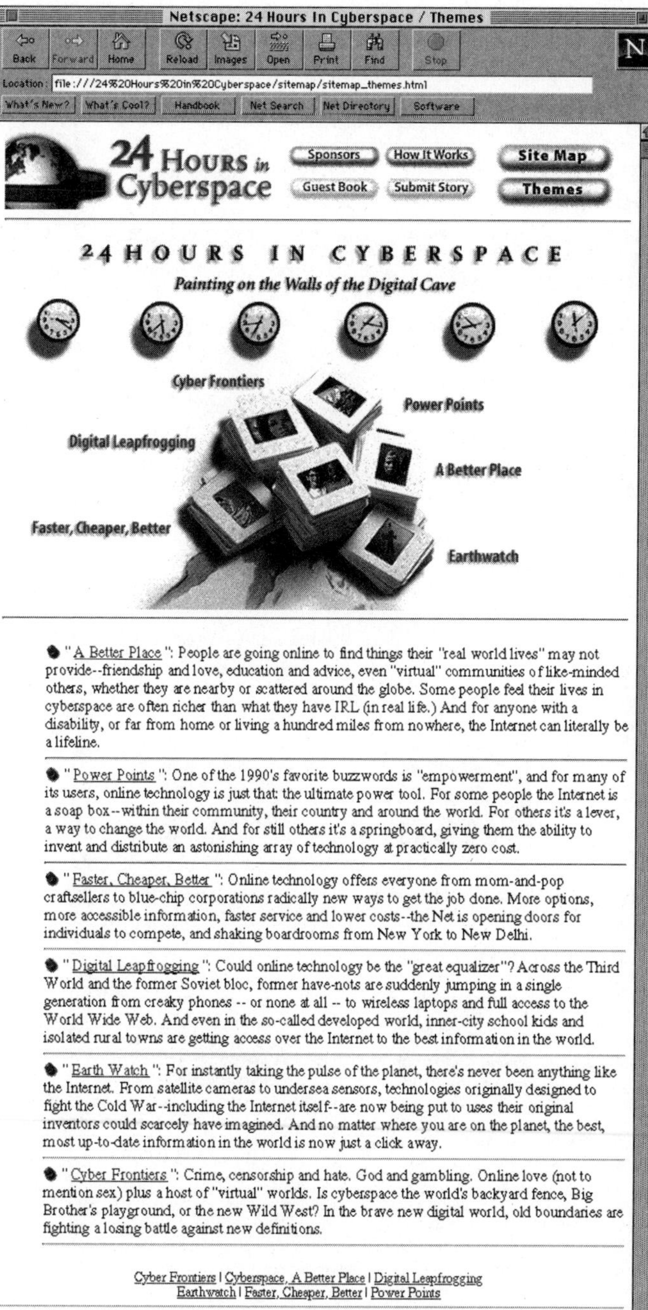

Figure 14:
The Themes page displays the six editorial themes and acts as a sort of table of contents for the site.

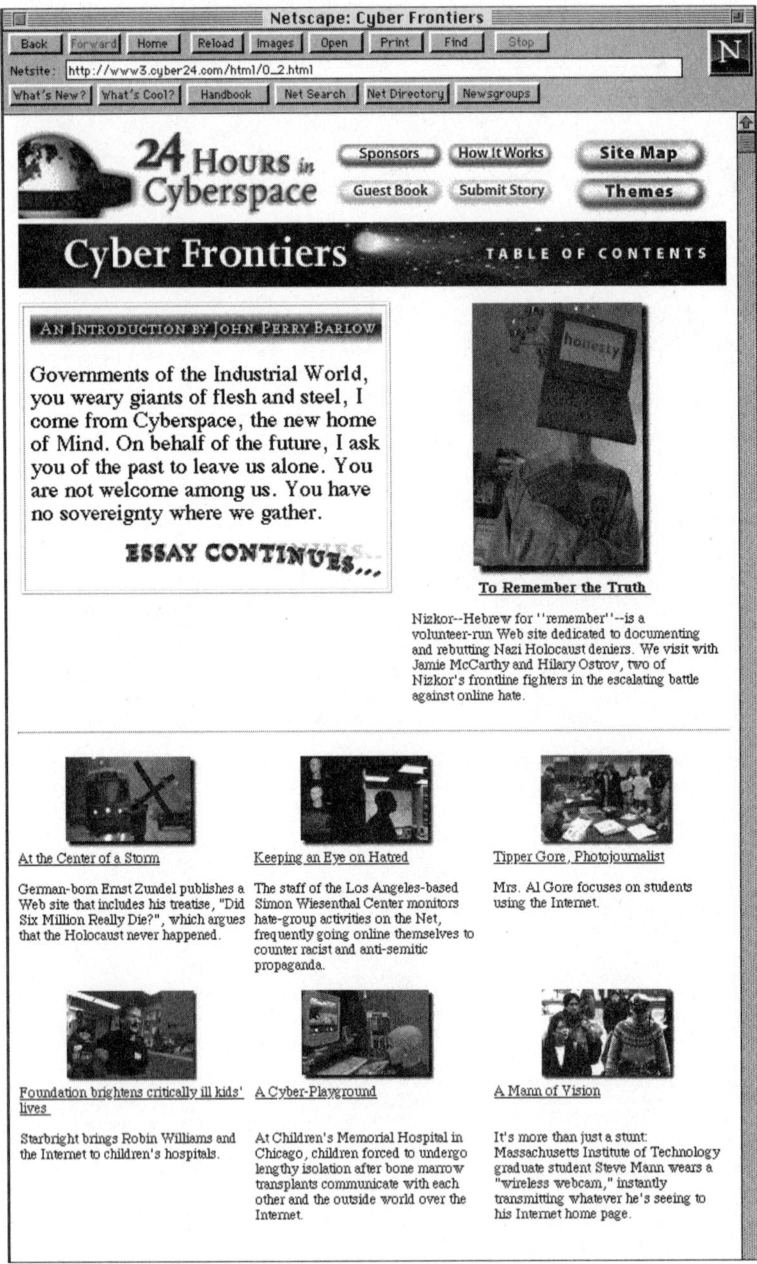

Figure 15: *Individual table of contents pages followed the Themes page.*

In fact, the near flawless execution of the day's events took us all by surprise. Thinking that the experimental nature of the project would likely result in numerous bugs to fix, we originally had planned to showcase the site only until midnight of Feb. 8. Then we would conduct a massive overhaul and relaunch on March 17 with the permanent *24 Hours in Cyberspace* Web site. Instead, the site was so clean that we left it up and, with the flexibility the Web provides us, continued to make adjustments until the permanent site was "completed."

Learning from Experience

With the World Wide Web evolving into an increasingly dynamic and interactive medium, perhaps the most significant notion for designers to keep in mind is their role as members of a larger team. No longer is it sufficient just to receive raw material and turn it into an attractive package for a particular audience. As *24 Hours in Cyberspace* clearly demonstrates, dynamic Web projects require collaboration with a much larger set of colleagues than ever before and, increasingly, a deeper understanding of those colleagues' actual work processes and work environments. I can't over-stress how critical that understanding was to the successful design and construction of the *24 Hours* site.

An additional caveat for designers approaching the Web: test, test, test. With technology driving design as never before, testing has to be a primary consideration. Basically, Studio Archetype is a Macintosh-based design house. But Netscape 1.*x* works slightly different on Windows than it does on Mac, and it works differently on Sun than on either of them. We had to test the designs on as many different computer systems as possible to ensure there were no unpleasant surprises for non-Macintosh–based visitors. And how did that influence design? Just one example: a well-placed image on a Mac might look perfectly dreadful on different system. We had to create flexible spaces for the images so that they would look good and sit well on the page regardless of the computer the visitor was using. Fortunately, this also produced a great design result. We had to leave lots of white space around the photographs, which, of course, showcased them nicely and pleased the photo editors.

Also, designers should keep in mind that while Web design is fundamentally no different than design for other media, the skills it requires do differ. Designing for the Web demands knowledge and experience with both print-based media and with computer-based multimedia. Experience in print media requires an understanding of that world's language and way of doing things. Raw artistic and design talent don't hurt. Designers in multimedia must understand graphical user interface design—that the viewer doesn't just see but also interacts with the information on a computer screen. The multimedia designer also must have a well-developed sense of how to construct a story in a time-based medium. A hybrid of the two worlds, the Web requires skills from them both.

Finally, designers must work with these key points when creating Web sites:

- Start with your audience's needs, desires, and interests.
- Remember your audience's technology limitations. Sophisticated graphics and images may take so long to download that your audience will just leave the site.
- Don't frustrate your audience. Provide easy-to-read maps when they enter the world you create.
- Remember that new technology may come along to change everything except remembering the audience.

What Will Web Sites Look Like in the Future?

Two years ago, there was no such thing as the World Wide Web. Until Feb. 8, there was no tested means of integrating volumes of newly generated, diverse kinds of material for pages to be created and seamlessly uploaded on the fly.

Already, publishers like Dow Jones are using the Web to create customized publications for subscribers who determine for themselves the kinds of information they want to receive. This is just a peek, I think, at what the future holds.

With computers' increased capability to integrate diverse media such as video, audio, text, and still images, and with the convergence of cable television and telephones, the imagination reels with possibilities.

While I hesitate to predict what the Web will hold in five years, I'd like to close by expanding on my original thoughts: that design is about bringing order to the world's chaos—particularly the chaos of information that is flooding us today. Our responsibility does not really change with the emergence of "new" media. While the Web is a new and evolving medium, there is, really, precious little that is new about what we are doing with it. The first records of humanity were informed by efforts to communicate beyond sightline and earshot, to pass on word about hunting grounds, or simply to defy mortality. Like much of the work being done on the Web, these efforts have blended word with image, movement with music. What is novel about reading poetry as you listen to somebody else read it aloud? What is new about blending animation with music, playing complex games with unseen opponents, or viewing a painting up close? Disregarding the absence of a nifty interface and clickable hotspots, most elements of this new medium are represented in the old. The packaging may change, and the vocabulary might shift—but there remains nothing new under the sun.

NetObjects

Company Profile

NetObjects was founded in November of 1995 by Rae Technology Inc. and Clement Mok Designs (now known as Studio Archetype). NetObjects was formed to create products, tools, and technologies that make it easier for people and businesses to communicate and deploy information on the Web. NetObjects' first set of products, lead by Site Publisher, will address the area of creating sites. Target customers include Internet and intranet Web designers, developers, publishers, and Web masters.

David Kleinberg, Executive V.P. in Marketing and Sales, has eleven years' experience in software product development, marketing, and sales. Prior to Rae, David spent three years with Macromedia. As Director of Product Marketing, he led the transition of Macromind Director 2.0 from an animation tool to the industry-leading multimedia authoring tool. Before Macromedia, David was at Apple Computer for five years, where he conceived of and managed the development and launch of KanjiTalk, the Japanese implementation of the Macintosh OS. He has an M.B.A. from Stanford and a B.A. from Georgetown University.

Essay

The New Web Publishing Paradigm and NetObjects

by David Kleinberg, Executive Vice President of Marketing & Sales, Founder

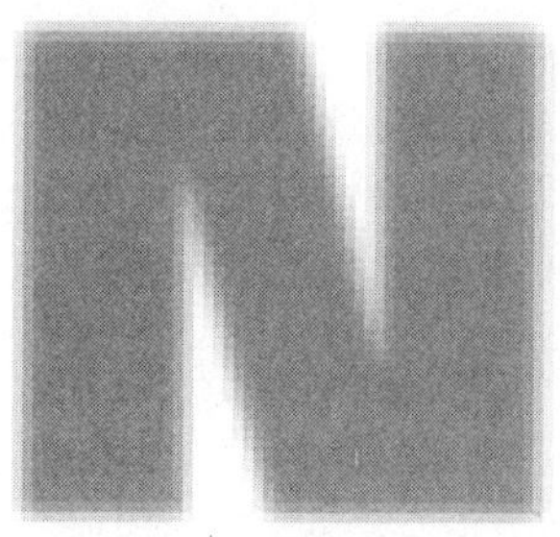

OW THAT COMPANIES such as Netscape have made it easy and inexpensive to view information on the Web, the new paradigm of Web publishing and production is emerging. This publishing model requires a new set of processes, roles, and tools. Current products, typically document- or database-centric, are either too hard to use or too limited in functionality to adequately meet the broad needs of Web publishers. People designing and authoring on the Web need tools to easily and automatically create and maintain sophisticated, high-quality sites. NetObjects' products will dramatically improve the ability of a broad range of authors to automatically design and produce their work on the Web.

To understand the unique value that NetObjects (**http://www.netobjects.com**) tools will provide, we will first review the special nature and challenges of creating content for the Web. The *24 Hours in Cyberspace* project, whose design was discussed in the previous essay, provides a case study to illuminate the issues of creating, publishing, and maintaining a relatively large, frequently changing, well-created site, we will walk through the entire production of the *24 Hours*

project and show how the NetObjects SitePublisher tool was used to automatically create, publish and instantly republish content on the Web. That process also applies to simpler sites. The essay concludes with a comparison of NetObjects' approach towards authoring and publishing tools to the approach of other companies.

Web Publishing: New Medium, New Challenges, New Process

While production for the World Wide Web has some similarities with authoring and publishing for other media, such as print, slides, video, TV, and CD-ROM, the differences are significant. These differences create the need for new activities, processes, skill sets, and tools to make authoring and publishing possible.

A Dynamic Medium

One of the most important factors about the Web is that it is a *dynamic* medium. Updating and maintaining a Web site is significantly more complicated than producing CD-ROMs or print, because most Web data and pages change on a monthly, weekly, daily, or even hourly basis. The tools used for creating and publishing sites need to squarely address the challenges of updating. These challenges include

- Gathering the content and maintaining version control and access
- Updating graphic images and text, inserting new pages in the site
- Updating links on and between all pages

Although updating the Web site occurs after the entire project is launched, we list it first because the complexities of updating are significant and often overlooked. In the long run, most of the time and expense involved in Web site production is spent in updating and maintenance.

As the sophistication of a site expands, so should the functionality of the tool set used to publish and republish it. For example, the tool should let the author easily create a few pages, but it also should allow them to create, manage, and update dozens, hundreds, and even thousands of pages. In addition to the scalability of the tool, the intention of the tool vendor should also be considered. If a vendor is focused on providing low-end tools, such as those for single-page authoring, the growth of the overall site created with those tools may be limited. On the other hand, tools designed specifically for the production of very high-end online publishing may lack the ease of use that will be required for the various contributors to the Web site.

Design: Structure and Navigation

Most authors of Web sites tend to ignore the need for—and the difficulties of—organizing content clearly and intuitively. Creating a simple, clear information structure and set of navigation controls is key for success. Small sites have little difficulty achieving clarity, but many sites are growing to hundreds or thousands of pages, making navigation and content management more important than ever.

Most current Web authoring tools provide virtually no support for organizing content into a meaningful information structure, nor for designing the navigation context and controls. Web tools should help the author envision, create, and manage the internal information architecture of the site. The tools should also help the author translate the internal information architecture into the visual graphic elements and their location and characteristics. This makes it easy for users to find information, to know their location within a site, and to locate other information.

The entire graphic and operational design of a site is a challenge, because the site needs to be consistent in terms of corporate identity, aesthetic design, and placement and functionality of buttons and other controls. In larger sites, individual pages are generally created by several different people. Tools should provide the facility for dealing with these design and quality considerations for a variety of individuals working on the same site.

A sophisticated Web site often contains a wide variety of content, including images, sounds, graphics, text from a variety of authors, and data from local and remote databases. All of this content needs to be coordinated by the designers and authors. Additionally, production is generally a team effort, as multiple production and design skills—text authoring, image editing, navigation design, graphics design, scripting, programming—are usually beyond the range of any one person. Tools must provide facilities to access and manage the content, track revisions, and coordinate team contributions.

Technical Considerations: Beyond HTML

The current HTML standard, while popular, is too complex for the average user. Future Web development tools must become dramatically more intuitive for average computer users to create reliable, exciting work. As an analogy, imagine if users of MacDraw or CorelDraw had to write special codes to boldface a word, or if users of Persuasion had to write a script to make one slide go sequentially to the next. Even though the brave have ventured to learn HTML in order to create a page, the complexity of manually creating and regularly updating 50 or 200 pages is too high for most time- or cost-conscious organizations. Hand-crafting pages is a challenge that tends to grow proportionally with the number of pages in a site.

Because of the inherent difficulties associated with learning, using, and maintaining HTML code, NetObjects believes that effective Web site authoring tools should require little if any HTML knowledge or use by the author.

The issue of using HTML is only the beginning. To add desired functionality such as animations or databases requires using other plug-ins or applets. Often, these require software programming expertise. Again, NetObjects believes that effective Web site authoring tools should make it extremely easy to add the functionality of plug-ins or applets.

Two-Way Communication and Transactions

An increasing number of organizations want to use Web sites for more than distributing information. They want a variety of two-way interactions with customers and vendors, ranging from simple registration and mail to commercial transactions. If the browser user needs to send information back to the site, an additional set of challenges exist for the author and designer.

A Web site supporting two-way interaction with users needs to be connected to a database. Even the simplest of user interactions via forms must be supported by programming, and sophisticated programming is necessary to send larger amounts of database data or entire pages to users based on their queries or status. Tools need to support the ability of authors and designers to easily create and integrate user forms in interactive Web site configurations.

Different Versions for Different Visitors

Web authors and designers do not have control of the environments in which users will be viewing Web sites. Different browsers, modem speeds, and graphics resolutions are factors that vary by user and affect the user's experience. Currently available browsers all "read" HTML differently, and a page authored for one may not look the same—in fact, may not be displayed at all—in another browser. Some users have relatively slow modems, limiting their ability to quickly view Web sites with a lot of large graphics. Because of these disparities, Web sites usually need to be created in several versions. Tools used to create and publish sites should help Web authors and designers create different versions of the Web site with minimal work.

Ease of Use

The overall ease of use of the tool for the author is a key factor. Most people responsible for a Web site are subject matter experts, not programmers or graphic designers. The popularity of the Web is leading more people to want to create sites. The authoring tools must address all of the issues discussed above and do so with ease. A tool that solves many problems but is difficult to learn and use may cost an organization more time in the long run.

Ease of use is not simply a matter of the number of icons in the interface and their shape. It is about the implicit process that the tool assumes the author(s) will follow, and the ease with which authors can complete that process and deliver the desired results.

Examples of easy-to-use tools for creating slide presentations are Microsoft's PowerPoint or Aldus' Persuasion. In these applications, the operation of and interaction with the tool closely matches the level of the user as well as the process used to create a presentation: start with an outline, decide on a general graphic style, then enter specific information and graphics.

The Web is so new that the process for creating and publishing a site has not been well defined in most organizations. In addition to considering the appropriate process and the previously mentioned design and development challenges, Web authors also need to consider how the tool(s) they select match the level of experience of the authors and/or contributors.

Putting Theory into Practice

Web production is new and unique, as are its challenges. New tools will be needed to publish for the new medium. An ambitious example of publishing for the new medium is the *24 Hours in Cyberspace* Web site (**http://www.cyber24.com**), created on February 8, 1996, using an early version of NetObjects' SitePublisher. We will examine how the *24 Hours* Web site was created and updated, beginning with the specific challenges facing the site's producers. These challenges, as it turns out, are similar to those facing producers in many other organizations.

While the project was high-end, the problems were solved with tools that will be highly applicable to producers of Web sites that contain a modicum of sophistication and complexity. Ultimately, the simplicity of the NetObjects tool belied its power. It made something very complicated very simple.

Building 24 Hours in Cyberspace

24 Hours in Cyberspace was one of the most ambitious real-time Web publishing ventures ever created. In the course of a single day, 100 of the world's top photojournalists from around the globe documented how the online digital revolution is changing people's lives. *24 Hours in Cyberspace* also was one of the largest photographic projects ever attempted. Thousands of photos, audio files, and text files were transmitted and converted into hundreds of stories published on the site. The results were released over the Internet on February 8th, making it the largest one-day online event in Internet history. The site is now a permanent record of the event.

The Challenge

As the *24 Hours in Cyberspace* producers began to think through their project, they identified several key requirements for evaluating tools to create and publish the project. Their needs, with a few exceptions, are quite similar to those of many other Web authors or content publishers for online news and content publishers, businesses, and government and education agencies.

Here are some of the major needs affecting the selection of tools for *24 Hours in Cyberspace*:

1. A large amount of content—digitized image files, digital audio files, and text—would be coming in from various sources. The content had to be assembled into stories for editing.
2. The producers of *24 Hours in Cyberspace* wanted a Web site whose design invited exploration and participation. They sought an easily understood navigational interface so that users wouldn't get lost as they browsed through hundreds of pages of stories and story themes.
3. Story editors would be coming in from all over the country on February 7th and would have only a few hours to learn the development tools before production actually started. Most of the editors were neither computer experts nor very technically experienced. Consequently, the tools needed to be extremely easy to learn and use, and could not require any HTML coding.
4. All the content would be stored in a database. The alternative to storing content in a database would have been to keep the content files in directories. One of the main reasons to use the database was to easily keep track of versions and maintain copyright information. In general, the more complex a Web site, the more important versioning becomes. Because of the number of editors that would be involved in producing each story, it was crucial for each person to be working on the correct version of a story.
5. The site would consist of several sections. The one that would change the most during the 24-hour period was Themes. The Themes section is similar to major sections in other Web sites; it contained six sections, each of which contained various stories. People who visited the site would choose a theme, and from there select a story to view. The major challenge this posed for the tool was that stories had to be assigned in real-time, and the order of stories within a theme changed throughout the day.
6. The site would need to be updated every half-hour with new stories and new arrangements of stories within themes. This meant that the internal information architecture of the site would be constantly changing.
7. Visitors to the site had to be able to click on the Next and Previous buttons on any story page to navigate to the prior or subsequent story. Because new stories would be coming at unpredictable intervals, the tool needed to provide a way to let editors easily place a story anywhere while minimizing (if not eliminating) the time needed to update the navigational links and

controls. This is, in fact, one of the most laborious tasks in updating Web sites, one for which there was no time in this site.

8. The site also needed to be *mirrored* (replicated) in several places around the U.S. and the rest of the world. For this reason, the final site would need to consist of actual pages that could be replicated, rather than a database that would serve pages to be viewed as the browser user made a selection.

It is worth mentioning that many organizations have similar needs:

- Online publishers, such as online newspapers, magazines, e-zines, and subscription-based information services, have needs that closely parallel those of the *24 Hours in Cyberspace* site, with stories and tables of contents requiring frequent updates.
- Financial and investment firms often want to publish frequently changing research reports on companies for their investors.
- In the manufacturing sector, companies want to publish engineering and product specifications to internal technical and marketing groups working on the products.
- Medium and large organizations may want to publish product and service descriptions, pricing and models, and resources available to internal and external constituents on the Web, using multiple authors and frequent updates.

The Solution

In addition to NetObjects' SitePublisher, the *24 Hours in Cyberspace* producers selected Illustra as the multimedia database to collect and assemble the content including story copy and photographs.

In the two months before February 8th, it became clear that there would simply be no time on the day of the event for editors to engage in the typical layout design and production activities that are common to preparing a publication. Since photos and text would be arriving in real-time, the *24 Hours* team concluded that all layouts would need to be created ahead of time in the form of templates for stories, themes, and tables of contents, and that story editors would be able to select from a variety of these precreated templates for their stories. Studio Archetype, formerly Clement Mok Design, built the templates for stories, themes, and tables of contents.

The process for the *24 Hours in Cyberspace* projects started at noon on February 7th when editors came in for training. At 8 PM, the first photographs came in and over the next 24 hours 63 stories were created and published. Here's a look at how it worked.

Site Publisher was used in a process that had several steps. Digital photos, sound files, and text files came in over modem and were stored and organized by story in the Illustra database. Photo editors and copy editors worked on the individual content for each story. Editors could double-click on a photo to edit it in Photoshop, and all changes to the photo would be saved back to the Illustra database. Text editing was performed directly in Illustra. Editors selected and assigned the top five photos to be used in each story. Each story was also assigned a default theme.

Each story editing workspace—called a *pod*—had four computers. Two computers were used for content and were running Illustra and Photoshop. The other two, Windows PCs running NetObjects' Site Publisher, were used for creating and editing stories. All the editors sat side by side to make artistic and journalistic decisions in real-time.

In each pod was a printed book of all the prebuilt HTML page templates created for the tables of contents for the Stories and Theme areas. There are different templates for each story, based on the number of photos in the story.

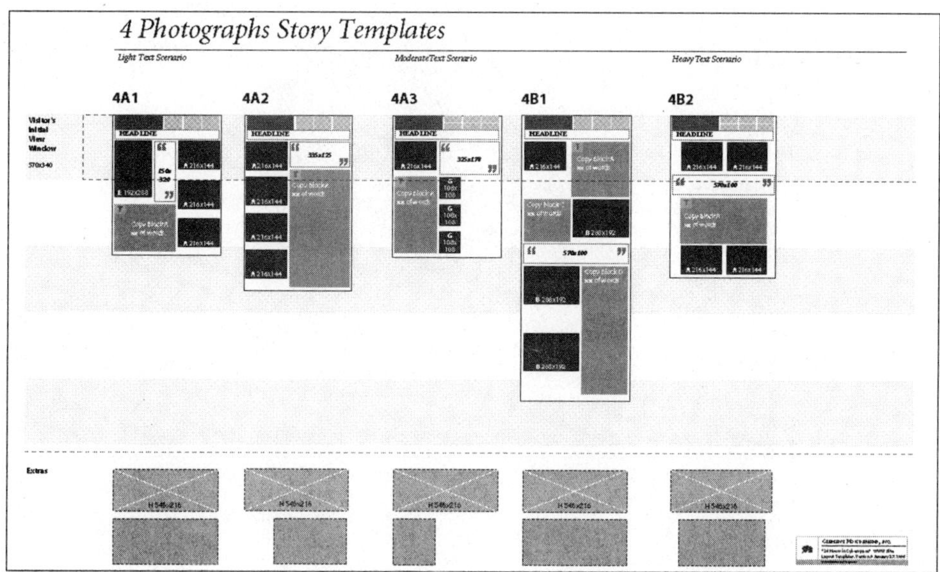

The Steps of the Story-Building Process

After the photos, text, and sound files had been edited, story editors used Site Publisher to create, edit, and publish their stories. The story building process had six steps.

1. Story editors select a story and a story template to be used to display the story.

2. Site Publisher retrieves the content for the story from the Illustra database and the template to display the story. Editors can edit text directly, with all changes automatically stored back in Illustra.

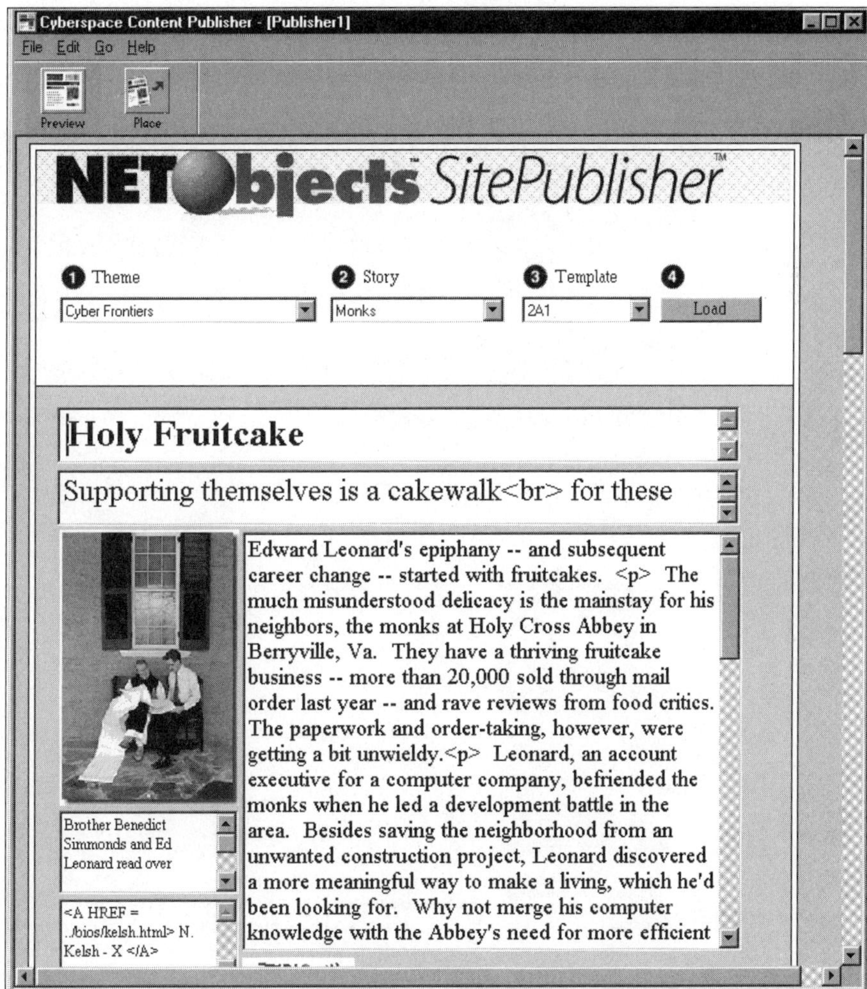

3. When the editor clicks on the Preview button, SitePublisher creates an HTML page containing the story with all its content and previews the story in Netscape Navigator. In displaying the story, SitePublisher has determined which images are needed from the Illustra database, (including the pictures that have been placed into the page along with the theme title bars) and has saved these images on the local hard disk.

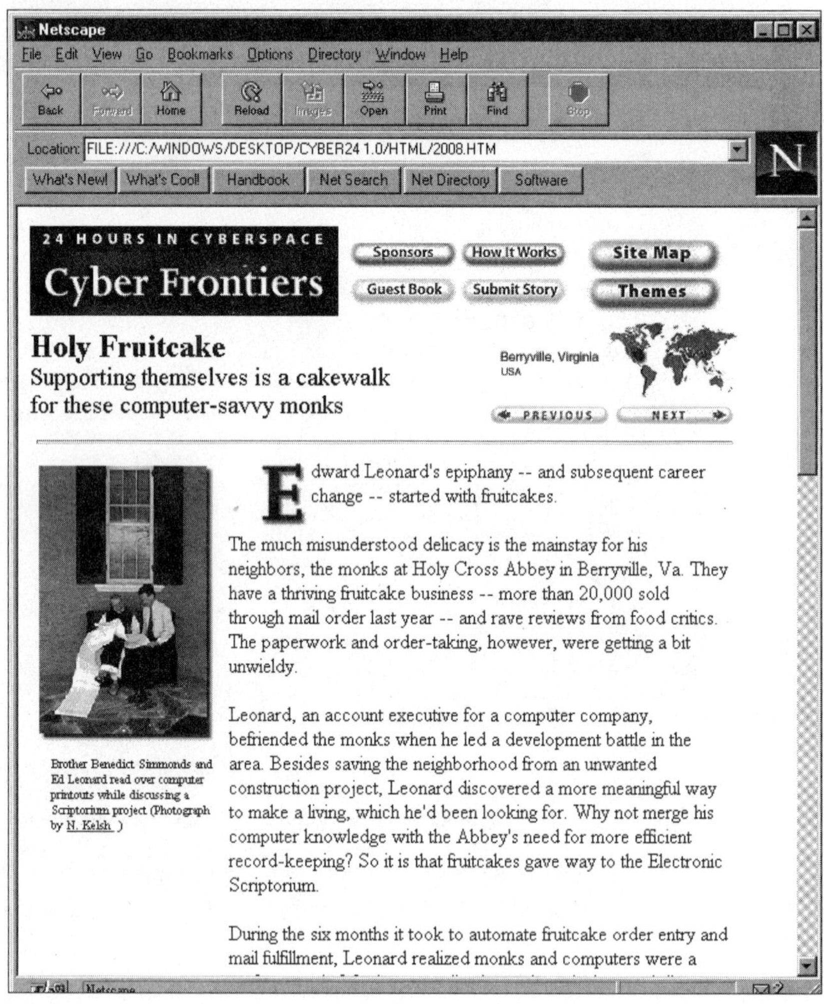

4. Editors select the theme in which the story will be listed. When they click on OK, Site Publisher marks the story as ready for publication, puts the page in the Illustra database, and tells Illustra which themes the story has been assigned to.

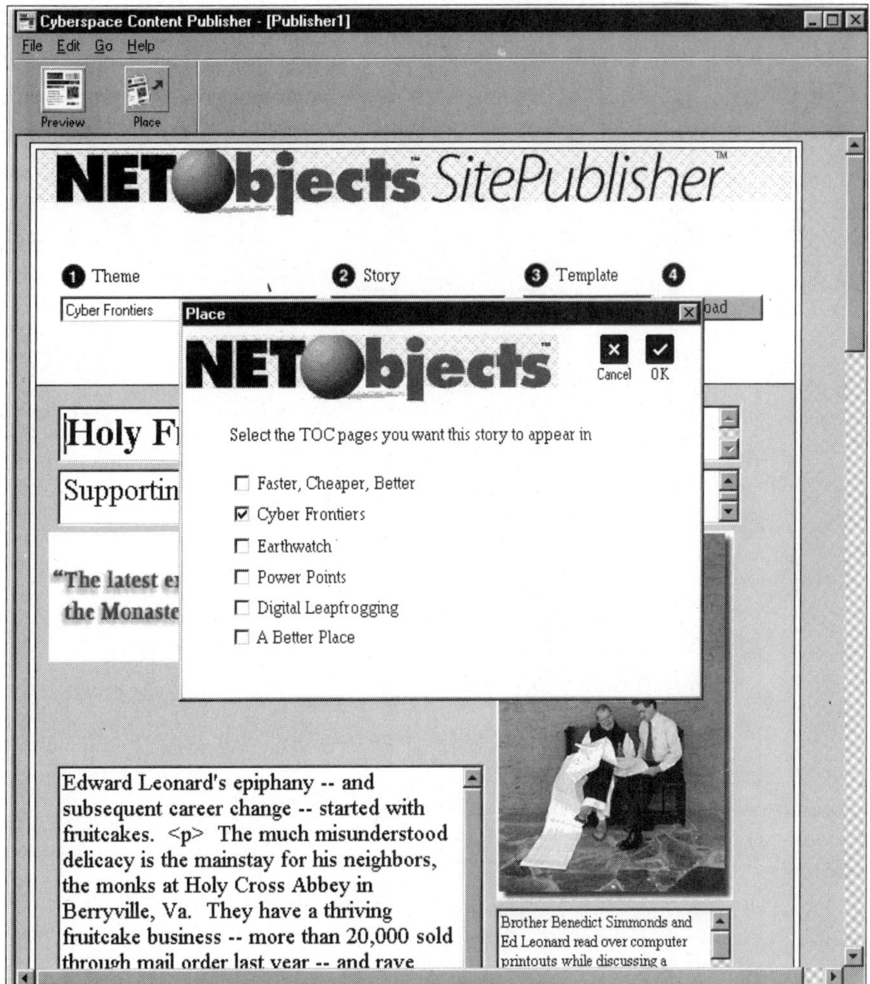

5. Editors for the table of contents pages decide the order of stories. The table of contents pages are also previously created templates, and the dialog box in the template lets editors easily order the stories that are assigned to each table of contents.

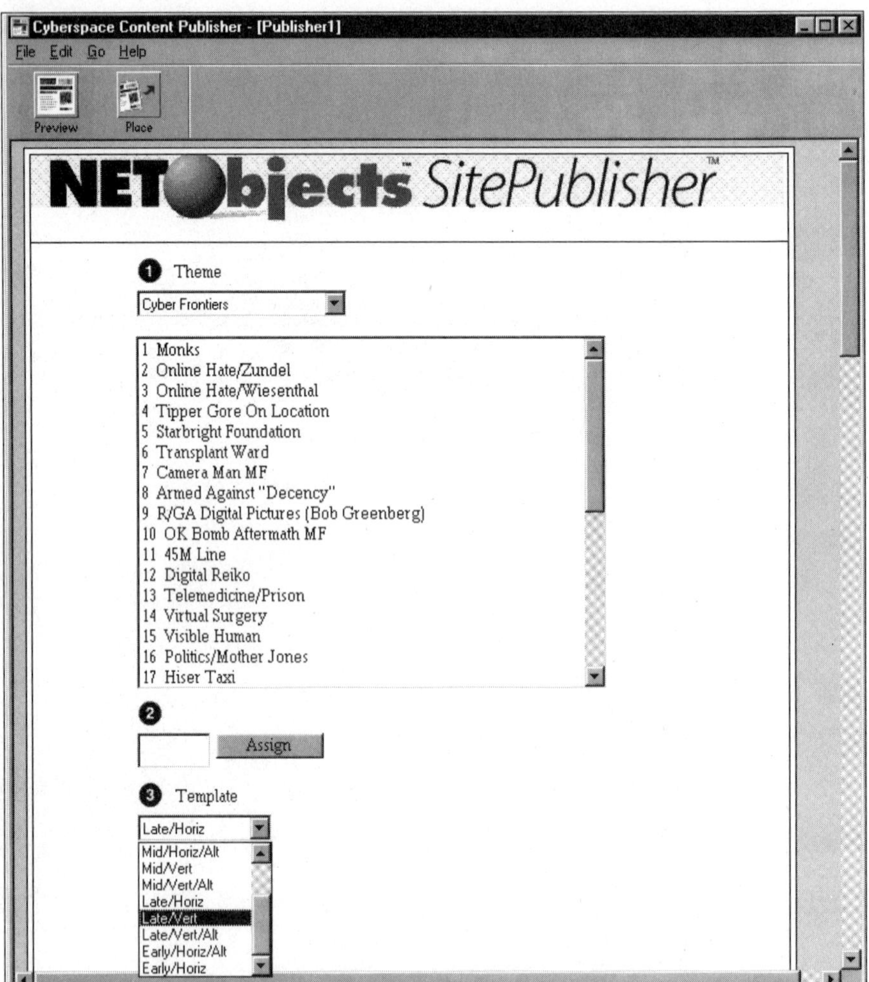

6. When the editor clicks on the Stage Site button, SitePublisher retrieves from Illustra all pages and data to be published along with all of the associated images and title bars, and builds the entire site, including all navigational links and controls, for final editorial review before mirroring it to the live Web servers. Site Publisher assembles the final site by placing all navigational controls on each page and by making all of the interpage links, including next/previous, up/down, and cross-links for the Next and Previous buttons. Site Publisher writes the pages and content into directories on the staging server.

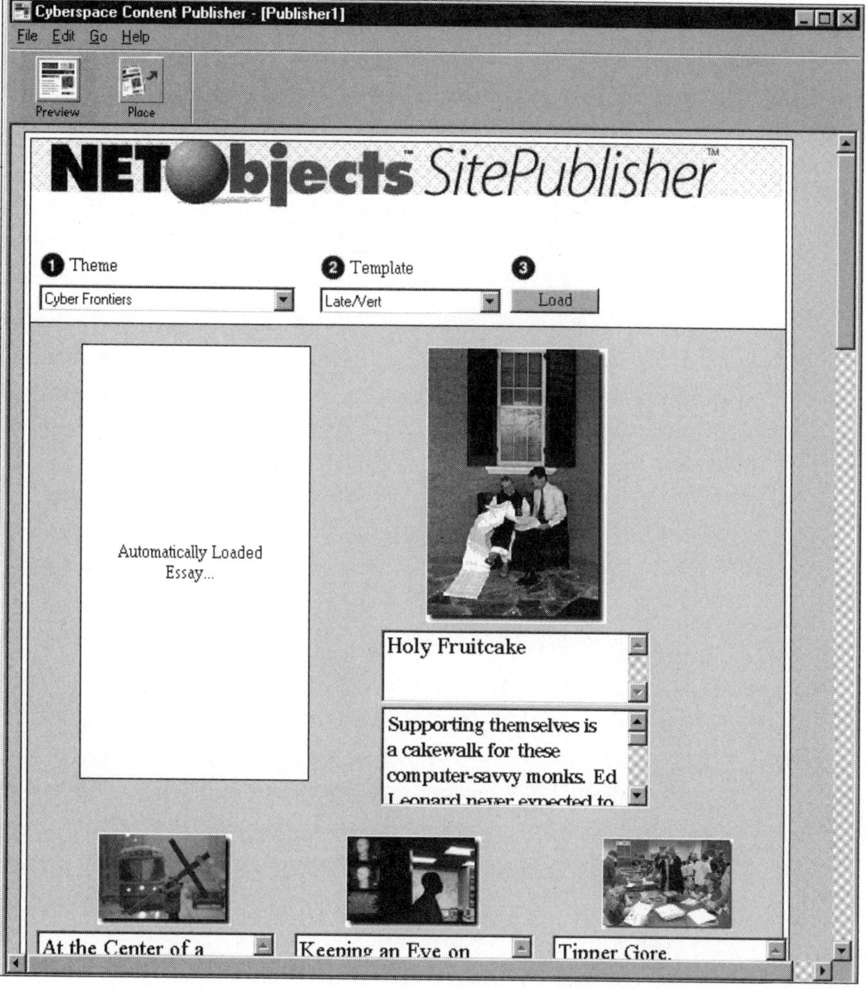

Creating a Story with SitePublisher

Reviewing the process for an actual story helps explain more precisely how the process really worked.

> *We could not have done the* 24 Hours in Cyberspace *project without NetObjects site-building and site management technology. None of the authoring tools we looked at, particularly the page-oriented tools, such as Vermeer's FrontPage, let us retrieve data, compose pages, and continuously publish and update the site with all navigational links automatically created and updated in the way NetObjects' technology does.*
>
> —Tom Melcher, Producer, *24 Hours in Cyberspace*

> *Although all the support from well-known vendors was critical to the [*24 Hours in Cyberspace *project's] success, we must highlight NetObjects as the linchpin technology. While the event itself is compelling, even more interesting is the future of NetObjects software. Any company that produces content, from Time Warner Inc. to Microsoft, will be looking at this technology, whether from the perspective of friend or predator. NetObjects is about to dance with some of the biggest elephants in the world.*
>
> —Dataquest *Quick Take*, 2/5/96

> *Perhaps the most interesting part about the process is how quickly the editors learned and began using the new tools they had never seen before. Most of the work was on content creation and editing, not learning how to use a particular tool. NetObjects provided a critical component for the editorial team on the Cyberspace project. The NetObjects tools, and the templates designed for them, made on-the-fly publishing for the Web possible. The extremely simple, WYSIWYG interface allowed us to concentrate on writing, editing, graphics, and proofing.*
>
> —Pat Soberanis, Editor, *24 Hours in Cyberspace*

NetObjects and Existing Web Production Tools

To help the reader understand the differences in our products, we'll comment briefly on the known available tools for creating and authoring for the Web. We'll also look at the approaches of the kinds of tools we know about and at our own distinctive approach.

Tools for the Web can be grouped into several categories. It is important to understand where a tool falls in relation to these categories in order to select the appropriate tool for your Web site.

Content Creation Tools

Content creation tools let authors create and edit particular pieces of media or content. Examples include Adobe Photoshop, Macromedia Director and Shockwave, RealAudio, and mFactory. These tools let the author create content that can be used on a particular Web page or Web site. They should not be confused with tools that primarily create pages or sites.

Database-centric Creation Tools

Database-centric creation tools let the author retrieve data from a database and display that data in Web pages. These tools typically may have some Web page authoring capability, primarily to facilitate getting particular database records published. These tools do not typically provide capabilities for information design, site design, or site management. Examples include Spider Technologies and Bluestone's Sapphire Web.

Document-centric Creation Tools

Document-centric authoring tools focus on letting the author create an individual Web page or a few Web pages. Examples include Microsoft's Front Page, Netscape's Navigator Gold, Adobe's PageMill, BB's Edit, and SoftQuad's Hot Metal Pro. These tools often have some facility or companion products to display the total set of literal pages and total set of external files and links. Examples of these file manager products include Adobe's SiteMill and Netscape's Navigator Gold.

Application Development Tools

Application development tools let authors build high-end sites that focus on sophisticated two-way communication and transactions between the browser user and the Web site. Examples include NeXT's WebObjects, and Haht's Haht Site. These tools are typically database oriented, offer scripting capability, and permit the creation of fully dynamic pages generated on the fly, depending on the browser user's profile and the response to a particular query.

Web Site Publishing Tools

Web site creation and publishing tools focus on letting the user design and develop a Web site with the site itself as the primary subject. The distinguishing features of this type of product is that they are centered on the site: data, design, information architecture, and navigation—and that they scale to support sites of many pages. Examples of these products include Netscape LiveWire and Microsoft Gibraltar.

A Concluding Thought

Web site authoring tools are in their first generation and have a ways to go before they catch up to their cousins in desktop publishing and other production areas. Because the tools are likely to change significantly, the key to determining whether an authoring tool will suit your needs is to evaluate the tool directly, to understand its feature set, and especially to understand its core paradigm and authoring model. Since it is virtually impossible for an authoring tool to change its core paradigm after it has come to market, these factors will indicate where the tool is likely to proceed in future versions. This, in turn, gives you a good sense of how the tool fits your needs for both the short and long term.

The Net Magazine

Company Profile

Shel Kimen is reviews editor for *The Net* (**http://www.thenet-usa.com**), a monthly print publication guiding new and experienced users through the Internet. Spending her childhood in a household with computer programmers for parents, she is no stranger to the binary landscape and has been online since 1989, first as a member of the Aurora BBS, and then through the channels of CompuServe, AOL, ISPs, etc., until now she has a T3 connection directly to her brain.

Besides tapping out wisdom for readers of *The Net*, Shel has written for *CD-ROM Today*, *Boot*, *Geek Girl*, various multimedia CD-ROM projects, and a series of online zines including *Spiv*, *Foxy*, and *Birdhouse.org*. In the last year, she has seen over 30,000 Web sites—far too many for any one person to be subject to—in a selfless attempt to filter the dizzying and oft-daunting entanglement that is the World Wide Web for surfers across the globe. Current projects include co-authoring a book about VRML with Mark Pesce (VRML founder) and taking over development of *The Net*'s Web site. If all goes as planned, she will be a fully digitized 3D Avatar, available for downloading, by 1997.

She can be reached at **shel@thenet-usa.com**.

Chapter Profile

The sheer proliferation of Web sites is a problem for both publishers and people surfing the Web. Publishers must constantly campaign against a barrage of other groups offering information. This is especially true of established name brand content providers who publish for the livelihood or their firms, not just as a hobby. Web surfers simply cannot see all the available information at any given time. In this environment, a third party must be available to filter sites for quality and fit them with a users interests. That is why the role of a Web site reviewer will become more important in the next few years as the growth of the Web continues to explode.

Addressing the above needs is *The Net* magazine's most valuable mission. It wins great respect for fulfilling these needs by reporting about new Web developments and explaining what they mean to Internet users. As reviews editor for *The Net*, Shel Kimen devotes considerable time to reviewing sites, distinguishing the great from the mediocre from the poor. She has become a reliable source to regular readers as they search for information to make their Web experience satisfying.

Shel has also built several of her own sites over the last few years and as a result, her insight in the field of Web design is for the professional designer who takes Web design personally. She is conscious of what attracts Internet users and what drives them away. Compared to other contributors to this book, she is less of a scientist and more of a theorist. She emphasizes approaching Web design from the perspective of the viewer rather than that of the creator. In this essay, she discusses potential pitfalls for first-time designers, strategies for enticing a new visitor to a site to return again and again, and sources of inspiration for the creative process.

Essay

Balancing Fun and Function

by Shel Kimen, Associate Editor

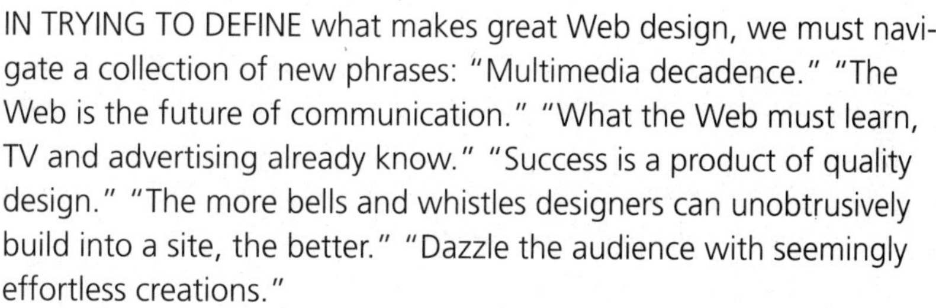

IN TRYING TO DEFINE what makes great Web design, we must navigate a collection of new phrases: "Multimedia decadence." "The Web is the future of communication." "What the Web must learn, TV and advertising already know." "Success is a product of quality design." "The more bells and whistles designers can unobtrusively build into a site, the better." "Dazzle the audience with seemingly effortless creations."

The "seemingly effortless" part is less a problem today than it was 12 months ago, but it still takes skill to master. When a page has a smooth layout, it reads like a creation in Quark: formatting, fonts, images. Because of the technological edge that underlies the Internet, design for the Web needs to be consistent with that technology. It is a myth that designers have to be programmers, just as it's a myth that programmers have to be designers. If the team works well together, no one needs to overstep the boundaries and mix up the gene pool. But let's not discount the fact that when an artist is at least familiar with programming and a programmer has at least a fraction of a sense for style and design, the project will be that much better.

Form Follows Function—Or Does It?

The traditional modern movements in art and design have relied heavily on the notion that form follows function. While this may be true in most present design arenas, it is not necessarily the case with HTML. HTML, while not extremely complicated, is a programming language. If the function of a Web site is to enchant Web surfers with snazzy graphics and a smooth layout, while simultaneously disseminating information, the designer must be very attuned to the concept of HTML form before expecting any sort of function. Improper handling of HTML can be a disastrous and dizzying mess.

All too often I run across sites that are reaching high for an artsy look to show off content. Unfortunately the images aren't aligned, the text wraps outside the browser window, or the tags (HTML commands) that are normally found in brackets behind the scenes are visible on the actual page. These are examples of poor copyediting skills and careless, though not completely inexcusable, errors. Detail is of significant importance in any programming language, as it is in design—which makes creating Web space doubly daunting.

The HTML standard, while quickly evolving, is still in its infancy. It will be a long while, which in the technology world can mean six to nine months, before designing Web sites is as easy as working in Quark, FrameMaker, PageMaker, etc. While many of these products do export to HTML, in most cases they do not export the actual placement, font, or font size.

HTML has just learned how to specify fonts and font size, create tables, and interlace images. But unless you know the code for these new snazzy tricks, you're out of luck in using them; most WYSIWYG (What You See Is What You Get) editors are incapable of executing these new commands because the standards evolve faster than the software can keep pace. This makes staying on top of the form part of the design process very difficult. Often, the most successful HTML pages are innovative more by mistakes than by intention. For these reasons, form is separate from function and, many times, the synthesis is purely coincidental.

Concept to Design

Some people read magazines from back to front. Some people create outlines after they've written a paper. Setting up a Web page relies more on individual thought processes than anything else. As in any design, whatever works best for the designer will probably work best for the design.

Having said that, however, I have found in my own page creations that organization and planning are very important. I think it's imperative to have at least a basic idea of what it is you want to do with the site and spend a while with a sketchbook planning it out.

Organization and Preparation

The beauty of hypertext is its ability to draw parallels between ideas at the click of a button. Unfortunately, hypertext is also what makes designing a nightmare. Pages leading to pages and still more pages make the top-level organization crucial.

Obsessive menu-maniacs may have a little trouble in this area. There is little that is more irritating in a Web site than an endless series of menus. Ten menu screens into the site, surfers might find the actual content they are looking for—if they have patience enough to make it that far. I try to maintain a broad organizational structure. I keep my menus short and rarely go beyond a three- or four-level organizational tier. I've also found it helpful to include a menu bar at the bottom of most of the pages on my site (see Figure 1). This is especially important if a site contains a large amount of content. The back arrow, while useful, is tedious after 20 or 30 clicks.

[eNdiX] [ego] [skandal] [klever] [virus] [woman] [mail]

Figure 1: *A menu bar is an invaluable aid to navigation around a Web site.*

Once you've decided the general concept and basic organization, gather the graphics. No matter how well you plan your image treatments, you will probably return to Photoshop, Paint, or whatever you use to build your graphics to resize, change colors, and attend to last-minute detail changes. Try to plan ahead for this stage as much as possible. Also find or create backgrounds that complement these graphics. Stay away from flashy graphics, as text can become difficult to read when superimposed on heavy backgrounds. (Take a look at Time Warner's Pathfinder site at **http://www.pathfinder.com** for an example of this visual chaos.)

A Few Pitfalls to Avoid

The biggest blunder in the first Web site I built was my obsession with Kai's Power Tools, the Adobe Photoshop plug-in. While I love Kai and his tools, they are generic. Everyone has them. Everyone has seen the metallic eerie alien glow. Everyone has seen the radial spiral. I abused poor Kai and splashed intense color all over my Web page backgrounds. While it looked pretty, the text was instantly lost to distracting shapes and blobs, which of course didn't match the shapes and blobs on my other pages. There was a lack of cohesion in my pages, which is fine for artsy-chaotic types like me, but potentially horrible for designers building corporate sites. It's very easy, especially for new Web surfers, to get lost online. If a site uses consistent backgrounds, link colors, and mastheads to remind users that they are still where they started, it will create a sense of safety and stability in a very unstable and random medium. Creating this level of safety for users greatly increases the likelihood of repeat visits.

Having the graphics ready will save you an incredible amount of time when it comes to actually laying out the page. I spent far too long designing and redesigning logos, icon buttons, and page graphics because I was too lazy to sit down and organize the process from the start. It is difficult to flip-flop between programming and designing graphics. I would get to a point in my page and realize I never made the art for the story. I'd have to save and close my editor, open Photoshop, and ultimately create a mediocre graphic.

My other big mistake in my first page was a lack of holistic concept. I wanted to tell people about me, splash my ego across the site, and at the same time have stories and ideas, places for people to post comments and questions, links, and lots of pictures. But the question I find myself asking now is Why? Why build this site? In my case it was purely for the sake of having a home page, because I was given server space and told I could create anything I wanted. It honestly

took about five tries before I got to the site I have now, one with a definite purpose: the Post Apocalyptic De(kon)structor (**http://www.thenet-usa.com/mag/staff/shel/shel.html**). It was built with the sketchbook planning model described above. Updates are considerably easier than in my past versions, and there is a unified voice and artistic theme that runs through the site. Each subsection has its own distinct flavor. Online visitors know whether they are in my women's resources section (see Figure 2) or in my story section by the colors and general layout of the pages. And they always know they are at the Post Apocalyptic De(kon)structor.

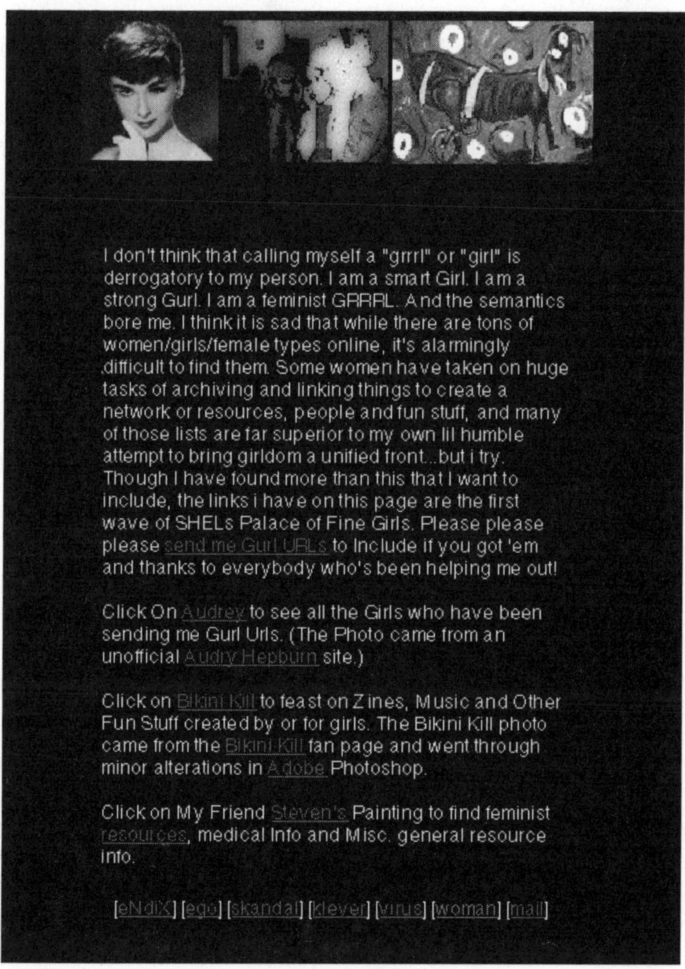

I don't think that calling myself a "grrrl" or "girl" is derrogatory to my person. I am a smart Girl. I am a strong Gurl. I am a feminist GRRRL. And the semantics bore me. I think it is sad that while there are tons of women/girls/female types online, it's alarmingly difficult to find them. Some women have taken on huge tasks of archiving and linking things to create a network or resources, people and fun stuff, and many of those lists are far superior to my own lil humble attempt to bring girldom a unified front...but i try. Though I have found more than this that I want to include, the links i have on this page are the first wave of SHELs Palace of Fine Girls. Please please please send me Gurl URLs to Include if you got 'em and thanks to everybody who's been helping me out!

Click On Audrey to see all the Girls who have been sending me Gurl Urls. (The Photo came from an unofficial Audry Hepburn site.)

Click on Bikini Kill to feast on Zines, Music and Other Fun Stuff created by or for girls. The Bikini Kill photo came from the Bikini Kill fan page and went through minor alterations in Adobe Photoshop.

Click on My Friend Steven's Painting to find feminist resources, medical Info and Misc. general resource info.

[eNdiX] [ego] [skandal] [klever] [virus] [woman] [mail]

Figure 2: *The women's resources page of the Post Apocalyptic De(kon)structor*

Where Do I Get Ideas?

The ideas for sites come from everywhere—other Web sites, to be certain. The beauty of the Web (and also its downfall) is that it creates itself. People see something they like and the source code is immediately available: most Web browsers make viewing the HTML code behind a Web site as easy as using a pull-down menu. About six months ago someone designed a background GIF with a sideline border. Within weeks, hundreds of sites were sporting the sideline border, with different colors and textures. Blinking text, scrolling title bars…trends come and go. The nature of the Web is a collective community decision. People use what they like and ignore what they don't. If you have a good or innovative design, expect it to be replicated, and quickly.

Inspiration is a completely different matter, however. It comes from internal or external influences, depending on individual experience. It can be as simple as seeing a shape in a cloud or as complex as a month-long journey through North Africa. I am inspired by most everything, and I find motivation within the things that are already around me.

The inspiration for my first site was shameless self-promotion. I wanted the world to know who Shel Kimen was and what she did. Needless to say, the site was inspiring to only me, and in retrospect, I'm not sure how much even I was inspired. Subsequent redesigns took on flavors of politics. I was inspired to rant about the world and why it was so unjust. I wanted to be the Gloria Steinem of cyberspace, networking women and flying the banner of feminism. While this attempt was slightly more noble, it still was far from captivating or useful.

Several recent personal experiences have spawned my latest and favorite Web design concept. I read a book by "avant-pop" artist/writer Mark Amerika called *The Kafka Chronicles*. I fell in love with a fictitious character in my own novel in progress. I discovered a site called Deconstruction23 demanding a new writers' movement. I found the Favela Organization the most inspiring of all art-related Web spaces. I had all these experiences within weeks of each other. The combination of art, philosophy, and emotion helped me get my most recent personal site off the ground. All of these entities weave through its pages.

I'd have to say that architecture, both in theory and aesthetics, is an important theme for me. Architecture is the synthesis of that form vs. function dilemma I talked about earlier. It is also very gratifying to me aesthetically, and the principles by which architecture is organized go hand and hand with Web design. I have a favorite architect, Lebbeus Woods, and I borrowed one of his images for the front page of my site (see Figure 3). Before starting a new page, I go back to the front, look at the art/building/anarchitecture of Lebbeus Woods, and go on from there. The tone of the overall site is much more consistent and inspired because of this. I also refer constantly to my own writing, Mark Amerika's book, and the Deconstruction23 page.

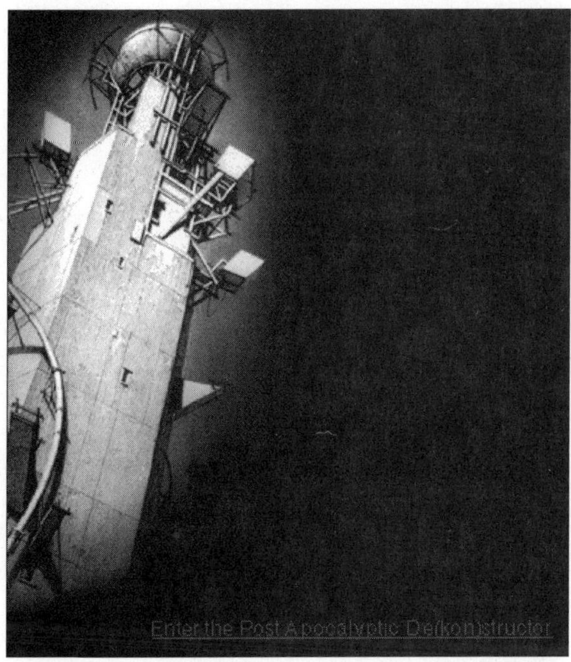

Figure 3:
Lebbeus Woods architecture on the front page of the Post Apocalyptic De(kon)structor

Inspiration is very personal, and it's easier to arrive at these ideas if you are creating your own personal home page. If you're designing for other people, pay attention to what inspires or motivates them. Ask questions. Listen keenly. And be as creative as the project allows.

Examples of Great Design

Of course, it never hurts to look around the Web to see what works—and what doesn't. I won't waste your time with bad designs here but will instead show you some of the best.

Voyager Company (http://www.voyagerco.com) The home page for Voyager Company, a CD-ROM manufacturer and distributor, has long been one of my favorite Web sites, residing somewhere near the top of my hot list. They have been consistently innovative and ready to take advantage of the new tricks and trials of HTML. The latest version of the Voyager Web site boasts speed and inventive, appealing graphics (see Figure 4). The organization of the new site is a bit chaotic for standard corporate sites, which is probably why it appeals to me more than a site such as Microsoft's. The twenty-something edge and feel is everywhere, from hip fonts to daring layouts.

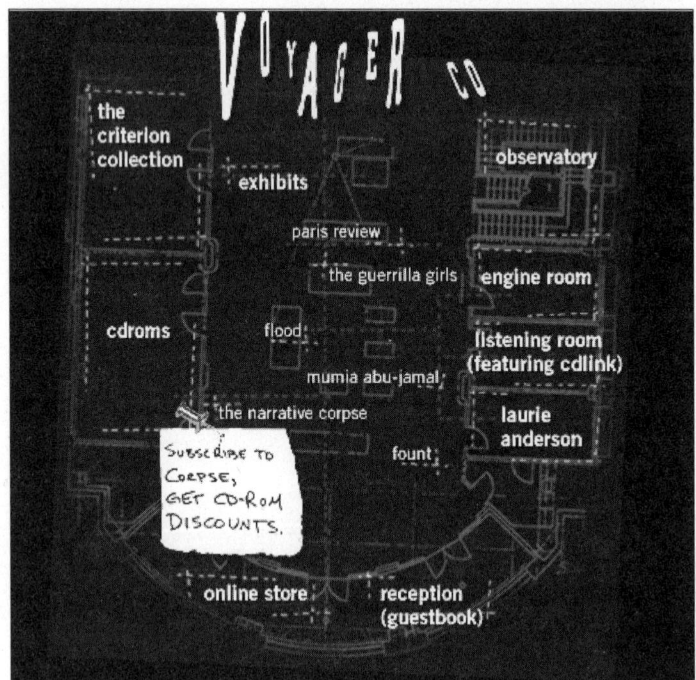

Figure 4: *Voyager's Web site is more chaotic than most corporate sites.*

The other wonderful aspect of the Voyager site is the original Web-only content Voyager has made available. Voyager has a priority to offer value-added content as a function of its primary purpose for the site, which is to sell CD-ROMs. They have forums for discussion on technology- and non–technology-related issues. They include regular thought-provoking essays and encourage active participation from readers with guest books, message boards, and so on. But if users are so inclined, it's easy to skip the philosophy and go straight to information about Voyager products. Phone numbers and ordering info are quick and extremely accessible (see Figure 5). You might be surprised by how many corporate Web sites I've found that forget to include their phone number.

online cd-rom store
Ordering online is easy. Below, click the box next to the titles you wish to purchase. Clicking on the name will take you to the catalog page (this page is a good one to bookmark). When you've checked off all the titles you want, submit your form. On the next page, you will select the number of copies you want, and for which kind of computer. 'M' means it's available for the Mac; 'W' for Windows. US Orders will be shipped to you within seven to ten business days.

Figure 5: *Voyager makes it easy to order their products.*

Favela (http://www.favela.org) The Favela Organization Web site (see Figure 6) is perhaps the most outstanding art-related Web site I've seen so far. It is visually beautiful and is miles thick with art to view, stories to read, and essays to provoke stimulating brain activity. I appreciate this site mostly because it achieves a level of conceptual thought and planning that is seldom accomplished online. It's obvious that no matter what section of the site you are perusing, you are in fact at the favela.org pages, though it never becomes staid or repetitious. They seem to save the most interesting design elements to carry through the entire site, and they pull in other elements to tie content within specific sections together. Incidentally, the art on this site is outstanding, with or without the Web.

MAIN MENU
THIS HUMILIATING AGE HAS NOT SUCEEDED IN WINNING OUR RESPECT

Figure 6:
Your entry to favela.org

Spiv (http://www.spiv.com) Turner Broadcasting has adopted the twenty-something "get hip" theme in its latest online venture, the Spiv. It is a site that caters to the whims, delights, intellectual needs, and desires of the Generation X crowd (see Figure 7). The most interesting and impressive aspect of this site is that it is created by the twenty-something folks involved in the current media movements, not some older Turner broadcasting executives in navy suits and power ties. The site is fresh and extremely appealing both in graphics and content. This is another site with exceptional top-level organization. While you always know you are at the Spiv site, it's also easy to draw distinctions between sections. It's an outstanding endeavor and it will stay in my bookmark file for as long as it continues its spare and tasteful use of advertising.

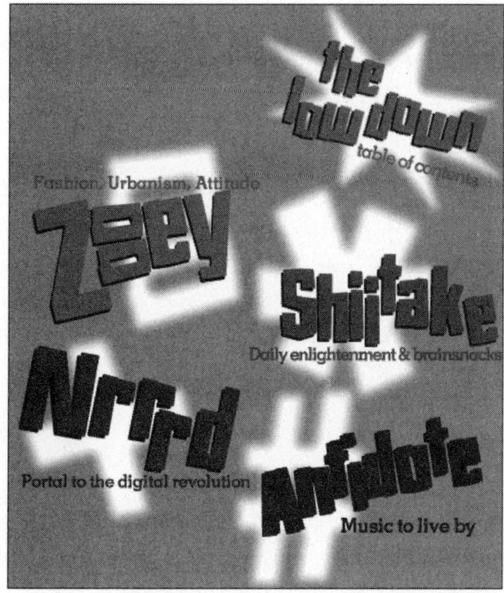

Figure 7:
All the topics are hip at the Spiv.

Urban Desires (http://www.desires.com) Urban Desires (see Figure 8) challenges viewers with in-your-face confrontation about art and culture, mesmerizing the metropolitan thirty-something crowd who wish they were still twenty-something. It's young and fresh, yet wonderfully sophisticated. The graphics use the same principles quite successfully.

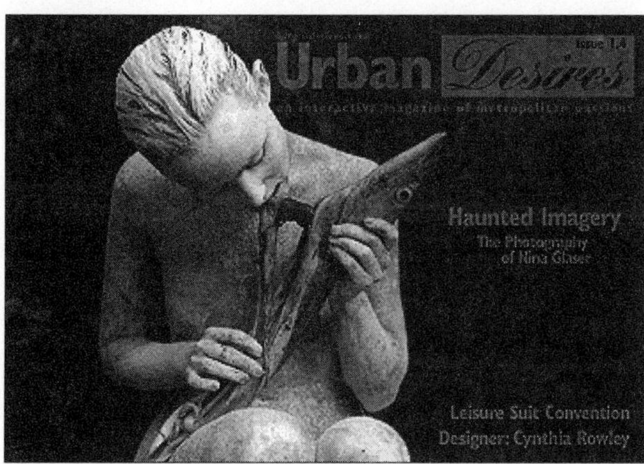

Figure 8:
In-your-face confrontation about art and culture await you at Urban Desires.

Urban Desires has stolen my heart more by content than by layout, although I'd be hard-pressed to find anything graphical about this site that I didn't like. They successfully use background color to distinguish between the various issues of the 'zine, which is a regular bimonthly creation.

While heavy on image maps (like all the sites I seem to enjoy), Urban Desires also makes sure to have visible text selections for those of us who either have slow modems or are too impatient to wait for high-resolution images to download. Unlike most snazzy 'zine sites, Urban Desires takes care of those of us still residing in the dark ages of the home computer.

Cybergrrl (http://www.cybergrrl.com) and FeMiNa (http://www.femina.com) Aliza Sherman, who is known online as Cybergrrl, could serve as an outstanding role model for all women online. She has single-handedly taken on the challenge of networking women's resources and has done this with exceptional passion and comprehensive detail. While her Cybergrrl site may not be the biggest and best site by way of super-hip graphics, her organization of a huge amount of content is one deserving extensive praise.

Aliza's FeMiNa database of women- and girl-related online resources, which is entirely searchable and dangerously quick, is another magnificent accomplishment (see Figure 9). FeMiNa is also wonderful because its aesthetics are simple and easy to understand, and they facilitate quick information retrieval, which is the site's purpose. Often, it seems, sites lose perspective of their intended goal. For example, the formerly quick and useful Lycos Web site index has evolved into a graphics-intensive, confusing behemoth that I hardly have patience to visit anymore. Sites such as databases are online to connect people to information, not to dazzle an audience with snappy graphics. Aliza seems to understand this well.

Figure 9: *The FeMiNa database is entirely searchable, easy to understand, and dangerously quick.*

Discovery Channel Online (http://www.discovery.com) While the Discovery Channel's Web site has a bit more of a formal organization and style than I normally prefer, I think it's important to show that a corporate site can maintain a visually appealing edge and still remain functional and valuable (see Figure 10). Discovery has added a few innovative services for free, which is always a good way to lure people to a site. They have a respectable Web search engine and also employ a service they call Knapsack. Knapsack lets surfers add a specific topic of interest to a personal profile, and the Discovery site will send weekly e-mail about new online sites addressing those interests. This feature is useful for people who don't have hours to spend cruising around hundreds of new Web creations each week.

Figure 10: *The Discovery Channel's site is both functional and visually appealing.*

Discovery also takes an innovative approach to content organization by devoting days of the week to specific topics: e.g., Saturday is technology day and Tuesday is nature day (see Figure 11). This concept gives readers a reason to return—guaranteed fresh content daily. It only takes surfers two or three visits to a static site before they decide they don't need to go back. Discovery knows how to captivate an audience; some of the other corporate Web pages could learn a bit from this site.

Figure 11: *Come back every day of the week for a different topic of discussion.*

The Future

The nation-state of Web space is growing at exponential rates. Even if we close our eyes really tight, it won't go away. Too many people have far too many marketing dollars and working hours invested in cyberspace for it to fade away like the Sony Betamax. As members of a new medium, we have an opportunity to set a few standards and help maximize the potential of Internet publishing. If we, as designers and creators of this new frontier, can elevate our expectations of what we want Web publishing to be, we can avoid the in-between stages of sloppy, useless pages and jump more quickly into an entertaining and valuable new medium.

Where do I see us in five years? It's hard to say, but I can only assume there will be a lot more people in the self-publishing business. Those of us reading this book now instead of later are probably going to be happy we did.

YAHOO!

New!
YAHOO!
EXTRA
ADD URL
NEW
COOL
RANDOM
HEAD LINES
YAHOO INFO
ADD URL

Hurricane Bertha
GoldMail zips TRIPS
GET PAID TO READ ADS!
Web Launch

CLICK HERE!

Search
options
Yahoo! Remote
Arts
Humanities, Photography, Architecture, ...
News [Xtra!]
World [Xtra!], Daily, Current Events, ...
Business and Economy [Xtra!]
Directory, Investments, Classifieds, ...
Recreation and Sports [Xtra!]
Sports, Games, Travel, Autos, Fishing, ...
Computers and Internet [Xtra!]
Internet, WWW, Software, Multimedia, ...
Reference
Libraries, Dictionaries, Phone Numbers, ...
Education
Universities, K-12, Courses, ...
Regional
Countries, Regions, U.S. States, ...
Entertainment [Xtra!]
TV, Movies, Music,
Astronomy, Engineering, ...
Government
Politics [Xtra!], Agen
ociology, Economics, ...
Health
Culture
Medicine, Drugs, Dise
nment, Religion, ...

Yahoo! Corporation

Company Profile

Yahoo! was founded in 1994 by Jerry Yang and David Filo, then graduate students at Stanford University. It is one of the most notable early successes in the Web industry, and it serves as a gateway for new and experienced users to search for specific sites or information in an incredibly vast array of sites.

David Shen is the manager of graphics and user interface at Yahoo!. He is in charge of all the "look and feel" issues of the main Yahoo! site and its forays into other media. David has a bachelor's degree in computer and systems engineering from Rensselaer Polytechnic Institute and a master's in computer science from Stanford University, along with extensive coursework in product design, also from Stanford. He is a veteran of Apple Computer's product design labs, where he was instrumental in the creation of Apple's ergonomic keyboard, the 1710AV monitor, and the QuickTake 100 digital camera. His most recent work prior to joining Yahoo! was as an industrial designer with frogdesign, an internationally acclaimed product design firm. During his studies at Stanford, David met Yahoo!'s creators. Since Yahoo!'s inception, David has helped his two school friends on Yahoo! site graphics until his actual hiring in September, 1995. He resides in Cupertino, California with his fifteen-year-old goldfish and works way too much for his own good.

Chapter Profile

Yahoo! has succeeded as a company for several reasons relative to design:

- First, the current Internet market is more wide than deep. Many Web surfers skip around from site to site, spending hours online but little time at one location. Further, with the rapid expansion of the Web, it is difficult to find specific information or a particular site. Yahoo! facilitates a broad, expanding market by providing Web users quick access to specific information.
- Second, the Yahoo! site is reliable and loads quickly. Yahoo! knows they have about thirty seconds to please every customer who comes to their site. If they fail to deliver, there are several aggressive competitors who will work hard to win new customers.
- Third, Yahoo! operates *beyond* the Web. In other words, they have diversified their product to other media, such as magazines, books, and CD-ROMs, while they have expanded their customers to include both large and small advertisers. Ultimately, Yahoo! will become far more than an online database and adopt a role as an arbiter of highly targeted media interests to individual users.

Each of these factors is reflected in Yahoo's design, which consistently focuses on the individual user. David is keenly aware of the user's experience of a site, as he has a background in industrial design for consumer and professional products. He recognizes that there are three primary audiences in any multimedia project: the user, the client or advertiser, and the designer.

- The focus on the user is the most important element of Web design because the medium demands it. If you as a designer fail to put yourself in your users' shoes, you are likely to lose them to any of hundreds of competitors. In this way, empathy is more powerful than artistic skills.
- If your site is supported by advertising revenue or represents a single client's products, its design must reflect a look and feel that is consistent with the demographic group to which they hope to appeal. This is a difficult goal to achieve because many commercial sites must appeal to multiple groups of people at once. Appealing to multiple audiences will determine the success or failure of many sites in the future.
- Finally, a site's design must be work you are proud to show, both for professional satisfaction of a job well done and as a testimony of your abilities as a designer. As one of the most highly visible companies on the Web, Yahoo! has proven itself highly capable in all these regards.

Each of the above priorities changes and grows daily in the Web world. Success is not just about following rules by rote; it is about learning new ideas and getting the most out of the ones that work.

Essay

Achieving Good Web Design

by David Shen, Manager of Graphics and User Interface

O ME, GOOD WEB DESIGN does not need to come from an experienced graphic designer or be programmed by the world's expert on HTML. Good Web design can be very simple in graphics, layout, and interactivity. Remember that every Web site has information a user needs to access, and ease of access is paramount. While we can appreciate that a site's graphics are incredibly beautiful and cutting-edge in layout, a site has failed if users cannot access the site to view these graphics or understand the navigation enough to access the site's information. It is the user interface as a whole that makes a great Web site design.

While many designers are extremely talented and want to express their talents online, some get caught up in the beauty of an image without considering whether it is confusing to the reader. The image may not convey what information is available at the site, or it may be too complex for the novice to interpret what it is attempting to communicate and where they should click on it to take an action. Great graphics are always attractive to the user, but using graphics in an intelligent and non-haphazard way will bring even more value to the user.

For instance, instead of randomizing color usage on text, it is much better if you pick certain colors to signify certain things, such as red for all hyperlinks and black for non-hyperlinked text. Keeping to consistent criteria helps users remember what your purpose is in using a certain image, text style, or design element—that way they will always know that looking for that element will allow them to accomplish their intended purpose.

A site does not need aggressive graphic design to be well-designed. A great site can be devoid of graphics. Consider the text-only version of Yahoo!. The fact that it contains no graphics does not at all detract from its ability to take you to your destination. That is because its user interface has been well thought out, incorporating much user feedback over a period of several months. It is very clear and explicit in communicating to the user what data is available at the site.

The number one goal of a Web site should be to allow users to get at the information at the site. Thus, the user interface comes before all other considerations. After you have worked out the navigation, you can introduce great design elements to dress up your site. At this point, the visual elements and the navigation will merge together, and both will have a synergistic effect on the final design.

Design Processes

Different projects demand different design processes; still, there are certain processes and guidelines I follow over and over again.

Use the Iterative Creative Process

I use the well-documented *iterative creative process* extensively. I will repeat it here briefly for the sake of completeness, but for more information I direct you to one of my favorite texts, *The All New Universal Traveler* by Koberg and Bagnall.

The iterative creative process has been shown to be a superior problem-solving method due to its ability to generate and explore a complete set of possibilities, minimizing the chance that a superior idea will be missed. The iterative creative process goes something like this:

1. **Define the problem.** Completely define the problem and determine the boundaries in which you must work.
2. **Gather information.** Research and obtain as much information as possible on the problem.
3. **Ideate.** Brainstorm and generate as many solutions as possible.
4. **Select and Test Idea(s).** From your brainstorming, select the most promising solutions and test them through physical manifestations and prototypes.
5. **Evaluate.** Determine which solutions are working and which are not. Run your working solutions through step 3 and repeat the process until a solution is found.

WARNING

In step 3, I use traditional brainstorming techniques to help stimulate my creativity. Space prohibits a lengthy tutorial on brainstorming techniques and games; however, there are some excellent texts on brainstorming and ideation. For instance, Roger van Oech's *A Whack on the Side of the Head* and *A Kick in the Seat of the Pants*, and James Adam's *Conceptual Blockbusting: A Guide to Better Ideas*. I encourage you to explore these texts in depth.

The number of times you can iterate is often bounded by schedule. Time is a luxury that few companies can afford; products need to ship on time to meet competitive milestones in the marketplace. Thus, you may have to look at how much time you have and set the number of iterations based on that factor. In business, iterating without end consumes resources and prevents products from being finished and ultimately getting to market.

As designers, we must discipline ourselves to know when to extend the schedule to make further iterations on the design and when to stop iterating and accept that the current state of the project is good enough. Often, the more you iterate, the less improvement each iteration brings to a product. Thus, a wise and seasoned designer knows how to balance the number of iterations on a project with schedule constraints—and how to prioritize which features or aspects of a project are most important to the final product.

Keep Sketches and Notes in Constant View

In many classes and texts that teach creativity, placing ideas down on paper is a key element in maintaining alternative idea generation within the participants of a brainstorming session. Why is this so? The human mind is funny: its thoughts can be very ephemeral in nature. The shortness of a certain idea's life can cause it to be lost for further idea generation. Thus, the best way to keep an idea in mind is to keep it in view where you can constantly refer to it.

Whenever I design, no matter what phase of the project I am working on, I am always sketching, drawing, or writing down my ideas as I come upon them. Then, I take these idea-laden papers and put them up on the wall of my office. Later, I will review these ideas and add new ones to the wall, or take two or more of the ideas from the wall and mutate them into new ideas. At some point, the wall becomes filled with ideas for designs. The more ideas you have at your disposal, the less chance there is that you will miss some design path or thought process. It is this completeness of analysis that is so valuable to this method of design.

Never EVER Design for Yourself

This is a key element in design philosophy and is also the least-used design concept. As designers, we tend to think that attending four years of college and working on many projects makes us experts in designing anything for anyone. It is this arrogance that we must be aware of and suppress as much as possible. When you do not consider the opinions and points of view of your design's users and customers, the potential for failure is huge. You are trusting that your own point of view is aligned with the millions of others in the general population. It is highly unlikely that you will be able to delve into that many minds, no matter how much experience you have.

To be successful in design, you must research your user audience. This research can take place in the library, in a store where potential customers come to shop, and/or in a market research test in which you watch end-users attempt to use your design. Take the time to create several prototypes and let users play with them. Observe them using those designs in their natural setting—at home, in the office, or on the road. Record their reactions. Listen to their comments on what they like and dislike. Conduct surveys—and try to conduct them yourself so that you can experience users' reactions firsthand. Nothing is as convincing as when you see several users do one thing when you wanted them to do something else.

Design Inspirations

I could mention famous painters or sculptors as my design inspirations, but instead I would like to credit some very talented designers with whom I have had the pleasure of working. While space prohibits mentioning every person I've worked with, I would like to mention a few who have taught me valuable design lessons.

Ray Riley of Apple Computer and Steve Peart of Vent Design, the industrial designers of the Apple Adjustable Keyboard, taught me to approach a design not only from an engineering perspective but also from an aesthetic one, and to fight for that which is both seen and felt.

Lisa Holzhauser, Apple Computer's user interaction specialist for the QuickTake 100 camera and the Apple 1710AV monitor, taught me the importance of user testing, surveys, and research in design. Many of the Apple projects I worked on were successful largely because I applied the knowledge and techniques of user interaction that Lisa taught me.

Amanda Ropa of Zanzara Design, a consultant whose expertise is interface design, taught me the importance of user interfaces on hardware and software—and the importance of including user interface development in every project. Through her, I have become extremely interested in interfaces on any kind of product, and I have learned many practical techniques of interface design, from using quick prototypes to creating easy-to-understand interaction paths.

Steven Holt, a mover and shaker at the product design firm frogdesign, taught me to look at design not from a microview but from a larger, holistic view. It is easy for us as designers to get caught up in the details of a project, forgetting to step back and take a fresh look at the design challenge. By taking a break from the problem, you can often find better solutions than your original one. Steven also taught me to build a database of knowledge and facts to which you can always refer. The more knowledge you have at your disposal, the better designer you will be. You can learn from the mistakes of past designers and apply past successes to new designs. In this way, you do not need to tread again on roads already worn by other designers, thus saving time and resources. While accumulating knowledge, you can also catch future trends and begin thinking about design on a more strategic level—how it may bring a company to the forefront of whatever industry it is in.

After mentioning all these designers from my life, I would like to mention one designer whom I have not encountered in real life but who has inspired me by his pioneering ideas in graphic design: David Carson, graphic designer extraordinaire and creative power behind *Ray Gun* magazine. His designs have broken every graphic design rule in the book. With his unorthodox views on imagery and type, Carson challenges your senses by destroying order and making beauty out of chaos. What inspires me most about his designs is that in order to create them, he had to free himself from the conventional bonds that hold each and every one of us to some extent, something all designers should experience. Within that freeing experience, designers discover new and individual means of expression. It is that opening up and unleashing of creative energies in David Carson's designs that appeals so much to me.

Design Considerations

There are many considerations for designing an effective Web site: its appearance, its navigability, its speed, the technology available, who will be using it and why. The following sections offer some practical advice for current and emerging designers.

Visual Design

Use graphics to enhance the experience rather than detract from it. Stay away from brightly colored backgrounds that are annoying to the eye. Make graphics small in Kbyte size so that users with slow modems as well as those with T1 lines can quickly download your entire page. Be clever with the use of text in your designs so that you can take advantage of the fast-loading capabilities of textual data versus image data. Be careful when translating high-end graphic designers' techniques to the Web; ensure that if the user does something as simple as resizing their browser window, they do not destroy the look of the page.

Interface Design

Make your navigation simple. Keep menus in the same location on different pages and use visual cues—color or a graphical element—to allow the user to easily find these menus. Be wary of using icons; while they are a fun and visually appealing way of representing menu items, they can also be very confusing if they are not designed well and/or if a neophyte user encounters them.

Users hate scrolling. Keep in mind that information may be better presented on several pages than on one large page. A caveat, however: it is easy to get lost on a Web site and not know how to return to the initial page. One way to solve this problem is to create a link on every page that leads back to a table of contents page so that users can easily regain their bearings. Another good way to solve this problem is to provide a menu at the top of every page so that users can always go directly to another location in the site. If your pages are long, include links to the top of the current page, or include menus at the top and bottom of each page so the user does not need to scroll all the way to the other end in order to leave the page.

Technological Considerations

When designing Web pages, you must think of the technology used on your server as well as on your user's computer. Herein lie many pitfalls that can be avoided with a little forethought.

Be aware of your server's technology. Can it handle the traffic that your site will bring? Can it handle the overhead of serving large graphics without bogging down to a crawl? If you are going with an Internet Service Provider (ISP), do they have enough computers to spread the load of multiple users and Web sites? Is their network connection a fast one, i.e., T1 or T3 versus 56K or ISDN? It may be that you will need to move to another ISP in order to get decent load times for your pages.

The user's end is even more varied. There is a proliferation of browsers in the marketplace, with each one implementing HTML tags in a slightly different way; some support new tags, while others support only those tags accepted by the HTML Standards Committee. Other browsers such as Netscape Navigator and Microsoft Explorer are forging new trails by implementing their own tags, which bring even greater flexibility in page design to the Web. Unfortunately, this means that you as the designer must consider how to deal with all the browsers out there. If you design your page to look good with Netscape 2.0, what do you do about visitors coming in through Spry's Mosaic browser or America Online's browser or even Netscape 1.1? Each one of these browsers will render the page slightly differently, and your original design intent may be tossed out the window as your images and text land in unintended locations or disappear altogether.

Probably the most effective way of dealing with this problem is to configure your server to redirect your users to different pages based on the browser they are using. Otherwise, if you care about accommodating all browsers, you may have to design for the lowest common denominator. Another way to deal with this issue is by warning users on your home page that your site is optimized for viewing with a certain browser.

Emerging Technologies

There are many exciting new Web technologies currently in the marketplace: Java, VRML, RealAudio, and Shockwave come to mind as four of the most visible. They offer the ability to do many great things, probably the most popular of which are animations and interactivity. However, I would caution the Web designer to use these technologies with care. Why? While impressive at first, these technologies can quickly seem stale. For example, it is easy to put up a "rebel yell" playback each time a user accesses a page; however, it becomes highly annoying when a user needs to access the page in order to jump to any other place on the site—and as a result hears fifty rebel yells. The same can occur with animations: imagine if the same looping video clip of a *Friends* episode were to play on a Web page minute after minute, day after day, without end. It was probably funny the first time around, but after the thirtieth or hundredth time, it will have lost its appeal.

Therefore, I encourage you as the Web designer to do your homework and learn about all of these technologies. Then, put some serious design thought into how each technology may be used to enhance your site rather than lowering its value.

Examples of Good Design

My favorite sites tend to have something unusual about them, whether it is content or design or both. The presentation of imagery and data pushes the limits of page layout on the Web, as does the interactivity. Also, in a few instances, the content is engaging and keeps you coming back to see if there is anything new. Typically, these sites require Netscape to view and, unfortunately, a high-speed connection to fully enjoy.

Organic Online: Levi Strauss & Co. (http://www.levi.com) The folks at Organic Online are true pioneers in Web design. As Web site designers for hire, they dabble in the latest Web technologies as soon as they are available, even before they are finished in development. They take their experience in traditional media, such as television, video, and print, and translate that to providing interactive experiences on the Web. If you visit their site (**http://www.organic.com**), you will find listed their many clients. I would encourage every Web surfer to check out those Organic sites, for in each of them there is something unique and special.

One unique Organically grown site is **http://www.levi.com** for Levi Strauss. Once you enter the site, you are presented with one of the most ambitious server-push examples on the Web, an exciting Web interpretation of the 501 jeans campaign and advertisement. Presented with continually flashing and changing imagery, the video-like bombardment of Levis propaganda is not to be found anywhere else on the Web. Amidst the flashing advertisements lies the interface to the site (see Figure 1). By clicking on some of those images, you travel to the many other areas of the site, which are also very hip in graphical layout. The Levis site remains the best example of Organic's ability to wrestle primitive interactive Web technology into doing something that perhaps the technology was not intended for.

Figure 1: *The Levi Strauss site pushes the envelope of Web advertising.*

The Spot (http://www.thespot.com) Just as daytime soap operas attract thousands of return viewers, some Web sites, aptly named "episodic Web sites," have achieved a similar loyal following. One such Web site, named *The Spot* (see Figure 2), spins a continuous tale of the lives of several beautiful Los Angeles residents, whose adventures are updated several times a week. Frequent visitors to The Spot find themselves getting engrossed with the characters living there and always wondering what they will do next, just as they do with their *Melrose Place* or *All My Children* counterparts.

The site also allows you many ways to interact with the characters. You can give advice to the Spotmates on what to do next in their personal adventures. There are calendars in which you can read the past adventures of Spot characters and a Spot Store where you can purchase Spot merchandise. As a Spot Virgin, you are introduced to The Spot via background stories and given a little tutorial on how to interact with the site. These instructions are great for those who may find the interface a little complex and are not sure where to find the juicy stories each day.

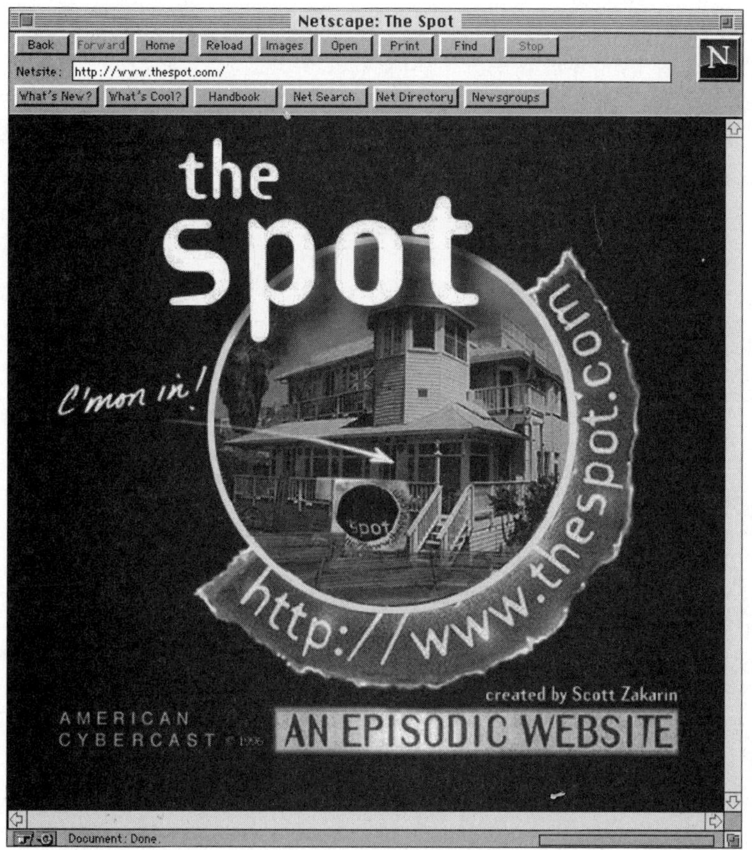

Figure 2: *The Spot invites you to explore its characters' lives.*

Of course, the story line is not the only thing that is great about The Spot. The images are great to look at. Each Spot character is depicted iconically, with a graphical representation of some aspect of their personality. "Trading cards" are created for each character showing important stats. The navigation is fun; for instance, to read a character's story for a certain day, you click on the character's icon, then choose the day from a calendar. If you are a frequent watcher of *Melrose Place* or other hip soap operas, you will not be disappointed with the adventures of The Spot crew.

Specialized Bicycles (http://www.specialized.com) Any avid bicyclist will enjoy the Specialized site (see Figure 3). Here you will find all sorts of bicycling information: there are features on everything from the entire Specialized bicycle line to technical information on bicycle components and Specialized-sponsored bicycling teams. You can even find mountain biking trail maps, special events, company press releases, and Specialized job listings. It remains one of the best resources of general bicycling knowledge on the Web.

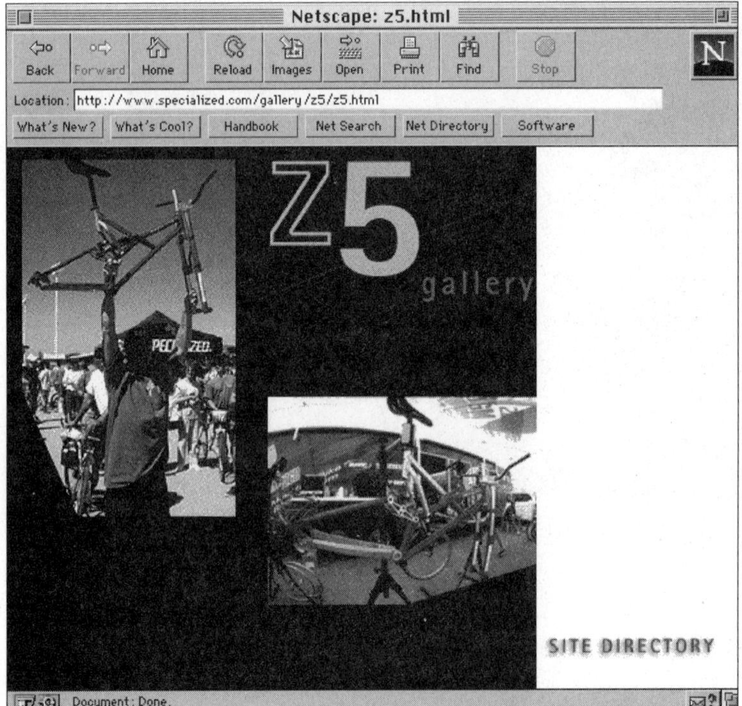

Figure 3: *There's all sorts of biking information to be found at the Specialized site.*

Information notwithstanding, I am impressed by the site's completeness in design. Not a single page of the site has broken from the overall design language. The interface is fun to use, presenting images and hypertext in many different ways. The color combinations and type treatment are sophisticated and characteristic of many examples seen in print. The site designers have clearly pushed the limits of Web page layout tools to produce this site, and it is definitely optimized for viewing by Netscape. Also, it cleverly uses server-push technology to flash images to help instill a sense of movement so characteristic of high-energy mountain bikers and racing cyclists.

The 11th Hour (http://www.vie.com/prodinfo/11th/home.html) At their site, Trilobyte promotes their CD-ROM adventure game, the 11th Hour. Designed by Claire Barry of Click Active Media, the site is rich in detail and successfully brings you into Henry Stauf's haunted mansion (see figure 4). Icons that throb like beating hearts help set the evil mood. And, if you dare, you can draw a tarot card online and see what the fates have in store for you.

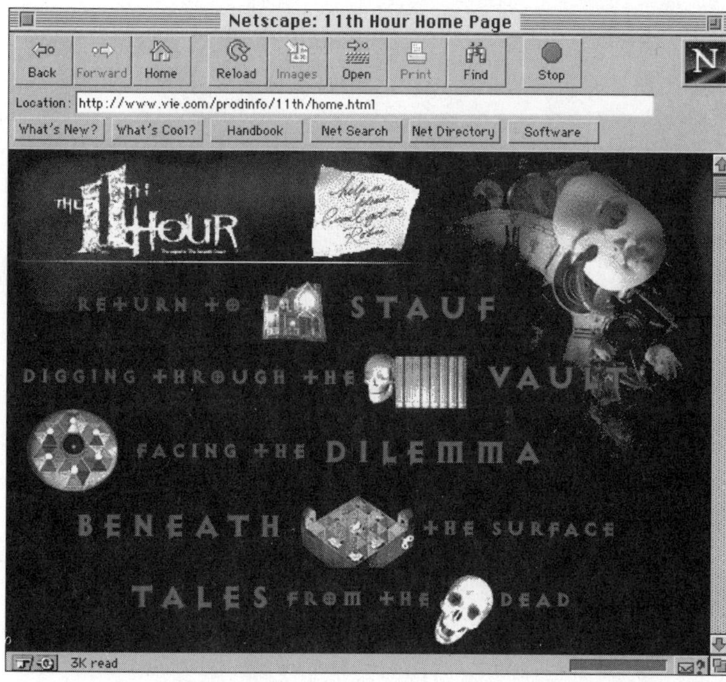

Figure 4: *The 11th Hour site features throbbing icons.*

The site also gives you many previews of the CD-ROM, showing you small video clips and sound effects from the game. Many images from portions of the CD-ROM are available for download. There are great stories to peruse, all of which originate from the game—from the background information on Henry Stauf's Wonderworld Toys to the journal of Robin Morales, a reporter who disappeared while investigating the rumors of grisly murders at Henry Stauf's estate. It also introduces you to many of the eerie puzzles you must solve to win the game, giving you hints along the way (see Figure 5). Also, the site acts as a "Making of 11th Hour" feature, where you can find video clips of the creators of the game and their development process as well as messages from the CEO and president of Trilobyte.

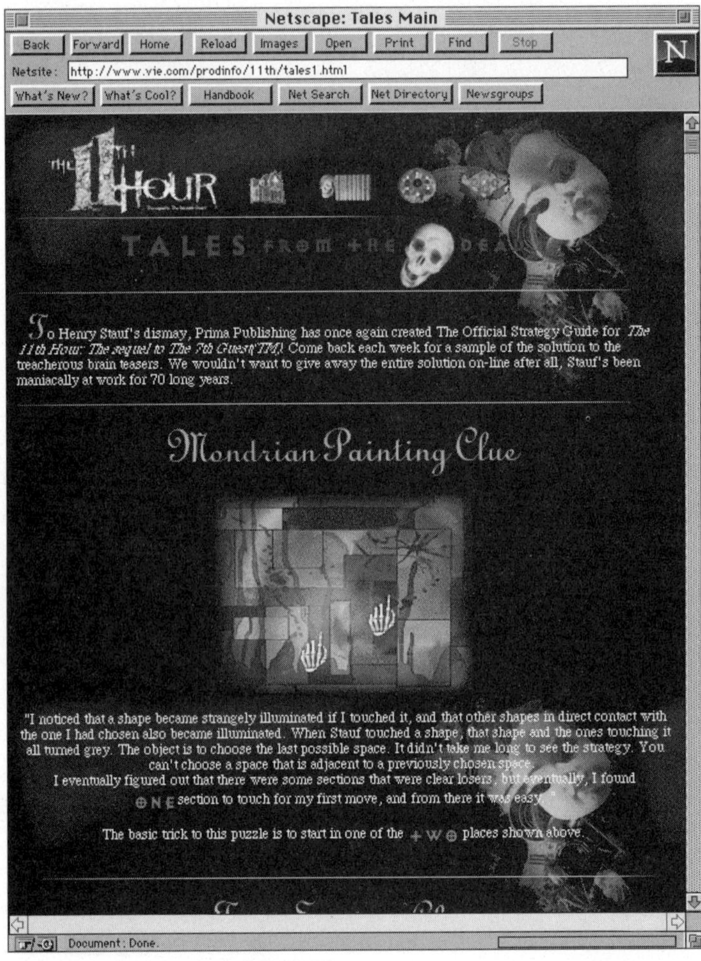

Figure 5: *The 11th Hour site previews puzzles you must solve to win the CD-ROM game.*

As a marketing tool, the site is excellent. It teases and tempts you with its great artwork and makes you wonder what is available with the full game. This site is a real treat, even if you don't buy the CD-ROM.

Web Design in Five Years

Two things will drive Web design into the next century: the improvement in users' speed of access to the Web from their home PCs, and the evolution of HTML to something beyond a simple page layout description language, along with the extension of Web page tools.

Speed of Access

Why is speed of access important? Anyone who has waited over 20 seconds to download a Web page knows why it is important. How many times have these same people simply clicked the Stop button to halt the download of the page and moved on to another, faster page? Lengthy downloads occur because the data used in the design of the page, whether it is text, images, executable code, or page-formatting information, occupies many bytes of information. As designers push the envelope of Web page design, they will bring traditional print design techniques as well as the interactive techniques of multimedia to the online page. Certainly, a designer can create cutting-edge graphics and interactivity using today's Web technology. However, the result is that an enormous amount of data is created in the process, and this data needs to be completely downloaded to the user in order for it to be viewed.

According to *The Yahoo! Jupiter Web User Survey* (Jupiter Communications, New York, 1995), the current population of Web surfers with 14.4 Kbps or less modems makes up approximately 70% of all Web users. At 14.4 Kbps. a good general rule for measuring speed of download is 1 Kbyte per second. For example, the home page of Yahoo! consists of a top banner of approximately 3.3 Kbytes and HTML of approximately 6.2 Kbytes. Thus, in approximately 9.5 seconds, you will have loaded the entire Yahoo! home page; not bad by Web standards—and, according to our user surveys, one of the most appreciated aspects of Yahoo!. Once the download goes from 10 seconds to 20 seconds to a minute or more, site designers need to contend with the low patience level of Web surfers to wait for data.

Over the last two to three years, companies like Apple Computer and Packard Bell have sold millions of personal computers bundled with 14.4 Kbps modems.

Just recently, the world has experienced a slowdown in the personal computer market (which has caused more than one computer manufacturer's stock price to drop steeply); after all, it is pretty difficult for consumers to keep paying $2,000 for a new multimedia PC every year. Thus, it may be that another few years may need to pass before the majority of the population turns over their systems and purchases new computers with faster Net access capabilities.

Upgrading modems may be easier. A purchase of a new modem ranges from $140 to $250 for a new 28.8 Kbps version. However, even that will take some time to filter down into the market; it will be at least a year until a sizable amount of the population of online users upgrade their modems and 28.8 Kbps modems become a fair percentage of the market. That means that a Web site will typically be viewed through the connection of a 14.4 Kbps or less modem for at least another year.

Given that designing graphics and interactivity to the level seen in interactive kiosks and CD-ROM titles consumes an enormous amount of data, and given that Web users are inherently impatient to wait for enormous amounts of data to be downloaded, speed of access to the Web for the general population needs to increase dramatically before users will be able to download this data in a very short amount of time. Thus, graphics- and interactive-intensive applications in the mainstream will require sweeping overhauls in many areas: installation of high-speed networks to our homes, increase in speed of modems to access these high-speed networks, and lowering of the cost of equipment and charges for high-speed networks.

HTML Evolution and Extension

In its current state, HTML remains a page formatting language. Herein lies both its strength and its weakness; as a simple page formatting language, HTML is extremely easy to learn and does not require programming knowledge to implement, but it is deficient in allowing users to create interactive designs easily. In order to create graphics- and interactive-intensive designs, a Web designer often needs to know not only HTML, but also programming languages such as Perl, C, CGI, and a host of other acronyms, which are frequently very difficult for the average Web page designer to learn and implement. Currently, there is not a single integrated programming/authoring suite with which to create extensive interactive Web applications.

The state of Web page design tools is constantly improving, with new technologies emerging every day:

- The Java programming language and its support by current browser manufacturers is a great step toward bringing full-blown multimedia to the Web. However, it is lacking in that it is a programming language and requires detailed knowledge of programming concepts both on and off the Web, which makes Java difficult to use for the majority of the population.
- Netscape Navigator Gold 2.0 is another application pushing Web design. It integrates many advanced Web and programming tools such as Java and scripting and makes them readily available to the designer in a single development application. At the time of this writing, Netscape Navigator Gold 2.0 has just been released.
- Shockwave technology from Macromedia allows Director documents to be played on the Web. Director is already familiar to most, if not all, interactive application designers and is an incredibly powerful multimedia authoring tool. Using the Afterburner application, Director programmers can compress and create Shockwave documents which can be viewed by any browser that has installed the Shockwave Plug-In.

This is only a small sample of the emerging technologies; many more exist or will be created. The difficulty comes when a Web designer attempts to integrate these varied technologies. The designer must expend substantial time and resources to learn how to use these technologies, then hope that the viewer has the correct browser and/or plug-ins to experience the site fully.

HTML is in dire need of improvement in functionality; otherwise, Web designers need to deal with many varied technologies and applications in order to create multimedia sites. In the future, HTML will evolve and combine with all these varied technologies so the unsophisticated Web designer will be able to create great interactive Web sites. Like Apple Computer's Hypercard and Microsoft's Visual Basic, HTML programming will become simpler and enable easy graphical interaction programming without needing to learn about complex low-level interfaces to programming toolboxes.

The Future Is Now

Let us assume that the above criteria have been satisfied, and that through our home computers we have near-infinite bandwidth to handle enormous amounts of data. HTML is now called HTML^3 and has incorporated the best elements of the UltraJava language and has the authoring capabilities of Macromedia's Director 10.1. So now what will Web design look like?

Total immersion is the name of the game. Taking what was formerly static text and images and transforming them into data experiences will be the next level of interactivity. Designers will be challenged by creating sites which affect several senses at once. Traditional interface design criteria will be strained, tested, and reconsidered when we are designing interfaces that involve the entire body. Not only will real physical activities be emulated electronically, but our search, retrieval, and analysis of information will be incorporated into data experiences. Web designers will push their creativity into the third and fourth (time) dimensions to produce sites whose interactivity is far beyond that of a flat two-dimensional page. Computers will be able to emulate human conversation to some extent, and therefore will be able to converse with users, determine their needs, and bring the appropriate data back to them. We will see currently theoretical "intelligent agents" become reality as we send these electronic servants out onto the Web to alert us to important news and events and help us find information when we need it.

As time progresses, processing power in personal computers grows by leaps and bounds. Each year sees incredible advances in chip technology over the previous year. Not too far in the future we will see things happen in technology and on the World Wide Web that seem incredible today. I am extremely excited to see these things happen in my lifetime.

POPPE TYSON

• *Agency of the Year* •

TOUR POPPE TYSON ADVERTISING

TOUR

THE DBM GROUP

P R

ABOUT BJK&E

ON-LINE SAMPLES & IDEAS

POPPE

poppe.com

TYSON

POPPE TYSON

Poppe Tyson

Company Profile

Poppe Tyson, a subsidiary of Bozell Worldwide, was founded in 1924 as a business-to-business advertising agency. Its core experience is selling to people who collect information before they buy—the "considered purchase." Its history of developing information-rich communications is ideal for online advertising. In addition to four offices in the U.S., the agency has locations in Europe and South America. Beyond its core advertising business, Poppe Tyson also operates a full-service PR agency and the DMB Group, a database marketing division. Poppe Tyson's clients include Chase Corporation, Chrysler, Hewlett-Packard, Netscape, Merrill Lynch, Silicon Graphics, the White House, and many others.

As the founder of Carlick Advertising in 1981, David Carlick developed one of Silicon Valley's largest independent agencies. In April of 1993, Carlick Advertising merged into the Poppe Tyson global network. As an ex-accountant turned creative director, David brings a unique business perspective to the marketing and advertising of Poppe Tyson's technology clients.

Craig Marr is Senior Vice President of Creative Services for Poppe Tyson's New York office. He helps to ensure that poppe .com's clients better understand the opportunities and challenges facing today's companies as they move into the digital age. He has designed successful Web programs for Valvoline, The White House, and Merrill Lynch.

Chapter Profile

The next five chapters, from Poppe Tyson, Rare Medium, CKSlInteractive, and Organic Online, each address an aspect of commercial design and branding on the Web. The strongest mainstream media focus in the last year has been consumers on the Web, yet many news organizations completely miss the bigger influence of business-to-business and other commercial applications. Whether we like it or not, it is advertising dollars and sales revenues, not good will and social ideals, that drive the largest growth of the Web. For this central force, firms with expertise in translating clients' product messages into digital form are hot property.

Poppe Tyson's message comes through clearly: design to serve customers, not just display product information. This concept extends the idea that good design must begin by understanding a client's relationships with its customers.

Most top designers have a transition in their careers when they learn to listen more than speak. You must observe this rule to understand the needs of any project's multiple audiences: the end user, the client, and the designers themselves. All must be satisfied with the end result in the same priority order. If the end user is happy, so is the client, and if the client is happy, the designer gets paid. End users' needs are successfully addressed by designers who see a Web experience through their eyes. The designer must begin with the following set of questions:

- Who are the end users?
- What are their ambitions/dreams?
- What are their fears?
- What is their experience with computers and/or this brand?
- How can a product message deliver value, not just marketing hype?
- What will keep customers coming back to the site in the future?
- What changes in their needs can we anticipate as designers/advertisers?

This last question says the most about the potential for advertisers and their designers to make an impact in the commercial world with the Web. The best service in any business, whether delivering a baby or building a skyscraper, is that which *anticipates* customer needs. Before you know you need something, it arrives. As boxer Muhammed Ali proclaimed many years ago, "I'm so fast, I can turn off the light and be in bed before it's dark!" Remember that empathy serves as a powerful form of creativity. Poppe Tyson (no relation to Mike) remembers it every day.

Essay

Building Brand Applications for a Global Audience

by David Carlick, Executive Vice President and General Manager, and Craig Marr, Senior Vice President of Creative Services

HE UNPRECEDENTED POPULARITY of the World Wide Web has occurred for a number of reasons, not all of which are necessarily understood by the companies rushing to build sites of their own. As the Web continues to mature as a legitimate business communications platform and the industry shakes out, this lack of understanding will mean that many sites that are poorly designed or lack a clear strategic purpose will disappear.

With technology moving forward at breakneck speed, understanding the elements that go in to making a successful Web site becomes all the more difficult, but then hitting a moving target is never easy!

Setting the Stage for Branding Applications

If we were to take a step back in time two years to when the Mosaic browser was introduced and businesses first became aware of the Web, we would see how much has changed since the first commercial efforts. In this short time, the Web has already gone through several transitional changes, and what was once the standard—or for that matter, cutting edge—has changed dramatically.

The Early Days of the Web

In the early stages of the "Web evolution," companies looked at the broad reach of the Web and the relatively low cost of entry and thought it was a great way to put their corporate brochures online where millions of people could see them. Since few commercial sites existed at the time, the novelty of being able to log on and surf the Web to see information about companies' products and services or to read their annual report was a novelty. Suddenly companies from almost every industry were putting up sites, and the Web was awash with sites that seemed to offer the visitor little of substance beyond a repackaged annual report.

What the Web really represents is a powerful and cost-effective means by which to build brand identity and develop one-to-one relationships with customers. The following is our description of branding and the ways in which to use the Web to help support an overall brand strategy:

> *The Internet is partly a medium, but more important, a vehicle for delivering service. The implications for brand builders are significant.*

In the advertising community, we have been treating the Internet as a new medium. We think of creating content that will attract users to the Web site in terms of traditional advertising information that could previously be found in brochures, data sheets, product literature, advertising, etc. We also think of attracting users with traditional incentives (promotions, coupons, contests, and rewards).

Each of these methods has its merits, and in fact these methods represent the way most organizations get started in creating a Web presence: putting information online that would have traditionally been delivered over other media to customers and prospects, and using incentive concepts borrowed from other media.

The Internet as an Applications Platform

The greater value of the Internet is as an applications platform that lets our clients deliver services that increase their brand equity. The Internet, and the computers connected to it, represent much more than the ability to deliver information, or even interactive information. It is really a collective, distributed computing system. The Internet also offers the ability to deliver applications (computer programs that deliver services) in a way that caters to the customer need for convenience and to businesses' need to lower costs while serving customers better. We call these *branding applications*.

Delivering a Service: Branding Applications

The pivotal example of a branding application is the home page for Federal Express at **http://www.fedex.com** (in its September 1995 incarnation). It does not present the visitor with a lot of slogans or snappy positioning themes. Instead, it first asks if you want to track a package.

This Web site presents an application—a computer program—to serve the user, instead of content. This concept represents a continuation of the fundamental shift in how we interact with customers and prospects, and how we, as marketing agencies, work with our clients to increase their brand equity.

Currently, *brand equity* is defined as that measurable increase in margins due to a price that exceeds commodity levels (*brand preference*), and due to a lower cost of selling because of increased repeat purchasing (*brand loyalty*). This simply nets out to a higher *gross margin*, and advertising's job was to help sustain those margins to enable a higher overall return than the advertising expenditure.

The advertising tools for Federal Express were brand awareness and brand image (including positioning). The home page of Federal Express succeeds brilliantly at increasing brand preference and increasing the company's gross margins by delivering a service, a branding application, over the Internet.

The customer wins because, for that rapidly increasing segment who are digitally connected to the Internet, tracking a package is truly a point-and-click event—no software to load, no dial-up or login, no telephone calls and hold music—just information on demand, any time, day or night, at the customer's convenience.

Federal Express wins because they are able to deliver this valuable package tracking service at a dramatically reduced cost, eliminating operators, switching equipment, telephone line charges, and a host of other internal costs while delivering fundamentally better service.

Enlightened Self-Service

This branding application that provides *enlightened self-service* has significant implications for marketing companies who wish to play a role in the branding efforts of companies as the Internet emerges. What is fundamentally important is that Federal Express is increasing brand equity by delivering a *differentiating service* over the Internet that sets them apart from other sites, as opposed to the media concept of content. In fact, the Internet is emerging as much as a service platform as a content medium, if not more-so! Today, the dominant Internet sites that sell advertising are services—Netscape, Yahoo, Prodigy, Webcrawler, and Infoseek.

The Internet currently delivers the following services that offer the enlightened self-service paradigm (in the case of brands, to increase brand equity):

- Banking
- Tickets and event information
- Package delivery, shipping, and tracking
- Automotive shopping, comparison pricing
- Personnel placement (want ads)
- Software and hardware support
- Stock listings, transactions, and portfolio management
- Industrial product listings and search engines
- Internet Advertising rate comparisons and analysis
- Education (there is now an accredited high school)
- Gaming and contests

- Software demonstrations (downloading)
- Catalog shopping and ordering
- News search and research services

Organizations are, in fact, discovering the Internet as a medium to *improve* service and lower costs compared to other options. Here are a few examples of traditional service venues that the Internet can improve upon:

- **Buildings**: Banks, brokerage houses, bookstores, and supermarkets, for example, can serve customers more inexpensively online, including home delivery. They can expand their customer base and franchises more cost-effectively by serving an online clientele than by expanding their brick and mortar investment.
- **800# operators**: Airlines, stockbrokers, hotel reservation systems, travel reservation systems, ticket reservation systems, and catalog operators can all offer better customer service and lower cost online, as in the Federal Express example.
- **Customer service representatives**: Computer companies already know, and other companies will follow, that customer satisfaction rises and costs decrease when the information customers need and the ability to communicate with the company are available online.

The definition of creativity will change in this shift from physical to digital commercial environments

In the traditional disintegrated media world, branding functioned as a funnel that took prospects from a general awareness in general media through the curiosity, interest, and purchase stages using different media (and different measures of creativity) at each level. For example, a person might see an ad in a magazine for a car (general awareness). They might contact a dealer through the phone book and speak to a sales rep on the phone (interest). If they were still intrigued with the product, they might go to the dealership for a test drive and possible purchase (purchase). However, in the Internet world of the *InterACTIVES* (firms that effectively use online media and their customers), the consumer can skip from browsing to buying at the click of a mouse. This brings different creative challenges. Over time, there will be a shift in emphasis from content to applications and services.

Web sites can offer a superb differentiating service as their branding application—as we found by including comparative shopping sections into the Web sites for Eagle and Jeep (**http://www.jeep.com**)—to help prospects and customers reach and reassure buying decisions in a complex world. They can also offer a sense of community for those prospects who attach more to a brand than the sum of its logical attributes. But it will be difficult for an advertiser, such as Jeep, to truly keep a site competitive for the time in people's lives against the increasing onslaught of interactive entertainment and information being published and sponsored by advertisers on the Web.

Keeping the Consumer Engaged

To counteract this sort of problem we will need, as Web site builders, to look beyond the Web site and understand that we need to build and measure traffic. We need to keep our message out in cyberspace to capture those who are entering the various stages of the purchase cycle, rather than depending on our ability to create a Web site that outpulls Hollywood, Las Vegas, Wall Street, and Main Street. To this end, Web sites must focus on the buying decision and the core brand identification activities, and turn to the professional entertainers (as we do with television) to help us scour the world for prospects. This scouring will be made easier by the inherent nature of the Internet to serve the advanced needs of the InterACTIVES. People will be able to enjoy advertiser-supported services with increased control. Consumers can

- Volunteer information about themselves so that the advertising they see can be customized to fit their interests
- Choose to select only advertising they like or are interested in
- Flame unpleasant advertisers instantly and easily
- Select from an increasing number of advertising incentives to interact with companies online

Creativity and the success of a site will be measured by our ability to

- Make it interesting and relevant to the prospect and customer
- Make it interactive—easy to use for beginners and stimulating for frequent visitors
- Make it valuable—a vehicle for services and applications (branding applications) that differentiate our clients to their customers and prospects

- Have it deliver and engage customers in the brands' core values
- Attract the right people to the visit at the right time
- Tailor the site to the user's needs
- Convince the user to favor our services
- Increase customer satisfaction and loyalty

All the above factors brought about by the Web are due to the vertically integrated role of the Internet in the awareness-through-purchase-through-support cycle for the customer. This cycle begins the first time a consumer has any contact with messages or images about a product, proceeds if they buy the product, and continues for the entire time they own it. With some products, such as soft drinks, this cycle might last about an hour: the consumer sees an ad, buys a six-pack, and shares it with friends. For other products, such as cars, this cycle may last for many years.

As more of the above innovations are implemented in the future, it will be exponentially more difficult for creative juries to evaluate the success of a Web site. The Federal Express site gets zero points for cleverness, and a billion points for delivering a differentiating service that increases Federal Express brand equity.

The role of the site in building the brand will become clearer, and buying links will become significantly more important. The notion that a site must be designed to generate repeat traffic is being modified as the nature of the content and services on the Internet become better understood. Certainly, a site must be interesting, but very few areas will compete successfully against entertainment for space in the customer's mind. The professional entertainment organizations and entrepreneurs clearly are recognizing the ability of this medium/platform/application to enable advertiser-supported sites.

Rarely can sites compete for space in a customer's mind if there is not an ongoing interest in the product. Golf club companies, for example, who understand that their customers regularly buy more products, may still find that "renting" awareness on huge golf content-oriented sites is considerably more cost-effective than creating their own content. Similarly, it is more cost-effective to advertise in golf special interest publications than to create and publish them.

The value of paid online advertising (sponsorships) is estimated to grow from $50 million this year to over $4 billion by the year 2000 (Forrester Research).

Strategies for Web Brand Builders

At Poppe Tyson, we view the Web as a computer application, not a medium. This definition has many implications:

- **Design**: Web creators must work from a perspective of a new application for computer users, not a means to convert television viewers.
- **Branding**: The Web is more about increasing services and lowering cost than about raising image.
- **Business**: Web design is about doing business in the most affluent, influential neighborhood around—the desktop of the digitally connected user.
- **An Offensive Model**: Lower costs, improve service, be proactive in reaching the networked psychological/demographic. Build a share in that group while the competition is leaner, and hold that share with preemptive application growth and service advantages.
- **A Defensive Model**: Don't lose top customers because you are behind in service. Build your share of the market at the same rate as the competition.

The Client's Shoes: Seeing Their Business on the Web

Before we can begin to understand what makes good Web design, we must first understand the purpose and the strategic goals that a company has established for their Web site. Companies have to make these base determinations before the design can be established, and before we can measure its relative success. So let us take a step back for a moment and look at a scenario that a typical CEO might face in determining the rationale for a Web site in the first place. From there we can better understand the issues facing businesses today and how it will impact their decisions in overall Web design. The number one question a manager needs to ask is, "Should my company have a Web site, and if so, what should it contain?" For the purposes of this exercise, let's assume the role of CEO of a major bank and look at the issues, challenges, and opportunities that face them.

A Sample Case Study

As CEO, we can make the following five assumptions, based on our own personal experience with the computer user world and Internet marketplace:

1. An increasing number of computer users (who represent a very affluent demographic) will have dramatically increasing expectations of the services that will arrive via their networked computers. These may be consumers or business buyers of our services. (It is within Poppe Tyson's own customer research capabilities to determine how many, but we would be tremendously surprised if the portion of many companies' total customer bases wanting these services was fewer than 5%!)
2. The cost of serving these people should actually be *lower* than the cost via traditional means (commissioned salespeople, telemarketing operators, printed literature) in the same way that automatic teller machines and videoconferencing kiosks lower our cost of delivering certain services.
3. If the market expects the services, and the cost of the services is lower, the market will get what it wants quickly. We call this the *digital service gap*. We can expect our competition to rush to fill this gap.
4. This digital service gap represents a very large potential for customers to shift their banking relationships, as banks will be able to significantly differentiate their services to the customers as the online marketplace sorts itself out.
5. There is the risk that if we wait for the research and the numbers, we will be left behind.

This kind of Web development for a company requires judgment; there is no easy precedent and there are no easy algorithms that return an automatic answer. However, there are some benchmarks on which we can safely base a decision as to what kind of site to build.

The first benchmark is the acceptance rate for self-service technologies. The automatic teller took 10 years to gain widespread acceptance. Presently, about 60% of bank consumers use automatic tellers.

The Internet is showing a more dramatic rate of acceptance in many areas, but let's be conservative and assume a 10 year curve, arriving at a 60% acceptance of Internet self-service technology.

So for the next five years, across both consumer and business lines, we should start with the assumption that a preference in the sophisticated business and consumer marketplace for interaction via computer will run at the rates listed in Table 1.

Table 1: A breakdown of the trends in services via computers

YEAR	1996	1997	1998	1999	2000
Online preference	5%	10%	15%	20%	25%
Revenues represented	$150M	$310M	$465M	$650M	$800M
Profit represented*	$28M	$45M	$63M	$90M	$125M

*Projected at a modest annual growth rate, based on historical growth rates. Business and consumer operations, while different in gross revenues, appear to contribute about equally to profit.

There is no reason to assume at present that the rate of preference for computer interaction will be higher or lower among business or consumer customers. The *Revenues Represented* and *Profit Represented* are the amount of business we should consider at risk to competitors who can come into our customer's "online neighborhood" with superior services.

What is the risk? In the near term, not much, as the online services are not powerfully differentiated. Beginning in 1997, the risk increases, as we can expect competitors to fill the digital service gap.

Of course, there is an upside: if we can learn to provide superior service to the percentage of our customer base who prefer online communications, we have the opportunity to *expand* those same services to customers of other banks.

Now, we have to figure out how much to invest. The answer should be *nothing*! After all, we are expecting the cost of serving people online to be less than the cost of traditional services. However, this will not happen by accident. It has to be integrated into operating budgets and capital budgets. Further, we must prime the pump—begin to fund the electronic effort while we lay the groundwork for a shift in operational budgets from traditional to online services.

Therefore, we should go to our product line managers and ask them to build the operating models for a world where a significant percentage of our customers want to do business online. We should tell them that we are prepared to begin work on online services while they build into their future operating budgets the shift from traditional resources to electronic resources.

We then would get the process rolling with 10% of the profits at risk in 1996 (from the table above), which would come to $2.8 million dollars. We use this amount because that is an amount sufficient to create a meaningful set of online services, and to measure and react to their impact on company operations.

But we will invest that money only based on the following management agreement:

- We are committed to serving the segment that prefers online interaction with the same operational excellence and total quality that we bring to our traditional services.
- We are committed to a constantly improving return to shareholders and, hence, must fund this set of services via a shift, and not an increase, in operating costs.
- Because of the nature of Internet Web sites, our bank will be able to present each user with the full array of financial products and services. For example, if we are serving the needs of a jumbo mortgage prospect and find their job is in money management, we can effectively cross-sell the commercial side of the business. Therefore, our Web site must make the various *silos* (significant areas of content and service) appear to the customer and prospect as an integrated offering.
- We must make some internal organizational adjustments to enable such a program to succeed. We recommend the following, based on our understanding of successful management of large Web sites:
    - Each significant silo should assign or hire a full time Webmaster. This individual is in effect a product manager, whose product is the Web site information and services that best enable the customers and prospects of that silo. This Webmaster will also be in charge of promoting the silo's service, and of the measurement and analysis tool that will enable the leadership of the company to understand the site's ROI (Return on Investment).
    - The corporation should hire or assign a full-time Integrated Marketing Webmaster. This individual will have three tasks: overview of the

integration of the site's "look and feel" so that the efforts of the individual product managers do not run off in different directions; *seamless integration*—a constant search for ways that the Web site can cross-sell services in order to best serve the customer; and overall ROI management and analysis.

- MIS should assign a full-time Web Liaison to manage the services of MIS in building and enabling the Web presence and to accelerate the integration of Web self-service applications with legacy applications (such as balances, interest rates, etc.).
- The balance of the work should be outsourced until we fully understand the organizational impact of our efforts.

Our preliminary objectives for each of the silo line managers (people responsible for managing site content) and their Webmasters is to perform an informal, personal survey of their customers. The purpose of the study is to gauge what services will be the most desirable. Then they must collaborate with the Web engineering team (internal and outsourced) in order to prioritize the services, ranking highest those that have high impact and low cost, and ranking lowest those that have low impact and high cost.

We would, based on instinct alone, create one pet project, which is to have our MIS team dedicate enough resources to create a product that provides the easiest, fastest, and most seamless connection between Quicken and Microsoft Money and the electronic services of a bank.

Within six to twelve months of our firm's initial investment, we should expect to have the following elements in place:

- A functional, cross-marketing Web team and outsource relationship, with a road map to site development.
- A functional, integrated site that offers the highest "bang for the buck" services to the computer-enabled customer segment.
- A set of measurement tools in place to enable us to track our progress.
- A consumer product that connects Quicken and Microsoft Money users to our services, with absolutely impeccable support. This will lose some money at first, until we have the product ironed out to be extremely easy to use; in the meantime, we must provide impeccable user support.

These steps will make our bank fully competitive in filling the digital service gap. We would then have our team address the following 1997 objectives:

- Based on our experience, how can we continue to improve the product for our customers?
- Based on our best customer experience, how can we raid other bank customer bases for those who prefer our high-quality, interactive computer services?

In the above scenario, we have looked at some of the business decisions that go into determining if a company, in this case a bank, should have a Web site, and what some of the major objectives and strategies should be if they decide to go forward. Next, we will review how different companies are presenting themselves on the Web.

Web Presentation Strategies

We have examined Web sites in three different areas—banking, mutual funds, and general interest/consumer—in order to provide an overview of how these different types of businesses present themselves on the Web. To help us to present our assessments, we have assigned a rating system, albeit arbitrarily. A score between 1 and 10 is used to measure such things as attractiveness and general feel, interactivity, frequency of updating, scope of the site, quality of the navigation features, links to other sites, ease of contacting someone at the host company, and the use of new Web technologies.

Banking Sites Go Online

In the August, 1995 issue of *Online Banking Report*, it was reported that the banking industry was racing to set up informational sites on the World Wide Web. According to their research, *Online Banking Report* believed that by the year's end, 425 banks would be online. They went on to predict that there would be 2,000 by the end of 1996 and over 7,500 by the end of the decade.

The reasons given for this extraordinary growth are both reactive and proactive. Banks fear losing market share to nonbank heavyweights such as Microsoft and AT&T. At the same time, banks recognize that for a relatively small capital investment, they can reach the 10% of U.S. households currently online. With more people working from home offices than ever before and with the increasing convergence of telephone, cable, entertainment companies, and Internet access providers, the number of people online will continue to grow dramatically.

While there are a number of banks currently on the Web, only a few of these sites stand out above the rest. One of the most glaring deficiencies is the attention paid to the graphical look of the sites. An argument could be made that selling an intangible service does not require the use of quality artwork because a consumer does not have to make a visual examination of the product in order to make a buying decision. This is true, but with more than 175,000 commercial sites currently on the Web and hundreds of new ones being added weekly, a site must stand out in a number of ways to be above the clutter. By investing in the up-front design, a bank makes the statement that their Web site is a serious business vehicle that has the full faith and backing of the institution, and is not simply an experiment or project.

Many of the bank Web sites seem like they are there simply to say that they have a Web site. With competition increasing for consumers' time, wasting their time by putting up an annual report and corporate statement online is a good way to lose consumers' interest. Because the Internet is such a powerful, information-rich resource, it follows that any business trying to attract users had better deliver more than a basic brochure.

We will take a look at those few sites that have begun to use the Web to its fullest potential. Several months ago, only one or two sites were getting close to being what could be considered an attractive, functional site. The good news for banks in general is that a few leading companies have redesigned their sites, and it seems only a matter of time until consumers respond favorably, in large numbers.

NationsBank

As a sponsor of the Olympic Games, NationsBank (**http://www.nationsbank.com**) has used their sponsorship effectively to attract visitors to their Web site. This seems like the perfect way to draw traffic to the site, especially around and during the games themselves.

As part of their sponsorship, they are offering information on the sale of Olympic coins. However, it seems that the logical thing to do in addition to providing information about the coins would be to allow visitors to the site to order and pay for their commemorative coins online. This would no doubt lead to greater sales and would provide a unique branding opportunity for NationsBank. In addition, this would be the perfect opportunity to mention the bank credit card and a perfect lead into an online application for a NationsBank card. It is this type of marketing synergy that needs to be mapped out in the early strategy and design plans.

NationsBank has selected some specific products to feature on their Web site and does a fair job overall of promoting them. Military bank service is one such featured area. This area has information on the services and products designed for members of the U.S. Armed Forces. This is a segment of the population that is represented in larger numbers than average on the Internet, and it makes sense to have an area of their Web site devoted to their interests.

Another feature offered is information on college tuition costs and an interactive tuition calculator. By entering a child's age and the number of years until college, the calculator will show the amount of money monthly, or weekly, that the customer must save in order to pay the tuition costs. A similar feature is used to calculate the amount of money to be saved for retirement.

Both of these areas of the site would be enhanced if, in addition to providing the costs or savings needed, they also contained relevant links to other areas on the Web such as colleges or universities that match the estimated tuition range or links to retirement planning newsletters or magazines. It might also make sense to create a newsletter that could be a regular feature on the site.

NationsBank has its own merchandise store area where they sell hats, T-shirts, and other logo merchandise, but again they did not allow for online ordering, which is sure to impede sales.

An area of the NationsBank site under development, called PC Banking Software, is quite informative and well-detailed. In addition, the visitor can submit their name, street address, and e-mail address so that the bank can notify them about product developments and software availability. This is a good example of building one-to-one relationships. When a person completes a form indicating their desire to receive information, the company then has the ability to develop two-way communications with them in a very responsive and efficient manner.

Overall, the NationsBank site is fair at best. It contains a number of interactive functions and addresses some unique product areas. However, the graphical presentation is poor and not very exciting. By not offering online ordering, the site loses several opportunities to build branding relationships with customers at their site.

CATEGORY:	RATING:
Attractiveness and general feel	3
Interactivity	5
Updating	5
Scope of the site	6
Quality of navigational features	6
Links to other sites	5
Ease of contact	2
New Web technologies	0

Wells Fargo

One of the top banking Web sites we looked at was Wells Fargo Bank (**http://www.wellsfargo.com**). They are doing a lot of things right on their Web site, shown in Figure 1.

In particular, they seem to be the only bank offering customers access to certain account information via the Internet (see Figure 2). Most banks are planning or implementing online banking either by an 800 number or with the use of custom-designed software. This seems an appropriate step until security concerns related to using the Internet can be adequately addressed. The limited access that Wells Fargo is offering does, however, give a glimpse of the future to their customers using the Web, and it shows a commitment on behalf of the bank.

Figure 1: *The Wells Fargo site ranks near the top of the online banking sites.*

In fact, Wells Fargo has an entire section devoted to online banking options, where they explain several ways to conduct electronic banking in detail. Wells Fargo is supporting their online banking through telephone, ATM machines, Prodigy, and the Web. Customers can use a number of different software options including Quicken, Microsoft Money, and Wells Fargo online software.

The site also gives interesting historical information about the early days of the West and Wells Fargo's role in bringing important supplies and information to the settlers. In fact, each day visitors are greeted on the home page with a "This Day in History" item that establishes the site as a continually updated resource. In addition, the site features a section called Web Trails that provides a number of links to various places of interest on the Web, under categories such as Kids and Education; Government, Federal, and State; and Financial/Economic Information and Services. Under each heading are hypertext links to at least 10 sites.

A mini online mall allows access to a handful of merchants that are supporting secure online transactions either through a Netscape secure server or by accepting cybercash. This service brings a sense of community to the site and helps to legitimize online shopping.

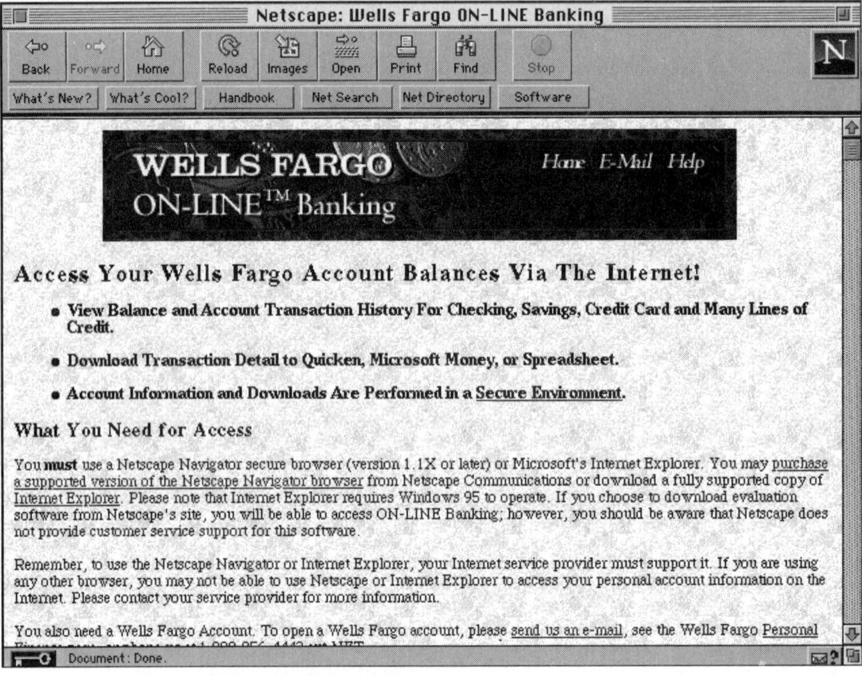

Figure 2: *Wells Fargo offers a glimpse into the future of online banking on their Web site with services such as account balance information.*

In all, the Wells Fargo Web site is informative, interactive, and a good resource for banking and finance, as well as a good starting point to find other interesting sites on the Web. In fact, in recent weeks Wells Fargo has once again redesigned certain parts of their site and added new features like Java applets to create up-to-date messages that scroll across the screen. It is this type of commitment and value-added features and information that ultimately will decide if a Web site is going to be worth visiting.

CATEGORY:	RATING:
Attractiveness and general feel	8
Interactivity	8
Updating	9
Scope of the site	9
Quality of navigational features	8
Links to other sites	9
Ease of contact	9
New Web technologies	8

CATEGORY:	RATING:
Attractiveness and general feel	8
Interactivity	9
Updating	8
Scope of the site	9
Quality of navigational features	8
Links to other sites	4
Ease of contact	9
New Web technologies	4

Offering Mutual Funds via the Web

Mutual fund companies are also finding the Web to be a very cost-effective place to offer their services and to develop strong relationships with customers and prospects alike. Mutual fund companies have developed some of the most interactive, information-rich sites on the Internet. With a little practice you can find almost the same level of information available to professional analysts and traders right on the Web. Much of this information can be found on the Web sites of the large mutual fund managers. Clearly the bar is being raised, and the need to provide significant amounts of information and to build strong one-to-one customer relationships is more important than ever.

One of the clear shifts taking place in our culture, especially as baby boomers enter their retirement years, is the desire for self-directed investing. Several factors enter into this, including the entry onto the scene some years ago of discount stock brokerages. Probably no single issue has been a greater influence, however, than the widely held belief that "Uncle Sam" simply will not be able to meet the financial obligations of its Social Security commitments when the baby boomers start to withdraw their retirement dollars in large numbers. This represents a huge audience, many of whom are technically savvy and looking for solutions on their own.

The Web then becomes the perfect place for these boomers to turn to and get information in a self-service environment. The companies in a position to meet the demands of this market stand to reap enormous benefits and the opportunity to build long-standing relationships with their customers.

Fidelity Investments

Fidelity Investments (**http://www.fid-inv.com/**) has made a real commitment to online access, establishing a presence on America Online, Prodigy, Microsoft Network, and the Web. Their Web site alone contains over 800 pages of information. The site provides a complete listing of account services and mutual fund information.

The Fidelity Investment Web site is truly an online environment that can serve the novice as well as the experienced investor. Information on market indicators, financial forecasts, fund performance (both current and historical), retirement (401k) and (403b) plans, and each of the Fidelity funds is easily found and is understandable, especially since an online glossary of terms is available.

Since the SEC now considers the electronic transfer of a prospectus to meet compliance requirements, Fidelity offers the option to download a prospectus directly from their Web site. This offers convenient and timely information for their customers while no doubt saving them significant dollars in printing and postage costs.

The site is extremely content heavy, so they could have made better use of graphics and design to provide a clearer sense of the topic section. The graphics simply do not lend themselves to the topic at hand. In addition, the gray background color offers a bland and stagnant delivery of the content. The general feel of the site is very corporate and does not appeal to the self-directed or potential investor except in content.

The interactivity built into the site, while a good beginning, could be improved upon. Within the site is a section titled "What's Your Savings Personality," but the interactivity is minimal. The user answers three questions and receives a canned response. The response introduces the next page of content rather than bringing the user into a section developed for their individual needs.

Fund prices are uploaded daily and the news section is updated several times a week. Otherwise, there does not seems to be significant up-to-date content. The site always has the same categories with little change in content or presentation. There is nothing new to see or do in the site, aside from following specific funds (which most financial sites provide).

The site is fairly easy to navigate. The common footer bar allows people to jump to an index or back to the home page, but it does not allow them to return to the beginning of a particular section. The user may be seven levels down and can only go back page by page or quickly return home—there is no happy medium. The use of Netscape frames in the Fund Profiles section allows for easy reading of the content.

The Comments section allows the user to send an open-ended e-mail to Fidelity, but does not guarantee a response, which seems pointless. Fidelity needs to allow the user to request information for specific products or services, and to receive order fulfillment kits.

CATEGORY:	RATING:
Attractiveness and general feel	7
Interactivity	6
Updating	8
Scope of the Site	9
Quality of navigational features	6
Links to other sites	4
Ease of contact	4
New Web technologies	7

The Vanguard Group

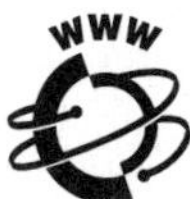

The Vanguard Group Mutual Funds site (**http://www.vanguard.com**) truly is in the vanguard. Vanguard is one of the most comprehensive, interactive, and graphically pleasing sites on the Internet, regardless of category. From the home page (Figure 5) on, you get a sense of a clean, crisp, and well-designed site.

One of the first things you will notice on the site, in bold letters, is the fact that the site is updated every day. As you travel through the site, you find so much useful information that there is a sense of excitement and anticipation in knowing that today's update will likely hold some relevance to your portfolio planning.

Talk about a value-added site: two features, the Vanguard University and the Library, contain enough information to arm even the most novice investor with the knowledge to become a savvy and self-directed mutual fund investor.

Like Fidelity, Vanguard offers downloads of prospectus kits (Figure 6). The level of interactivity is significantly higher than Fidelity's, however, as Vanguard offers several ways in which to contact the company, invites feedback on various site sections, has several online quizzes located after each lesson in the Vanguard University, and provides three interactive planning tools.

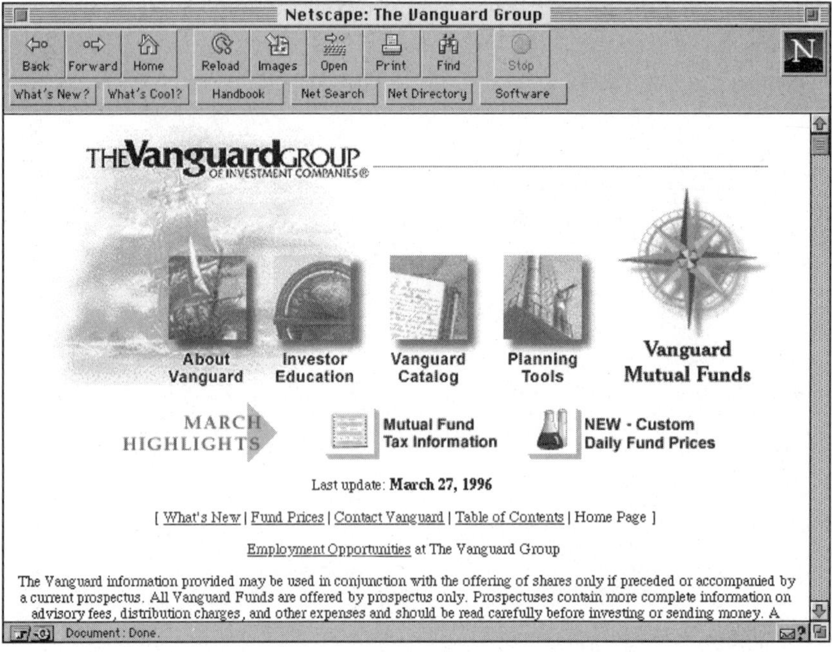

Figure 5: *The Vanguard Group site delivers content and quality in a visually pleasing format.*

Finally, the site is currently previewing a new section called the Laboratory, an area that is going to feature demonstrations and testing of new Web technologies. Unfortunately, this section is still in development, but if it is done correctly, it is sure to be an often-visited feature.

CATEGORY:	RATING:
Attractiveness and general feel	9
Interactivity	9
Updating	10
Scope of the site	9
Quality of navigational features	9
Links to other sites	7
Ease of contact	9
New Web technologies	8

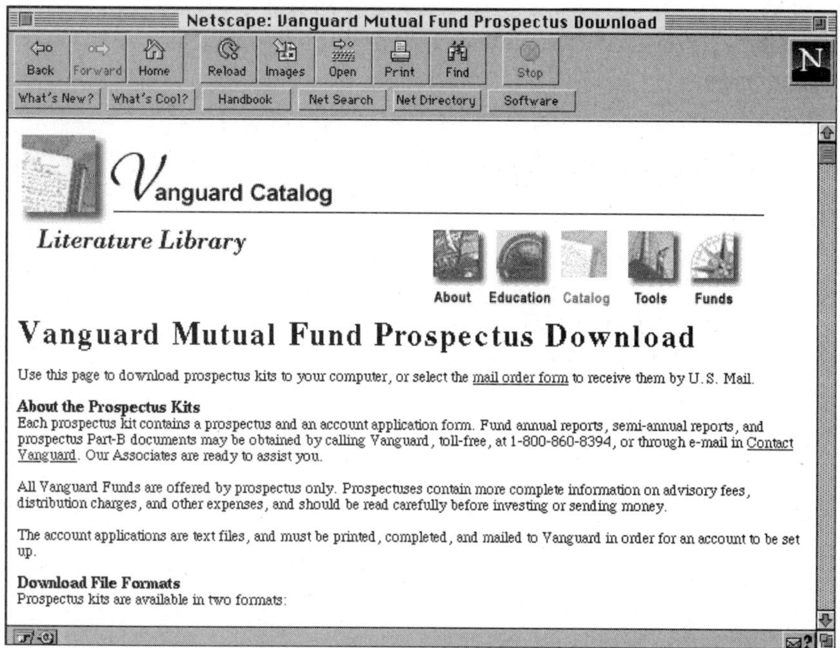

Figure 6: *From the Vanguard Library, the visitor can download prospectus kits in two different formats.*

T. Rowe Price

T. Rowe Price (**http://www.troweprice.com**), recognizing the need to provide personalized service, has taken a unique approach to their Web design. Visitors to the site are given the option of creating their own personalized "watch lists" that track the activity of specified mutual funds within the T. Rowe family of funds (see Figure 7). Each time a user visits the site, they can sign in with their e-mail address or personal password, and they are immediately taken to their personal watch list page with a "Welcome (user's name)" header.

T. Rowe is currently working on adding a dynamic graph generated from individual fund performances; the graph will show both current and historic trends. The graph is being created using Java programming and will take them another step toward providing custom-tailored information.

The T. Rowe site (you can see their home page in Figure 8) also contains all the information, in an extremely well-designed navigational path, that a person would need to go from novice to a savvy, self-directed investor. T. Rowe assumes that their Web site should be used as a decision support center.

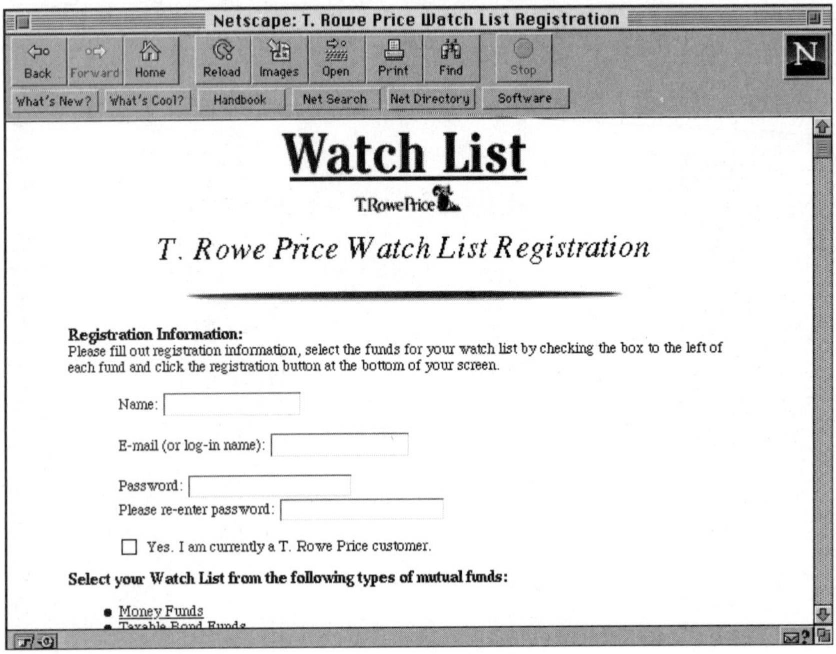

Figure 7: *T. Rowe Price allows visitors to create personalized watch lists to track the activities of specific funds.*

As with the other mutual fund sites that we reviewed, T. Rowe is offering the option to download prospectus kits. They also offer the option to receive additional information or prospectus kits by mail and make a point of ensuring their immediate response and the use of first-class mail, further instilling the sense of quality customer service.

CATEGORY:	RATING:
Attractiveness and general feel	9
Interactivity	9
Updating	10
Scope of the site	9
Quality of navigational features	9
Links to other sites	2
Ease of contact	9
New Web technologies	8

Figure 8: *The T. Rowe home page*

General Interest/Consumer Sites

With more than 30 million people accessing the World Wide Web in 1996 and over 1,000 new Web sites going live every week, companies representing virtually every industry are investing in ways to take advantage of the enormous marketing opportunities that the Web offers. Many companies, even those with consumer products, are using the Web as a marketing and communications tool for promoting their products or services. What we have learned, however, is that if you are going to use the Web as a brand promotion vehicle, you need to do more than simply put up a display case of products. Whether you are a designer or a client, you will need to create a theme or online environment to support products in addition to offering the consumer some value-added feature such as coupons or new product information.

Companies promoting products such as Ragu sauces and Valvoline motor oil have developed effective Web marketing plans that draw from two common elements: they both provide timely and relevant information in a fashion that is welcomed by the visitor.

Pleasant design and the ability to navigate through a site to find specific information easily is critical. A Web site may provide several features and functions that at different times can attract different users. In addition, the ability to develop one-to-one relationships with customers is perhaps the most powerful, and often overlooked, aspect of a successful Web site. This interaction with customers and prospects gives you the opportunity to instantly send product news and information, providing the customer has expressed their desire to receive it, and allows them to contact you at their convenience. Both will offer significant cost benefits to you.

Ragu Foods

With an award-winning Web site (**http://www.eat.com**), Ragu's Mama's Cucina has established a creative, interactive, and entertaining product-oriented site. The site has the theme of an elderly Italian grandmother's kitchen (see Figure 9), thus emphasizing the authenticity of the product at hand.

Figure 9: *Visitors to Ragu's Mama's Cucina are greeted by an Italian grandmother.*

A recipe book filled with glossaries and a search engine allow the user to browse any of the Italian food specialties featured in Mama's Cucina, often providing a picture of the finished dish. Ragu products are an ingredient in each recipe, and additional information can easily be found by following a hypertext link. Often the product link provides visually creative labels.

An interactive contest invites visitors to answer a series of questions; correct entries are then entered into a pool from which winners are selected to win a free trip to Italy. The site also features a "Family Reunion" contest, in which winners are invited to fly 20 people to any U.S. city with all the food provided for a family reunion-style party.

The Ragu site provides two very good examples of interactive branding applications (see Figure 10). Coupons are offered to visitors of the site, and signing up for them is made easy. Registered visitors simply look in their e-mail for the savings coupons, print them, and take them to the local market. This helps reinforce brand loyalty and ensure repeat visits to the Web site. Visitors are also invited to

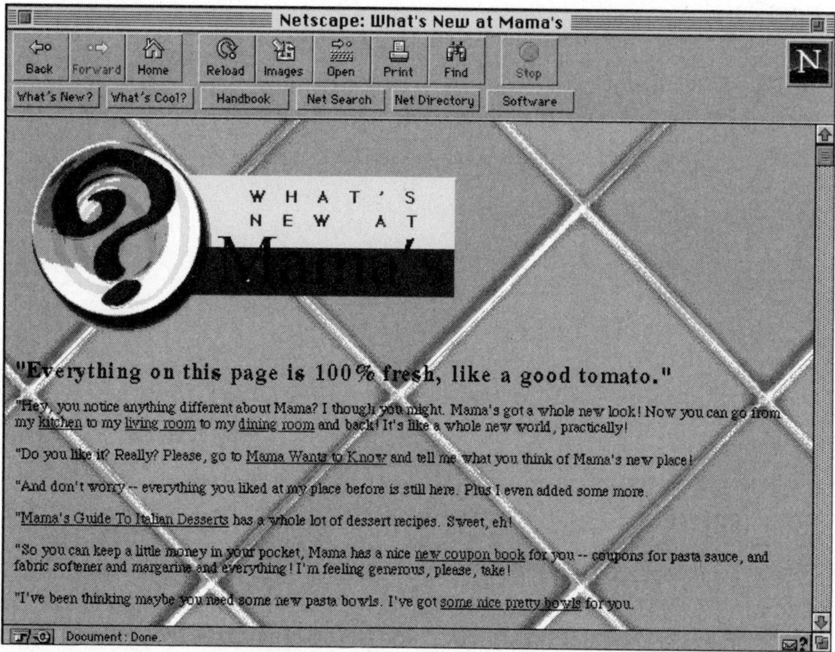

Figure 10: *Visitors can register for coupons on the Ragu site.*

submit their e-mail addresses if they would "like to hear from Mama when she's got something new to talk about." This creates the opportunity to instantly contact customers with new product announcements, special promotions, or any other product news without incurring additional marketing expenses. At the same time, they are reaching an audience that is predisposed to buy.

The site provides several links to other sites that may be of interest to the visiting "Italian." In addition, there is a link to an Italian Art and Architecture section that includes a comprehensive photo tour of New York's Little Italy. For the truly adventurous, why not learn to speak Italian? The site offers an entertaining way to learn some basic Italian phrases using a popular phrase sound interface.

The Ragu's Mama's Cucina site offers an array of resources and service-oriented areas that are very innovative in presenting their products. One of the first Web offerings from a packaged goods company, the Ragu site is a good example of innovative thinking and creative use of a new medium.

CATEGORY:	RATING:
Attractiveness and general feel	7
Interactivity	8
Updating	7
Scope of the site	7
Quality of navigational features	8
Links to other sites	8
Ease of contact	9
New Web technologies	5

Valvoline

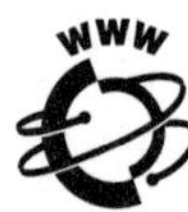

The Valvoline Web site (**http://www.valvoline.com**) has succeeded in using great brand identification by taking a commodity, motor oil, and creating a complete online environment revolving around auto racing, with which Valvoline has long been associated (see Figure 11).

Because Valvoline has a long history of sponsorship and involvement in the auto racing circuit, they have leveraged their high profile among racing fans into a fun, interactive Web site. The site was first launched in the spring of 1995 to coincide with the annual Indianapolis 500. Visitors to the Web site were able to log in and receive up-to-the-minute reports on the time trials and positioning of their favorite race car driver.

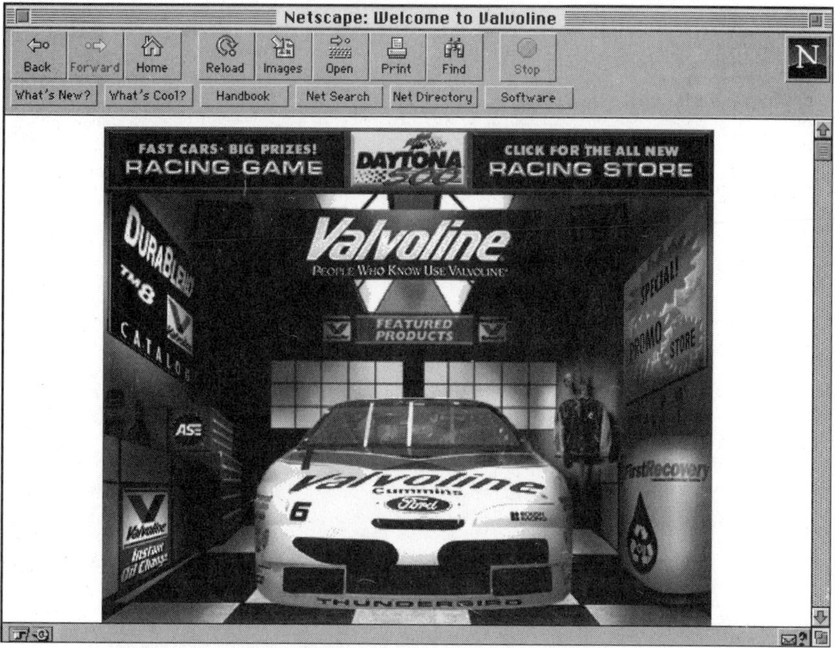

Figure 11: *The Valvoline home page emphasizes their auto racing connection.*

The site carries the racing theme throughout in a visually appealing design that maintains consistency with Valvoline's traditional advertising campaigns and image. In fact, you can even view a video clip of one of their television commercials right on their Web site, if you have the patience for the download time

The Valvoline Racing Store (see Figure 12) is another area on the Web site where racing fans can purchase hats, T-shirts, racing jackets, and other Valvoline logo merchandise.

The Valvoline Racing Store is going to begin taking orders online within the next several months with real-time credit card processing rather than expecting visitors to call an 800 number, as is currently the case.

Of course, selling racing paraphernalia is not the sole mission of the Web site. Valvoline manages to impart a significant amount of product information in a friendly non-sales-oriented style. Interested visitors can read about Valvoline's commitment to the environment and learn tips from professional auto mechanics.

Figure 12: *Racing fans can order their favorite racing merchandise in the Racing Store section.*

Because of the immense popularity of their Web site, Valvoline has redoubled their commitment to the Web and is aggressively pursuing the second phase of their Web development. New Web technologies are being added to enhance the interactivity and entertainment features.

Following last year's success, Valvoline added an interactive racing game and live camera shots from inside the Valvoline car during the running of the Daytona 500. Using the latest Shockwave technology, visitors to a section set up to look like the driver's seat of a race car were able to answer racing history questions by turning the wheel or shifting the gear shift. Correct answers moved the player along the race track in competition with other visitors to the site. Players who completed a lap in the least amount of time had their names posted on a leader board and were entered into a drawing to win a trip to the Indianapolis 500.

Valvoline represents a good example of taking the medium to another level. The Valvoline business is in no way similar to Wells or Vanguard; however, regardless of the product or service being sold, creative and strategic uses of the Web can be a powerful marketing tool.

CATEGORY:	RATING:
Attractiveness and general feel	9
Interactivity	9
Updating	8
Scope of the site	7
Quality of navigational features	8
Links to other sites	8
Ease of contact	7
New Web technologies	9

What Does It All Mean?

Throughout 1996 and 1997, we expect the interactive and online marketplace to continue its migration to the open, standards-based network platform, the Internet. We expect the tools and bandwidth to develop rapidly, which will in turn enable richer interaction and more useful Internet-based service.

We predict that the Internet will be increasingly viewed as a worldwide applications platform, and not as a mere medium, although the Internet can certainly function as a medium. In its more important role as an applications platform, the Internet is capable of delivering significant services and customer support—a role with far more impact than just delivering content.

Web designers and developers and the companies they are marketing will become more sophisticated in measurement, two-way interactivity, customer service and support, online advertising, and calculating return of investment. We believe that over the next two years, the Internet will emerge as the most measurable communication expenditure, and as a result, we expect advertising and promotional dollars to shift significantly to the Internet, and follow the measurable behavior of consumers and businesses.

The barriers to direct selling over the Internet will disappear, and we will see highly sophisticated "catalog" sites, which will enjoy worldwide reach, dramatically lower production costs (no printing or mailing costs, which accounts for up to 40% of cost of goods sold for the catalog industry), and more effective stocking (dynamic electronic marketing eliminates the cost of promoting out-of-stock items).

We will also see a strong trend in applications that allow customers to make their own travel reservations, buy and sell securities, and perform other actions without using a travel agent, broker, or other mediator. Customers can access services 24 hours a day at their convenience, leading to greater customer satisfaction, while significantly lowering the commissions, cost, and telephony infrastructure of the current business models.

We are convinced that the fear of using credit cards over the Internet will evaporate as customers realize that there is no more risk than with any other credit transaction. Credit card use will also increase as the number of services and products available online grows significantly.

We expect significant new services to enrich the Internet, coming from virtually every important sector, including automotive, consumer, entertainment, financial, government, media (publishing and broadcasting), telecommunications, service, and technology. This explosion of new services will continue to fuel the increased use of the Internet. We expect that the growth rate for Internet use, both at work and at home, will continue at a brisk pace. Further, we believe that at the end of five years, a digital Internet connection will be viewed as mandatory for virtually every job and as a necessity for the home, in all economically advantaged (or industrialized) sectors of the world.

That growth rate, and the attendant worldwide reach, will affirm and fuel the continued development of Internet-based applications that fundamentally re-engineer the relationship between companies, their customers, and their prospects in much the same way that automatic tellers have driven a re-engineering of the architecture of banking. We see the Web continuing along its path as an interactive communications platform allowing broadcast capabilities with *narrowcast* (highly specific audience) focus.

With all these changes in such a compressed time frame, it should be first and foremost in the minds of those planning and designing a successful site to have clear goals and objectives as the first step in the development process. It is also important to remember that a plan needs to address the direction and development process the site will follow after the launch. Too often we set our sights on the immediate goal, such as a site's launch, and we forget that it is only the beginning in the life-cycle of the site. Proper care must be given to plan for future additions to the site, since rarely will everything be put up at one time.

Building a Screenplay for Site Development

We find that by first looking at our intended strategic destination, we can work backwards, setting realistic goals along the way. In planning this way, we reduce the risk of trying to achieve everything at once, which frequently reduces the chance of launching at all. Building a screenplay for site development in order to create the site in stages or acts works best.

Act One is the initial launch phase and will serve to establish the look and feel of the site and set the overall tone. It is always a good idea to provide an opportunity for users to give developers feedback—if possible, with some incentive to do so. We have also found that open-ended questions are not as useful as creating a framework with a series of questions directing the focus of the feedback.

Act Two should be used to introduce some new features and should make any adjustments based on both user and internal feedback.

Act Three is the process of continual maintenance and management of the Web site and is an ever-evolving program. As new technologies become available, such as Java and Shockwave, the need to keep upgrading and adding new features will continue unabated. None of us can accurately predict what the future will bring, only that it will bring change at a faster rate than at any previous time in our history.

Remember, a Web site cannot be all things to all people. Find out all you can about your customers and your target audience and plan a site that speaks to their wants, needs, and desires. If planned properly, the design of a the site will ultimately perform a function or service that is of value or convenience to your user group. If it does not, all of the flashiest graphics, new technologies, and whiz-bang special effects will not bring you any closer to your customer.

Give us anything- We'll make it interactive
Give us anything- We'll make it interactive

PROJECTS
TOOLBOX
THE CHEFS
rare medium
EYE CANDY
EYE STRAIN
FREE STUFF
RARE STUFF
rare medium

rare medium

Rare Medium, Inc.

Company Profile

Rare Medium, Inc., has created interactive projects for such leading companies as Sony, General Mills, USA Networks, Prodigy, Polygram Records, Major League Baseball, and many others. Located in the heart of New York's historical Flatiron district, Rare Medium has over 25 collective years of multimedia experience among its five founding partners. The company's goal is to create visually striking yet functionally sound interactive products; focusing on the creation of Internet Web sites, CD-ROMs, and other digital media.

Most recently, Rare Medium has been working with several entertainment companies, including ABC Multimedia, to develop online gaming and related programs. Rare Medium has taken advantage of the entrance of Macromedia's Shockwave technology along with their extensive experience in Director programming to create highly integrated programs for the Web. In addition, Rare Medium and its principals have worked with the digital publisher Voyager to create five commercial CD-ROM titles. In short, Rare Medium is a content developer, proficient in creating interactive projects for virtually any digital media.

You can reach Rare Medium at **Raremedium@interport.net**.

Chapter Profile

Weaving an existing, branded product into the Web is one of the toughest tasks for any designer. The legacy of an established product with a history of traditional advertising methods sets a precedence of expectation in a consumer's mind. Clients tend to protect their expectations, challenging designers to work with restricted messages and ways to deliver them. General Mills, Inc., makers of several highly successful breakfast cereals, has such a legacy. Rare Medium took the challenge of creating a site for GMI, managing a legacy through some simple techniques available to all designers.

Smart Web creators know that our medium means a different relationship to customers. This shift can be described as *pull-selling* rather than *push-selling*. Push-selling techniques come in several well-known forms:

- Fast-talking sales people who dodge questions and cleverly avoid complete answers
- Television, radio, or print ads that use a lot of special effects but provide little honest information about a product
- Ad blitzes which hammer markets with repetitive messages

In contrast, pull-selling allows for, but does not always demand, a more involved role of a customer in order to deliver a more valuable message. On the Web, pull-selling comes in three primary forms:

- *Immersion* is the closest cousin to push-selling; it can be overt or subtle. Overt examples include VRML or other 3-D Web-based worlds and rich graphics or animations that incorporate a product message or logo. This approach frequently demands high production costs and the most download time. While some clients see value in large budgets, some target audiences, such as kids, have little patience to wait for the fun to arrive.
- *Suggestion* is an approach used by a number of advertisers who realize that information about their products alone may not be enough to entice customer attention. Examples include topical 'zines with content that suggests the use of a given product, such as Toyota's *alt.terrain* site. Despite the value of the content, the message can have high impact by what it does not say in addition to what it does say.
- *Community/Dialog* is the most risky but successful technique to date. This approach must match closely with a target audience, usually young and playful. Molson Breweries, which uses message boards to connect visitors, is an example.

A synthesis of these three techniques manifests in Rare Medium's General Mills site. It combines immersive graphics, games with suggestive messages, and postings/e-mails for community development.

Bear in mind that this recipe can function with new ingredients for different clients. As chef, you must match the meal with the message. Come and get it!

Essay

General Mills on a Web Adventure

by Nate Brochin, Co-Creative Director, and David Grossman, Producer

HE CURRENT STATE of professional interactive Web design is a large equation that precariously balances contradictory impulses: one of glamour and acclaim, and another of practicality and accessibility.

Generally, clients expect the richest design, the latest technology, and immediate accessibility and download time, all for a budget that would normally accommodate half the original vision. In fact, many of the most important factors in determining a paradigm for good Web design are inherent contradictions. The essential contradictions are between a rich graphical style and quick download times. Global accessibility and the latest technology are also contradictions because of the proliferation of different browsers and viewing environments. Deciding on a percentage of resources to be allocated to the back-end infrastructure is, itself, a battle, given the modest experience and knowledge of most current Web users.

The General Mills site (**http://www.youruleschool.com**) is the perfect example to demonstrate large, state-of-the-art Web site design. As with any project, we had to ask ourselves two primary questions when designing the site:

- Do we produce a site that looks great but does not maintain a user/server dialog?
- Do we create a site that is full of client-side feedback, but is quicker and leaner on the visual end?

The answers to these questions form a valuable study in the creation of effective and engaging Web site design. Of course, these balances and compromises do not occur without the limitations imposed by both the well-meaning client and the current state of technology. What follows is a discussion of the factors that led to our final decisions regarding allocation of resources in designing a site that had the greatest impact on the largest number of people.

Designing the General Mills Site

The project began in earnest with our first client meeting subsequent to winning the assignment. This first meeting was called to develop the creative strategy for the Web site. For us, this was really a set of goals and benchmarks against which both client and developer would ultimately measure the site. It was important in this meeting for us to understand the tone that the client needed to communicate. We clearly defined issues such as style, movement, attitude, accessibility, and technology. Listening was the key.

General Mills' advertising agency, Saatchi & Saatchi, worked with us to shape the strategy and set specific goals. Their first goal was to establish a framework around which we could provide General Mills' product and brand information in a lively and entertaining way.

Back to School

After briefing ourselves with the original concepts submitted by Saatchi & Saatchi, we focused on an appropriate but somewhat offbeat metaphor for the Web site. This metaphor would ultimately touch on every kid's dream of going to a school where fun was the rule. Saatchi & Saatchi called it *You Rule School.* After a few sketches and decisions regarding the attitude and look of this environment, we began to design the site with interactivity in mind (see Figure 1).

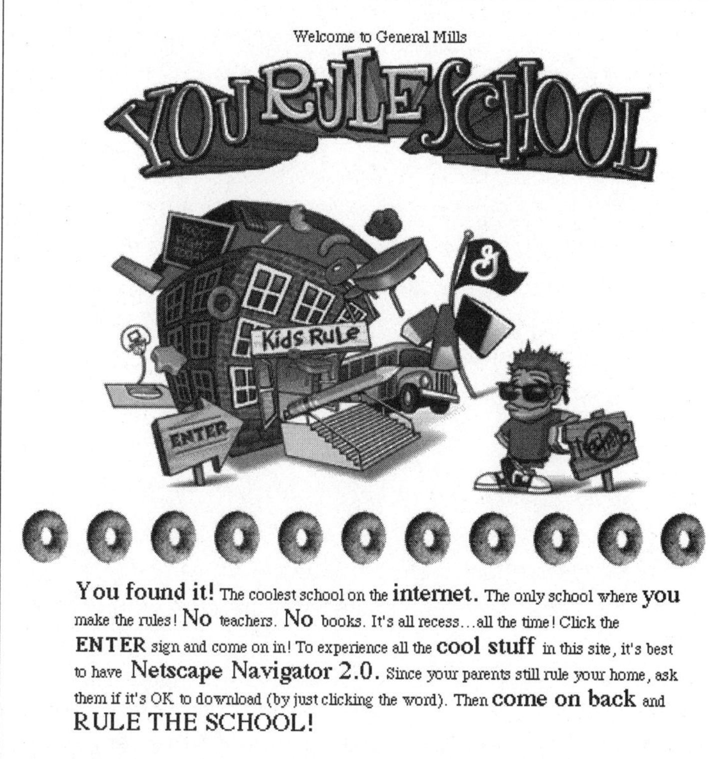

Figure 1: *The You Rule School home page*

In addition to creating the name and defining the tone, Saatchi & Saatchi contributed by providing their professional expertise in copywriting, along with their intimate knowledge of GMI's core businesses. It was helpful for this project that Saatchi & Saatchi also has a specific division, the Kid Connection, geared toward the development of children's educational research and age demographic information.

The You Rule School concept was built around the following areas:

- The Hall, for entrance and registration
- The Home Room, to send mail and get character bios

- The Yumnasium for fun workouts and games
- The Laugheteria, with games related to specific characters
- The Library, a resource for animation cels, fun sounds, and other kid stuff on the Web

Within each of these areas, there are literally dozens of sublevels that kids can access. Because of the navigational devices we included, however, each page is never more than two clicks away from one of the main rooms. More about that later.

These initial content issues helped us develop a visual framework to which we could apply what we thought were the key ingredients to creating a successful site for kids. We listened to the client to balance the design philosophy of the site with the technical and programming factors outlined above. We felt that there were four crucial elements to successful development of a kids-oriented Web site, regardless of the impact made on either the aesthetic or technical issues:

- Creating a virtual environment
- Making the experience of the site goal-oriented
- Giving important feedback based on initial user input
- Reinforcing the product and character branding through online activities and games

As a cognitive technique for site design, we ultimately adopted the *challenge-achievement-reward* (C-A-R) model frequently used in children's educational software. This model made the site as interactive and meaningful as possible.

Equally important was the clear identification of the target audience for whom we built the site. Initially, the target audience was seven- to eleven-year-olds. However, it was mandated that the site still appeal to older children as well. As a result, we positioned the site to appeal to the young teenager. Our experience developing products for kids suggests that the youngest audience tends to reach a little higher than expected, while teenagers still find the interaction amusing and engaging.

Now we had a road map with an accepted creative strategy. At this point, our Web team—the creative directors of design and illustration, the technology director, and an assortment of artists, programmers, and account people—met internally and tried to envision a site that would integrate the appropriate elements from the creative strategy sessions. It was clear that our mission was to create a cool interactive environment for kids to hang out in, filled with surprises, game-play, and personalization.

We agreed upon the metaphor, type of interaction, and scope of the site. Next, we decided that the site needed one clearly identifiable theme that addressed all the above goals and encouraged deeper exploration of the site. With a solid theme, we could explore other design ideas and concepts while maintaining the users' overall interest. If any of the secondary concepts generated activity, they would be brought to the fore and developed further at a future date. In keeping with the C-A-R model, we chose a treasure hunt to be the main theme of the site (see Figure 2). This concept helps to address several of the secondary level goals, such as repeat visitation and the branding of the General Mills characters.

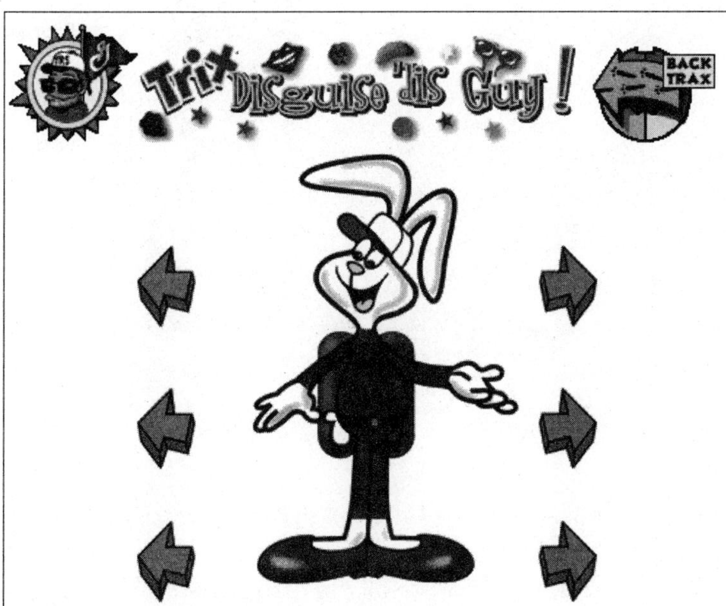

Trix Disguise 'is Guy!
BACK TRAX
The rabbit needs your help! He's tired of hearing "Trix are for kids. Trix are for kids!. "Here's your chance to find the perfect disguise so that, maybe, he can finally get a bite of his favorite fruity cereal. When you find one you like, print it out. It's yours to keep. And, who knows, maybe the disguise you choose will help the rabbit get Trix!

Figure 2: *The site's main theme is a treasure hunt.*

In an effort to weave General Mills' equities into the fabric of the site, we chose one of their lead brands to highlight the treasure hunt: Lucky Charms provides the mechanism for the search in the guise of digitally re-created "magic charm" cereal pieces (see Figure 3). We decided to bury these charms throughout the site, often utilizing several levels of integration. For instance, directions to some charms are revealed only when the user completes a Macromedia Shockwave-based game.

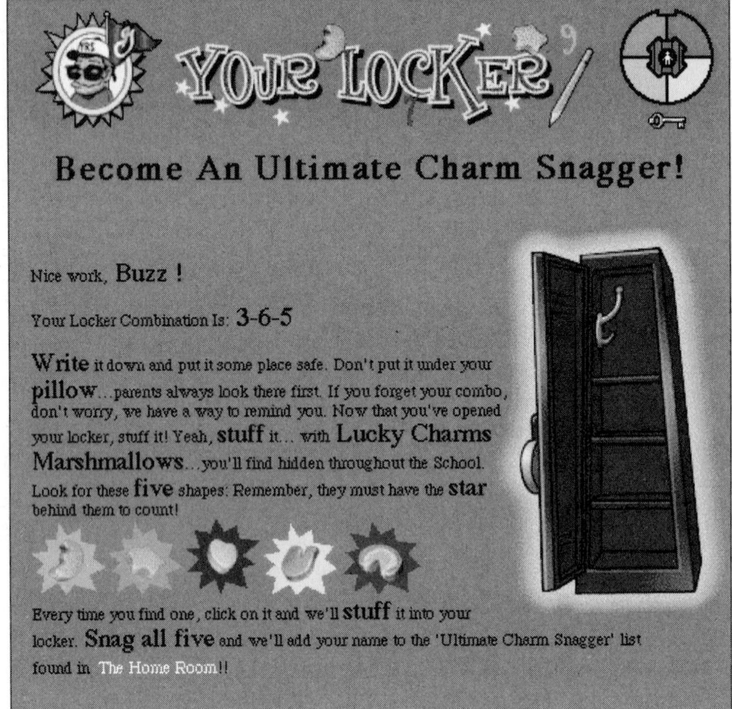

Figure 3: *We hid charms throughout the site for the user to discover.*

The site fulfills the challenge part of the C-A-R model by having users acquire the charms through site exploration and game-play. Achievement, is satisfied by users completing the hunt and finding all the magic charms. The General Mills folks provide the reward in the form of a promotional giveaway. The giveaway, together with a personalized, printable diploma and the posting of the user's name to a V.I.P. honor roll, make for an exciting end to a truly interactive Web experience. This concept encourages both site navigation and repeat visitation for users who do not find all the charms on the first pass. It should be noted that the task of finding all the charms is actually quite difficult.

The treasure hunt motif gives site navigation a new meaning; it becomes an integral part of the design concept over and above basic navigational programming (see Figure 4). Both the designers and the programmers picked an online map as the most appealing solution to the problem of tying in the search for treasure with users' need to recognize their status or position at all times. This dynamic map appears on the main headers on all top-level screen sections and shows users not only where they are located, but also their history (see Figure 5). For example, if a user has been in the Hall and the Home Room, but not the Yumnasium, their path is reflected as a cross-hatched area on the map. In this way we provide a road map for users who have found the charms in certain rooms but not yet in others. (This idea required programming savvy—creative CGI scripting and a few C++ routines called by various scripts—and some design ingenuity to implement.)

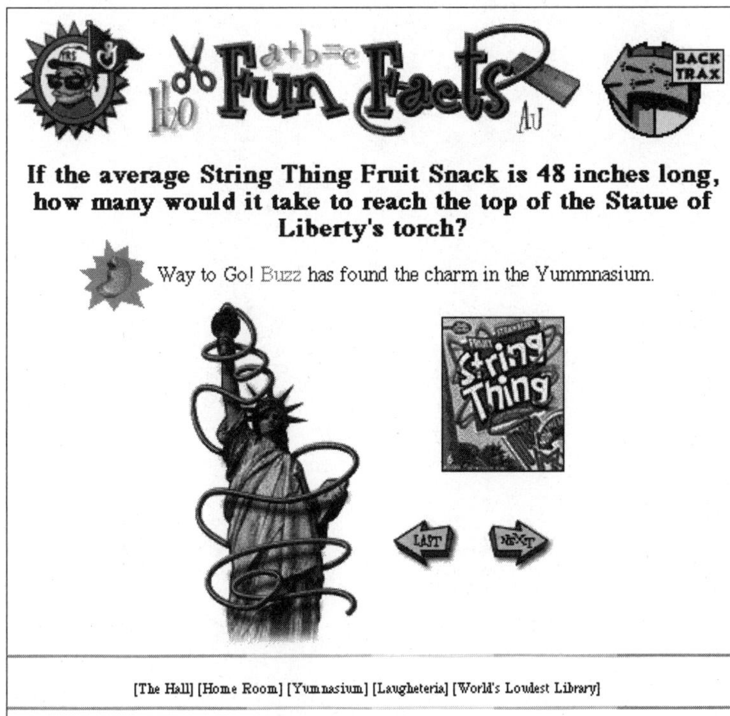

Figure 4: *Navigation becomes part of the design concept.*

The map is also an intriguing decorative element that prompted almost immediate interaction and curiosity in all the focus group tests. Because we provide a key just below the map itself, the mystery element quickly disappeared and the map became the navigational method of choice for about 80% of our focus group users. It's also important to mention that depending on which room the user is in, there can be as many as four ways to navigate through the immediately adjacent pages or rooms.

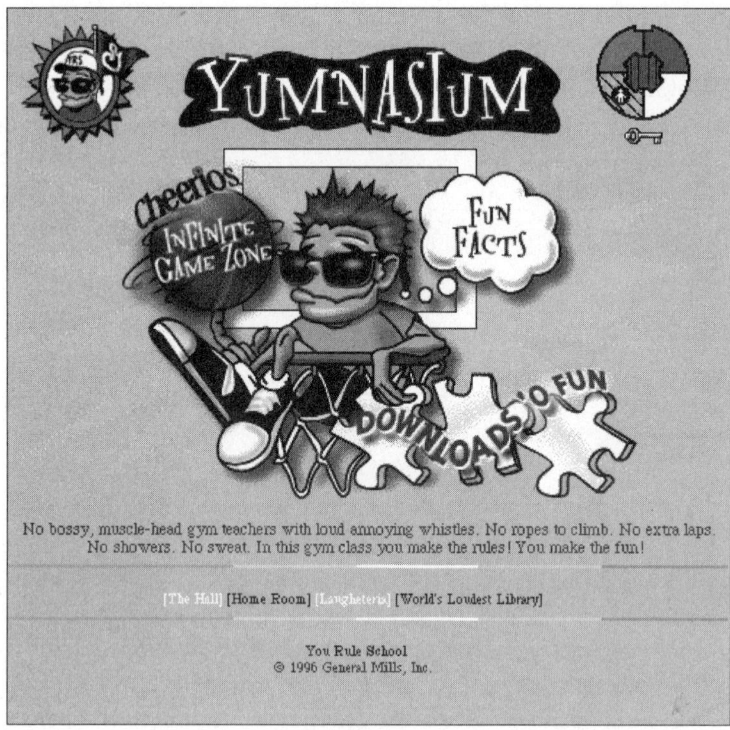

Figure 5: *The map in the upper-right corner lets the user know their position in the site.*

Personalization=True Interactivity

The battle between the dreamers (designers) and the realists (programmers) is one that takes place within most creative media. With interactive applications, the friction between design and programming takes on added significance because of the disparate nature of the tasks involved. In the General Mills case, however, we challenged and forced ourselves to think creatively on both ends. In fact, we broke from the typical development paradigm of designing within current technology. Instead, we asked ourselves what we *wanted* to have happen, forcing ourselves to figure out how to stretch the current limits of technology or to seek new methods for our concepts. A paramount concern was how to raise the level of personalization on the site. We finally addressed that issue through some clever back-end programming and nifty visual tricks.

At the site, users register brief information to get the combination to a virtual locker. Each locker has a temp file on the server that records the registrant's information and creates an environment that is unique to the viewer. In the file, this information is stored along with the number of charms the user has gathered, their location in the school, and their locker combination. Users place magical charms inside the locker by clicking on them when they appear in the course of the treasure hunt. The personalized locker also serves several other purposes:

- It gives us an opportunity to collect user information, essential to the personalization process (see Figure 6).

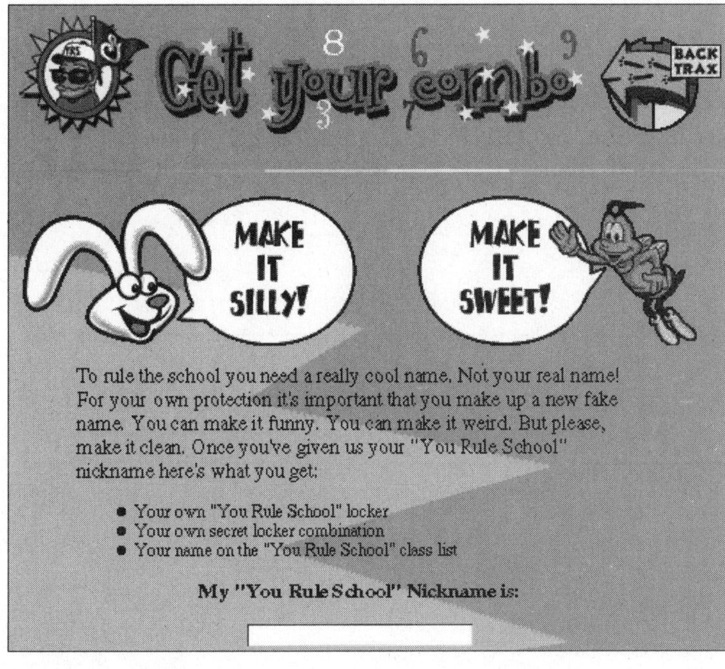

Figure 6: *The locker area allows us to collect user information.*

- It gives us a reference area to update new information as it happens. For example, if there is a new announcement or a new offer from General Mills, we prompt users to go check their lockers to see the new information, graphics, or offers.
- It gives us a place to send personalized e-mail to the user. We programmed various sections of the site to automatically send mail to the user, generally a note from one of the General Mills characters containing a secret combination that the visitor could use to open up previously inaccessible lockers (see Figure 7). Ultimately, the e-mail not only created a more personal experience, it generated repeat visits, encouraging kids to take the mystery locker combination and come back online.

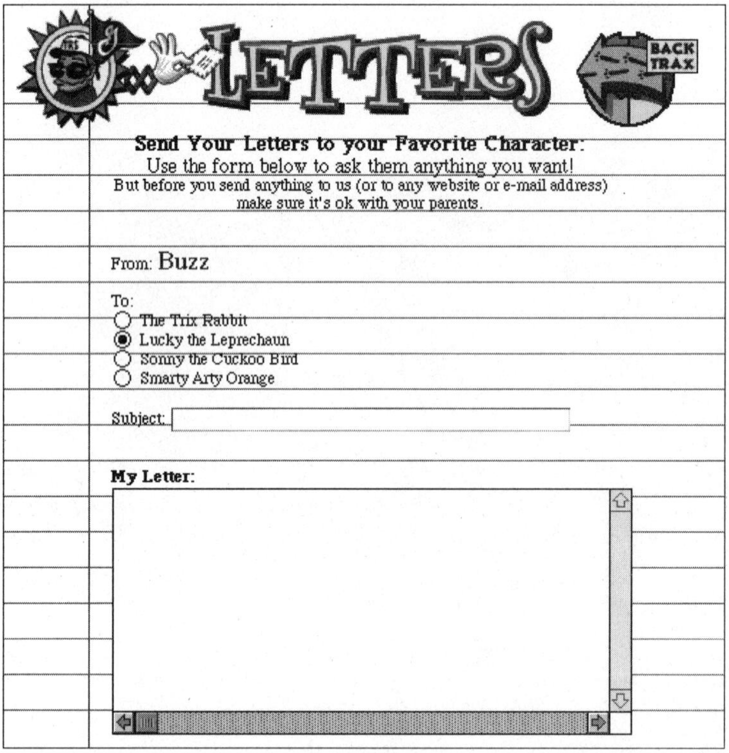

LETTERS

BACK TRAX

Send Your Letters to your Favorite Character:
Use the form below to ask them anything you want!
But before you send anything to us (or to any website or e-mail address) make sure it's ok with your parents.

From: Buzz

To:
- The Trix Rabbit
- Lucky the Leprechaun
- Sonny the Cuckoo Bird
- Smarty Arty Orange

Subject:

My Letter:

Figure 7:
We can send personalized e-mail to users.

Artistry and Patience

In the real world, an artist needs a definitive style to excel. The same is true for Web site design. Although we presented three options for the General Mills site, all were variations of the same basic illustration style.

The first option was a flat, 2D, lightly stroked version, which, while not very exciting, made for very quick downloading. The second was more of a 3D, airbrushed look. This option looked terrific but severely handicapped loading times and functionality. The last option was what we call *2½D*. This is a hybrid of 2D illustration and digitally optimized 3D–like shadowing. We ultimately made the decision to go with the hybrid. Our next challenge was to optimize this look even further in an effort to speed up loading times. Once we rendered all the 24-bit images using the Netscape default palette, we used Debabelizer to create 7-bit or 128-color custom palettes for each page, all within the Netscape default 256 colors.

Now that our illustration and production techniques were set, we had to think about layout and design issues. Making what was probably the easiest decision to date, we decided to re-create the look and feel of the General Mills' cereal boxes. The classic Lucky Charms and Trix packages provided us with much of the inspiration for type style and color scheme and are a good start for inspiration for any kids-related site.

As developers, we did take a calculated gamble by skewing the optimized nature of the site towards those with Netscape 2.0-compatible browsers. We made this choice because of Netscape's 85% market share and the convergence of other browsers to emulate its benchmarks. (We did allow for the lowest common denominator browsers, but they aren't able to see all the extras.) In an effort to differentiate the site from other kids-related sites currently on the Web, it was also essential to adopt a standard with the greatest flexibility in terms of new tricks, techniques, and browser-based enhancements.

Ultimately, the propensity for doing everything to be the biggest, boldest, newest, and most hip subsides into a realization that the World Wide Web is still in its infancy. With the advent of graphical browsers just a few blinks ago in 1993, there is still a millennium of experimentation and exploration ahead. It is important to recognize, however, that every project, from a single user's home page to a monolithic site like Time Warner's Pathfinder, all start with the same basic technology.

As in most media, the impact of a Web experience depends upon the power of the tools and the clarity of the message. For General Mills' You Rule School, we established clear-cut goals, conveyed the appropriate message, and used the best possible resources to ensure that the client's vision was fulfilled. We drew visual inspiration from the company's core business, cereal boxes, and created a site that included the lowest common denominator of Web browsers for an engaging interactive experience.

At Rare Medium, we believe that the most important problems dealing with Web design stem from developers producing cookie-cutter sites that do not relate functionally or aesthetically to the client or product at hand. No one can successfully design within a vacuum. Because the parameters and possibilities for successful Web design change on a weekly basis, that vacuum is always getting larger and more eager to swallow up developers unwilling or unable to keep up with the latest tools, technology, and techniques. Keeping pace with changes in technology and design will propel the World Wide Web from its current state as a graphic advertising billboard to an immersive, interactive, animated experience.

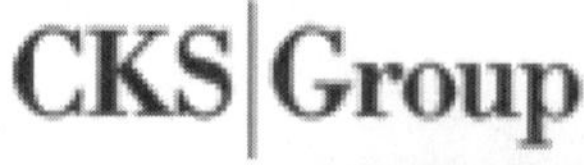

www.CKS.com

Our address is turning up on everything.

Check out our latest web sites under Services & Clients

What is CKS?
Services & Clients
People & Places
Making the News
Connect to CKS
Site Map

CKS | Interactive

CKS|Interactive

Company Profile

CKS provides its clients with an integrated menu of services, ranging from strategic corporate positioning to traditional television advertising and media placement to interactive advertising via the Internet. The CKS|Group combines the strength of its marketing communications firm CKS|Partners with its new media divisions CKS|Interactive and CKS|Pictures, along with support from CKS|Media and CKS|Onsite. These companies bring together experts in communications, marketing, and technology to shape marketing communications in a rapidly changing media landscape. CKS is a master of integrated marketing communications, creating brand awareness and consumer interest, educating potential customers with interactive software demonstrations, touch-screen kiosks, and the Internet, including effective packaging and secure, Internet-enabled transactions. Its clients include United Airlines, MCI, McDonald's, Sony, Yahoo!, Quarterdeck, Time Warner Interactive, NBC, General Motors, Apple Computer, Prudential, Clinique, Transamerica, and National Semiconductor. You can see a complete portfolio of their work at **http://www.cks.com**.

John Holland is a veteran creative director in Silicon Valley and the driving force behind all of CKS' Web and multimedia projects. He can be reached at **holland@cks.com** or 408.342.5400.

As one of CKS' leading designers, Tom Walter puts a "face" on the concepts. He has designed sites for The Prudential, CKS Group, Concentric Network, and many other companies and can be reached at **walter@cks.com**.

Chapter Profile

The Web took most of the "traditional" advertising community by surprise when it began in late 1992. The reaction was mostly one of fear: suddenly agencies had to wrestle with a two-way, interactive medium with immediate mechanisms for measuring effectiveness. Further, this new medium demanded a tight integration between media types: no single one could stands alone, so messages had to have crossover impact.

The new "relationship" that companies had to develop with their customers had a basic rhythm: listen (to the messages in the market), communicate (with a useful innovation), listen again (to customers' feedback), iterate (the message communicated), listen again, and so on.

An old Chinese proverb says, "We have two ears and one mouth because we should listen twice as much as we speak." This concept drives most of the successful designs on the Net. The Web is, for now, still a "quiet" medium, so listening is just as important as communicating. Nowhere is this idea more important than in the relationship between consumers and advertisers that exists on the Web. CKSlInteractive and its matching CKS divisions drive this idea forward by creating a "Brand Experience" in every project they build.

CKS' position as an "integrated marketing" agency is perfect for this environment, as they balance print, television, and the Web together as a cohesive system. Repetition alone is not enough—people must have immersion across the multiple environments they experience every day.

These two elements together—relationship and integration—form a "Brand Experience". To extend the proverb, "We have two ears and one mouth because we should listen to our Web customers twice as much as we speak to them."

Essay

Blending Strategy and Aesthetics Online

by John Holland and Tom Walter

HEN WE FIRST SAT DOWN to discuss this chapter on designing for the World Wide Web, we felt somewhat overwhelmed. After all, until a few years ago, the Web wasn't a commercial medium at all. Most commercial Web design "experts," ourselves included, have only a few years of focused Web experience. Nonetheless, after much work and discussion, we found a lot to say about designing for this new environment.

John's current role as the online strategist for CKS|Interactive challenges him to think every day about how to design a Web site for the users—the many guests we hope will visit the site. On the other hand, Tom's role as one of CKS' leading designers provides a wealth of daily experience and wisdom for the designer.

With these different perspectives in mind, we divided this chapter into halves. In the first half, John talks about the strategic components of design: objectives, strategies, and technologies. In the second half, Tom focuses on the creative process of Web design: aesthetics, issues, and techniques.

We hope this thinking and instruction benefits Web designers as they explore new frontiers and express their creativity in this compelling, emerging medium. We welcome your feedback via e-mail!

Design Strategies & Tactics

When you design a site, you must ask yourself a series of questions. What do you want your home page to communicate to the user? How can you imprint your brand image on the user's mind? Will content or presentation be the focus of the site? How will the user navigate the site? What new technologies will you use? These are some of the most important questions to answer when designing a Web site—questions we'd like to elaborate on here.

Digital Branding

Networked technologies such as the Internet and the World Wide Web are revolutionizing the way companies and their customers interact and communicate. These new media offer new opportunities for creative breakthrough advertising and marketing communications. Understanding the unique qualities of the Internet are critical to creating a successful brand presence online.

The first, and perhaps most important opportunity, is the ability to reach your audience wherever they are, 24 hours a day. This direct line of communication allows customers to interact with your company and your brand at their convenience. If that interaction is fulfilling, you've enhanced your product brand with the consumer.

Second, on the Web, unlike in traditional print and broadcast media, the user has total control over their experience. That means most opportunities to communicate with your audience are initiated by the consumer. Whether your Web site visitors find you through an Internet directory, a banner ad, a traditional print or broadcast ad, or even an e-mail from the friend, they all have one thing in common: a genuine interest in your service and product. Since consumers "self-select" themselves when they visit your site, every hit to your site is an opportunity to create and influence a brand loyalist.

Third, the Internet facilitates an instantaneous dialog between the company and the consumer. Customers can provide immediate feedback, helping you improve your products or even your communications itself. This kind of interaction increases the value of each customer relationship. As these relationships increase in value, so do the equities in your brand.

Finally, the Internet enables the fulfillment of every step of the consumer/company relationship, all in one place: you can build awareness through advertising and promotional content on your own site. You can educate the consumer and generate trials. Ultimately, you can complete secure sales transactions and provide service and support after sales. How well you perform these functions online ultimately contributes to defining the entirety of your brand for consumers.

The Brand Experience

Traditional advertising and marketing communications build toward creating a *brand image* in consumers' minds and a *brand identity* in the marketplace. Typically, this image and identity is the product of a series of one-way communications from a company to the consumer. This series might include television or print advertising to create awareness, brochures to educate the consumer, point-of-purchase sales, and so on.

But the interactivity and interaction on the Internet offer a way to transcend the independent staccato of traditional brand-building materials. The unique qualities of networked new media create the possibility for a real-time, dynamic brand property that we call a *brand experience*. A brand experience could be a user making a one-time visit to your site seeking product information for a considered purchase. It might be a user repeatedly visiting your site to get updates on new products or services. Regardless of its form, your ability to provide a positive brand experience to your users is essential to create a successful Internet presence.

Creating a Positive Brand Experience

You might have multiple objectives for creating a positive brand experience: to create brand awareness, to build and reinforce brand loyalty, to qualify leads and shorten sales cycles, or to improve service and reduce costs. You might even be launching a new brand over the Internet. How can a positive brand experience successfully accomplish these objectives?

- A brand experience should begin before a visitor hits your site. To successfully attract visitors, make sure you're registered with the major search engines, and describe your site in a way that makes it sound valuable to users. Publicize your site on- and offline. Make sure your site contains content that creates a "buzz" and is worth talking about.
- Deliver high-quality, brand-building content. Make sure information is easy to find. If you're trying to be entertaining, make sure that you provide real entertainment value. If you provide services and transactions, make sure they are simple and secure.
- Add value to your product or services by providing content that involves your user more actively with your product. Always position your brand as the fulcrum of the added value.
- Listen to your customer by enabling them to give you feedback from anywhere in the site. Nothing is more frustrating to visitors than not being able to talk to you about your brand. Actively solicit feedback for market research on your brands and products.
- Build relationships with brand loyalists by encouraging repeat visits to your site. Update your site with valuable content and offer an e-mail broadcast that notifies brand loyalists when a site has changed.

The defining question for a positive brand experience is, "Did the visitor take something positive away from this interaction?" Granted, you may have more specific strategic and tactical objectives. But your implementations to achieve these objectives will define the overall brand experience. With that in mind, you can move on to considering the many other Web design issues that affect a user's experience.

The Home Page

Surfing the Web is a naturally exploratory experience. Each click presents surfers with new possibilities, and the Back button enables them to back out of a site if it doesn't interest them. Because it's so easy for surfers to backtrack, the home page needs to deliver enough information about the content and benefits of a site as quickly and attractively as possible.

Your first contact with a home page should be like walking in the door at a cocktail party: you can tell what your experience will be like almost immediately. The host greets you and gives you the lay of the land. You can smell food, you can hear music, and you start to size up the people. Even though you might not know specifically what types of food, music, or people you might encounter, you have a good idea of what the party might be like.

A home page needs to deliver the same kind of first impressions about its site. Make sure the title of your site and any logo or brandmark cleanly greet the visitor, as demonstrated in the Tonight Show home page (**http://www.nbctonightshow.com**), shown in Figure 1. Use graphics and hypertext to communicate the possibilities and benefits of your site to first-time visitors. Tell repeat visitors what's new and make it easy for them to find their favorite areas on your site. Introduce a navigation system that orients visitors and helps them move through the site quickly and easily, as you can see in the Clinique home page (**http://www.clinique.com/maps**), shown in Figure 2.

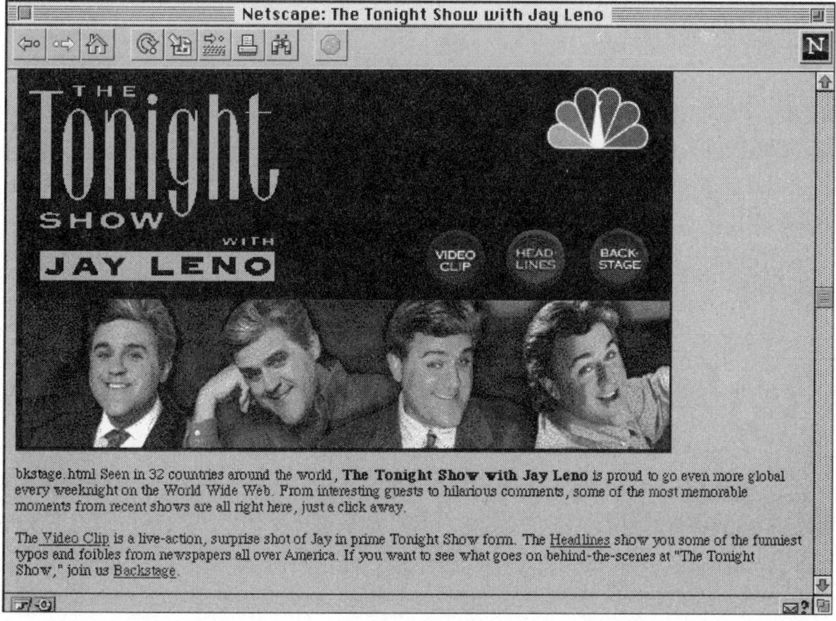

Figure 1: *Your brand's logo should immediately catch the user's eye.*

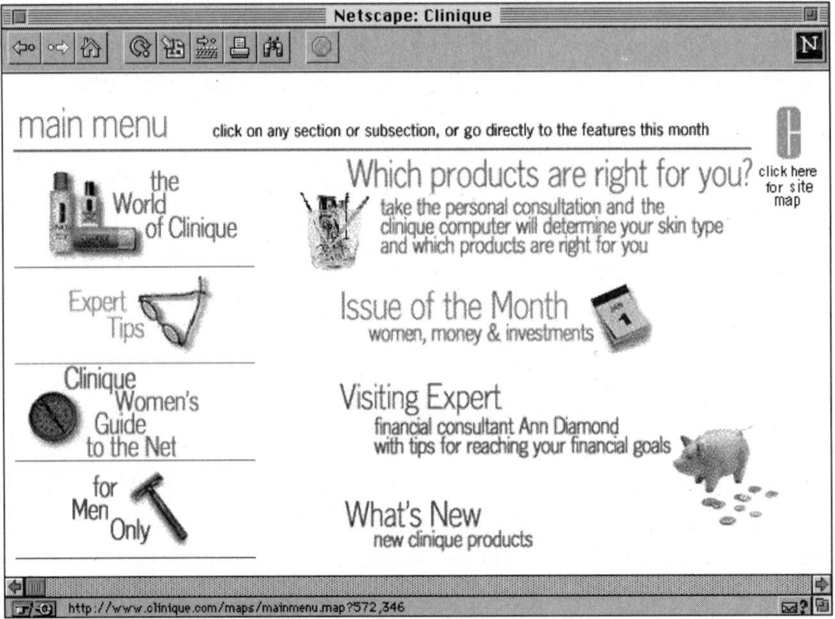

Figure 2: *Help your visitor get oriented quickly.*

Finally, a well-designed home page uses text and graphics to begin to tell your story—to communicate your key message. This doesn't have to be an explicit communication, but it should be carefully crafted nonetheless. The important thing is to make sure that your visitors start to form positive impressions about your site at the beginning of their surfing experience.

Content, Content, Content

There are two components of Web design: content and format. Because Web use is information driven, content is more important. You may create the most compelling design ever seen on a Web site, but if you don't deliver valuable content, you'll lose your visitors to the Back button. That's not to say good design on a Web site isn't important, but you must understand what visitors really want when they surf the Net.

So before you start to design, identify the content that will be of most interest to site visitors. For example, most visitors would find a rich description of a new high-tech product more interesting than a message from the CEO. Once you've identified the most valuable content, design to make sure that it's the most accessible item to the user.

Copy as Design

In traditional publishing, copywriting is a separate component from design. With the advent of hypertext, however, the copy on your Web site is not just writing, it is an *interface*. Whether you're writing copy yourself or designing the layout for copy that has already been written, keep these rules in mind:

- Try not to embed important links within prose. Instead, position them in bulleted lists when possible.
- Hypertext should read like poetry. Strive for efficiency; squeeze as much meaning out of each word as possible.
- Avoid the passive voice; active verbs energize hypertext.
- Active hypertext links should describe the destination as completely as possible (e.g., "Check out our low prices," rather than "Click here to check out our low prices").
- Think in broad strokes, not minute details. Assume that visitors are surfing, not reading, so you need to get as much of the marketing message across as quickly as possible.

Navigation and Exploration

Different people like to find information in different ways. It's important to accommodate these multiple preferences when designing tools to help your visitors locate specific information easily.

The best tool you can offer your visitor is an intuitive user interface and navigation scheme:

- Design interface elements to appear *hot*, or clickable.
- Provide a universal button bar that appears on every page of your site, as you can see in the pages of the CKS|Group site (**http://www.cks.com**) shown in Figure 3 and the internetMCI site (**http://www.internetmci.com**) shown in Figure 4.

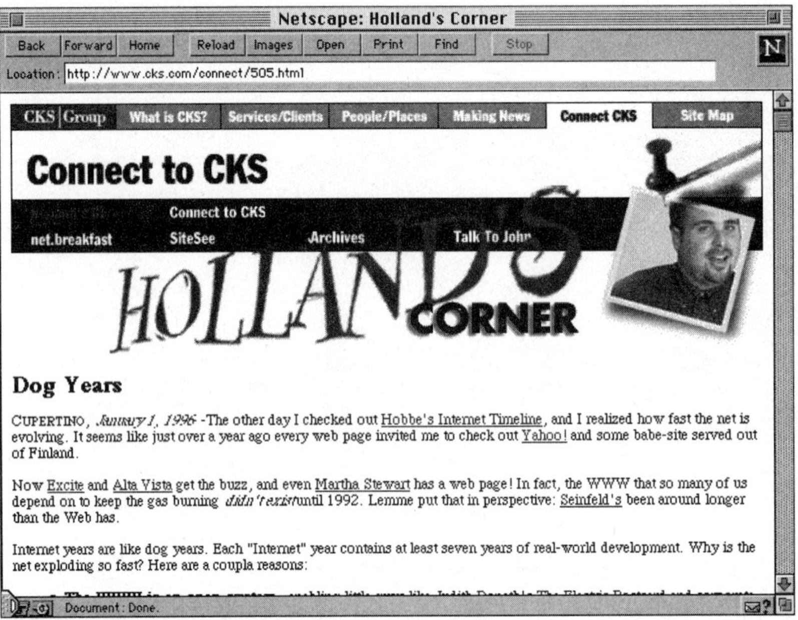

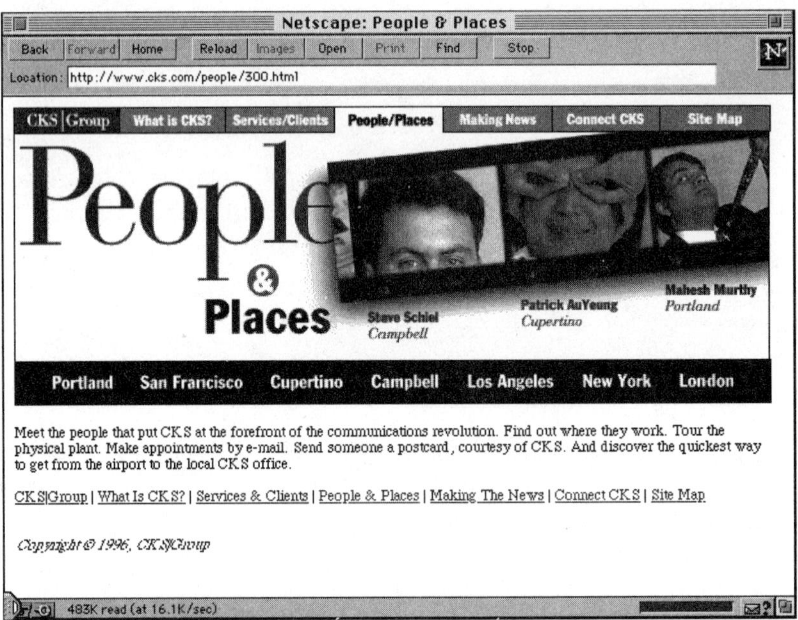

Figure 3: *CKS|Group uses a universal navigation bar both to allow readers to jump quickly to other areas and to know where they currently are in the information.*

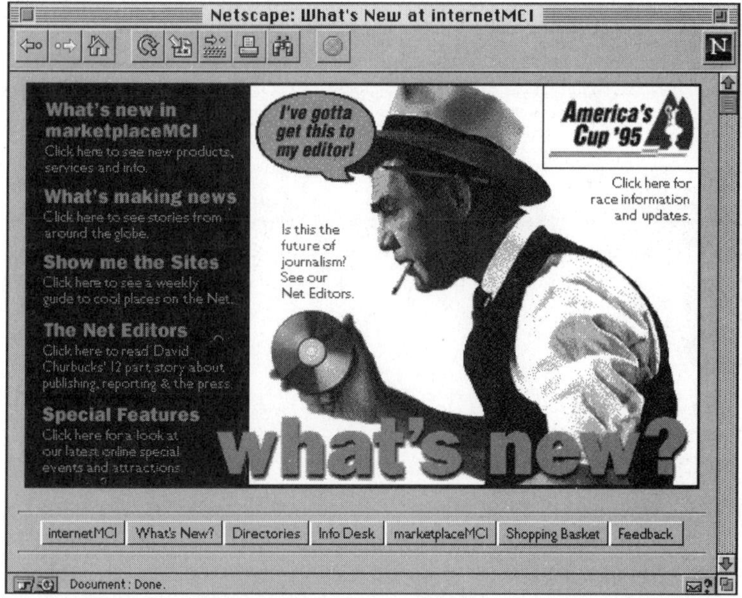

Figure 4: *The internetMCI button bar presents the user with a clear set of navigational tools.*

- Make it easy for visitors to get back to the home page if they get lost.

These guidelines will go a long way in helping your visitors feel comfortable on your site. If you're really interested in creating superior navigation, you might want to consider obtaining a book on user interface design. Two you might try are *The Art of Human-Computer Interface Design* (edited by Brenda Laurel and published by Addison-Wesley), and *Tog on Design* (by Bruce Tognazini).

Besides creating intuitive navigation, there are three tactical methods you can use to help visitors find information on your site:

- A *map*, which is a graphical representation of the content and organization on your site, such as the one for CKS (**http://www.cks.com/map/map.html**) shown in Figure 5.

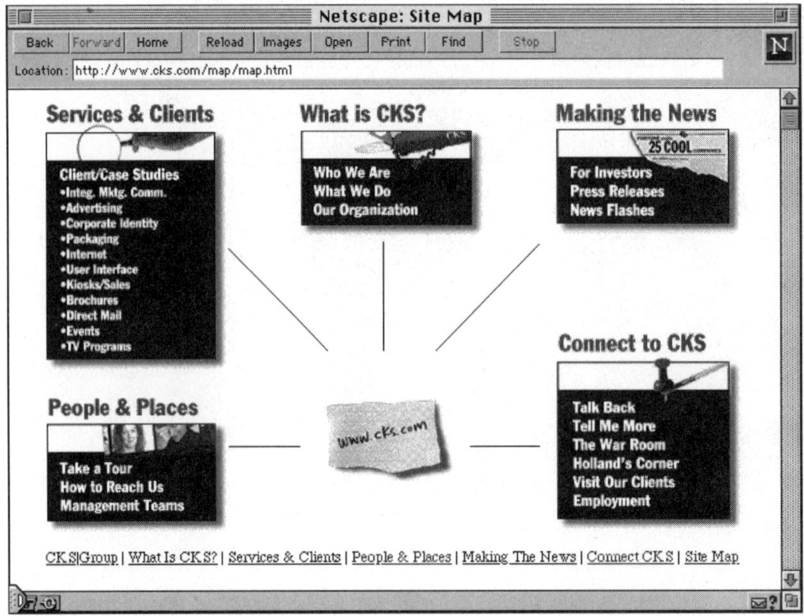

Figure 5: *Give users a map of your site to help them navigate.*

- An *index*, an alphabetical list of the content on your site.
- A *search engine*, where users can type a search query into a text field and receive a list of matching pages in return (such as Yahoo! at **http://www.yahoo.com**).

Maps and indexes are easy enough to create on your own. A map can be a graphic with an image map attached to it, and an index can be HTML text, like The Prudential's (**http://www.prudential.com/maps**), shown in Figure 6.

Integrating a search is a little trickier. Usually, installing a search engine requires some degree of Unix or Windows NT experience, as well as special access to the file server that you plan to use for your site. Fortunately, the process is relatively simple, and there are several excellent freeware search engine applications available. If you don't have the expertise or access to install an engine yourself, your systems administrator can usually help with selecting and installing the necessary software.

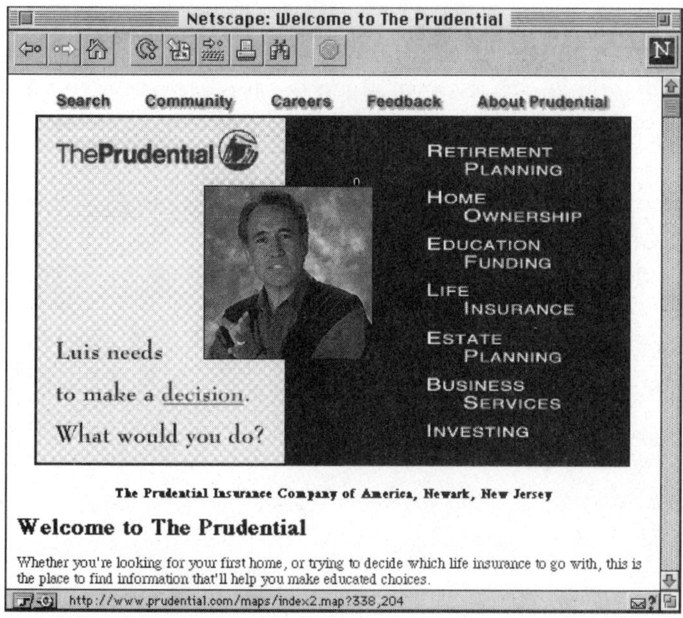

Figure 6:
An index can be HTML text the reader can click on to move to a new area.

Designing with New Technologies

New Internet technologies emerge on a daily basis, and Web sites are beginning to come alive with sound, video, and animation. These innovations excite designers with the ability to move beyond the static page.

However, new Internet technologies are experimental by nature, and you should carefully consider their application when designing your site. You can design the most visually stimulating, most technologically advanced site on the Internet, but if it doesn't accomplish your objectives, all that hard work will have been for nothing.

Misapplied technology can ruin a user experience and limit the efficacy of your Web design. There are two questions you should ask yourself when choosing a technology to enhance your Web site:

- Is this technology appropriate for my content?
- Is this technology compatible with my visitors' capabilities?

Choosing Appropriate Technologies

Though it may be tempting to use everything but the kitchen sink to enhance your Web design (see Table 1 for a representation of the types of technology out there), think carefully before using technology for its own sake. Sometimes a low-tech solution is better than a high-tech solution. For example, a text version of a speech may be better than a streamed audio version. It's searchable, printable, and it doesn't commit your visitor to a linear listening experience.

Table 1: Types of technology

CATEGORY	EXAMPLE
Media	RealAudio, VDO Live, Shockwave
Development	Java
Demographic capture and application	I/Pro
Database	Illustra
Transaction	E-cash
Interaction	Global Chat, Net Gen

Maturity of Technologies

It's true that cool technology can bring your site alive. However, new technologies often present a Faustian bargain: the more advanced and intriguing they are, the less likely it is that all your visitors will be able to enjoy them. So, in addition to thinking about applying the right technology to the right content, you should consider whether or not your target visitor will be able to view the technology you use.

These are the three compatibility issues you can expect with new technologies:

- Browser compatibility: new technologies often require the visitor to use a special browser or plug-in to enable the technology.
- Bandwidth compatibility: typical home modem connections may not be fast enough for some technologies, degrading the user experience.
- Platform compatibility: a new technology might not be available for all hardware or operating systems.

You can chart the evolution of technological adoption into three basic stages: established, emerging, and elite technologies. Each stage of a technology has its own appropriate application.

- *Established technologies* are those a majority of Internet users can use. Some examples of established technologies are e-mail and HTML forms. You should feel comfortable using these kinds of technologies for any appropriate application.
- *Emerging technologies* offer compelling new functionality, but have not achieved a standard position in the industry. As of this writing, RealAudio and Macromedia Shockwave represent emerging technologies. Because some users won't be able to use these technologies, they're best used for tactical purposes. For example, a Shockwave movie might be used to animate the circulation system of the human body. But don't forget to create a redundant, low-tech substitute, such as a static graphic of the human body, for those who cannot see the ideal presentation.
- *Elite technologies* often require high-bandwidth and/or powerful workstations. High-bandwidth streamed video is a type of elite technology. Because many Internet users don't have access to these technologies, they don't have much measurable value in terms of return. However, elite technologies can position your Web site as sophisticated and advanced, helping to generate PR and enhance your image. Because these technologies have limited reach and questionable marketing value, reserve them for when you really need to create a "buzz".

Table 2 summarizes these technological stages.

Table 2: Stages of technological adoption

STAGE	APPLICATION	EXAMPLES
Established	Broad	Forms, tables
Emerging	Tactical	RealAudio, Shockwave
Elite	"Buzz"	Xing Streamworks, Java

As technologies mature, they move up this ladder in level of acceptance and application. RealAudio is an excellent example of a technology that is successfully migrating through these stages. Once an elite technology, RealAudio is now an emerging technology on its way to becoming an established standard for streaming audio over the Net.

Web Design Aesthetics

When you tackle the role of design on the Web, the concept of aesthetics gets turned on its side. While everyone believes they know what it takes to make good design, these parameters usually do not coincide with what the Web was inherently created for—to transfer and disseminate large amounts of information. The most efficient way to transfer much of this type of information is text. But viewing a text-only Web site is about as much fun as watching paint dry. So graphics are added and the question of design arises.

Aesthetics—what makes good design and bad design—is so subjective that no single designer or company can truly define what is best. The goal here is not to critique various sites and decide if the person creating it knew the first thing about design or simply threw something together. Such a discussion would be counterproductive. The thornier and more difficult question is to see how design is affected by the transfer to the new medium: the World Wide Web.

Graphic File Sizes

Bandwidth is the term we use to describe how much information the Web is capable of pushing through the line—whether it be text or graphics, it's all reduced to zeros and ones and electronically transmitted through the telephone line. The major problem is that, in its current state, the transmission lines for the Web (and the modems connected to them) are incapable of handling the load we would like them to. They're just too slow in their data transfer rates to accommodate all the cool graphics and other stuff we want. To give you a more visual metaphor, it's like pushing a load of concrete through a drinking straw.

Thus, the first, most important, and most daunting aspect of designing and creating graphics for the Web is file size. Making graphics as small as possible, but still of acceptable viewing quality, is the tightrope any designer for the Web must continually walk. There will be occasions when you'll spend as much time and effort on reducing the file size of the graphic as you spent on creating it. It's the way of the Web, and small file size is the mantra by which you live.

There are many tricks and devices to reduce the file size, and as soon as one is divulged there's someone standing by to tell you that they know a better way. As a general rule, if the design uses flat color, try to keep the colors to a minimum. Also, try to use as few graduated tones as possible. This will give you a good starting point but should by no means be the only way you design. Multiple color and a myriad of grades can be displayed on the Web—it just takes more savvy.

Slice 'n' Dice: Cutting Up Your Graphics to Minimize Load Time

To help give the appearance that your page is loading faster, you can cut graphics into smaller pieces and load them separately. For instance, load a banner first, then a main graphic, then a menu bar or an icon. Your viewer will think they've spent much less time waiting if they get little rewards as the page goes along. It seems as if it's faster to wait for six 10K graphics than one 60K graphic. Go back through many of the pages you like on the Web. Download the various graphics that make up the page. Odds are you'll find that what you thought was one huge graphic is actually five or six well-placed graphics, as you can see on the CKS home page (**http://www.cks.com**) shown in Figure 7.

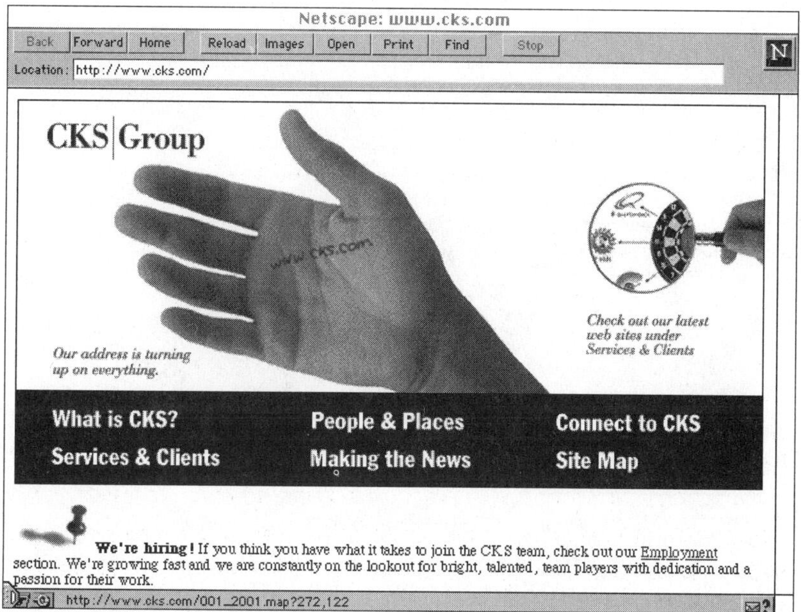

Figure 7: *Cut large graphics into small pieces to make them load faster.*

How you cut up your graphics can also reduce how many graphics you actually have to create for a Web site. That menu bar at the top of the page can be used over and over again by the HTML documents you generate. (This tip may seem remedial to some, but it is often the simplest things that need to be repeated.) Cut your graphics up well and expeditiously, and your page will seem like a breeze to load.

One way to ensure your cut-up graphics load the way you intended when you so carefully designed them in that multilayered Photoshop file is to use invisible tables. Tables can be used for much more than chunking up a lot of text into a more aesthetically pleasing, eye-catching manner; you can also place graphics in them as shown in Figure 8, the General Motors home page (**http://www.gm.com/index.htm**), locking up the graphics' position on the page. No matter how large or small the viewer makes the browser window, your graphics will stay just where you, the design megalomaniac, want them to appear. And you can get rid of those unsightly table borders by making them invisible. Some people won't even know you're using a table, but instead will think you've somehow gained incredible control over HTML programming. Let 'em think what they want.

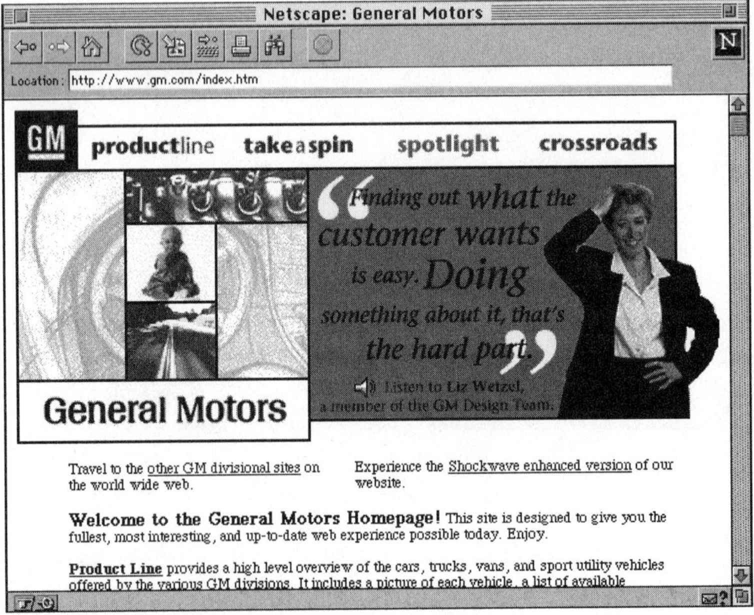

Figure 8: *Tables aren't just for text. Use them to organize graphics you've cut up.*

GIF vs. JPEG: Must It Be War?

When discussing the topic of whether the GIF or JPEG format is better, people often become near-zealots. There are those who will use only GIFs because of their widespread popularity and browser integration, and there are those who insist only JPEGs will do the job because of their richness in color, tone, and detail. They both have their place, time, and specific uses.

The GIF Format It has been my experience that the GIF format's compression algorithm works better when there are large portions of the graphic where the pixels are the same color. That makes it best for type and large graphic elements with little or no variance in tone. Also, if your design calls for a Web page with an intricate design (often done yet seldom needed), you will want to use a GIF so you can make portions of the graphic transparent, allowing the background to show through. (Transparency is achieved through many programs, including an export plug-in in Photoshop, and allows the creator to select certain pixels and, in effect, drop them out of the graphic, making those areas transparent.) The GIF format is also the most widely supported inline graphic format—the lowest common denominator.

The JPEG Format On the other hand, the JPEG compression algorithm is best suited to graphics where there is an abundance of colors and subtle, varying tones—as in a photograph. Depending upon the quality setting you choose (which can vary widely from no loss to nearly unusable), you can have your graphic displayed in pure, rich tones with little or no quality sacrifice. While it compresses all those tones wonderfully, the JPEG format does a terrible job of rendering large expanses of color, making them look muddy—as if they had been filled in with marker pens or watercolor paints. This means that if your graphic sits on a white background, JPEG will never give you a true white but rather a mixture of off-whites and pale pinks. And you will be unable to turn the background transparent as with GIF. Also, there are still browsers that do not support inline JPEGs, although as each day passes, these antiquated viewing programs become phased out.

TIP

You can make your file size smaller in both formats: with a GIF you can reduce the bit-depth or crunch down the palette the graphic was made with, and with a JPEG you can reconvert the graphic using a lower quality save setting, resulting in a more *lossy* image with higher generation degradation. In other words, the smaller the amount of memory an image takes, the lower the image quality. As always, you'll walk the tightrope between what is acceptable to your viewer in file size and what is acceptable to you in appearance.

Below are some very general guidelines to help you determine which file format is best in certain situations. As always, the caveat is that these are basic rules, not religious dogma.

It is best to use a GIF when

- Your graphic contains large areas of flat color
- You want to make sure your graphic can be viewed by all browser platforms
- You need to make an area of the graphic transparent

It is best to use a JPEG when

- Your graphic has areas of graduated tones
- Your graphic is a full-color photograph

The Single-Screen vs. Scroll Design Methods: Is One Better Than the Other?

Just as the brouhaha of GIF vs. JPEG rages, another debate is being fought in the design trenches. This new disagreement centers on the single-screen vs. scroll methods of design. The *scroll* method is the way most Web pages are laid out: the content is chosen for a particular page, and if it's longer than the display, you simply scroll down to view the rest. The *single-screen* method works in a way that more closely resembles the page metaphor. This design takes into consideration the default screen sizes for browsers (in most cases, Netscape) and derives a height and width pixel dimension within which all the information and graphics are disseminated. When you're done viewing one screen, a click takes you to another, in effect turning the page.

Single-Screen Page Design The single-screen method is definitely more graphics-intensive, usually relying on type set into a graphic for everything from navigation to content. These sites usually have more visual bang for the buck and for the most part are lighter in content, at least on the higher levels.

While the screen ideal is more pleasing to most designers, more closely echoing their experiences in the realms of print and multimedia, it fails to take into consideration the main strength of the Web and the Internet. This strength is the ability to impart large quantities of information in a small area. It also tends to rely more heavily on graphics which do not load as fast as hypertext, and as a result, the pages themselves load more slowly.

The Scroll Page Design The opposite end of the spectrum is the scroll design model. It relies on fewer graphic elements—mainly banners and icons—and more on hypertext to deliver the message. Since it's more text-heavy, the obvious conclusion is that the viewer will be forced to scroll down the page. Scrolling down, and even to the right, should not be a problem for the reader because the Web by its very nature demands the ability to scan information by scrolling.

The fine line to walk here is knowing when a little scrolling becomes too much. Have the viewer scroll through what is the equivalent of three or four typewritten pages and you might as well give them a shot of sodium pentathol. Knowing when and how to break up your pages is just as important as how many beautiful graphics you upload.

So, once again, the question must be asked: which is better? And, once again, the answer is neither. Both are valid and both have their place and time. A Web site whose main objective is to impart information—and lots of it—would be better off with the scroll design. Likewise, a site in which the style of presentation is the main objective would be better served by the screen design. The client and/or type of site will drive which method you employ in your design; most often, it will be a combination of the two.

Color Testing: 256 vs. Thousands of Colors Is Quite a Difference

As mentioned above, there are many times as you design for the Web when you must take into consideration the lowest common denominator. While it would be ideal if everyone had nice graphics cards and great monitors, that is not always the case. Since the Web is the ultimate cross-platform media, this makes color a particularly thorny issue. What looks great on a PC can look terrible on a Macintosh and what looks good on the Mac can end up looking like a Day-Glo velvet poster on the PC.

How do you control how your work is viewed and perceived when you have little or no control of the hardware on which it is being viewed? It's like asking a Hollywood director to control the look of their film when every movie theater is using a different projector, color balance, and screen size. With very few standards that cross platforms, consistency in look and feel can be difficult—but not impossible.

The best way around this is to test your colors throughout the project. Test them on whatever platforms are important to you: PC, Macintosh, Unix, etc. There are certain colors (of course too numerous to mention by name or RGB value) that translate from one platform to another much better. To get some ideas about good color use on the Web, check out **http://www.lynda.com/hex.html**. The links on this page will give you great ideas about browser-safe, non-dithering colors. The creator of the site, Lynda Weiman, has written an excellent book about color on the Web, which is also discussed on this site.

And when you test, make sure you test in both 256 and thousands of colors. The difference between the two, even on the same machine, can be striking. That color you thought perfect in full color can suddenly look like a Technicolor snowstorm when reduced to 256 colors. Even standard hexadecimal background colors can tweak off into the color netherworld when making the transition from full to 256. So test early and often to insure good color balance throughout viewing platforms and color resolutions.

Browser-Specific Design: Pick a Browser, Any Browser

Although by now it may seem as if only a few people on the remotest parts of the earth have not yet heard of Netscape Microsoft Internet Explorer, there are still quite a number of other browsers left out there.

The best-case scenario is one in which you only have to design for one browser: that's the only one you think the people interested in your site will be using or that's the only one you care about. Unfortunately, most clients want their site and their content to be viewed on as many different browsers as possible. This request is somewhat like telling a designer that the same piece of work must be used on television, in print, and on radio without any alteration. My metaphor is fairly ham-handed but realistic nonetheless and, considering the current state of the Web, a necessity for most sites which would appeal to a broad viewer base.

While the task of designing for multiple browsers is difficult, it can be done. Make sure, however, to use one browser as your lead browser, the one that defines how your site should look—the *control* browser. You might need to tweak individual pages or even generate duplicate pages to satisfy a specific browser, but that's just the nature of the beast as it stands today.

Beyond the technical aspects, designing for the Web is ultimately much the same as designing for any other medium: some things work and some things don't and much of it is purely subjective. The best way to determine good design, and what will work best for you individually, is to surf the Net relentlessly and decide for yourself what is appropriate. So load up that browser and get that mouse finger clicking.

Designing for the Web requires thinking "outside of the box" in order to achieve the objectives set by you and your clients. It is truly a collaborative effort. It requires the talents of a marketing/online strategist such as John to determine the objectives and the content of a given site, and the talents of Tom to give the site order and personality.

process thirty-nine

process thirty-nine

Partner in Design, Development, and Production

Process 39 is an experienced multimedia development group helping **authors**, **publishers**, and **corporate clients** take newmedia projects from concept to finished product. Melding traditional design with technical expertise, Process 39 functions as a **digital workshop** – a place where bold ideas really get built.

Process 39 has collaborated on projects for **education**, **home entertainment**, **interactive television**, **corporate multimedia**, and the **Internet**. As a strong development partner, we have learned how to effectively contribute to **all phases** of development – from the first storyboards through the final audio tweaks.

Process 39

Company Profile

Process 39 is an experienced multimedia development group helping authors and publishers take all kinds of new media projects from concept refinement to finished product. By melding traditional design with technical expertise, Process 39 functions as a digital workshop—a place where bold ideas get built. Clients include 3COM, Apple Computer, Viacom, and Macromedia.

Process 39's founding partners—who wrote the following piece—are functional designer Joe Speaks and senior designers Dale Horstman and Joe Lachoff. They can be reached at **info@process39.com**. Joe Speaks—a technical writer, functional designer, computer consultant, production manager, book author, and award-winning multimedia producer—brings a rare clarity to issues of software design and development. Dale—a veteran design professional who has won awards in such fields as illustration, corporate identity, and computer interfaces for consumer products, to name only a few—is intimately versed in the running of a design studio and the effective motivation of creative teams. His work has appeared in publications such as *MacWorld*, *HOW*, *Communication Arts*, and *New Media* magazine. Joe Lachoff, a software interface and content designer, has also had successes in animation, illustration, video, and page design.

Chapter Profile

Process 39's chapter focuses on a variety of issues: design process, finding an Internet Service Provider, client relations, editorial voice, scheduling, graphics management, HTML programming tips, and testing. Joe, Dale, and Joe bring the perspective of seasoned multimedia professionals and entrepreneurs. Defining good Web site design is as much about aesthetic and technical concerns as it is about running a profitable project. It is difficult to run a profitable independent Web design firm while building cutting-edge work. The history of the multimedia business is littered with the corpses of many small firms that simply could not be technically competitive while managing their bottom line.

Process 39 has succeeded at both, and their contribution reflects this experience. If you are an independent designer who hopes to take on bigger projects and build a firm, or if you run a multimedia division for a large, diverse, successful corporation, you will be able to gain several gems from the following pages.

A common mistake among design firms is overpromising deliverables while underestimating costs and schedules. To become proficient at striking a balance between design and profit takes experience. Web site development has the benefit of being incremental—a small start can still become a large and powerful venture. Growing a site over time allows developers and their clients to test ideas, make corrections, and determine a workload that is sustainable and profitable for the designer.

Five factors determine success in the dual roles of designer and entrepreneur:

- Solid design and technical skills
- Good time management
- Rapid adaptation to new markets and "rules"
- The ability to articulate ideas
- Determination

Building your design and technical skills are the obvious reasons you are reading this book, but a healthy combination of the two is rare. The relationship between designers and programmers is similar to the dynamic between editorial and management teams of newspaper, television, or radio firms: they need each other but often work in very different ways. In each of these businesses, people who have experience in both areas are especially valuable. The Web business is the same: designers need to have technical knowledge and programmers need to appreciate the factors that make good design. It is the people trying to use a Web site who lose when either team fails in its individual task or fails to cooperate with the other.

Time management is difficult to master but vital for success. I have seen few other businesses where people work as hard as they do as in Web development. Most people are trying to succeed in an exploding business, but some people are just wasting time. Dr. Fred Brooks developed the operating system for the IBM 360 mainframe products in the 1960s. He wrote a seminal book about software development and time management called *The Mythical Man-Month*, in which he says the efficiency of most businesses suffers from too many meetings. I saw Dr. Brooks' ideas recur several times as designers and programmers ran in frustration from meeting to meeting, knowing they did not have enough time to get their most important work done. There are several good books and courses available on time management; many use the same ideas. If you don't know your own bad habits, learn them and change your behavior! No amount of design knowledge or technical skills can compensate for being late or working harder than you have to. Make a plan and stick to it!

Stay agile and ready to adapt to changes in technology and the market. The Web is the greatest single example of this principle in American business right now. Many firms that have prospered for years are having to revise their ways of doing business because of the Web. Some will survive and some will not. Even within the multimedia industry, many firms have been surprised by the rapid change in skills and business models the Web requires. Some companies have invested in platforms or product families that do not have viable, near-term growth prospects, such as broadband interactive television. ITV, which assumes a centralized, closed architecture, is likely to die out as cable-modem access to the Web booms in the next few years. Other businesses have established market niches with high overhead facilities that are difficult to sustain as service companies. Create a stable but nimble development environment for yourself—bigger is not always better.

People who articulate themselves well are powerful and rare. In Web development, articulation generally works in three ways:

- Developers to their clients
- Designers to programmers
- Programmers to designers

Entrepreneurs who cannot articulate their qualifications and ideas to clients will not be successful. This is true from the moment you pick up the phone to contact a prospect to the final sign-off and project approval. There are many programmers in the computer business who simply cannot speak well or in a way that nontechnical

Chapter Profile

clients understand. There are also designers who don't know how to communicate their visions well or cannot translate a client's words into pictures and technology. Both are limited in their ability to achieve.

Internally, designers must learn that programmers work with technology that is unforgiving of ambiguity. They need precision and specifics, not just dreams and aesthetics. Programmers must respect that designers use a language primarily of images. Designers often work well with magazine snippings, photos, and illustrations, instead of numbers, statistics, and esoteric technical terms. The respective teams must speak the other's language, not just their own. Architect Frank Lloyd Wright once said, "Talking about architecture is like dancing about painting." In other words, use language that is appropriate for your medium and audience.

Many of my peers have heard me say, "Determination is a mixture of persistence and impatience." Nothing is as powerful as determination. Everyone who has succeeded personally or professionally has lived this idea. Developing Web sites is not rocket science, but it will test your desire to complete a project with integrity and professionalism. The United States Marine Corps teaches it troops, "Never do nothing." Even if you do something and it is wrong, you can fix it and keep moving toward success. Quitting achieves nothing.

Essay

Running a Digital Design Studio

by Joe Speaks, Dale Horstman, and Joe Lachoff

T PROCESS 39 WE CALL OURSELVES a digital design studio. This means that most of our design work ends up as the organized bits of electrons that make software interfaces, multimedia CD-ROMs, the Web, and other things viewed on your computer monitor, video game, or TV screen. Technical mastery of electronic technology is only one of the many factors required to do our jobs, but it is the process of design on which we concentrate most. It is our ability as practitioners of this process—and the results we get—that attracts our clients. Like any craftsperson, we find it impossible to separate the design process from technique and technical skill, so we've chosen to write about it all as an intertwined whole.

Understanding the Design Process

Like others in the design community—architects, photographers, clothiers, graphic designers—we will spend our entire careers learning and mastering the subtleties and techniques we employ in the process of design. The process in its simplest form usually involves the steps shown in Figure 1.

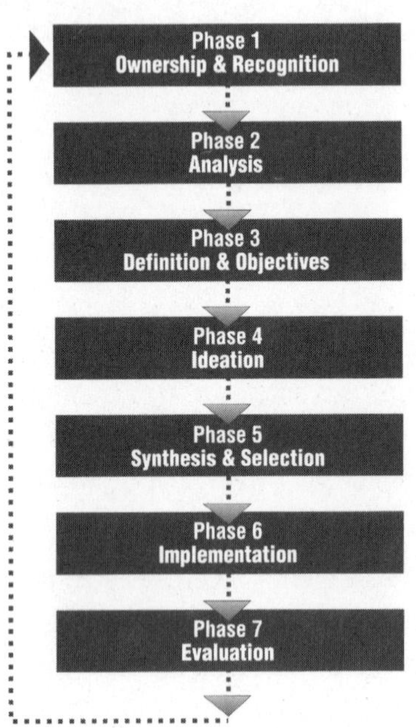

Figure 1:
The design process. The order of the steps that make up this process is crucial; no step should ever be skipped. Design is an iterative activity, so the end of the process is just the beginning of another cycle. If the results from one step seem inconsistent or unsatisfactory, repeat it, or even the previous two steps, but never skip a step.

Phase 1: Ownership & Recognition

As a designer, you must accept your responsibility to a new project: a Web site that must be changed, improved, or created altogether. On your first project, this means coming to understand how the Web works. Why do sites work the way they do? What are the ramifications of maintaining the status quo or making changes?

Phase 2: Analysis

In the analysis phase, you really get to the heart of the details involved in the situation. What are the limitations and unrealized opportunities? What's the difference between good sites and bad?

Phase 3: Definition & Objectives

In this phase, you take the information gained in analysis and form the backbone objectives and needs of the situation. At this stage there has been no generation of ideas, only a clear and exhaustive process of working with the situation.

Phase 4: Ideation

In this phase, pencil finally hits paper. Many, many (we can't stress this enough) ideas get generated. Have far-fetched ideas and keep things open; you can identify and select ideas in phase 5.

Phase 5: Synthesis & Selection

Taking all the ideas generated in phase 4, you start to critically assess the possible solutions, weeding out the less appropriate ones (based on the objectives and a little luck) and synthesize ideas together to make stronger solutions. At Process 39, we usually attempt to create two or more complete strategies and ways of looking at the challenge.

Phase 6: Implementation

Some sage said many years ago, "Once you have decided what you need to do, the doing becomes effortless." That may be true sometimes, but in this complex, interdependent world, it usually doesn't get you all the way to your solution. Phase 6, the actual creation of the project, involves a clear production plan, a good dose of technical knowledge or advice, and a lot of hard work.

Phase 7: Evaluation

The dust of production has settled and your site is up, but that isn't all there is to do. Evaluating the process and where it has brought you is one of the most important issues for designers; it is the element that affords the most potential for learning. Also, there will be continuing issues of performance, maintenance, and site usage. This is where your service provider may be able to help out, giving you much needed hard data about the performance of your site. Part of the solution for a Web site should be a maintenance or future development plan.

Phases 1 through 5 often get shortchanged; skipping these steps on any project always affects quality. Usually when a project is over it leaves your desk forever, but Web work is like the design process itself—an iterative cycle. One ending is the next round's beginning.

Facilitating the Designer/Client Experience

As a good Web designer, you should advise your clients to do more than publish their existing brochures using HTML—that's simply not appropriate. A site should challenge the client to provide more factual, in-depth information about their organization than has been developed for other media. Constructing the client's message is a task that even the best outside design firm might not be up to.

Questions to Answer Early

Before you bring a bunch of people together to talk about the contents of the Web site, ask the following questions. The answers to these questions, and the process of getting them answered, will help you understand the Web-making process and make those first meetings more productive.

- Who is the service provider and what are their services? (See "Choosing an Internet Service Provider" later in the chapter if this hasn't been decided yet.)
- Who is available internally and what are their skills?
- Who is the target audience? (The Web is one medium that lets you have several!)
- What do Web users expect from this site?
- What is the initial budget and what will that buy?
- What is the ongoing budget?
- Where will the Web site be built and how will we view it in progress?
- Where will the Web site live permanently and how will it be updated?
- Where do we get the Web address (URL) and what should it be?
- When do we want the site to launch?
- Why are we doing this Web site anyway? (You should have a good reason; make sure this reason becomes your primary objective.)

It's likely that a Web site is a client's first foray into a digital representation of their organization. Regardless of how established a client's print identity, a Web site often provides unanticipated challenges to their established identity. You will have to work closely with the client to walk them through this identity crisis.

The client needs to realize that when the site goes online, they are not done! A good site requires updates and maintenance, and this is the responsibility of whoever has their name at the top of the site.

Budgeting Resources

As a group of designers, Process 39 believes that the key to a successful project is *process*—a good plan. Enough money, the right people, and a realistic schedule ensure the success of that plan. The hard part is knowing what's enough, right, and realistic when dealing with a new technology like the Web. The advice in this section applies to sites with budgets ranging from $1,000 to $100,000.

First, the initial plan for a Web site must include the ongoing monthly budget and resources. A Web site is not something you make and then it's done. You must plan for the ongoing development or the site will quickly become outdated. Even Web sites that are initially cool (and expensive) can decay in a matter of months due to lack of maintenance. An undersized ongoing budget is often what dooms the best kind of Web content—current events and up-to-the-minute news about the client's organization.

In order to ensure long-term maintenance, the initial plan should include someone's ongoing time to generate new information. The plan should also secure the service provider's involvement in regular updates. Don't build what the client can't maintain.

Once you realize the scale of a site that the client can maintain, work with the client to make a brief outline of all the content areas that they might want included in their site. Consider the involvement of inside resources. Who can do what in how much time? Does some of this material already exist?

Here's a short list of items you might forget when creating the initial project plan:

Copywriting New material will need to be created; whose responsibility is it to write the text?

HTML coding Who's making the Web-ready documents and when do they need "raw" text? The client's service provider will not automatically assume that they are helping with this task.

Approval Who wants to approve the site and how long will that really take? How will they review it? First-time Web publishers be warned: the big cheese in your organization might like to be a part of your first online foray.

Troubleshooting This is technology development, so it won't be right the first time. Include a team member who is familiar with the potholes of software development.

Graphics for the Web Just because you have some graphics on disk doesn't mean they're ready for the Web (see the sidebar "Using Digital Graphics").

Using Digital Graphics

So you have a corporate logo, a picture from a brochure, or an info-graphic designed for print. How do you convert it for use on the Web?

Don't be naive and assume that simply taking the electronic files you have already produced for print and converting them automatically to lower-resolution bitmap-based versions will preserve the original intent. It is important to take those materials, convert them, and *alter* them so that they will look onscreen as they do in other media.

First, the computer screen is relatively low-resolution compared to print. A skilled computer artist can often convert graphics from other sources and make them look good, but some graphics simply cannot hold enough detail on the computer screen to make them useful.

Second, computer color is not like print color. Pantone colors and the four-color CMYK process both work in a *subtractive* manner—light hits the paper and the ink subtracts every color except those you see. TV and computer monitors are *additive*—they emit colored light. Individual monitors display a wide range of color spectrums; lower dot-pitch monitors will seem softer than higher dot-pitch

Continued on next page

monitors. There are even differences between platforms and browsers. Getting it right for all possibilities can be an overwhelming challenge.

Color consistency is still a big issue on the Web. Sitting in front of a monitor with a color swatch book and making a decision about a color onscreen is not a perfect method, but it is one way to start. Alter all colors and images on one monitor to closely match each other. Then take that art to other monitors and, if you have access to them, other platforms. Another good way is to create a series of tests using different techniques and then try them out. This can also be useful for future projects, as you will start to develop a matrix of tests and results to refer to when something new comes along.

As you continue to develop materials for the Web, you will find that few solutions are perfect for all platforms and browsers, but one solution is usually best. Always try to test graphics you create for your Web site on a wide variety of systems before you consider them Web-ready.

Be realistic about your resources. Maybe you start small and only have a home page with a few key messages on it. A small but complete site is far better than having a huge site planned with lots of unfinished items all over the place. Start small, but plan an upgrade path. The Web is expandable and flexible. What can't be in the site when you launch can be connected next month.

Don't Go with Your First Solution

The excitement of getting a Web site published may inspire an amazing amount of creative energy. Use this energy wisely, however, by spending some time exploring many ideas before settling on a final solution. After all, how many things have you ever gotten right the first time?

Ideation is the process of exploring all the ideas that will contribute to your final design solution. You need to come up with a whole bunch of different concepts before the best one becomes obvious, and most often that concept is a combination of originally unrelated ideas rather than a single epiphany. (Every epiphany is a product of the auto-ideation that goes on constantly in your subconscious mind.)

How you ideate depends upon the tools you are familiar with. For example, if you are a writer and not a visual problem-solver, you will probably be more comfortable describing your ideas with words. This approach is fine—work in words if you are more comfortable expressing yourself in that realm. At the same time, though, don't hesitate to make drawings, even if you think they are pathetic. Don't be put off by an apparent lack of artistic ability; a bad drawing will help to symbolize an entire idea, thereby freeing you to keep coming up with other ideas. The whole point is to go for quantity at this stage.

A good place to start ideating is with that first killer idea—remember, the one that you almost went ahead with before reading this book? Write or sketch a diagram, illustration, or synopsis of this idea. Use a whole sheet of paper, more if you need it. I usually torture about 30 sheets of paper before I'm satisfied. Treat yourself to a new pad of paper if that makes you happier.

Now try something crazy: fold in something from recent experience that you might normally dismiss as unrelated. Think of your current task as an idea free-for-all. You aren't concerned with the viability of the ideas here, just the raw material. If your first idea is a dog, don't put a leash on the dog; that's not a new idea. Instead, try dog + melon. How about just melon? What about other fruit? Maybe you're more in the mood for cheesecake. Whatever! The point is, take a lot of turns and you'll find a mess of interesting stuff just begging for attention. This is the desired effect.

Luxuriate in the product of this exercise. Spread the ideas out in front of you and start to weed out the deadwood. Get some help from a friend, coworker, or relative. Intellectualize now—discuss the viability of the ideas that stand out. This impromptu critique will yield one or more concepts that deserve further exploration. Let your own sensibilities take over from there.

Fit the Message to the Medium

The Web is truly different from print, TV, radio, or any other traditional communication medium. So don't treat it the same; don't take content you have developed for some other medium and put it directly on the Web. Your site will simply disappoint Web surfers.

Two things make the Web different. First, the Web is a functional (or interactive) medium. That means users are expecting a high level of choice from the Web. Simple reproduction of static promotional or advertising materials will be ignored on the Web and will leave the user wanting more. Second, there's more room for information. The limits of 3-column brochures or 15-second sound bites are gone.

Together these two differences translate into a lot of choices and material to choose from. What's still limited, however, is the audience's time and attention. Combine these factors with the educational and income demographics of the typical Web surfer, and you quickly realize that only clear messages with significant content rise above the Web's natural din of information.

So what's appropriate content for the Web? With the ousting of sound bites went low-substance advertising copy. Users expect more specific information that directly addresses their needs. As a content provider on the Web, you are supposed to use its expanded capacity to offer users navigational choices for the more in-depth information they expect to find.

For people used to tailoring one small message to appeal to the broadest band of "average" consumers, the Web is a large adjustment. For example, politicians and large advertising agencies will have to earn their broad appeal with substance, not just paid exposure. Now anyone can inexpensively deliver an in-depth message to a smaller audience, but deliver it with greater meaning and purpose. It's just possible that the reality of the Web could change politics and advertising as we know it.

Don't fight the reality of tighter, more in-depth messages on the Web. Instead, join in. Tailor lots of specific messages to the array of interested Web surfers. Use good menuing to attract each individual with content that interests them specifically.

Use Web-Specific Information Structures

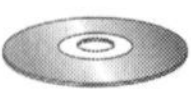

Here are some example content structures with accompanying examples on CD. These examples reveal some of the more popular information structures on the Web.

FAQs This standard format for answering Frequently Asked Questions allows users to view a list of questions, find the one they want answered, then go right to the answer (see Figure 2). Since skimming is not practical on the Web, this FAQ format has become its electronic equivalent. This editorially-prepared skimming has applications far beyond FAQ presentation.

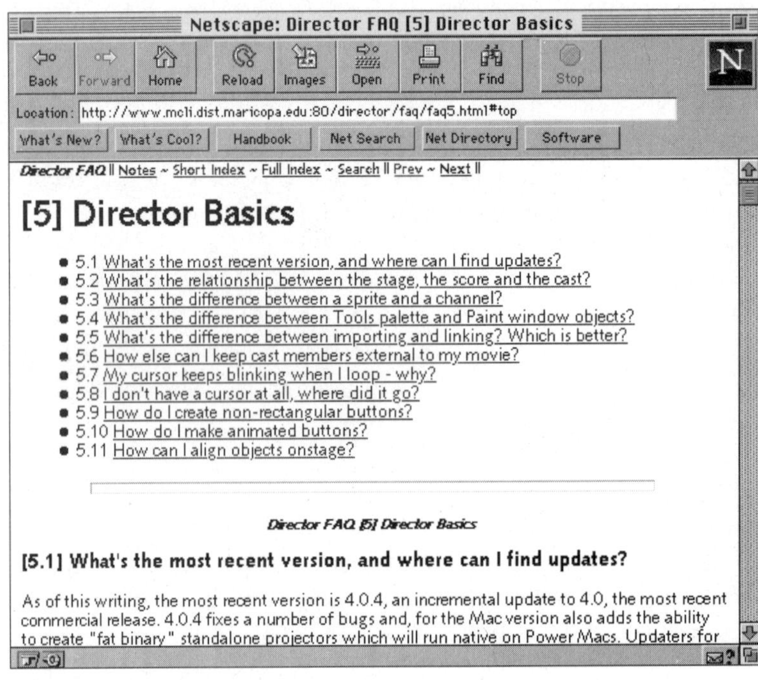

Figure 2: *An FAQ-formatted page*

Long home pages A linear story is often still the appropriate format for many messages delivered over the Web. With no limit on the length of a Web page, one long page is a reasonable way to present a message where one point logically follows the point before. Hyperlinking and menuing can still be extremely useful tools for navigation on this page, but maintaining a linear format gives the user context for the information at hand (see Figure 3).

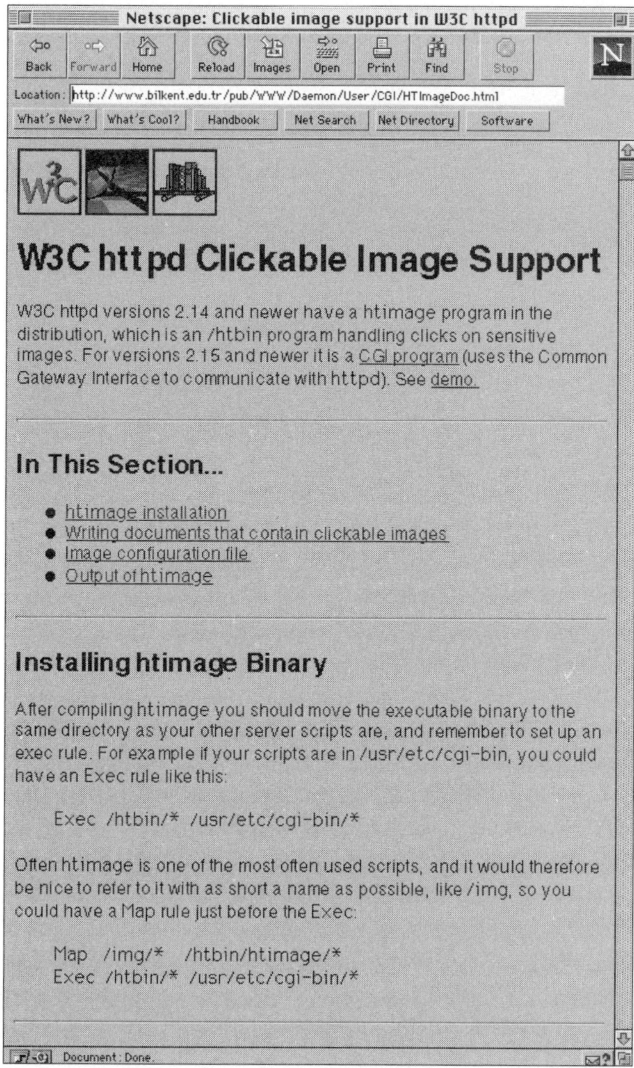

Figure 3:
A long-formatted home page

Menu home page and supporting subpages The beauty of the Web is that users can prioritize your site for themselves. If the site presents a variety of unique sections of content, use a top-level menu to allow the user to jump right to the information they find most interesting. An older version of the Process 39 Web site made use of this technique by presenting a variety of subjects on design and development and allowing users to determine their own areas of interest (see Figures 4 and 5). The text of the menu items also serves as a list of the services we provide, a useful melding of content and functionality.

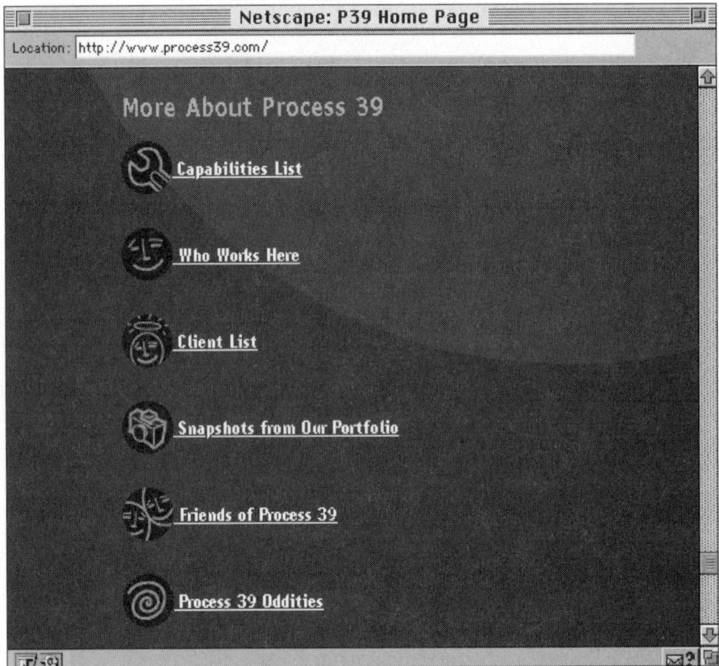

Figure 4: *A menu home page pointing to supporting subpages*

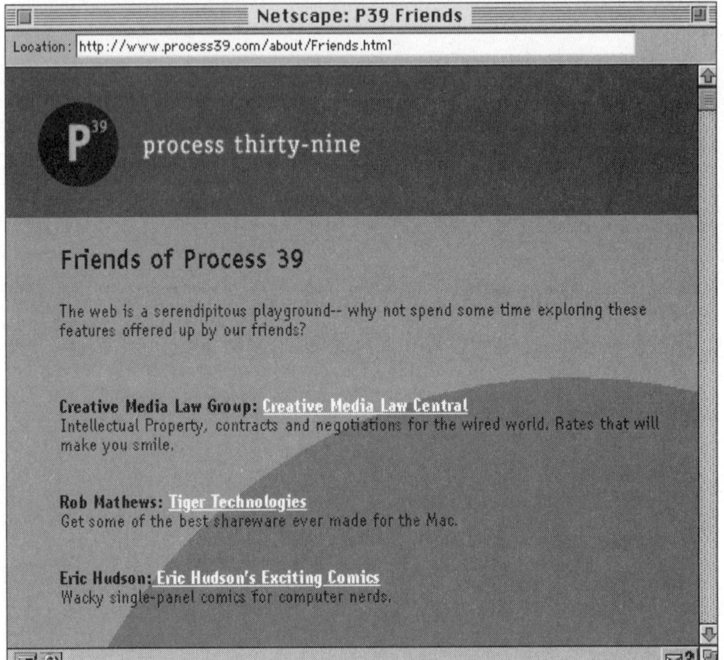

Figure 5: *One of the supporting subpages from the menu home page*

Separate graphic pages Don't assume the graphic you want to show is the graphic the user came to see. It's rude and conceited to assume that a user wants to wait more than a few seconds for a download that they didn't choose. If you're rude, a user is likely to leave. Be courteous by keeping your pages quick to download and offering the user the option of waiting to see more detailed info of their choosing.

For example, take the Process 39 portfolio page. Rather than force the user to endure the download of large graphics that they may or may not care about, this page provides a small graphic with supporting text. The user invests their download time only in the graphics they decide are worthwhile. Small thumbnail graphics are often used as buttons to select larger, more detailed graphics (see Figures 6 and 7).

Various sites with different quantities of data Many Web sites offer the user a choice of two or more versions of their site—usually fast or slow. The

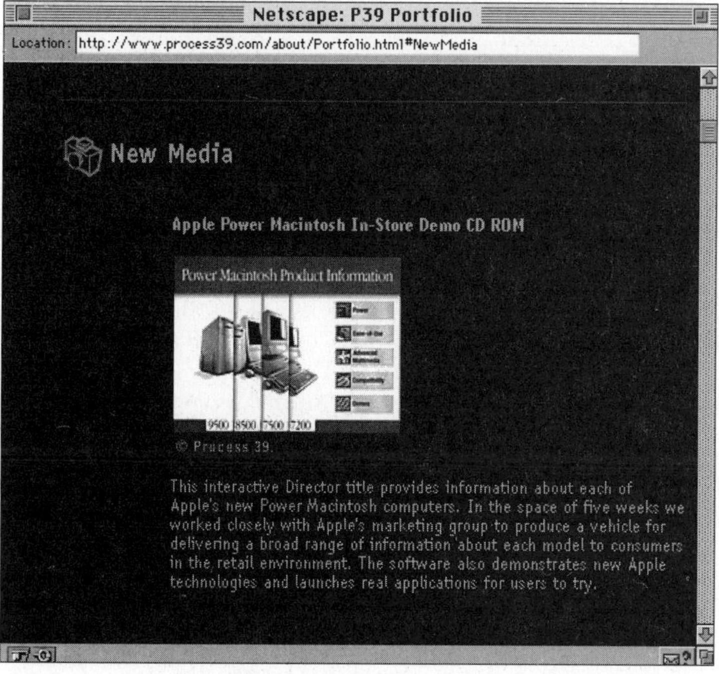

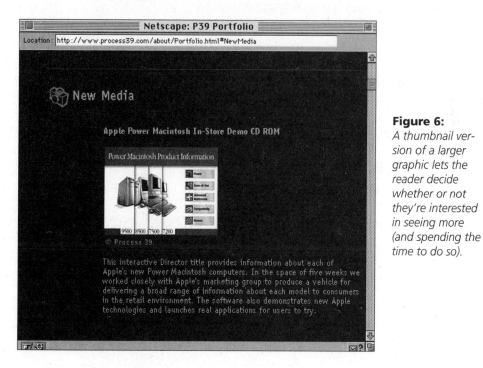

Figure 6: *A thumbnail version of a larger graphic lets the reader decide whether or not they're interested in seeing more (and spending the time to do so).*

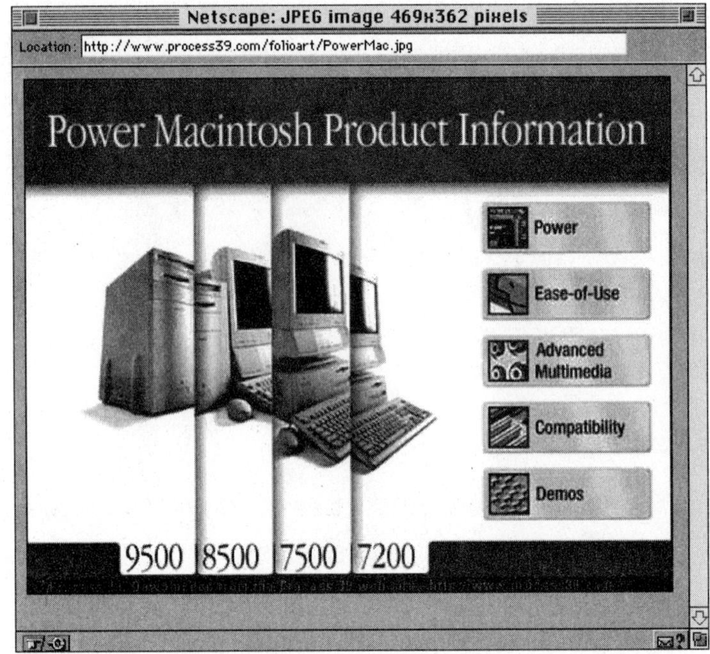

Figure 7:
The larger linked graphic, viewed at the user's discretion

site versions differ in the amount of digital information used to present the site, usually by making a graphical and nongraphical version of the same content. Why? Users come to any given site using all kinds of hardware, software, and connections. Web designers often want to show off the coolest graphics and the latest technology, but they run the risk of alienating users with slower connections and less advanced browsers. Offering different versions gives users the opportunity to participate at their own level (see Figure 8).

Also, many sites have competing missions. For example, sometimes a site is supposed to present marketing information *and* answer technical support questions. The tech support users already own the product and don't care what it looks like, so they'll be willing to skip the fancy graphics. Besides, they saw it the first two times they came to this site.

Figure 8: *Cybergrrl offers text-only, graphics-intensive, and Netscape-enhanced versions to choose from.*

Have Something to Say!

The traditional rules for good content and a clear message still apply in designing material for the Web. Doing a Web site just because you think you should might not be a compelling reason that will result in success.

Don't create a site without a mission. In other words, don't create a useless site unless *that* is your mission (see Figure 9). Try to generate a clear understanding of what you or your client want to say and how you wish the site to be perceived before you begin construction. The technical considerations alone might befuddle a site that has a shaky intent.

We often see Web sites with several "This area under construction" signs. For some commercial sites this technique is useful for advertising new features. But more often than not it only serves to give the user the feeling that they are missing some information or experience—the wrong impression to make at a

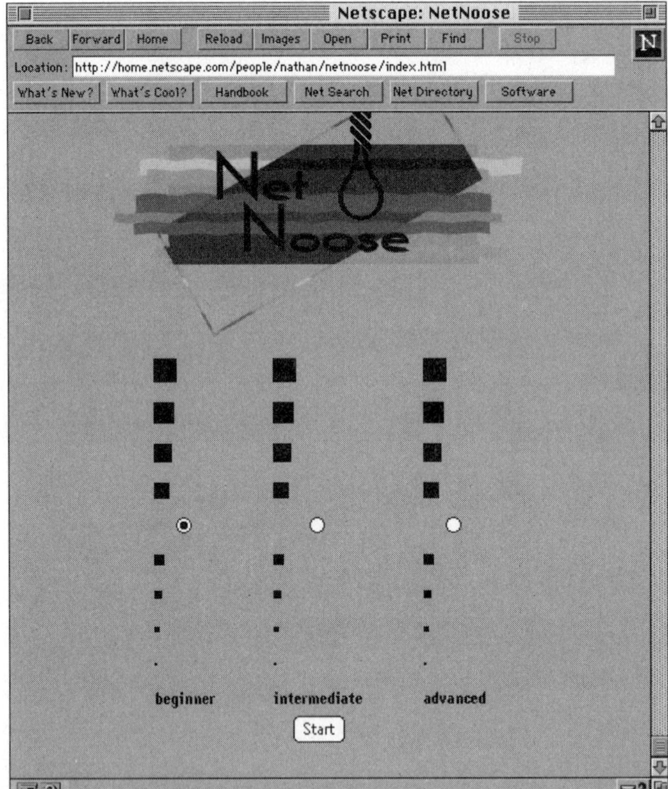

Figure 9:
An intentionally useless site

commercial site (see Figure 10). If you were developing a corporate brochure, would you leave the last four pages blank with a line of type on the bottom saying, "Material to come"? Probably not. Make sure an unfinished area is a useful strategy before you make it, or don't make it at all.

A more elegant approach to this issue is to incorporate a promise for future features in the body of one of your completed pages. Support it with graphics if you like, but don't lead people astray. HTML allows for a very organic construction method and, once you've realized this, you can free yourself from the constraints of thinking about putting up a complete site. Instead of creating a seemingly deep and complex site that is populated with numerous ghost town pages, start small with good materials and a good message; grow only when you have a new and completed branch to add.

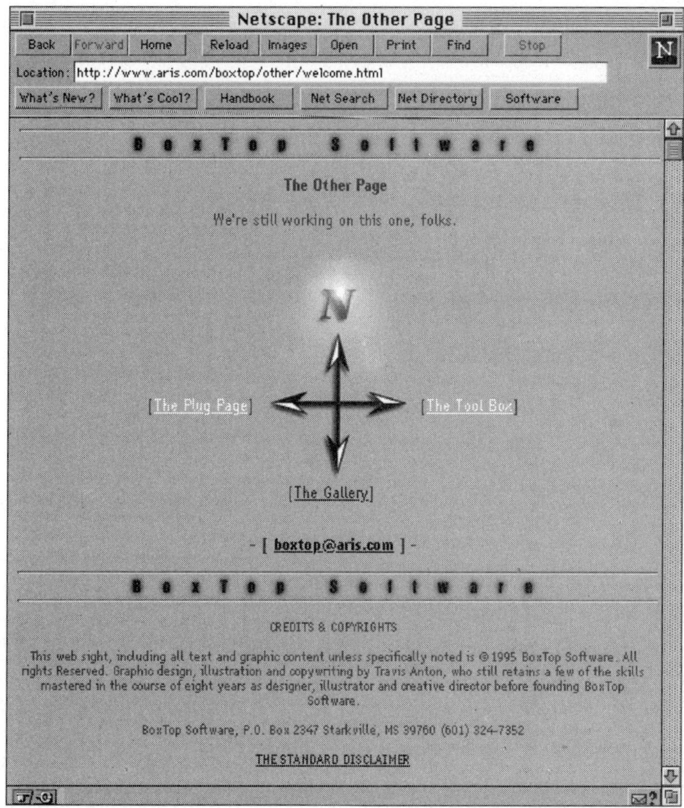

Figure 10:
An example of the "This area under construction" letdown

The Text/Graphics Trade-Off

A pretty picture may be worth a thousand products sold, but a clear, simple, and well-crafted message may be worth the world. Lush photography and graphic decoration surely have their place on the Web, but as a designer, don't assume they're the first tools you should pick up. If you can't effectively explain what your Web site has to offer to a friend or associate, it may need more development before you place it in the visual realm.

One of the easiest and most efficient transmissions of information on the Web is text (see Figure 11). With the letter-writing renaissance currently underway, due in part to e-mail, the beauty and effectiveness of the written word should not be dismissed. People still read, and Web users are surely no exception. Some of the best material that we have discovered on the Web and the Internet has been text and e-mail. Take ASCII art, for instance. It is the Internet's origami. It says something about the common forms of expression on the Internet, and thus is one of the many keys to understanding the dynamics of the Internet and the Web (see Figure 12).

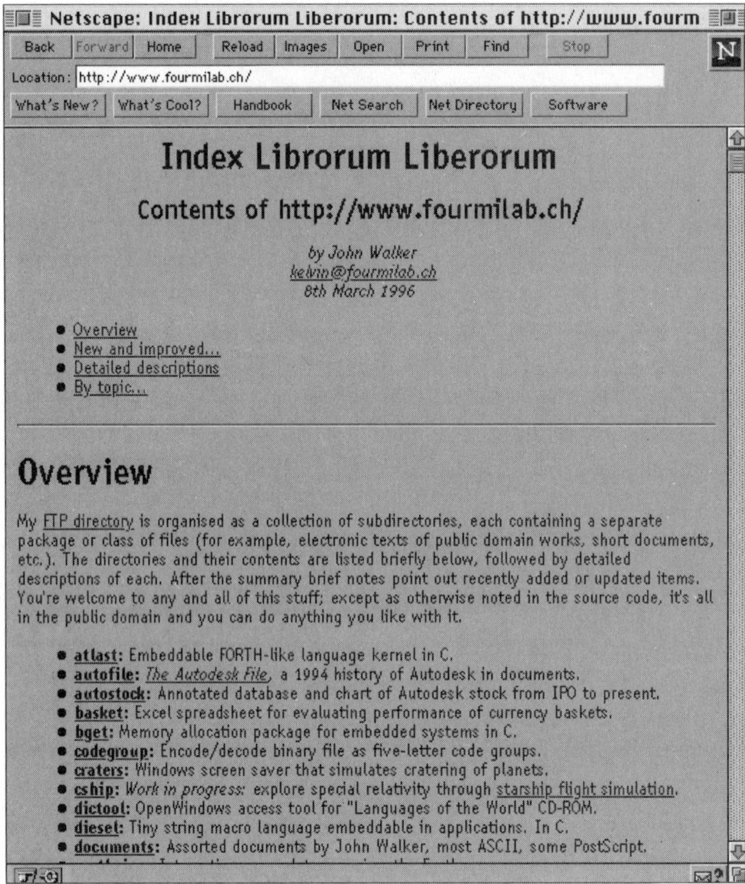

Figure 11: *A good, text-only home page*

Keep an eye out for the ultimate modernist credo "Less is more." The time it takes to download material directly affects the user's quality of experience. Each situation must determine its own level of comfortable finger-tapping time. *HotWired* (**http://www.hotwired.com**) and *c|net* (**http://www.cnet.com**) are both good examples of sites with a lot of materials that balance graphics and text for speedy transmission and effect.

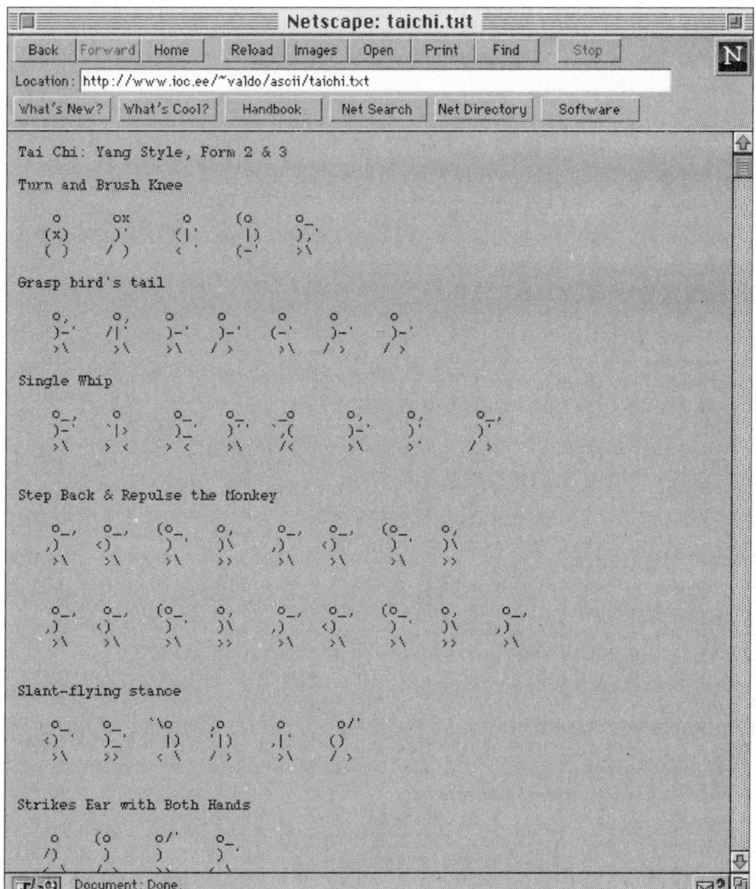

Figure 12: *ASCII art*

Here's an anecdote: I got on the Web to look for business check printing services. I searched and found two sites that I wanted to investigate. The first site was a company I had previously bought from, but never visited on the Web. Their home page took well over a minute to download a high-quality version of their simple two-color company logo. What a waste of my time! I wasn't about to try to browse photos of their checks. I left. The other company had no images on their home page, just a simple directory of check styles with small thumbnails to preview, with larger versions available to help you make your final decision. The more detailed versions took longer, but thanks to the previews, I only downloaded one, then ordered my checks right there.

Don't Clog the Internet with Junk

The Internet has been called the *information superhighway*. The word *information* should be taken very seriously in this context, because it doesn't mean "just any bits." For example: you look into your mailbox to find a stack of junk mail and a letter from a friend. Which is more desirable? Why?

Cable companies and telephone giants will sell you cable modems and interactive digital television faster than you can scream for the snake-oil police. But let's get something straight once and for all: the Internet is *not* an infinite resource. Nobody likes a traffic jam, and if you don't see this one coming, my friend, you're in denial.

Net bandwidth doesn't grow on trees, at least not this year. For now, most people get their dose of Net media via slow dial-up lines, or via nice big high-capacity lines shared with a bunch of coworkers. Either way, the result is limited bandwidth. "No problem," you say, "just grab a fatter connection; upgrade to ISDN or a T1 line. Right?" Well, maybe.

Let's move up the food chain a notch: let's talk about the main arteries of the information superhighway. What kind of connection does *your* service provider use? What about the connection upstream from them? Most of these pipes are already state of the art, representing the biggest, highest capacity data tarmac that corporate bucks can buy. You don't have to be a genius to recognize that we have trouble in toyland—if the Web is your gravy train it may be derailed by issues of bandwidth.

Is digital video good for the Internet? What about Internet telephony? How much data can the current system deliver before someone runs fiber to every address on the planet? These are the questions that surround the issue.

Understanding that these issues even exist can inform the quantity of content you put on your Web site. In this case, quantity is inversely proportional to quality; fewer bits equals a better experience. If your target user is viewing your site via America Online or even Netscape Navigator over a 28.8 dial-up connection, you should strongly consider leaving that digital video out. Most people would prefer not to wait 20 minutes for a small, low–frame-rate digital version of a talking head video to download; instead, they'd rather read a transcript of the video, especially if you spend some time formatting it nicely with some key stills taken from the video. The time your users spend reading the document will leave a nice little patch of open lane on the infobahn, making way for the bozos downloading bad quality digital video on the "bleeding" edge.

For more on the issue of Internet clog prevention, check out the Bandwidth Conservation Society at **http://www.infohiway.com/faster/index.html**.

Choosing an Internet Service Provider

The mass popularization of the Internet has spawned a rapid growth in Internet Service Providers (ISPs). These are the companies that maintain a constant connection to the Internet so you don't have to. If you are designing a Web site that will be hosted by an independent ISP, this section will provide you with some tips to inform your search for an ISP.

Assuming you are primarily interested in finding optimal Web service, some ISPs offer services that set them apart from the others as better choices to host Web sites.

Bigger Isn't Better

As a general rule, stay away from giant ISPs, especially if you are going to publish an intelligent site (any site that employs server-side technology such as CGI scripting). For the time being, these companies are primarily interested in profit margins, a goal that is at odds with what normal people consider good service. Big ISPs typically offer cookie-cutter solutions with minimal technical support; they don't give you the kind of custom, personalized support you'll want and need as you begin to publish Web material.

Instead, look for a small company with a solid reputation. The good news is that there are a whole slew of hardworking, ambitious entrepreneurs out there just salivating at the prospect of garnering your Web-bucks through good old-fashioned honest service.

Of course, things change (constantly, as it turns out), and it's only a matter of time before one of the smaller, more Web-savvy ISPs grows large and manages that growth with elegance.

If you can't get a referral for a small, reliable ISP from someone you know, try a Web directory such as Yahoo! or try posting a request to the appropriate Usenet newsgroups. Remember, the ISP you choose doesn't have to be right around the corner from you. This is an important point, because some areas of the country (notably California's Silicon Valley) are host to an inordinately high number of very good ISPs. On the other hand, you may get a warmer feeling from supporting local business—the choice is yours.

Narrowing the Choices

Once you have a list of potential service providers, you'll need to weed out the deadwood. Start by exploring the candidate ISP's own Web site. Service providers are notorious for having aesthetically flat sites of their own, so don't judge an ISP by their home page.

A good ISP will have a directory page on their Web site pointing to the sites that they host. If the candidate ISP *doesn't* have one of these directories, well, you've just eliminated them! If they do have a directory, explore some of the sites listed. Do they seem quick? Are the connections dependable? Do you have to wait an inordinately long time when you go from page to page within the site? Send e-mail to the people who maintain these sites. Try to set up a telephone conversation. A brief conversation with an existing client can tell you a lot about the ISP in question.

If you are satisfied that the ISP is still in the running, now is the time for a phone call to them. Be prepared to take notes, and definitely be ready to describe your needs in detail. If an ISP refuses to communicate via telephone, eliminate them from the list. This sounds harsh, but it's not. Some ISPs claim that telephone communication is passé. That's a load of hogwash. If the service provider you are interested in doesn't have the time to discuss technical and business matters with you in real time, there is something very wrong with their business model—either they're overextended and don't have the time (in which case they shouldn't be accepting new accounts anyway) or they don't understand what it means to be in a service industry.

Hardware makes less of a difference than you might think. Sure, fast computers and a big connection to the Internet are important, but it's the configuration, load balance, and quality control of these services that make the difference between a fast Web server and a dog-slow one. Suffice it to say that you probably don't have the technical expertise to keep up in the conversation about these issues, but by asking a few good questions you can stimulate the ISP representative to discuss their viewpoints. The fact that they even *have* viewpoints on these issues helps to qualify them further.

What kind of computers are being used as Web site hosts? What kind of connection does the ISP maintain? Who's upstream from them? How is the staff configured? Can you get tech support with a phone call? How much experience do they have configuring and maintaining their hardware? What is their policy regarding security? Do they offer secured transactions? How do they monitor reliability? How many customers do they host per machine? Do they provide popular CGI scripts and the support to help make them effective? What sort of special services, like CyberCash, do they offer?

If you still feel good about an ISP after this conversation, you're probably in good shape. You still need to evaluate their fee structure and billing practices to make sure you can afford what they have to offer.

Finally, remember that Web sites are portable. If your ISP turns out to be a dud you can always move your Web site to another service provider.

Some Technical Advice

So far in this essay we've talked about design processes and philosophies. The following sections offer practical advice about some of the more technical aspects of Web design: working with graphics, HTML, and FTP.

Making Graphics Faster

Why do some graphics seem to show up so much faster than others? How can I guarantee that my pictures will draw quickly?

You can't control the speed of the Internet at the moment a user is downloading your Web site's graphics, so you should always make your images as small as possible. This point cannot be emphasized strongly enough, so let me put it another way: from a performance standpoint, the best graphic you can make for use on the Web is a graphic that is zero in size—that's right, *zero*.

Unfortunately, it is impossible to create a graphic that is represented by zero data. I will gladly stake the family farm on this claim. Luckily, there are several ways to make your pictures take up almost zero space. The closer you come, the faster you are. It's that easy.

Most popular browsers support inline graphics in both GIF and JPEG formats, so the following discussion will focus on techniques for deciding which format is best to use for a given image and how to optimize the effects of their respective compression methods on your images. Both of these formats have strengths and weaknesses, so understanding them will help you to create the smallest files possible on a case-by-case basis.

GIF

GIF files use a type of compression called *Lempel-Ziv-Welch* (LZW), named for the three people who developed and refined it. LZW compression works by finding frequently used, recognizable patterns in your picture, such as large areas of the same color. When it finds a popular pattern, the pattern is stored in a special dictionary and given a short code name. Now, every time that pattern is encountered throughout the picture, the compressor knows to symbolize it with the short code name. The potential for creating small files with this technique is pretty good.

For example, to describe a 100 by 100 pixel image that is all one color, let's say blue, you could store the information for each pixel by saying "blue blue blue blue blue blue blue blue" etc. until you had said "blue" a total of 10,000 times—once for each pixel in the image. For an 8-bit image, which uses 8 bits of data to say "blue" each time, that's 80,000 bits, or 8 Kbytes, of data. That image will take most people about 5 or 10 seconds to download. Not very close to zero.

However, a GIF file, which uses LZW compression, simply identifies this redundancy as a pattern and symbolizes it with clever shorthand notation. Instead of saying "blue" so many times in a row, a GIF file says "I noticed 10,000 blue pixels in a row, so if I see this pattern later, I'll just call it 'Frank.' Frank!" Pure genius. This file might only take up 1024 bytes (1 Kbyte), much less than its uncompressed sibling, and would take most people less than one second to download—approaching zero, which is good.

Testing Compression

Try this: create an RGB bitmap in a paint program like Photoshop. Make the canvas 2000 by 2000 pixels in size. Fill the canvas in any color you like. Convert the image to 8-bit, indexed color. Save the image in GIF format. You will notice that the file only takes up a tiny amount of space on your hard disk.

Now save a copy of the same file in an uncompressed format, such as BMP. Compare the size of this file, which stores a complete set of information for each pixel in the image, with the GIF file of the same image, which uses LZW compression to eliminate the redundant information. Quite a difference, no?

Of course, you probably want your pictures to contain some content beyond one color. This content will invariably ruin the continuous pixel values that gave us such a sweet, tiny file size (almost zero!). This doesn't necessarily cancel the positive effect of LZW compression, but it can. The more random pixel values become, the fewer recognizable patterns there are. Fewer patterns equals less compression.

Understanding how this type of compression works can help you create images that are surprisingly small on disk. It should be obvious to you by now that gradations (with the exception of perfectly vertical gradations), basically kill the effect of LZW compression. Anti-aliasing also has a negative effect, because it introduces a boatload of single pixels that are unique in value, thereby sabotaging LZW once again. Dither patterns are not necessarily bad—if the pattern is regular. Adding noise to an image usually reduces compression, because the noise is rarely organized in a regular pattern.

You may find the idea of designing images with jaggy, flat-colored shapes distasteful and constricting, but you can make the best of this situation. Here's how:

Reduce the pixel depth. Most images don't use as many colors as you may imagine. Sure, you can select colors from a palette of 16 million+ colors. Once you're done painting, though, the actual number used is often quite small.

Working on a copy of your image, convert it to indexed color, trying successively lower bit depths until it "breaks"—until you can't stand the idea of broadcasting the image because it's just too ugly. Then step back to the last acceptable bit depth—that's your palette. Make sure you use the adaptive color option when you convert to indexed color. This will insure that you don't accidentally introduce dither patterns into your image. Also, make sure that you always start with a fresh copy of the original RGB image; going from 24-bit true color to 5-bit adaptive indexed color will give you a result far superior to the one you achieve by downsampling an 8-bit adaptive image to 5 bits.

Don't anti-alias unless you really have to. Using adjacent colors that are low contrast will minimize the aliasing effect you see when anti-aliasing is not used. To prove this, try the following experiment: create a white circle on a black background without anti-aliasing. Now create a 20% gray circle on an 80% gray background, also with no anti-aliasing applied. The gray circle looks smoother than the white one.

Paint with broad areas of flat color. This will help reduce the sizes of your GIF files, and that will make them small and quick to download. Try painting with the pencil tool rather than the airbrush or paintbrush tools. This may constitute the development of a new style for your artistic repertoire.

Try JPEG instead. If your illustrations are riddled with complex forms, anti-aliasing, and photo-realistic effects, try leaving them in 24-bit true color mode and saving them as JPEG files instead of GIF.

JPEG

As you may have guessed, LZW compression, and therefore GIF files, don't offer much relief for 24-bit photographic images, even after you reduce them to 8-bit color or less. This is because photos rarely have predictable, repeating patterns. (Even a simple photograph of a perfectly blue backdrop will have random noise and subtle gradations throughout.) Enter the JPEG file format, which uses a combination of compression techniques optimized for photographic images.

There are three main steps in JPEG compression:

1. It throws out half of the color information in a picture, while preserving all of the luminance (gray value) information. This saves 50% right off the top.

You may find it disturbing that the data is being thrown out—sorry. JPEG is known as a *lossy* compression technique because it actually loses image information in an attempt to achieve better performance. GIF files are *lossless*, but they don't perform well on photographic images. No pain, no gain. The good news is that the human eye can't really tell the difference at this stage.

2. Next, it cuts the image up into 8 by 8 pixel cells and applies a DCT (you asked—*Discrete Cosine Transform*) to each cell, and then quantizes the resulting values. The amount of quantization depends on the Quality setting you pick when you save the image. This step loses even more image data, but it loses more information the human eye *can't* see than stuff it can see.
3. Finally, it compresses the output from step 2 using Huffman encoding. This step doesn't lose any more data (phew!); it just recognizes redundant patterns and stores them more efficiently.

Even if you don't understand how JPEG works, you should recognize that it is only suited to photographs or images that contain a photographic level of complexity. Simple images with flat colors simply don't benefit from JPEG compression as much, and they tend to look worse, because the artifacts created in the compression process stand out more in simple images.

Save your image with JPEG set to maximum compression/minimum quality. Always work on a copy of the image—remember, JPEG will irreversibly damage your artwork. Now open the compressed image. How does it look? Is it acceptable? Check the file size on disk. A good general rule is 1 second per Kbyte of image data, so a 10 Kbyte image will take roughly 10 seconds to download. (This rule is only for estimation purposes. Keep in mind that actual throughput on the Internet depends upon many variables.) If the image looks OK, it's ready to use. If you're unhappy with the quality, try starting over with a lower compression/higher quality setting.

If you just can't stand the sight of low-quality JPEG on your image, try increasing the quality setting when you save the image. The trade-off will be a larger file size, but the bump in quality may be worth it.

As a last resort, you can always try converting a photograph to 8-bit indexed color and then saving it as a GIF file. Because compression varies from image to image, using GIF may make an image smaller and better looking.

NOTE

Don't be fooled by the file size listed in a Macintosh Finder list view. You have to choose Get Info on a file and read the File size on the disk number to see its true size. The list view size shows the amount of space the file is taking up on your hard disk, which is not the same thing as the real number of bytes in the file.

HTML Tips

We all know that HTML tags are used to add formatting, graphics, and interactivity to the otherwise boring ASCII text that is displayed in a Web browser. What makes the difference between a bad page of HTML and a page that you'd be proud to show your mom (assuming she could actually understand it)?

Several popular word processors and page layout programs provide style sheets and parsing engines that will convert their documents into HTML-tagged text. While these tools are convenient for converting reams of existing documentation, they fall short of the mark for serious site development and design.

WYSIWYG Web tools such Adobe's PageMill and Netscape's Navigator Gold show promise for the future, but are still in their adolescence as far as software goes. While they do offer easy setup of Web pages with standard elements, there isn't much they can do to help you create a page that stands out in a crowd.

For now, you should expect to buckle under and learn the tags that make up HTML pages. This knowledge separates the dabbler, who may be satisfied with an off-the-shelf page design, from the designer, who must understand all of the medium's constraints in order to synthesize great solutions. Your knowledge of tagging today will translate into expertise tomorrow.

HTML text editors such as HoTMetaL are usually simple ASCII text editing programs that have a number of features added to make the task of tagging easier. These programs work in concert with one or more off-the-shelf Web browsers so you can preview your pages as you create them. There's simply no point in previewing your work anywhere but in a true Web browser. Pick an HTML editor and use it regularly.

Tagging with an HTML editor doesn't guarantee well-formatted HTML, however. You must form good tagging habits. Luckily, this is pretty easy. Here are some tips:

Develop a consistent template. Certain elements should appear consistently on every individual page in your Web site. Rather than starting each page from scratch, try creating a template and then starting each new page from a copy of the template. This isn't just fussy behavior for its own sake: it serves to ensure that your site performs reliably and consistently, page after page.

Here's a minimal template:

```
<HTML>
<HEAD>
<TITLE>Title</TITLE>
</HEAD>
<BODY>
Body
</BODY>
</HTML>
```

Use white space to your advantage. Because white space is ignored by browsers but interpreted by text editors, you can use it to separate logical breaks in your text. For example:

```
<HTML>

<HEAD>
<TITLE>My Page</TITLE>
</HEAD>

<BODY>
This is a Web page. Yippee!
</BODY>

</HTML>
```

Compare the above example with the following one:

```
<HTML><HEAD><TITLE>My Page</TITLE></
HEAD><BODY>This is a Web page. Yippee!</BODY></
HTML>
```

The second example is interpreted exactly the same way as the first. But because you have to look at this material in your HTML editor in order to work with it, it makes sense to spend some extra time formatting it so that you can see what's what.

NOTE

The first example leaves an extra blank space between major structural elements (use more than one if you like), and each major tag lives on a line by itself. Using white space to connote structure and hierarchy in your text will make it easier to work with later.

Use Comments. Comments are notes that you leave to yourself or others who might read your HTML later. Remember that anyone browsing your Web page can also view your HTML by saving the document on their local drive. While this presents an opportunity for others to copy your formatting (so what?) it also gives you a chance to communicate with them via embedded comments.

A comment looks like this:

```
<--!  Comment -->
```

Comments can be as long as you want, but some browsers lose track of additional lines if the comment is longer than one line, so make sure you test your comment structure with your target browsers.

One useful comment is copyright information about your page. For example:

```
<--!  Copyright 1996 by Meme Itself. All rights
reserved. -->
```

Another useful comment is information about a link. For example:

```
<--! This is the link to the donut site. -->
```

This comment may appear a little obvious at first glance, maybe a little unnecessary. Looked at in context, however, it becomes much more valuable:

```
blah blah blah blah blah

<--! This is the link to the donut site. -->
```

```
<A HREF="http://my_local.server.edu:70/00/internet/
library/e-journals/jnl/pop-o-matic/journals/
selected/tree/donuts/index.html"><B>Donuts</B></A>
blah blah blah blah blah blah blah blah blah blah
```

NOTE

We're using white space to our advantage here as well. Isolating the link and beginning it with a comment turns it into a neat, portable package that can be identified and moved around without too much attention.

Title-tag your documents appropriately. The title you create for your page will be stored in people's hot lists and displayed in their Web browsers. Don't use titles that are overly long or start with irrelevant words (see Figure 13). Try to think of names that will sort as you would hope in a hot list.

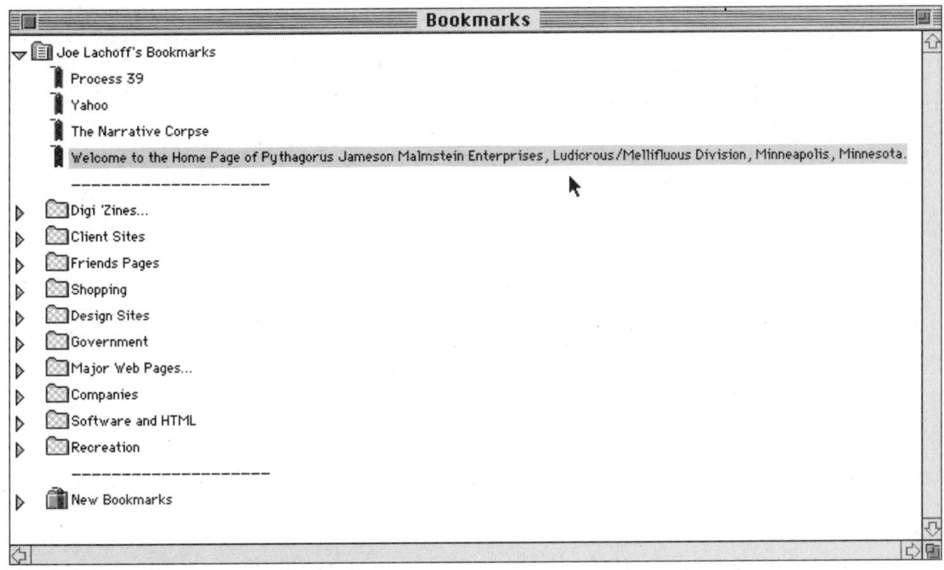

Figure 13: *An example of a poorly thought-out title, as seen in a hot list*

Learn to recognize problem characters. All Web browsers on all computer platforms will correctly display the standard ASCII characters. These include the upper- and lowercase alphabets, standard punctuation, and math symbols (see Figure 14).

<table>
<tr><td>!</td><td>"</td><td>#</td><td>$</td><td>%</td><td>&</td><td>'</td><td>(</td><td>)</td><td>*</td><td>+</td><td>,</td><td>-</td><td>.</td><td>/</td><td></td></tr>
<tr><td>0</td><td>1</td><td>2</td><td>3</td><td>4</td><td>5</td><td>6</td><td>7</td><td>8</td><td>9</td><td>:</td><td>;</td><td><</td><td>=</td><td>></td><td>?</td></tr>
<tr><td>@</td><td>A</td><td>B</td><td>C</td><td>D</td><td>E</td><td>F</td><td>G</td><td>H</td><td>I</td><td>J</td><td>K</td><td>L</td><td>M</td><td>N</td><td>O</td></tr>
<tr><td>P</td><td>Q</td><td>R</td><td>S</td><td>T</td><td>U</td><td>V</td><td>W</td><td>X</td><td>Y</td><td>Z</td><td>[</td><td>\</td><td>]</td><td>^</td><td>_</td></tr>
<tr><td>`</td><td>a</td><td>b</td><td>c</td><td>d</td><td>e</td><td>f</td><td>g</td><td>h</td><td>i</td><td>j</td><td>k</td><td>l</td><td>m</td><td>n</td><td>o</td></tr>
<tr><td>p</td><td>q</td><td>r</td><td>s</td><td>t</td><td>u</td><td>v</td><td>w</td><td>x</td><td>y</td><td>z</td><td>{</td><td>|</td><td>}</td><td>~</td><td></td></tr>
</table>

Figure 14:
The standard ASCII "safe" characters

We all use characters from the extended character set from time to time, however. These characters are not standard from platform to platform, which is why you sometimes see odd characters or the mysterious square box in a formatted word processing document from another platform (see Figures 15 and 16).

```
<HTML>
<HEAD><TITLE>Illegal Characters</TITLE></HEAD>
<BODY>
This text uses characters from the upper 128 ASCII range, including:
<P>
• Bullets;
<P>
• "Curly Quotes;"
<P>
• Many Symbols, such as ß, ∂, ƒ, œ, Σ, ¥, and ø;
<P>
• Foreign accent characters, such as á, ç, ü, ñ, ¿, and ô
|
</BODY>
</HTML>
```

Figure 15: *The source HTML for a page using "unsafe" characters*

To avoid problems with these extended characters, the HTML specification dictates a number of escape code sequences that look like gibberish but are interpreted by Web browsers as single characters from the extended character range. For example, `é` in HTML translates to é when viewed in a browser.

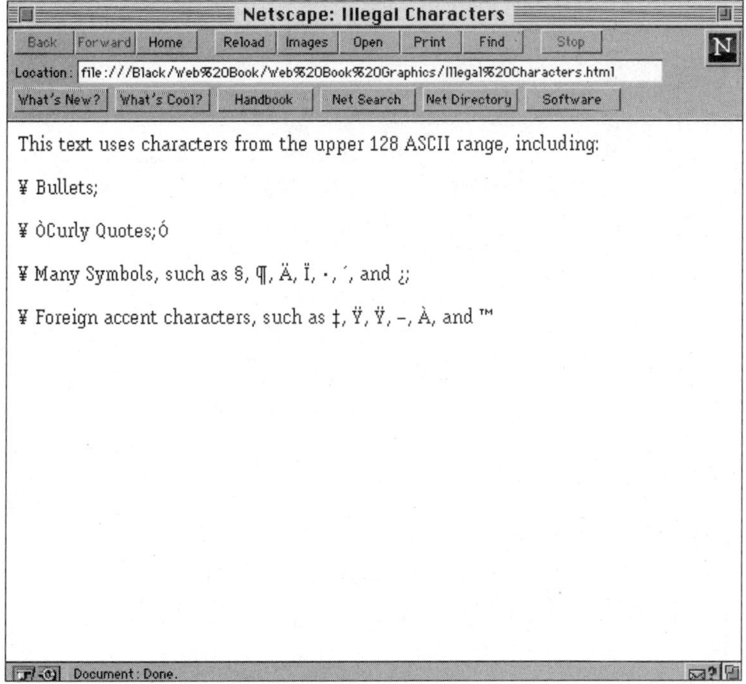

Figure 16: *The page as it appears in a browser*

If you're using an HTML text editor, it probably has the ability to scan a document for extended characters and convert them to escape code sequences. In a normal text editor, use the Find and Replace feature to automate the process of converting frequently used extended characters.

Ultimately, though, there's no replacement for actually proofreading each page in each target browser.

Understanding FTP

Unlike publishing in traditional media, Web publishing is a dynamic format that can be changed and updated easily, even after it has been released for public consumption. This is one of the strongest features of Web publishing, but it can have a darker side: changes that seem to have nothing to do with your work can affect it, even break it, without your knowledge. It's also possible to break links as you post your files by inadvertently renaming, reorganizing, or changing file permissions.

When you copy a file from your local desktop computer to its final destination on a Unix-based Web server, you use an FTP client to accomplish the file transfer. If you are serving your Web material from a PC or Macintosh you can skip this section—lucky you!

Although FTP can be used from the command line of a terminal emulator on your desktop machine, it's much easier to use a graphical FTP client such as Fetch on the Macintosh or WS-FTP on Windows. These simple, powerful tools are available as shareware.

Using a graphical FTP client is convenient and quick, giving you the familiar feeling of using the Windows or Mac interface when you are actually moving files around using Unix commands. Unfortunately, there's trouble to be had if you don't learn just a little more. Here are some details that you should be aware of in order to make your transfers go smoothly.

File Formats

A digital file is made up of data. There are two basic flavors of data: *ASCII* and *binary*. ASCII (American Standard Code for Information Interchange) files contain text data that humans can understand, so they are often referred to as *text files*. Binary files contain data that computers understand—these files look like gibberish to normal people.

A program on your computer's hard disk is stored in binary format. A letter to your mom is stored as a text file. The difference is important when it comes time to upload your files to a Web server, because your Web data must conform to file format standards that can be interpreted by all computing platforms. HTML files are text files. GIF, JPEG, and almost all other graphics formats are binary files.

When you upload your files using FTP, you need to specify which format they're in. From a Windows machine this is pretty straightforward—text is text, binary is binary. There aren't any other choices. File formats can be a little more tricky if you're developing on the Macintosh, however. Here's why: some Mac files can really be two different files. These two files are called *forks*—the resource fork and the data fork. To confuse things even more, you can't tell which Mac files are really two files just by looking at them in the Finder, because the Mac OS hides this information from you.

This is fine (actually, this little-known fact is one of the reasons why the Mac OS is such a powerful operating system), because the whole two-files-in-one strategy is really pretty inconsequential...except when you want to use your Mac files on other platforms such as Windows, DOS, or Unix. These platforms don't understand the two-forked Mac files, and they usually break the forks up into separate files, or just ignore the resource fork entirely. Depending on the specific type of Mac file in question, the split can be fatal or completely inconsequential.

The Macintosh versions of file formats that are popular on the Web are usually well-behaved—they don't put anything too important in the resource fork, so when it's stripped away, the data in the data fork still works.

Your FTP client may offer some choices that are confusing, however: the *Binary* and *Raw Data* settings are good; using these settings will strip away the resource fork and post only the information that everyone in the world can use. *MacBinary*, *MacBinary II*, *BinHex*, *AppleDouble*, and *AppleSingle* are all formats designed to preserve the Mac's two-forked features. This is good if you are trying to send a file to a buddy with a Mac, but bad for Web publishing.

File Permissions

The Internet is still primarily served by computers running some form of the Unix operating system. Unlike personal computers, which developed as single-user systems, Unix-based computers have always been multiuser. The file permission system employed by Unix makes it possible for lots of people to share the same computer equipment without giving up their ability to keep some files private. A general understanding of this permission system will help you solve problems that can arise when your Web site is not behaving as expected.

In Unix there are three types of users and three types of permission:

- Users can be you, your group, or everyone in the whole world.
- Permission can be to read, to write, or to execute (as in running a program, or opening a folder, which is considered executing it).

I count 56 possible combinations of these permissions, ranging from you alone being able to just read a file to everyone being able to read, write, and execute a file.

If you are publishing your Web site for public consumption, all of the files and directories (folders) within it must have read permission granted to everyone. Folders must also have execute permission granted to everyone.

But the Unix box that serves your Web site may be configured so that when you transfer your files using FTP, they don't have these permissions by default. To test this, upload your files to the server and then try your site. If you get an error like this:

```
Error blah blah. File Permission Denied
```

your *umask* is set incorrectly. Luckily, you can correct this by modifying your umask.

Your umask is actually a Unix file that dictates what your default file permissions are. If you have access to the server, you can change the umask settings yourself. If you don't have access to the server, you'll have to ask your system administrator to make the changes for you.

Testing the Web Site

Testing your site is an ongoing process: it begins as you tag each page, continues as you expand the site to include several interlinked pages, and extends well into the post-publication period of the site.

Did you check every page of your site on every browser you care to support? Get in the habit of previewing your pages in more than one browser before you commit to standards that might not work in all browsers (see Figures 17 and 18). For example, if you design a site that depends on the `FONT SIZE =` tag, you may be in for a surprise when you see the site in another browser. Developing site-wide standards is a good idea, but don't wait until after they are implemented to test them.

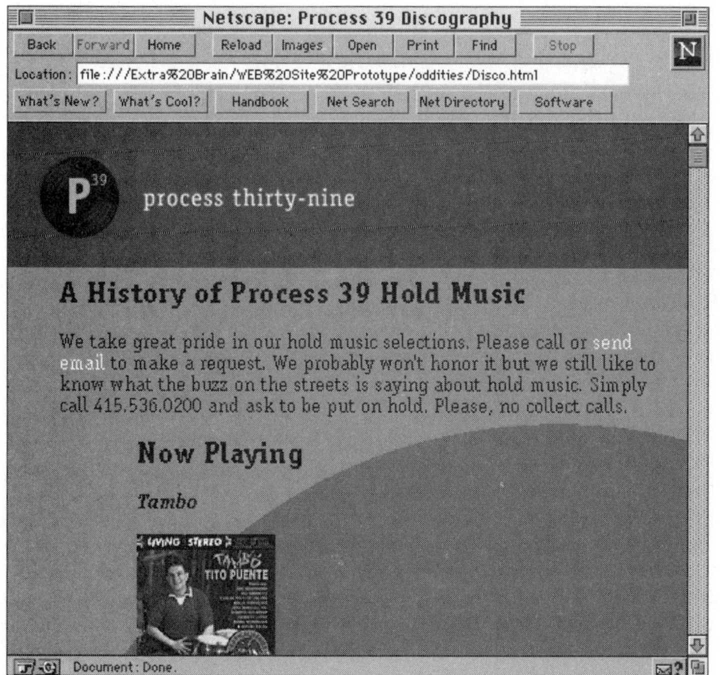

Figure 17: *A great-looking page designed and previewed only in Netscape 2.0. Nice!*

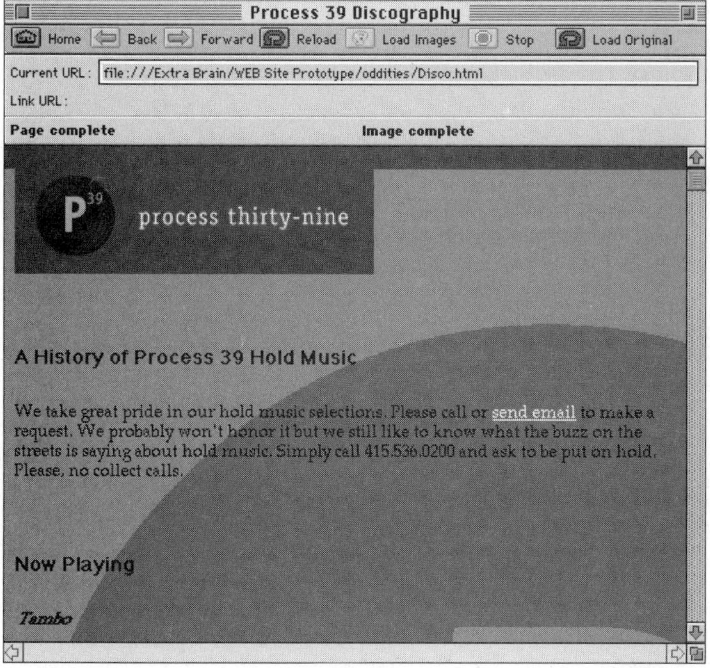

Figure 18: *That same "great-looking page," as viewed in the eWorld/AOL browser. Yuck!*

Did you make a well-behaved site with relative links on a local drive? If so, did you test everything again when you uploaded it? This may seem tedious, and it may be easier to skip this step, but the cost might be a loss of interest by visitors as they encounter broken graphics and links that don't work.

One of the coolest things about Web development is that page design can occur on local machines—your home computer, for instance. Entire sites can be assembled on a local volume. This is a powerful way to develop a site, but it can cause problems if you don't structure the local site with well-designed relative links and a robust directory structure.

Did you ask a bunch of (preferably good, kindhearted, generous) friends to check out your site and give you feedback? Make a list of people who owe you a favor, whose opinions you trust, and whose computers are different from yours. If you developed on a Mac, get some people with PCs and Unix boxes to check out your site and report any broken stuff they find. Even if you've been thorough in your efforts to test a new site, this testing process may reveal quirks on other people's systems.

TIP

You can enlist the whole world to participate in this system by including a MAILTO: link at the bottom of each page in your site (some sites just put them on the home page). This link gives users a convenient way to send you feedback via e-mail as soon as they see something broken (or something they like).

Some Major Process Milestones

As a digital design studio, Process 39 is often asked to lead clients through the process of creating a Web site—and it's different every time. The exact process we take with one client is never the same as the process we take with another, but the sequence of milestones is usually similar. Below are the major milestones pulled from a real schedule we recently performed for a client. Consider what milestones might apply to your own process.

Wed 1/10–Tues.1/30: Preliminary work

- The client approaches Process 39 with rough objectives and a budget.
- Process 39 gives the client a proposal detailing what type of site they can expect to build with their budget.

It's important to establish the client's rough objectives and the development budget before gathering everyone together for a meeting. The designer should give the client a proposal so they will know what to expect.

Wed 1/31: Project launch meeting

Process definition and creative refinement with Joe Speaks of Process 39:

- The client's Web site objectives are confirmed.
- Process 39's Web development proposal is reviewed.
- The client's content intentions are refined.

This is the first real working meeting. It confirms the client's objectives and maps their content ideas to an appropriate Web site design.

Mon 2/5: Background materials distributed

- Additional collateral materials and the client's background information are disseminated to the project team.

It's important for everyone on the development team to understand what the site is about. Even the person doing the HTML tagging should have an understanding of the overall site message. Assembling a background information packet with relevant information is crucial.

Wed 2/7: Web site brainstorm

- Process 39 and the client wildly experiment with lots of ideas.

The process of sharing those ideas helps refine objectives and spawn creative solutions.

Wed 2/14: Design presentation

- Process 39 presents three creative approaches, including content structure, sketches showing possible banner graphics/animations, navigational icon examples, and example subpage banners.
- The client chooses one direction for further refinement. This direction sets the context for overall site development past this point.

At some point you need to decide what you're actually going to build. Process 39 likes to present a few different design directions to show the client a variety of ideas to meet their objectives. Even if you're not using an outside designer, you should come together and agree on the look, feel, and organization of your site to ensure that everyone who's contributing is building the same thing.

Mon 2/19: Refinement materials prepared

- Based on the chosen design direction, the project team gathers appropriate content materials, including text and graphics.
- The team prepares a complete list of content to be included in the site and a site map based on this list.

Once the design direction is chosen, a final content plan needs to be created and examples of that content need to be made available to the implementation team.

Mon 2/26: Design refinement presentation

- Process 39 implements the chosen design throughout the site.
- The site is presented to the client online and includes the following elements:
    - Banner graphics/animations
    - Home page HTML text
    - Navigational controls
    - All subpages available for navigation to test site layout
    - Other unique or complex HTML text and tables
    - Examples of the complete set of HTML formatting styles to be used throughout the site

Think of this as a beta version of your eventual Web site. You should be able to see approximately what you want to build and make some adjustments before you're too far along.

Wed 2/28: Text materials delivered

- The client delivers text to Process 39 to be included in the Web site. This is not final text, merely the text that Process 39 will use to launch the site. Text changes beyond this point will be handled as site updates between the client and the service provider. This gives Process 39 the opportunity to monitor the revision process and ensure its effectiveness.

You should set a date when content materials are due from all contributors. But remember, the site is never finished. By making the final refinement process the same as the revision process, you can ensure that future revisions will go smoothly once the site is up and running.

Mon 3/1: Web site beta

- The beta site is online for review. It will include 85% of all material to be in the site.

Since the site will be available constantly online starting back at the design refinement on 2/26, this milestone is merely a target date for a significant level of completion. As you get near the end, ask for final review.

Mon 3/8: Site launch

- The final site is made public.

The client should incorporate user feedback into the continuing evolution of the site.

Designing into the Future

The main rule for design on the Web is *think on your feet.* At this time, the medium has few common practice standards, and with changing technology, standards are moving targets.

If you want to build an office building and you want to hire a top-notch architect, you can find out roughly what the industry's going rate is. Right now, for Web design and implementation this is very hard to do. Clients and individuals are unsure of what the going rate is for *anything*. There are hidden costs in serving a site that not everyone will know of. An offer from one service provider may be significantly different than another, yet cost the same. People, including designers, are not sure what to expect. You have to take each instance on its own.

This lack of common practice standards has one upside, though, and that is opportunity. People are unsure of what to expect, so the designer has a great opportunity to innovate and develop something surprising and wonderful. Today's Web site may not look like next week's. Technology, user tastes, and understanding are all on the move. The Web is a plastic medium, ever-changing. Keep up to date with what's out there and who's doing what. It's a big world—get moving.

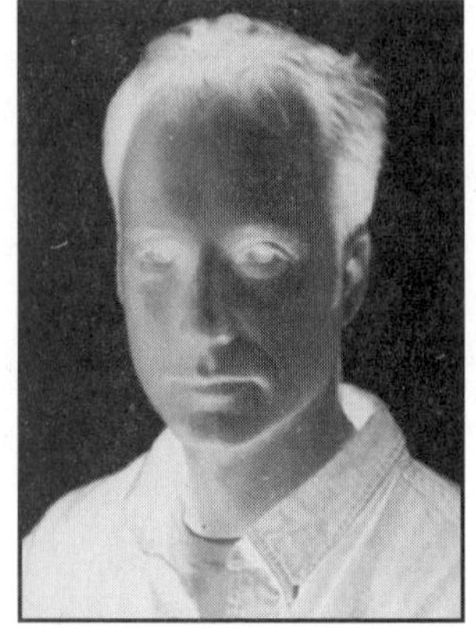

Founded in 1993, Organic Online has grown to become one of the premier full-service World Wide Web development companies. Organizations choose Organic because we apply our unparalleled experience to create innovative and effectiv sites. We utilize technology to meet the needs of our clients while building informational databases that are intuitive, informative and interesting.

Organic Online: In Brief

The Organic Announcements Mailing List

Personnel

Press Releases

Job Openings

Organic's Thoughts on Content Negotiation

what's new | services | information | playground | our clients | non-profits

home

We welcome your comments and feedback. To reach us send email to www@organic.com or call (415) 284-6888.

Organic Online

Company Profile

Founded in 1993, Organic Online has become one of the premier full-service developers of the World Wide Web. Organic's staff includes the most diverse, experienced, creative, and dedicated talent in the industry, whose résumés read like a who's who of Silicon Valley, Madison Avenue, and Hollywood. Organic has developed programming for clients including Levi Strauss & Co., Microsoft Corporation, Netscape Communications, Advertising Age, Saturn Corporation, and many other global brands.

Jonathan Nelson was evangelizing the Web before most people knew of its existence. In addition to his executive duties, Jonathan is involved with the creative department and all elements of interface and graphic design. Prior to Organic, he was involved in the start-up of Wired magazine, HotWired, and also worked in the music industry as a producer with 35 album credits to his name.

Chapter Profile

Most Web sites fit into one of three categories: academic, hobby, or corporate. Of these three, corporate sites got the most attention in the last year because their development provided the revenue to drive hardware and software sales while employing legions of designers. Many corporate sites are just electronic brochures online, but a few make statements about the companies and the way they market themselves. It is naive to assume the Web will completely replace all other forms of corporate marketing in the near future. Yet several firms will gain or lose prominence in their markets by the relative effectiveness of Web marketing strategies.

There are three primary challenges facing new and established firms doing business on the Web for the first time.

- First, brands are perceived by how they transact their sales. For example, Netscape's products are intimately bound to the Web, so the Internet is the central focus of their marketing effort. Chevrolet must use the Web to complement their existing strategies, driving customers into the showroom. Sony must connect people to an experience of their products and even sell some of them directly over the Web.
- Second, how can a firm change its relationship to its customers? The old model of advertising, to coin a phrase, is wide, shallow, expensive, and mostly unaccountable. The new model, on the other hand, uses the Web to be wide but focused, deep, and detailed, has a higher level of integrity, and arrives on a user's screen far more cheaply. There has been considerable discussion in the last year about when the boom in developing corporate sites will end. Some think it will occur this year. If this is so, many of the firms leaving the Web are those that cannot market themselves effectively because they are forcing the old model on a new medium.
- Third, Web marketers must integrate their online efforts with their other communications tools. Very basic forms of this integration have already been used, with print and TV ads including a firm's URL, for example. Many corporate sites are already generating content of their own, giving people a reason to visit and stay. Large content producers will sell *streams*, ongoing portions of their own sites, to advertisers who must deliver their message to a focused audience.

It is these three challenges that Organic seeks to win for its clients. The following interview, which elaborates on Organic's role in these challenges, was conducted by John McCoy with CEO Jonathan Nelson at the Organic offices in San Francisco.

Essay

Global Brands in the Digital Age

John McCoy with Jonathan Nelson, President/CEO

JOHN McCOY: How do you define great Web design?

Jonathan Nelson: To me, good design on the Web is something that takes designers who are thinking in multiple dimensions at once. And the dimensions are numerous and changing. It is sort of like you've got to force it through a lot of filters. It has got to be small; it has got to be fast. Small *is* fast in the online world. Form and function need to dovetail together, and it needs to fit the demographic objective of the site.

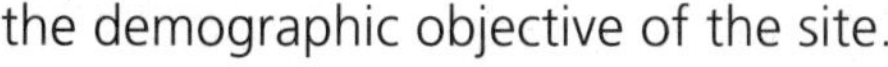

For instance, the focus of the Levis site [**http://www.levi.com**] is very well defined: global youth culture, 18- to 24-year-old people, worldwide. And everything goes through that filter for that site. That is the creative direction, and the design trickles out of that. The design of that site is very different from something like Saturn Motorcars [**http://www.saturncars.com**], which, by the way, was designed by Doris Mitsch at Hal Riney & Partners. It is very Saturn in design, and it caters to an older, much more, I don't want say *staid*, but ah…

JM: Conservative, established…

JN: Yeah, conservative, established car-buying audience. It is more middle-of-the-road and middle-America. For that site, navigation and design dovetail together completely so that the graphics download very, very quickly and very elegantly. You always know where you are. It is very, very specific, whereas the design for Levis is much more elusive. It is much larger and in K [kilobyte] size, much flashier. So I think that this idea of K size is one of the filters through which you need to fit good design.

Another filter you have to fit it through is demographics. The design, of course, has to fit whoever the audience is. You also need to match this idea of form and function into it. Who is going to be looking at this? Generally, the older the audience, the more you sort of need to lead them with very clean, clear navigation. Always tell them where they are. Perhaps you can even show them where they've been and how they got there. Whereas the younger audience has probably a little bit more time on their hands, is willing to explore, wants to be engaged and entertained, and the design is a function of that. So the filters are K size, navigation, and demographics…those are the key things for me.

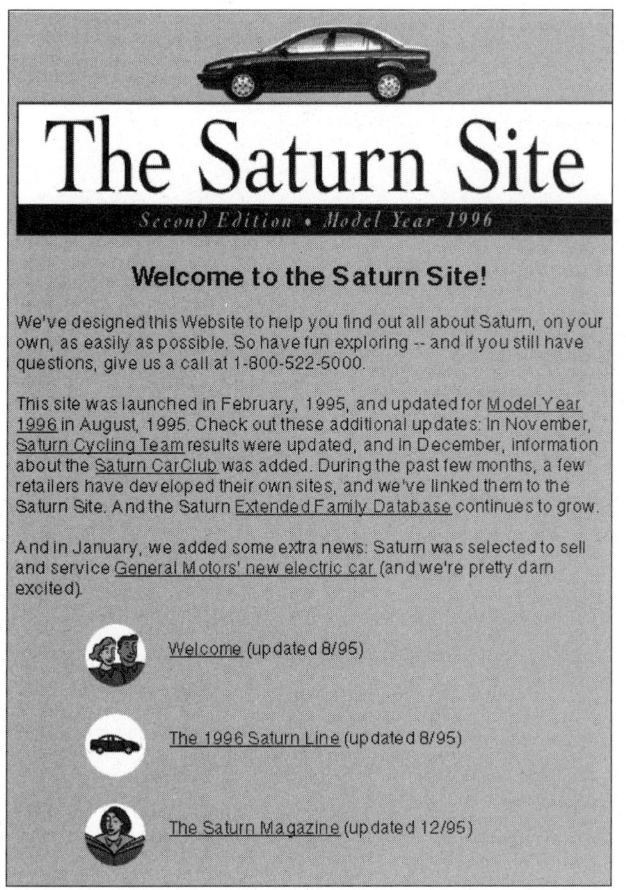

Another thing that starts impending on the reality of the design is color palettes. We're designing across platforms here. We don't know what the person is going to be looking at this on. It could be a 2-bit, LCD laptop screen, which is basically black and white, and/or 16-color grays, 256-color grays, 256 colors, or 16 million colors. We don't really know, so it lowers the common denominator between platforms. You know Macintoshes treat colors very differently than most Windows machines, and this affects design very, very much. It is just a major impediment. Likewise, browsers treat colors differently. So all of these things affect design to a great extent.

JM: In terms of the younger audience, they seem to be more willing to go with an unusual design or be willing to explore the site even if they do feel momentarily confused.

JN: Absolutely. A lot of young people want to say, "Surprise me, take me somewhere." Entertainment plays a big role for them, whereas I think information is a bigger use for older, more mature audiences. I know that during the day, when I'm looking for something online, and I'm at work, I want to get from A to B as quickly as possible, and the design should be subsumed to function. Whereas at night, that same computer becomes more like a television set for me. I'm looking for entertainment, I'm looking to be engaged. And I'm looking at that box as my window to the world of entertainment, not information.

JM: That actually brings up a good point which is apparent on the Levis site: an intersection between advertising and entertainment. There have been some discussions of where entertainment and advertising could go specifically relative to Organic. Could you elaborate on where you see entertainment and advertising intersecting both now and in the future? Do you see there being much distinction between the two of those?

JN: I'm not sure that there will be a distinction between entertainment, design, and marketing. Once again, it trickles out of the target audience. You start at point D and you work back to point A, which is "What are you marketing?" One of the things we try to do is to pick clients that have something interesting to say or a product that is interesting. With Levis it was very clear how to use this medium. Other clients of ours are a little bit more conservative, but we always try to infuse a little bit of entertainment or at least a really high production value into every site.

For instance, we designed the Internet tutorial for Microsoft, the Microsoft Network. The first thing you see when you come onto the Microsoft Network's Internet section is a guide to the Internet [**http://www.msn.com/tutorial/default.html**], which Organic developed. Now, here the interface is mostly text-based and informative, but the design elegantly plays with the Internet. What we're trying to do is lower expectations as well as impediments and barriers—make it more fun. Most people are afraid of computers. They don't need to be afraid of computers. So what we try to do is make it a little bit more playful—take the edge off of the learning experience.

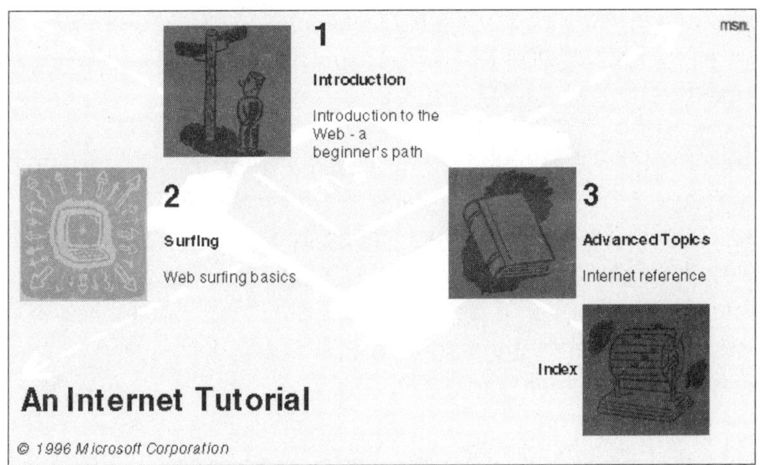

Other companies are trying to come across as very straightforward and slick—powerful. Montgomery Securities, for example: this is a securities company. They're a bastion of solidity and their Web site portrays this [**http://www.montgomery.com**]. So with each one it really depends on who the audience is and what you're trying to portray.

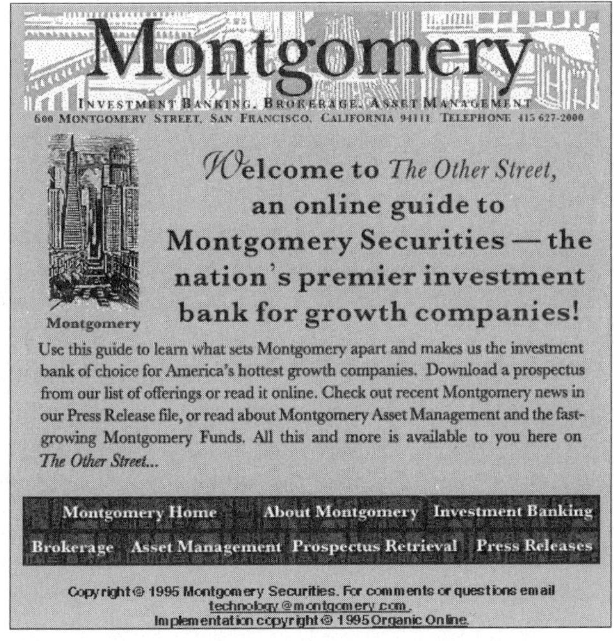

JM: Do you feel that you'll be creating sites with a range of conservative to almost total entertainment in the future—sites that would display a tailored experience to each individual user?

JN: Oh, dynamic. Dynamic designs that have matched demographic material—yeah, absolutely. Organic has been doing a lot of work with database technology that can build dynamic pages on the fly depending on consumer demographics. Some of the stuff we've done for Netscape [**http://www.netscape.com**] has been dynamically generated out of an Oracle database. And while the design doesn't change, the information does. You'll see the design start to change in the future to a national demographic or consumer profile.

N DEVELOPMENT PARTNERS

NETSCAPE DEVELOPMENT PARTNERS

Whether you're developing shrinkwrapped software or custom solutions for your enterprise, building Internet sites with Netscape Server software for commercial or communications uses, or designing Internet content best viewed with Netscape Navigator, you need the tools and technical information to succeed. With the Netscape Development Partners Program, you'll be only a click away from these resources.

The Netscape Development Partners Program is an annual subscription service for US$495 that gives you the software, tools, information, and support you need to develop products and services based on open, secure Netscape technology. You'll have the most up-to-date information on Netscape products, as well as the best tools available, to help you develop and deploy business solutions or commercial applications for your customers.

If you have had trouble accessing the Partners' Net site or have any questions, please read our FAQ.

JAVAONE DISCOUNT DEADLINE EXTENDED TO APRIL 22
Netscape is co-sponsoring JavaOne, Sun's first worldwide conference for Java developers May 29-31 in San Francisco. If you attended the Netscape Internet Developer Conference or are a Netscape Development Partner, save $300 when you register by April 22. To receive the discount, register by phone by calling 1-800-488-2883 or 415-578-6900 outside the U.S.

SGI TO FOCUS ON VRML, WEB AT UPCOMING DEVELOPER/COSMO FORUM
Internet and intranet developers planning to incorporate VRML, Java and interactive audio and video into their products, won't want to miss Silicon Graphics' Developer and Cosmo Forum. This is the conference to attend for those wanting to learn about next generation, cross-platform tools that bring interactivity to the web. Forum '96 is May 21-23 at the San Jose Fairmont. **Early registration ends** April 19 - save $150 off the Forum price of $845.

CAN'T GET ENOUGH JAVA?
Netscape is co-sponsoring JavaOne, Sun's first worldwide conference for Java developers May 29-31 in San Francisco. If you attended the Netscape Internet Developer Conference or are a Netscape Development Partner, save $300 when you register by April 15. Be sure to register by phone to receive this discount. Call 1-800-488-2883 or 415-578-6900 outside the U.S.

DEVELOPER CONFERENCE PRESENTATIONS NOW AVAILABLE
View over 27 slide presentations from Netscape's Internet Developer Conference now the conference site. Transcripts of keynote addresses and general sessions are also available including Marc Andreessen's SuiteSpot server announcement.

NAVIGATOR GOLD FOR MACINTOSH GOES ALPHA
Macintosh developers can download Navigator Gold 2.01 Alpha for the Mac from our

JM: You are talking about your design process—working from B to A, as opposed to A to B. Can you flesh that out a little bit? Obviously, you have to understand your audience. But what are the steps you use in your design process?

JN: I think that it is hard to say. I can't completely quantify how I think about a consumer. I do a lot of reading of different magazines, newspapers, and books. You've got to crawl inside the head of the consumer. I've been spending quite a bit of time traveling to foreign countries, trying to figure out how people deal with multimedia computers in Sweden or Vietnam or wherever. And that to me is fascinating because it is a cultural issue. You know, different ages deal with computers differently and different cultures deal with them differently. I am trying to figure out personally how people react. You can do all kinds of market research, which we certainly pay attention to. We look at what other designers have done.

I think Organic is a company of consensus where we really try to listen to each other and we also try to understand that each person has a different and very valid point of view. And through a certain consensus with an array of ideas and raising of the bar of design, I think we've been pretty successful.

JM: Tell me about the ways you handle your creative development.

JN: Organic will commonly do what we call a *brand immersion*, which means that we'll talk to either the client or the ad agency and really try and, once again, get inside the minds of the client and their customers. I've looked at hours and hours of television commercials, print ads, billboards. I've looked at market research, product, gone shopping myself. We were doing a car company and I went to the auto dealer and pretended I was going to buy a car, just so I could get that experience—you know, test drive the car. I really get into the products and how they've done their marketing before. I see the Web as an extension of marketing campaigns. You know, we don't need to completely rewrite who the company is. We certainly don't rewrite who Levi is or some of our other clients are. But often we are marketing to a different demographic. We have different tools at our disposal. We are usually bringing this into people's homes, and we're trying to make it compelling and interactive—and at the same time tell a story and make it fun. It is a pretty complex set of things that we're doing, and we can't do it unless we understand both who the audience is and what they want, as well as who the client is, what they've got, and why a consumer would want it.

The Web is merely a transmission medium. I want to make the Web as transparent as possible. The more the consumer can understand our client or a product, the better we've done our job. Whether we use humor or entertainment or basic text—just basic information—we've succeeded if the Web disappears and that person can understand what we're trying to get across. I think a lot of people think the Web is about technology. Yeah, it is about technology, but it is *really* about people; it is about communications.

JM: You mentioned the international site earlier. What is your experience internationally, in terms of the Web being able to communicate to a global audience—and being able to design for a global audience?

JN: Well, we certainly don't have all the answers here, but it is completely fascinating to me. For the first time in history, companies essentially have the ability to have a channel, so to speak. We can have a single point of communication where the world can tune in, in their own language if they'd like. For instance, we just designed a site for Kinko's Copies [**http://www.kinkos.com**], once again with Hal Riney & Partners, and I think we have eight or so languages—Chinese, Japanese, Spanish, French, German, etcetera. And yes, we are serving this from a single point, out of our offices here in San Francisco, but the whole world is tuning in to see what is going on with Kinko's on their WWW site.

Once again, the content needs to adapt to the consumer. We've talked a lot internally about general core content and localized content. So to use the Levis example, you might have a global youth culture. We have core content that fits that demographic, but then we've customized content, localized for the European audience [**http://www.eu.levi.com/menu**]. So the Europeans see the European styles of jeans. They see the European advertising; they see things that are tailored to them. And I think this is going to be a huge trend in the Web of the future: building core content and localized content as the medium expands globally. It is going to be huge.

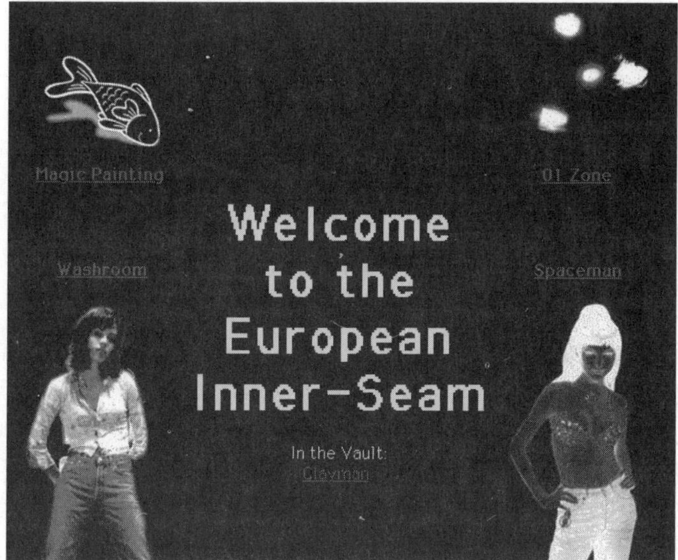

JM: I agree. In terms of localized design, do you try to work with people who are in the target markets that you're trying to address, to make sure the design has a look, feel, and function that's going to make sense to them? Something that makes sense to somebody who is living in Northern California might not make sense to someone else with a geographic, cultural, or language difference.

JN: There is a point where this happened. I went traveling in the far East—I had been over there a couple of times—in China. I was recently in Vietnam and Cambodia. You go into a restaurant, and oftentimes if you don't speak the language; they'll just take you back to the kitchen and you can point at what you want. So you go back there and say you want to order squid soup or something.

They've got a bowl of squid sitting there and they've got broth. And you'll point at the squid and you'll hold up one finger meaning *one*, right? Well, in China, most of the people will look at you like, "What does this guy want?" And you realize how ineffectual even gestures can be. I mean if you can't communicate verbally, you know sign language almost always works in the Western world, but it really hammers home your cultural bias when you can't communicate verbally and sign language doesn't work either.

I think Web design is similar to that kind of gross analogy in that certain things just don't work in foreign countries. One of the fortunate things is that people are starting to adapt to Western ways because most of the technology is Western and the software is Western. Other cultures are starting to gravitate more towards the West as the world shrinks. English is getting to be more and more predominant, and cultural biases are diminishing. But I think one of the really interesting challenges is to adapt. For us, as a Western company, we just do our job better by understanding those cultures.

JM: Do you feel that you owe a certain respect to their own design parameters and cultural traditions?

JN: Oh, absolutely. At the end of the day we're trying to communicate, and if we can't get our point across, I don't have any squid soup and I starve. I'm not here to say, "Look, be like an American," or "Be like a Westerner." It is a trade-off here. I'll talk to you the way you want to be talked to if you'll listen to me. Or I'll make it easier for you to listen; it is a voluntary thing, the Web.

JM: Do you usually undergo testing so that you don't have scenarios where people try to do the Web equivalent of using a mouse as a foot pedal?

JN: Well, if somebody is using a mouse as foot pedal I think...[*laughter*]...they will need a pretty detailed splash page explaining how to use a computer! No, we have seen that people are fairly computer literate. I'm talking more design issues. I wish I had the time and the money to do focus groups in 142 countries or whatever, but I don't, so all I can do is travel and keep my eyes open and try to understand.

JM: That actually leads to my next question, which is What are your design inspirations, from history, art, personal experience...?

JN; Well, at Organic we're a young company that is playing with a new medium. And we're constantly trying to push the envelope in terms of design and technology. And it is really the fusion of design and technology that makes these things fly, as well as marketing and just general creativity. These things all need to fit together to be a good Web site. You know, the narrative and the copyrighting of a story affect the design pretty dramatically. Personally, I affect it by hiring the best people that I can find, people who have open minds and are really willing to push boundaries within themselves—but who are really trying to examine the issues and understand that Organic is not just one person or even a small group of people. It is a lot of people adding very valid opinions and fusing them together.

I have a degree in history and a degree in art. And have looked a lot at all different types of art, from the Etruscans, before Christ, to very modern art. I look a lot at modern magazines: *Ray Gun* and *Wired*. A lot of my personal taste is much farther out than what actually comes out in our work, but I'm certainly looking at the cutting-edge and the avant-garde. I am a big fan of pop art. The designs of Warhol and Roy Lichtenstein work very well online and affect my thought process. I like incredibly detailed medieval art, but it doesn't really work online.

JM: What do you think are some examples of your best work and why?

JN: The first set that we ever designed was very elegant. We did the first Volvo design, which at the time was all squares—very blocky [**http://www.volvocars.com**]. But there was no transparency on the Web, so that's what we had to play with. I thought it was extremely successful, even though now it looks like a dinosaur.

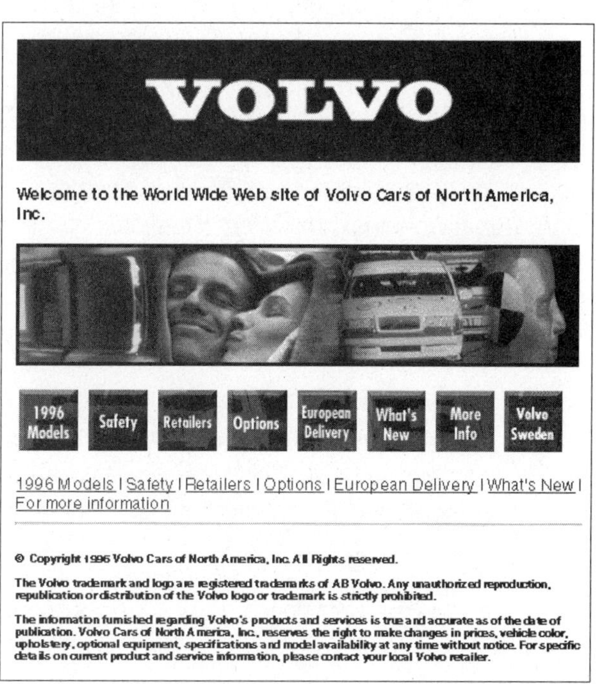

Saturn I think is great, but once again Doris over at Hal Riney designed it and did a lot of the implementation.

We did a site for Apple [**http://www.apple.com**] that was straight out of the Apple design book. It was a little bit different where we used Garamond Bold, which is Apple's font, so we kind of ripped a page out of the print manual and put it online, which was very challenging and it was a technical thing. The funniest thing about it was one of the people who looked at it said, "What you did is so simple—why did it cost so much?" [*laughter*] I almost went through the roof, because we worked so hard to get it to work. It was a strange backhanded compliment, in that we worked so hard that it looked completely elegant, completely simple, completely Apple.

We've just launched a site with Colgate-Palmolive. Once again, it is trying to tell a story. It is not completely avant-garde, cutting edge, but it is very good in the way that it tells its story.

JM: We have a lot of products that are coming out to allow people to do multimedia on the Web. How do you see it being integrated?

JN: Well, I think that it is just going to make it more fun and more engaging. You could draw a spectrum of print to television, overlaid as cold to hot. Right now, the Web is more on the print side, but it is definitely not print. It is more kinetic than print. It is quickly moving—getting warmer. As it is moves towards TV, it is moving towards a really fulfilling, engaging experience. And, of course, at some point computers and televisions will merge completely so that they're really one. But the Web is certainly going to take you there, and each of these multimedia applications, whether it be Java or Shockwave or even server-push, is a step towards making the media more engaging, more compelling, or more entertaining.

It is not all just flash. Java can help you build a spreadsheet too, which for that killer mortgage calculation site could be great if you're buying a house. It presents you with what we call *media value*, which is about how this stuff relates to me as an individual. If I'm going to buy a house, the mortgage is going to affect my life to a pretty substantial degree. So, I think these things just help the Web grow.

JM: If you were coaching or giving some time to mentor a young designer, what do you think would be the best advice you could give them in terms of their skill development, the kind of things that they can study, the kinds of things they should incorporate into their designs…?

JN: I've talked to a number of designers over time. I think you've got to find your own voice, but you also need to play by the rules in the early days. You've got to know the rules in order to break them. Look at a lot of work. I'm not just saying go to every Web site you can find; although that would be kind of fun, it would be a long process. But look at everything; everything should affect your design.

One of the things I wasn't that familiar with was corporate design—some of the classics, like the Tide box. It's straight out of pop art and looks like contemporary graphics even though it is 20 or 30 years old at this point. There is incredible corporate equity in brands—any brand, whether it be soap or shoes or pants or cars. There is a lot in there to be looked at, and there is a lot to be pulled out that actually relates to the Web in a perverse way.

Now it is up to you to build those bridges, to see how everyday life effects Web design. Understand dynamic systems of Web design. Understand how relational databases can be your friend and help you out. Understand how Java can animate things. Understand how server-push can animate things, how Shockwave can animate things, or whatever the latest new technology is. The more you have a 360-degree view of the world around you when you are home, and the more you have a 360-degree view of the world around you when you are sitting at your computer terminal, the better job you'll do as a designer.

JM: Lots of tools are coming out that make it easier for nontechnical people to build technology. To what degree do you think the designers will have to become more or less technical as time goes on?

JN: They're going to have to become more technical certainly. I think you are starting to see the rise of some really good companies and individuals. The thing that is interesting about design on the Web is that it is totally open—there are no superstars yet; there's no Picasso of the Web right now. You know, it is a wide open field and, quite honestly, it is probably going to be an 18- to 22-year-old kid who is going to be the Picasso of the Web. It is a wild new medium. The world is watching us do this stuff.

It is also very interesting right now that you have a very limited palette, but the palette is bigger than almost anything else. You are limited by colors; you don't have the unlimited colors that an oil painter would. But you have an unlimited palette of audiences, of technologies, of animation, of sound, of multiple pages, of experience, of narrative, of all of these things—emerging new technologies. All of these things can be brought to bear on an issue, whether that is a commercial issue like building a Web site for Levis or a noncommercial issue like putting your vacation pictures online in the most compelling way possible.

JM: What are the kinds of brands do you feel are going the most successful in the next century by using the Web?

JN: There is a thing in marketing that they call the *considered purchase*. The considered purchase is something like a car. Basically, the idea is that either something is really expensive so you're going to think about it a lot before you buy one, or it can fit your image. Like I'm a macho guy smoking Marlboro cigarettes; I might buy a Chevy Blazer. If I'm a sophisticated gigolo, I might buy an Alfa Romeo. There are also other considered purchases, such as music. When you think about the group, you're buying into a culture. Those things sell very well on the Web because they have a story to tell of themselves and people are interested.

There are other things that are not so interesting, like toilet paper or sheet rock. What are you going to say about toilet paper, other than "ours is softer than theirs"? And you can start getting into technical explanations of two-ply or three-ply or pillow-soft or whatever. These are incredibly complex issues for a designers such as ourselves, but actually they are incredibly liberating: the reality is you really can't say much about it, so you've got to say something else if you want to be there on the Web. I think that these people with considered purchases will be very successful in the way that the *Hallmark Hall of Fame* was very successful in the 50s as a television program, because they sponsored programming. They built content that was associative in nature, not direct in nature. And it actually is freeing us up to develop content and to just let our minds wander. Once again, we start at B. Who is your audience? Are they on the Web? Can we get across to them? How can we get across to them? What are we going to say?

Maybe the big sheet rock audience is not online and it is not the appropriate venue. Maybe people would rather read about sheet rock by going to Walmart or Home Depot. It is consumer goods, products that people use a lot, that are actually the most exciting to me because I don't need to tell the story of the car. I don't need to tell the story of a music group. That is an obvious story. It is not so obvious when you're developing programming from scratch.

JM: What kind of entertainment do you think will be on the Web? In the sheet rock example we might have the Web equivalent of Home Improvement. *What kind of entertainment experiences do you think designers need to think about creating?*

JN: You can look to the real world as opposed to the virtual world for a lot of examples. Good designers are going to mix and match and permeate and evolve some new examples. You're going to see narratives; you're going to see more soap operas like *The Spot* [**http://www.thespot.com**]. They've obviously looked to afternoon soaps as their thing, or *Models Inc.* or *Melrose Place*.

I think there are informative examples of people who are creating documentaries or windows into the world. One of the things about the Web is that because it is an inherently disposable medium, you can do broadcasts. But you don't need to be the world figure skating championships or the Olympics to get prime-time coverage. You're going to see home football games broadcast on the Web. The magazine metaphor with *HotWired* [**http://www.hotwired.com**] and *Pathfinder* [**http://pathfinder.com**] is pretty well evolved. You will see people going on trips and beaming back information in real time. We've done this ourselves with our AIDS Ride [**http://www.aidsride.org**]. We sent out a correspondent on the AIDS Ride and they beamed back actual digital pictures of the ride as well as a text narrative of what they were experiencing. You will have how to's—like home improvement shows—which are educational while they are entertaining and engaging. Say you're building your house or fixing your car or programming your VCR to stop that blinking 12:00. There are ways to do that with an eye for design and humor or narrative that will help you tell the story and get your point across.

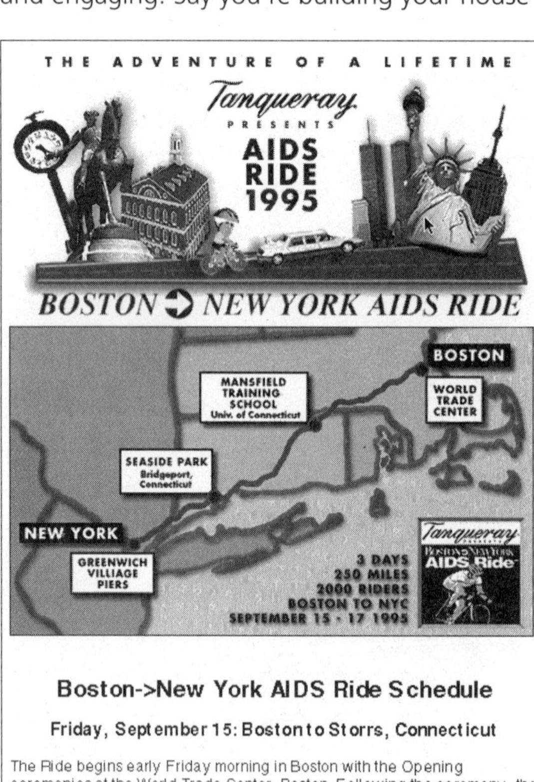

JM: What do you think the Web is going to look like in five years—which I realize is an eternity? What do you think it is going to be like? Can you give a description of what a given user's experience might be?

JN: Well, one, the Web will start customizing itself to the user. If you give me a little information about you, I will start customizing your experience towards you and show it to you the way you want, whether that be textually, narratively, graphically. I might give you coupons or inducements or comarketing campaigns. Microsoft might own the Super Bowl at that point [*laughter*]. If I'm a 16-year-old kid in Topeka, Kansas, I might get a graphic within the broadcast that is customized to me.

I think it will become much more dynamic—more animated, more three-dimensional, more engaging and compelling. It will suck you in more. Interfaces will get much more complex. It is kind of like we're developing a new language here. Not only are we trying to develop a new language so that we can talk to people, but other people are trying to figure out the language that we're trying to develop so that they can understand it. And we're raising the bar for everybody, both producer and consumer. Right now, we have to make buttons that are obvious. They look like buttons because people don't know to press them otherwise. In the future, people will just know that little blurb of text or that little icon is a button. We won't need to tell them that or make it so obvious that a brain-dead person can figure it out.

It is going to move further and further towards TV. It is going to surpass TV. It is going to bring in better sound technology, in stereo or in surround sound. It is going to become more and more engaging. It is going to become high-definition. It is going to be yet another way that people connect to their world.

JM: What do you think of the discussions that the Web is not just a broadcast medium anymore, but many-to-many.

JN: That's the whole idea. This is a new medium. It is not print; it is not TV. It has elements of both of those. These are real-world things; the Web is its own thing and there will be new terms to describe it. It will take its own evolutionary path. It will customize itself to the user. It will connect users in foreign countries who don't even speak the same language; it will have translation programs so people can have a conversation even though they don't speak the same language. You know, technology creates and reduces barriers at the same time. And one of the things is this globalization. I think design and technology used together can reduce barriers.

JM: Who do you think are going to be the people or companies with the greatest potential to shape the Web—to contribute to its evolution?

JN: I think a lot of young people have a leg up because they've just been immersed in media. A lot of us are the *Brady Bunch* generation or the *Smurf* generation or whatever. It is second nature for me to go home and turn on the TV, the radio, have the phone ring, have faxes spinning out, get my news by pager, and have my computer running all the time, sitting right next to me. I don't even think about it anymore. I'm just constantly soaking in stuff.

I think it is a very, very different perspective than my grandmother has. If you talk while the TV is on, she wigs out because two things are happening at once. Was it Gerald Ford who couldn't walk and chew gum at the same time? It was sensory overload. There is a whole generation of kids who say, "Oh yeah, I can save the planet on Nintendo, be watching TV, have the radio going, and be thinking about my homework at the same time." It is this crazy multitasking that we're all forced to do in a modern society. It's funny. People have an incredible propensity to be engaged on a number of different levels all at once. What is sensory overload to some people is boring to others. So I think a lot of young people are built to understand the Web as design. They understand that it is about design and technology and narrative and marketing and creativity all at once. You know all of these things need to fuse together.

But you need some older people who have the right business connections, the right money or clout, or who have a business that has already evolved in this direction. Some of the obvious players are the networks, the cable TV companies, Hughes satellite, Microsoft, some of the database companies. I think there are going to be some ad agencies that do very well in this world. I think there are going to be a million Organics that come up and do really well. It will be a very interesting time.

In the early days, there was print, and then radio came along. So there was print and radio. Then TV came along and everybody said it was going to replace radio. Well it didn't. It mutated radio. But now there is print, radio, TV, billboards, and Web. And Web and TV might merge in the future. Who knows?

But the reality is that all of a sudden we've got a two-way mass communication going on, which is something that has never happened before.

JM: What do you think were the most important things for you in getting Organic from being an idea to actually getting your first client? Do you think it is because you were one of the first?

JN: I think timing is certainly a big one. More than anything, it was blind perseverance. I knew that this was going to be big. I always did; I never questioned it. (I questioned my *business* when I was about to go bankrupt in the early days, but I never questioned the Web itself.) It was obvious the minute I saw it that it had every element of the new medium—graphics, text, audio, and video—being integrated on a network platform that cut across PCs, Apples, and Unix. It is kind of a strange dream.

I also think we've been very fortunate. We have a great geographic location in San Francisco. The key companies are right in our own backyard. There is a great group of very intelligent people here, in San Francisco, who are both within the office as colleagues and outside the office as advisors or just friends. It is not just one thing, you know—design is not all we do. It is design fused with technology fused with networking fused with many other things. It just goes on and on and on. It is the sum of the parts, not the discrete parts themselves that makes Organic fly.

JM: Is there anything else you think you'd like to contribute to the designers who maybe don't even know they're designers yet, who are up and coming?

JN: One of the main things that I'm constantly saying is that everybody thinks this game is about technology. And yes, it is about technology, but it is really about people and it is about communication. Almost everything I said—you know, going from A to B—is about a company talking to a person. In order to be a good designer on the Web, you need to really understand your audience and not loose sight of that. So don't forget it is a person at the end of the line; it is just a computer that you are talking through.

**Aaron Marcus
and Associates, Inc.**

Consulting and Planning
Design and Development
Evaluation and Documentation

User Interface for Productivity Tools
Multimedia and Training
Web and Print Publications

Feedback

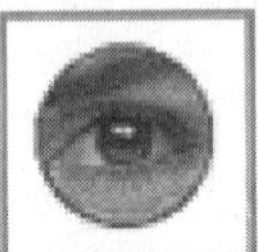
Overview

Tutorials

Publications

Projects

1144 65th Street, Suite F
Emeryville, California
94608-1053 USA

Telephone: 510-601-0994
Facsimile: 510-547-6125
E-mail: mail@AMandA.com

AM+A

Aaron Marcus and Associates

Company Profile

Aaron Marcus and Associates, Inc. (AM+A), has designed, developed, and evaluated user interfaces, multimedia (including CD titles and computer-based training), and electronic publishing documents/presentations for American Airlines, Apple, AT&T, General Motors, Hewlett-Packard, IBM, Microsoft, Random House, Reuters, and many other companies.

Aaron Marcus received a B.A. in physics from Princeton University (1965) and a B.F.A. and M.F.A. in graphic design from Yale University Art School (1968). He coauthored *Human Factors and Typography for More Readable Programs* (1990) and *The Cross-GUI Handbook for Multiplatform User Interface Design* (1994), and he authored *Graphic Design for Electronic Documents and User Interfaces* (1992), all published by Addison-Wesley. He is the only graphic designer to receive the National Computer Graphics Association (USA) Industry Achievement Award for his contributions to computer graphics (1992). In 1995, AM+A was cited as one of the Top 100 Multimedia firms by Multimedia Producer.

E-mail: **Aaron@AMandA.com**; Web: **http://www.AMandA.com**.

Chapter Profile

Aaron Marcus is a well-established and highly respected multimedia designer. He and his firm are living proof of the value of a balance between solid design skills and foresight of technical innovations in the marketplace. He brings several years' experience of human factors and user interface design to the Web. This is an important perspective, because many Web designers do not have solid experience with the science of user interface design. They frequently make fundamental mistakes by ignoring this knowledge. This factor will be especially important in the next several years for two reasons:

- First, the Web is rapidly becoming a consumer medium. For many consumers, the only interfaces they have known are the dashboards of their cars, the flashing *12:00* on their VCRs, and telephones. None of these consumer products gives designers a consistent metaphor for designing online information. This situation is further complicated by the global design of the Web, as millions of future Web users may not even have experience programming a VCR.
- The second reason traditional user interface design methods are important to know is the exact opposite of the first. Young, smart Web surfers very much want to be challenged as they explore information spaces. For people who grew up with Sega/Nintendo, PCs, and MTV, the notion of navigation, especially for entertainment products, must be constantly pushed to new boundaries. In this regard, a Web designer needs to know what the rules are so they can be broken in clever and visually appealing ways.

For the above reasons, Aaron's background of academic research, fine arts, and many years of designing interfaces for consumer products, software, and education tools bears great significance for Web design.

Essay

User Interface Issues In Web Design

by Aaron Marcus, President

SINCE THE EARLY 1980s, hypertext and hypermedia systems began to flourish. In the last few years, the spectacular growth of Internet use—in particular, the World Wide Web—has focused attention on the possibilities and challenges of good communication in Web sites. During that same period beginning in the 1980s, graphical user interface (GUI) designers have been sensitized to an increasingly complex set of design issues that promote utility, appeal, and productivity—in short, *user-friendliness*.

Because of the perceived need for Web sites and the availability of tools, even if some are still in a rudimentary stage of development, many neophytes have suddenly found themselves assigned the task of building a Web site and have begun to call themselves Web site designers. In addition, many professionals from related fields such as illustration, technical editing, computer science, and graphic design, to name a few, have jumped into this new area of computer-based visual communication. The situation is similar to the early days of desktop publishing.

Too often, analyses of Web sites have focused on technical issues of setting up and maintaining systems. Articles in industry publications often focus on the extent of information content and links, the functional capabilities of the sites (whether they have chat rooms, bulletin boards, interactive forms, transaction capability, etc.) or appeal (whether their imagery grabs viewers). Beyond these considerations lies the user interface design of the Web site—the sum total of its controls and displays, which affect the appeal to the user but which also affect the user's ease of learning, ease of use, and productivity.

User interface research and development have given considerable attention to user interfaces for business productivity tools, training environments, and consumer products, on applications as well as interactive documents or hypermedia search/retrieval environments. Both neophytes and professionals can learn valuable lessons by applying some of the insights gained in the user interface design community to Web site design. The legacy and ongoing research undertaken in the user interface design community is extensive and easily available. Resources for information, user interface-oriented design organizations, and new technology sites on the Web, plus a bibliography on the subject, appear at the end of this essay. This article introduces some key issues and provides examples of what can make the user interface design of a Web site more successful.

What Are User Interfaces?

User interfaces are a mixture of functional and formal content. One definition of user interfaces is the physical display of informational, aesthetic, and persuasive content affording the means for interacting with that content. For the purposes of specific users and their tasks, user interfaces provide metaphors, mental models, navigation, appearance (including sound, for example), and interaction. These components may be defined in this way (Marcus, 1995):

- *Metaphors:* the essential terms, images, and concepts
- *Mental model:* the organization of data, functions, tasks, roles, and people
- *Navigation:* the movement through the mental model afforded by menus, dialog boxes, control panels, etc.
- *Appearance:* the verbal, visual, and acoustic characteristics of the displays
- *Interaction:* the means by which users input changes to the system and the feedback supplied by the system

Note that an application, its data, the graphical user interface (GUI), the hardware platform, the network, and the input and output display devices all contribute to the user interface.

The Beginning and the End of the Design Process

User interface design is a process that begins with getting to know the target user community. The user interface design community has placed increasing importance on knowing as much about the user as possible: cognitive habits, educational and cultural background, perceived needs and desires, and the nature of jobs, roles, and tasks within an organization of work or play. Focus groups and usability tests have become valuable sources of information to determine the task specifications or requirement documents that help to generate a user interface design solution.

In many Web design situations, insufficient attention is given to determining precisely who is going to access the information, what their goals might be, and what responses should be provided for special needs. This situation has occurred with many corporate sites that began to build Web sites primarily as trophies or because of some sense of urgency to make a corporate presence known on the Web and to provide corporate documents, with little or no consideration of what might be useful to novice or expert "cybernauts." One example is a paper company that provided details of corporate financial documents but did not provide sufficient information about paper stocks, their prices, and recommended uses that would aid graphic designers in making good selections. This situation is similar to the early years of multimedia when some publishers merely poured books onto CD-ROMs with little or no consideration for the user interface of interactive access to content.

Once a Web site design is determined, the design rules should be captured in documents that describe and explain the essential elements. Too often, designs are retained only in the heads of a few key people who have set up a Web site. Even if specifications are prepared, they may not provide sufficient information on user interface design components. Some user interface design specification documents for Web sites have begun to appear. One exemplary Web-oriented

resource is the Yale University Web site (**http://info.med.yale.edu/caim/C_HOME.HTML**). In *Graphic Design for Electronic Documents and User Interfaces* (Marcus, 1992), a chapter devoted to user interface design specification documents helps to introduce the topic. Let us now turn to the essential components themselves.

Metaphors

Metaphors concern the essential themes, concepts, imagery, and terms of the Web site, especially the top-level labels and images provided to users, by which they are expected to understand the fundamental organization and purpose of the site. Because the entire world of Web sites is so new and growing so fast, conventions are not particularly stable. For example, is a Web site a bulletin board, a treasury, an archive, a tool, a store, an adventure, or a meeting place? Each approach might lead to very different imagery, themes, and terminology.

The essential categories of content and functions beyond those provided by established browsers vary widely, making it difficult to know where to go for certain needs, especially for a novice user. A What's Cool button in one site may be labeled What's Hot in another. The example in Figure 1, a home page for a Nynex Yellow Pages site (**http://www.niyp.com**), shows a More Stuff button whose semantics are somewhat vague: is it more content, more functions, both? Note also that the page has a Business Name Search button as well as a Business Type Search button. When pressed, each of these leads to essentially similar functions and content, suggesting that a Search button alone might have been more useful and would have simplified the construction of these essential choices.

In designing good metaphors, designers should seek well-established terms and images if they want users to recognize and use buttons and labels immediately. Novel, unique terms and images should be checked carefully with representatives of the user community to determine whether the elements are undesirably obscure, annoying, or even offensive.

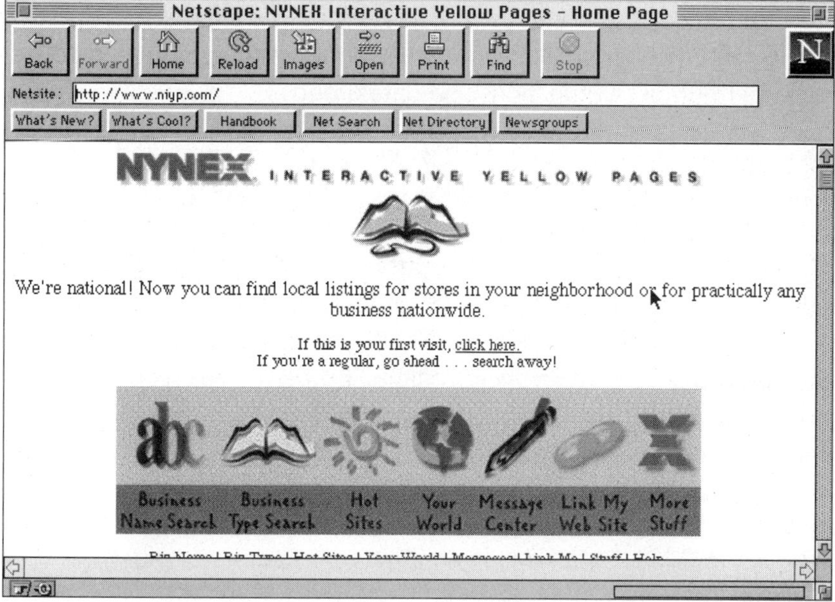

Figure 1: *The home page screen from the Nynex Yellow Pages site, showing main choices*

Mental Models and Navigation

The mental model is the organization of functions and data within the site, especially that among the layers below the first home page. Navigation concerns the means by which the user can move within and among layers to reveal new content: buttons, lists, tables, etc.

One of the primary challenges of Web site design is to organize the content in useful ways so that users can intuitively understand the site and can easily find what they seek. Designers should allocate a significant amount of time to designing alternative approaches to organization and navigation, then evaluate with typical users what seem to be simple, clear, approaches. Often many surprises will result: what the designer thought was obvious may be obscure to the user. One typical trade-off is simplicity of higher levels vs. the consequent complexity of lower levels for a given system of content. Generally, novice users (e.g., consumers) prefer simpler organization, while experts (e.g., professionals familiar with the content subject matter) prefer getting more immediate access to a larger number of functions and data groups.

The navigation controls (also called *widgets*) for Web user interfaces often do not follow standards of classical graphical user interfaces (e.g., Windows, Macintosh, and Motif) or multimedia collections of content (e.g., games and titles on CD-ROMs). For example, the way buttons are drawn, the location of buttons within an area for dialog, the use of underlined text as buttons, or the absence of default next-action symbols are all differences between the Web user interface and other interactive environments. In the future, Web user interfaces will have a greater variety of widgets, raising many of the design issues that other kinds of user interfaces currently face. For those interested in considering the widgets of classical GUIs and pondering how Web sites might provide them, *The Cross-GUI Handbook for Multiplatform User Interface Design* (Marcus et al., 1995) provides a fairly complete taxonomy of all the widgets of all classical GUIs.

Consider Figure 2, which shows one portion of Xerox Corporation's Web site (**http://www.xerox.com**). A visitor to the Web site soon encounters a fairly long list of items that might be of interest. These entries are broken into a few groups, but no group titles appear. In addition, the organizing principle of the lists may not be readily apparent, and no information about the timeliness or size of the possible next link is provided. In other words, many cues that would assist a user in deciding where to go next are missing.

In general, areas of a page or form should be clearly and consistently labeled so that novice and even intermediate or occasional users will not have a problem understanding what kind of functions or content is being displayed. Lists, and especially tables, should have simple, clear, and consistent column labels. Long heterogeneous lists should be broken up into smaller groups wherever possible. Long homogeneous lists should be clearly organized by time, space, alphabetical sequence, ordinal number, or some other simple means. Ideally, lists (and tables) ought to be sortable by different means. It would be useful, for example, to see the topics in the Xerox list organized by several categories, including the time-stamping of the entry when added to the list. In this way, users can have some flexibility in their strategies for searching and evaluating content, then taking action.

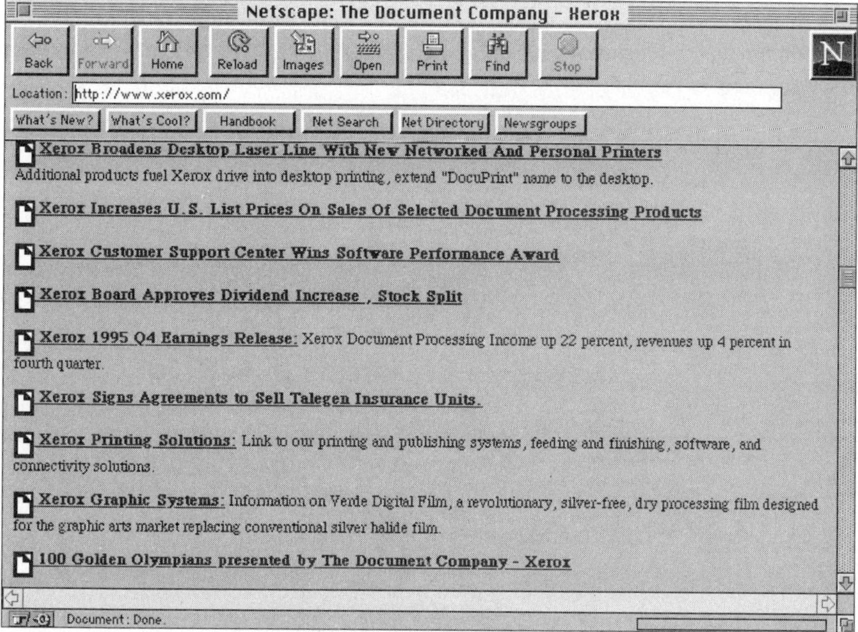

Figure 2: *The home page screen from the Xerox Corporation's Web site, showing a list of subordinate links of possible interest to users*

Appearance and Interaction

Appearance covers all aspects of the *look* of the user interface: not only typography, symbolism, color, layout, and animation, but also verbal appearance, that is, the language choice (English, Spanish, etc.) and the terminology choice (informal, technical, etc.). Interaction concerns the *feel*: the input and feedback techniques, including mouse vs. keyboard input, any future drag-and-drop functionality, highlighting for location or selection, etc.

Each of these attributes is itself a complex set of design choices and trade-offs. Many Web sites routinely ignore traditional human factors and ergonomic concerns about appearance and interaction. For example, in Figure 3, the CNN Web site's home page (**http://www.cnn.com**), presents major news topics in condensed all capital letters, a choice that guarantees decreased legibility. Words set in all capital letters do not have distinguishing descenders and ascenders, and in this case, several words are approximately the same length. These rectangular blocks of symbols must be read in detail, rather than by word shape, as is typically done. (In the Nynex example in Figure 1, note that the cursive black letters on medium green buttons are not a particularly legible typeface and color choice; they are made even less legible on a color that reduces the contrast between text and background.)

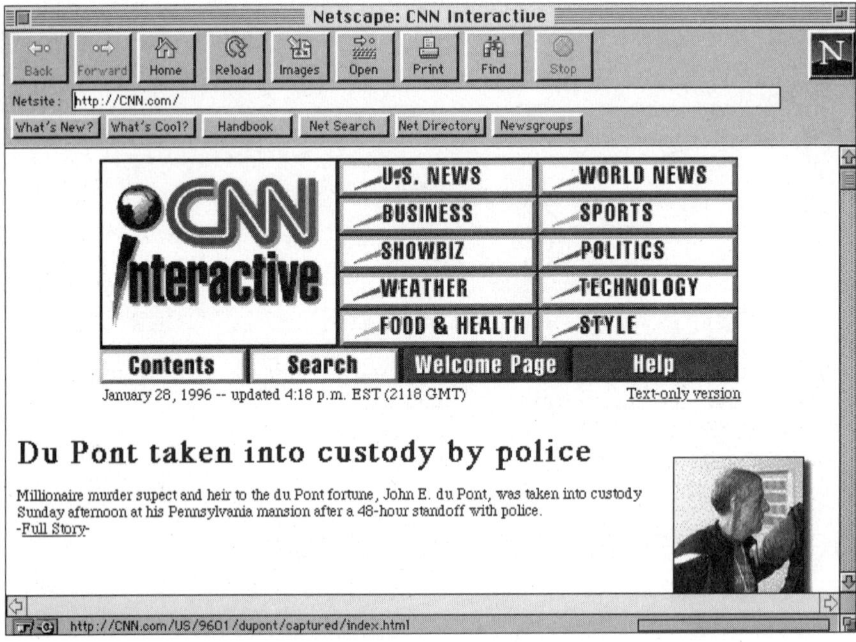

Figure 3: *The top of the CNN home page, showing major categories of news*

Lower down in the CNN page, as shown in Figure 4, text and photographs are presented in several layouts that compete for attention in the viewer's mind. Notice that no standard layout grid seems to govern these areas. Similar contents ought to be presented in similar layouts, unless there is a compelling reason to be inconsistent. In this example, even the two-column areas at the top and bottom of the screen have varying column widths. Within these set off areas, the illustrations appear at the far right, at the far left, and also centered, again an inconsistency that can distract the viewer. Notice also that text appears for the most part flush left, ragged right (generally useful for pieces of noncontinuous text), but one text block at the upper-right is centered. Inconsistencies like these cause the viewer to be uncertain about visual cues and to waste effort in trying to understand what may well be differences of appearance with little or no significance.

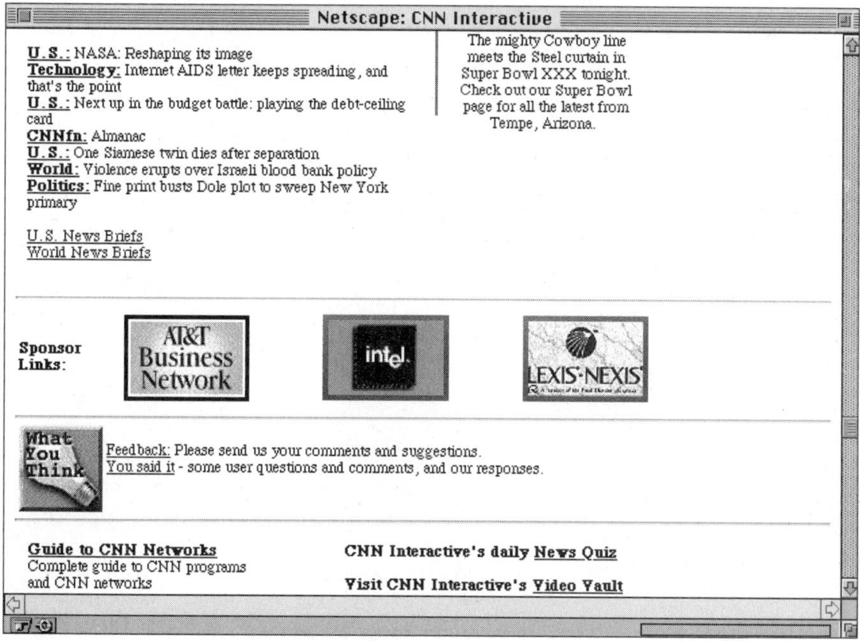

Figure 4: *The bottom of the CNN home page, showing subordinate groupings of content*

In general, designers should choose a limited number of legible typefaces, type sizes, locations, symbols, illustration styles, and layouts with which to present all content. *Graphic Design for Electronic Documents and User Interfaces* (Marcus, 1992) and "Metaphor Mayhem: Mismanaging Expectation and Surprise" (Marcus, 1994) provide some essential principles for effective use of information-oriented graphic design in making some of these design decisions.

Bear in mind also that designers must establish clear paradigms for providing feedback to the user that items are selectable, have been located by the pointer, are being selected, and have already been selected. The conventions for establishing these interaction states also vary widely in the world of Web sites.

Even the original color sets proposed by Netscape for available and already-viewed links contains a non-ergonomic color choice: blue has become a convention signifying available selection, while red means already selected. From a communication design perspective, hot red on a white background seems a more suitable, legible color for links that must be highlighted, noticed, selected, and reviewed, while the cool color blue seems more appropriate for already-selected links, just the opposite of the current industry convention that has already influenced many Web site designers.

Another challenge to designers is continuity of the use of mouse and keyboard. Currently, many Web sites make extensive use of scrolling to get to additional downloaded content and buttons. The Web designer must examine carefully whether this manipulation of screen contents is a satisfactory alternative to waiting for a hyperlink to connect.

Web site designers will be challenged to reinvent many of the widgets that traditional GUI designers have spent a decade or more perfecting. Often, relatively little time and money is available to redesign or reinvent these widgets. Consequently, designers must analyze in a practical manner the appearance and interaction schemes, then evaluate them with users to determine optimum choices.

An Example: Planet SABRE™

Each of the components described above requires significant time to perfect for any user interface to online services. In many cases, too little time is provided by the project developers. One example in which significant time was provided is the Planet SABRE™ project, a new design of the user interface for American Airlines' SABRE Travel Information Network (STIN), one of the largest private online information and transaction systems in the world. Figure 5 shows a scene from the opening screen. The author's firm, in conjunction with the staff of STIN, is developing a new user interface specifically oriented to travel agents (Steyer-Coyne, 1996). In the limited space available, I will consider just one aspect of the system in this essay: metaphor design.

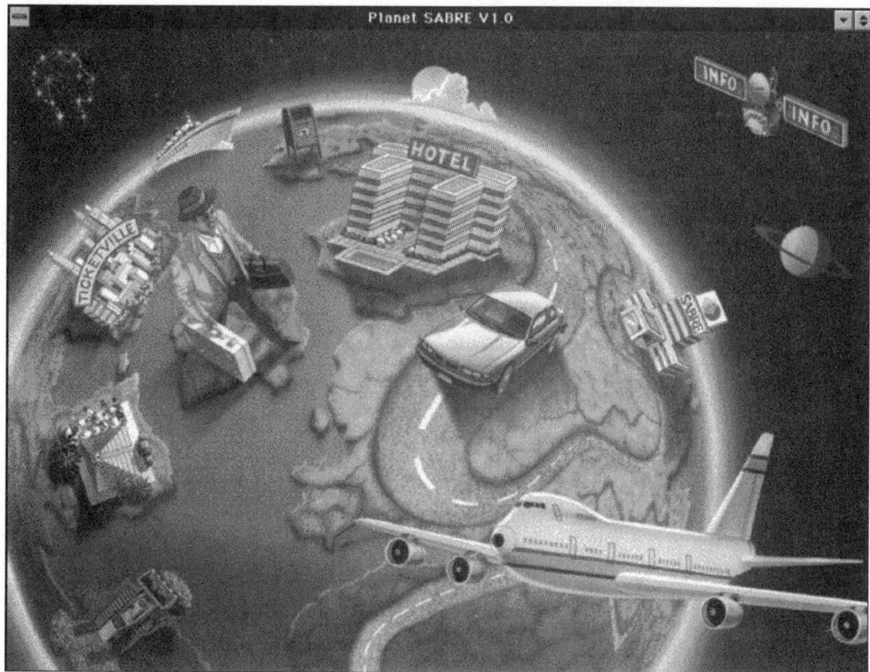

Figure 5: *An opening screen for Planet SABRE, a new means of presenting the functions and data of the American Airlines SABRE Travel Information Network to travel agents*

The developers considered for some time how better to represent the core functions of a complex database system for reservations to travel agents. In think-tank sessions, several different metaphorical scenes emerged (e.g., depicting all the primary functions as an airport environment or a cityscape). One approach seemed promising as both novel yet intuitive: the functional modules depicted as three-dimensional objects on the surface of a planet viewed from outer space. Once this Planet SABRE metaphor was determined, the design team tried many styles of depiction (e.g., pictographic, cartoon-like, and representational) for the modules—application suites for reserving flights, car, and hotels—and eventually decided on representational, intuitive icons.

The large land mass or planet metaphor is useful for depicting elements of an operating system or a suite of applications. In a sense, this image is a very large extension of the concept of the desktop, which is in a room, in a building, in a city, in a country, on a continent, on a world.

Notice that some of the items are culturally biased. For example, the mailbox representing an electronic mail application makes sense for a user in the United States, but a British user would expect to see a red, columnar British postbox. The Planet SABRE design standards actually provide for a variety of icons to be available to represent items that differ among countries and cultures. In this manner, the user interface design is attempting to make differences not only of language, but of symbolism and illustration suitable for a truly worldwide user group. This diversity in user interface design will eventually need to be considered for most Web sites as they become visited by more varied and international groups of users.

Conclusions

With each passing day, more Web sites, more sophisticated browsers, and more elaborate Web authoring and designing tools emerge. As with previous developments in technology, these advances do not guarantee good user interface design. There are many opportunities for creative invention of metaphors, mental models, navigation, appearance, and interaction; there are also many opportunities to thwart clear and effective communication. As object-oriented construction of these user interfaces becomes more widespread, designers may be able to develop user interfaces more efficiently, but the underlying challenge to communicate effectively remains.

Designers must not only give extensive energy to the design of appealing illustrations and opening scenes of Web sites, they must also grapple with the extensive verbal naming and conceptual organization issues as well, then go on to determine the appropriate similarities and differences of layout, color, lines, textures, illustrations, sounds, and music in user interfaces. Because Web sites demand so much effort to build and maintain, the ability of designers to develop a systematic set of user interface elements means that items can be reused or managed in effective ways without damaging the freshness of Web sites and that changes in fundamental design characteristics can be implemented more efficiently because of the systematic nature and inheritance of change that occurs in a large system of signs.

Designers will contribute significantly to the invention of new forms of communication, especially to the means of formulating queries and to displaying results visually. These efforts should be acknowledged, valued, and protected. One way to encourage better design is to take the time to evaluate Web sites and to prove in a quantitative manner some significant benefit to implementations. Web site design has much to contribute that is new and fresh; on the other hand, Web site designers can benefit greatly by learning lessons from the recent history of the user interface design community.

Web Resources

If you're looking for more information, the Web itself is probably your best source for general Web knowledge, Web design organizations, and advanced Web technology.

Information Resources on the Web

The following Web sites provide information of general interest and use to Web site designers. The Web site's URL appears in parentheses.

AM+A (http://www.AMandA.com) Aaron Marcus and Associates, Inc., maintains a Web site that provides links of interest to Web designers focusing on user interface design and information visualization.

C|net Online (http://www.cnet.com) A well-organized site, covering new WWW and multimedia technologies and products.

DesignOnline (http://www.dol.com/Root/welcome/welcome.html) An information and conversation hub for designers.

HCI Index: Links to Newsgroups (http://is.twi.tudelft.nl/hci/communication.html) A thorough set of links to Human-Computer Interaction and related newsgroups from a large archive of user interface design resources.

MIT Media Lab (http://www.1010.org) Innovative research and technology. Designers should look into Design Interactions Paradigms Home Page (**http://design-paradigms.www.media.mit.edu/projects/design-paradigms**), a product of MIT's Visible Language Workshop.

The Yale Center for Advanced Instructional Media: WWW Style Manual (http://info.med.yale.edu/caim/C_HOME.HTML) A well-organized and thorough guide to WWW design.

UI-Design Web (http://duto02.tudelft.nl/uidesign) An excellent site, formerly known as UIWORLD, containing over 175 valuable resources for multimedia and interaction design professionals, e.g., tools, books, editorials, events, studios, jobs, and Net sites.

Design Organizations on the Web

The following sites provide information about user interface design and related topics, together with information about tutorials, publications, and events.

ACD (http://www.design.chi.il.us/ac4d) The American Center for Design, a national design organization that emphasizes technologies, systems, and information. Links to conferences, membership information, and areas of interest.

ACM-SIGCHI (http://www.acm.org/sigchi) The Association for Computing Machinery's Special Interest Group on Computer-Human Interaction. Links to local SIGs, annual conference, and user interface design resources on the WWW.

ACM-SIGGRAPH (http://www.siggraph.org) The Association for Computing Machinery's Special Interest Group on Computer Graphics. Links to design resources, publications (including SIGCHI videos), local SIGs, and annual conference. AM+A has presented keynote lectures and tutorials at SIGGRAPH annual conferences since 1980.

AIGA (http://www.dol.com/AIGA) The American Institute of Graphic Arts, a national organization promoting excellence in graphic design. Links to membership information, events, publications, and local chapters.

HFES (http://www.hfes.vt.edu/HFES) Human Factors and Ergonomics Society, an international organization with many specialized SIGs and an annual conference. See also Human Factors Perspectives on Human-Computer Interaction (**http://www.cis.ohiostate.edu/~perlman/hfeshci/contents.html**), selected proceedings from HFES Annual Meetings 1983–1994.

IICS (http://www.dnai.com/~sfiics) The San Francisco Bay Area Chapter of the International Interactive Communications Society, an organization that promotes, informs, and represents multimedia professionals. Links to an online gallery, calendar, publications, and other local chapter home pages.

MDG (http://www.mdg.org) Multimedia Development Group, an international trade association that promotes growth within the industry by linking developers, producers, and tech firms. Links to monthly calendar and an MDG bulletin.

Advanced Technology on the Web

To keep up with some of the latest technology, consider the following sites providing information or demonstrations.

Java (http://www.sun.com) Sun's new approach, with its own programming language, to support communicating small applications, or *applets*, on the Internet presents a major alternative to the way information is stored and distributed.

Shockwave (http://www.macromedia.com) This software adds Macromedia Director's functionality to the Web.

VRML (http://www.virtus.com) A viewer for virtual reality displays on the Web is available for the Macintosh platform.

Caveats and Acknowledgments

Because Web sites are in constant flux, comments made about a particular site's design may no longer be valid. The reader should bear this in mind upon examining any Web sites referenced. The text of this essay attempts to clarify the design issue without reference to the current status of the site.

In preparing this essay, I would like to acknowledge the assistance of the staff and associates of Aaron Marcus and Associates, Inc., particularly Mr. Anthony Sokolowski and Mr. Hank Duderstadt, and to acknowledge AM+A's client, American Airlines SABRE Travel Information Network, for permission to reprint an image from an ongoing project.

Bibliography

The following references, some of which are cited above, are useful resources for further investigation of the issues addressed in the essay.

Albertson, Rick, Jeffrey Fine, Mike Zender, et al. *Designer's Guide to the Internet*. Hayden Books: Indianapolis, 1995.

Marcus, Aaron. "Principles of Effective Visual Communication for Graphical User Interface Design." *Readings in Human-Computer Interaction*, Second Edition. Ed. Baecker, Grudin, Buxton, and Greenberg. Morgan Kaufman: Palo Alto, 1995.

Marcus, Aaron. "Metaphor Mayhem: Mismanaging Expectation and Surprise." *Interactions*, Vol. 1, No. 1 (January 1994): 41–43.

Marcus, Aaron. *Graphic Design for Electronic Documents and User Interfaces*. Addison-Wesley: Reading, MA, 1992.

Marcus, Aaron, Nick Smilonich, and Lynne Thompson. *The Cross-GUI Handbook for Multi-platform User Interface Design*. Addison-Wesley: Menlo Park, CA, 1995.

Steyer-Coyne, Stephanie. "The ACD Conference: Design for the Internet," *Communication Arts*, Vol. 37, No. 8 (January/February 1996): 137–142.

THE WALL STREET JOURNAL * * *

INTERACTIVE

EDITION.

No. 1 © 1996

vol. CCXXVI

* * *

The Interactive Edition gives you a continually updated view of business around the world. You'll find nearly every story from all the print editions of the Journal, plus the Interactive Edition's own non-stop breaking coverage and in-depth background. Its Personal Journal section gathers all the information relevant to you in one place.

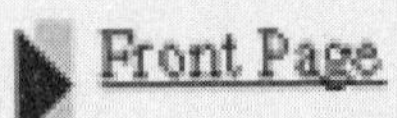

WSJ Services

Advertising

Asia Europe

Journal Links

Access to the Interactive Edition remains free until August 31 for anyone registered before July 31. Money & Investing Update readers: You do not need to re-register to read the Interactive Edition. Just use your existing user name and password and go directly to the front page or any other page. Read us as much as you like before August 31 at no charge.

The Wall Street Journal Interactive Edition

Company Profile

The Wall Street Journal Interactive Edition provides continually updated news and global financial information. It encompasses the full range of business and world news found in the printed edition of *The Wall Street Journal*.

Working with *The Wall Street Journal* Interactive Edition team puts Jennifer Edson at the forefront of the electronic age, where her contributions help define and shape how business people receive, process, and use information. As the Art Director for Money & Investing Update and *The Wall Street Journal* Interactive Edition, Ms. Edson's creative direction incorporates graphic intelligence and functionality. These two elements combine to create a fluid and easy interface for readers. The polished, graphical "look and feel" of the publication complements the high quality news content and helps make it one of the busiest, "coolest," and most successful Internet sites for business news.

Sharon Denning has worked on the design of *The Wall Street Journal* Interactive Edition since its inception. Her focus is on how readers approach the interactive edition and find their way through the news while retaining a sense of "space" and an awareness of where they are. As assistant art director, she coordinates production of the many news graphics for *The Wall Street Journal* Interactive Edition, and also designs special reports and other packages—all on tight deadlines.

Chapter Profile

This chapter poses several challenges for any Web designer:

- Conceive, produce, and deliver a site for one of America's oldest and most prestigious daily business newspapers.
- Create a look and feel that reflects the original paper while taking advantage of the smaller size and lower resolution of a computer screen.
- Build a transition between the experience people have of the paper to one they can enjoy with pixels.
- Take advantage of as many new technologies as are appropriate while keeping the traditional structure of the core product and maintaining accessibility for all users.

The team at Dow Jones & Company's *The Wall Street Journal* Interactive Edition met the above challenges and continues to operate under the design authority of Art Director Jennifer Edson and Interactive Multimedia Designer Sharon Denning and a staff of six dedicated artists. Though readers may consider the look of *The Wall Street Journal* to be old-fashioned and rigid, it blazes a trail that other papers around the world follow as they make the transition from 19th- to 21st-century technology. With the long history of pioneering technology in the service of news delivery—it founded the leading business newswire in 1897 and has printed editions of the paper via satellite for more than a quarter-century—Dow Jones continues to be a dominant player with a unique position from which to maximize its brand in the digital age. This dominance comes from two primary factors.

First, the vital need for immediate and accurate business news and analysis forms a core audience demand every minute of every business day. A business newspaper's greatest challenge is that it must present a static impression of dynamic information. Stock prices, bond rates, and hundreds of other indexes change literally every second. Deep analysis of trends must reach readers with timeliness and a clear, distinctive voice. For the professionals (and even amateurs) whose livelihoods depend on this information, speed, precision, and access often determine success or failure. Getting today's news tomorrow is not an option for future champions. *The Wall Street Journal* must prove its dominance every day by fulfilling these needs, and the *The Wall Street Journal* Interactive Edition delivers fast, high-impact, credible information to a discerning audience.

Second, *The Wall Street Journal* Interactive Edition team creates a product that successfully makes the transition between traditional print and new digital publishing paradigms. The team knows that simply installing an electronic version of a printed product on the Web is a recipe for disaster. Multiple audiences, brand equity, advertising models, information ergonomics, and changing technologies all converge successfully in *The Wall Street Journal* Interactive Edition every day. For current and future designers, these challenges play some part in nearly every new project built.

Essay

The Wall Street Journal Interactive Edition

by Jennifer Edson and Sharon Denning

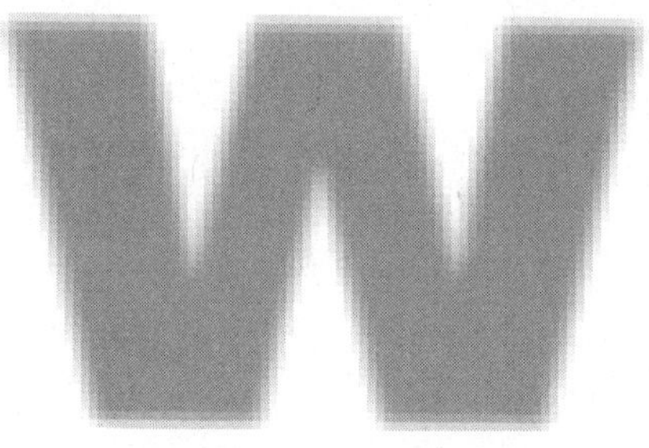

ITH A REAL GOAL of efficiently communicating business information, design is often described by its beauty and its ability to translate a concept into images, but the biggest challenge we faced was how to balance aesthetics and economics. What defines the best work on the Internet in 1996 with all its limitations? Where we are today with design on the Internet is comparable to the early days of desktop publishing: clunky design tools, big promises for ease of use, and the allure of entering the new technological age. This scenario yielded bad design back in the early '80s when everyone jumped in and became designers overnight. The current state of primitive design tools for the Web has forced designers to take a step back. In both the print publishing and multimedia arenas, designers have made great strides in controlling the design process and ultimate output. For this new age of online design, our eyes must remain wide open as we grasp this truly great opportunity to pioneer how information is presented and designed for a globally wired audience.

On June 12, 1995, *The Wall Street Journal* launched its first effort on the Internet. With a dedicated staff of over 25 News Editors, a Webmaster, a Managing Editor, a Business Manager, an Art Director, an Interactive Multimedia Designer, two design interns, and two freelance artists, the third section of the paper, "Money & Investing," was transformed from its printed roots to an Internet site called Money & Investing Update. As of March 1996, Money & Investing Update boasted over 100 pages, updated 24 hours a day. Within three months, The Update had registered over 200,000 subscribers. On any given day, over 20,000 readers visited the site.

Designing for and putting The Update online, however, was really a learning experience. The next effort was our real test. On May 1, 1996, Dow Jones (the parent company of *The Wall Street Journal*) launched the entire *The Wall Street Journal* Interactive Edition, including the three sections of the print edition: Front Section, Marketplace, Money & Investing, and two additional exclusive sections: Sports and Personal—with many times the amount of information in The Update. Before we launched, we promised ourselves and our subscribers a site that would match the integrity of the name *The Wall Street Journal* and equal the value of its journalistic content. As a news organization, our goal is to furnish readers with fresh information as continually as possible, 24 hours a day. As designers in a news organization, our goal is to provide this information in an interesting way. The Internet gives us the limitless ability to offer more information (in both length and depth) and on a continuous and timely basis. Utilizing these distinct advantages of the Web, *The Wall Street Journal* Interactive Edition will distinctly offer value for our readers, as well as attract a new audience. We must deliver on our commitments 24 hours every day.

In this chapter, we have set out to share our experiences and perspectives with you, knowing our work is nascent and ongoing. We (Jennifer and Sharon) have collaborated to write this piece because we felt that combining two different professional experiences and perspectives would benefit you, the Web developer or designer, as our professional experiences and perspectives are different. Both of us contribute tremendously to discern the realities of designing for the Web. Jennifer's perspective is from multimedia and marketing communications, and Sharon's perspective is from the print and traditional design side.

Ask Questions, Make Rules, and Break Them

Designing for the Internet is a set of paradoxes; challenging, dynamic, frustrating, and limiting. The rules of the Internet change constantly and the tools relative to both print and multimedia are primitive and clunky. Despite these limitations, we have found designing on the Internet extremely challenging and, in fact, very creative. A designer must fluctuate between holding on tightly and stubbornly to traditional design principles that work in other media, and letting go of everything that worked in the past in order to find that sliver of creative hope. Designing well for the Internet is hard work, but it forces a designer to readdress and redefine issues of importance, priority, elegance, and beauty.

We maintain certain a priori design rules that work for us. The process starts with a series of very basic questions:

- Why create a Web site?
- What corporate communications objective is the company fulfilling by creating a Web site?
- How do we want our audience/readers/users to benefit by coming to our Web site?
- How are we going to direct our audience to our Web site?

The answers to these questions highlight the function that the Web site will serve both internally (how it is viewed and perhaps used within the company) and externally (how it is used by your users or customers). The answers to these very fundamental questions will allow you to define the purpose of the site. You must decide if the site's function is to

- *Inform* (as in databases or catalogs of information)
- *Educate* (as in libraries)
- *Sell* (as in stores, catalogs, and direct mailers)
- *Entertain* (as in a computer game)
- Perform a combination of any of these characteristics

For *The Wall Street Journal* Web site, we have the luxury of knowing who our audience is from studying our print edition's demographics. With a Web version of our paper, we have the potential to capture a younger audience, one which is more connected, more digital, more wired. Capturing a younger audience, however, is a by-product of our offering *The Wall Street Journal* online. The overall objective has always been to offer business users extensive access to rich information, updated business news, and background resources on thousands of companies worldwide with an editorial commitment 24 hours a day.

The Mission: Make It Wide, Deep, and Personal

We knew we wanted a look and feel that could maintain the integrity of *The Wall Street Journal* print edition, while still appearing contemporary, fresh, sleek, and cool. We set out to create an interface that met these stringent criteria. For the rest of this chapter we will discuss the process for both the Money & Investing Update and *The Wall Street Journal* Interactive Edition.

As a department of six full-time people, we address the daily graphics needs of *The Wall Street Journal* Interactive Edition. Simultaneously, we explore new technologies; experiment with layout possibilities offered by different browsers, ShockWave, animated GIFs, and Java; and design *The Wall Street Journal* Interactive Edition. It is a life full of contradictions. On one hand, it is challenging yet frustrating because of the primitive tools and the limited bandwidth, which causes information to move slowly over the Internet. On the other hand, the Web is an extraordinary publishing medium with which to distribute content-rich information. However, to be successful, it must be constructed in a form that readers can access and use immediately. As a developer, designer, and information publisher, you must always keep this responsibility to your readers foremost in your mind.

A mission statement is one way to answer the questions we mentioned earlier and to clarify the goals of the project and the group. The following is *The Wall Street Journal* Interactive Edition design department's mission statement:

> *Our goal is to provide an interface with clear and concise navigation, sleek and clean design, which allows easy access and readability of information. Overall, our commitment is to create an environment that focuses on the user's experience. While currently using a newspaper metaphor to display the information, we are committed to a design look and feel that aligns with the journalistic elegance and integrity of* The Wall

> Street Journal *content. The design department is a group of designers, multimedia and video producers, illustrators, and new media professionals. In order to achieve our goals and stay on track, we systematically analyze, review, and keep up with the constant emerging technologies, discerning appropriateness for* The Wall Street Journal *Interactive Edition from a functionality perspective. These are the specific questions we should continuously ask: Will this new technology give the user a beneficial experience? Is accessing information in a different way more efficient and effective?*
>
> *We are sensitive to the fact that our user is deluged with information and not only are we competing for the user's time and attention (from ANY other activity he/she may be engaged in), we are also respectful of the time/information overload stress and thus aim to provide information that quickly downloads, has a purpose, and allows the user to gain a deeper understanding of the information provided.*
>
> *For the daily* The Wall Street Journal *Interactive Edition we are committed to collaborating closely with the news department (our content providers) in the efforts of providing relevant graphics in a timely manner—all in the interest of creating an environment and experience for our audience—the user.*

We must determine how our audience will use our site. There are users who only read *The Wall Street Journal* online. Then there are users who have the printed edition sitting right next to them and only use the online service for quick updates and references. We already know from research that people have strong individualistic approaches to *The Wall Street Journal* in the ways they read it, relate to it, and interact with it. An online version of *The Wall Street Journal* must possess much of the same quality and sensibility. We do not in any way want to cannibalize the print edition's readership. Instead, we want to give the readers/users an information-rich experience that will complement their experience of the printed *The Wall Street Journal* and stand on its own as a valuable resource.

At the time we are writing this chapter, we have just launched the full version, so many of our findings are based on Money & Investing Update. We know the readers of The Update are not casual visitors. Tens of thousands come to us daily for reliable updates and easy access to extensive information. We get visitors because we are the most respected brand name in the world for accurate business coverage. This makes our job easier because we need to focus less on attracting people to our site than on creating an environment that enables information to be accessible at a keystroke.

We approach design as a way to tell a story. This story happens to be about business news. We focus on giving the user an experience that reaches beyond what print can do. Decisions are made about organization, navigation, and layout on the pages. Structural layout relies upon the presentation and layering of information. An interesting aspect of the information age is the sheer quantity of information and how quickly this avalanche becomes overwhelming. The Web offers astounding possibilities for accessing, tying together, taking apart, referencing, and indexing information. The Web also offers opportunities that print cannot provide. The Briefing Books are a good example of this. Simply checking on any highlighted company name will open a resource that allows the user to access the history and current financial state of a company.

It is the designer's job to magnify the areas of interest and make them accessible. Find out why your audience would want to access your site and create a visually compelling reason for keeping them there. Make the reasons obvious to them. *The Wall Street Journal* Interactive Edition in its most basic structure is a big database with a newspaper interface and the editorial precision that unites the content.

Form and Function

There are four rough forms that structural design can take:

- The index style
- The table of contents style
- The guided style
- The edited style

The *index* style emphasizes the idea of accessibility. Envision it as a warehouse of information where the user has an idea of the topic they want to find. Topics are usually hidden from the user and accessed with a search engine. To a veteran user, these sites are seen as similar to an encyclopedia: quick and convenient. But to the novice, the index style can be overwhelming. We use this style in our search section shown in Figure 1 (**http://wsj.com/edition/resources/documents/search.htm**), where users can access quick information about companies or topics.

Netscape: SEARCH MENU -- WSJ Interactive Edition

Location: http://interactive2.wsj.com/edition/resources/documents/search.htm

What's New? | What's Cool? | Handbook | Net Search | Net Directory | Software

THE WALL STREET JOURNAL INTERACTIVE EDITION. SEARCH TEXT SEARCH

HELP SEARCH QUOTES VOICES

FRONT SECTION
MARKETPLACE
MONEY
SPORTS
PERSONAL JOURNAL

Search the Interactive Edition archive

Locate articles from the past 14 days that contain the words you enter below. For more information and examples, select Help above.

Search for articles containing the following words:

Search archive

Must contain all words entered above.
Must contain at least one of the words.

Advanced text search: Use additional features to search the archive.

Search for a Company Briefing Book

Briefing Books include background information, a financial overview, stock performance charts and data, recent news and press releases.

To find a Briefing Book, enter company name or stock symbol, select the button for which one you entered, and click Get Briefing Book.

SNP

Stock Symbol Company Name

Get Briefing Book

More ways to find information in the Interactive Edition

- Quotes
Get delayed composite prices for U.S. stocks or mutual funds.
- Table of Contents
A list of all regular features in the Interactive Edition.
- Index to Market Data
A list of markets data and tables.

Tools for finding information on other Internet sites

- Other business Web sites
A list of other places on the Web that offer business information.
- Free annual reports
Order reports from selected companies via The Wall Street Journal Annual Reports Service.
- Internet Search

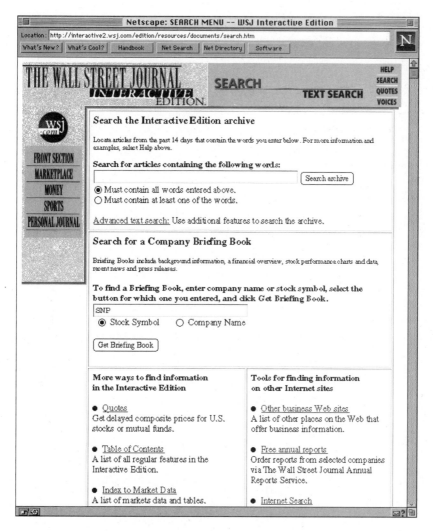

Figure 1: *An example of the index style in* The Wall Street Journal *Interactive Edition's Search section*

The *table of contents* style lists topics, as you can see in Figure 2, our Table Of Contents section (**http://wsj.com/edition/resources/documents/toc.htm**). The major benefit of this style of design is that every item is presented up front and is available for the user to select. These sites resemble reference books, as they are usually designed around one general topic broken down into smaller subtopics.

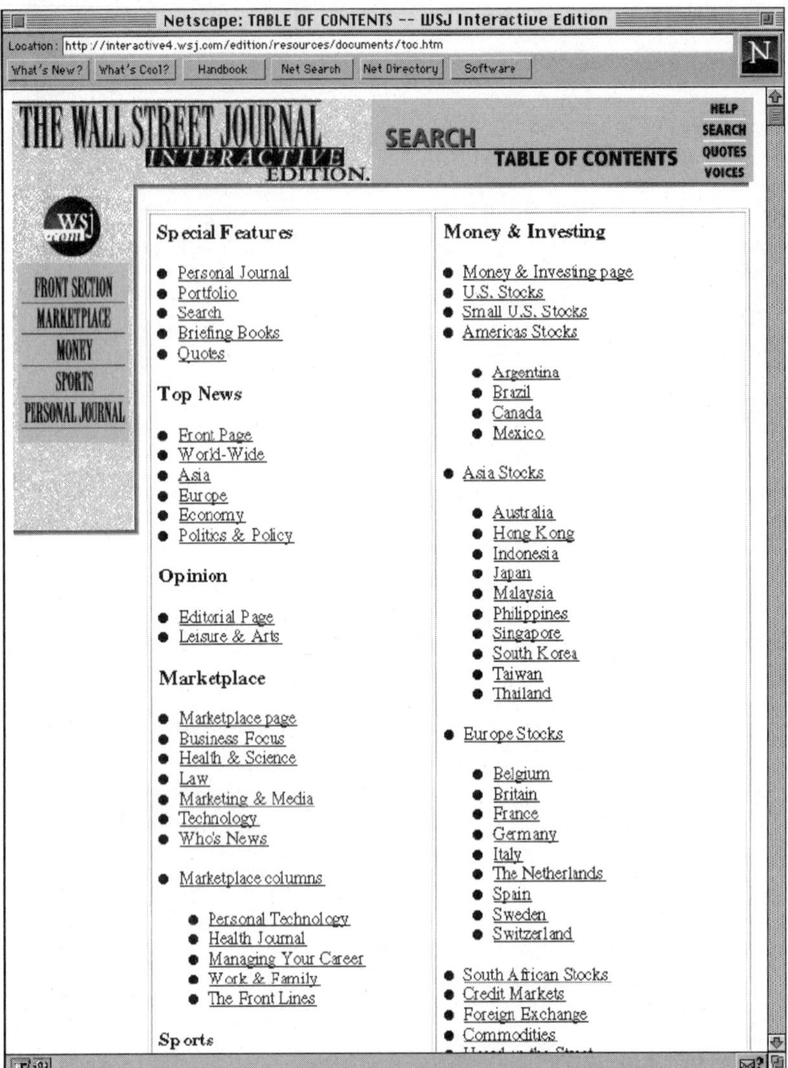

Figure 2: *The table of contents style presents every item for the user to select, very much like a reference book.*

Take care to limit the list of subsections or else a design will appear as a wall of information with all topics presented at about the same importance. As a designer, you may use this effect intentionally, but you must keep these lists relatively small and manageable. The design paradigm is often clunky and unwieldy, forcing the viewer to scroll down to find their topic, occasionally missing it completely.

A controlled navigational scheme works the best for a designer to completely guide the unfolding of an idea. In the *guided* style, users are guided through one specific route. These paths may branch a bit, but they tend to return to the same main storyline. The structure is fairly linear and is useful for presenting experiences or any topics that must be understood in stages, such as training manuals. We use this approach in our interactive tour of *The Wall Street Journal* Interactive Edition (**http://wsj.com/tour.htm**), as you can see in Figure 3.

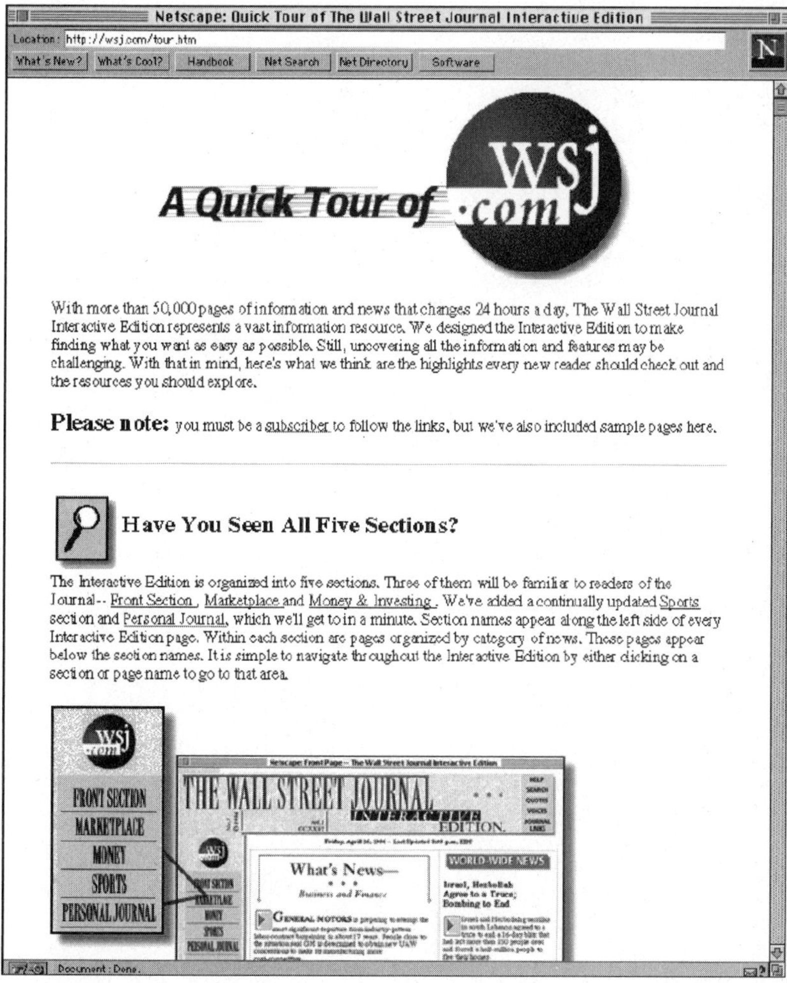

Figure 3: *The guided style directs users through a specific route.*

The Wall Street Journal Interactive Edition primarily uses the *edited* style, which offers the viewer various paths while maintaining the visibility of other options. You can see an example of this style in the Front Page section (**http://wsj.com/edition/current/summaries/front.htm**), shown in Figure 4. Much like a newspaper, it is often divided into sections, which have further subsections within them. Articles and information are organized around very general

Netscape: Front Page -- The Wall Street Journal Interactive Edition

Back | Forward | Home | Reload | Images | Open | Print | Find | Stop

THE WALL STREET JOURNAL INTERACTIVE EDITION.

No. 1 ©1996 vol. 1 CCXXVI

HELP
SEARCH
QUOTES
VOICES
JOURNAL LINKS

Thursday, May 2, 1996 -- Last Updated 9:12 a.m. EDT

wsj.com

FRONT SECTION
MARKETPLACE
MONEY
SPORTS
PERSONAL JOURNAL

WORLD-WIDE
ASIA
EUROPE
ECONOMY
POLITICS & POLICY
LEISURE & ARTS
EDITORIAL
WEATHER

TABLE OF CONTENTS

What's News—

* * *

Business and Finance

GDP GREW at a robust rate of 2.8% in the first quarter, showing the U.S. economy is gaining strength after struggling through the end of 1995. Consumer spending and business-equipment purchases led the advance, which came despite severe winter weather and the government shutdown.

* * *

American Express is launching a major effort to persuade banks to issue its credit cards, even though it would mean direct competition for the banks' own Visa cards and MasterCards. Visa currently prohibits member banks from offering American Express and Dean Witter Discover cards. MasterCard has no such ban.

* * *

HFS unveiled plans to acquire Coldwell Banker for $640 million and the assumption of $100 million in debt. The purchase would make HFS by far the nation's largest real-estate franchiser.

* * *

BellSouth has formed an alliance with Pacific Telesis and SBC Communications to combine their orders for long-distance service with an eye toward commanding bigger discounts from AT&T and other providers.

WORLD-WIDE NEWS

Arafat Receives Statesman's Welcome At the White House

Arafat was received by President Clinton, capping his transition to a statesman. The Palestinian leader was once shunned by the U.S. as a terrorist, but Wednesday's meeting had the trappings of a state visit.

PAGE ONE

Steelmaker Built Up By Buying Old Mills Finally Hits Trouble

When British steelmaker Ispat bought Kazakstan's largest steel plant it also inherited a KGB office, a bloated 38,000-person work force, and hundreds of employees in the habit of coming to work drunk.

Document: Done.

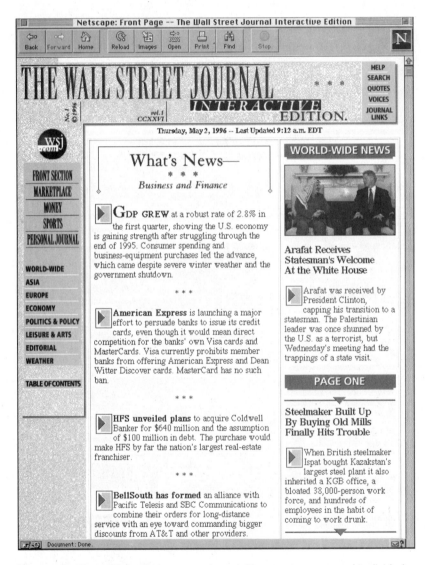

Figure 4: *The edited style is arranged much like a newspaper, and is divided into different sections.*

topics, with certain stories featured while others are contained in subsections. This design principle works well for sites that consciously offer opinions and ideas.

Remember the users' expectations when designing a site's organization. A good online reference tool allows users to access information quickly and leave. Someone accessing a reference book will want to find their topic quickly and bookmark it for the future. Someone accessing a book or a magazine will want a sense of comprehension and completion. Comprehension means that a user has a fair idea of where articles or data about a given topic appear. Visitors want to know they have read or seen all the factual information about a current event, as well as the opinions of their favorite, and least favorite, columnists. Complete access to the information must be possible, whether the visitor uses it or not. Using the edited style allows the user to understand that there are five sections. Links within the sections allow the user to move vertically as well as horizontally to explore the text. In addition to the core content, users may enjoy reading letters, sending e-mail, and participating in a debate about a particularly interesting subject, as demonstrated in Figure 5.

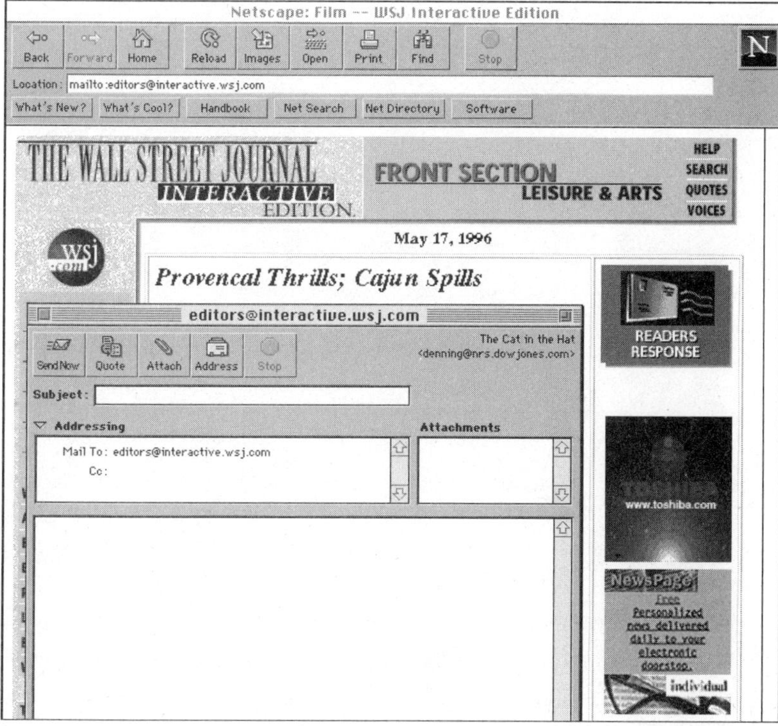

Figure 5: *Remember to provide users the opportunity to participate in your site.*

The Web should connect readers to outside sources. Readers must not feel they are navigating in isolation. The edited style rarely presents design problems in a strict adaptation of a linear text, but more circular or branched information structures raise new challenges. This problem may decrease as users become more accustomed to the Web, but as it stands now, users want to feel a sense of closure. Whatever the amount of flexibility or freedom built into a system, users must have a clear sense of their location in the information, what they are exploring, and where you are sending them. Let them see where they've been and where they are going, as shown in Figure 6.

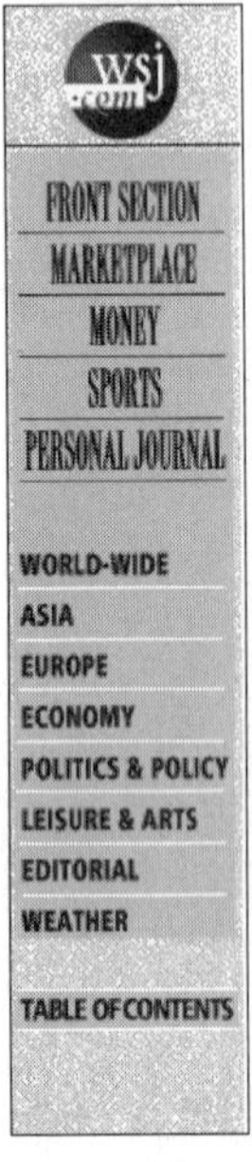

Figure 6:
Give readers a strong sense of their location in the information.

Navigation

Despite the hype about the hyperconnectivity of the Web, poor navigation design means your users will be lost in information space. After spending hours designing every pixel of a site, it is hard to imagine that a first time viewer to your Web site could have no idea of its message. But if you are not blatantly clear up front, you will lose your readers immediately. A user may have arrived on your site by chance. Even a user who knows your company or product may see information in an unfamiliar form with an unknown intent. They may have no immediate way of knowing if your site is an ad, a brochure, a press release, a game, or a story. A designer must clarify this issue for the user.

The first screen (home page) should set the mood, both visually and structurally—the look and feel; see the Money & Investing Update home page in Figure 7. It must outline the intent of the site and offer something that interests or intrigues your viewer. It must be viewable at 640 x 480 proportion. Our experience has shown us that a large graphic is not always the best home page. The viewer should be able to quickly identify where they are and whether they want to be on your site. For example, *The Wall Street Journal* Interactive Edition's home page (**http://wsj.com**), shown in Figure 8, presents the users with clear information about where they are and what they can access. Viewers will quickly leave if the design fails to meet these criteria. A Web site must have as much of an identity as a well-designed printed newspaper or magazine.

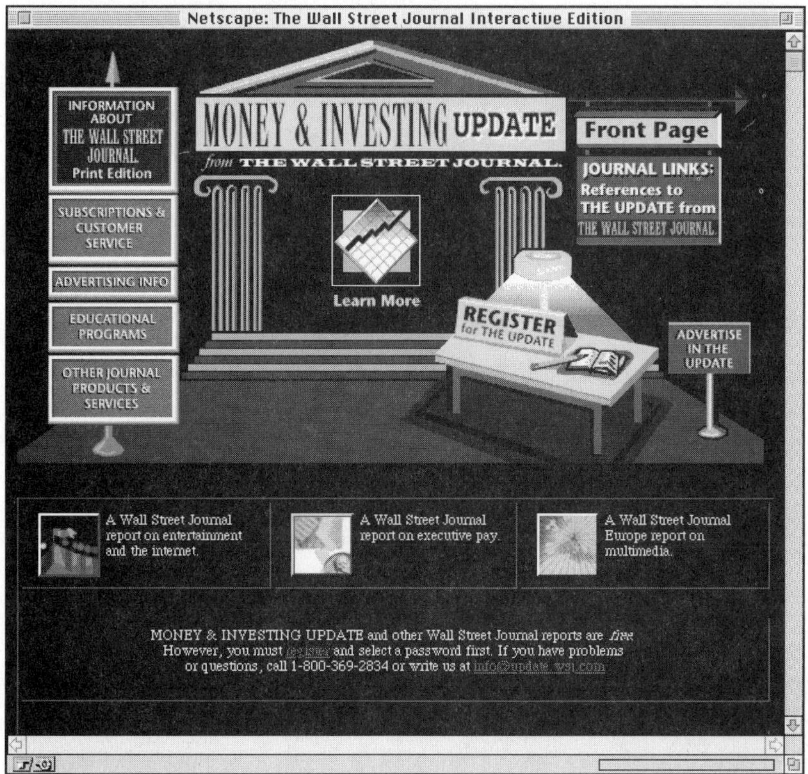

Figure 7: *A home page should set the mood both visually and structurally for the site.*

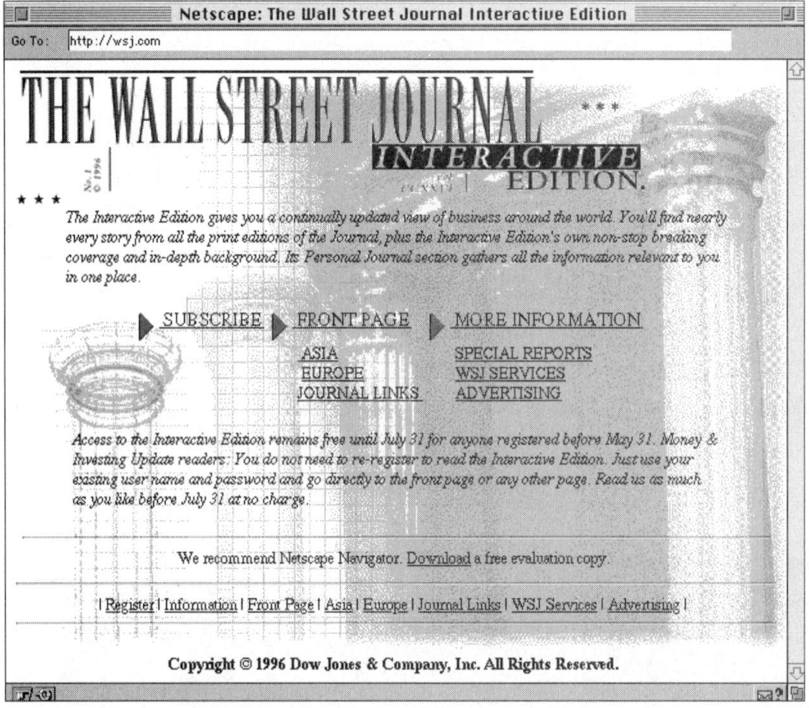

Figure 8: *Users should be able to immediately identify where they are and what information is available from a home page.*

The navigational scheme includes the choice of metaphor and what options the designer has chosen to present to the viewer. The choice of options is a delicate matter. Too few and you will hide the depth of your site's content. Too many and the user may become overwhelmed, confused, and frustrated. As mentioned above, we chose the obvious: a newspaper metaphor. Currently, it seems easiest for us as designers, and most importantly, for our audience, to understand and engage.

The navigational structure controls the mood and the flow of the site. Visual clues within the interface may include colors, styles, and groupings of objects. The choice of metaphor provides clues to the hierarchy and importance of topics, and it informs the viewer's idea of space and boundaries. Is the metaphor an architectural reference, such as a town or room? Or does it mimic an everyday object such as a tape player? The profusion of buttons on the Web relates to people associating access to electronic information with devices such as VCRs, radios, and TVs. Designers can use accepted ideas of perspective and actual physical changes, such as shapes that get bigger or smaller or colors that get brighter or dimmer. Using a 640 x 480 screen limits design but compels creative solutions in order to build attractive, meaningful environments (as you can see in Figure 9).

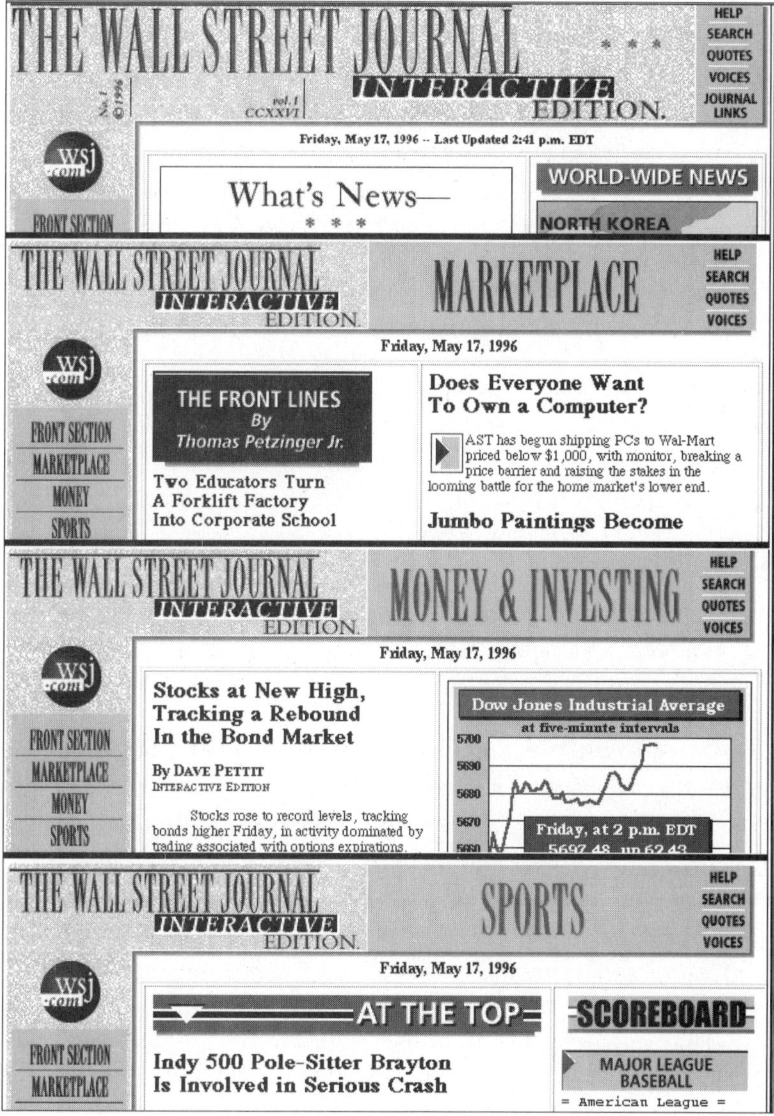

Figure 9: *A good design combines navigation metaphors with other visual clues to control the flow of the site.*

Most navigation does not indicate a move inward (toward the viewer) or outward (away from the viewer). More often it is depicted as scrolling up and down to show movement forwards and backwards through information space. Until bandwidth opens up and tools like VRML are more than experimental, creating three-dimensional and virtual environments will remain difficult. Most of this difficulty

is due to technical limitations, but it is also at least partially due to both users' and designers' physical familiarity with the two-dimensional environment as a platform for presenting information. Virtual Reality has given us a taste of what it would be like to live in virtual environments. The popularity of games such as Myst has proven that people are willing to step into these worlds, especially if they are guided and left with satisfaction, not confusion and frustration.

So how do we think creatively about metaphors and navigation? The most obvious way is from personal experience. Sharon comments:

> *My best inspiration comes from travel. There is a unique feeling when entering a country where you don't speak the language and carry a background of past experiences. I usually feel a certain awe, coupled with a big sense of dislocation. It all can feel very surreal. I can feel right on the edge of being truly lost too. You are relying on past experience, something familiar in addition to signs to guide you. It is most often marked by the need to know the necessities: Where is the most important information? How do I save? How do I quit?*
>
> *The desire to explore a unique and unknown area fades when you just want a cup of coffee and can't seem to communicate the idea. Many of the absolutely essential elements of an interface must be designed with this idea in mind. Your user is newly arrived and would like to explore. Make sure you have a map or a code to give them, and that your site is well laid out and integrated. It might be done in grids like New York City or tangles like Tokyo, but there must be an internal structure the user can learn.*

Just about everything we see can be an inspiration for interface design, metaphors, and navigation. You can drive down a street and see buildings, street lights, and stop signs. You walk into a home and there are familiar sights: rooms, bedrooms, a kitchen. Even taking an elevator to get somewhere, you have to make a decision—click either up or down—then wait for the elevator to come, then tell it what floor to go to. As we design our interface, we are extremely aware that the user does not want to keep clicking their mouse to get to the information. We try to keep as much information accessible on a 640 x 480 screen at any given time without making it too crowded. It is interesting to note that we are willing to wait for an elevator, but with information retrieval, we have little tolerance for waiting at all. Why? We have become so spoiled with information gathering, it will never be fast enough.

The design process for an interface is not an easy one. As a result, *The Wall Street Journal* Interactive Edition Design Department has created over one hundred interfaces. We have held two workshops at different times to take an objective step back so we could analyze the interface, the most important part of designing a Web site. In the Money & Investing Update, we had to navigate to 14 choices at any given time. For *The Wall Street Journal* Interactive Edition, we had to integrate four times the amount of navigation into the interface. We had to break things down to shapes and strip away any unnecessary information, as you can see in Figure 10. We analyzed, we looked at negative and positive space, we tried all sorts of solutions to build depth…all in search of the right look and feel for a product from *The Wall Street Journal*.

Hierarchy goes hand-in-hand with structure. Often every topic included in a Web site is considered important, which tends to result in everything being emphasized. When everything is big and bold it doesn't make anything clearer; it just raises the level of hysteria. Worse than everyone in a room talking at once, it is the same as everyone shouting at once. Viewers' eyes adapt to the overall look of the site. If the design differences are subtle, small changes are more easily recognizable. If the design is big, bigger, and biggest, it takes a great change to command attention.

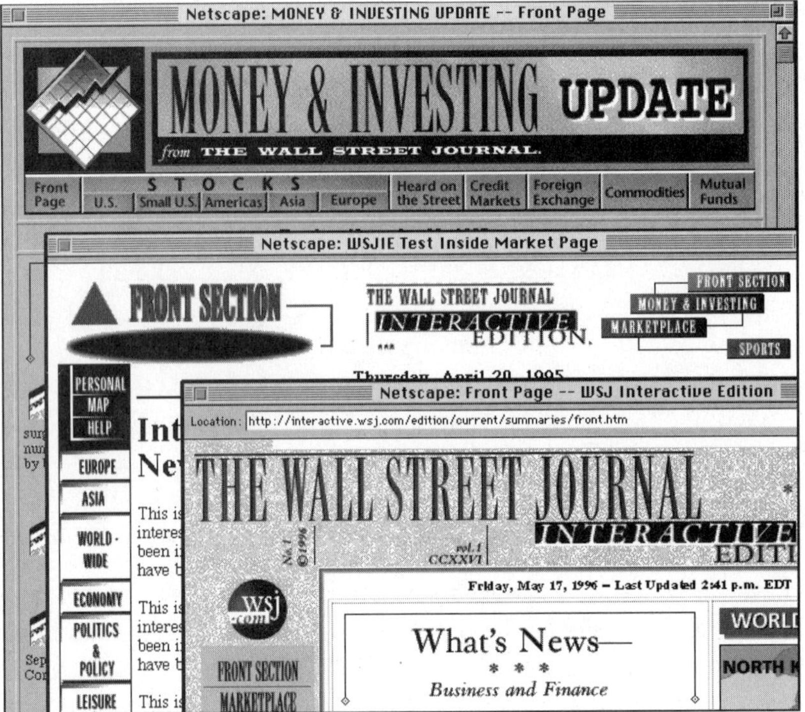

Figure 10: *An interface with the right look and feel is one of the most important aspects of Web site design.*

Time also has become a very important design element to deal with on the Web. Download time is the first experience users have with your site and is one of the most important factors you need to be conscious of when you design. It will determine the accessibility of your site, how many people will look at it and how often, and if they will return to look at it. Since download time is an ugly fact of the Web, can this trait be used to any sort of advantage? It can certainly build anticipation.

Colored flash screens and downloading a low resolution image before the final one will let your user know that more is coming. Usually the low resolution images are simply poorer copies of the original, but there's no reason why they need to be. They can be images for entertainment, teasers, or ads.

Production Issues

As a Web designer you have much less control over design and layout than in a print medium. Font choices and sizes are left to the viewer's discretion, layout is often up to the specifications of a particular browser, and colors are affected by the quality and type of a user's monitor as well as the specifications of a browser. Most designers are tempted to consolidate their development work out of frustration, building a site specifically for one browser on one platform. While ultimately the design will probably be perfected for a specific browser/palette/monitor combination (usually the lowest common denominator of your users' equipment), it is important to continue to keep other possibilities in mind. The layout possibilities of specific browsers are very attractive, but make sure your site is usable in other popular browsers. From the beginning of the design process, check other browsers and look at your designs in other platforms. It will be impossible to make the design perfect in all browsers and on all monitors, but the design must remain attractive and navigable in other browsers.

Some sites make a decision to support users who turn off graphics. This means that users get an alternative text-only version of the navigation path to access the site. At the launch of *The Wall Street Journal* Interactive Edition we determined that Netscape would be our preferred browser, and we would not support turning off graphics. Graphics help users navigate and enable an enriched experience, sometimes at the expense of performance.

A good designer must design for optimum cross-platform visibility. While most computers used today are PCs, Mac users form a disproportionately active segment on the Internet. (No one said this would be easy.) Most computer users are fanatically loyal to their chosen platform, but designers don't have that luxury. At *The Wall Street Journal* we do most of our actual design work on the Mac, but keep a PC loaded with Photoshop, Premiere, Director, and various browsers close at hand. We've come to use it more and more for design work, but its most important function is for viewing works in progress and checking finished projects. The PC has a 15" monitor and is set to 256 colors at the lowest possible resolution. Affectionately known as *The Worst Case*, it is a source of great frustration, but a check point we couldn't do without. Another important factor is to have PCs and Macs access the same files. When using the "Sneakernet," it is simply too easy to copy the wrong file and not the one that was approved.

After many months of trial and error, we have a color palette that works fairly well on both the Mac and the PC. While not perfect, it works with predictable results, as opposed to very dithered and ugly alternatives. This has saved us an incredible amount of time and has given us back some measure of control. When a graphic must be fairly simple or we must pick a frequently used color, we make our selections from that palette exclusively. Images that are more like illustrations are done according to our own aesthetic choices and then converted to a GIF using a custom palette.

The palette problem is especially difficult for designers, most of whom work on Macs, because the colors in the PC palette tend to run to the blues and greens, and on the PC screen colors often appear darker than on Macs. While we do occasionally feel constrained by color choices, we must guarantee that the design appears consistent across platforms, thus the strict adherence to the predetermined color palette.

After losing all control over colors, fonts, and layout, what elements can a designer use to maintain a feeling of identity and give their Web site project the feeling of beautiful design? Color, line, shape, form, and texture are still the basics. You can distinguish parts of the site by the background using a GIF, a color tag, or big image maps. They all have benefits and drawbacks. The designer and part of the larger team must explore these benefits of communication weighed against the drawbacks in performance. For example, when we do a special report, we often experiment with different ways of communication, like the one in Figure 11 with one big image map for our Entertainment+Technology section.

Given the nature of the medium, users of the Web do not have the grounding experience of someone reading a magazine or book. A site on the Web needs to feel self-contained, because if the design changes radically, users may wonder where they are. To avoid this, when we change the layout for a site like Entertainment+Technology, we keep the interface familiar. For the same reason, it is important to indicate when a link is taking the user outside a site. Maintain continuity of design, as it allows users to know where they are and identifies the space of the site. Maintaining a high visibility of navigation is an important and practical way to ensure that visitors are constantly seeing the sites identity. Keep them grounded in this dazzling and often confusing new world experience.

THE WALL STREET JOURNAL INTERACTIVE EDITION.

ENTERTAINMENT + TECHNOLOGY

TABLE OF CONTENTS

FRONT SECTION · MARKETPLACE · MONEY · SPORTS · PERSONAL JOURNAL

Thursday, March 28, 1996

See what many readers wrote to us about this section.

Editor's Note

A couple of years ago, talk of entertainment and technology was all about interactive TV. But promises of 500 channels, movies-on-demand, and shopping from the couch have yet to materialize. Now, a new circus has rolled into town, offering everything from Hollywood gossip to 24-hour-a-day news to do-it-yourself publishing. It's called the World Wide Web, and it's here *today*.

Welcome to our tour of the World Wide Web. Read what may lie in store for the Web -- and, if you have RealAudio capability, listen to what some of the players in this fast-moving medium think the future may hold.

The potential of on-line entertainment has inspired hopes and fears alike.

Journey with John Blanton into the new world of on-line fiction. Most of what's out there now isn't worth reading. But this is the birth of a whole new type of fiction, and it promises to be one of the most creative corners of the on-line world.

TV vs. PC!

Up and Running

Why did the Web replace interactive TV as the new mantra? A simple reason: It's here.

***

Off the Dial

TV networks have a ready-made audience for their on-line offerings. They just have to find a way to capitalize on that.

***

Best Guesses

Two experts give their best guess on which technologies will dominate home entertainment in the future.

***

ROUNDTABLE

Web Forum

Join four industry players for a discussion of what the future of the World Wide Web may hold.

RealAudio DOWNLOAD

Hear the News!

Our tour of the World Wide Web contains audio clips which you can play by clicking on the corresponding RealAudio icon. If you don't have this capability, you can download RealAudio by clicking here.

Try Your Luck!

Wanna Play?

Figures 11: *Maintain some consistency while introducing a new look.*

As a designer it is important to keep an eye on this form of communication as evolutionary. We are in a renaissance and lucky to be living and working as part of it. If we take a playful view of the design process, it may be easier to find places to be creative. Any sport has a rigid set of rules, constraints, and regulations to follow. On the Web, the rules set the environment for a certain kind of creativity to emerge freely. Remember the site's purpose, and then design within those objectives. Think of it as putting pieces of a giant puzzle together, with the designer's role being to make those pieces feel coherent, compelling, and approachable.

Too

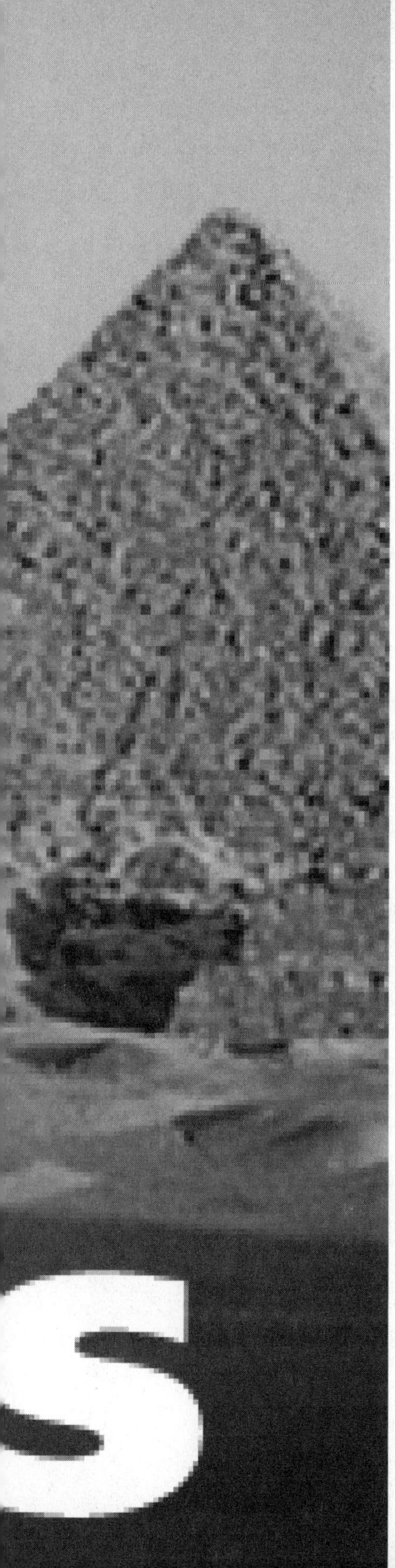

Part 2

Now that you have a deeper sense of what makes great Web design, this second part of the book will give you some of the skills you will need to make your visions into a reality. Part 2 is a compilation of tutorials on some of the best tools for Web development currently available.

Each section has two parts: a Chapter Profile and a Tutorial. The Chapter Profiles will help you understand the positioning and value of each tool relative to the others. But the real benefit of Part 2 is in the tutorials themselves. Each tutorial is designed to work in conjunction with the CD-ROM in the back of the book and with the Web itself. A good technique for getting the most out of the tutorials is to load the software and work through the lessons as you read. This will give you a chance to get hands-on experience with the tools that will use as you implement the Web design theories from Part 1.

GNNpress

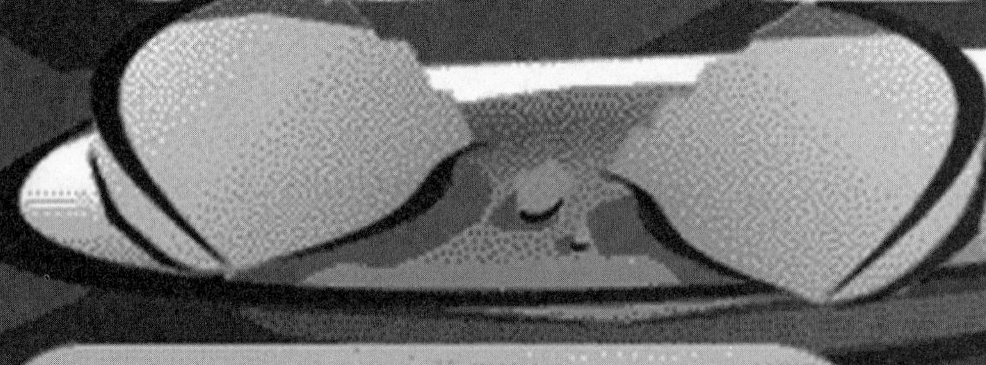

A Delicious Adventure Awaits Yo
Grab Your Chopsticks!
A Taste of China

GNN

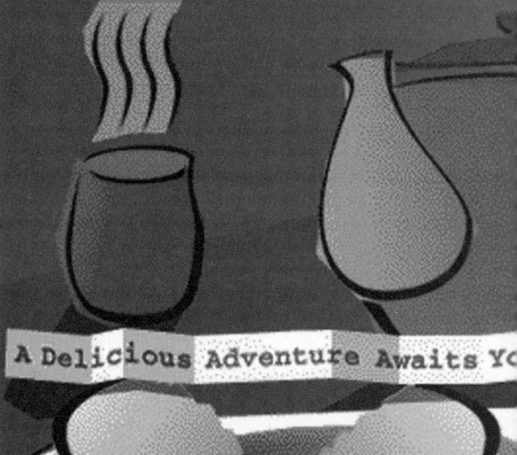

GNN and GNNpress

Company Profile

NaviSoft was founded in 1991 to create authoring tools and server technologies for online communications. Their lead products, NaviPress and NaviServer, use a unique publishing model: local authoring with immediate remote publishing. NaviSoft was acquired in 1994 by America Online. In 1995, AOL bought GNN, The Global Network Navigator, a dial-up, hosting, and online content developer. Shortly afterward, NaviSoft revised and re-released NaviPress as GNNpress, designing it to work with GNN's subscriber base. This is a powerful combination of technology and publishing, as the GNNpress tool gives average, nontechnical people the ability to create and publish in one compact environment.

Chapter Profile

The GNN service allows you to access the Internet and publish your pages on the World Wide Web with the help of a variety of tools: GNNworks is the browser you use to surf the Web, and GNNpress is the tool you use to publish your pages on the Web. GNNpress was created by the folks who brought you NaviPress. GNNworks was created by the people who developed Internet Works. Together, they create a comprehensive Internet software suite that is one of the most powerful available to the home consumer. The GNNpress software (version 1.1) is provided on the CD-ROM that accompanies this book.

GNNpress makes Web publishing available to Web newcomers and masters alike. As an authoring tool, GNNpress renders HTML transparent, allowing you to perform all of the most common formatting actions (such as working with text, headings, tables, and images) using menu selections and toolbar buttons. In addition, GNNpress supports many HTML 3.0 formats that aren't directly available through the menus. Along with the authoring features, GNNpress offers the MiniWeb tool, which acts as a graphical file manager that you can use to organize and manage all the files and pages on your Web site.

GNNpress and the GNN service give you an integrated publishing system for the World Wide Web that is easy to use. The computer system on your desk connects to GNN's Web servers, where you can publish your pages The GNNpress software, the tutorial below, and the GNN service enable you to join the thousands of people who have made their presence known on the Internet.

Currently, GNN's primary market focus is individuals who want to install their own personal sites on the Web. This focus is changing fast to become a place for small businesses to do the same. For emerging Web developers, this shift provides an opportunity to build sites for their own clients with GNN's software.

This tutorial will take you through everything you will need to know about GNNpress to get started building your own sites. You'll get step-by-step instructions on creating a simple page from a template, organizing a MiniWeb, and publishing your page through the GNN service. Beginners will also find useful sections on Web basics and the inner workings of HTML, and a reference section provides detailed information about adding tables, links, and images to your pages. Dive in, ramp up, and go for it!

Tutorial

User's Guide to GNNpress 1.1

by Jeff Dozier, Yvonne DeGraw, Ralph Chaney

HE WORLD WIDE WEB has fueled the explosive growth of the Internet and the emerging software and services industries that surround it. The Web lets individuals, companies, and institutions—anyone with an Internet connection—publish electronically.

GNNpress is an interactive authoring tool that helps you create and publish Web pages. The tool is a custom version of NaviSoft's NaviPress, and has been optimized to work with the GNN service. Before you start building your own pages, you'll need to have all of your software and services set up properly. We'll explain how to do this in the first part of the chapter, and then move on to learning how to use this powerful tool.

About This Tutorial

We realize there is probably no "typical" reader of this tutorial or user of GNN-press. Some of you are novices; some have considerable experience. If you can use a word processor, you have the skills to use GNNpress. How you will use this chapter depends on what you already know, and how we explain things depends on what we assume about you and your system. In this section, we'll let you know what assumptions we made when we wrote this tutorial.

We assume your computer connects to the GNN Internet access service from GNN, and that you are subscribed to the GNN service, not simply someone who reads the GNN home page on the World Wide Web. If you are not a subscriber, please see the instructions printed on the card in the CD-ROM sleeve at the back of this book.

We assume you know how to use your computer and its operating software:

- You know about files and directories (sometimes called *documents* and *folders*), how to create them, rename them, move them, and delete them.
- You know how to use your computer's operating system to run programs.
- You have experience with Microsoft Windows.
- You know how to use your computer's mouse. You can move its cursor and use its button(s).

We assume you have used one of the popular word-processing software packages, such as Microsoft Word. The editing conventions in GNNpress are similar to those used in word processing. The file-saving operations in GNNpress look similar, but they allow you to save files over a network.

We do *not* assume that you are an expert on the World Wide Web and the concept of navigating through information with hypertext, but we recognize that many of you are familiar with these services and concepts. If you are already familiar with Web navigation, skim the text to see how GNNpress lets you browse the Web, then work through the examples to create a Web page.

Using This Tutorial

We urge you to *use* this tutorial, not just read it. Throughout the tutorial, we'll show you how to accomplish a variety of tasks—work through the instructions to learn.

Following the heading that introduces a task are either sequential steps or optional steps, each with its distinctive style:

1. Numbered paragraphs, like this one, designate step-by-step instructions. Follow them to learn how the tools work.

- Paragraphs with a bullet, like this one, are optional steps. Usually there is a sequence. Do one or more of the steps to cause the designated action or actions.

After you have gained experience, you will find that the tutorial serves as a working companion and a source of more detail.

Considering our experience with many software packages, we recommend that you go through the tutorial thoroughly after you have used the software for a while. You will discover useful features that you breezed over the first time.

NOTE

In this chapter, underlined words indicate hyperlinks. **Boldfaced** words indicate text that you should key in.

Online Help

There are many online help pages available throughout the application. Most dialog boxes have a help button that you can click to get assistance with a specific task. You can search for specific topics using Help ➤ Search For Help On. This will bring up a dialog box where you enter a term to search for in the online documentation.

What's New in v1.1?

This tutorial describes GNNpress v1.1. If you are using an earlier version of GNNpress (such as v1.01), some of the v1.1 features will appear differently or will not be available. "New" Icons like the one to the left identify features added in v1.1.

Coming Soon in Version 1.2...

In late summer 1996, a new version of GNNpress will be available: version 1.2. This version will offer new and improved features in areas including browsing, MiniWebs, tables, and HTML and Java support. For information on how to download version 1.2 when it becomes available, check out **http://www.gnn.com**. Here's a quick preview of some of the features you can look forward to in version 1.2:

Browsing

- To load or reload the images in a page, you can use Browse ➤ Load Images.
- To open a page that was displayed in a window you closed during this session or a previous session, you can open that page from the File ➤ Open Recent list.
- In the Windows version, the toolbar and Location, Title, and Home Page fields have been moved out of the Page and MiniWeb windows and made part of the main GNNpress window. This saves screen space when you use several Page and MiniWeb windows at once.
- The new toolbar buttons are smaller to match the size of buttons in other applications.
- If you place the mouse cursor over a toolbar button for a second, you will see a "Tool Tip" that tells you the function of the button. To turn these tool tips off, uncheck the Help ➤ Show Tool Tips menu item.
- The Short Menus are no longer available.

Text and Content

- GNNpress now has a built-in spell checker. You can check pages or entire MiniWebs by choosing the Tools ➤ Spell Check menu item.
- You can change the color of selected text by choosing a color from the Format ➤ Type Color menu.
- The Bigger and Smaller options have been moved out of the Format ➤ Type Style menu and into the new Format ➤ Type Size menu.
- You can rate the contents of your pages by choosing the Format ➤ Page Attributes menu item and typing a PICS label or selecting a SafeSurf rating. The rating you add can be used by several browsers that let parents and teachers control the level of potentially offensive material children can see.

Images, Image Maps, and Toolbars

- You can resize images by double-clicking on them and dragging the image handles.

Continued on next page

- You can uncheck the Border field when you insert an image if you don't want a border around linked images.
- You can create client-side or server-side image maps with GNNpress.
- You can create circles and polygons in image maps, as well as rectangles.
- GNNpress highlights linked areas defined in a client-side image map when you move the cursor over the map.
- You can add toolbar buttons that link to pages like your Home, Next, and Index pages. Each page can have whatever set of toolbar button you want to add. Many browsers do not currently display these additional toolbar buttons, but for browsers that do display them, you can make navigation much easier. Choose the Format ➤ Page Attributes menu item and select a type of Toolbar Link.

Tables

- You can add or delete rows and columns within a table by using the options you see when you choose Table ➤ Alter Table.
- If the text and other items you want to place in the table are already in your page, highlight them before you create the table. When you create the table, the table cells will be filled with the paragraphs you selected (from left to right and then from top to bottom).

Java Support

- You can add Java applets to your pages by choosing the Element ➤ Java Applet menu item or by copying and pasting a Java applet in your page. (GNNpress currently does not display and run Java applets.)
- You can create Java source files within a MiniWeb by choosing the File ➤ New Java menu item.
- You can decide whether you want place holders for Java applets displayed in your pages using the Show Java Windows box in the Tools ➤ Preferences ➤ General dialog box.

HTML Support

- GNNpress supports HTML 3.2. You can choose to have your pages conform to Netscape's standards or HTML 3.2 in the Tools ➤ Preferences ➤ General dialog box.
- The HTML you see when you choose the Tools ➤ Show HTML menu item is now formatted nicely and the tags and attributes are color-coded.
- GNNpress does not erase any <FRAME>, <FRAMESET>, or <NOFRAMES> tags in the files you edit.

Continued on next page

- GNNpress supports a number of new tags and attributes if they are contained in the HTML you are viewing or if you add them directly to the HTML.
- If you directly edit HTML and do not wish GNNpress to conform it (so that GNNpress pages are always in strict HTML compliance), you can save your changes directly from the HTML editor. Similarly, reloading from the HTML editor allows you to edit HTML before it is conformed for display on the GNNpress browser.

MiniWebs

- You can assign icons to files in a MiniWeb by choosing the Edit ➤ Set Icon menu item. You can use an image as the icon for its own file by choosing the Edit ➤ Make Icon menu item.
- You can set titles for page files and other types of files in a MiniWeb by choosing the Edit ➤ Set Title menu item.
- You can assign help pages to files in a MiniWeb by choosing the Edit ➤ Set Help menu item.
- You can decide whether you want GNNpress to open the MiniWeb, the home page for the MiniWeb, or both windows when you access the URL for a MiniWeb.

Publishing

- GNNpress stores backup copies of pages you have edited but have not saved. When you restart GNNpress after a crash, it opens these copies and tells you that it is recovering old files. You can continue editing these files without losing much of your work.
- GNNpress helps you avoid conflicts when several people edit the same Web pages. When you publish a page, AOLservers (v2.1 or higher) make sure no one has saved changes to the page since the last time you loaded it. If someone else has changed the page, the server sends you a message. (Other servers that check content versions may provide similar messages.)
- If you want to warn other people in your group that you are making changes to a page, you can lock the page by choosing the Tools ➤ Administer Page Lock menu item.
- You can save files in Rich Text Format (RTF) or in Java source format.

NOTE

For information about GNN and its products, call 1-800-879-6882, or send e-mail to **interest@GNN.com**.

Short Menus vs. Long Menus

A number of features are not available through the default short menus in GNNpress. These features include MiniWebs, Style Sheets, and various dialog boxes for setting preferences. To see these features, you must activate the long menus by choosing Tools ➤ Preferences and unchecking the Short Menus field in the dialog box that appears. Click on OK, and the hidden features will be available.

When you use the long menus, you will see some menu items that are not currently supported with the GNN service. These menu items would be supported if you had your own Web server from NaviSoft, the makers of GNNpress. You should ignore the following long menu items that are not documented in this tutorial:

Format ➤ Form	Format ➤ Style Sheet
Tools ➤ NaviLinks	Tools ➤ Search Server
Tools ➤ Administer Server	Tools ➤ Administer Page
Tools ➤ Administer MiniWeb	Tools ➤ Preferences ➤ Network
Tools ➤ Preferences ➤ Animation	Tools ➤ Preferences ➤ NaviServers

Installing GNNpress

GNNpress must be installed on your computer before you can use the software. This section explains how to install GNNpress on Microsoft Windows 3.1, Windows 3.5 NT, Windows for Workgroups, and Windows 95.

System Requirements

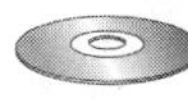

As we said above, we expect that your computer connects directly to the GNN Internet access service from GNN, and that you are a subscriber to the GNN service. If you are not currently a GNN subscriber, you are in luck! The CD-ROM in the back of this book includes a complete copy of the GNNpress application software and a free 30-day trial membership on the GNN service. You can sign up by following the installation instructions below and those on the card inserted with the CD-ROM itself.

You can still use GNNpress to author and access local files when your computer is not connected to the Internet. For example, while you create pages, you may want to leave your modem off and then connect to the Internet when you are ready to publish your pages. When your modem is off, you have access to all the features of GNNpress, but cannot open, save, delete, or browse on network locations.

You need the following to use GNNpress:

- Intel x86 microprocessor:
    - 386 minimum
    - 486 or above recommended
- 4 Mbytes RAM minimum; 8 Mbytes recommended.
- 5 Mbytes free disk space required for installation.
- 1.4 Mbytes floppy drive and an Internet TCP/IP connection
    - Windows NT and Windows 95 have support for Internet connectivity built in. Windows NT and Windows 95 users do *not* need to install third-party software.
    - The Windows 3.1 and Windows for Workgroups 3.11 operating systems do *not* have built-in support for Internet connectivity, and you have to install one on your system if you plan to search the World Wide Web. Sources of commercial products include FTP, Inc, Microsoft, NetManage, Novell, Digital Equipment Corp., and Spry.

Installing the Software

To install GNNpress on Windows 3.1, Windows NT, Windows for Workgroups 3.11, or Windows 95 from the CD-ROM that accompanies this book, follow the steps listed on the cards inserted with the CD-ROM. Before you can install GNNpress, however, you must install the software to connect you to the GNN service.

Connecting to the GNN Service

Here's how to get hooked up to the GNN service:

1. Put the CD-ROM into your CD-ROM drive.

2. If you have Windows 3.1 or Windows for Workgroups 3.11, open the File Manager and select the CD-ROM. If you have Windows 95 or NT, use the Explorer to open the CD-ROM.
3. Open the GNN folder, then open the second GNN folder.
4. Click on SETUP.EXE.
5. When you see an Install button, click on it.
6. The software for connecting to the GNN service is automatically installed in the C:\GNN directory.
7. Click on OK to start the registration process.
8. If you wish to register with GNN, follow the instructions that appear on your screen, using the registration number and password included on the card that comes with the CD-ROM. You can also click on Cancel and just install GNNpress without connecting to the service, but you will not be able to use all of the GNNpress features covered in this tutorial.
9. Click on OK to close the registration dialog box.

Installing GNNpress on Windows 3.1 and Windows for Workgroups 3.11

Follow these steps to install GNNpress on Windows 3.1 or Windows for Workgroups 3.11:

1. The CD-ROM should still be in your CD-ROM drive.
2. Start your system's File Manager tool and double-click to activate your CD-ROM drive.
3. Double-click to open the GNN folder, then double click on the GNNpress folder.
4. Double-click on SETUP.EXE to automatically install GNNpress.

Installing GNNpress on Windows 95/NT

Follow these steps to install GNNpress on Windows 95/NT:

1. The CD-ROM should still be in your CD-ROM drive.
2. Double-click on the My Computer folder.
3. Double-click on the CD-ROM icon.
4. Double-click to open the GNN folder, then double-click on the GNNpress folder.
5. Double-click on Setup to automatically install GNNpress.

Updating GNNpress

When new versions of GNNpress are introduced, you can update your version via the GNN Web site (**http://www.tools.gnn.com/index.html**), instead of having to reinstall it. From the home page, select File ➤ Upgrade GNNpress from the menu bar. You will be prompted for subscriber information, and then an upgrade will be downloaded to your computer.

Starting GNNpress

To start GNNpress in Windws 3.1, double-click on the GNNpress icon in the Global Network Navigator program group. (In Windows 95/NT, select Run from the Start menu, click on Browse, and open the folder where you installed GNNpress. Double-click on the GNNpress icon and click on OK to start GNNpress.) By default, GNNpress starts with a *Page window* (see Figure 1) with helpful pointers to documentation, support, and authoring assistance. We'll take a closer look at this window later.

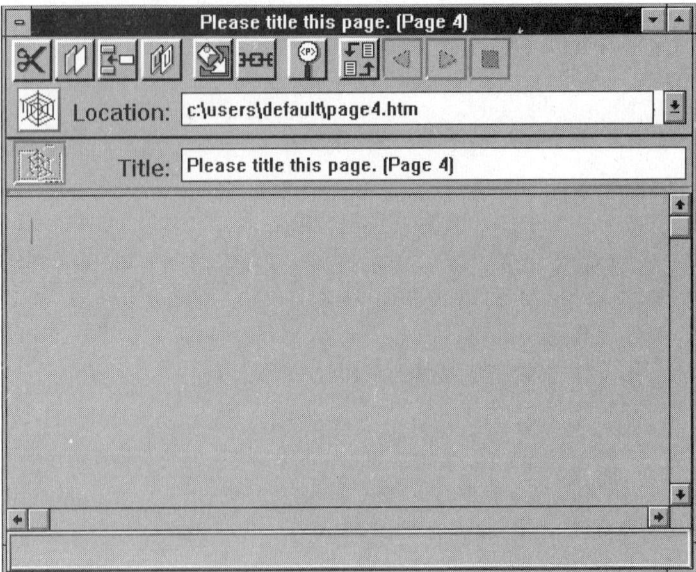

Figure 1: *When you first open GNNpress, you'll see a Page window.*

NOTE

You can also set your Preferences (by selecting Tools ➤ Preferences) to bring up an empty Web page, a specific page, or a MiniWeb. We'll explain more about how to do this later in the chapter.

Now that you have your software in place, we can get to work with GNNpress.

The GNNpress Workspace

The GNNpress user interface lets you work with Page windows and MiniWeb windows, choose commands, drag and drop, work with local or remote pages, and more. This section will give you an overview of the software, to help you use it more efficiently. This section also presents an overview of how to find your way around the online help system.

Browse and Author

GNNpress has a different interface than other Web browsers—it is both an editor and a browser. The editing and formatting features have not been available in other Web browsers.

Because we integrate authoring and browsing, you can integrate reading and editing. If you are browsing (reading) a page on a server where you have permission to change pages, you can correct an error that you see and republish the page.

You can copy material from pages you are browsing—text, images, hyperlinks, and full URLs—and paste them into a page that you are authoring.

GNNpress and the GNN service give you an integrated publishing solution for the World Wide Web. As a subscriber to the GNN service, you can publish your pages on the Web server GNN provides.

Pages and MiniWebs

GNNpress uses two kinds of windows: *Page* windows and *MiniWeb* windows. You use Page windows to browse and author individual Web pages, and you use MiniWeb windows to work on collections of related pages. When GNNpress starts, by default, you see a Page window, as we explained above. Page windows and MiniWeb windows are visually distinct from each other and have different menus and commands. However, basic principles about the interface work the same in both windows.

You can open many Page windows and MiniWeb windows at the same time. The number is limited by the amount of memory on your machine. Each Page window maintains its own history, so that you can retrace your steps in each individual window.

NOTE

To access MiniWebs, you must first make advanced features available by choosing Tools ➤ Preferences and unchecking the Short Menus item, as we explained above. From here on, we'll just tell you to deactivate short menus when necessary.

Your Hard Disk and the GNN Service

GNNpress can be used without the GNN service to browse the Web and to develop Web pages. However, you see the full power of GNNpress and when you use both of them together.

GNNpress lets you create Web pages whether or not you are not connected to the GNN service. You can save the pages as files on your own hard drive. When you are ready for the rest of the world to see your pages, just connect to the GNN service and save the files in your publishing space.

This next section describes the window and menus you see when GNNpress starts up. It explains major elements on the screen and explains how to distinguish between the two kinds of windows used in GNNpress—the Page window and MiniWeb window.

GNNpress Windows

Figure 2 shows the major parts of the GNNpress screen. We'll look more closely at these parts, the Page window, and the MiniWeb window a little later.

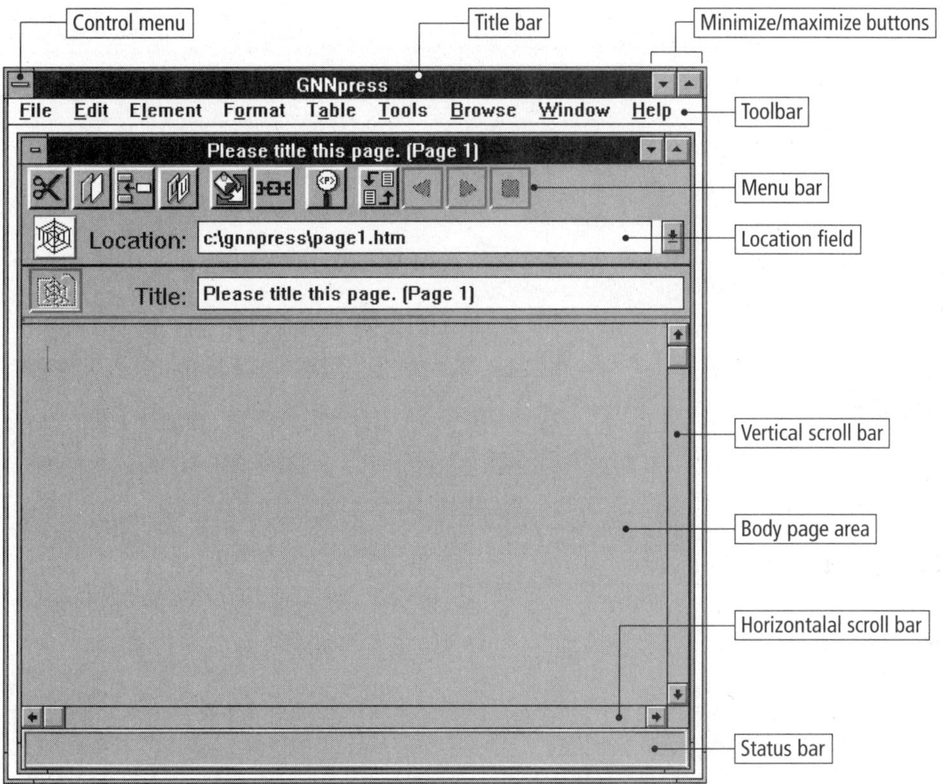

Figure 2: *The GNNpress opening screen*

TIP

You can resize Page and MiniWeb windows by dragging the window border or corner.

These are the parts of a window:

- Title bar: The title bar is at the top of the window. It contains the title of the page or MiniWeb. The title bar lets you find the window you want when you have more than one window open.
- Menu bar: Just beneath the title bar is the menu bar. The menus in it give you access to the tools that the application provides. In the Page window, the menus are File, Edit, Element, Format, Table, Tools, Browse, Window, and Help. In the MiniWeb window, the menus are File, Edit, View, Tools, Browse, and Help.

Edit	
Undo	Ctrl+Z
Redo	Ctrl+Y
Cut	**Ctrl+X**
Copy	**Ctrl+C**
Paste	**Ctrl+V**
Clear	
Select All	**Ctrl+A**
Copy URL	**Shift+Ctrl+C**
Paste URL	Shift+Ctrl+V
Find / Replace...	**Shift+Ctrl+F**
Find Next	Ctrl+G

NOTE

The available menu choices are shown in bold. Some choices are grayed out; they are unavailable for this particular page or MiniWeb.

- Toolbar: Below the menu bar is the toolbar, which has buttons for the most common commands. The toolbars for the Page and MiniWeb windows contain different buttons.
- Location field: Below the toolbar is the Location field. It contains the URL (Uniform Resource Locator) of the page you are viewing. You can view another page by typing its URL in this field.
- Title field: Below the Location field is the Title field. It contains the title of the page you are viewing. It shows the same text as the window's title bar. You can use the Title field to change the text in the title bar. Just type a new title in the field and press ↵.

- Home Page field: The MiniWeb has a Home Page field instead of a Title field. It contains the title of the home page in the MiniWeb you are viewing. You can select a different home page in this field by clicking on the arrow to the right of the field and selecting a page from the list.
- Scroll bars: On the bottom and right side of the windows are scroll bars, which function like scroll bars in any word processing application.
- Status bar: At the bottom of the window is a status bar. As you work, messages appear there so the application can let you know what it is doing. (For example, if you click on a hyperlink to cause a page to be transferred over the network, the status bar will continually update information about the transfer.) If the mouse cursor is over a toolbar button, the status bar shows the button's function.

The Page Window

When you start GNNpress as we explained above, you see a Page window. Page windows and MiniWeb windows have many features in common, but they also have some individual elements as well.

The Page Window Toolbar The Page window toolbar gives you quick access to frequently used commands such as Cut, Copy, Paste, and Copy URL. The buttons and their names are shown in Figure 3.

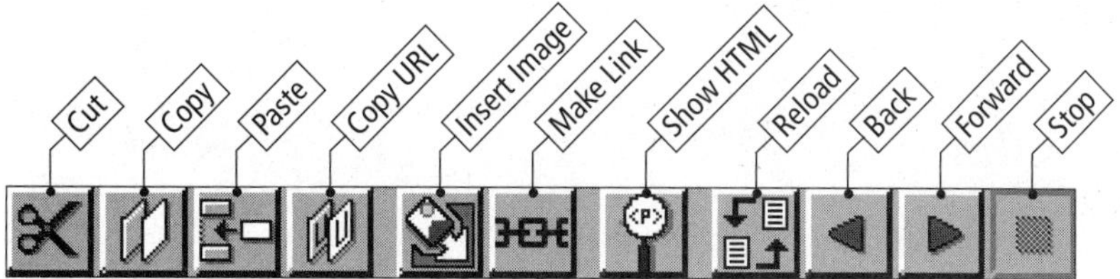

Figure 3: *The Page window toolbar buttons*

Page Window Menus Here is the menu bar for the Page window.

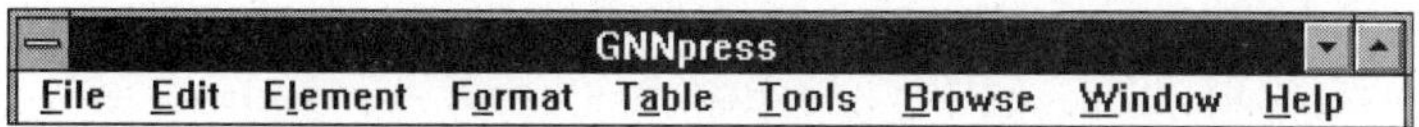

Click on any menu to see the choices it offers. The File menu operates on Pages either locally or remotely over the Web. Edit, Element, Format, and Table are all used to author pages. The Tools menu has special utilities and functions. Browse has viewing capabilities. Window lets you rearrange multiple GNNpress pages on your screen, and Help provides access to documentation, search tools, and examples.

The MiniWeb Window

The MiniWeb is like a file manager for your Web pages. It helps you organize and manage the files that make up your Web site. It gives you a graphical view of the collection of files showing all the pages and any other files (such as images and sounds) and the connections between them (see Figure 4). One page is designated as the home page (it is displayed with a special icon—a spider at home in its web). If a page links to other pages outside your directory, those pages are also shown.

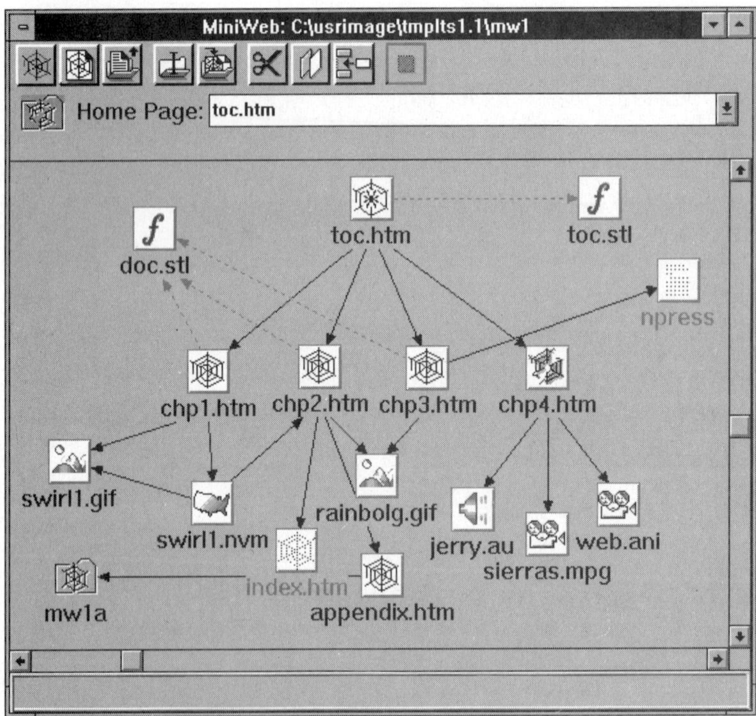

Figure 4: *A MiniWeb helps you organize your site, using icons and arrows to represent pages and links.*

NOTE

When you have a MiniWeb window open, you should not switch back to short menus, or you will not have access to many useful menu items.

A MiniWeb uses icons to represent files (pages) and arrows to represent the links between them. Icons can be dragged and dropped into other MiniWeb windows and into Page windows. Arrows between icons represent links between the files. MiniWebs are color coded to show the status and relationships of the files in the MiniWeb.

The MiniWeb Window Toolbar The MiniWeb toolbar gives you quick access to frequently used commands such as Open, Import, and Save As. You can see the buttons of the MiniWeb toolbar and their names in Figure 5.

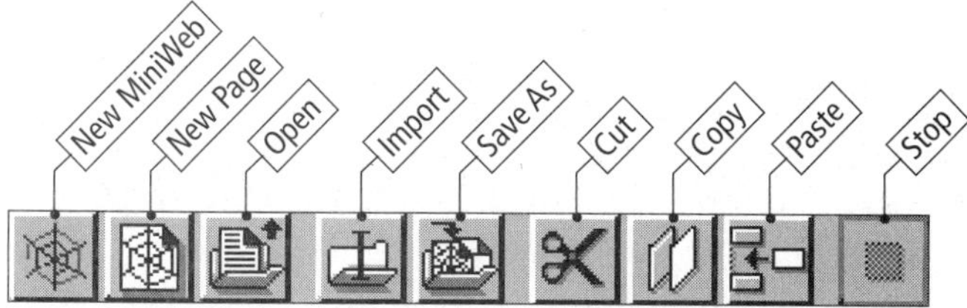

Figure 5: *The buttons of the MiniWeb toolbar*

MiniWeb Window Menus The File menu operates on both Pages and MiniWebs—opening, saving, closing—either locally or remotely over the Net. Click on any entry to access tools associated with the application. The Edit menu is used to copy URLs from or to the MiniWeb. The View menu controls the viewing scale and redraws the MiniWeb. The Tools menu has utilities or functions to access special services. Browse examines the history and the Hot List for that window. Help provides access to documentation, search tools, and examples.

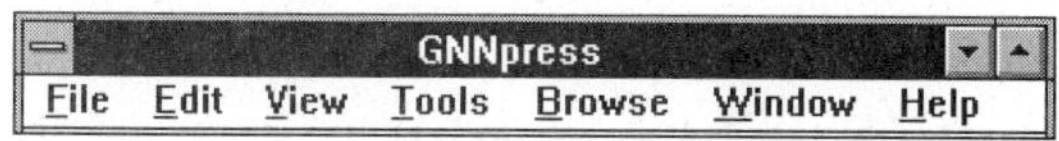

Working in the Windows

The GNNpress interface is much like that of a word processing or desktop publishing application, with dialog boxes, online help, and standard file management capabilities.

Dialog Boxes

Selecting a pull-down menu item that has three dots at the end (for example, File ➤ Open…) displays a dialog box where you type text or click buttons. Some dialog boxes require you to close the dialog box (generally by clicking on OK or Cancel) before you can continue other operations in GNNpress. Your computer will beep if you need to close a dialog box before moving to a different window.

Getting Online Help

GNNpress provides several ways you can find answers to your questions—you can click on the Help button in various dialog boxes, or you can use the Help menu.

- To get online help in a dialog box, click on the Help button, or press Help or F1 on your keyboard. This displays specific help about that dialog box.
- To search the Help table of contents, choose Help ➤ Contents. You will see a page that contains and describes links to various help files. For example, you can click on the link to the online User Guide to search the online version of this tutorial.
- To search for Help by looking up a word, follow these steps:

  1. Choose Help ➤ Search For Help. You will see a page with links to the GNNpress online documentation.
  2. Click on the link to search the GNNpress documentation. If you are not connected to the GNN service, the dialer will appear. Once you are connected, you will see the Contents page shown in Figure 6.
  3. Type a word or words in the field, and click on the Search button. You will see a list of sections that contain those words. You can click on a link to move to that section.

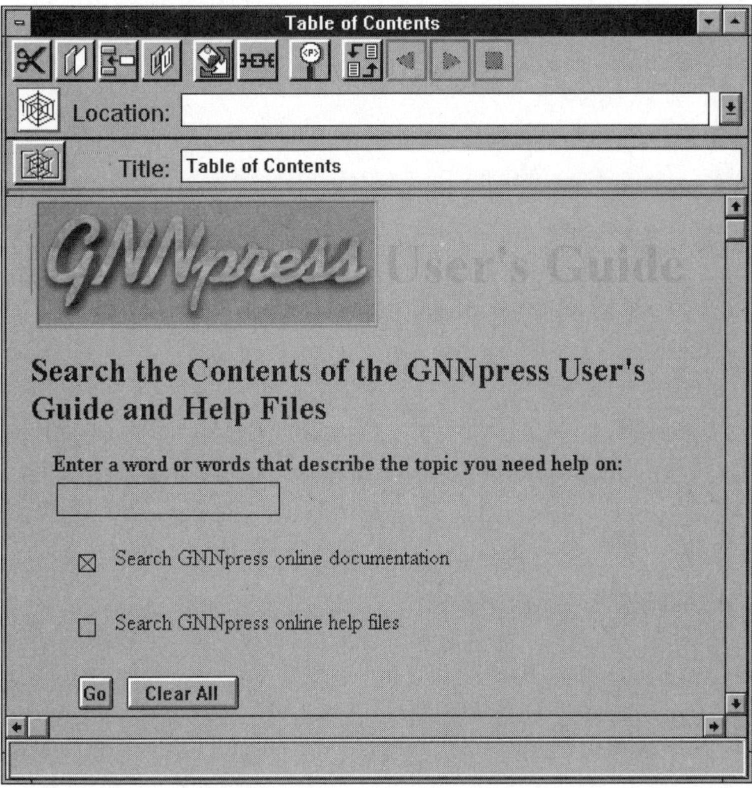

Figure 6: *The Contents page, where you can search for specific words and topics*

- To open an example Web page that you can modify to use for your own site, follow these steps:
  1. Choose Help ➤ Templates.
  2. Select a template from the list. Each template is a group of pages and images.
  3. A page will appear, and you can modify it as you wish.

NOTE

We'll discuss templates more completely later in the chapter in the "Templates" section.

- To look at the list of Frequently Asked Questions (FAQs), choose Help ➤ FAQ.
- To get contact information for help with technical questions, choose Help ➤ Technical Support.

File Selection and Network Operations

The following commands in the File menu open file selection dialog boxes: Open, Save, Save As, Import, Copy File, and Delete. In addition, the Browse buttons in various dialog boxes open similar dialog boxes. These file selection dialog boxes allow you to manipulate files on both your local disks and on your GNN directory. When you save or open a file on your GNN directory, you may be prompted for a user name and password if the file or location is protected.

The file selection dialog boxes are much like file selection dialog boxes in other Windows applications, as you can see here:

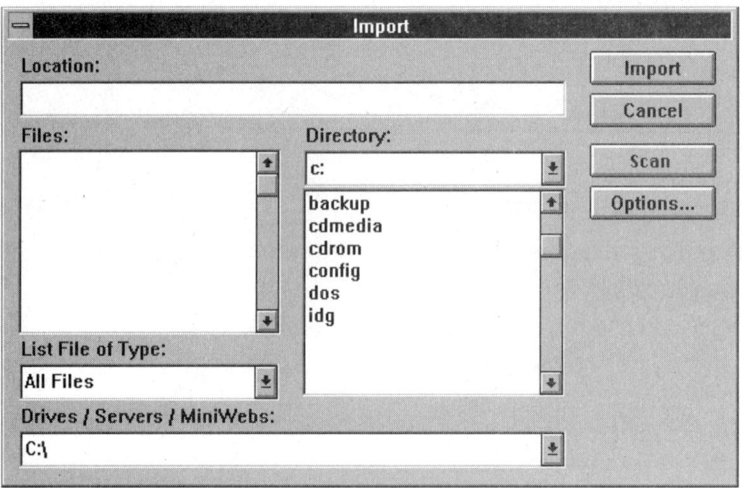

In addition to selecting local disk drives (such as C:\), the Drives/Servers/MiniWebs field lets you select the GNN server, which is **http://members.gnn.com**.

The Location field uses Windows file paths, such as C:\MYDIR\INDEX.HTM for local files. For files on a server, the Location field uses URLs, such as **http://members.gnn.com/netname/index.htm** For pages, use the file extension .HTM (for example, **mypage.htm**). For MiniWebs, use no file extension.

MiniWebs are stored both as directories and files, so they show up in both lists. Double-click on a MiniWeb in the Directory list to see a list of the files in the MiniWeb. Double-click on a MiniWeb in the Files list to perform the dialog box's action on the MiniWeb.

Choose Commands

GNNpress gives you several options for choosing commands to execute. You can use the toolbar buttons, the pull-down menus, or command keystrokes. These options give you speed when you know the command you want and a complete view of the commands when you need it.

Short Menus One of the choices when you select Tools ➤ Preferences ➤ General is Short Menus. Short menus are the default setting in GNNpress. You can uncheck this field to switch to the longer menus, which allow you to create MiniWebs and style sheets, and to set a number of additional preferences. In addition, the longer menus include menu options for advance features that are not currently supported by the GNN service. The sections that describe the menus in detail show specific differences between short menus and full menus. You can ignore menu items that are not explained in this tutorial.

Undo Commands The first items in the Edit pull-down menu are Undo and Redo. Each Undo command backtracks another step through the changes you have made. Redo reverses the last Undo.

Names for Pages and Directories

You can name page URLs, MiniWeb URLs, and directory URLs anything you want, but you will find your Web pages easier to manage if you give them distinctive names. Page URLs should end with .HTM. Directories should not have an extension.

Using GNNpress as a Browser

GNNpress is both a browsing and an authoring tool. As a browser, GNNpress offers many of the same capabilities you enjoy with the GNNworks browser. In this section, we'll give you a brief introduction to using the browser. In the section

"Browsing the Web," below, we'll go into more detail about what you can do with the GNNpress browser and how it differs from other popular browsers.

NOTE

The steps in this section assume that your modem is connected to the GNN service. You *can* use GNNpress to create and access local files when your computer is not connected to the Internet. For example, while you create pages, you may want to leave your modem off and then connect to the Internet when you are ready to put your pages up.

To test out GNNpress as a browser, try the following steps:

1. In the Location field in the Page window, type **http://gnn.com/gnn/GNNhome.html** and press ↵ to check out the GNN home page.
2. The small animation in the upper-right corner of the window tells you that the computer is transferring information. In addition, as with other browsers, messages at the bottom of the page in the status bar tell you when the connection is made and the size of the files that are being transferred. Figure 7 shows the home page as it appeared at the writing of this tutorial.

   This page changes every week, so don't worry if it doesn't look like the picture. The instructions that follow lead you to a gallery of paintings that includes the Mona Lisa. If you find links to something else that interests you, go ahead and try those links. The exact path to the gallery of paintings may change, too. If the path changes, go ahead and explore on your own.
3. Look for the text that says *Whole Internet Catalog* or *WIC*. Click on this text to open the home page for the catalog.
4. Click on *Webcrawler Select*.
5. As with most browsers, hyperlinks are colored and underlined. Move the cursor to the *Arts and Entertainment* hyperlink and click on it.
6. Scroll down and click on the *Arts Exhibits* link.
7. Scroll down the page until you find the *Leonardo da Vinci Museum* link (in the "Artists" section). Click on this link.
8. A page entitled *Leonardo da Vinci Museum* appears. Click on the *Leonardo da Vinci Museum* link.

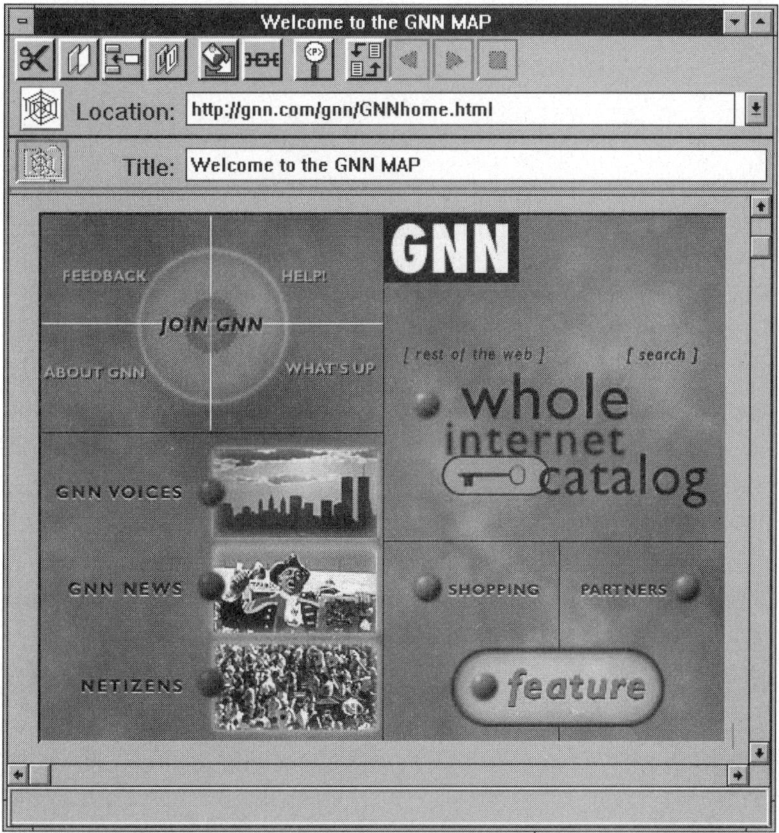

Figure 7: *The GNN home page, as viewed from the GNNpress browser*

9. Scroll down to the *Enter the Main Gallery* hyperlink and click on it.
10. Click on the *East Wing* link. Miniature images of famous paintings appear.
11. Scroll down the page until you see the *Mona Lisa* and click on it. After a time delay, she fills a big part of your screen.
12. Now traverse backward by clicking on the Back button at the top of the Page window twice. You can choose another wing of the museum to visit if you like.

As you browse the Web, you may see messages like "Could not contact server." This means the Web site you are trying to reach is either busy or not running. You can try the link again later.

NOTE

For more on using GNNpress as a browser, see "Browsing the Web," later in the chapter.

Creating Web Pages in GNNpress

Now that you're familiar with what GNNpress looks like, this section will take you through the very basics of how to create a simple page from a template. It also shows you how to use GNNpress to author a Web page and publish it. You'll create a simple Web page with text, links, and a way for people to send you e-mail. And, you'll be surprised how quickly you can create all of this.

TIP

Before starting, create a directory on your hard drive for saving files for your Web site. The name on your local drive could be **C:\MYDIR** or **C:\WEBSITE**. On the GNN service, you save your pages in a subdirectory that matches your *netname*, the name you use to connect to the service.

To create and edit your personal Web page, start by creating a blank page:

1. Choose File ➤ New Page. You'll see a blank window with the words *Please title this page* in the Title field and the title bar (see Figure 8). This window is just like a blank document in a word processor.
2. Let's start by giving the page a title. In the Title field above the blank area, type ____**'s Page** and fill in your name. For example, type **Joe's Page**. Press ↵, and the new title appears at the top of the window.

Next, type and format text in your page:

1. At the top of the page, type **Welcome to _____'s Home Page!** and fill in your name again. For example, type **Welcome to Joe's Home Page!** Then, click on the welcome message you typed to make sure the cursor is in this line.

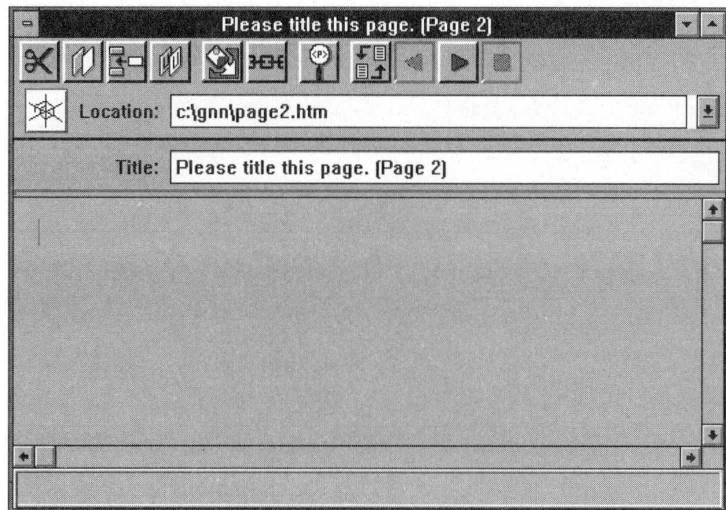

Figure 8: *Creating a blank page*

2. Choose Format ➤ Heading ➤ Hdg 1 and click. This makes your welcome message into a level one heading, big and bold. Your welcome message will look like this:

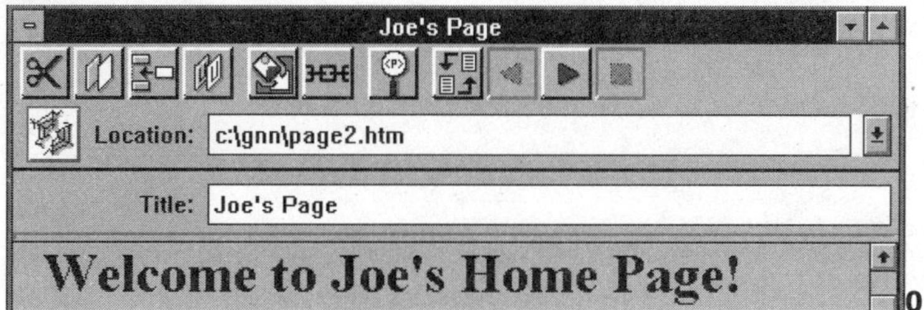

Now create a list after your welcome message:

1. Press ↵. Below your welcome message, type **These are my favorite links:** and press ↵. Then type **GNN** and **Webcrawler,** pressing ↵ after each. Your page should now look like this:

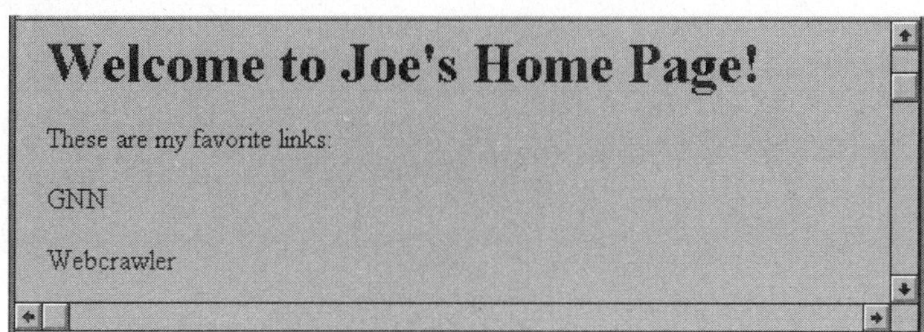

2. Use your mouse to highlight the GNN and Webcrawler lines. (Be sure to highlight all of both lines, including the paragraph returns.)
3. Choose Format ➤ List ➤ Bulleted List to make these two lines into a list. Your page should now look like this:

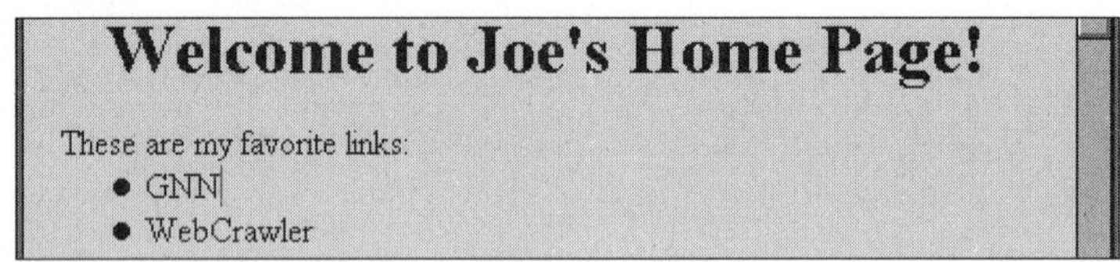

Now create some links to other pages:

1. Use your mouse to highlight the word *GNN*. Then choose Element ➤ Link.
2. In the Link dialog box that appears, type the URL for GNN's home page (**http://www.gnn.com/**) in the Link To Page field, then click on OK. The word *GNN* is now a link to GNN's home page.

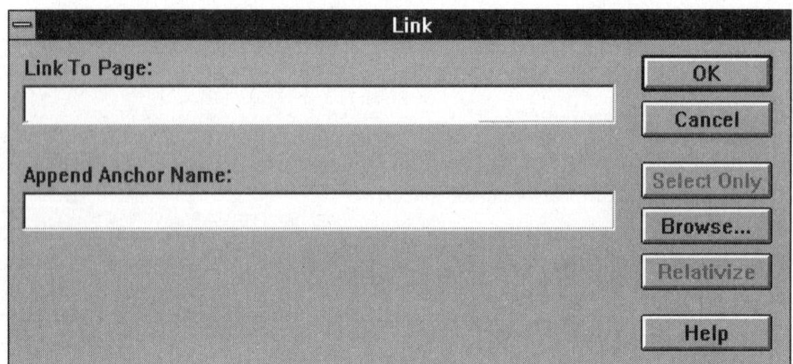

3. Double-click on the link you just created to the GNN home page. Double-clicking opens a second window.

NOTE

You must be a registerd GNN member to link to the Internet with this program. Don't worry if you accidentally single-click on the link. You can use the Back button later to move back to the page you are editing. Your changes to the page will still be there unless you click on the Reload Page button.

4. Follow the link on GNN's page to the Whole Internet Catalog, as we tried out above.
5. From the Whole Internet Catalog, follow the link to WebCrawler (see Figure 9).

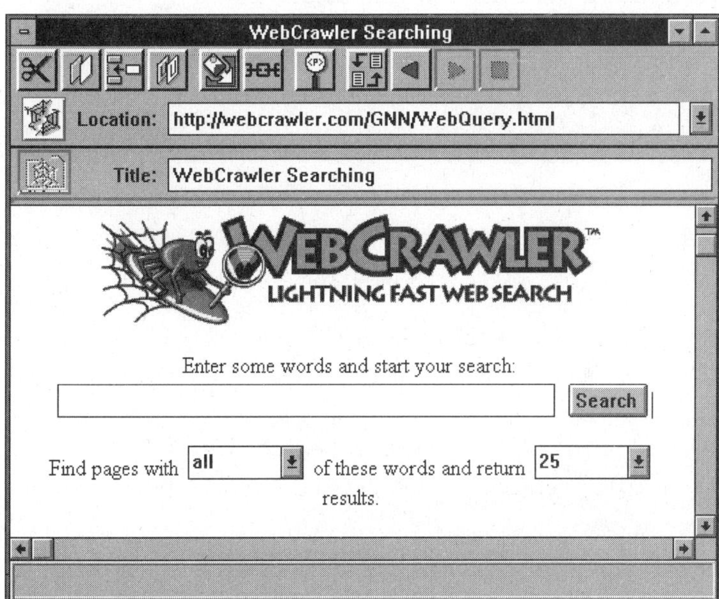

Figure 9: *Follow the links in the Whole Internet Catalog to get to WebCrawler.*

6. Click on the Copy URL button in the toolbar of the WebCrawler Page window.
7. Now move back to the window you were editing and use your mouse to highlight the word *Webcrawler*. Then choose Element ➤ Link to display the Link dialog box.
8. With the cursor in the Link To Page field, press Ctrl+V to paste the URL you copied from the WebCrawler page into this field. Then, click on OK. The word *Webcrawler* is now a link, too.

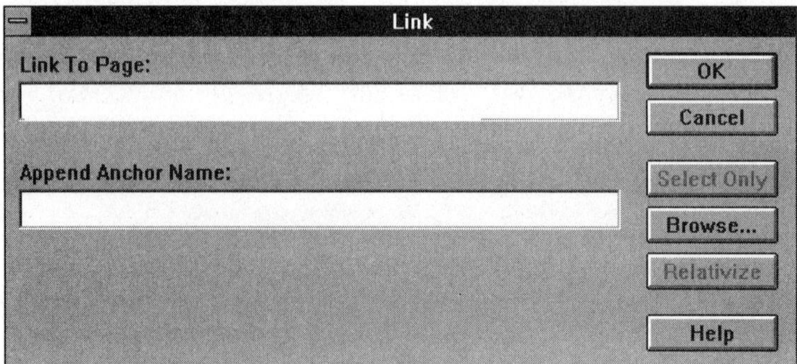

You may want to give the people viewing your page a way to get in touch with you via e-mail. To do this, you'll need to create an e-mail link:

1. After your list of links, type **Send me mail**.
2. Highlight the word *mail* and choose Element ➤ Link to open the Link dialog box again.
3. In the Link To Page field, type **mailto:** and then enter your e-mail address (see Figure 10). Then click on OK to close the dialog box.

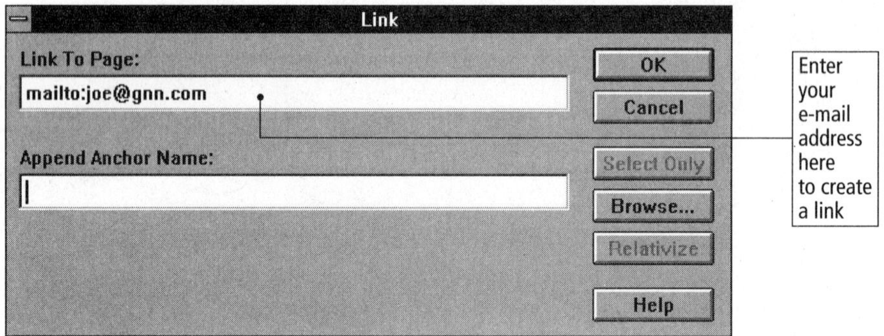

Figure 10: *Create an e-mail link using the Links dialog box.*

4. Click on the link you just created to try sending mail to yourself. You will see a page that looks like Figure 11. Go ahead and send yourself some mail.

NOTE

You must have set your Mail Address Host in Tool ➤ Preferences ➤ Network for this to work.

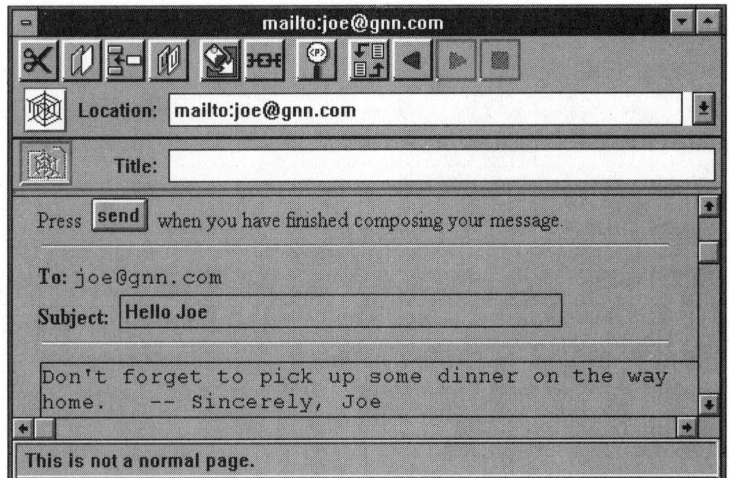

Figure 11: *The page for sending mail to an e-mail link*

Now try adding a background color and graphics to jazz up your page:

1. Click on the Back button until you are back at the page you have been creating.
2. Choose Format ➤ Body Attributes to display the Body Attributes dialog box, which lets you select colors for the background and text in your page.

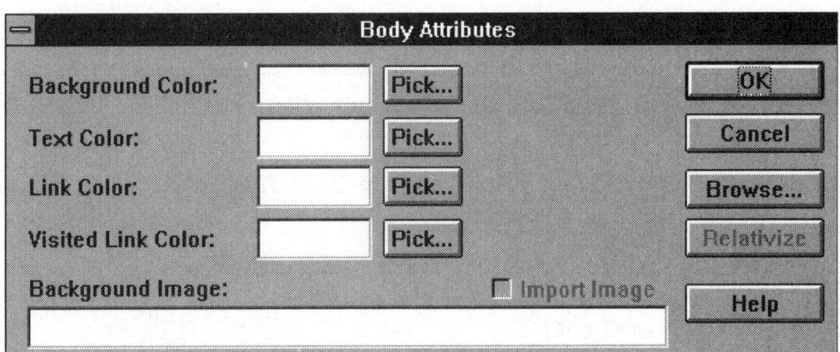

3. Click on the Pick button to the right of the Background Color field. You'll see the Color dialog box (see Figure 12). Click on a light background color like white or yellow. Then click on OK to close the Color dialog box. The hexadecimal code for the RGB color you selected will be shown in the Background Color field.
4. Click the OK button in the Body Attributes window. The background of your window will change to the color you selected.

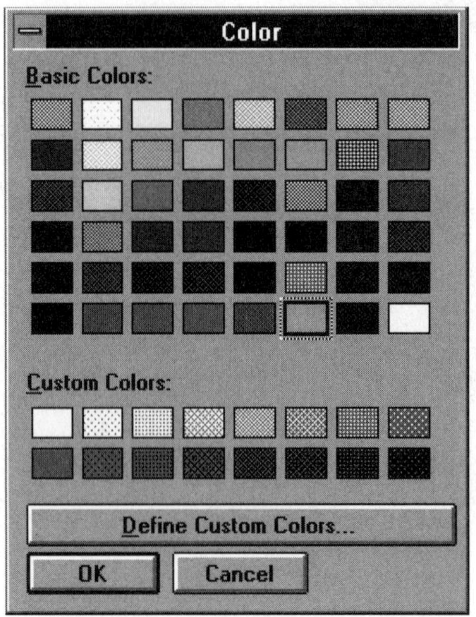

Figure 12:
Pick a background color for your page from the Color dialog box.

5. Now your page has a background color, but you probably want to add graphics to it, too. GNNpress comes with a library of clip art you can use in your pages. (Or you can use graphics you create with any other software.) To see the clip art library, choose Help ➤ Templates.

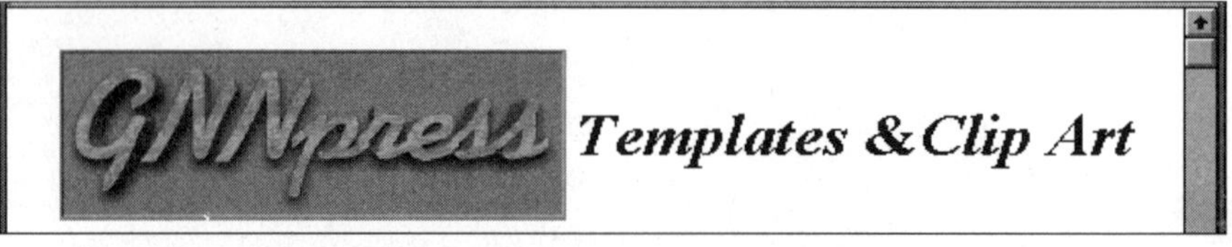

6. Scroll down and click on the link to the Clip Art Library.
7. Scroll down until you see the list of Rules in the clip art collection. Click on the <u>*Full Collection*</u> link to see all the horizontal rules.

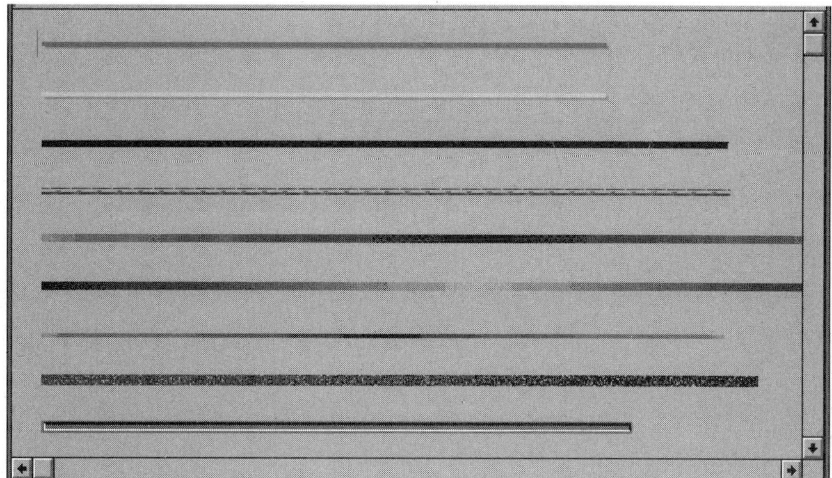

8. Find your favorite rule and drag your mouse across it to highlight it. Then press Ctrl+C to copy the rule.
9. Move back to the window for your page. (It should be under the clip art window.) You can use the Window menu to select it.
10. Place the cursor in your page where you want the line inserted and press Ctrl+V to paste the rule you selected. Your page should now look like the one in Figure 13. You can copy and paste graphics from any Web page to your page.
11. An Option box appears. Leave Relative checked and click on OK.

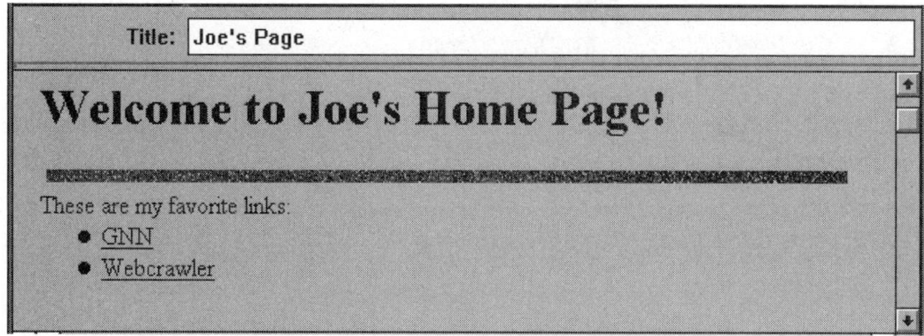

Figure 13: *A rule pasted into a page from the clip art window*

Saving to Your Local Drive

As you create Web pages, you should save copies of them to your local disk drive. In fact, you can use GNNpress to create and save Web pages even when your modem is not connected. Then, when you connect to the Web, you can publish your pages as we'll describe in the next section.

To save your home page to your local disk, follow these steps:

1. Choose File ➤ Save As. A file selection dialog box appears (see Figure 14).

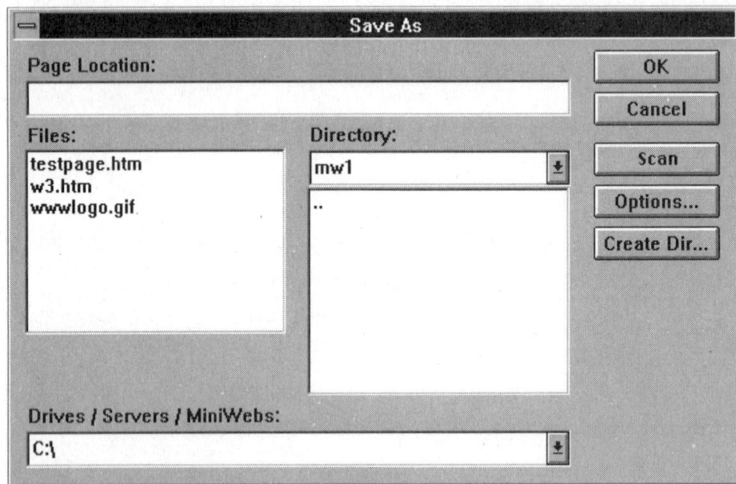

Figure 14: *The Save As dialog box, where you can save pages to your local disk*

2. Select your local drive in the field labeled Drives/Servers/MiniWebs.
3. In the Directory list, double-click on the directory where you want to save your page.
4. Move the cursor to the Page Location field. Replace the existing file name with **INDEX.HTM**. (Use the file name INDEX.HTM for your "home page"—the first page you want people to see when they visit your pages. If people don't specify a file name when they visit your page, most Web servers use INDEX.HTM as the default HTML file to load.) For example, the location on your local drive could be C:\MYDIR\INDEX.HTM.
5. Click on OK when you have finished setting the location.

Publishing to the GNN Service

Publishing with GNNpress is as easy as saving a Web file to your local computer—the three steps are the same, except you save to the GNN server instead of to your local disk drive, and you need to enter your username and password.

To publish your personal home page to the GNN Web server, follow these steps:

1. Choose File ➤ Save As. The file selection dialog box you saw when you saved the file locally appears.

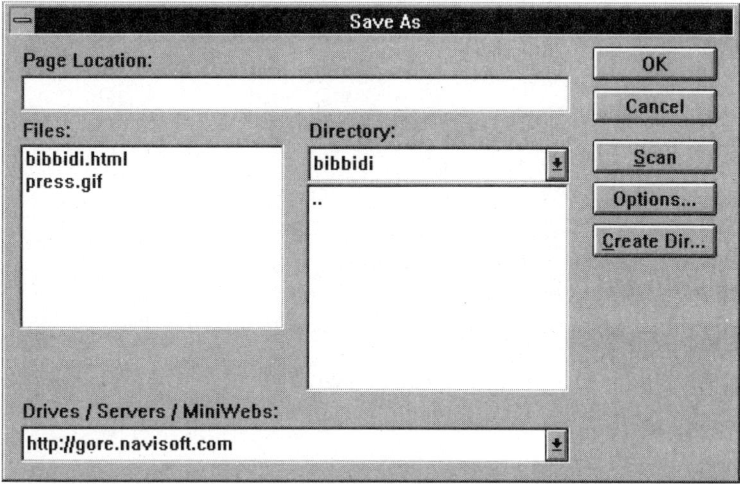

2. Click on the arrow to the right of the Drives/Servers/MiniWebs field to open a drop-down list.
3. Select **http://members.gnn.com/**, which is the location of the GNN server. If this location is not listed in the field, type it directly into the Page Location field.
4. In the Directory list, scroll down to the directory with your username and double-click on it to open it. The page location changes to **http://members .gnn.com/netname/**
5. Move the cursor to the Page Location field and add the file name **INDEX .HTML** to the end of the page location, just as you would to save your home page to your local drive.
6. Click on OK to save your page. Type your username and password if GNNpress prompts you for them. GNNpress will save the page and all the

image files (lines, bullets, photos) associated with it. Saving the file across the network may take a few seconds.

- If a page with the file name you typed already exists (for example, if you typed INDEX.HTM), a dialog box will ask you whether to save the file, don't save it, or rename the page.
- If any of your images already exist in this directory, GNNpress asks you if you want to save it, don't save it, rename it, or cancel.

Now your page is on GNN's Web server! Your friends with Web browsers can see it if they look at **http://members.gnn.com.netname/**, substituting your username for *netname*.

TIP

Don't forget to add your page to your own Hot List so you can get to it easily. We'll explain how to create a Hot List in the section "Browsing the Web," below.

If you want to change your page in the future, just display your page with GNNpress. Make your changes with GNNpress, then choose File ➤ Save to publish your changes.

Basics about the World Wide Web

This tutorial covers many details about the Web: how to author pages, manage and arrange them, and publish them to a server. In this section, we cover a few basic concepts that appear in several places in the rest of the text.

NOTE

If you are already familiar with the World Wide Web, you may want to skip this review section and go ahead to the section on "Browsing the Web," later in this chapter.

Hypertext Markup Language (HTML)

The *Hypertext Markup Language* (HTML) is the standard language that Web pages use to specify the links and structure of a document. The Web itself is independent of the data transferred, but all current browsers can render HTML into a readable page on your screen.

Detailed information about the HTML standard is available on the Web at **http://www.w3.org/pub/WWW/** (follow the hyperlink to HTML).

In this tutorial we cover only a few of the details about HTML, because GNNpress makes most of them transparent to you. You edit with GNNpress much as you would with a traditional word processor—you don't have to learn complicated HTML codes. However, understanding how HTML works will help you design better pages.

There are some limitations to Web publishing because of HTML's inability to support some common attributes of publications (like nicely formatted equations), but there are compensating benefits, mainly the ability to create a link to a page anywhere in the world. After you have created a page, GNNpress helps you package and save it onto a friendly server near you, and anyone with access to any Web browser can access it.

Structure and Layout of HTML Documents

There is an important difference between Web pages and the documents you create with a typical word processor. With a word processor, you assign appearances to elements that make up your document. For example, a document contains various levels of headings, paragraphs, bulleted lists, numbered lists, page headings, and page numbers.

When you create a Web page, you cannot have this much flexibility. You specify only the structure of the page—six levels of headings, three types of paragraphs, three kinds of lists, a few fonts. GNNpress lets you create a Style Sheet that defines the appearance of each structure, but people browsing with another tool can define these relations differently. In short, the reader controls the appearance of the page, not the author or publisher.

Markup Tags

HTML contains several categories of "tags" you use to structure pages. The minimum set of tags you need to create a page are *Titles*, *Headings*, and *Paragraphs*. This section just gives you an overview of the types of formatting HTML allows; GNNpress handles the syntax of the tags for you.

Titles Every HTML page file must a title. A title is generally displayed above the page in the Web browser and is used to identify it in other contexts (for example, the title appears in the Hot List). Choose about half a dozen words that describe the document's purpose. Moreover, various Web search engines use the title for search indexes.

Headings HTML has six levels of headings, numbered 1 through 6, with 1 being the most prominent. Headings are displayed in larger and/or bolder fonts than normal body text.

Paragraphs Most of the text in Web pages is in paragraphs. Browsers handle the lengths of the lines. If you change the size of a window, the lines on the pages rewrap correctly.

Additional Markup Tags Your document can also have various kinds of lists (unnumbered, numbered, term-definition pairs) that you can nest. You can also include quotes, addresses, and text that is *preformatted* so that the spacing and line breaks will not change.

Character Formatting HTML allows formatting of specific words or characters. You can designate words to be emphasized, underlined, italicized, and more.

Links to Other Documents

HTML's distinctive feature is the *hyperlink*, which is a link to other documents. These appear in a distinctive font, and clicking on one will fetch the page it references.

Link addresses can be relative to the current page or absolute. You can have links to other locations in the same page and links to specific places in other documents.

Images, Graphics, and Other Special Features

HTML includes mechanisms for transmitting *inline* images—that is, images included on the page—and *external* images, which you click on a link to display.

Documents can also include graphics, animation, sound, and other special files by associating an external program that can display or play them.

Uniform Resource Locators (URLs)

The cryptic strings of characters (like **http://www.sybex.com)** you keep seeing in advertisements are addresses on the Web. These addresses are called *Uniform Resource Locators* or *URLs*. Browsers use these addresses to find Web pages and other files on the Internet.

You can think of a URL as being a little like a file location on your disk drive. However, the URL also tells the location of the file on the Web and how to read the file.

Anatomy of a URL

URLs contain three types of information. (Well, if you start writing programs for the Web, they can contain more than that. But, we won't get into that here.)

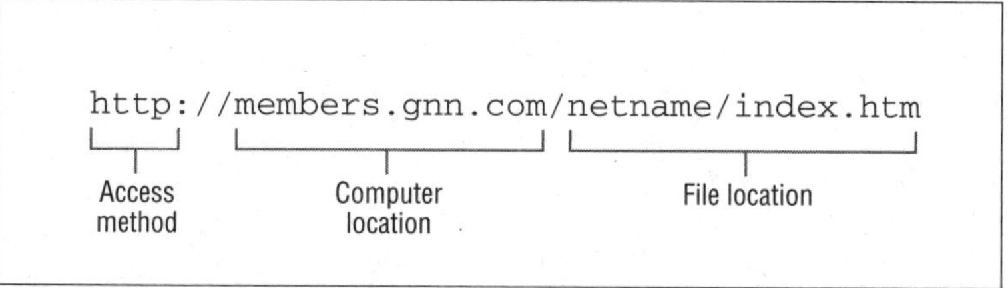

- Access method: Most URLs you see have an access method of http, which stands for *Hypertext Transfer Protocol*. This is the standard protocol used to send Web pages across the Net. (That's really all you need to know about it unless you want to write programs for the Web.) If you see a

Web address starting with something like **www.mycompany.com**, you need to put **http://** before that address to read that page with GNNpress.

- Other common access methods are: file, ftp, and mailto. Read the **http://www.ncsa.uiuc.edu/** page if you want to learn more about URLs for other access methods.
- Computer location: The next part of the URL tells which computer holds the file. The location is usually **www.** plus the *domain* name you see in e-mail addresses from this location (such as **aol.com** or **gnn.com**). Some URLs contains a different prefix or no prefix before the domain name. You may occasionally see a number following a colon after the domain name. This is called a *port number*.
- File location: The last part of the URL tells where to find the file on the computer. The file location can contain a directory path and/or a file name. If you omit the directory, the top-level directory on the Web server is used. If you omit the file name, the default "home page" file name on the Web server is used. On most Web servers, the default home page is **index.htm** or **index.html**. Table 1 explains how the file locations in URLs work.

Table 1: File locations in URLs

LOCATION IN URL	DIRECTORY	FILE
.../subdir/file.htm	Use the **subdir** directory below the top-level directory.	Use the **file.htm** file.
.../file.htm	Use the top-level directory.	Use the **file.htm** file.
.../subdir/	Use the **subdir** directory below the top-level directory.	Use the default home page name for this Web server.
.../	Use the top-level directory.	Use the default home page name for this Web server.

With GNN, you save your pages in a subdirectory that matches your *netname*, the name you use to connect to the service. Your default home page is **index.htm**.

Browsing the Web

You've already taken the GNNpress browser for a quick spin above, but the browser has many more capabilities. In this section, we'll go into more detail on how to use GNNpress to navigate and read information on the World Wide Web. While GNNpress is primarily a tool for creating HTML and publishing to your GNN directory, it is also a browser. Familiarity with GNNpress and its differences from other Web browsers is also important when you create pages.

NOTE

To use the GNNpress as a browser you first must subscribe to the GNN service.

Opening Pages

To use the Page window as a browser when you know the URL, type the URL in the Location field in your Page window. Position your cursor in the field and edit the current URL. You can use the Backspace key to get rid of the current URL and type in a new one, or you can move the cursor and edit specific parts of the current URL.

For example, to look at the Global Network Navigator home page, type **http://www.gnn.com/** and then press ↵.

What You See When the Page Opens

A small Web animation appears in the upper-right corner of the GNNpress Page window. This animation indicates that GNNpress is searching for and loading the page. The status bar at the bottom of the window shows what GNNpress is doing. The page you requested is shown when it has been loaded.

Notice several changes while the page is loading:

- The Stop button in the toolbar becomes "active" and is no longer fuzzy. If you want to stop the current function—for example, loading a new Web page—click on this button. To resume loading after you have stopped it, select Browse ➤ Reload Page or click on the Reload Page button. This transfers the page and images again.

- The status bar at the bottom of the window shows a message about the current state of the current action, or, if your cursor is pointing to a toolbar button, displays the button's function.

- If you have set your preferences so that pictures are loaded by default, you may see hour glasses appear in the page, soon to be replaced by images. The hour glass appears while an image is being loaded, and is replaced by the image when it is ready to be displayed. If your system and network connection are fast enough, images may load before you see the hour glass.

- If you have set your preferences so that pictures are not displayed, a question mark appears and the image does not appear automatically. This is a useful option if your modem is not very fast. In this case, you click the mouse on the question mark to cause the image to appear.

- A lightning bolt appears if the image cannot be loaded. This usually occurs because a hyperlink has broken.

Multiple Windows, Multiple Pages One of the more useful features of GNNpress is the ability to open multiple Page windows and browse in all of them. The number of windows you can open is limited by the amount of memory (RAM) your computer lets GNNpress use. You will see a message if you do not have enough memory to open another window.

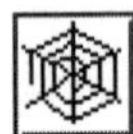

Cloning a Page Double-click on Page button to the left of the Location field to open another window showing the same page. Select Window ➤ Cascade to view them both.

Unsuccessful Openings

Sometimes the URLs or pages you request do not open successfully. When GNNpress cannot open a page, the server usually gives a helpful message. Some of the reasons for the lack of success are beyond your control.

TIP

You should always check the URL you entered first to make sure you typed it correctly.

A common cause of problems is that the link you tried to follow was incorrect. Sometimes a URL connected to link has moved, yet the link is still there. You can sometimes figure out bad links. Look for the following possibilities if you typed the URL correctly:

- Some URLs require a trailing slash at the end of a directory.
- Sometimes the file name requires the .HTML file ending and the author forgot to use it. Try .HTM as well.

Here are some messages you might see:

- **Retrieve Failed**: Usually the result of a server error, which may be out of your control. Browse ➤ Reload Page may produce the correct result.
- **Couldn't Find Server**: GNNpress couldn't find the URL that contains the page. Either the URL is wrong or the server that contains the page is down.
- **Not Found**: The file name is wrong, even though the server may be correct. Sometimes this occurs because a link points to a file that no longer exists.
- **Couldn't Find File/Page/MiniWeb** or **Forbidden**: The file is not available. Sometimes this is because there are too many people trying to access the server that contains the page you want to see. Access to a particular page may also be forbidden.

Different Ways to Navigate

As you'll see, there are several ways to find and display the page of a URL in GNNpress:

- If you know the URL, you can type it directly into the Open dialog box that appears when you select File ➤ Open.
- You can follow a hyperlink in an open page to a new page (a new URL).

- Each GNNpress Page window keeps a history of the current session. Using the Back and Forward buttons in the toolbar at the top of the window, you can traverse to any page in the list of pages that GNNpress has displayed in this Page window in this session. You can also scroll through the list of available pages.

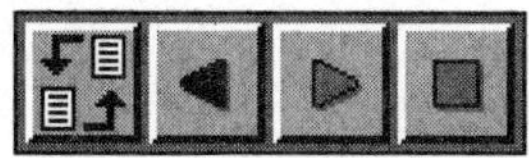

- The GNNpress Hot List keeps track of addresses that you have placed there. You can use the Hot List (by selecting Browse ➤ Add To Hot List) to "remember" names of interesting Web pages, and consult your Hot List (by selecting Browse ➤ Hot List) when you want to return to a URL you previously found.

NOTE

We'll explain more about Hot Lists later.

- GNNpress also keeps a Global History of the current session. You can jump back to any page in the list of pages that GNNpress has displayed in any Page Window by selecting Browse ➤ Global History and selecting from the list that appears.

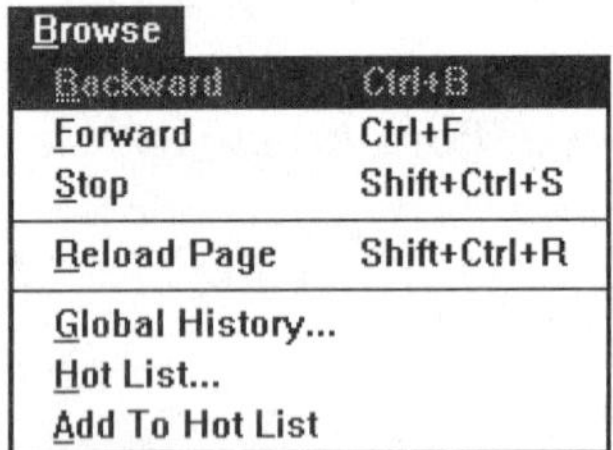

NOTE

There are also many Web pages that provide information services for the World Wide Web. You can use these to search for information. We'll take a look at some of these later in the chapter.

If you have moved all the way back to the first page of your browser selection, you should notice that the Back button is no longer fuzzy. To move backward a page, click on the Back button. The backward function is also available when you choose Browse ➤ Backward.

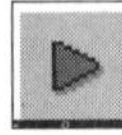

If you have moved all the way back to the first page of your browser selection, you should notice that the Forward button is no longer fuzzy. To move to a Web page you have just come back from, click on the Forward button. The forward function is also available when you choose Browse ➤ Forward.

Notice also that the underline for the hyperlink you followed is purple instead of blue, and the underline is now dashed. Purple text means that the page that this link points to is *cached* (stored in local memory). Hence it is much faster to use that link again, because GNNpress no longer has to download the page across the Internet.

NOTE

The network link to the URL is not kept open after the page is transferred.

Reloading Pages

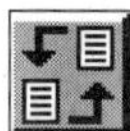

When you load a page, it is cached (that is, it is stored in your computer's memory). If you open the same page again, it does not have to be transferred over the network again. However, if for some reason you need to reload the current page you are viewing in the Page window (perhaps because you think the original page has changed), you can use the Reload button in the toolbar or the menu item Browse ➤ Reload Page. This causes the page to be transferred over the network again, even if the page is locally cached.

When you reload the page, GNNpress shows any changes that have taken place in the document since you last visited it. Some Web pages change often, sometimes by the minute. Weather or time Web sites reload the current page with the current data.

If you are also editing pages with GNNpress (in addition to browsing), you should save any changes to your pages before you reload. Attempting to reload an unsaved page that has been edited produces a dialog box asking you to save your changes or reload and lose changes.

Stopping the Current Action

If you want to stop the current function (for example, to stop loading a new Web page or image), click on the Stop button in the toolbar. The status bar at the bottom of the Page window says *aborted http://....* To resume loading after you have stopped, select Browse ➤ Reload Page. This causes the URL to be transferred again.

Viewing Locations within a Page

Some pages have links to *internal* anchors, which look like hyperlinks that have been already been used. They simply point to a location within the same page. You can read a page by just scrolling upward and downward, but these anchors let you move to specific sections. Click on the link to jump to the anchor it points to.

History—Remember Where You've Been

You can open URLs that your have viewed before during this session using GNNpress' history:

- Window History: Click the down arrow to the right of the Location field to see a list of all Web pages you have visited during this session in that Page window. You can reopen any page in this list by selecting it. This menu only lists pages opened from this window; it does not list pages visited from other windows you may have opened.
- Global History: A similar list of all Web pages viewed by any Page window during this session is available if you choose Browse ➤ Global History (see Figure 15). A list of Web pages appears. If the list is too long to fit in the small window, use the scrolling arrows on the right side of the window. To view a page from this history, double-click on it to select it from the list, then click on the Fetch button.

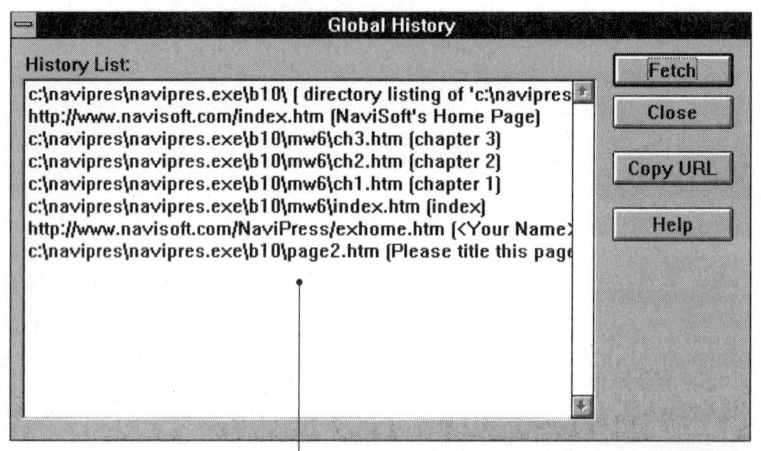

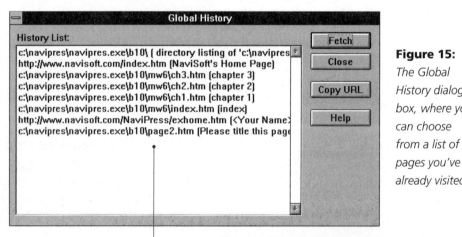

Figure 15: *The Global History dialog box, where you can choose from a list of pages you've already visited*

Closing the GNNpress application automatically clears your global history. Each launch of GNNpress begins a new global history.

Hot Lists—Keep Track of Interesting Web Pages

GNNpress also allows you to keep a *Hot List* from session to session. This is a list of Web sites (URLs) that you think you might visit frequently, or that you want to remember and access easily. Unlike the history list, the Hot List is maintained after you finish your session and exit GNNpress.

This list is stored in your GNNpress preference file, which GNNpress creates internally when you use the Preferences option under the Tools menu.

WARNING

Deleting this file erases your Hot List.

Adding or Opening a Page Here's how to add or open a page to your Hot List:

1. Go to that page in the Page window (enter the URL in the Location field, or if you have visited it already, choose it either by selecting Browse ➤ Global History or by scrolling the arrow to the right of the Location field).
2. Choose Browse ➤ Add To Hot List to add the page to the list. To see the list, choose the menu item Browse ➤ Hot List. The Hot List dialog box will appear, as shown in Figure 16.
3. Double-clicking on any entry in the Hot List brings up that page in the Page window. Alternatively, you can single-click on any entry to select it, then click on the Fetch button. If no entry is selected, the Fetch button is inactive.

TIP

You can open a Global History or Hot List item without opening a new page by using the Copy URL button to copy the URL of an item to the clipboard. Then, in a Page window, paste the URL into the Location field. Delete the URL in the location field. Paste the new URL into the Location Field. Press ↵.

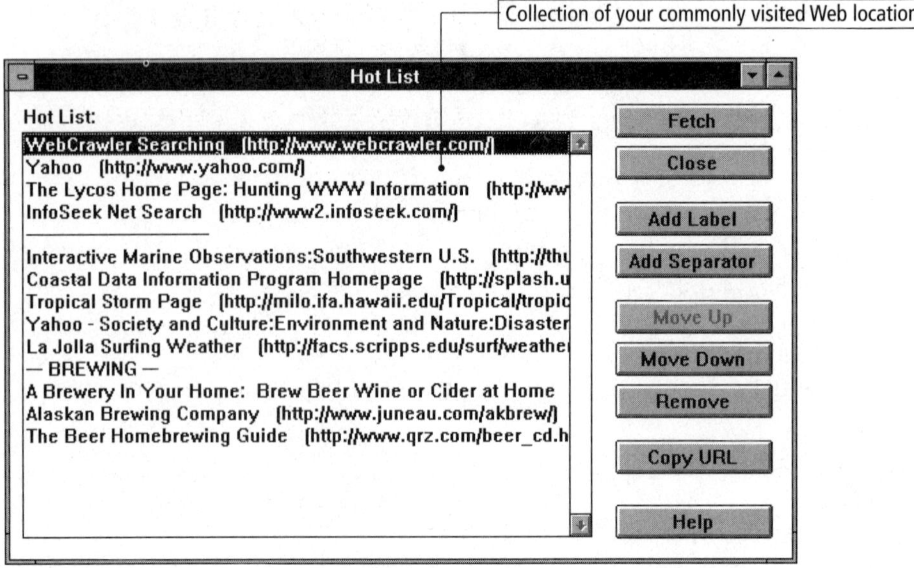

Figure 16: *You can choose among all the entries in your Hot List in the Hot List dialog box.*

Editing and Formatting the Hot List When you add a page to your Hot List, it is added to the end of the list, but you can edit and rearrange your Hot List. The buttons in the Hot List have these functions:

Fetch	Causes the selected page to be displayed in the Page window. Click on Fetch after you have selected an entry from the list.
Close	Closes the Hot List dialog box.
Add Label	Allows you to add a label above a selection in the list. When you click on Add Label, a dialog box appears and asks you for the name of the label. Type the name in the box indicated.
Add Separator	Adds a line across the list above the selected item.
Move Up	Select an entry, a separator, or a label. Click on Move Up to raise the selection one notch up the list.
Move Down	Select an entry, a separator, or a label. Click on Move Down to lower the selection one notch down the list.
Remove	Removes the selection from the list.
Copy URL	Copies the URL of the selection. You can then paste the URL.
Help	Invokes the help window about the Hot List.

Directory Services—Finding Things on the Web

Normally you find information on the Web by following links. While this mechanism often leads you to unexpected treasures, it is not efficient. The Web has a great navigation architecture, but it lacks an information architecture. The normal method of browsing is somewhat like using a library whose main search mechanism is to pick up a book and then follow references from book to book. Moreover, the books' titles relate only vaguely to their content. Without indexing services and ways to search for information, Web pages are strewn throughout file systems all over the world with no relationship to each other except through URLs.

Fortunately, several institutions and companies have filled this void by creating Web pages whose main purpose is to catalog and provide search mechanisms to find other pages on the Web. Because they were created independently, their search mechanisms are different, so we do not describe them here. Some of the more popular sites are listed here (there are many, many more):

- Global Network Navigator and the Whole Internet Catalog (**http://www.gnn.com/**). This site gives you news, articles, and an online community called "Netizens."
- WebCrawler (**http://www.webcrawler.com/**), a keyword searcher of Web pages.
- Yahoo (**http://www.yahoo.com/**), a catalog and search engine.
- Infoseek (**http://www.infoseek.com/**), a full-text commercial search service.
- Lycos (**http://lycos.cs.cmu.edu/**), an Internet catalog served by Carnegie-Mellon University.

Printing a Page

Once you've found the page you are looking for, you can print it out on your printer. Choose File ➤ Print to print the current page. Selecting File ➤ Print Setup lets you specify various printing options—size of page, orientation, scale, and color.

A Summary of Commands for Browsing the Web

Here is a quick summary of commands you can use while browsing the Web:

To Get Pages

- When you know the URL, type it into the Location field at the top of the page, or select File ➤ Open and enter it into the Location field of the Open dialog box.
- Use hyperlinks: Single-click on the hyperlink (double-click to get the page in a new window).
- Follow window history: Click on the drop-down arrow beside the Location field in Page window to display a list of the pages you've visited in this window.
- Follow global history: Select Browse ➤ Global History, and click on the Fetch button in the dialog box that appears.
- Use your Hot List: Select Browse ➤ Hot List and pick a page from the list you've created.
- Use the Back button: Click on the Back button in the toolbar to view the previous page.
- Use the Forward button: Click on the Forward button in the toolbar to see the next page.

To View Pages

- If you don't want to see images: Select Tools ➤ Preferences ➤ General and uncheck Load Remote Images.
- If you don't want to wait for a page to finish loading: Click on the Stop button in the toolbar.
- If the page didn't load properly or you want to load it again: Select Browse ➤ Reload Page or click on the Reload Page button in the toolbar.

To Use the Hot List

- To add a URL to your Hot List: Select Browse ➤ Add To Hot List.
- To edit your Hot List: Select Browse ➤ Hot List.

Creating More Complex Pages

Earlier in the chapter, you created a very basic home page to test out some of the GNNpress features. But you can create much more complex pages, complete with tables, graphics, and other special elements. The remainder of this chapter serves as a quick reference for how to create and implement different effects and elements using GNNpress.

Design Guidelines

Creating HTML is easy—witness the proliferation of Web pages—and GNNpress makes it easier. The following hints will help you plan and create better pages.

Headings

- Do not use a header level smaller than Hdg 3 for text that you want to be read easily or in the main part of the document.
- Use the various Hdg styles as headers. To make text dark or boldface, select Format ➤ Type Style ➤ Bold or Format ➤ Type Style ➤ Strong.

Images and Graphics

- In the Alignment dialog box that appears when you select Element ➤ Image, check the Bottom, Left, or Right button for images, so text wraps nicely for those readers who make their windows narrow. If you use Middle or Top, there will be a large gap between lines.
- Some readers still use browsers that don't display images. You should add some text in the Text For Non-graphic Browsers field for these readers. For non-linked images, this field should describe the image. For hyperlinked images, this field should say what page the hyperlink goes to or the name of the linked page. Use brackets to surround the text in the Text For Non-graphic Browsers field; for example, *[Lightning bolt image]*. This has a nice look on browsers that don't show graphics (like Lynx).
- Keep image files smaller than about 30 Kbytes.

Structure of a Set of Web Pages

- When including textual or pictorial navigation aids, place cues on the left side to go back or to the previous page. Use the right side to go forward or to the next page.

Continued on next page

- When doing slide presentations, use Prev/Next links, instead of Next/Prev, to match the organization of browser navigation buttons.
- To keep the reader from getting lost, organize the information in a hierarchical format with a shallow depth (about five layers maximum), and a wide base.
- Let readers move down the hierarchy quickly by providing bulleted/graphical indexes or main menus with textual and/or visual clues about the pages to which you link.
- Typically, the title of the page should also be in the text of the page as a Hdg 1.
- Bulleted graphics or image maps can exist on your page and are often next to the Hdg 1 title.
- Provide header and footer navigation bars (text or graphics) for moving up and down throughout the hierarchy.

HTML vs. Word Processors

When the Web was created, people first wrote pages by typing HTML tags by hand—just as they would write computer programs. GNNpress lets you create pages without worrying about the HTML tags. You edit Web pages as you would edit documents with a word processor.

You'll need to remember that HTML does not give you as much control over page layout as a word processor. The reader also has some control over how your pages look. The reader decides how big to make the browser window, and often the reader can even change the font your pages use.

Here are some tips about how to design around the limitations of HTML:

- Paragraph Formatting: In some word processors, if you want to grab paragraph formatting when copying a selection into so that you can paste it, you grab the entire line at the end of the paragraph. In GNNpress, you need to grab the blank line before the paragraph, instead. (In HTML, the information about the paragraph is stored in a tag before the paragraph.)
- Bulleted lists: Bullets are not characters that can be selected. Think of them as part of the line break between paragraphs. The only way to select

or delete bullets is to select or delete the line break.

- Titles: Every HTML file has a title. This is different from the file name. The title is what will be placed at the top of a window displaying the page. Changing the title will not change the URL, nor will changing the URL change the title.
- Images: GNNpress can display GIF, JPEG, and XBM files as inline images at the moment. Other graphic file formats require an external viewer.

TIP

For more information, see the Web page **http://www.w3.org/pub/WWW/MarkUp/**. Follow any of the links in the "Specs, Drafts, and Reports" section.

Starting Points

You can start your Web page from scratch, or you can import information from another Web page and use it as the foundation for your own page.

Starting from an Empty Page

If you do not have documents in another format that you can import or transfer into your Web pages, you can always create them from scratch. There are several ways to open an empty page:

- In a Page window, choose File ➤ New Page.
- In a MiniWeb window, choose File ➤ New Page. Or, click on the toolbar's Page button.

Setting the Start-Up Page Default

If you always want to begin with a certain kind of page, you can set your GNNpress start-up preferences to reflect this. For example, if you are a designer, you may want to set your preferences so that you get a blank page to begin working on every time you start GNNpress.

Here's how to set this up:

1. Choose Tools ➤ Preferences ➤ General.
2. Select one of three choices for the Startup View:
    - Home Page: opens with the page you specify.
    - Blank Page: opens with a new, empty page.
    - MiniWeb: opens with a new MiniWeb and a new empty page in the MiniWeb.

Now, whenever you start GNNpress, the kind of page you specified will be displayed, and you can get right to work.

Opening an Existing Page

Probably the most useful attribute of browsing with GNNpress is the tool's ability to browse and author pages at the same time. You can edit a page as you browse and then either save the file to your GNN directory, or to your local files for further editing. Pages at Web sites you visit can be used the same way. Saving the file to your local directory provides a quick way to reformat the page as you wish and then publish it on your GNN directory.

You can also copy an existing page to a new file using File ➤ Copy File. You can then edit that new file without making changes to the existing page.

Importing HTML Text and Graphics

You can also import text from another Web page:

1. Place your cursor where you wish the imported file to be inserted.
2. Choose File ➤ Import. You will see the Import dialog box (see Figure 17), from which you can select files to import. The dialog box has the following choices:
    - Import: Imports whatever file is selected in the dialog into the document where your cursor is placed.
    - Cancel: Closes the Import dialog box.

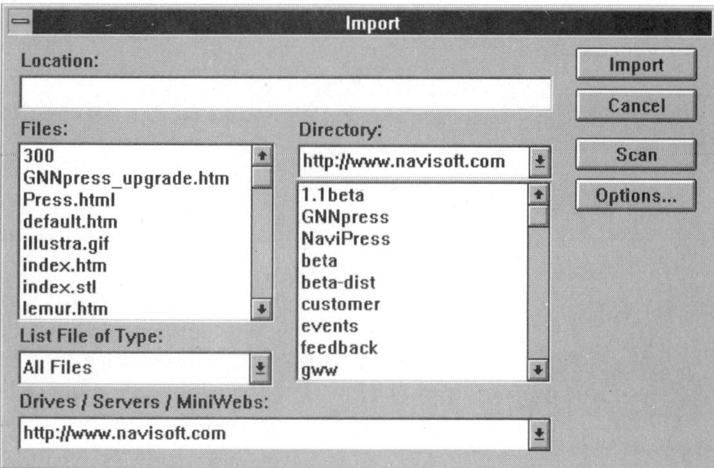

Figure 17: *The Import dialog box, where you can choose files to import into your Web page*

- Scan: Browse your local files or your GNN service directory. If you enter a site that you don't have permission to browse, the message "Cannot Browse Location" appears in the box where the file names would otherwise appear.
- Options: Click on the Options button to display the Options dialog box (see Figure 18).

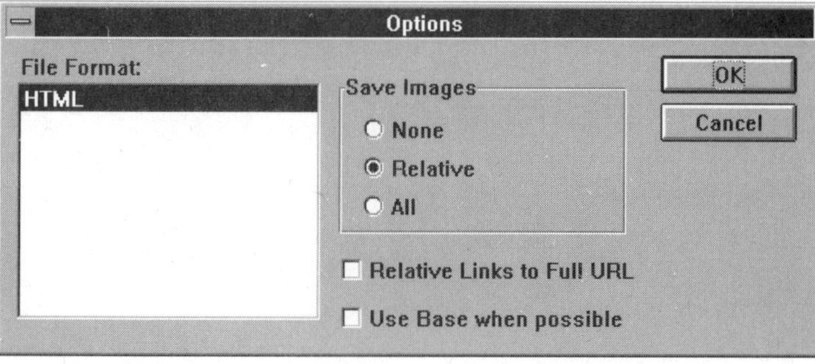

Figure 18: *The Import Options dialog box, where you can select options for files you are importing*

3. The Options dialog box contains the following choices:

- None: If there are any images in the page you are importing, they are not imported to the same directory that contains the page. If you want the imported page to reference the images in their original location, check the Relative Links To Full URL field.
- Relative: All relative images are saved locally into your directory, and they are linked within the text of the document as local images.

NOTE

See the "Links" section later in this chapter for an explanation of relative and absolute references.

- All: All image files in the document are copied to your directory.
- Relative Links To Full URL: All relative links in the imported page are converted to absolute URLs.
- Use Base When Possible: Some HTML files use a base parameter. If found, use this in calculating URLs.

4. When you are ready to import the file, click on Import in the Import dialog box, and the file will be placed at the location of the cursor in the original page.

Working with Text in Web Pages

Once you have started the page you want to work on and have given it a title, you are ready to start entering text. When you click the mouse pointer in the text, a flashing I-beam cursor marks the point where text will be placed when you type. Once you have positioned the cursor, there are several ways to add text to your page.

The most basic way to add text to your page is to simply type it in using the keyboard. The text you type appears at the cursor position, and you do not see any HTML tags around it.

TIP

If you want to see and edit the HTML code, choose Tools ➤ Show HTML. We'll talk more about looking at the HTML source code in the section "Viewing and Editing HTML," later.

You can also paste text into your page from almost any source. For example, in Microsoft Word or PowerPoint, select the text you want to paste and then choose Edit ➤ Copy (or press Ctrl+C). You can then paste the text into your Page window at the cursor location by choosing Edit ➤ Paste (or by pressing Ctrl+V).

If you have multiple Page windows open, you can drag and drop text between them:

1. In any GNNpress Page window, highlight the text you want to move. (You cannot drag and drop text from other applications to GNNpress.)
2. Drag the text to the page and location where you want to place it.
3. Release the mouse button. The text is moved from where you selected it and placed in the new location.
4. The text is actually cut and moved. If you wish, choose Edit ➤ Undo, and the original text will be replaced in the source document without affecting the destination window.

Selecting and Editing Text

You can edit the text in your pages much as you can with any word processor:

- To delete text, select it, then press the Backspace or Delete keys on the keyboard, or select Edit ➤ Clear or Edit ➤ Cut.
- To drag and drop text, highlight it, hold the mouse button down, move the cursor to the desired new location, then release the mouse button.
- Alternatively, you can cut and paste text, either using the Edit menu (select Edit ➤ Cut, then select Edit ➤ Paste) or the Cut and Paste buttons on the toolbar.
- To replace text, select it using the mouse, then type or paste over it.
- To move a line of text up or down, place the cursor above the line or at the left margin, then press Delete or ↵ to raise or lower the line.

You can also edit text using the keyboard:

- Holding down Ctrl while pressing the Copy key copies the URL.
- Pressing ↵ starts a new paragraph in the appropriate style—in a list it creates a new list item, in a header it exits the header and starts a new paragraph, etc.

- Pressing Linefeed or Ctrl+J (at the end of a list, header, or form) exits the current format (list, header, or form) and starts a new paragraph in the appropriate style.
- Pressing Backspace (or Ctrl+H) deletes the last character.
- Pressing Ctrl+D deletes the next character.
- Pressing Delete normally deletes the character to the right of the cursor, but you can change it to delete the character to the left by choosing Tools ➤ Preferences and checking the UNIX Style Delete field in the dialog box that appears.

Finding and Replacing

You can find and replace text in your GNNpress pages just as you would with a word processor. Selecting Edit ➤ Find/Replace opens the Find/Replace dialog box (Figure 19), where you can search for text in the current page.

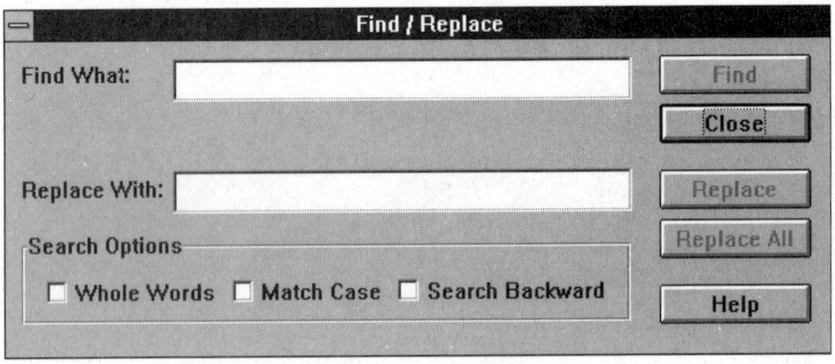

Figure 19: *Use the Find/ Replace dialog box to search for and replace text in the current Web page.*

To find and replace text, follow these steps:

1. Type the characters to search for in the Find What box at the top of the Find/Replace dialog box.
2. Type the characters to replace these in the Replace With box.
3. Optionally, select one or more of the following Search Options:
   - Whole Word: Checking this box makes the match find only whole words that match the text you type. When this box is not checked, GNNpress matches your text even if it is a part of a word. For example, if you check this box, searching for *cat* will match *cat* only, and not words like *catalog*.

- Match Case: Checking this box makes the match case-sensitive. When this box is not checked, GNNpress finds matches that use either upper- or lowercase letters. For example, if you check this box, searching for *ZIP* matches *ZIP*, but not *zip* or *Zip*.
- Search Backward: Checking this box makes GNNpress search backward through the page, beginning at the cursor position. The default is to search forward.

4. Use the buttons on the right to control the search.

   - Find: Finds and selects the next match.
   - Close: Closes the dialog box.
   - Replace: Replaces the current selection with the characters in the Replace With box.
   - Replace All: Finds and replaces all the characters that match in the entire page.
   - Find Next: Finds the next match (this may be up or down depending on whether you checked the Search Backward field).
   - Wrap & Find: Same as Find Next, but starts over at the beginning of the page if it gets to the end of the page.

Copying Text from Other Pages

You can copy and paste text between Web pages:

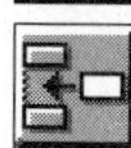

1. With the mouse, highlight the text you want to copy.
2. Click on the Copy button in the toolbar.
3. Return to your Web page, position the cursor where you want the text to appear, and click on the Paste button.

Copying and Pasting URLs

Copying and pasting isn't just for text. You can create links to pages by copying the URL of a page and pasting it into your page.

First, you must copy the URL:

- If you've already opened the page whose address you want to copy, choose Edit ➤ Copy URL Of Page (or click on the Copy URL button in the toolbar). This copies the URL of the current page so that you can paste it.

- If the page you want to link to is listed as a link on another page, highlight that link and choose Edit ➤ Copy URL In Selection (or click on the Copy URL button in the toolbar). You can hold down the Ctrl key on your keyboard while you highlight a link to prevent GNNpress from opening that page. This copies the URL of the link so that you can paste it.

Next, you paste the URL into your page to create a link:

- If you want GNNpress to fill in the text for the link, position the cursor where you want to create the link, and choose Edit ➤ Paste URL (or click on the Paste URL button in the toolbar). This creates a hyperlink to the URL you copied. If you copied the URL of a page, GNNpress adds the title of that page as the text for the link. If you copied the URL of a highlighted link, GNNpress adds the URL of the page as the text, instead.
- If you want to turn existing text into a link, highlight the text you want to link, and choose Edit ➤ Paste URL (or click on the Paste URL button in the toolbar). This makes the highlighted text a hyperlink to the URL you copied.

Spaces, Line-Breaks, and Horizontal Rules

There are several ways you can arrange material in your pages.

Spaces

One method to arrange material is to use spaces. Generally, you can't use multiple spaces to move text horizontally in HTML. However, there are some ways to get around this restriction and move text horizontally:

- You can add horizontal spaces by choosing Tools ➤ Preferences ➤ General and checking the Non-Breaking option in the Text Edit Spacing field. Then, you can type multiple spaces. However, some browsers show these non-breaking spaces as * * instead of as a space. If you select the One option in this field, you can only type one blank space at a time.
- Another way to add spaces is to highlight the paragraph and choose Format ➤ Paragraph ➤ Preformatted to change the paragraph to a fixed width font and allow you to align text by adding spaces.

- However, the best way to align text into columns is to use tables. We'll cover tables later in this chapter.

Line Breaks and Forced Line Breaks

You can also use line breaks and forced line breaks to format text in your pages. To create a *normal* line break—a new paragraph, placed two lines below the point of insertion, do either of the following:

- Press ↵.

- In the middle of any list, you can add a line break without creating a new list item by choosing Format ➤ Paragraph ➤ New.

To create a *forced* line break—a new line that is part of the same paragraph, one line below the point of insertion—press Shift+↵ or choose Element ➤ Forced Line Break.

A line separated by a forced line break is still part of the same paragraph as the line above and is subject to that paragraph's formatting.

Horizontal Rules

You can use the horizontal rule, which by default spans the full width of the page, to divide areas of the page.

To insert a horizontal rule, follow these steps:

1. Position the cursor where you want the rule to start.
2. Choose Element ➤ Horizontal Rule.

To reposition or duplicate a horizontal rule, you can do either of the following:

- Use the basic editing conventions—select, cut, copy, paste, and drag and drop.
- Use the Cut, Copy, and Paste buttons in the toolbar.

Character Styles

Characters can be given distinctive styles, like **boldface**, *italic*, `fixed pitch`, and more. To format the style of text you have selected, choose Format ➤ Type

Style. Character styles are applied to individual characters (and strings of characters like words and sentences), as opposed to whole paragraphs or other page elements.

Some paragraph structures (such as Headings and Quotations) also affect how the characters within them look. You can use these character styles to further modify the type style of a Heading or other paragraph structure.

GNNpress provides two categories of character styles: formatted (physical) styles and logical styles.

Formatted Character Styles

Formatted character styles are styles that have a specific meaning, for example, **boldface** or *italic*. Regardless of the browser used to view your page, characters with formatted styles always appear in that style.

GNNpress has these formatted styles:

STYLE	RESULT
Plain	Plain text
Bold	Boldfaced text
Italic	Italicized text
Underline	Underlined text
Fixed Pitch	A monospaced font such as Courier
Superscript	A smaller point size of the current font, elevated above the base line
Subscript	A smaller point size of the current font, moved slightly below the baseline
NEW Bigger	A larger font size than the surrounding text. Font size changes are cumulative. You can apply this style multiple times to text to increase the font size further. The actual font size varies on different browsers.
NEW Smaller	A smaller font size than the surrounding text. You can apply this style multiple times to text to decrease the font size further.

Logical Character Styles

We recommend using *logical* character styles, rather than formatted styles, to describe how a particular word or phrase is used. Logical character styles, like page elements, have no "standard" appearance, and are displayed according to the optimum system for a particular browser. Different browsers may display these styles in different ways.

These are the logical styles:

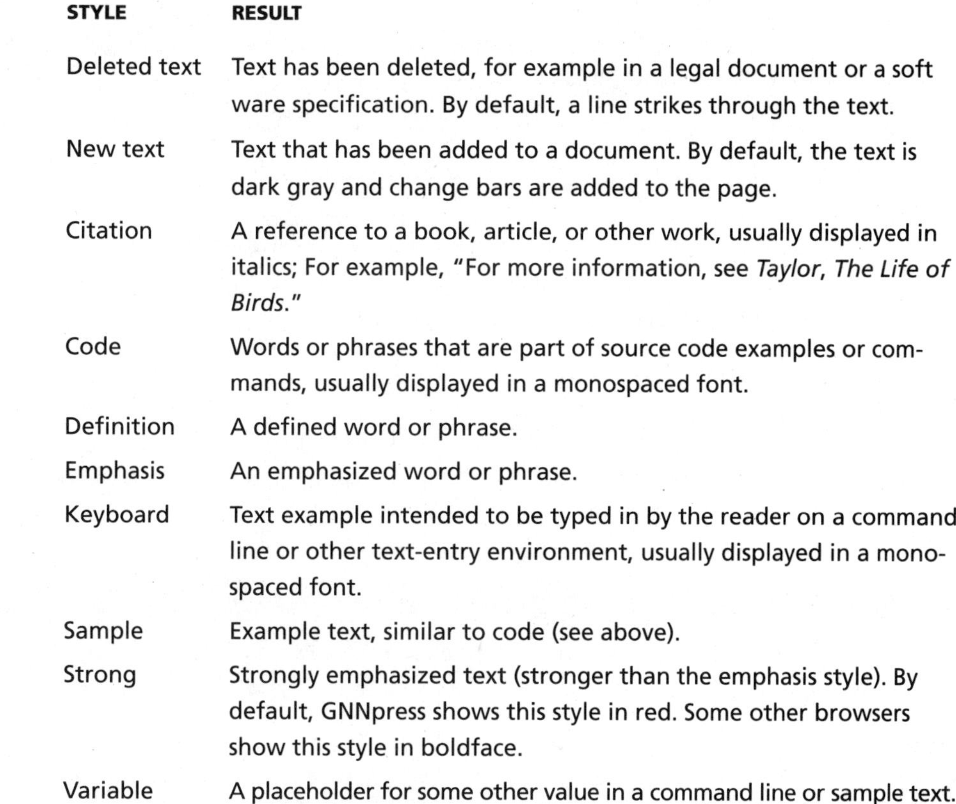

STYLE	RESULT
Deleted text	Text has been deleted, for example in a legal document or a soft ware specification. By default, a line strikes through the text.
New text	Text that has been added to a document. By default, the text is dark gray and change bars are added to the page.
Citation	A reference to a book, article, or other work, usually displayed in italics; For example, "For more information, see *Taylor*, *The Life of Birds*."
Code	Words or phrases that are part of source code examples or commands, usually displayed in a monospaced font.
Definition	A defined word or phrase.
Emphasis	An emphasized word or phrase.
Keyboard	Text example intended to be typed in by the reader on a command line or other text-entry environment, usually displayed in a monospaced font.
Sample	Example text, similar to code (see above).
Strong	Strongly emphasized text (stronger than the emphasis style). By default, GNNpress shows this style in red. Some other browsers show this style in boldface.
Variable	A placeholder for some other value in a command line or sample text.

Applying and Removing Character Styles

Both formatted and logical styles are cumulative—that is, you can apply several styles to a selection. When a style has been applied to a selection, that style name has a check next to it in the Format ➤ Type Style menu.

To apply a character style, follow these steps:

1. Select the characters to which you want to apply a style by highlighting them with the mouse.
2. Choose a character style from the Format ➤ Type Style menu.

TIP

You can apply more than one style at a time to characters. To do this, repeat step 2 while the selected characters are still highlighted.

To remove a single character style from a selection:

1. Select the characters that have the style you want to remove.
2. Choose the character style (checked) you want to remove using the Format ➤ Type Style menu.

To remove all character styles from a selection:

1. Select the characters you want to revert to plain text.
2. Choose Format ➤ Type Style ➤ Plain. The characters you selected revert to the default style of the surrounding text.

NOTE

Use Edit ➤ Undo if you want to correct a recent formatting choice.

Creating Paragraphs and Lists

Paragraphs can be assigned a specific structure—like *Heading*, *Numbered List*, or *Quote*—to set off text and organize your page. You use the Format menu to give paragraphs structure.

Normal Paragraphs

Normal paragraphs, the default, are almost unstructured. They start at the left margin with no indenting or character styles.

To change a structure back to a normal paragraph, follow these steps:

1. Place the cursor in the paragraph or structure that you want to change back.
2. Choose Format ➤ Remove Format.

Changing Paragraph Alignment

You can make any paragraph, heading, or list centered, right-aligned, or fully justified on both the left and right. In fact, you can even align text that wraps next to an image that is left- or right-aligned with text.

NOTE

To enable this feature, you must disable short menus.

To align a paragraph, follow these steps:

1. Place the cursor in the paragraph, heading, or list you want to align or justify.
2. Select Format ➤ Paragraph, then choose Align Left, Align Right, Align Center, Flush, or Align Default. (Align default removes any previous paragraph alignment.)

NOTE

Note that some browsers do not support text alignment. For example, Netscape currently supports only Align Left and Align Center.

Headings

GNNpress provides six levels of headings, from Hdg 1, the largest, to Hdg 6, the smallest. Usually you use headings to title a section. They are set off from the text through a larger font or other form of emphasis.

To apply a heading to text you have not yet typed, follow these steps:

1. Place the cursor where you want the heading to start.
2. Choose a heading type from the Format ➤ Heading menu.
3. Type your heading text.

You can also apply a heading to existing text:

1. Position the cursor in the line of text you want to affect.
2. Choose a Heading type from the Format ➤ Heading menu.

You can change an existing heading's format:

1. Select all of the text in the heading.
2. Choose the new heading level you want to use from the Format ➤ Heading list.

To remove a heading format, position the cursor anywhere in the heading text, then choose Format ➤ Remove Heading Format.

NOTE

You can also use Edit ➤ Undo to undo a recent formatting choice.

Block Quotes, Preformatted Text, and Address Signatures

Block Quotes are used for long passages of quoted material and as such are, by default, offset from regular paragraphs.

Preformatted text is used when you want tabs, spaces, and carriage returns in the text preserved; for example, in code samples or examples that must appear as they are typed. GNNpress displays preformatted text in a monospaced font like Courier.

Address Signatures are typically used at the top or the bottom of the page to indicate the owner of the document, when it was last changed, any copyright information, or any other administrative information for the page. Address signatures are usually in italics and offset, by default.

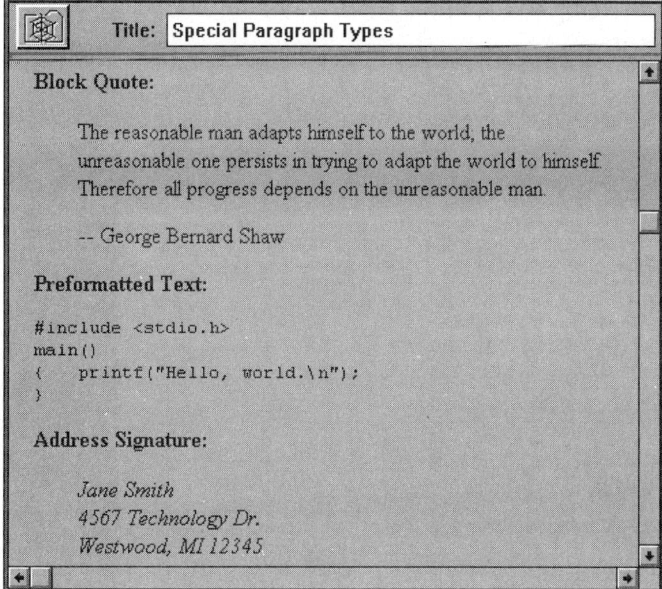

To apply block quotes, preformatted text, and address signatures, follow these steps:

1. Place the insertion point where you want the structure to begin, or position the cursor in the paragraph you want to affect.
2. Choose one of the three structures from the Format ➤ Paragraph menu.

To change block quotes, preformatted text, and address signatures:

1. Position the cursor in the paragraph you want to affect.
2. Choose BlockQuote, Preformatted, or Address from the Format ➤ Paragraph menu.

To remove block quotes, preformatted text, and address signatures, position the cursor in the paragraph you want to affect, then choose Format ➤ Remove Paragraph Format.

Lists

Lists are useful for organizing related text. They combine a group of lines, all separated by line breaks, into a single structure. There are three types of lists:

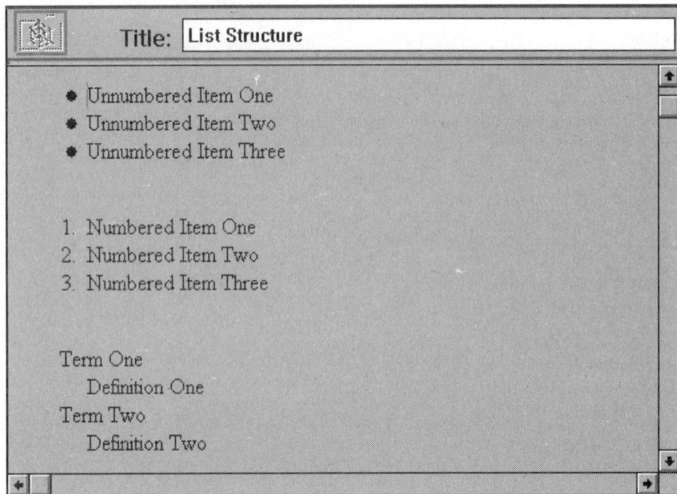

- *Bulleted* lists are indented, with bullets marking each item.
- *Numbered* lists have sequential numbers.
- *Definition* lists have a *term* line followed by a further-indented *definition* paragraph. The term and definition structure is repeated throughout the list.

You can add, delete, and rearrange list items. You can also nest lists. *Nested* lists have multiple levels of sublists and can be mixed. For example, a numbered list can be nested within a definition or bulleted list, or another numbered list.

Bulleted and Numbered Lists

Bulleted lists are useful for listing items that can appear in any order. This structure indents and indicates items by bullets or squares. Numbered lists are best for items that are ordered in a specific sequence, as with procedures.

To apply a bulleted or numbered list structure, follow these steps:

1. Place the insertion point where you want the bulleted or numbered list to begin when you type. Or, select the text you want to turn into a list.
2. Choose Bulleted List or Numbered List from the Format ➤ List menu.

NOTE

You cannot select the numbers or bullets associated with a list. They are part of the structure, but not part of the context.

To end the current list structure, place the cursor anywhere in the list, then choose Format ➤ Exit List Format. Do not hit ↵ after the last list item or an additional unwanted entry is generated. The cursor moves to the line below the list, and leaves it unstructured. Exiting from a nested list takes you out one level. Repeat the Exit command to continue to move out. To move completely out of the list, place the cursor below the list and click.

To remove a list structure (that is, make it unstructured), place the cursor in the list, and choose Format ➤ Remove List Format.

NOTE

Individual items in a list cannot be unstructured. You must unstructure the whole list at once.

Adding, Deleting, and Rearranging List Items

To paste or type new items into an existing list, follow these steps:

1. Place the cursor at the end of the line before the new item you want to add.
2. Press ↵ to provide a line for the new item.
3. Type text or Paste previously typed list items.

Several list items can be pasted in at once. The items below the new items shift downward to accommodate the new list members.

To delete or move items within the list, use basic editing conventions. If you add or delete an item in the middle of a numbered list, all the items below it are automatically renumbered to reflect the change. (If the numbers look odd, scroll up and down to refresh the screen.)

Normally, when you press ↵ within a list, the bullet or number for the next item is added automatically. However, sometimes you want to add a second paragraph to a single list item. To add a second paragraph within a list, choose Format ➤ Paragraph ➤ New.

Definition Lists

Definition lists contain indented *terms* followed by their *definitions* which are indented further (see Figure 20).

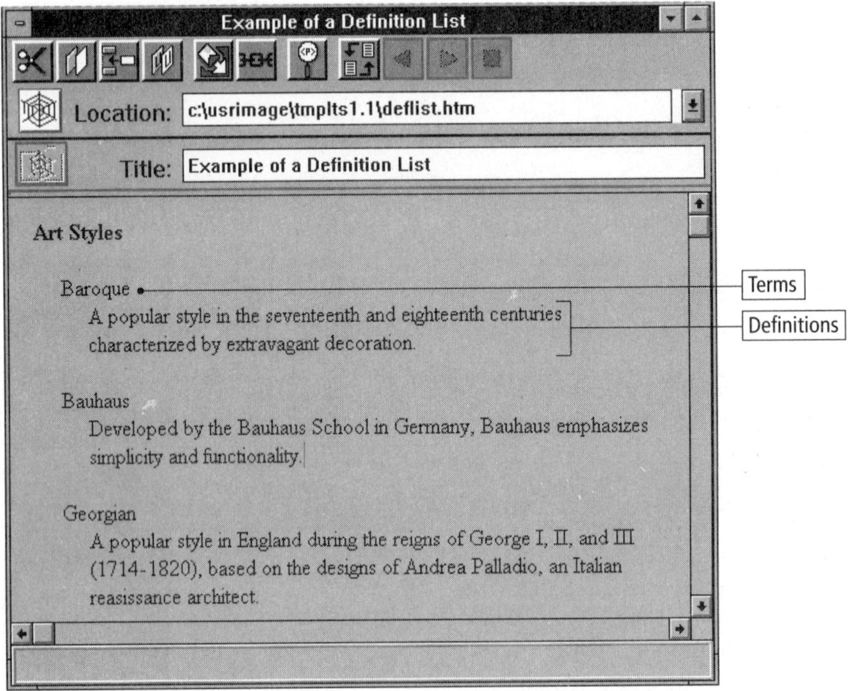

Figure 20: *Definition lists contain terms followed by their definitions.*

Definition lists follow the same basic rules as bulleted and numbered lists. The differences are presented below.

To apply a definition list structure, follow these steps:

1. Place the insertion cursor where you want the definition list to begin. Alternatively, select text you want to turn into a definition list (see Figure 21).

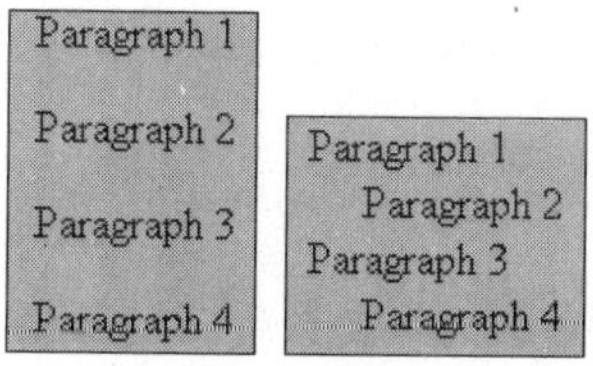

Paragraph 1
Paragraph 2
Paragraph 3
Paragraph 4

Paragraph 1
Paragraph 2
Paragraph 3
Paragraph 4

Figure 21:
Select text and use the definition list style to format it as a series of terms and indented definitions.

NOTE

Terms and definitions must be on separate lines. The term item must be first, then the definition line.

2. Choose Definition List from the Format ➤ List menu.
3. Type your text. Create new a term line by pressing ↵ at the end of a definition, then press ↵ again to create a new definition line.

If you convert selected text to a list, the first paragraph becomes a Term, the second a Definition, and so on until the last paragraph in the selection.

You can change the relative positions of term and definition lines:

1. Place the cursor within or highlight the term or definition you want to change.
2. Choose Term or Definition from the Format ➤ List menu.
3. When you are finished, select Format ➤ Exit List Format to end your list structure

If you place the insertion cursor in a line or at the beginning of a line, all the text to the right of the cursor moves down one line and changes to a term or definition (depending on which you choose). There is still a line for the term or definition where your cursor started, even if your cursor was at the beginning of the line.

Placing the cursor in a line and pressing ↵ has the same effect as placing the cursor in a line and selecting the opposite line type from the Format ➤ List menu (see Figure 22).

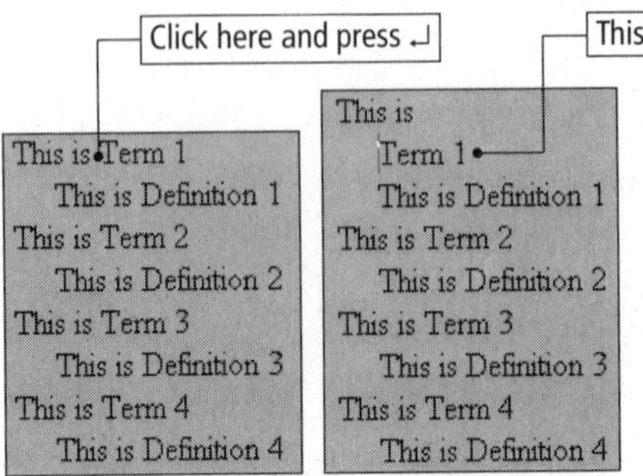

Figure 22: *Pressing ↵ in a line has the same effect as selecting the opposite line type from a menu.*

You can choose Format ➤ List ➤ Term when the cursor is already in a term line to create two terms in a row (see Figure 23). Likewise, you can choose Format ➤ Definition when the cursor is already in a definition line to create two definitions in a row.

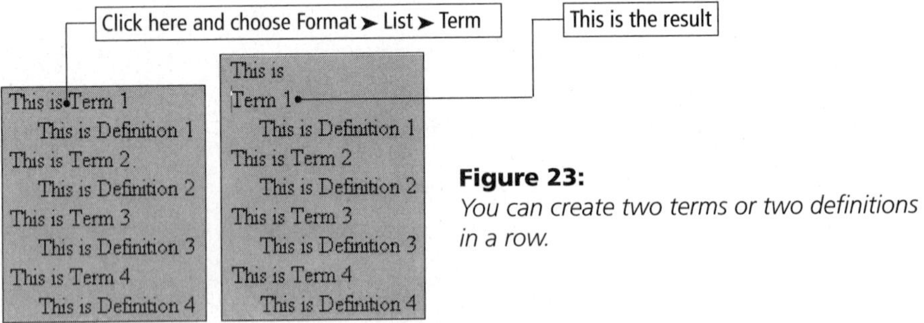

Figure 23:
You can create two terms or two definitions in a row.

If you highlight the entire term or definition line and select an option from the Format ➤ List menu, that line slides left or right to become a term or definition (depending on which you choose) without moving down a line or affecting any other lines (see Figure 24).

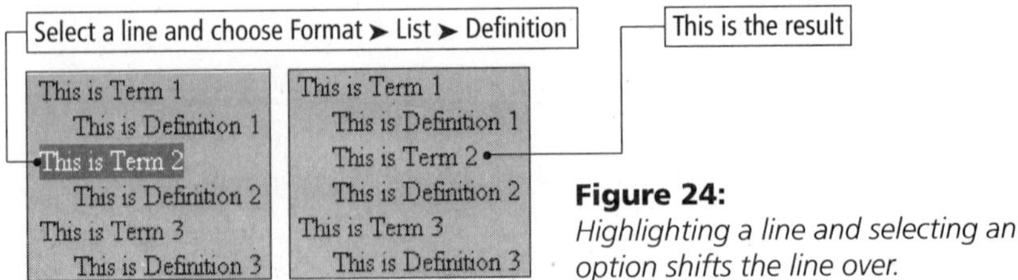

Figure 24:
Highlighting a line and selecting an option shifts the line over.

Nested Lists

At any point in a list you can create a *sublist* or *nested* list, which is indented further then the current list item (see Figure 25).

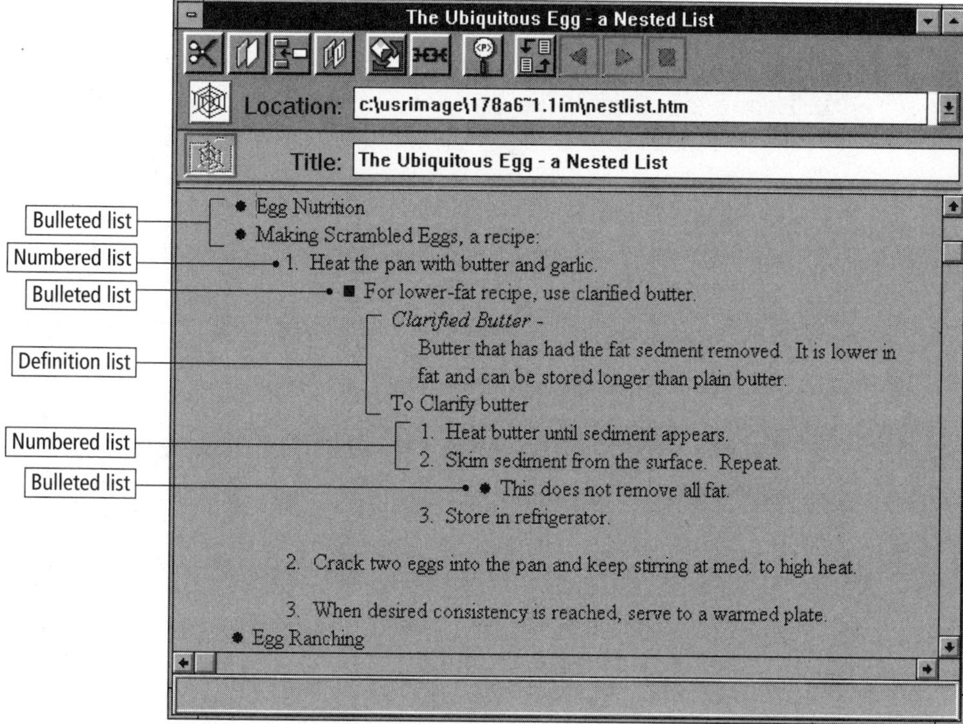

Figure 25: *You can create nested lists to further structure text.*

There is no limit to the number of nested list layers and the kinds of primary and nested lists that can be mixed. Nested lists can carry markers that are different from the primary lists that contain them. These markers may not look the same to all browsers.

TIP

As with all lists, the nested list is itself a distinct list that adheres to basic list rules. See the list rules above to understand how nested lists work.

To nest an existing list item(s), follow these steps:

1. Select the item(s) you want to nest.
2. Choose the list structure you want to use from the Format ➤ List menu.
3. Continue the nested list by pressing ↵ at the end of the nested list.

There are two possible results, depending on how you select the item in step 1.

- Placing the cursor in the item line shifts everything to its right to a new indented line. Everything to the left of the cursor remains in the original item position in the primary list. This is true even if the cursor rests to the left of all text in the line.
- Selecting the entire line moves the entire item line to a nested position and erases the original item position.

You can nest a new list with typed or pasted items:

1. Place the cursor at the end of the item line you would like to nest below.
2. Choose the desired list structure from the Format ➤ List menu.
3. Type or Paste new items, as many as you want.

Removing Formats

You can remove character styles and paragraph structures, leaving the text in a plain format. Use Edit ➤ Undo if you want to correct a recent formatting choice.

To remove all character styles from a selection, follow these steps:

1. Select the characters you want to change back to plain text.
2. Choose Format ➤ Type Style ➤ Plain.

To change a heading into a normal paragraph, place the cursor in the heading you want to change to plain text, then choose Format ➤ Remove Heading Format. To remove block quotes, preformatted text, or address signatures, place the cursor in the paragraph you want to affect, then choose Format ➤ Remove Paragraph Format. To remove a list structure, place the cursor anywhere in the list and choose Format ➤ Remove List Format.

NOTE

You cannot remove the format of more than one list level at a time.

Adding Borders

To help show the structure of a page, you can add border lines above and below lists.

NOTE

To enable this feature, you must first disable short menus.

To show borders, choose Format ➤ Show Border. These lines are not part of the page. They exist only to help you edit the page and are only shown in GNNpress.

To remove the borders, choose Format ➤ Hide Border.

Images and Colors

Images give the Web its lively look and exploit the capabilities of electronic media. Though many pages use hypertext effectively without them, pictures can make information clearer and the page more appealing. This section covers inserting, positioning, and sizing images and changing the colors used by a page.

Images on the World Wide Web

Inline images are graphic elements that load automatically with a Web page. GNNpress and most common Web browsers support several image formats:

- GIF (Graphical Interchange Format). File names normally have the .GIF suffix. GIFs can use up to 256 colors and are best for images with large areas of a single color. GIFs compresses files without loss of information.

- JPEG (Joint Photographic Experts Group). File names normally have the .JPG or .JPEG suffix. JPEGs can use many colors and are best for photographic or painted images. You can specify the amount of file compression. Some of the information is lost during JPEG compression proportional to the compression amount chosen and the number of colors.
- XBM (X bitmap format). Files normally have the .XBM suffix. XBM images use only two colors.

Images in these formats are shown inline—the image is shown as a part of the page itself. There may be a transmission delay after the page appears and before the image fills in, perhaps slowly if the image is large.

A common technique for displaying large images is to create a small version of the image called a *thumbnail*. Make the thumbnail an inline image and link the thumbnail to either a page containing the full-size image or to the full-size image itself.

If a browser cannot display a particular image type, the image is represented by an *undisplayed image* icon (or text) on the page. Double-clicking on the icon or text opens your external viewer, which displays the image. For example, you can use Microsoft Imager or Paintbrush. If no external viewer is set, and the image is in GIF, JPEG, or XBM format, GNNpress displays the image on a separate page. The external viewer must exist on your PC and be associated to GNN.

Inserting Images Inline

There are several ways to insert an image into a page:

- Insert it as an *element*
- Insert it as an *imported file*
- Copy and Paste or drag and drop it from another page in the same MiniWeb.

- Use the right mouse button to drag an icon for an image from a MiniWeb to a page. The image is added to the page. (If you use the left mouse button to drag the image instead, your page is replaced by a blank page containing the image. You must save this page before you can edit it.)

As an Element

This is the recommended way to insert most images (because the dialog box provides more options that apply to images than the File ➤ Import dialog box). To insert an image as an element, follow these steps:

1. Position the cursor where you want the image to be placed.
2. Choose Element ➤ Image to bring up the Image dialog box, shown in Figure 26.

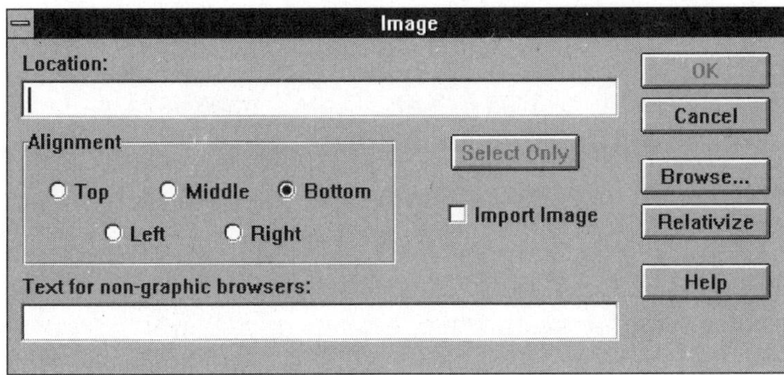

Figure 26: *The Image dialog box, where you can choose an image to add to your page*

3. Enter the location of the image in the Location field:
   - Type a URL or the local file name in the Location field, or
   - Click on the Browse button to browse for the file on your local disks, your GNN service directory, and MiniWebs. Click on OK when you have selected the file you want.

4. Click on a Text Alignment option—Top, Middle, Bottom, Left, or Right—to choose how the image is aligned with the adjoining text. Text aligns with the image. You can also align the text next to a left or right-aligned image by using the Format ➤ Paragraph menu item.
5. Optionally, you can check the Import Image box to copy the image file to the page's MiniWeb. If you do not check this box, the image stays where it is and the reference to the image in your page uses a full URL.

NOTE

This box is dimmed if the image is already stored in the page's MiniWeb or if the image is stored on your local disk and the page is on a server. You can use File ➤ Import, instead, to import images if you want them automatically copied from your local disk to a MiniWeb on a server.

6. You can click the Relativize button to change the reference to the image to a relative URL. If the reference is already a relative reference, you can click the Absolutize button to change the reference to an absolute reference.
7. In the Text For Non-graphic Browsers box, type the text you want to appear instead of the image for readers using browsers that do not display graphics.
8. Click on OK, and the image appears where the cursor was positioned.

As an Imported File

Normally, using Element ➤ Image is the recommended way to insert images because the dialog box provides more options that apply to images. However, File ➤ Import has the advantage of making it easier to copy images from your local disks to a MiniWeb on a server, so you may want to use this second method in that situation.

To insert an image as an Imported File, follow these steps:

1. Position the cursor where you want the image to be placed.
2. Choose File ➤ Import to see the Import dialog box.
3. Enter the location of the image, either by typing a URL or the local file name in the Location field, or by using the directory list and file list to find and select the file.
4. Click on Import, and the image appears where the cursor was positioned. You can ignore the Options button; it provides options that apply to importing HTML and text files.

Copying Images from Another Page

If you are working with more than one page in the same MiniWeb, you can copy images from one Page window to another. The image files are already saved in a common directory.

- To copy an image from one page to another, either copy and paste it using the menus or toolbar buttons, or drag and drop it between the windows.

For example, you can copy and paste images from the clip art library provided with GNNpress. Just choose Help ➤ Templates and follow the link to the Clip Art Library. These files are stored on your hard disk when you install GNNpress.

Replacing and Modifying Images

Once images are in a page, you can replace images, realign text to them, reposition them, or delete them.

Replacing Images or Changing Alignment

You can replace any image on the page with another image. The procedure here is for inline images.

To replace or change the text alignment of an image, follow these steps:

1. Select the image by double-clicking on it or dragging across it. It is OK to select both an image and some of the associated text.
2. Choose Element ➤ Get Attribute to open the Image dialog box.
3. Enter a URL in the Location field or click on Browse to find the new image.
4. Change the Text Alignment option if you want to change the way the image aligns with the adjoining text.
5. Click on OK.

Repositioning Images

To reposition an image, you can do any of the following:

- Cut and Paste it. You can use the commands in the Edit menu, the buttons in the toolbar, or the keyboard equivalents.
- Drag and drop it into place.
- Change the vertical position by placing the cursor above the image and adding or deleting lines to move the image.

TIP

To move an image down a single line, press Shift+↵ to create a forced line break.

You can also indent the image:

1. Select Format ➤ Paragraph ➤ Preformatted to preformat the image's paragraph. This changes the font of the text in the paragraph as well.
2. Press the spacebar to indent the image.

Copying or Deleting Images

You can use this procedure to place a graphic element, like a bullet or a line, several times on a page. To copy an image, use the copy and paste commands via the Edit menu, the toolbar, or the keyboard.

To delete an image from your page, you can use the Backspace or Delete keys on the keyboard, or the Cut button.

Deleting an image from a page does not delete the actual image file. In addition, deleting a page file does not delete image files associated with it. If you want to delete files that are associated with another file, you can delete them separately using File ➤ Delete or by selecting and deleting the file icon in the MiniWeb view.

External Viewers for Images

Images are one of the categories of objects linked to the page that often require an external viewer. When you click on the link to the image, typically a thumbnail-size icon, GNNpress launches the right external viewer if it cannot view it, and the image appears on your screen.

Image Maps

Image Maps are a special kind of link, based on an image. An image is divided, or *mapped*, into regions, and each region functions as a separate link. A single image, such as a diagram of a truck, can be clicked in different places to link to information about that part of the image. Clicking on the truck's hood could link to an engine specification page, or clicking on a wheel could link to a tire wear comparison. Image maps work well for geographic maps, general diagrams, or any large image that functions as an index to more information.

NOTE

We'll talk more about image maps later in this chapter in the section on links.

Setting Colors and Background Images

You can change the colors used for the background and text of a Web page. In addition, you can use an image file for the background of a page. Select Format ➤ Body Attributes to set colors and select a background image. Any browser that allows background color changes will display the colors you set.

To set background and text colors for a page, follow these steps:

1. Choose Format ➤ Body Attributes to display the Body Attributes dialog box shown in Figure 27. This dialog box allows you to select colors for the page background, the normal text, text with an unused link, and text with a link that you have already used.

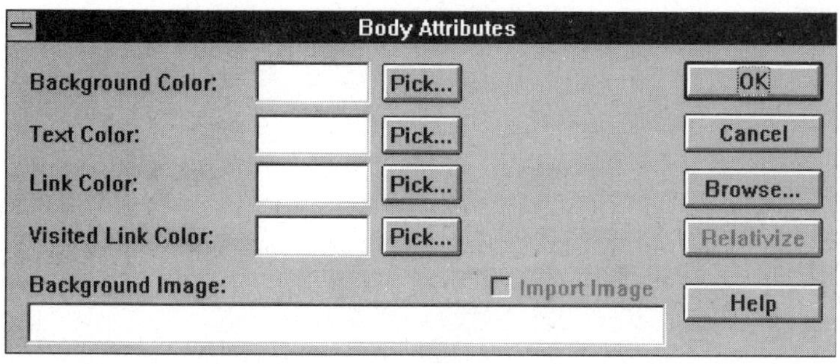

Figure 27: *The Body Attributes dialog box lets you set background and text colors.*

2. Click on Pick next to the item whose color you want to set. You will see the Color dialog box.
3. Select a color from this dialog box. You may want to choose one of the standard colors so that the background will not be dithered on screens that can only display 256 colors.

NOTE

Another way to set a color is to type the RGB value for the color you want (in hexadecimal numbers) into the field directly. The first two characters are the red value, the next two green, and the final two blue. Therefore #ff0000 is red, #00ff00 is green, #0000ff is blue, #ffff00 is yellow, #000000 is black, #ffffff is white, and #808080 is medium gray.

4. Click on OK to close the Color dialog box.
5. In the Body Attributes dialog box, you can set another color or click on OK to see the effects of your changes.

If you set any color, we recommend that you set all four colors to prevent conflicts with settings your readers may have. For example, if you set a light background color and use the default text colors, a reader with a default background of black and light text may not be able to read your page because the text may appear light on a light background. These are the default colors for GNNpress:

- Background: Gray (#c0c0c0)
- Text: Black (#000000)
- Link: Blue (#0000ff)
- Visited Link: Deep Purple (#400080)

You can also use an image as the background for your page. To select a background image, follow these steps:

1. Choose Format ➤ Body Attributes to display the Body Attributes dialog box.
2. Type a URL in the Location field or click on Browse to find the new image. If the image you select is smaller than the browser window, the image will be *tiled* to fill the whole space. You should use an image with edges that match up when the image is tiled. Tiling allows you to specify a small image that will load quickly.
3. You can click on the Relativize button to change the reference to the background image to a relative URL. If the reference is already a relative reference, you can click the Absolutize button to change the reference to an absolute reference.
4. Click on OK to see your changes.

If you use a background image, we recommend that you also set the colors to avoid conflicts with your readers' settings. In most cases, the colors in your background image should contrast strongly with the text colors you choose and the background image should be simple enough that it doesn't distract from the text.

Example: Inserting an Image into Your Page

This section lets you step through the process of inserting an image:

1. Choose Element ➤ Image to display the Image dialog box:

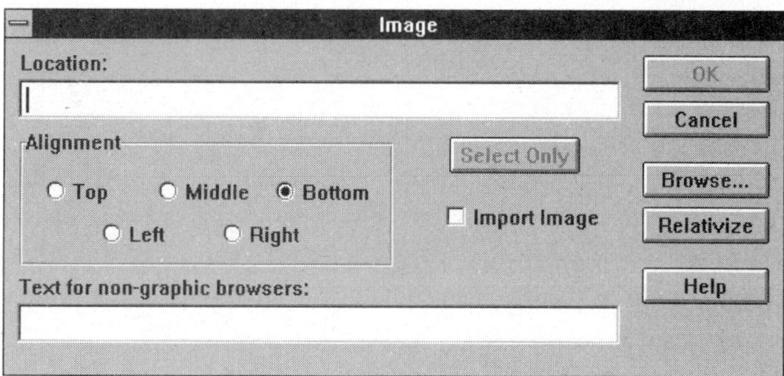

2. If you know the URL for the graphic you wish to import, you can just type in into the Location field in this dialog box. Otherwise, if the graphic is on or on your local file system, click on Browse to find it.
3. Click on Browse to see the Insert Image dialog box:

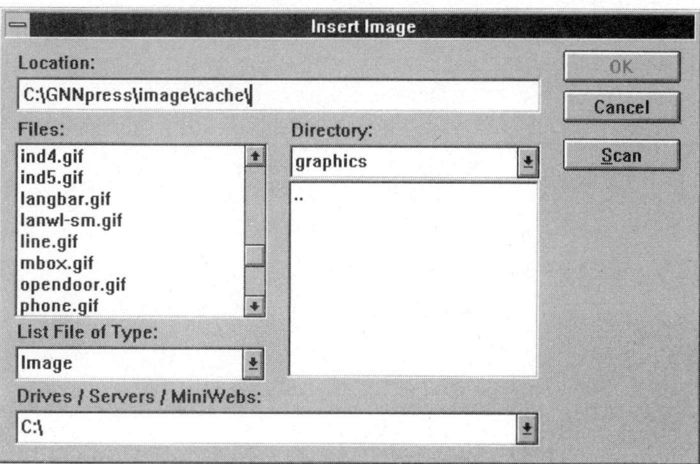

4. Choose a local drive to search, either by entering the location in the Location field at the top of the dialog box, or by choosing a location from the Drivers/Servers/MiniWebs list that appears when you click on the arrow to the right of the box.
5. Set the List Files Of Type field to Image. The Files list now shows file names ending with .GIF and .JPG.
6. Select from the file list and click on OK to return to the original Image dialog box.
7. The five radio buttons—Top, Middle, Bottom, Left, and Right—allow you to select how the graphic aligns with the text. Select Middle, then click on OK.
8. Your image should now appear in your page as you've specified.

A Quick Summary of Commands for Images

Here is a quick summary of commands you can use with images:

To insert images inline

- To insert an image as an *element*, choose Element ➤ Image.
- To insert image as *imported file*, choose File ➤ Import.
- To insert an image out of line, choose Element ➤ Link.
- To copy images from page to page, choose Copy and Paste or drag and drop them.
- To view the GNNpress clip art library, choose Help ➤ Templates and follow the links to the Clip Art Library.

To replace and modify images

- To replace an inline image, choose Element ➤ Get Attribute, then select the new image from the Image dialog box that appears.
- To change an image's alignment with text, choose Element ➤ Get Attribute, then select a new alignment in the Image dialog box that appears.
- To reposition an image, use Cut and Paste or drag and drop.
- To copy an image, use Copy and Paste or drag and drop.
- To delete an image, use the Delete or Backspace keys, the Cut button on the toolbar, or the Tools ➤ Cut menu option.

To modify page colors

- To change background colors for most other browsers, choose Format ➤ Body Attributes and make selections in the Body Attributes dialog box.
- To change background colors for GNNpress browsers, choose Format ➤ Style Sheet.

Tables

Tables allow you to align text and images into columns and rows like the one shown in Figure 28.

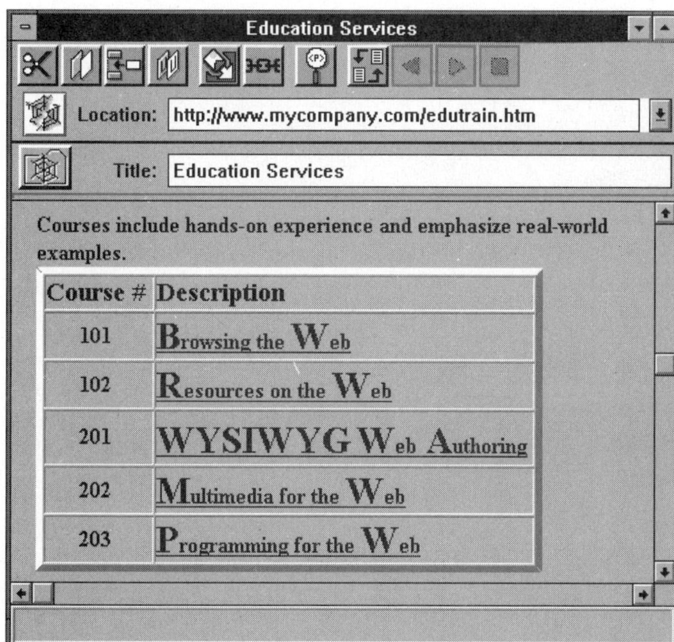

Figure 28:
Use tables to align text and images into columns and rows.

GNNpress gives you control over the look of your tables:

- You can set and modify the number of rows and columns in your table.
- You can add headings and table captions to your table.
- You can set the width of your table's border and the amount of space in the margins of individual table cells.
- You can merge cells to create areas that span any number of rows and columns.
- You can align the contents of cells both horizontally and vertically.
- You can put almost anything inside a table cell: text, images, headings, links, forms, horizontal rules—even other tables.

Creating and Formatting Tables

To create a table in a page, follow these steps:

1. Place your cursor where you want to create the table, and choose Table ➤ Create Table. You will see the Table dialog box, shown in Figure 29.

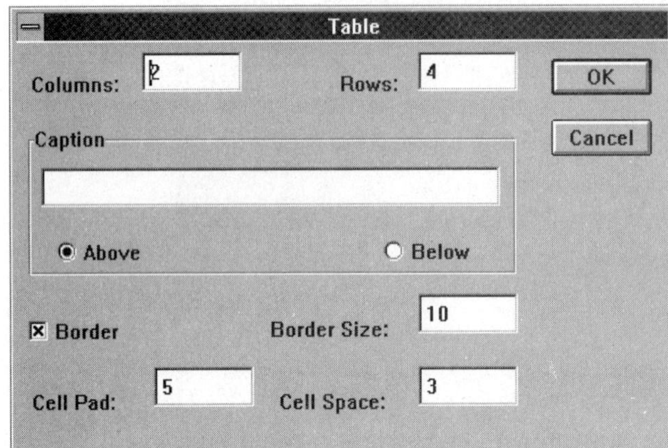

Figure 29: *The Table dialog box, where you can specify how you want your table set up.*

2. Set the number of vertical columns and horizontal rows you want in your table. (It's easy to change these numbers later.)
3. If you want the table to have a caption, type the text for it in the Caption field. The caption will be centered horizontally to right either above or below the table, depending on which radio button you select.
4. The fields at the bottom of the dialog box control the borders and spacing of the table:

    - If you want to hide the borders of the table, uncheck the Border box. (It's actually easier to edit a table with borders, so you'll probably want to leave this box checked while you are creating the table. When you are finished editing the table, you can hide the borders if you like.)
    - The Border Size field lets you set the width (in pixels) of the outside border of the table. If you make the Border Size a larger number (for example, 10), the table will look like it has a picture frame.
    - The Cell Space field lets you set the width (in pixels) of the borders between the individual cells in the table.

- The Cell Pad field lets you set the amount of blank space (in pixels) between the text or other contents of a cell and the borders of that cell. You can think of this field as setting the margin widths of the cell. Figure 30 illustrates these options in a table.

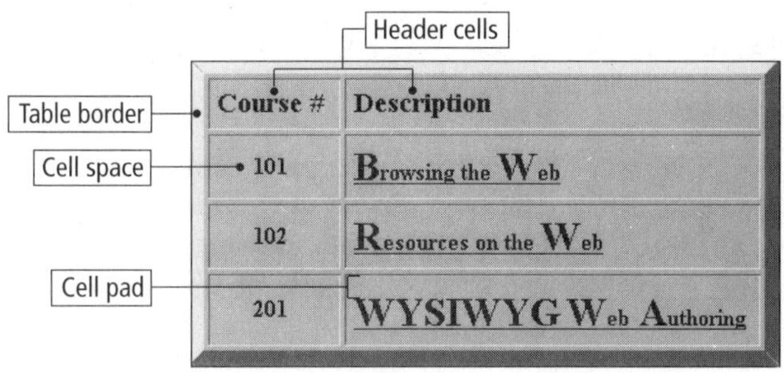

Figure 30: *Border and cell options for a table*

5. Click on OK when you are ready to create the table.
6. If you want to change any of these settings later, just put your cursor inside the table and chooe Table ➤ Alter Table.

NOTE

If you have a background graphic file for your Web page, it can affect the look of the table.

Putting Elements into Tables

You can put text, graphics, and other elements into table cells the same way you would add them anywhere else on a page. Just position your cursor and type text. You can also use the menus to add text formatting, images, headings, links, forms, horizontal rules—even other tables.

You can use the arrow keys to move the cursor from one cell to another.

You can start new paragraphs by pressing ↵. You can force text to wrap to the next line by choosing Element ➤ Forced Line Break.

Cells automatically expand as you add text and other elements. Once the table is as wide as your page window, text automatically wraps to the next line in the cell. When your readers view this page, wide tables are automatically adjusted to fit in the width of their browser windows. We recommend that you test the formatting of your tables with various page window widths.

Formatting Table Cells

A special way of formatting table cells is to make them into *header cells*. By default, the text in header cells is shown in boldface. You might want to change the cells in the top row or the left column of a table into header cells. Another way you may want to format cells is to align the contents vertically or horizontally.

To create a header cell, follow these steps:

1. Place the cursor in the cell that you want to be a header cell.
2. Choose Table ➤ Header Cell. The cell becomes a header cell, and the text is boldfaced and centered vertically and horizontally in the cell.
3. If you want to change a header cell back to a normal cell, choose Table ➤ Normal Cell.

You can also align the contents of cells:

- To change the vertical (top-to-bottom) alignment of the contents of a cell, place your cursor in the cell and choose Table ➤ V Align Cell. You can choose to align the contents to the Top, Middle, or Bottom of the cell.
- You can choose Table ➤ V Align Row to vertically align the contents of all the cells in a table row. (If you align the contents of a cell, that setting overrides the alignment of the row.) You can align all the contents of the row to the Top, Middle, Bottom, or Baseline.
- To change the horizontal (left-to-right) alignment of a cell, highlight the text you want to align and choose Format ➤ Paragraph. You can choose Align Left, Align Right, Align Center, Align Flush, or Align Default to align the paragraphs. (If you highlight the entire table, you can change the alignment of all the cells in the table.)

NOTE

To enable this feature, you must first disable short menus.

- To align an image with text, highlight the image and choose Element ➤ Get Attribute. In the Image dialog box that appears, choose a Text Alignment option—Top, Middle, Bottom, Left, or Right—to align the image with the adjoining text.

If you want to align the entire table to the left, center, or right of the page, choose Tools ➤ Show HTML. Find the `<TABLE>` tag. (It may already contain attributes like `BORDER`, `CELLPADDING`, and `CELLSPACING`.) Add the boldfaced text shown below inside the existing `<TABLE>` tag.

```
<TABLE ALIGN=left>
<TABLE ALIGN=center>
<TABLE ALIGN=right>
```

Then, choose File ➤ Parse to apply your changes to the page window.

Merging and Splitting Table Cells

You can merge table cells to create areas that span rows and columns. For example, you could create a table like this one:

WARNING

Merging cells deletes the contents of all the cells you merge, except the contents of the upper-left cell. To keep the contents of the other cells, you should cut and paste or drag and drop them into the upper-right cell of the area before you merge cells.

To merge table cells, follow these steps:

1. Move your cursor to upper-right cell in the set of cells you want to merge.

WARNING

If you get a message box that says "This cell would stretch beyond the bounds of the table," decrease the number of columns.

2. Choose Table ➤ Merge Cell. You will see the Merge Cell dialog box shown in Figure 31.

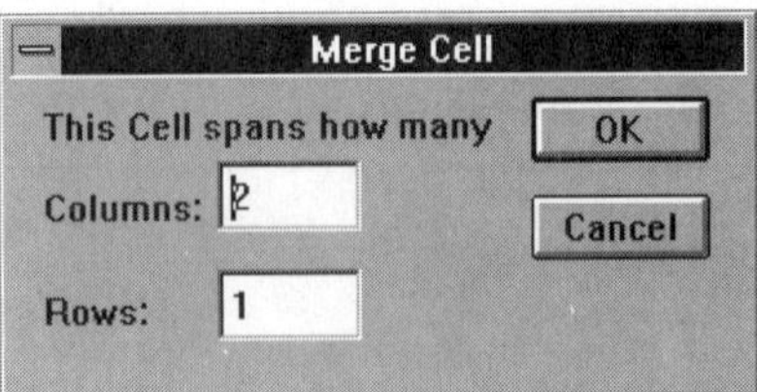

Figure 31:
The Merge Cell dialog box, where you can choose options for combining table cells

3. Type the number of Columns and Rows the cell should span, and click on OK to merge the cells. For example, if you place the cursor in the upper-left cell of a table that looks like this:

and merge that cell to span two columns and two rows, the result will be a table that looks like this:

4. If you want to unmerge cells, choose Table ➤ Split Cell. The merged area will be split into the number of columns and rows that were merged. However, any information destroyed in the merge is not restored, only the structure of the table.

NOTE

You cannot split cells unless they have already been merged.

HTML 3.0 Tables vs. Netscape Tables

There are minor differences in the ways tables are defined in the HTML 3.0 and Netscape specifications. GNNpress creates and displays HTML code using the current selection in the Conform To field in the General Preferences dialog box. To check or change this setting, choose Tools ➤ Preferences ➤ General. If most of your readers will use Netscape to browse your pages, you will probably want to conform to Netscape conventions. Otherwise, HTML 3.0 may be a better choice.

Changing this setting affects the following defaults for tables:

- With Netscape, text in table cells is aligned vertically to the middle of the cell by default. With HTML 3.0, text is aligned to the top of the cell by default.
- With Netscape, tables are aligned to the left of the page by default. With HTML 3.0, tables are centered on the page by default.
- With Netscape, table widths are specified in pixels by default. With HTML 3.0, table widths are specified in *ens* (the width of the letter *n*) by default. You can add table width specifications by editing the HTML directly.

NOTE

Changing the Conform To field doesn't control how other browsers display your table. You may want to set the vertical alignment of table cells even if you want to use the default to make other browsers align the text correctly.

The HTML 3.0 and Netscape specifications provide additional attributes for formatting tables. You can use Tools ➤ Show HTML to add such attributes. For example, you can add the `WIDTH`, `UNITS`, `COLSPEC`, and `NOWRAP` attributes to the `<TABLE>` tag. Select File ➤ Parse to implement these changes into your file.

Links

Links are probably the single most important elements in Web pages. They allow your readers to move from page to page and site to site, finding all kinds of new information along the way. Let's start by taking a look at the parts of a link.

Hyperlinks

As we've explained above, a hyperlink is a cross-reference to another file or target location in a file. Other files and anchors are the targets of hyperlinks. A link can be either an absolute link or a relative link.

- Absolute links specify the exact location or complete URL of a file. Relative links can only link to a file on the same server or disk.
- Relative links omit part of the file specification and use the current location as the default. (For example, **http://www.gnn.com/news/news.htm** is an absolute reference. A relative reference to this file from the directory above would be **news/news.htm**.)

It's usually best to use relative links within your own Web site. Relative links allow you to move the entire directory tree to a new location without breaking your links. You should try to use absolute links only to reference files outside your own Web.

GNNpress can automatically change references from absolute to relative references and back for you. If you see a Relativize button in a dialog box for creating links or setting image attributes, the link is currently an absolute link and you can click this button to make it a relative link. If you see an Absolutize button, you can change the relative link to an absolute link. Also, when you choose File ➤ Save As, the Options button provides a dialog box that allows you to convert all relative references to absolute references by checking the Relative Links To Full URL box.

Anchors

An *anchor* is a target location in a file. Links point to anchors, which can be in the same file as the link or in another file. An important distinction is that anchors are not clickable, they are only placeholders to be linked to.

Creating Links with the Link Dialog Box

You can create a hyperlink using the Link dialog box:

1. Select the text you would like to make into a hyperlink, either to another Web site or another page within your MiniWeb.
2. Choose Element ➤ Link to bring up the Link dialog box, shown in Figure 32.

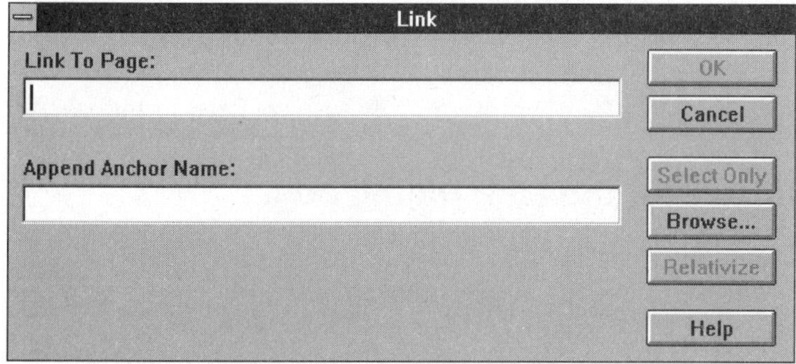

Figure 32: *The Link dialog box, where you create hyperlinks for your page*

3. To link to a page, type its URL in the Link To Page field (for example, **http://www.gnn.com/**).
4. Click on OK.

Your selected text is hyperlinked to the URL in this field. The text you selected in your document is now in color, italicized, and underlined. This is a hyperlink. Clicking on your newly created link takes you, in this example, to GNN's Web page.

If you wish to link your selected text to a location within a document, you can append an anchor name to the URL in the Link To Page field.

1. In the Link dialog box, type the URL in the Link To Page box.
2. Type an anchor name in the Append Anchor Name box. This is the same name that you give the target anchor, described below.

3. Click on OK.

The text you selected in your document is now in color, italicized, and underlined, identical to the hyperlink described above. Clicking on this newly created link would fetch the Web page whose URL you specified, at the part of the document where it is anchored.

NOTE

Typically, you will have assigned some text in a document with anchor names before you create the hyperlink to that anchor, but you can still set them using this dialog box.

To select links from URLs in the Link dialog box, double-click on them, or highlight the selection and click on OK.

The text you selected in your document is now in color, italicized, and underlined. If selected now, it takes you to the URL you selected in this scrolling menu.

Other Buttons in the Link Dialog Box

The Link dialog box also contains these buttons:

- Cancel: Closes the Link dialog box without making changes.
- Select Only: If the text you selected already contains a link, then that link URL is displayed in the Link To Page field and the Select Only button is enabled. Because selecting text by dragging and highlighting is inaccurate, selecting this button ensures that you select only the text that was the previous link.
- Browse: Allows you to browse your local files or for files to choose as links. If you enter a site that you cannot browse, you get a message "Cannot Browse Location."

- Relativize or Absolutize: Click on the Relativize button to change the link reference to a relative URL. If the reference is already a relative reference, click on the Absolutize button to change the reference to an absolute reference.
- Help: Provides an online Link Help Page.

Making Anchors Within a Page

Anchors allow you to use plain text in a document and link to that exact part of the document. The anchor is not a hyperlink and cannot be clicked on. It is used as a target text, for example in a long page with an index or a table of contents.

To make an anchor within a page, follow these steps:

1. Type or select some text in your page, the choose Element ➤ Anchor.
2. Type an anchor name in the text field of the Anchor dialog box. For convenience, use an anchor name that is related to the text you selected. For example, you could type **Top** if you are placing an anchor at the top of the page so that hyperlinks within a long page can jump back to the top of the page.
3. Click on OK. The text you selected in your document changes appearance. It is not underlined, because it is not a clickable hyperlink.

You can check anchor names or remove anchors:

- If you forget an anchor name and want to create a link to that anchor, select the anchor text and choose Element ➤ Anchor. You will see the anchor name in the dialog box.
- If you erase the anchor name from this dialog box and click on OK, the anchor will be removed from the page. Edit ➤ Undo will restore the anchor.

Copying and Pasting URLs

In addition to selecting text to link to, you can copy-and-paste URLs from almost any source, including Hot Lists and Web pages. To copy a URL from the Hot List, follow these steps:

1. Choose Browse ➤ Hot List.
2. Select a URL in the Hot List menu and click on the Copy URL button. You can then paste this copied URL into a document for an instant link to your Hot List item.
3. Place your cursor where you want the URL to be placed in your document. Choose Edit ➤ Paste URL or click on the Paste button on the toolbar. The

URL you copied is pasted into your document. If you highlight the text, that will be the underlined link; otherwise, the name of the HTML file will be substituted.

You can also copy a URL from a Web page:

1. Select a hyperlinked URL from a Web page by holding down Ctrl and then selecting the text. Choose Edit ➤ Copy URL In Selection or click on the Copy URL button on the toolbar.

2. Place your cursor where you want the URL to be placed in your document. Choose Edit ➤ Paste URL or click on the Paste button on the toolbar.

Image Maps—Links to Images

As we mentioned above, image maps are images that, when clicked on, act like hyperlinked text. The difference is that you can map URLs to different parts of the image. For example, you could create an image map with symbols for parts of your business (support, sales, products). When readers click on a part of the image, they are taken to a page on that subject.

Because image maps require readers to download an extra image, you should use them only when they present a distinct advantage in navigating your Web pages. By using the GNN service along with GNNpress, you can create quick and easy image maps. Moreover, image maps function differently on various Web servers and browsers.

The browser (in this case, GNNpress) queries the Web server for a page that contains an image map. It also requests the image and displays it along with the text. The reader clicks on the map image. GNNpress sends the coordinates of the click to the server, which processes the coordinates and decides which *hot spot* the mouse was in when it was clicked. It then returns the URL associated with that spot. If the spot is not mapped, the default URL is returned instead. GNNpress retrieves the page designated by the URL and opens a new window.

TIP

When you delete an image map from a page (by highlighting it and pressing the Delete key), the actual image and image map files are not deleted. To delete the files, you can use File ➤ Delete, or you can select and delete the file's icon in the MiniWeb view.

To create an image map, follow the steps below:

1. Select an image in your document that you would like to function as your image map.
2. Choose Element ➤ Image Map to see the GNNpress Image Map dialog box shown in Figure 33. The dialog box contains the following options:
   - Map Name: This is the name of your map file, which is different from the name of the image. Map names end with .NVM, which replaces the ending of your image file (for example, .GIF). You can rename it if you wish.
   - Create Rectangle: The image you have just selected is located in this box. This is the work area where you draw rectangles that will be hot spots.
   - Rectangle List: This is a menu list of your map hot spots. The coordinates of the rectangle are listed along with the URL of the item.
   - Location: Type the URL you want the rectangle to link to.
   - Rectangle In Pixels: When the Image Map dialog opens, the four pixel boxes have zeros. After you select a rectangle in the Create Rectangle box, the pixel boxes show the coordinates of the rectangle. You can also make rectangle selections by entering the exact pixel coordinates.
   - Selection Type: Choose Rectangle to select rectangle hot spots. Choose Default to select the default link (the URL that appears if no selection is clicked on the image map).
   - Add: Adds a new selection or hot spot to the image map.
   - Change: Allows you to edit any URL selection you have made.
   - Remove: Removes the rectangle or hot spot selected.
   - Up: Moves the rectangle or hot spot selected up one line.
   - Down: Moves the rectangle or hot spot selected down one line.
   - Browse: Allows you to browse your local files or for choosing map links.
   - Help: Provides an online Image Map Help Page.

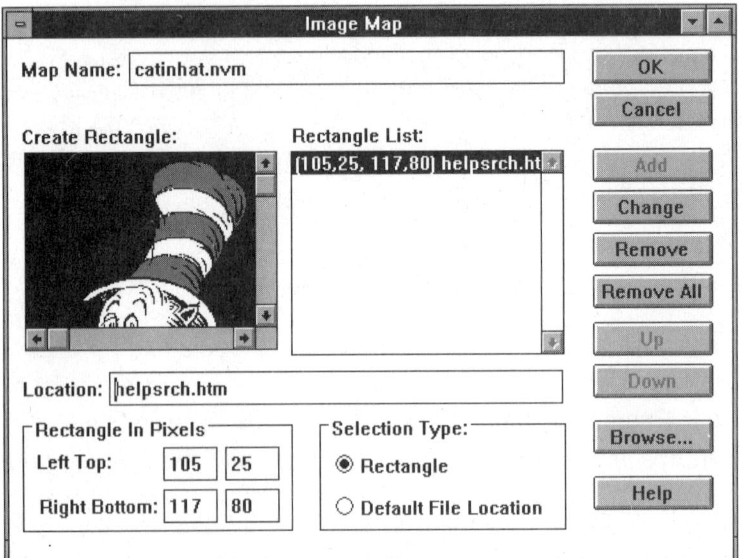

Figure 33: *The Image Map dialog box, where you can create an image map for a graphic*

TIP

You will probably want to resize the Image Map dialog box to be able to see the entire image. You can do this as you would for any window.

Here's how to insert a specific image map:

1. Set the default location by clicking on the Default button under Selection Type. You can use the Browser button to search.

NOTE

If nothing is chosen for default, clicking outside all hot spots has no effect.

2. Enter a URL in the Location field (for example, **http://www.gnn.com/**) for the default selection. You can use the Browse button to search.
3. Click on the Add button. The default location has now been set. If a reader clicks on a spot that has not been mapped, this default URL page appears.
4. Click on the Rectangle button under Selection Type.

5. Click on the parts of the image you wish to select. Hold down the mouse button and draw a rectangle to select a hot spot.
6. Enter the URL in the Location field (for example, **http://www.aol.com/**) for the first map selection.
7. Click on the Add button. Don't be afraid if you make mapping mistakes at first. Mappings that have been added can be removed by clicking on Remove. Try the map again.
8. Repeat the above steps for each URL you wish to be mapped. When you are done, click on OK.

The image map you have just created has a fine blue line surrounding it, which indicates that the image is a link—possibly an image map, but it could also link to a normal page. Click on the hot spots you have just created, and the hot spot's page appears.

Links to Other Media

Links to audio or video files are just like hyperlinks to other pages. However, audio and video are not viewed or heard when first displayed. An external viewer (for video) or player (for audio) is required to use these types of links. Currently, the extensions include either the Mime view or the RealAudio Player (available at: **http://www.realaudio.com/**).

NOTE

This chapter assumes you already have audio or video files if you plan on incorporating them into your Web document. It does not explain how to create these other media files.

Here's how to insert an audio or video link:

1. Select the text or image you would like to be hyperlinked to your audio or video file.
2. Choose Element ➤ Link to display the Link dialog box.
3. Either type in the URL if you know it or browse your files to locate the file you wish you link.
4. Click on OK.

The selected text is now blue, italicized, and underlined and is hyperlinked to the file you chose. You can click on this link, and if you have the external player or viewer, you will see or hear the file.

Changing Links

You can also modify an existing link:

1. Hold down Ctrl and click on an existing link, or, if the link is one word, hold down Ctrl and double-click on the link.
2. Choose Element ➤ Get Attribute or Element ➤ Link.

You can now make any changes to your link just as you would if you were creating a new link from plain text.

Here's how to remove a link:

1. Hold down Ctrl and click on an existing link, or, if the link is one word, hold down Ctrl and double-click on the link.
2. Choose Element ➤ Unlink.

The selected text now appears in the state it was before it was a hyperlink.

TIP

Selecting Edit ➤ Undo reestablishes the link if you make a mistake.

Checking Links

You should use this GNNpress function to make your Web information as accurate as possible. *Check Links* gives you the ability to select a GNNpress page and check most of the hyperlinks it contains. GNNpress finds links that are not working, for whatever reason. You can then edit your document and links as needed. Without Check Links, you would have to click on each link in the document to verify it.

Here's how to check the links in any Web page:

1. Open any Web page, either in your local directory or on a Web server.
2. Choose Tools ➤ Check Links to display the Check Link dialog box shown in Figure 34.

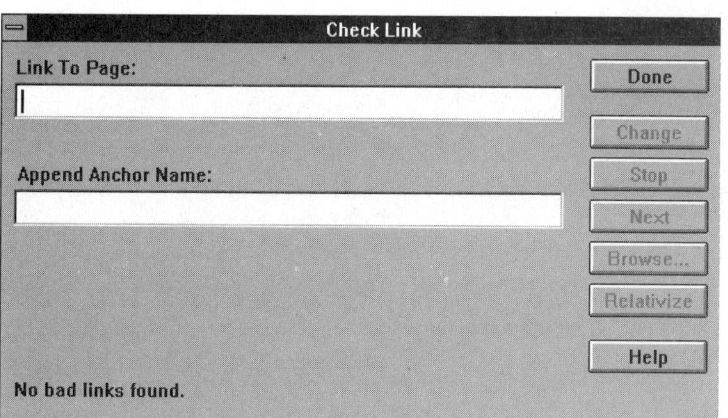

Figure 34: *The Check Link dialog box automatically checks all the links in the current page.*

GNNpress scans all links to the page and verifies that they exist. A status message at the bottom of the dialog box keeps you apprised on GNNpress' activity. If it finds a bad link, the status message changes to indicate the problem. If no bad links are found you get a "No bad links found" message. If you get a "Could not find 'http://....'" message, you can edit the URL.

NOTE

You can cancel the link checking while it is in progress by clicking on the Done button.

If you find a bad link, you can edit the URL:

1. Edit the URL as necessary in the Link To Page field.
2. Click on the Change button.

This corrects the link in the page and moves on to check the next link.

From the Check Link dialog box, you can also append an anchor to the URL:

1. Type in an anchor name in the Append Anchor Name field.
2. Click on the Change button.

This changes the link, adds the anchor, and moves on to check the next link.

Closing the Check Links Dialog Box

While the Check Links dialog box is open, your page is locked. You cannot browse any links until you close the dialog box. If you try, you get a "This page is temporarily locked..." message at the bottom of your Page window.

To close the Check Links dialog box, click on the Done button.

Stopping Link Checking

To abort the link checking, click on the Stop button. This gives you an "aborted 'http://....[name of link currently being checked]'" message and allows you to change the link.

Checking the Next Link

To continue link checking after you've clicked on Stop, click on Next. You can also use the Next button when you wish to leave in a link that is currently unavailable.

Browsing to Choose Links

If you want to change the URL of a link, you may want to browse your local files or your GNN directory from the Check Link dialog box.

To browse files or a server, follow these steps:

1. Click on Browse.
2. In the Locate File To Link To dialog box that appears (see Figure 35), click on the down-arrow to the right of the Drives/Servers/MiniWebs field to choose a drive, server, or MiniWeb to browse.

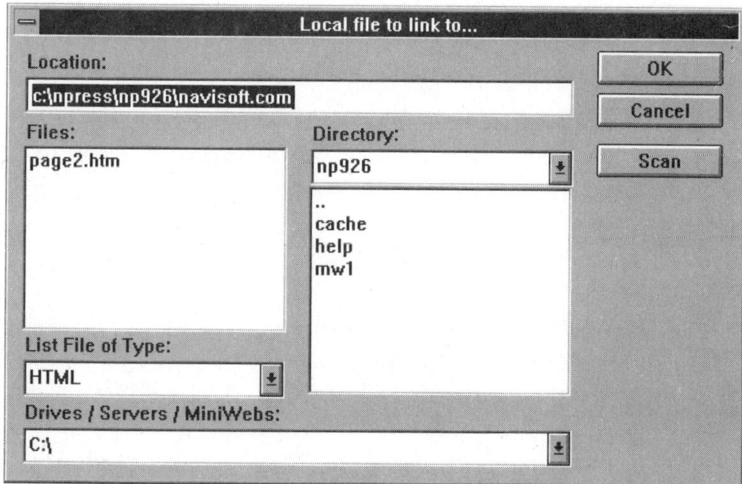

Figure 35: *The Locate File To Link To dialog box, where you can browse to choose a link*

3. Click on the down-arrow to the right of the Files/Directories field to browse files and directories once you have chosen a drive, server, or MiniWeb.

NOTE

If you enter a site you cannot browse, you see a "Cannot Browse Location" message.

A Quick Summary of Commands for Links

Here is a quick summary of commands you can use with links:

- To create links, select the text you want as a link, then choose Element ➤ Link.
- To create anchors, select the text you want as an anchor, the select Element ➤ Anchor.
- To change links and anchors, hold down Ctrl and click on the link or anchor, then select Element ➤ Link or Element ➤ Get Attribute.

Saving Your Web Page

Once you have finished your page (or at least gotten it started), you need to save the page and give it a title by choosing File ➤ Save and saving the page to a directory on your local disk. Because this is a new page, this action invokes the Save As dialog box. If you've already saved this page, choosing File ➤ Save will save your page without displaying this dialog box.

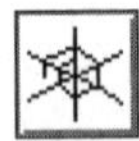

Notice that the Web icon next to the Title field in your Page window changes to reflect the status of your page. If the icon looks like this, you are working in a new, unsaved page.

If the web in the graphic appears broken, you have unsaved changes.

When you save the page, the icon looks like this.

Viewing and Editing HTML

If you know the source language for Web pages, HTML, or if you want to learn about it by example, you can use the Tools ➤ Show HTML command or the Show HTML button on the toolbar to display the actual document with its HTML tags.

GNNpress lets you edit the HTML source directly and then test your changes quickly. You might want to edit the HTML source to add tags for which GNNpress does not provide direct authoring support. For example, you can add the `<P CLEAR=ALL>` tag after a paragraph that wraps around an image to make sure the next paragraph or image starts below the first image.

You might also want to view the HTML source to find out how a particular page was created so that you can create similar pages.

Viewing the HTML Source Code

Here's how to open a window showing the HTML tags:

1. Open a Web page. The page need not be part of a MiniWeb.
2. Choose Tools ➤ Show HTML to open a window containing the HTML for that page. If any text in the Page window was highlighted, the HTML window automatically scrolls to show that highlighted text.

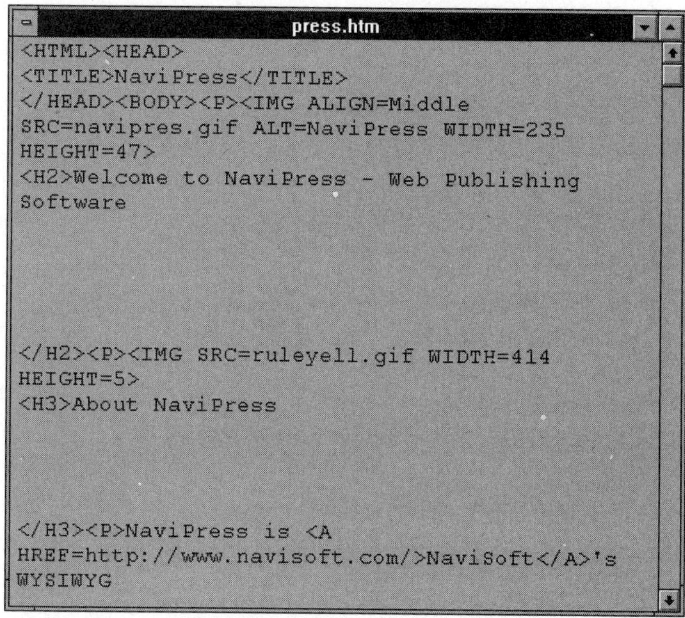

press.htm
<HTML><HEAD>
<TITLE>NaviPress</TITLE>
</HEAD><BODY><P><IMG ALIGN=Middle
SRC=navipres.gif ALT=NaviPress WIDTH=235
HEIGHT=47>
<H2>Welcome to NaviPress - Web Publishing
Software
</H2><P><IMG SRC=ruleyell.gif WIDTH=414
HEIGHT=5>
<H3>About NaviPress
</H3><P>NaviPress is <A
HREF=http://www.navisoft.com/>NaviSoft</A>'s
WYSIWYG

3. You can open multiple HTML windows for different Page windows at the same time, if you like. (Select Window ➤ Tile.)

To close the HTML window, do one of the following:

- Choose File ➤ Close from the HTML window.
- Edit the page in the Page window. The HTML window closes automatically when you edit the Page window so that the contents of the Page window and the HTML window will not conflict.

Editing the HTML Source Code

You can edit the HTML source and load the changes you make into the Page window. For example, you might want to add HTML extensions for which GNNpress does not provide WYSIWYG authoring support.

Here's how to edit the source:

1. Open a GNNpress page.
2. Choose Tools ➤ Show HTML.
3. You can edit the HTML by typing text directly or by using any of the commands in the Edit menu.
    - If you cut and paste from an HTML window to a Page window, you will be able to see the HTML tags in the Page window. You can use this technique if you want to create a Web page that explains how to use HTML tags.
    - If you cut and paste from a Page window into an HTML window, the tags will not be pasted.
4. To save changes you make in an HTML window, choose File ➤ Parse. GNNpress checks your HTML code for errors. If any errors are found, you will see a message explaining the error. If no errors occur (or if you choose to ignore the errors), your changes will be shown in the Page window.

NOTE

You can also choose File ➤ Save As to save your HTML changes to a separate file.

Use File ➤ Reload if you want to discard changes you made to the HTML and start modifying the HTML again using the current code for the Page window.

Additional HTML 3.0 Tags Supported

In addition to the HTML tags you can add through WYSIWYG editing in GNNpress, the HTML 3.0 tags shown in Table 2 are supported by the GNNpress browser. See the HTML 3.0 specification for details. Other browsers may not yet support these additional tags.

Table 2: Additional HTML tags supported by GNNpress

TAG	DESCRIPTION
<LINK REL=>	Adds buttons to the toolbar for links such as *Home*, *Next*, and *Index*. For example, <LINK REL=PreviousHREF="mydoc2.htm">, and <LINK REL=Bookmark TITLE="Buy" HREF="b.htm">
<TAB>	Sets tab stops and indents text. Attributes supported are ID, TO, and INDENT. For example, Item 1: <TAB ID=T1> description, <P><TAB TO=T1>2nd description paragraph
<AU>, <PERSON>, <ACRONYM>, and <ABBREV>	Identify the following types of content: authors, people, acronyms, and abbreviations.
<INPUT TYPE=RANGE>	Creates a sliding range field inside a form.
<INPUT DISABLED>	Prevents the reader from setting a value in a field.
<P CLEAR=> and <BR CLEAR=>	Moves text down to clear space after an image. If you use LEFT or RIGHT alignment for images near each other, you will probably want to use this tag. The CLEAR attribute can be set to LEFT, RIGHT, or ALL.
<P NOWRAP>	Prevents the text in a paragraph from wrapping.
<TABLE> attributes: WIDTH, UNITS, COLSPEC, and NOWRAP	Provide additional control over width and formatting of tables.

Working with MiniWebs

As we mentioned earlier in the chapter, MiniWebs help you manage the files that make up your Web site. You can think of a MiniWeb as being similar to the Windows File Manager. MiniWebs provide a visual structure for organizing and manipulating your Web pages. In addition to letting you visualize and edit your Web structures, one of the real strengths of MiniWebs is that they help you manage and maintain your Web structures.

NOTE

To create and use MiniWebs, you must first disable short menus. When you have a MiniWeb open, you should not switch back to short menus, or you will not have access to many useful menu items.

Things to Know about MiniWebs

Each MiniWeb shows the contents of a directory on your local machine or on your remote GNN Web site (see Figure 36). When you create files in a MiniWeb, you are also creating files in that directory.

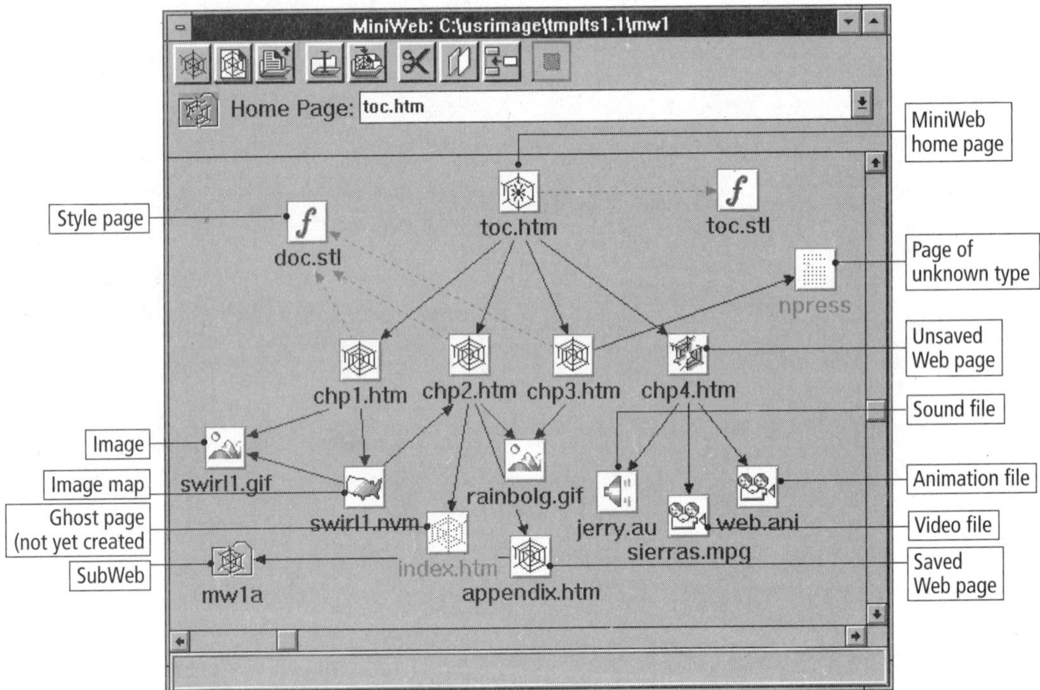

Figure 36: *Anatomy of a MiniWeb*

You can put one MiniWeb inside another MiniWeb to reflect the directory structure of your entire site. These nested webs are called *SubWebs*.

MiniWebs are excellent tools for creating Web sites with multiple pages—even if you expect your readers will be using browsers other than GNNpress.

Because MiniWebs are unique to NaviSoft, you cannot view MiniWebs with other browsers as you can with GNNpress. In addition, you cannot use MiniWebs to view directory structures on servers.

Viewing MiniWebs

MiniWebs provide a visual structure for organizing and manipulating your Web pages. You can view MiniWebs as a web, as a tree, and as a list of files sorted by name, title, or type. These views make it easy to find broken links, pages not linked to other pages, pages you have links to but have not yet created, and more. You can also show or hide both links to files and links from files, and you can hide groups of files so that you can focus on other files.

Creating MiniWebs

To create a new MiniWeb choose File ➤ New MiniWeb.

If your current window is a MiniWeb view, the new MiniWeb you create using this method (or the New MiniWeb button in the toolbar) will be a SubWeb of that MiniWeb.

Webizing Existing Directories

You may already have a set of files you want to publish on the Web. GNNpress makes it quick and easy to convert directories containing pages and other files into a MiniWeb. We call this *Webizing* the directory.

You can Webize a directory on your hard drive or one of your GNN directories (in **http://members.gnn.com/netname**).

NOTE

You cannot Webize someone else's Web site.

You should re-Webize your directories if you add pages or other files to the directory with a product other than GNNpress. GNNpress can't add icons to your MiniWeb automatically if you create them outside GNNpress. Also, if your MiniWeb doesn't match the files your directory contains, you can re-Webize the directory anytime.

Here's how to convert existing directories to MiniWebs:

1. From any Page or MiniWeb window, choose Tools ➤ Webize. The Webize Directory dialog box will appear, as shown in Figure 37.

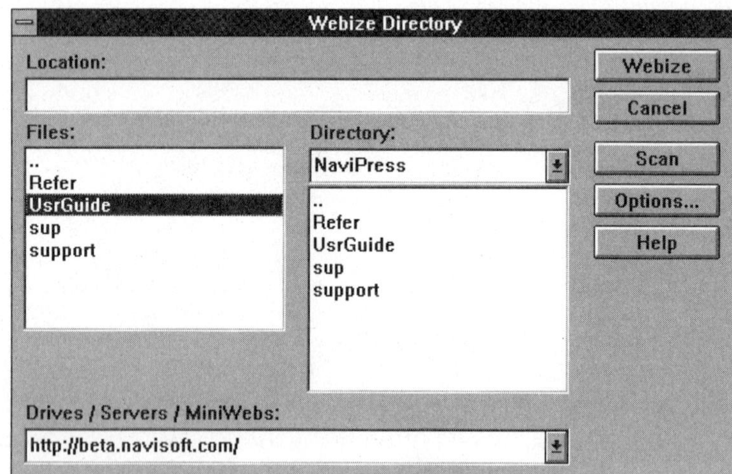

Figure 37: *The Webize Directory dialog box for converting existing directories to MiniWebs*

2. If the directory you want to Webize has subdirectories (or folders) that you want to turn into SubWebs, click on Options. You can choose whether you want to Webize subdirectories that are not already MiniWebs, and whether you want to Webize subdirectories that are already MiniWebs. If you check both boxes, all subdirectories are Webized. If you uncheck both boxes, no subdirectories are Webized.
3. Browse to find the directory you want to convert to a MiniWeb.

TIP

If you want to Webize a directory and its subdirectories, select the highest-level directory you want to Webize.

4. Double-click on the directory name in the list of Files. Or, select the directory in the Directory list and click on Webize.
5. If a MiniWeb already exists for a directory, you will be asked whether you want to regenerate the MiniWeb. Click on Regenerate to update the MiniWeb.

Opening Existing MiniWebs

MiniWebs can be stored on your local disks or on your GNN directory (**http://members.gnn.com/netname/**). There are several ways to open existing MiniWebs:

- Choose File ➤ Open. Select MiniWeb in the List Files Of Type field. Select the MiniWeb you want to open. Then, click on Open. (If the MiniWeb is not listed as a separate file, select its directory and erase the file name NEW.HTM at the end of the Location field.)
- Click on the Open button in the MiniWeb toolbar.
- Type the MiniWeb URL you want to open in the Location field of a Page window.
- Click on the MiniWeb icon to the left of the Title field in a Page window. You can click this button any time you are viewing a page that is part of a MiniWeb. The button is grayed out if the page is not part of a MiniWeb.

Templates

Templates are existing example MiniWebs we have created for your use. You can simply view them to get ideas or a better understanding of how MiniWebs work, or you can create your own copy of them and adapt them to suit your own purposes.

To adapt a template for your use, follow these steps:

1. Select Help ➤ Templates to open a page that lists MiniWeb templates available from GNN.
2. Click on the Templates link to move down the page to the list of templates.
3. Click on the Resume link to see the resume template.
4. Click on the Show MiniWeb icon to the left of the Title field. You will see the MiniWeb for the resume template.

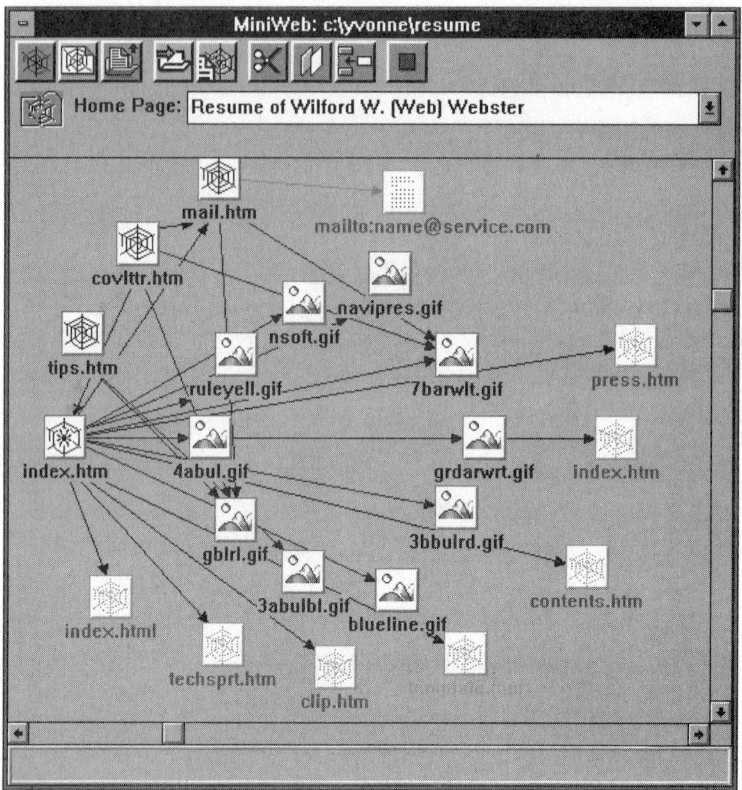

5. Choose File ➤ Save As.
6. It's a good idea to save the template MiniWeb to your local hard drive while you're working on it. Select the drive from the Drives/Servers/MiniWebs field and find the directory you want to contain the MiniWeb. A new subdirectory will be added to that directory to contain the MiniWeb when you click on OK.

The status bar of the MiniWeb displays the names of all the MiniWeb files. It then briefly displays the word *Publishing…* and then the word *Saved*, indicating a successful copy and save of the template to your local files.

Selecting a MiniWeb View

The default way to view a MiniWeb is with the Web view (Figure 38). The Mini-Web is shown with icons for all the files in a series of concentric circles. The icons are connected by arrows that show the connections between files. You can view MiniWebs in several other formats. The Tree and Name views are shown in the Figures 39 and 40.

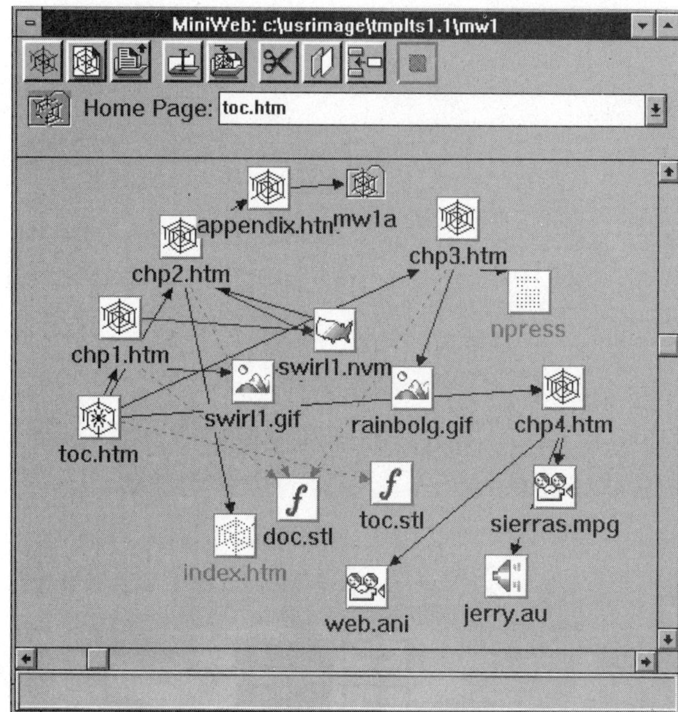

Figure 38: *A MiniWeb in Web view*

To select a MiniWeb view, follow these steps:

1. Choose View ➤ Name. The window will list files by file name. Links to files are indented below each file.
2. As you work, you can switch the MiniWeb view between Web, Tree, Name, Title, and MIME Type (which is similar to the file type).
3. Notice that each type of file has a different icon, and that there are several colors for arrows and text. The next sections explain these icons, arrows, and colors.

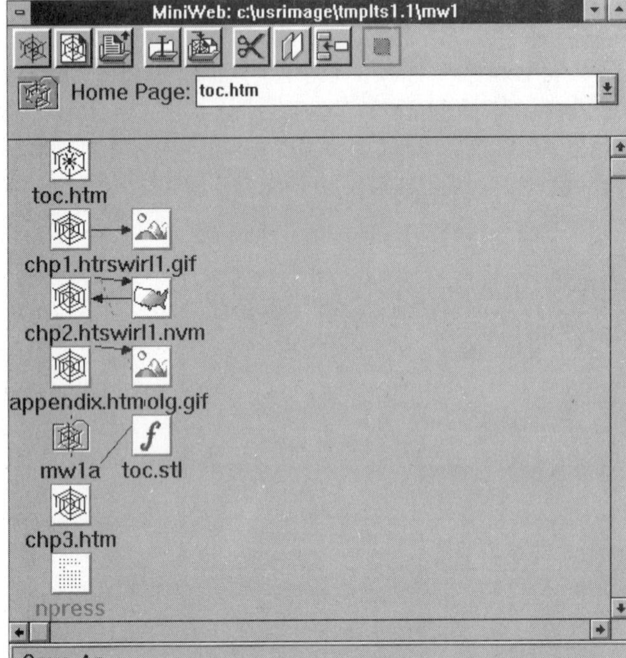

Figure 39:
A MiniWeb in Tree view

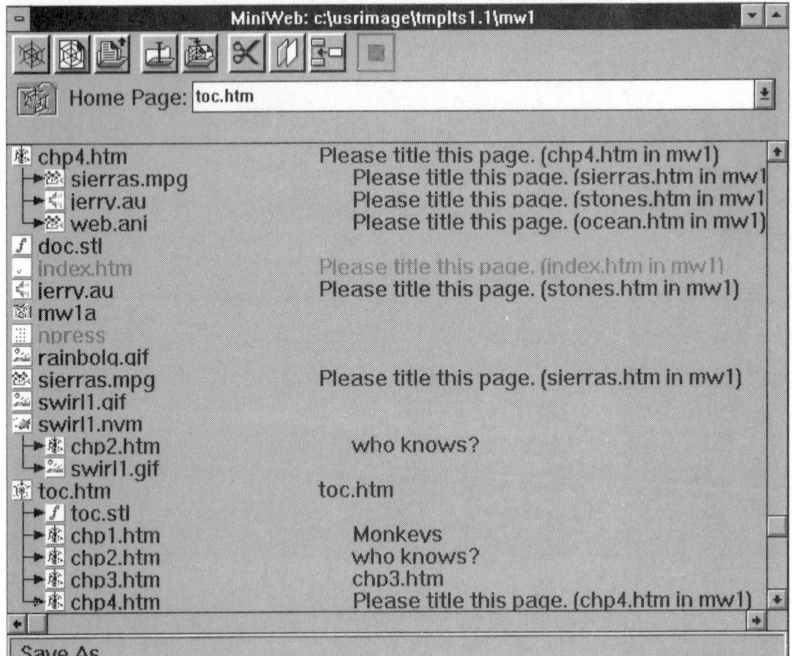

Figure 39:
A MiniWeb in Name view

Icons in MiniWebs

One page in the MiniWeb is designated the home page (it is displayed with a special icon—a spider in its web); any file in the directory that can be reached through a series of links from the home page is shown in the web. Some pages may not be "reachable"; they are displayed either to the right or below the main graph.

Pages that are referenced but have not yet been created are grayed out. References to the external Web have another type of grayed icon, and their names are green. Files other than pages (images, sounds, etc.) are shown with different icons: page icons are webs, image icons are a landscape, sound icons are a speaker, video icons are a projector, style icons are an italic *f*, and image maps icons are a map of the United States.

HTML pages come in three states: new, modified, and normal. The normal icon is a full web, the modified icon is a broken web (until the file is saved), the new icon is a very small web. Pages and images come in several states with similar icons.

Home page

External image

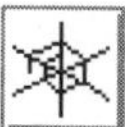
New page

Ghost image (file not yet created)

Image

Unsaved page

Arrows in MiniWebs

When you use the Web or Tree views, arrows between the icons indicate the relationships between them.

- Black arrow: A normal, one directional link.
- Double-ended cyan arrow: Each page refers to the other.

- Blue arrow: Link to an inline image.
- Green arrow: Link from a page containing a form to the form handler program.
- Gray dotted arrow: A link that does not appear in the page when it is displayed (for example, a link to an image map file).

Color Codes in MiniWebs

MiniWebs icons are color coded to show the status and relationships of the files in the MiniWeb:

- Solid: The file is physically located in the MiniWeb.
- Dithered: The file is a relative link, but is not physically located in the MiniWeb.

NOTE

See the "Links" section earlier in this chapter for an explanation of relative and absolute references.

- Green text: The file is an absolute link and is not physically located in the MiniWeb.
- Broken: The file is physically located in the MiniWeb but has unsaved changes.

Focusing the View

GNNpress provides several ways to focus on the files you are working on, even if your MiniWeb contains lots of files.

One method is to hide various file types:

1. Choose View ➤ Display Control to open the Display Control dialog box.

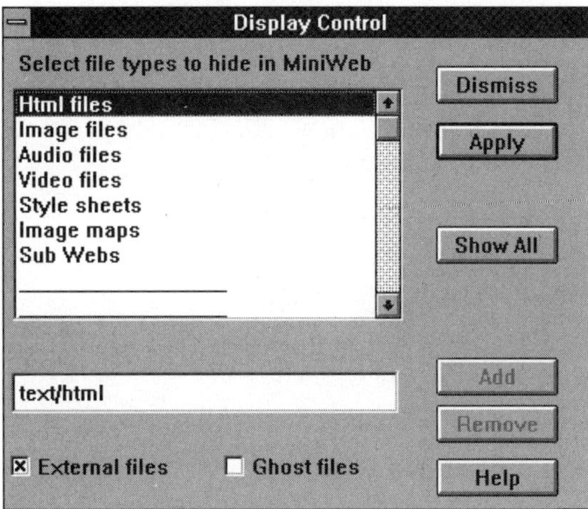

2. Select the types of files you want to hide. You can hold down the Shift key to select several types in a row, or the Ctrl key to select any set of file types.
3. Click Apply to hide the file types you selected.
4. You can check the External Files box to hide files outside your MiniWeb or the Ghost Files box to hide files that are linked to but do not exist.
5. If you want to add kinds of files to the list, type a MIME type in the field and click on Add. The new type will be added above the Anything Else type. (To see a list of MIME types, choose the Tools ➤ Preferences ➤ Extensions/MIME menu item.)

To hide or display links in the Name, Title, or MIME type view:

- If the Name, Title, or MIME Type view does not show links to other files, you can display them by choosing the View ➤ List Links To menu item.
- If the same view does not show links from other files, you can display them by choosing the View ➤ List Links From menu item.
- If a type of link is shown, you can hide those links by reselecting the menu item.

You can find a file in a MiniWeb by following these steps:

1. If you want to find a particular file in a large MiniWeb, choose Edit ➤ Find Page.
2. In the Find Page dialog box that appears, type the full name of the file you want to find. The file can be a page or any other file in the MiniWeb.

3. Click on OK. The file you named will be highlighted in the MiniWeb.

You can zoom in or out in the Web or Tree view. You can view part of the MiniWeb at a larger size by choosing the View ➤ Zoom In menu item. You can view more of a MiniWeb by choosing View ➤ Zoom Out.

Using the MiniWeb View

Pointing the mouse at an icon in MiniWeb view displays the page's title (or URL if it has no title) in the status bar. Clicking on an icon selects it. In the Web or Tree view, you can drag the selected icon around to reposition it.

Opening Pages and Files

Dragging and dropping an icon from a MiniWeb view into a Page window opens the file in that Page window.

Double-clicking on an icon generally opens the file in a new Page window. GNNpress performs the action that makes sense for each type of file:

- Page: If the page exists in the MiniWeb or there is an absolute link to the page, it is opened in a new Page window. If the page has not been created (light dithered icon), GNNpress asks you if you want to create it. If there is a relative link to the page, you should first find the SubWeb that contains the page and open the page from that SubWeb.
- Graphic: GNNpress attempts to launch an external viewer. If no viewer is available, and the image is either a GIF, JPEG, or XBM, then it opens a Page window containing just the image. Otherwise, you are asked if you want to save the file.
- Video or Sound: GNNpress attempts to launch an external viewer or player. If no viewer is available, you are asked if you want to save the file.
- Image Map: The Image Map window is opened for the image.
- Style Sheet: The Style Sheet dialog box is opened.
- Form: There's no useful result if you double-click on a form icon; you get a "Not Found" message, or something similar.

Editing MiniWebs

You can use MiniWebs to help you create, save, and delete pages and other files. MiniWebs also help you create a variety of links between files.

Creating New Pages in MiniWebs

You can create a new page or file in a MiniWeb by doing any of the following:

- Choosing File ➤ New Page.
- Clicking on the New Page button in the MiniWeb toolbar.
- Double-clicking on any "ghosted" icon in your MiniWeb. (These icons show you which files are linked to but do not exist.) You will see a prompt that asks if you want to create the file.

You can also define a page template (or *stationery*):

1. Highlight the page you want to use as a template in the MiniWeb window.
2. Choose Edit ➤ Set Stationery. When you create a new page, the page you selected will be used as the starting point for your new page.

Copying Pages and Files to MiniWebs

GNNpress gives you several ways to copy files to your MiniWebs. To copy a file from one location to another, follow these steps:

1. Choose File ➤ Copy File. You will see the Copy File dialog box:

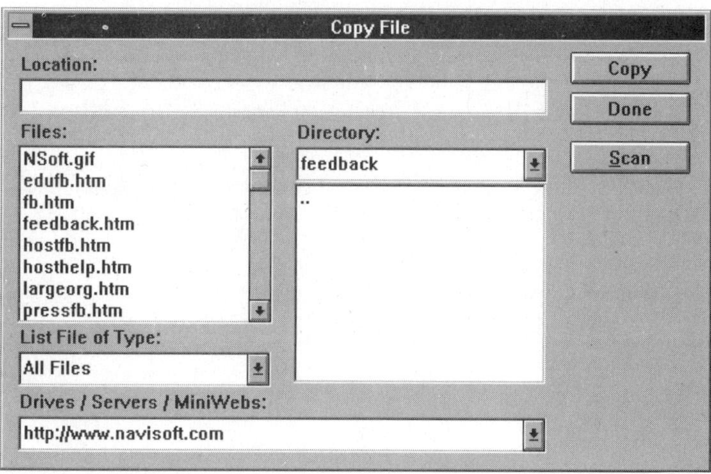

2. Choose the file you want to copy. The file can be any file on your local disks.
3. Click on Copy when you have selected the file. You will see this dialog box:

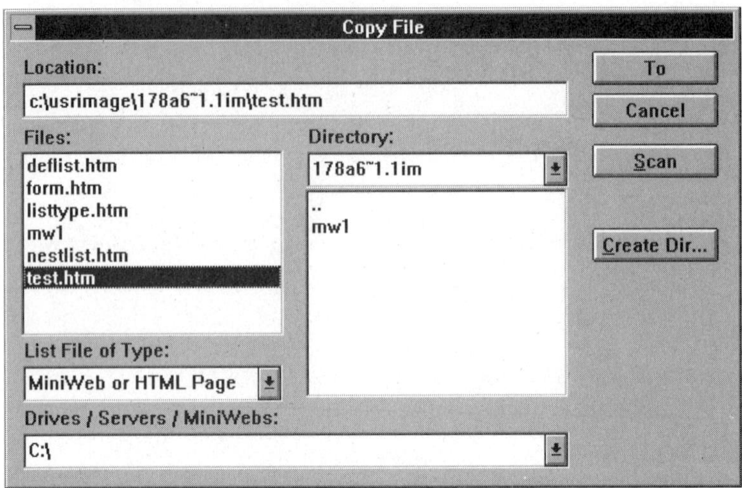

4. Select the directory where you want to save the file and add a file name. You can copy the file to a local disk or to your GNN directory.

This method copies a single file. It doesn't copy images within pages or other linked files to the new location. If you want to copy the images too, select File ➤ Save As and click on the Options button to choose how to deal with images.

Here are some other ways to copy files to your MiniWeb:

- Edit a page and choose File ➤ Save As to save the page to your MiniWeb with a new file name or location.
- Drag and drop a file icon from one MiniWeb to another. This copies the file to the second MiniWeb.
- Import an existing file into the MiniWeb by choosing File ➤ Import. Importing a page into a MiniWeb puts a separate copy of the file in your MiniWeb.
- Paste a page into a MiniWeb by pasting its URL. You can use this method to copy a file anywhere on the World Wide Web to your MiniWeb:

    1. Move to a Page window, highlight a link inside a Page window, or highlight an icon in a MiniWeb.

2. Click on the Copy URL button in the toolbar or choose Edit ➤ Copy URL. (Double-clicking on a MiniWeb icon while pressing Ctrl also copies the URL so you can paste it.)
3. Move to a MiniWeb window and choose Edit ➤ Paste URL.

Options for Copying Links and Images If you use any of the previous methods (except File ➤ Copy File) to copy a page to a MiniWeb, you will either automatically see the Options dialog box, or you can open the Options dialog box by clicking the Options button in the file selection dialog box.

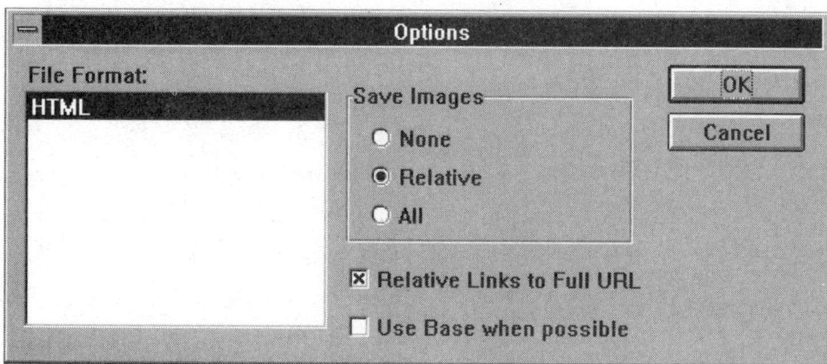

This dialog box allows you to set the following options:

- File Format: Normally, pages are imported or copied as HTML pages. If you choose File ➤ Save As, you can change the format of the file that is saved to "Text without line breaks" or "Text".
- Save Images: When you copy a page, you can choose what you want to do with any images inside the page:
    - None: Choose None if you do not want to copy any of the images. If the images are not already part of your MiniWeb, also check the Relative Links To Full URL box so that the links to the images will still work.
    - Relative: Choose Relative if you want to copy images with relative links to your MiniWeb. You should also uncheck the Relative Links To Full URL box.
    - All: Choose All if you want to copy all the images in the page to your MiniWeb. You should also uncheck the Relative Links To Full URL box.
- Control Links: If you want to convert relative links in the page to absolute links, check the Relative Links To Full URL box. For example, check this box

if you copy a page from some other server and want the links in that page to continue working.

- The Use Base when possible box is ignored when you are copying a file into a MiniWeb.

Saving MiniWebs

When you save a MiniWeb, GNNpress also saves all files in the MiniWeb that are open and have unsaved changes.

To save a MiniWeb, do one of the following:

- From the MiniWeb window, choose File ➤ Save. This saves the MiniWeb in its current location along with any unsaved pages.
- From the MiniWeb window, choose File ➤ Save As. You can use this dialog to move the MiniWeb to a different location on your local disk or on the Web. The files in your MiniWeb are copied to the new location you choose.

The Options button opens a dialog box that lets you choose whether or not to save all the SubWebs under this MiniWeb, and whether or not to convert any relative references to other files to absolute references. By default, relative links to files in the same MiniWeb are still relative in the new location and SubWebs under the MiniWeb are also copied to the new location.

Deleting Files in MiniWebs

When you delete a file from a MiniWeb, you are also deleting the file from your disk or from the server's disk. If other files in your MiniWeb link to the file you delete, you will still see a "ghost" image of the file icon.

Deleting an image or image map from a page does not delete the actual file. Likewise, deleting a page file does not delete files associated with it—such as images and image maps. If you want to delete files associated with another file, you must delete them separately using one of the following techniques:

- In a MiniWeb view, highlight an icon and press Delete or Backspace. You will not be prompted, and there is no way to undo this action.

- In a MiniWeb view, highlight an icon and choose Edit ➤ Cut. You can choose Edit ➤ Paste to restore the file.
- In a MiniWeb view, choose File ➤ Delete to open the Delete dialog box. Select the file you want to delete and click on Delete. A prompt window will ask if you are sure you want to delete the file.

Creating Links Using MiniWebs

MiniWebs give you many ways to control links between pages and files.

If you rename a file within a MiniWeb, the links to that file within the current MiniWeb (but not the SubWebs) are automatically fixed. From a MiniWeb window you can also use the Check Links feature to check the links in all the pages in your MiniWeb and in all of its SubWebs at once.

To create links in a MiniWeb, you can do any of the following:

- From the Window ➤ Cascade menu, use the right mouse button to drag a page icon from a MiniWeb to a page.
- Use the right mouse button to drag an icon for an image from a MiniWeb to a page. The image is added to the page. (If you use the left mouse button to drag the image, instead, your page is replaced by a blank page containing the image.)
- Paste a link into a page by pasting the URL:

  1. Move to a Page window, highlight a link (by Ctrl+clicking) inside a Page window, or highlight an icon in a MiniWeb.
  2. Click on the Copy URL button in the toolbar or choose Edit ➤ Copy URL. (Double-clicking on a MiniWeb icon while pressing Ctrl also copies the URL so you can paste it.)
  3. Move to a Page window and position the cursor wherever you want to place the link. If the text or image you want to act as a link is already in the page, highlight it. If you don't highlight any text, the title of the page you are linking to is automatically added to your page as a link.
  4. Choose Edit ➤ Paste URL.

Managing MiniWebs

In addition to letting you visualize and edit your Web structures, one of the real strengths of MiniWebs is that they help you manage and maintain your Web structures.

Setting the Home Page

The "home page" is the page where readers start in your directory. If a reader uses a URL with no file name (such as **http://www.company.com/mydir/**), the GNN server automatically sends the home page in that MiniWeb to be displayed.

If you use a URL without a file name in GNNpress, you normally see the MiniWeb view for that directory if there is one. However, if you are using the short menus, you will automatically see the home page.

To set a home page for a MiniWeb, follow these steps:

1. Click the arrow to the right of the Home Page field below the MiniWeb toolbar. You will see a list of the titles of pages in your MiniWeb.
2. From this list, select the title of the page you want to be the home page of your MiniWeb. The icon for that page in your MiniWeb will change to have a spider in the web.

Finding and Replacing MiniWeb-Wide

When you are in a MiniWeb window, you can find text anywhere in your MiniWeb and make global changes to the MiniWeb.

To find and replace text, follow these steps:

1. Choose Edit ➤ Find/Replace to display the Find/Replace dialog box.

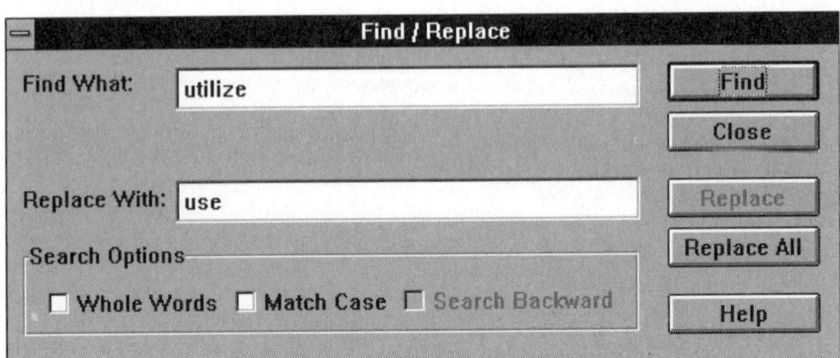

2. Type the text you want to search for in the Find What field.
3. If you want to change that text, type the new text in the Replace With field. You can also check one or more of the following Search Options:

   - Whole Words: Finds only whole words that match the characters you type. The default is to match any characters, even parts of words.
   - Match Case: Makes the match case-sensitive. The default is to ignore case.
   - Search Backward: Causes the search to move backwards from the current cursor location. The default is to search forward.

4. Use the buttons on the right to control the search:

   - Find: Finds and selects the next match.
   - Close: Closes the dialog box.
   - Replace: Replaces the selection with the text in the Replace With field.
   - Replace All: Finds and replaces all the occurrences in the entire MiniWeb.

Printing Pages and MiniWebs

To manage a MiniWeb, you may need to create printed documentation about the MiniWeb.

To print all the MiniWeb pages, move to the MiniWeb window and choose File ➤ Print. This will send all the pages in your MiniWeb to your current printer.

You can also print just the current MiniWeb view:

1. Move to the MiniWeb window and display the MiniWeb in the format you want to print.
2. Choose File ➤ Print Graphs. This sends the view of your MiniWeb to your current printer.

Using SubWebs

Larger Web sites use several related directories instead of a single directory. This makes maintaining the Web site easier in some ways, because you can make the directory structure match the structure of your site. For example, you might store customer support pages in a CUSTSUPP directory, sales pages in a SALES directory, and images in an IMAGES directory.

You manage multidirectory Webs in GNNpress using SubWebs. Each subdirectory is its own SubWeb. A folder icon for each SubWeb is shown in the MiniWeb for the directory containing the SubWeb.

In general, you use SubWebs the same as any other MiniWeb. For example, you can drag and drop files from one SubWeb to another SubWeb. The differences are the additional ways files in a SubWeb can interact with files in other SubWebs.

To create a SubWeb, do any of the following:

- Select Tools ➤ Webize to create a main MiniWeb and SubWebs for all of your existing directories.
- Display the MiniWeb that will contain the SubWeb, and choose File ➤ New MiniWeb or click on the New MiniWeb icon in the MiniWeb toolbar. The new MiniWeb will be a SubWeb of the MiniWeb you were viewing.
- Drag and drop a SubWeb icon into another MiniWeb window.
- Create an empty MiniWeb. Then, choose the File ➤ Save As menu item to save the MiniWeb inside another MiniWeb.
- Import one MiniWeb into another MiniWeb.

To open a SubWeb, try any of the following:

- Double-click on the SubWeb's folder icon in the MiniWeb above the SubWeb in the directory tree.
- Choose File ➤ Open.
- Click on the Open button in the MiniWeb view.
- Type the SubWeb's URL in the Location field of a Page window.

References between SubWebs

It's usually best to use relative links within your own Web site. Relative links allow you to move the entire directory tree to a new location (for example, from your hard disk to the Web) without breaking your links. You should try to use absolute links only to references files outside your own Web.

A relative reference to a file in the same directory is simple—just use the filename and omit any information about the Web location and the directory. For example, use OTHER.HTM instead of **http://members.gnn.com/netname/other.htm**.

You can also use relative links to reference files in different SubWebs within your site, but they are a little more complicated. Suppose you have a directory tree like this:

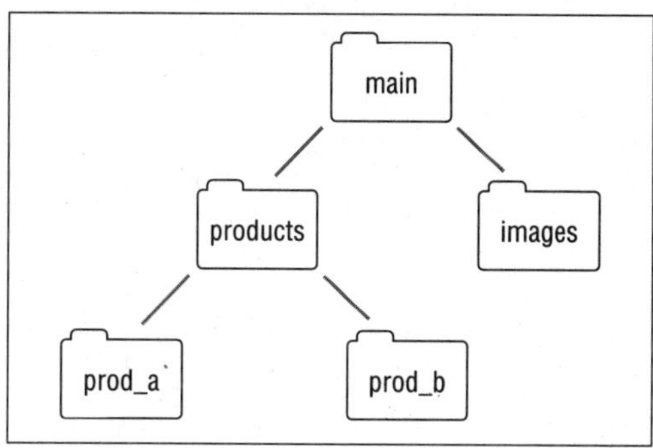

Relative references between files in these directories would have the following syntax:

REFERENCE BETWEEN...	RELATIVE LINK FORMAT
"main" to "products"	products/file.htm
"main" to "prod_a"	products/prod_a/file.htm
"products" to "prod_a"	prod_a/file.htm
"products" to "main"	../file.htm
"products" to "images"	../images/fig.gif
"prod_a" to "products"	../file.htm
"prod_a" to "prod_b"	../prod_b/file.htm
"prod_a" to "main"	../../file.html
"prod_a" to "images"	../../images/fig.gif

A Quick Summary of Commands for MiniWebs

Here is a quick summary of commands you can use with MiniWebs:

- To open a MiniWeb, choose File ➤ Open or select the Open button in the MiniWeb view.
- To open a new MiniWeb, choose File ➤ New MiniWeb or select the MiniWeb icon in the MiniWeb view.
- To open a file, choose File ➤ Open or select the Open button in the MiniWeb view.
- To open a new page, choose File ➤ New page or select the Page button in the toolbar.

Templates

- To open a template, choose Help ➤ Templates. Click on the Templates link and select one of the templates. Then, click on the MiniWeb icon.
- To save your own copy of the template, choose File ➤ Save As.

Directories

- To convert a directory into a MiniWeb, select Tools ➤ Webize.

Modify MiniWebs

- To add pages, choose File ➤ New Page or choose the Page button in the toolbar.
- To set the home page, Click on the down arrow to the right of the Home Page Title field.
- To copy a URL, select Edit ➤ Copy URL or choose the Copy URL button in the toolbar.
- To delete pages, highlight an icon and press the Delete or Backspace key; or highlight an icon and choose Edit ➤ Cut or File ➤ Delete.
- To save a MiniWeb, choose File ➤ Save or File ➤ Save As.

Authors: Jeff Dozier, Yvonne DeGraw, Ralph Chaney

Special Thanks To: Thomas Storm, Dave Bourgeois, Jim Davidson, Linda T. Dozier, Cathe Gordon, Dave Long, Doug McKee, Jeff Rawlings, Joel Thames, and George W. Williams, V.

To Contact Us For information about GNNpress and GNN service:

- See GNNpress' home page—**http://www.tools.gnn.com**.
- Call (800) 819-6112.
- Check out the Primehost forum on America Online at keyword Primehost.
- Send e-mail to **info@tools.gnn.com**.

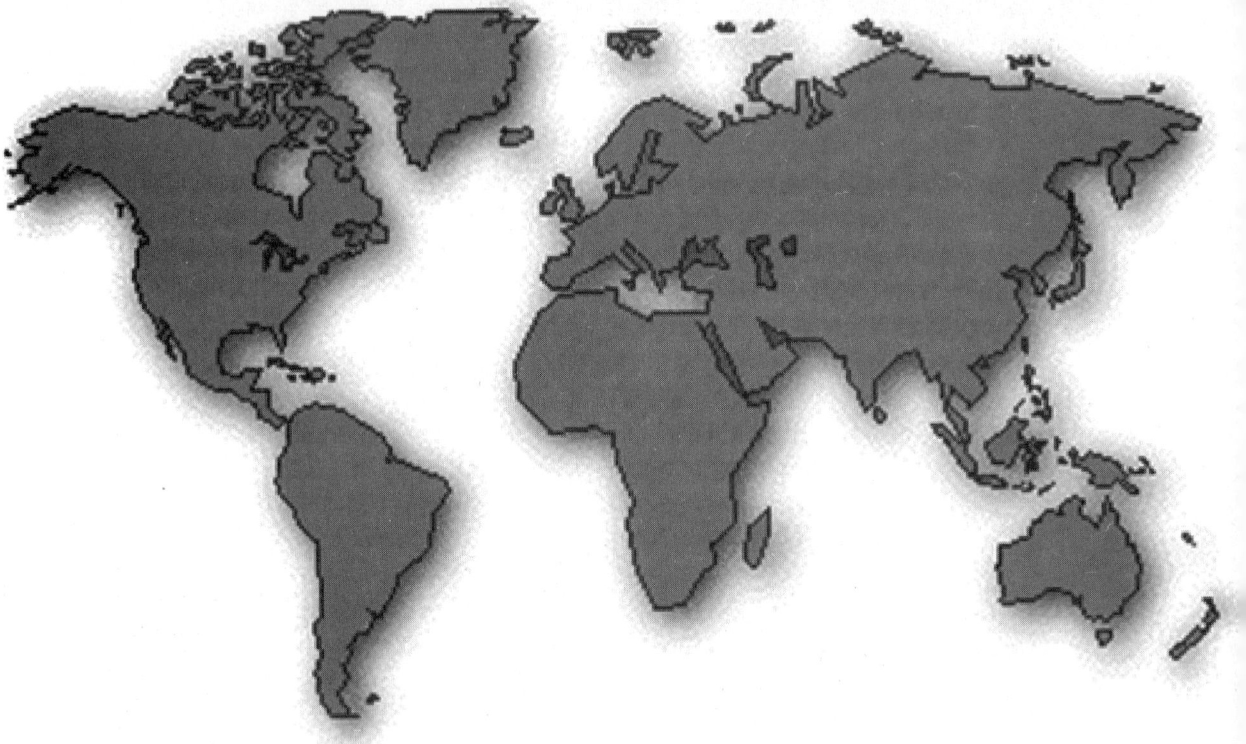

Adobe Acrobat

Adobe

Adobe Systems

Adobe Acrobat Exchange and Reader

Company Profile

Adobe Systems Incorporated (**http://www.adobe.com**) is the world's leading publisher of desktop publishing and visual communication tools. Its lead products include Adobe Photoshop, Adobe Illustrator, Adobe PageMaker, Adobe Acrobat, Adobe FrameMaker, Adobe PageMill, Adobe SiteMill, and Adobe Premiere. Its products are essential components to nearly every Web or print designer in the United States and abroad.

Adobe Acrobat is a cross-platform tool for electronic publishing. With Acrobat, you can create, view, and navigate documents in electronic form, print them, or distribute them electronically to others. All documents created with Acrobat are PDF (Portable Document Format) files, based on Adobe's PostScript language, which allows for consistent presentation of content on Macintosh, Windows, Unix, and DOS platforms. There is an exciting new distribution channel for Adobe Acrobat documents: The Web. The new Adobe Web strategy has a two-tiered approach to distributing elaborate graphics and files across the Net: the freely distributed Adobe Acrobat Reader, included on the CD-ROM, which allows for any PDF document to be identically viewed from within the Netscape browser; and the Adobe Acrobat Suite of PDS development tools, which includes several new features and much deeper Web capability, including custom programming with Microsoft ActiveX, which allows for inclusion into the Microsoft Internet Explorer.

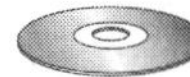

Chapter Profile

Many technology pundits have written about "convergence" of telephony and computing or the "transition" from print to digital media in the last few years, but few have given concrete examples of what people can do to actively *participate* in such changes. This tutorial fulfills that opportunity.

This tutorial covers the Adobe Acrobat Exchange version 2.1, which assembles PDF files complete with Web links, Hypertext controls, graphics, and multiple document controls. This chapter will get you up to speed with the application, but is not definitive. Once your PDF files are created and linked, the Adobe Acrobat Reader, which is freely distributed, allows many different platforms to display and print the files in an identical fashion. The Acrobat Distiller functions as a printer driver, which intercepts postscript output and formats it into the PDF format for inclusion into documents via the Acrobat Exchange. For the current version of Exchange, you can embed PDF files into a HTML page. New versions of Acrobat 3.0 available in Fall 1996 will permit direct Web authoring. For upgrades and more product information, visit the Adobe site: **http://www.adobe.com**.

The big boom in the '80s was desktop publishing: suddenly, everyone was a publisher...well, maybe. Several of the same hype-masters returned in the last few years, running up and down the streets of Silicon Valley like Paul Revere spouting the same message with a World Wide Web spin to it. Few understood that the shift in industries assured neither immediate success or good design, ergo the creation of this book. But what several of them may not have known is that their messages, taken together, actually made some sense. Opportunity would reward people who could master *transition*, not just each new level of "publishing." In other words, people who could balance talents of both print and digital publishing would be valuable, as the shift from paper to screen would not be immediate.

Smart carpenters know the old phrase, "measure twice, cut once." This phrase pertains not only to attentiveness, but to the choice of proper tools as well. In the current shift from print to screen, one such tool is Adobe Acrobat. It allows for a wide variety of creativity, while taking advantage of some of the best capabilities of each medium.

Bear in mind that the Web is already, to a limited extent, a "print" medium, as most screens can be printed from within browsers. Yet the presentation of the materials that come out of your printer is likely to be mediocre—HTML is not the world's best page layout tool by a long shot. If a project requires materials to look good in both media, Adobe Acrobat is a great choice for the tool to use. It gives you control over the printed page, while allowing for wide distribution over the Web at a very low cost.

The next transition is already nearing: the convergence of print and screen with video and animation (see the Dimension X chapter in this book). If you feel the itch to be a pioneer, go for it! If you choose to be a "settler" instead, wait for Adobe Acrobat 3.0!

Tutorial

Getting Started with Acrobat for the Web

ELCOME TO ADOBE ACROBAT. The Adobe Acrobat product family consists of the following products: the freely available and freely distributable Adobe Acrobat Reader, Adobe Acrobat Exchange, Adobe Acrobat Pro (available in version 2.1 but not in 3.0), Adobe Acrobat for Workgroups 2.1 (called *Acrobat for Ten-User License* in 3.0), and Acrobat Capture—designed to bring electronic documents to a wide range of users. These cross-platform documents, which are created in Adobe's Portable Document Format (PDF), are called *PDF documents*.

NOTE

This tutorial covers version 2.1 of Adobe Acrobat Exchange. At the time of this writing, version 3.0 had not yet been released, but many of its features and much of its functionality should be very similar to version 2.1.

Adobe Acrobat Software allows you to create and add value to electronic documents and then share them with other Acrobat users. You can view and print PDF documents, as well as annotate, build navigational links, and add security controls to PDF files. This product includes everything most business users need to create, use, and distribute electronic documents:

- *Acrobat PDF Writer* is a driver that enables you to "print" common business documents, such as word processing or spreadsheet files, to a PDF file (instead of to a printer).
- *Acrobat Search* provides full-text search capabilities for PDF files that have been indexed using Acrobat Catalog software.
- *Acrobat Reader* enables Windows (and Windows NT), Macintosh, DOS, and Unix users to view, navigate through, and print any PDF document. Currently, Reader 2.1 can be freely distributed to Macintosh, Sun SPARC, HP-UX, Silicon Graphics IRIX, and Windows users. Reader 1.0 is available to DOS.

Acrobat Pro includes all of the components of Adobe Acrobat plus Acrobat Distiller.

- *Acrobat Distiller* converts any PostScript language file into PDF format. You can use it with files from drawing, page layout, or image-editing programs, as well as with documents that contain high-resolution or Encapsulated PostScript (EPS) language artwork or images, or documents with complex blends or gradient fills.
- *Acrobat for Workgroups* contains everything a workgroup of up to 10 people needs to create, share, and review documents electronically. It includes a 10-user license for all Adobe Acrobat products, plus Acrobat Distiller software and Acrobat Catalog for creating indexes for full-text cross-document searches. (Acrobat Catalog is also available in the new Acrobat 3.0.)
- *Adobe Acrobat Capture* enables you to scan and OCR paper documents to PDF documents, ASCII text, or popular word processor document formats.

Acrobat 2.1 Features for the Web Designer

Acrobat has several features valuable to Web designers who want to build cool sites for the Web. Many of these features, such as multimedia on the Web, anticipate the development efforts by several other tool companies. These features include the following:

Movies. Add QuickTime and AVI movies and sounds to your PDF file; the movies and sounds can be played back using the movie tool plug-in.

Link PDF documents to the World Wide Web. Add links from PDF documents to documents on Web servers anywhere on the Internet using the Weblink plug-in.

Automatic compression selection. Acrobat Distiller determines the best compression method for your images (JPEG or LZW) and applies the correct setting.

Power Macintosh-native. Acrobat Exchange 2.1 joins Acrobat Distiller and ATM as Power Macintosh-native applications.

Windows NT 3.5 support. Acrobat Exchange 2.1, Reader, Distiller, and Catalog are compatible with Windows NT 3.5 or later.

QuickDraw GX support. The Macintosh version of the Acrobat Exchange program runs under QuickDraw GX and uses GX fonts when QuickDraw GX is running.

Search capability. Windows, Unix, and Macintosh users can conduct full-text searches of PDF files that have been indexed using Acrobat Catalog software.

Acrobat Catalog. Enables users to manage large volumes of information by building online indexes for PDF documents on either platform.

Security. You can add password protection to your PDF document and limit access to document features such as printing, selecting text and graphics, and adding or changing notes.

Linking to other PDF documents or files. You can create bookmarks and links to other Acrobat documents and to other application files.

Editing with thumbnails. You can use thumbnails to move, copy, insert, replace, and delete pages in a PDF document. You can edit within a single PDF document or between PDF documents.

Page insertion and page replacement. You can combine two or more PDF files into a single document by inserting specified pages (or the complete document) into one of the documents. You can also replace pages without affecting the bookmarks and links.

Text flows, or articles, for reading a PDF document. In documents in which text is in columns or otherwise separated, you can guide the reader from one part of the article to the next. Readers click to advance to the next view.

TrueType font embedding. You can use PDF Writer to embed TrueType fonts into your PDF documents so that Acrobat Exchange and Reader programs can display and print the same fonts on computers that do not have them installed (instead of substituting the fonts).

Multiple master font embedding. Acrobat Distiller embeds an instance of any multiple master fonts used in a document. This instance is a valid Type 1 font and is compatible with Acrobat Exchange and Acrobat Reader, versions 1.0 and later.

Device-independent color for PostScript Level 2 printing. Acrobat Distiller 2.0 and later adds device-independent color (DIC) information to all PDF files that contain RGB color or grayscale information. Printing of DIC is supported by the Acrobat viewers (Acrobat Exchange and Acrobat Reader 2.0 and later) when printing to PostScript Level 2 devices.

Fit Visible. This magnification option automatically selects the appropriate zoom level to display the visible elements of a page. Fit Visible eliminates white space in the margins.

Full Screen. Ideal for presentations: you can display PDF documents across the full monitor screen without any user interface. In this mode, pages can be set to advance automatically.

Page Cache. This feature speeds up the display of PDF documents, such as presentations, by rendering and caching the next page.

Text Notes. Acrobat notes can now be customized with a personal label and color, and each note is time- and date-stamped. This information is included in a Notes Summary file. You can export your notes from a PDF file into a file that consists of only notes, and you can send this notes-only file to the author to be imported into the PDF document.

OLE (Object Linking and Embedding). PDF documents can be incorporated into documents created by any OLE 1.0 or OLE 2.0 application. By supporting OLE and Lotus Notes/FX (Field Exchange), Acrobat allows users to search, view, modify, and print PDF documents distributed by Lotus Notes on both the Macintosh and Windows platforms.

Application Programming Interfaces (APIs). Acrobat's open architecture supports Lotus Notes/FX, AppleScript, Apple events, OLE, and Dynamic Data Exchange (DDE). An extensive API is available for creating plug-in modules, customizing the user interface, adding new features, and integrating Acrobat with other products. The Acrobat Software Development Kit, which includes software, technical documents, and examples, helps developers extend and integrate Acrobat software into other applications.

About This Tutorial

This tutorial is written for both Windows and Macintosh users, and uses the convention that Windows commands precede Macintosh commands. For example, Ctrl/Command+C equals the Window's Ctrl+C command and the Macintosh's Command+C command. In addition, this tutorial uses the term *folder* for both Macintosh folders and Windows directories.

Acrobat 2.1 Requirements

To use the Windows version of Acrobat Exchange, you need the following hardware and software:

- A 386-, 486-, or Pentium-based personal computer
- Microsoft Windows 3.1, Windows for Workgroup, Windows 95, Windows NT 3.5, Windows NT 3.51, OS/2 2.11 or later (running in Windows compatibility mode), OS/2 Warp (running in Windows compatibility mode)
- A minimum of 4 megabytes (MB) of RAM
- A CD-ROM drive

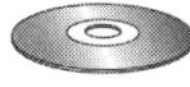

Only the freely distributed Acrobat Reader is provided on the CD-ROM in the back of this book; you must purchase a copy of Acrobat Exchange and install it according to the documentation that comes with it. For information on how to get a copy, visit the Adobe Web site at **http://www.adobe.com**, telephone them at (415) 962-4800, or write to them at 1585 Charlston Rd., Mountain View, CA 94043.

To use the Macintosh version of Acrobat Exchange, you need the following hardware and software (in addition to a purchased copy of Exchange):

- A Macintosh computer (a 68020 or later processor)
- Apple System 7.0 or later
- 2 MB of application RAM (for 68020-68040 computers), or 4 MB of application RAM (for Power Macintosh computers)
- A CD-ROM drive

Installing Acrobat Reader

Here's how to install Acrobat Reader from the CD-ROM in the back of this book:

Open the Adobe Folder. Double-click on Acroread.exe. Follow the onscreen instructions. Read the agreement. Accept it if you agree. If you don't agree, you won't be able to use the utility. You may select a directory for the reader, the default is C:\acroread. Click Install. Fill in your name and the organization. Click OK. Click OK when the installation is complete. You can then register this program with Windows to open PDF files and/or add it as an extension to your Web browser. Your particular Web browser will have specific extension installation requirements.

Using Acrobat Exchange

This section introduces you to the Acrobat Exchange screen and tools, and to the basic concepts of viewing Acrobat documents, which are electronic, cross-platform documents in the Portable Document Format (PDF). In these next few sections, you will learn Acrobat basics, such as navigating through PDF documents and adding comments and hypertext links to documents.

Starting Acrobat

Before beginning the steps below, you may need to use the Custom Install option of the Acrobat Exchange installer to install the tutorial files if you did not do it during initial program installation.

First, you'll need to open the tutorial files:

1. Open the Adobe Acrobat program group or folder and double-click on the Acrobat Exchange program icon.
2. For Macintosh users only, if this is your first time running Acrobat Exchange, personalize your copy by entering your name, organization, and serial number.
3. Select File ➤ Open. In the Open dialog box, select the Tutorial folder, and click on OK (Windows) or on Open (Macintosh).

4. Select MRKTPLAN.PDF from the list of file names, and click on OK (Windows) or on Open (Macintosh).

The first page of the brochure appears in the Acrobat window, as you can see in Figure 1.

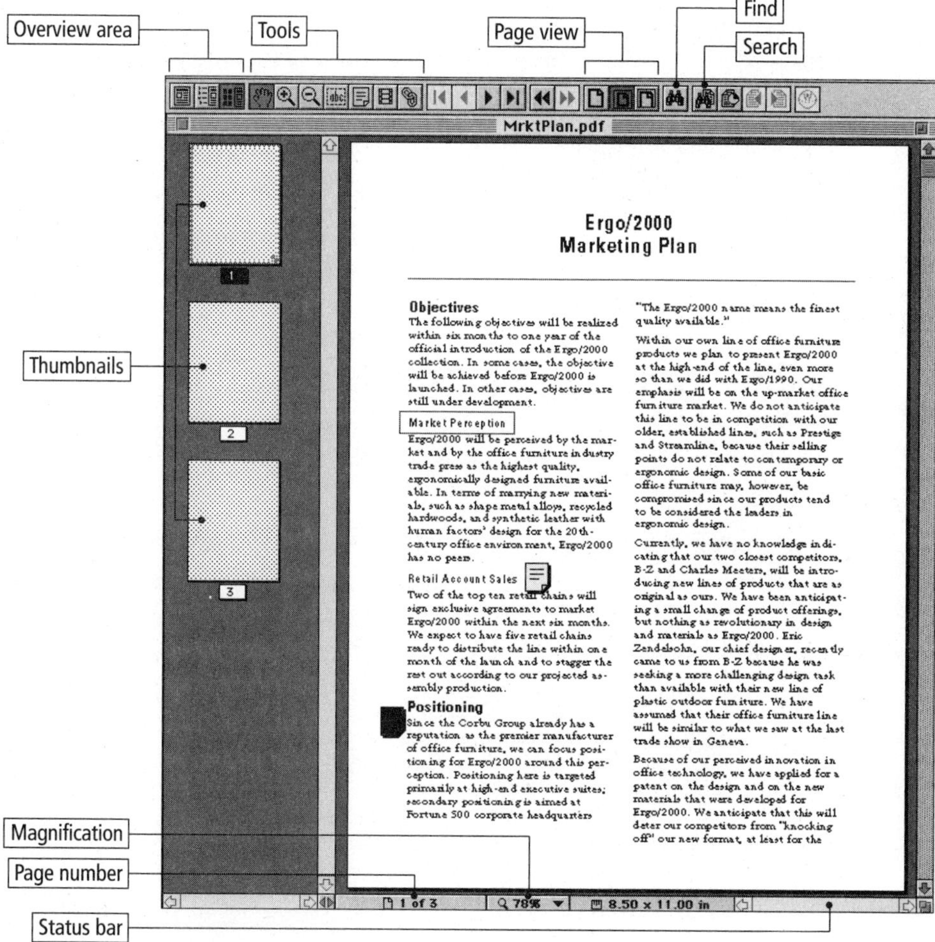

Figure 1: *The Marketing Plan brochure in the Acrobat window*

About the Acrobat Window

The Acrobat window is divided into three areas, as the preceding illustration shows—the document area, the overview area, and the toolbar area. The document area is where you view documents.

The overview area displays bookmarks or thumbnails for the document. *Bookmarks* allow you to go directly to a topic by clicking on the bookmark text. *Thumbnails* are miniature views of pages that you can click on to display the associated page.

The toolbar provides tools for tasks such as viewing, navigating, browsing, and searching documents. To select a tool, click on its button or choose it from the Tools menu.

Browsing through the Document

Now, try reviewing the marketing plan using the browse buttons and the zooming and magnification options.

1. Position the pointer on the status bar at the bottom of the Acrobat screen. The status bar displays general information about a document. The marketing plan consists of three 8½ x 11-inch pages that are displayed in the window at actual size (100%).

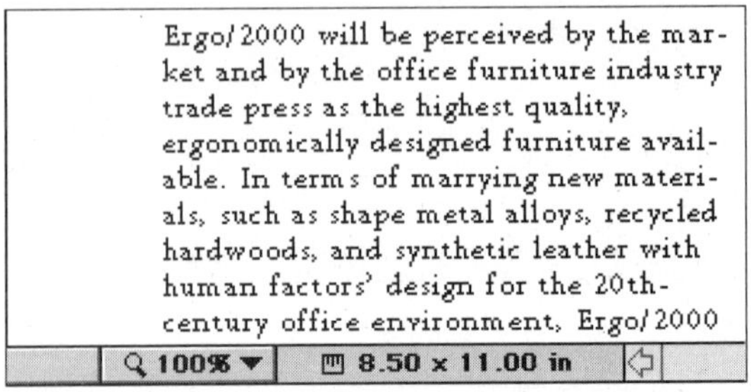

Ergo/2000 will be perceived by the market and by the office furniture industry trade press as the highest quality, ergonomically designed furniture available. In terms of marrying new materials, such as shape metal alloys, recycled hardwoods, and synthetic leather with human factors' design for the 20th-century office environment, Ergo/2000

100% | 8.50 x 11.00 in

2. Click on the magnification box in the status bar, and select Fit Visible from the menu that appears. (The Fit Visible button in the toolbar is also highlighted.) The marketing plan is enlarged to fill the document window.

3. Click on the Next Page button in the toolbar or press → on the keyboard to advance through the marketing plan page by page. All of the pages are displayed at the Fit Visible zoom level.
4. Choose View from the menu bar. The Fit Visible item is checked to show that this is your current page view. The view remains enlarged at this level until you change the zoom option.

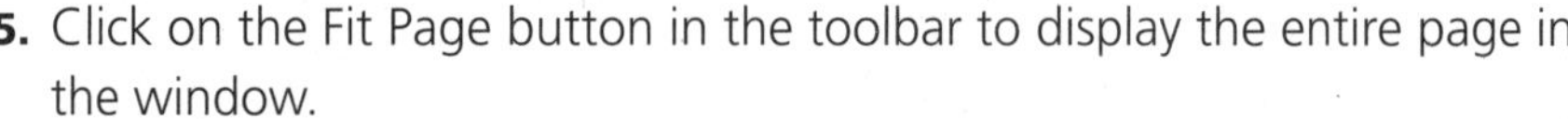

5. Click on the Fit Page button in the toolbar to display the entire page in the window.

6. Click on the Actual Size button. The document is now displayed at 100%.

7. Click on the First Page button to return to the first page.

8. Click on the Go Back button. Clicking on Go Back reverses the sequence of page and magnification changes. You can also click Go Back when you lose your place in a document.

Annotating the Document

Notes provide a way for you and document reviewers to add comments to a PDF document. Each reviewer can add notes to a PDF document just as any number of reviewers can write notes on the same printed document. Each reviewer's notes can be associated with a different label and color for easy identification. This annotation feature is helpful to Web designers mostly as a production tool. As a PDF progresses through multiple stages of refinement, it is helpful to have a version control mechanism and method by which several people can collaborate on a single piece of work.

Reading and Deleting Review Notes

Now, try opening, reading, and deleting a note:

1. Click on the First Page button. The marketing plan already has a graphic of a reviewer' s yellow sticky note affixed to the first column of the first page.

2. Double-click on the note icon in the first column to open this note.

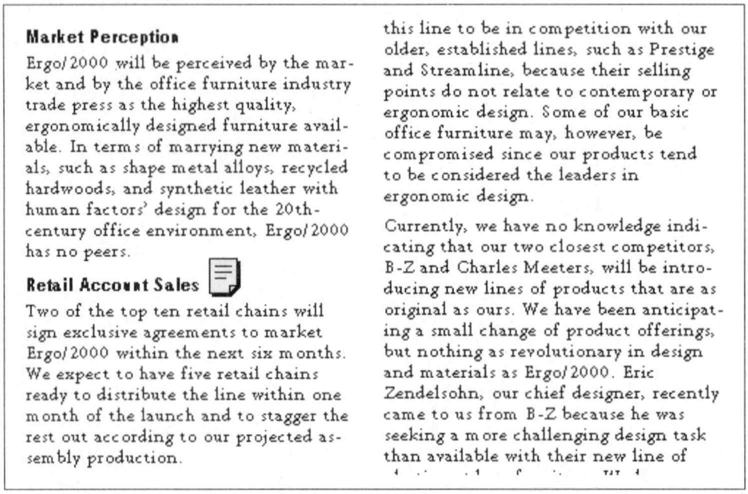

Market Perception

Ergo/2000 will be perceived by the market and by the office furniture industry trade press as the highest quality, ergonomically designed furniture available. In terms of marrying new materials, such as shape metal alloys, recycled hardwoods, and synthetic leather with human factors' design for the 20th-century office environment, Ergo/2000 has no peers.

Retail Account Sales

Two of the top ten retail chains will sign exclusive agreements to market Ergo/2000 within the next six months. We expect to have five retail chains ready to distribute the line within one month of the launch and to stagger the rest out according to our projected assembly production.

this line to be in competition with our older, established lines, such as Prestige and Streamline, because their selling points do not relate to contemporary or ergonomic design. Some of our basic office furniture may, however, be compromised since our products tend to be considered the leaders in ergonomic design.

Currently, we have no knowledge indicating that our two closest competitors, B-Z and Charles Meeters, will be introducing new lines of products that are as original as ours. We have been anticipating a small change of product offerings, but nothing as revolutionary in design and materials as Ergo/2000. Eric Zendelsohn, our chief designer, recently came to us from B-Z because he was seeking a more challenging design task than available with their new line of

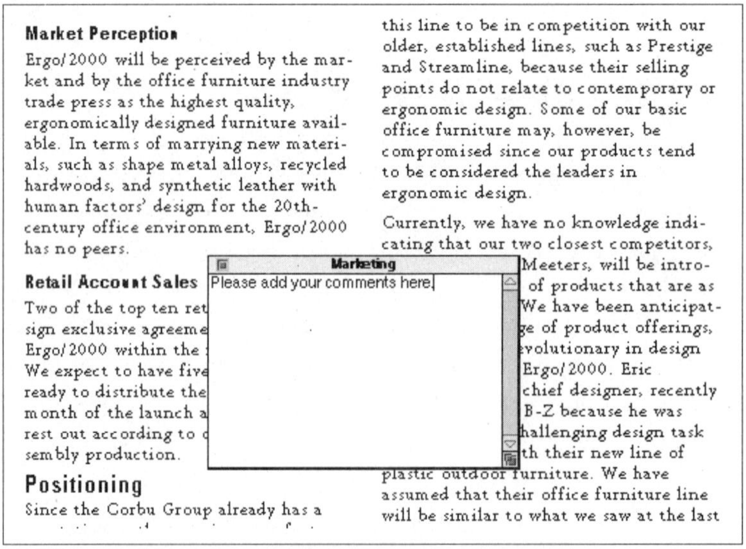

Market Perception

Ergo/2000 will be perceived by the market and by the office furniture industry trade press as the highest quality, ergonomically designed furniture available. In terms of marrying new materials, such as shape metal alloys, recycled hardwoods, and synthetic leather with human factors' design for the 20th-century office environment, Ergo/2000 has no peers.

Retail Account Sales

Two of the top ten ret sign exclusive agreeme Ergo/2000 within the We expect to have five ready to distribute the month of the launch a rest out according to c sembly production.

Marketing

Please add your comments here.

Positioning

Since the Corbu Group already has a

this line to be in competition with our older, established lines, such as Prestige and Streamline, because their selling points do not relate to contemporary or ergonomic design. Some of our basic office furniture may, however, be compromised since our products tend to be considered the leaders in ergonomic design.

Currently, we have no knowledge indicating that our two closest competitors, Meeters, will be intro- of products that are as We have been anticipat- ge of product offerings, evolutionary in design Ergo/2000. Eric chief designer, recently B-Z because he was hallenging design task th their new line of
plastic outdoor furniture. We have assumed that their office furniture line will be similar to what we saw at the last

3. After reading the note, click on the close box to close it.
4. Go to the next note in the document by choosing Tools ➤ Find Next Note. You can also press Ctrl/Command+T.
5. Double-click on the note to open it. A note stays attached to a PDF document until it is deleted. You will delete this one.
6. Click on the Close box to close the note, and then click on the note icon to select it. The note is highlighted.

7. Press the Delete key.
8. Click on OK in the confirmation box to remove the note from the document.

Customizing the Note Properties

Before adding notes to a document for the first time, you can customize the notes' appearance:

1. Choose Edit ➤ Preferences ➤ Notes.

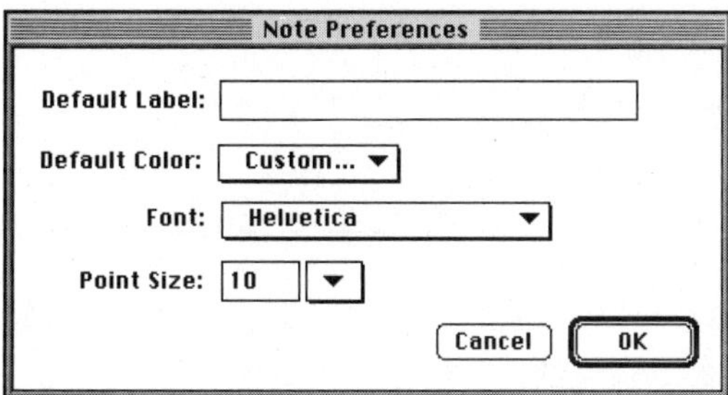

2. In the Default Label text box, type your name and company name.
3. Choose your preferred note color by selecting a color from the menu, or a custom color from the system's color selector.
4. If desired, select a font from the Font menu to change the font of the notes.
5. To change the point size for the notes, select an option from the Point Size menu.
6. Click on OK.

Creating Notes

Next you will add your comments to the marketing plan.

1. Click the Note tool in the toolbar to select it.
2. Move the pointer to the last paragraph in the first column of page 1, which discusses product positioning. If necessary, drag the vertical scroll bar to scroll the page.

3. Click to create a default-size note window (3 inches by 4 inches).

Retail Account Sales

Two of the top ten retail chains will sign exclusive agreements to market Ergo/2000 within the next six months. We expect to have five retail chains ready to distribute the line within one month of the launch and to stagger the rest out according to our projected assembly production.

Positioning

Since the Corbu Group already has a reputation as the premier manufacturer of office furniture, we can focus positioning for Ergo/2000 around this perception. Positioning here is targeted primarily at high-end executive suites; secondary positioning is aimed at Fortune 500 corporate headquarters

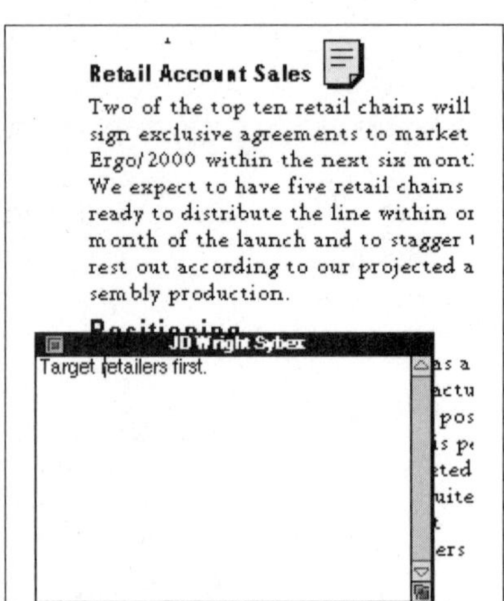

4. Type some text in the note window (for example, **Target retailers first**).
5. Close the note window by clicking on the Close box.
6. Drag the closed note icon so that it does not obscure text.

Retail Account Sales

Two of the top ten retail chains will sign exclusive agreements to market Ergo/2000 within the next six months. We expect to have five retail chains ready to distribute the line within one month of the launch and to stagger the rest out according to our projected assembly production.

Positioning

Since the Corbu Group already has a reputation as the premier manufacturer of office furniture, we can focus positioning for Ergo/2000 around this perception. Positioning here is targeted primarily at high-end executive suites; secondary positioning is aimed at Fortune 500 corporate headquarters

7. Click on Last Page to go to the last page of the marketing plan.
8. Holding down Ctrl (Windows) or the Option key (Macintosh), select the Note tool. Holding down the Ctrl or Option key keeps the Note tool

selected so that you can create more than one note in a row without having to reselect the Note tool.

9. Create two more notes. Add text to the first, and then close the note window. Leave the second note open.

Creating a Notes Summary

Acrobat's Summarize Notes command enables you to collate your comments, as well as those of other reviewers, into a separate document for viewing or printing. As mentioned above, these documents will be inserted into your Web page with the EMBED HTML tag. Bear this in mind with regard to creating a notes summary for your PDF—it functions within the PDF document rather than within HTML itself.

In this section, you will copy text from the PDF document into your notes, add your comments, and then create a notes summary. Text from the document helps place your comments in context.

Creating Notes from Existing Text

You can use the Text Selection tool to copy text from a PDF document and then paste the text into a note or bookmark where it can be edited.

You can copy text into the Clipboard in three formats: plain text, styled text (Macintosh only), and rich text format (RTF). You can choose which format to apply to the pasted text. You can also use the Text Selection tool to copy text into a document in another application, such as Microsoft Word, for editing.

1. Click on the Last Page button in the toolbar to go directly to the end of the document. Increase the magnification so that you can read the text.
2. Click on the Text Selection tool in the toolbar to select it.
3. Go to the Summary heading (last page, second column).
4. Holding down the Ctrl/Option key, drag down and to the right to highlight several sentences from this column of text. The Ctrl/Option key is used with the Text Selection tool to select text in only one column of a multicolumn document.

All of these ideas and more are being actively pursued by PR. The roll-out will be launched with as much publicity as we can attract. The trades guilds in San Francisco and the Future Office Consortium promise to provide additional publicity. Our President is addressing a convention on office furniture that will be held in Paris two months after the roll-out.

As we devise novel ways to bring this product line to wider public attention, we are considering a joint-advertising venture with several of our retailers. Details will be made available as soon as we have finalized them.

our normal capacity is not a venture we should undertake, since a normal leveling off of demand is to be expected within the first six months of even the most successful product launch.

Summary

Planning for the distribution of the Ergo/2000 product line is beginning to take shape and will be further developed when this Marketing Plan is reviewed by all of the key people involved in the product line's launch and initial sales.

The Corbu Group believes that the Ergo/2000 line is its finest yet and anticipates that the quality we have built into the line will be readily perceived by

5. Choose Edit ➤ Copy (Ctrl/Command+C) to copy the text.
6. Move the cursor to the appropriate note and choose Edit ➤ Paste (Ctrl/Command+V) to paste the text in the note.

Marketing

Planning for the distribut ion of the Ergo/2000 product line is beginning to take shape and will be further developed when this Marketing Plan is reviewed by all of the key people involved in the product line's launch and initial sales.

TIP

If you need to increase the note's size, drag the size box in the lower-right corner of the note window.

7. Add some lines, such as a row of asterisks or a row of equal marks, to separate the document text from the comments. These lines will make comments easier to see on the notes summary.
8. Following this separation line, type any comments.
9. Close the note by clicking on its Close box.

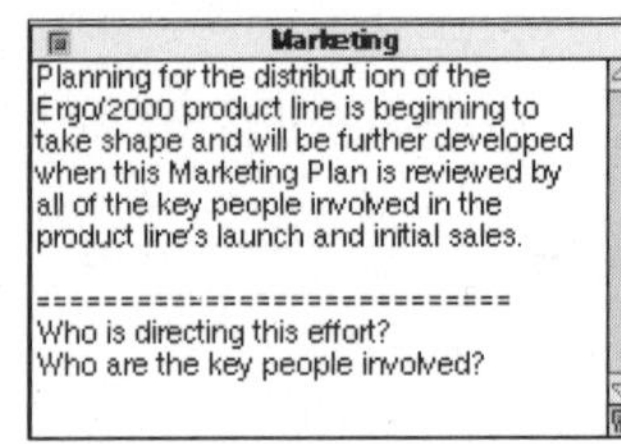

Generating the Summary

The Summarize Notes command creates a PDF document of all the notes in your file.

1. Choose Tools ➤ Summarize Notes (Ctrl/Command+Shift+T). A listing of the notes by page is displayed in a new PDF document named *Notes From MRKTPLAN.PDF.*

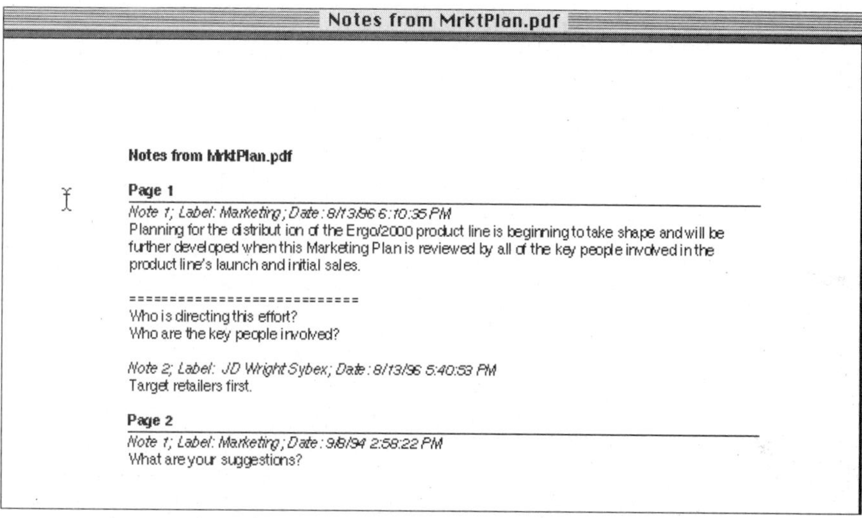

Notes from MrktPlan.pdf

Notes from MrktPlan.pdf

Page 1

Note 1; Label: Marketing; Date: 8/13/96 6:10:35 PM
Planning for the distribut ion of the Ergo/2000 product line is beginning to take shape and will be further developed when this Marketing Plan is reviewed by all of the key people involved in the product line's launch and initial sales.

============================
Who is directing this effort?
Who are the key people involved?

Note 2; Label: JD Wright Sybex; Date: 8/13/96 5:40:53 PM
Target retailers first.

Page 2

Note 1; Label: Marketing; Date: 9/8/94 2:58:22 PM
What are your suggestions?

2. Save and close the summary document.

TIP

You can use the Edit ➤ Notes ➤ Export command to extract your comments and send a file of only your notes to the author. These notes can then be imported into the original PDF document via the Edit ➤ Notes ➤ Import command. You can also collate notes from multiple versions of a file into a single document.

Adding Hypertext Links

Hypertext links are navigation tools that make it easier to read PDF documents online. A *link* is a selected area of a document that you click to jump to another area of the same document, or to another document.

You can add links to direct readers to related topics. This method is similar to creating hyperlinks between HTML pages, but instead creating them between PDF files.

Creating a Link

In this section, you will link the heading *Market Perception* to the summary on the last page of the marketing plan.

1. Click on the First Page button to go to the first page of the marketing plan.
2. Click on the Link tool in the toolbar.
3. Place the cross-hair pointer at the upper-left corner of the heading *Market Perception* and drag a rectangle around this text. When you release the mouse button, a box with handles and the Create Link dialog box appear.

Market Perception

Ergo/2000 will be perceived by the market and by the office furniture industry trade press as the highest quality, ergonomically designed furniture available. In terms of marrying new materials, such as shape metal alloys, recycled hardwoods, and synthetic leather with human factors' design for the 20th-century office environment, Ergo/2000 has no peers.

Retail Account Sales

Two of the top ten retail chains will

Market Perception

Ergo/2000 will be perceived by the market and by the office furniture industry trade press as the highest quality, ergonomically designed furniture available. In terms of marrying new materials, such as shape metal alloys, recycled hardwoods, and synthetic leather with human factors' design for the 20th-century office environment, Ergo/2000 has no peers.

Retail Account Sales

Two of the top ten retail chains will

4. In the Create Link dialog box, make sure that Visible is selected so that the link rectangle is displayed. Change the Color to Red, the Width to Thin, and the Style to Solid.
5. Select Go To View as the Action Type.

6. Select Inherit Zoom as the Magnification so that the linked page appears at the document's current magnification.

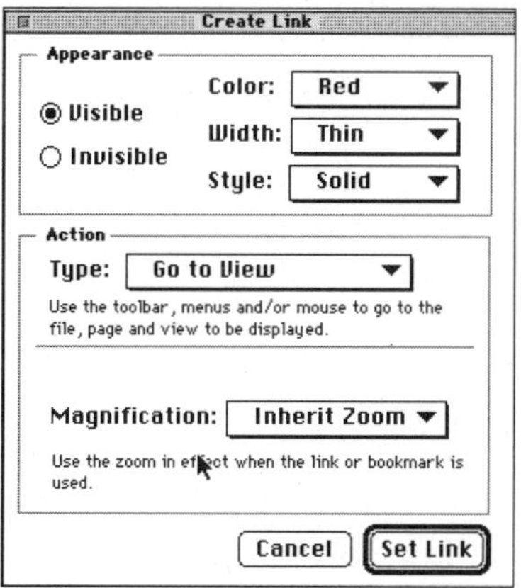

NOTE

The default magnification option, Fit View, causes links to be displayed at different magnifications on different monitors.

7. Click on the Last Page button to go to the last page. Then click on the Set Link button in the Create Link dialog box to set the link destination and return to the link rectangle.
8. Position the pointer over the link rectangle. The pointer changes to an icon of a pointing finger.

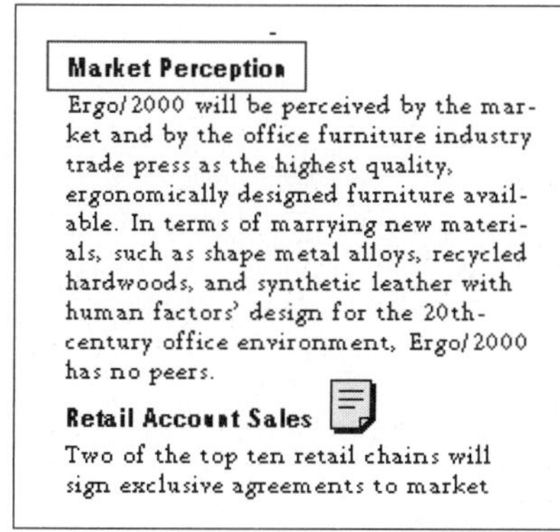

9. Click on the rectangle to jump to the Summary page.

Finding a Phrase to Link

The Find tool allows you to search for a word, for part of a word, or for a phrase in a PDF document. In this section, you will use the Find tool to search for a phrase that you want to link to another document.

1. Click on the Find button to display the Find dialog box.
2. Type **Annual Budget** in the Find What dialog box and select Match Case to tell Acrobat Exchange to find a phrase with the same capitalization.

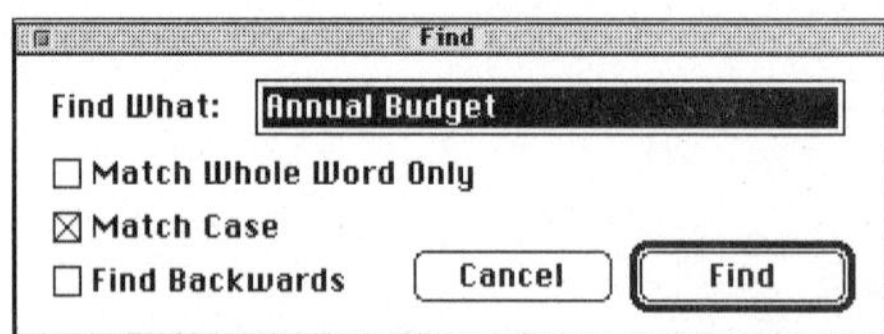

3. Click on Find, and click on Yes or Continue.

Page 2 appears with the phrase *Annual Budget* highlighted.

Creating a Cross-Document Link

Next you will create a cross-document link from the heading *Annual Budget* in the marketing plan to another document, a spreadsheet.

1. With the MRKTPLAN.PDF document open, open the BUDGET.PDF document in the Tutorial folder. You will create a link to this spreadsheet document.

NOTE

When creating cross-document links to be shared by Windows and Macintosh users, you should name your files according to the DOS file-naming convention of an eight-character file name followed by a three-character extension. Avoid creating links across volumes (that is, separate disks or tapes, or a hard disk divided into separate volumes).

2. Make MRKTPLAN.PDF the active document by selecting it from the Window menu.

3. Click on the Link tool and draw a link around the heading *Annual Budget* on page 2.

achieved during a similar period with the Ergo/1990 line.

Annual Budget

The projected annual budget prepared by Finance is attached.

Promotion

In addition to our formal announcement at the Future Offices show this spring in San Francisco, we have been providing timely press releases and developing public relations kits to send to the press, our usual retailers, and

4. Make BUDGET.PDF the active document, and go to page 2.
5. In the Create Link dialog box, select Fit Width as the Magnification option.
6. Click on Set Link. The Create Link dialog box closes, and you are returned to MRKTPLAN.PDF.
7. Test the link by clicking on it. The second page of the spreadsheet is displayed across the width of the document window.

8. Return to the marketing plan document by clicking on the Go Back button. Keep this document open.

9. Go to the spreadsheet document and close it.

Creating an Article Flow

Certain documents, such as newsletters and magazines, contain articles that start on one page but continue several pages later. This is helpful for creating a document within a Web site that has the elegance of desktop publishing without the trouble of DTP tools. Though more advanced functionality is coming fast to Web tools, creating a PDF file in Acrobat is much faster for now.

In this section, you will use the Article feature to create an article flow that guides the reader through selected parts of a document. An article flow enhances the readability of the marketing plan with its two-column text.

Defining Article Boxes

First you will create the article flow path for the marketing plan.

1. Click on the First Page button to go to the beginning of the marketing plan.
2. Click on the Fit Page button to display the entire page in the Acrobat window.
3. Choose Tools ➤ Article. The mouse pointer becomes a cross-hair pointer.
4. Position the cross-hair pointer in the upper-left corner of the first column of text, and drag it to create a rectangular outline over the column. When you release the mouse button, the cross-hair pointer changes to the article flow pointer. The newly created box is selected and has four corner points for resizing, an article number (1-1), and a box tab (see Figure 2). To resize an article box, drag the handles in the corner of the box. To redraw the box, press Delete, click on Box in the confirmation message, and drag the cursor again.

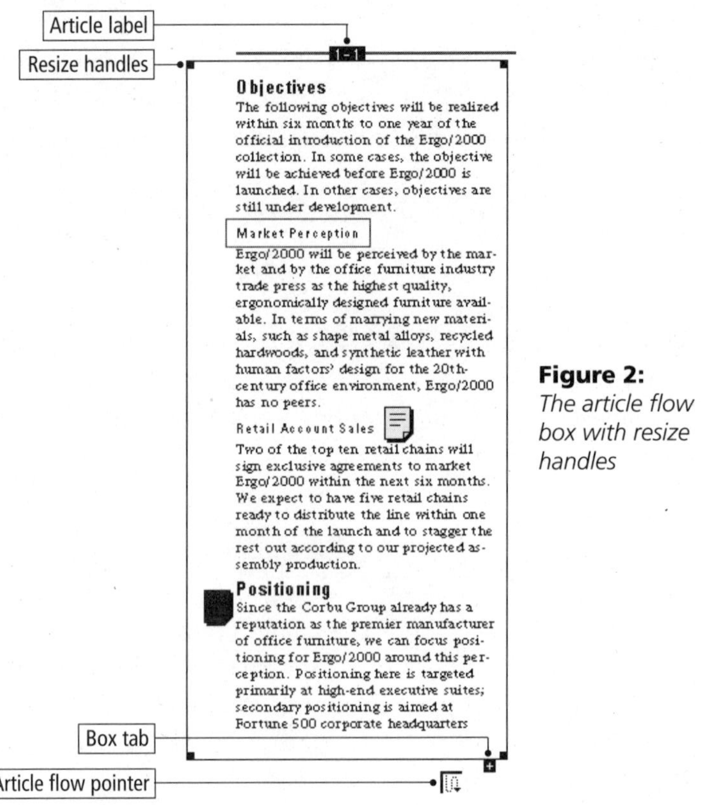

Figure 2: *The article flow box with resize handles*

5. Draw a box around the second column. The second article box you create is labeled 1-2. Each article box is labeled with its article number and its box sequence within the article. To select an article, click inside its article box.

6. Click on the Next Page button, and continue to create article boxes until you have created article box 1-6, which encloses the document's sixth and last column.
7. Click on End Article in the status bar at the bottom of the window, or select another tool.

8. Type **Marketing Plan** as the article title, **Ergo/2000** as the subject, and your name as the author.
9. Click on OK to create the article.

Reviewing the Article Flow

Next, you will follow the text view by view. As you read an article, the text is automatically magnified to fit the width of the Exchange Window. Each time you click on the article, the next portion of the article flow is displayed.

1. Click on the First Page button to go to page 1, and click on the hand tool.

NOTE

If a document contains one or more articles, you can select Articles from the View menu, and then select an article name in the dialog box.

2. Move the pointer over the first column. The pointer changes to indicate that this text is part of an article (see Figure 3).
3. Click anywhere in the article to start reading the article.
4. Continue to click anywhere in the article until you reach the end of the article.
5. Click again to exit the article. You can also hold down the Shift key and Ctrl+click (Ctrl key and mouse click at the same time for Windows) or Option+click (Option key and a mouse click for Macintosh) to exit an article at any time.

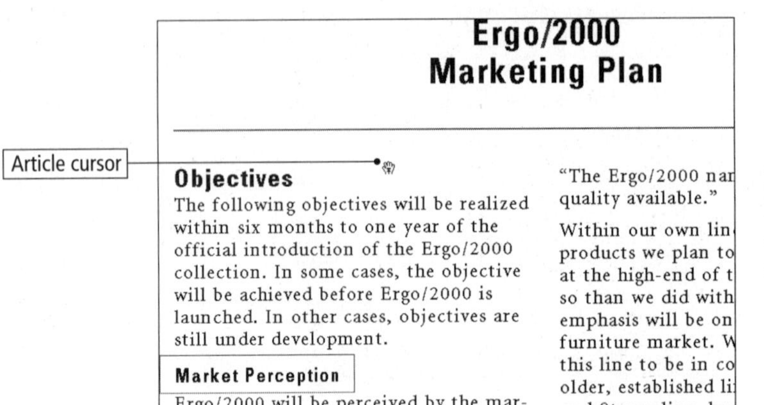

Article cursor
Ergo/2000
Marketing Plan
Objectives
The following objectives will be realized within six months to one year of the official introduction of the Ergo/2000 collection. In some cases, the objective will be achieved before Ergo/2000 is launched. In other cases, objectives are still under development.
Market Perception
Ergo/2000 will be perceived by the market and by the office furniture industry
"The Ergo/2000 nar
quality available."
Within our own lin
products we plan to
at the high-end of t
so than we did with
emphasis will be on
furniture market. W
this line to be in co
older, established li
and Streamline, bec

Figure 3: *The pointer indicates that text is part of a longer article.*

Whenever you exit an article, you are returned to the original page view and magnification that you set before you started reading the article.

Combining Two PDF Documents

You may want to combine two PDF documents instead of creating cross-document links. You can combine any two PDF documents, regardless of their length or page sizes. In this section, you will prepare a PDF version of a brochure and then attach it to the marketing plan. Again, the value of this process to a Web designer is the elegance of desktop publishing design within a Web page.

Zooming in on an Area

The BROCHURE.PDF document has been designed for printing and so contains type that is too small to view on the screen at 100 percent. To read the brochure, you need to magnify the document:

1. Open the tutorial file BROCHURE.PDF in the Tutorial directory. The document is displayed at the default magnification of 100 percent.

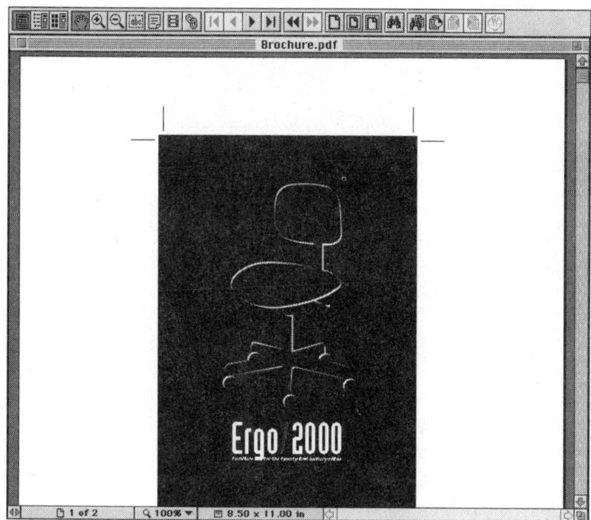

2. Select the Zoom-In tool and position it over the text *Ergo/2000*. Click once to increase the magnification by a factor of two.
3. To magnify the text more exactly, use the Zoom-In tool to drag a rectangle around this text; this action is called *marquee-zooming*. When you release the mouse button, the enlarged text fills the document window (see Figure 4).

Figure 4: *Use marquee-zooming to magnify just a portion of the text.*

Cropping a Page

Pages or presentation screens may have unnecessary amounts of white space in the margins, especially if a document was designed to be printed or trimmed. You can eliminate this white space using the Crop Pages command. Cropping margins speeds scrolling through documents.

In this section, you will crop the white space surrounding the brochure:

1. To display the entire brochure page in the Acrobat window, select Fit Page from the magnification box in the status bar.
2. Choose Edit ➤ Pages ➤ Crop (Ctrl/Command+Shift+C).
3. Drag the Crop Pages dialog box to the side of the document window.
4. Click on the arrows to adjust the margins. Click on an inside arrow and continue to click until the cropping line touches the crop marks. If you go too far, click on an outer arrow. As you click, the current margin measurements and cropping lines indicate the margins in the document window (see Figure 5).

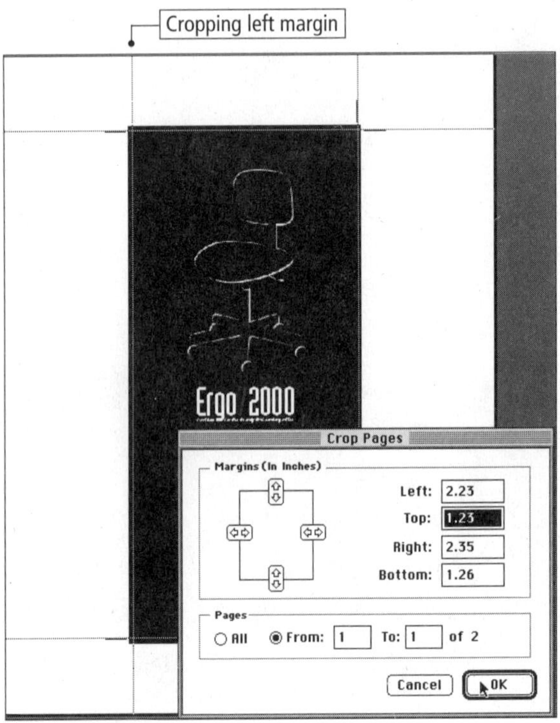

Figure 5: *Cropping the margin of the brochure*

NOTE

If you know the measurements for the margins, you can enter these values in the text boxes and fine-tune the cropping using the arrows and dotted line.

5. Repeat this adjustment for all margins.
6. When the new margins are correct, click on All in the Crop Pages dialog box to crop all pages, and click on OK. Confirm that you want the pages cropped by clicking on OK. The document page appears with the new margins.
7. Choose File ➤ Save As and save the brochure as **NEWBROCH.PDF**.
8. Close the file.

Attaching the Brochure

You can use the Edit ➤ Pages ➤ Insert command to combine PDF documents. You can also use the Edit ➤ Pages ➤ Extract command to divide a PDF document into smaller documents that can be reviewed and annotated individually. When documents are combined, the notes, links, and bookmarks in each file are retained.

1. Open MRKTPLAN.PDF and choose Edit ➤ Pages ➤ Insert (Ctrl/Command+Shift+I).
2. Select NEWBROCH.PDF, and click on Select.
3. Select the options After and Last, and click on OK. When the progress bar is finished, the brochure is attached.
4. Page through the combined documents to verify that the document has been correctly attached.
5. Use the Save As command to save the PDF document as **REVIEW.PDF**.

Creating Bookmarks

Bookmarks are often included in documents to provide readers with an automated table of contents. Readers can also create bookmarks to mark pages or to mark specific page views (such as a zoomed-in section of a page).

Creating Bookmarks within the Document

In this section you will add bookmarks to the document (REVIEW.PDF) you just created.

1. With REVIEW.PDF displayed in the document window, click on the Bookmarks And Page button or choose View ➤ Bookmarks And Page (Ctrl/Command+7).
2. Adjust the page view and resize the document window, if necessary.
3. Click on the First Page button in the toolbar to go to page 1.

4. Click on the Text Selection tool, and select the text *Marketing Plan* in the title.

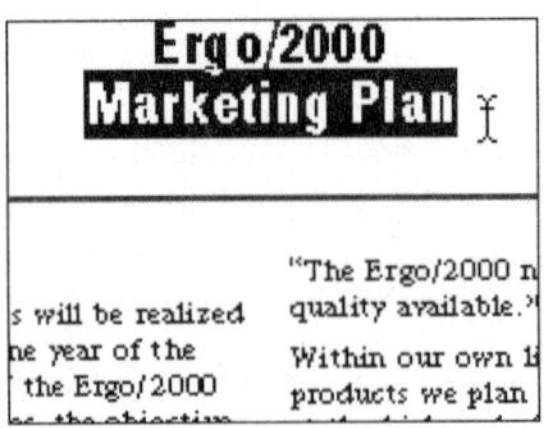

5. Choose Edit ➤ Copy (Ctrl/Command+C) to copy the text.
6. Choose Edit ➤ Bookmarks ➤ New (Ctrl/Command+B). (If the Bookmarks command is not visible, choose Edit ➤ Full Menus.) A new, untitled bookmark appears in the bookmark list.

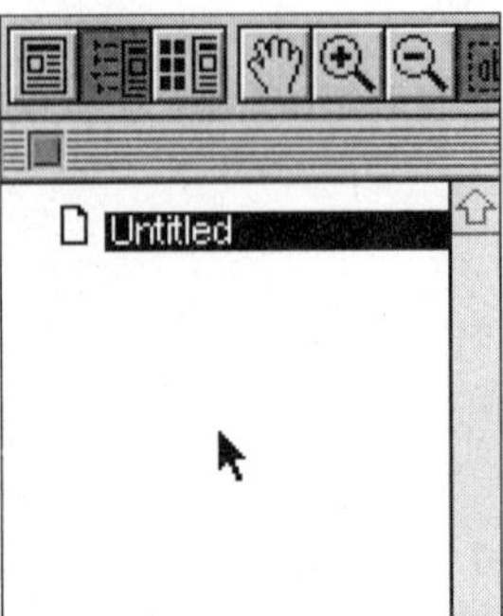

7. Choose Edit ➤ Paste (Ctrl/Command+V) to paste the text into the bookmark.
8. Drag the window splitter—the vertical bar separating the overview and document areas—to resize these two screen areas (see Figure 6). Select the window splitter and drag left or right as necessary.

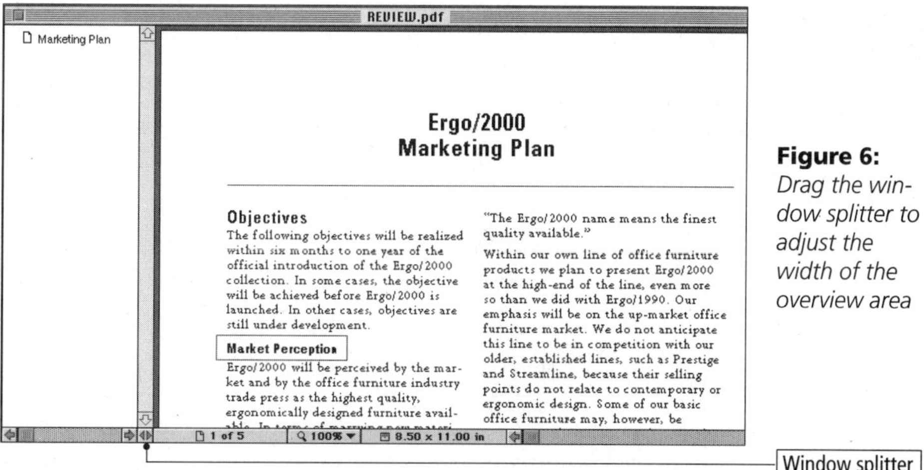

Figure 6: *Drag the window splitter to adjust the width of the overview area*

9. Click on the scroll box in the vertical scroll bar to the right of the document window, and drag until page 4 appears in the pop-up window (see Figure 7).

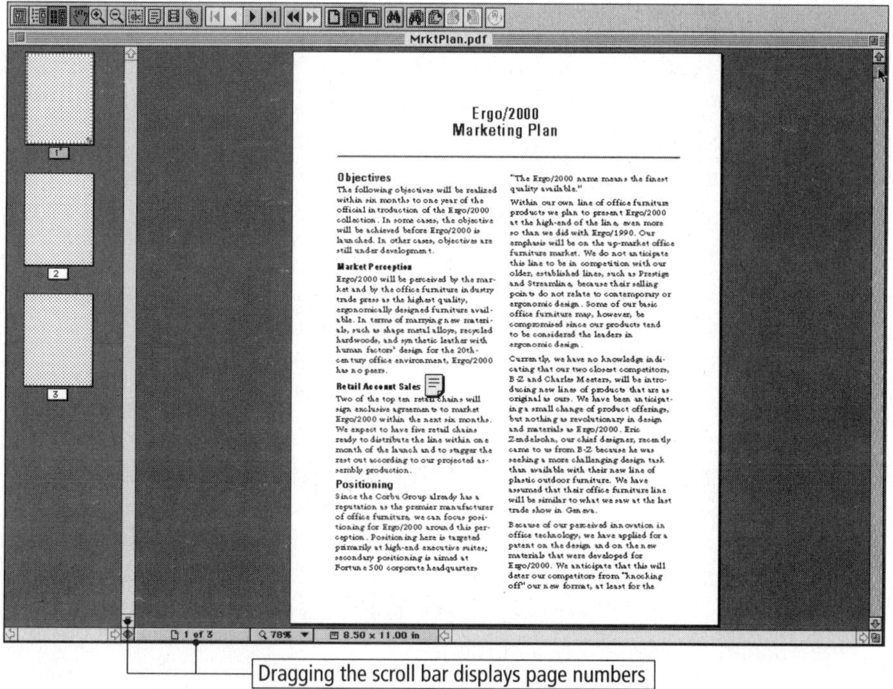

Figure 7: *Drag the scroll bar to move between pages*

10. Choose Edit ➤ Bookmarks ➤ New.
11. Type **Brochure** as the bookmark name.

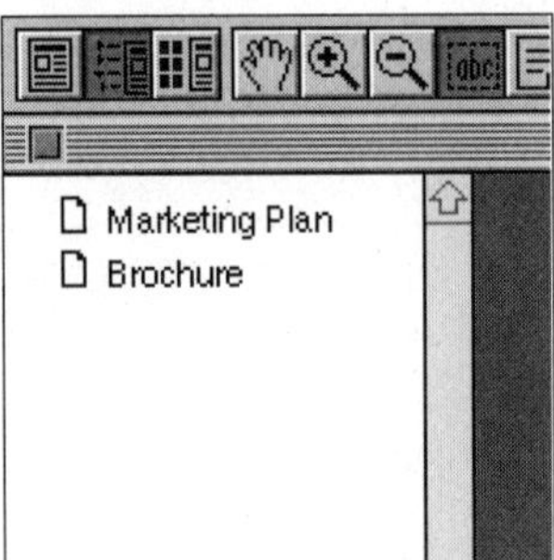

Changing the Default Bookmark Magnification to Inherit Zoom

The page view at which your document is read depends on how the reader adjusts the page view for the monitor's screen. To have a bookmark link to a page at the reader's current page view, you need to set Inherit Zoom as the bookmark's default magnification. Subsequent bookmarks you create in the document will assume the default magnification of Inherit Zoom.

1. Click on the page icon to the left of the *Brochure* bookmark to select it.
2. Choose Edit ➤ Properties (Ctrl/Command+I) to display the Bookmark Properties dialog box.
3. Click on Edit Destination.
4. Select Inherit Zoom as the magnification option.
5. Click on Set Action.

Creating a Bookmark for the Spreadsheet

As with links, you can create bookmarks that jump to other PDF documents. This is useful when you want your bookmark list to display a set of related documents. In this case, the spreadsheet is linked to the marketing plan but can be maintained as a separate document.

1. Choose Edit ➤ Bookmarks ➤ New (Ctrl/Command+B).
2. Type **Spreadsheet** as the name of the bookmark.

3. Select the bookmark by clicking on its page icon. Choose Edit ➤ Properties (Ctrl/Command+I).

NOTE

You must select bookmarks before you can edit or move them.

4. With Go To View selected in the Action Type menu, click on Edit Destination.

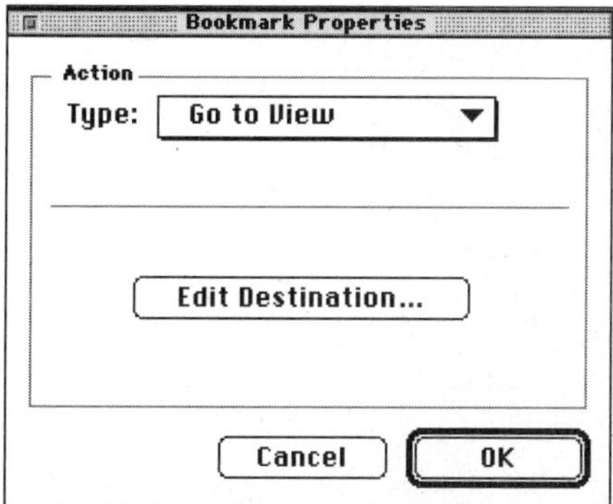

5. Open the BUDGET.PDF document. The Bookmark Properties dialog box displays the destination properties.
6. Select Fit Width from the Magnification menu.
7. Click on Set Action. You are returned to the *Spreadsheet* bookmark.
8. Click outside of the bookmark's name to deselect it.
9. Double-click on the *Spreadsheet* bookmark to return to the spreadsheet.
10. Close the BUDGET.PDF file.

Editing Pages Using Thumbnails

Thumbnails are miniature views of each page in a PDF document. You can use them for navigating through a document, and for moving, copying, deleting, and replacing pages in one or more Acrobat documents.

Creating the Thumbnails

In this section, you'll create thumbnails for REVIEW.PDF and then for a file named MEMO.PDF, so that you can edit these pages using thumbnails.

1. With REVIEW.PDF displayed in the document window, select Edit ➤ Thumbnails ➤ Create All.
2. Drag the scroll box to the right of the thumbnails to display the thumbnail for page 1 (see Figure 8).

Figure 8:
Drag the scroll bar to display the thumbnail for page 1.

3. Open MEMO.PDF in the Tutorial directory.
4. Choose Edit ➤ Thumbnails ➤ Create All.
5. Choose Window ➤ Tile Vertically to arrange both documents side-by-side.

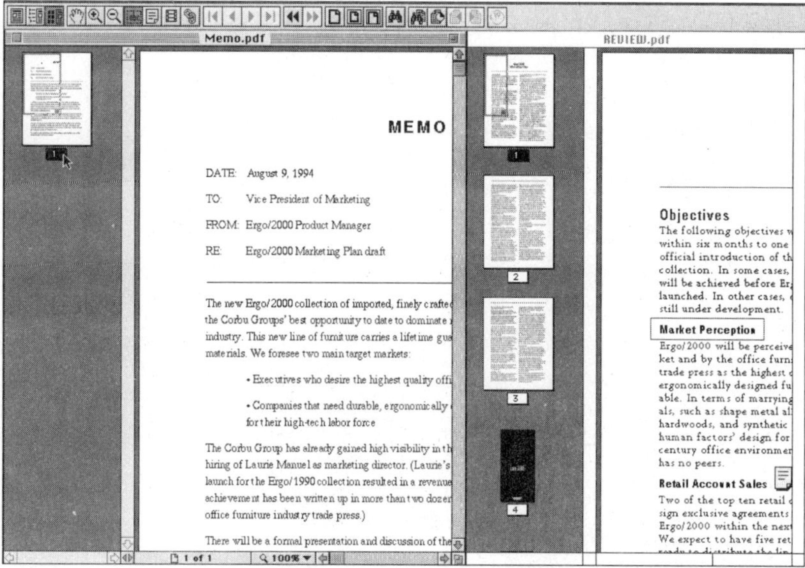

Copying a Page from Another Document

You can use thumbnails to copy a page from one document into another:

1. In the MEMO.PDF file, click on the page icon beneath the page 1 thumbnail. A box appears around the page.

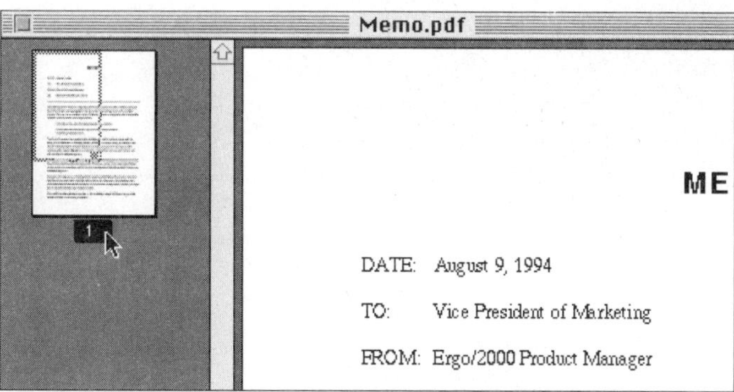

2. Position the pointer on the page number of the selected page. Drag the thumbnail to the overview area of REVIEW.PDF, and move the thumbnail anywhere in the thumbnail list.
3. When a bar over or under a thumbnail is highlighted, release the mouse button.

Moving a Page

You can also use the thumbnails to reorganize pages within a document:

1. Move the pointer to the REVIEW.PDF document overview area.
2. Click on the page icon beneath the thumbnail for the MEMO.PDF. A box appears around the page.

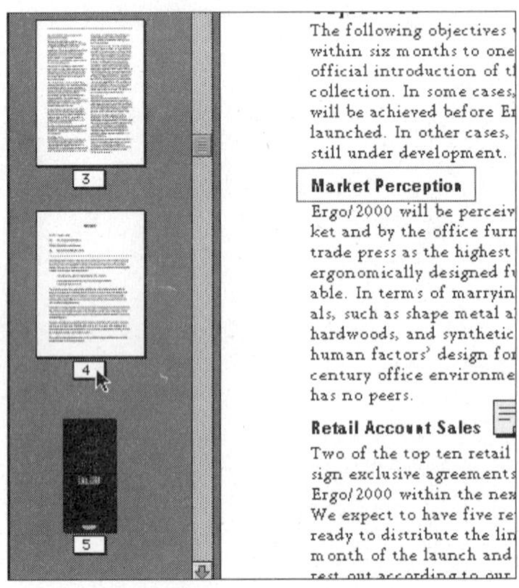

3. With the page icon selected, drag the page to the beginning of the thumbnail list. As you drag upward, the bar above the thumbnail shows where the page will be inserted.
4. When the bar appears at the very top of page 1, release the mouse button. The memo is now the first thumbnail as well as the first page of the review document.
5. Click on the thumbnail of the memo to jump to that page.
6. Close MEMO.PDF without saving changes.
7. Save REVIEW.PDF.

Creating an Acrobat Presentation

You can use the full-screen feature to create slide show presentations that are displayed on the entire monitor screen. These presentations can be used to accompany lectures, or as kiosk displays.

Preparing the Presentation Document

To facilitate printing, the presentation file was created with the pages oriented vertically. First, you'll open the presentation document and rotate the pages for viewing. Then, you'll edit the Acrobat program preferences to set Exchange to cycle through the pages.

1. In the Tutorial folder, open PRESENT.PDF.

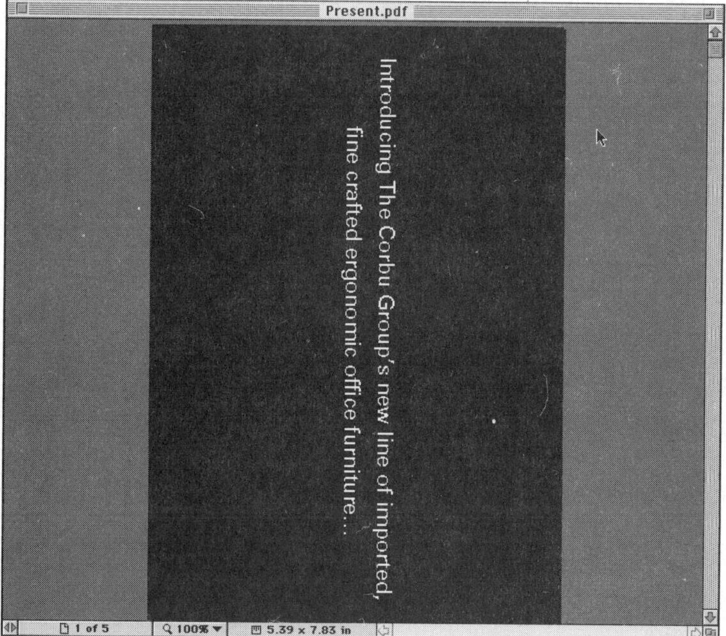

2. Choose Edit ➤ Pages ➤ Rotate.
3. Select Left and All pages, and click on OK. Click on Yes (Windows) or OK (Macintosh) in the alert dialog box.

4. Choose File ➤ Document Info ➤ Open.
5. Select Full Screen as the Show option, and click on OK.
6. Save the file as **KIOSK.PDF** and close it.
7. Choose Edit ➤ Preferences ➤ Full Screen to display the Full Screen Preferences dialog box.

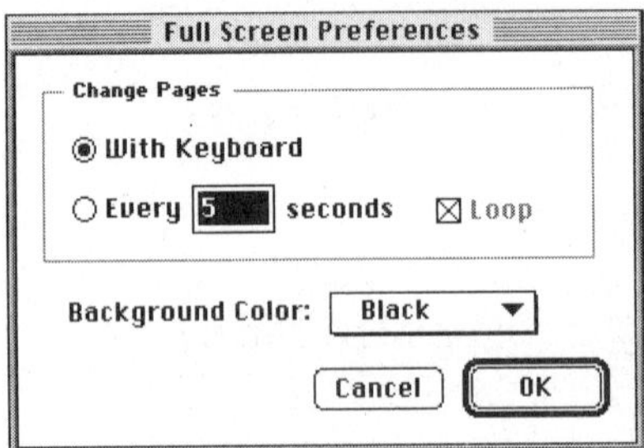

8. Set Change Pages to Every 3 Seconds, and select Loop.
9. From the Background Color menu, select Black and click on OK.

Linking the Presentation to the Review

Now you will link the presentation document KIOSK.PDF to the review document. The REVIEW.PDF file should still be active; if not, open it.

1. Use the Find tool to locate the heading *Promotion*.
2. Click on the Link tool in the toolbar to select it, and draw a link around the word *Promotion*. The Create Link dialog box appears.
3. Select Open File as the Action Type, and click on Select File. The Open File action type links to the first page of a document or to the beginning of a file.
4. Select KIOSK.PDF and click on the Select button.
5. Click on Set Link. The marketing plan is now linked to the presentation.

Viewing the Presentation

Now that you have created a presentation, you can watch it.

NOTE

KIOSK.PDF should be closed before you begin the presentation.

1. Click on the newly created link to start the presentation. The presentation pages loop continuously.

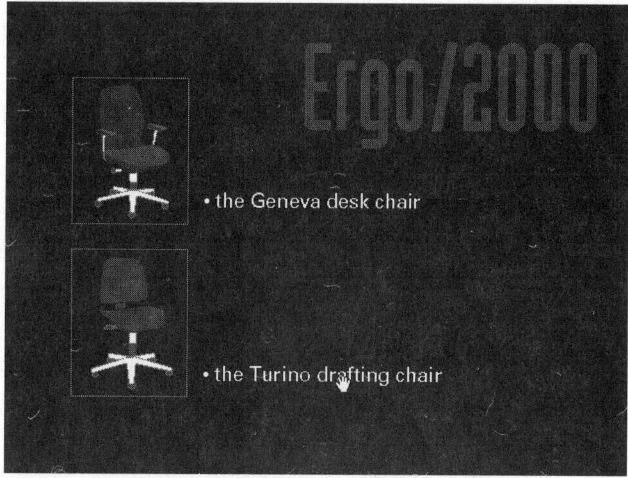

2. Press Escape to exit from the full-screen display.
3. Close KIOSK.PDF without saving changes.

NOTE

When looping is not set, you can change pages using the Page Up and Page Down keys or the arrow keys on the keyboard.

The pointer remains active during full-screen mode so that you can click on links and open notes. In addition, the following commands are accessible through shortcut keys:

- View menu commands except Page Only, Bookmarks And Page, and Thumbnails And Page. (See the shortcut keys listed in the menus.)

- Hand (Shift+Ctrl+1 for Windows; Command+Option+1 for Macintosh)
- Zoom In (Shift+Ctrl+2 for Windows; Command+Option+2 for Macintosh)
- Zoom Out (Shift+Ctrl+3 for Windows; Command+Option+3 for Macintosh)

Setting Document Security

You can assign passwords and other controls to a PDF document to limit access to the document using the Security dialog box. PDF documents with passwords or limited functionality are called *secure* documents. When documents have limited access, the restricted tools and menu items are dimmed. These secure documents allow access control on an otherwise open Web site. Users may download the files, but need the passwords to open and modify them.

1. With REVIEW.PDF open, choose File ➤ Save As.
2. Click on Security.
3. In the Open The Document text box, enter the password that will be required to open the document. The text appears as bullets.
4. Press the Tab key to go to the Change Security Options text box, and enter another password required to change the document's security options. The text appears as bullets.
5. In the Do Not Allow section, select the desired restrictions to prevent readers from printing, changing the document, selecting text and graphics, or adding and changing notes.

NOTE

If you set any of these restrictions, you must also set a password unless it is acceptable for others to change the document's security settings.

6. Click on OK.
7. Retype the passwords in the confirmation dialog boxes, and click on OK.
8. Name the document SECURE.PDF, and click on OK (Windows) or Save (Macintosh) to save the document.
9. Close the SECURE.PDF file.
10. Open SECURE.PDF and enter the password as requested. The review document is now a secure, password-protected file.

WARNING

The password used must be typed exactly as entered, including uppercase and lowercase letters as entered.

11. Close the SECURE.PDF file.

This section completes the Acrobat Exchange portion of this tutorial. You are now ready to open and view any Acrobat document.

In the next section, you'll learn to create PDF documents.

Making PDF Documents

This section describes how to make PDF documents using the two Acrobat document creation tools—PDF Writer and Acrobat Distiller. It also discusses when to use PDF Writer and when to use Acrobat Distiller, and provides tips on reproducing fonts and minimizing the file size of documents.

Using PDF Writer

To use PDF Writer, select PDF Writer as your printer driver and "print" the document to a file instead of to a printer.

NOTE

Acrobat PDF Writer 2.1 is not compatible with QuickDraw GX. When the QuickDraw GX extension is enabled, the PDF Writer icon does not appear in the Chooser.

Here's how to use PDF Writer on the Windows platform:

1. Start your application and open the document.
2. Choose File ➤ Print.
3. If the current printer listed in the Print dialog box is not Acrobat PDF

Writer On DISK, click on the Print Setup button. The Print Setup dialog box appears. Select Acrobat PDF Writer On DISK from the Specific Printer list, and close the dialog box.

NOTE

In some applications, you can also choose File ➤ Print Setup to select Acrobat PDF Writer On DISK, and then repeat step 2.

4. In the Print dialog box, click on OK.
5. Name the PDF file, and select a destination folder.
6. If desired, choose one of two options:
   - To view the PDF file in the Acrobat Exchange window, select the View PDF File option.
   - To enter information about the file, select the Prompt For Document Info option. Click on OK. In the General Information dialog box, enter the document's title (do not enter the PDF file's name unless it is the same as the title), subject, author, and keywords. Acrobat Search users can enter these data fields, which are saved with the document, as search criteria.
7. Click on OK.

The PDF file is generated and appears onscreen in the Acrobat Exchange window if you selected the View PDF File option; otherwise, you are returned to your application.

Here's how to use PDF Writer on the Macintosh:

1. Start your application and open the document.
2. Hold down the shortcut key (the Ctrl key by default) and choose File ➤ Print.

NOTE

If the PDF Writer dialog box does not appear, select Acrobat PDF Writer from the Chooser. The PDF Writer shortcut key may not work with all Macintosh applications. Make sure PDF Writer is in the System/Extensions folder.

3. Select the Select Short (DOS) File Names to truncate the default file name in the Save dialog box to a DOS file name consisting of eight characters

followed by a period and a two- or three-character file extension (such as .PS or .PDF).

NOTE

If you plan to distribute the PDF file over a network or via an electronic mail system, Adobe recommends that you use the MS-DOS file naming convention. This is particularly important in the Web environment of portability.

4. If desired, choose one of two options:
   - To view the PDF file in the Acrobat Exchange window, select the View PDF File option.
   - To enter information about the file, select the Prompt For Document Info option. Click on OK. In the General Information dialog box, enter the document's title (do not enter the PDF file's name unless it is the same as the title), subject, author, and keywords. Acrobat Search users can enter these data fields, which are saved with the document, as search criteria.
5. Click on OK. The Save As dialog box appears with the name of the PDF file.
6. Rename the file, if desired. Select a destination folder, and click on Save.

The PDF file is generated and appears onscreen in the Acrobat Exchange window if you selected the View PDF File option; otherwise, you are returned to your application.

Selecting PDF Writer Compression and Font Options

You can specify options to control how the PDF Writer formats and compresses files, and whether certain Type 1 or TrueType font outlines are included (embedded) in PDF files.

Selecting Options from Windows

To select options for your Windows system, follow the steps below:

1. Choose File ➤ Print, and click on Setup in the Print dialog box.
2. Select PDF Writer On DISK from the specific Printer list, and click on Options. (In Windows 95, open the My Computer folder, click on the

Printers folder, and right-click on Acrobat PDFWriter. Select Properties ➤ Details ➤ Setup).

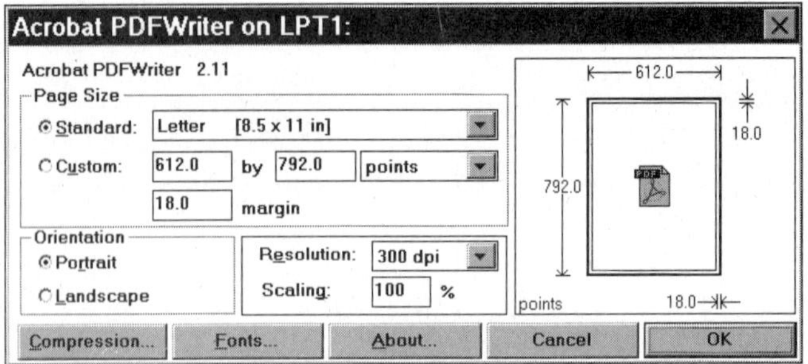

3. Click on Compression to change the PDF Writer compression options. Select the desired compression options, and click on OK.

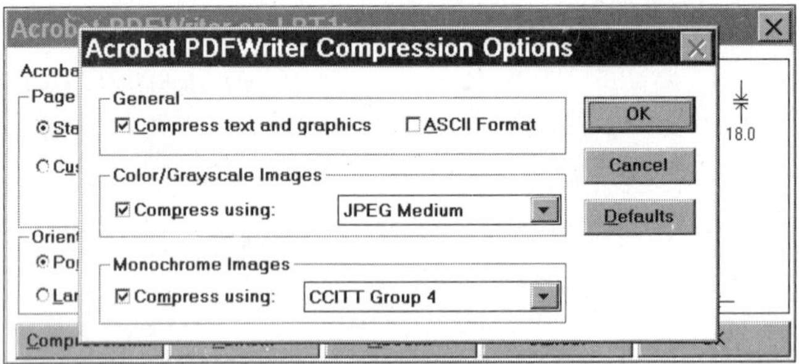

4. Click on Fonts to display the Font Embedding dialog box. Select the desired options, and click on OK.

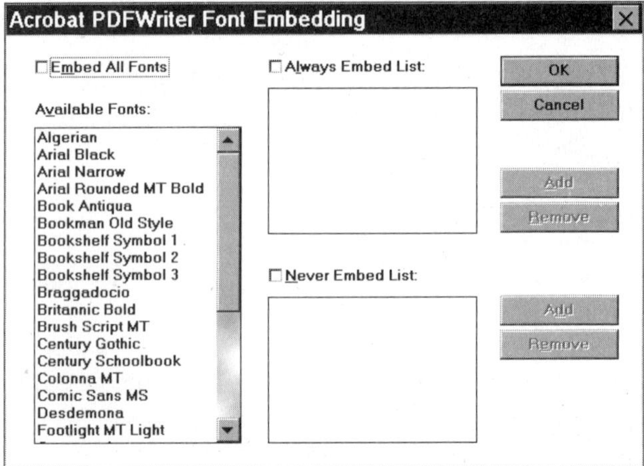

Selecting Options from the Macintosh

If you want to select options for your Macintosh system, follow the steps below:

1. Hold down the PDF Writer shortcut key and choose File ➤ Page Setup, or select Acrobat PDF Writer from the Chooser.

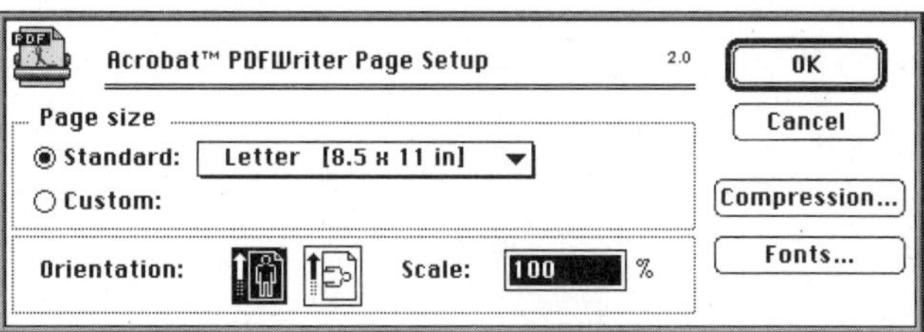

2. Click on Compression to change the PDF Writer Compression options. Select the desired options, and click on OK.

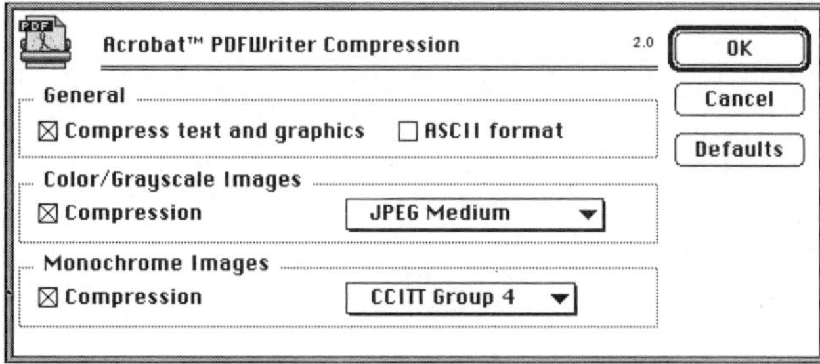

3. Click on Fonts to display the Font Embedding dialog box. Select the desired options, and click on OK.

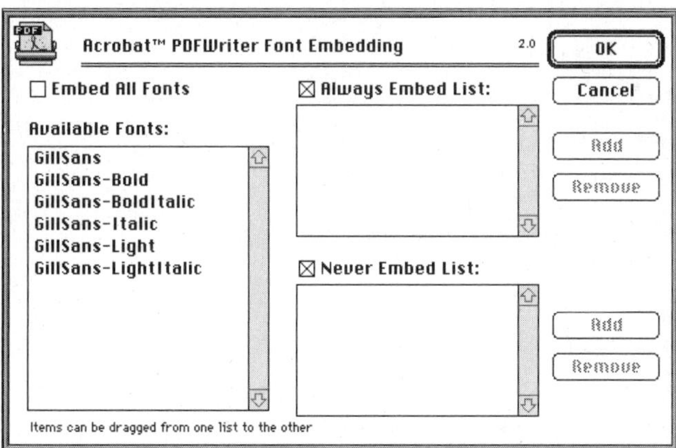

Creating PostScript Language Files

You create a PostScript language file from your document by selecting a PostScript printer driver and printing the document to a file. The following instructions are for users of the Adobe PSPrinter driver.

Before creating a PostScript language file from your document, make sure that the document prints correctly on a PostScript printer. Documents that do not print correctly cannot be properly distilled.

TIP

To create a PostScript language file and a PDF file in one step, save your PostScript language file directly to the Acrobat Distiller In folder.

To creating a PostScript language file from a Windows document, follow these steps:

1. Start your application and open the document.
2. If your default printer is not a PostScript printer, choose a PostScript printer from the Specific Printer menu. Click on OK.
3. Choose File ➤ Print.
4. Select the Print To File option, and click on OK.

NOTE

If your application Print dialog box does not include a Print To File option, you must set up a PostScript printer driver to print to a file.

5. Enter a path name and file name for the PostScript language file, and click on OK. By convention, PostScript language files are named using a .PS extension (for example, Q1REPORT.PS).

To creating a PostScript language file from a Macintosh document, follow these steps:

1. Start your application and open the document.
2. If you do not normally use a PostScript printer driver, select the LaserWriter or PSPrinter driver from the Chooser, and click on OK.

3. Choose File ➤ Print.
4. Select File as the destination.
5. If the document is a color document or contains grayscale images, click on Options to display the Print Options dialog box, choose Print ➤ Color/Grayscale, and click on OK.
6. Click on Save in the Print dialog box. The Save As dialog box appears.
7. Unless you are sure that Acrobat Distiller has access to all the fonts you use in your document, select All But Standard 13 from the Font Inclusion menu.
8. Select the destination folder and enter a name for the PostScript language file. By convention, PostScript file names are named using a .PS extension (for example, Q1REPORT.PS).
9. Click on Save to create the PostScript language file and return to your application.

Embedding and Substituting Fonts

Acrobat Exchange and Reader programs reproduce each font in a document in one of three ways:

- By using the same font installed on the viewing computer
- By creating a substitute font using information in the PDF file
- By displaying a font that has been embedded in the PDF file

When a font has been embedded, Acrobat Exchange and Reader can display and print the font on any computer without relying on font substitution. Both the PDF Writer and Acrobat Distiller automatically embed non-ISO Type 1 fonts—that is, fonts with nonstandard character sets. Embedding these fonts ensures that they will be displayed properly even when they are unavailable on the current computer.

Embedding Type 1 Fonts

You may want to set up both programs to embed additional Type 1 fonts and avoid font substitution for any of these reasons:

- You are using decorative fonts, such as Adobe Wild Type fonts, or script fonts, such as Park Avenue. Substitute fonts for these types of fonts do not look like the originals.

- Users will print the document on early model PostScript printers with little memory. Font substitution may require more printer memory for each font that is substituted.
- You want to ensure that a font will display like the original on Macintosh, Windows, Unix, and DOS systems.

NOTE

A font embedded using PDF Writer typically requires between 25K and 40K of storage; a font embedded using Acrobat Distiller with the Make Font Subsets option (the default option) typically requires 10K to 25K of storage.

To embed all fonts, follow these steps:

1. Display the Font Embedding dialog box, as described in the Windows or Macintosh procedure in "Selecting PDF Writer Compression and Font Options" previously.
2. In the Font Embedding dialog box, select Embed All Fonts.
3. Click on OK.

To embed specific fonts, follow these steps:

1. Display the Font Embedding dialog box, as described in the Windows or Macintosh procedure in "Selecting PDF Writer Compression and Font Options" previously.
2. In the Font Embedding dialog box, deselect the Embed All Fonts check box. Select the Always Embed check box.
3. From the Available Fonts list, select the names of fonts that you want to embed in all PDF documents. Click on Add to embed the selected fonts in the PDF document.
4. Click on OK when you have finished adding fonts.

You can also embed all fonts except specific fonts:

1. Display the Font Embedding dialog box, as described in the Windows or Macintosh procedure in "Selecting PDF Writer Compression and Font Options" above.
2. In the Font Embedding dialog box, select the Embed All Fonts check box. Select the Never Embed check box.

3. From the Available Fonts list, select the names of fonts that you do not want to embed in all PDF documents. Click on Add to exclude these fonts from the PDF documents.
4. Click on OK.

NOTE

You can embed Adobe Originals and fonts owned by Linotype-Hell AG, International Typeface Corporation, Agfa-Gevaert, Fundición Typográfica Neufville, and Monotype Typography, Ltd. that are available from the Adobe Type Library. You may need permission from the font supplier to distribute PDF files containing other embedded fonts.

Embedding TrueType and Multiple Master Fonts

Like Type 1 fonts, TrueType fonts can be embedded in PDF documents. If a PDF file of a document containing TrueType fonts is created using PDF Writer, Acrobat Exchange and Reader use the original TrueType font when the document is displayed on the same platform (Windows, Macintosh, Unix, or DOS). The TrueType font, however, must be embedded in the PDF file or available to the operating system for Acrobat Exchange and Reader to use it.

TrueType fonts are converted to either Type 1 or Type 3 PostScript language fonts when a document is saved by a PostScript printer driver and converted to PDF format by Acrobat Distiller. This means that any PDF file created by Distiller always has font substitution performed. This is the case even if the named TrueType font is available to the operating system, because that font is designated as either a Type 1 or Type 3 font in the PDF file.

In addition, Acrobat Distiller embeds an instance of any multiple master font used in a document. This instance is a valid Type 1 font, and is thus compatible with all Acrobat 1.0 and 2.0 viewers.

Tips for Minimizing PDF File Size

This section offers suggestions and guidelines for keeping the size of PDF files to a minimum. Keep in mind that the smaller your graphics, whether in HTML or PDF, the faster they will load for your users.

Using the Save As Command to Save Changes

After changing a PDF file with the Acrobat Exchange program, save the changes with the Save As command (not Save). The Save command saves incremental changes by, for example, marking deleted pages as invalid but not removing them. The Save As command rebuilds files by removing all deleted objects.

Don't Use the ASCII Format Option

By default, both the Acrobat Distiller and PDF Writer programs create 8-bit binary files. This is the recommended setting because many electronic-mail, file-transfer, and network programs add characters and otherwise corrupt ASCII-formatted PDF files. Acrobat Exchange or Reader may not be able to read such corrupted files.

However, in some cases, you may have to select the ASCII Format option because some older versions of file-transfer programs cannot successfully copy 8-bit binary files. (Almost all recent versions of file-transfer, electronic-mail programs, and network copy operations can successfully transfer 8-bit binary files.)

Compress Text and Graphics

Both the Distiller and PDF Writer programs have options for compressing text and graphics to reduce the file size when they create a PDF file. In addition, the Distiller also lets you downsample (reduce the resolution) of bitmapped images when you compress them. See the next section on downsampling files for low-resolution and online use for more information.

Text and graphics include any figure, illustration, or graphic that is not a bitmapped image. Bitmapped images include images created by paint and photo-retouching programs, scanned images, and screen shots created by screen capture programs. Bitmapped images require much more storage space than text and simple drawings—and high-resolution images, such as 24-bit color images obtained from a scanner, require even more. A 2 x 3-inch 24-bit color image, for example, requires several megabytes of storage space.

Keep in mind the following when selecting compression options:

- The Distiller lets you specify separate compression options for color and grayscale images, but the PDF Writer does not.
- Acrobat Distiller determines the best compression method for your images (JPEG for halftone images and LZW (GIF) for screenshots) and applies the correct setting. You can choose the JPEG compression setting to be used only if JPEG is selected in the Job Options dialog box.
- The LZW (GIF) method compresses images without reducing image quality; these compressed images view and print exactly as uncompressed images.
- The JPEG compression method reduces image quality, but can compress images far more than the LZW (GIF) method.
- Monochrome image compression does not reduce image quality. You should always compress monochrome images if file size is an issue.

Downsample Files for Low-Resolution and Online Use

Most users view PDF documents with 96-dpi or lower resolution monitors, and print the documents with 400-dpi or lower resolution printers. To minimize PDF file size, consider downsampling bitmapped images to match the resolution of the laser printer used to reproduce them. If the document is mainly for online use, consider downsampling the images to match the highest resolution monitor your readers will use.

Convert Color Images

To reduce PDF file size and speed display, convert CMYK images to RGB. RGB images require less storage, display faster, and their colors often look better onscreen. The Acrobat Distiller is set, by default, to convert CMYK images to RGB for online viewing.

You may also want to try converting color EPS images to TIFF. For some applications, color TIFF images require less storage space than color EPS images. (Grayscale TIFF and EPS images are about the same size.)

Adobe Photoshop can convert EPS images to TIFF. HiJaak by Inset Systems can also convert many graphic formats, including EPS, to TIFF.

Embed Your PDF into an HTML Page

Now that you have learned how to assemble a basic PDF file, you need to build it into your Web page. This is a simple process. In your HTML editor, create the following set of tags:

```
<A HREF="yourfile.pdf"><IMG SRC="youricon.gif"
WIDTH="53" HEIGHT="38" ALIGN="top" BORDER=0></A>
```

Once you have uploaded your pdf and gif file to your server, include the above HTML tags. When the user of an Internet browser clicks on the graphic, 'youricon .gif', then, the PDF yourfile.pdf will be downloaded to them. Both of these files should be in the same directory as the page that references them. You will have to change the file references to include different directories if these files are located elsewhere.

Some newer version of Acrobat will require a server capable of byte serving capability to deliver the complete functionality of Acrobat 3.0. Ask your Internet provider if your Web server has that capability, or if you maintain your own Web server, check the Adobe site http://www.adobe.com for the correct server patches.

Once you name the PDF you have questioned, maintain it on the server where the page is published and it will be called up automatically for the user when the HTML page is loaded.

Copyrights

Adobe Acrobat Distiller™, Adobe Acrobat Exchange™, Adobe Acrobat Catalog™, Adobe Photoshop™, Adobe Illustrator™, Adobe PageMaker™, Adobe Acrobat™, Adobe FrameMaker™, Adobe PageMill™, Adobe SiteMill™, Adobe Type Manager™, and Adobe Premiere™ are all trademarks of Adobe Systems Incorporated.

d i m e n s i o n

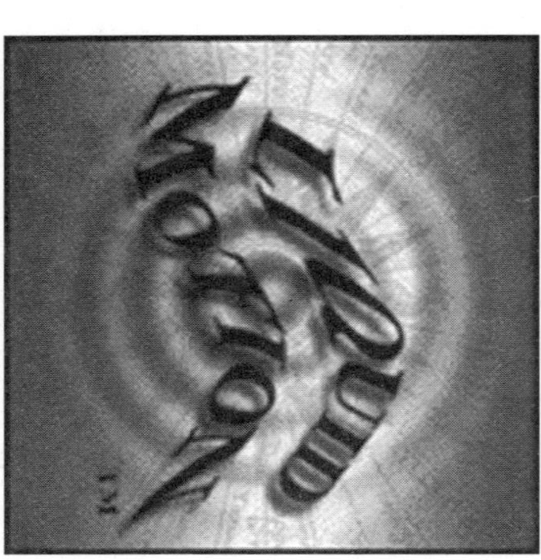

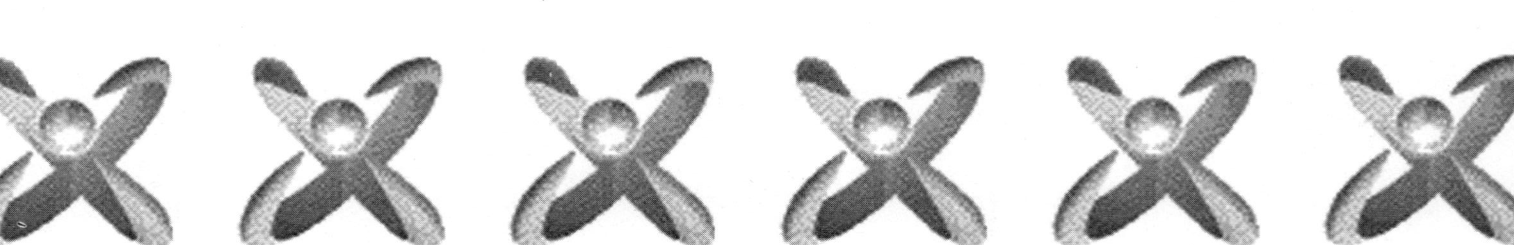

Dimension X and Liquid Motion

Company Profile

Dimension X, founded in February of 1995, was the first to blend the Java programming language from Sun Microsystems with VRML (Virtual Reality Modeling Language), unifying disparate Web technologies and creating powerful tools for users. A licensee of the Java language, Dimension X works as both a design studio and a tool builder. Clients include Sega of America, MCA Records, Intel, Fox Broadcasting, AT&T, Kenwood, and Entertainment Radio Networks.

Liquid Motion is the first product from Dimension X. It is a Java-based tool for creating 2D animations for your Web site, providing a more dynamic and interesting site for visitors. Because Java is a language that enables media to *stream* or move over the Web continuously, content appears immediately upon arrival, without the need to download. This rapid accessibility to site visitors, combined with ease of use of Liquid Motion itself, will enable you to build cool features for your site *today*. The following tutorial, designed for Windows 95 and Windows NT users, will give you a good taste of the application and enable you to embed an actual animation in a site. The application itself, with all the supporting files, is on the CD-ROM that comes with this book. If you want to learn more about Liquid Motion after you finish this tutorial, visit the Dimension X Web site at **http://www.dimensionx.com/**

Chapter Profile

By early 1993, when the Web first gained the wider recognition of the multimedia industry, bandwidth was considered the key issue of its growth and survival. At the time, several broadband trials were under development, all of which promised an array of visually rich services for consumers. Two years later, the Web is booming, ITV is all but dead, and the tables of "survival" have turned. There are lessons to remember from this transfer of power.

The first lesson is that consumers value visually stimulating content. In my opinion, the current state of the Web loses hands down to television and film for sheer storytelling power and immersive entertainment. But the Web has its own storytelling power, one which works in a very different way and likely will push storytelling to new heights. Yet there are few creative tools that allow people to tell stories on the Web using moving pictures instead of just words.

The second lesson is that bandwidth is likely to be scarce for the short-term future (one to two years). Broadband is "dead on arrival" because the cost of wiring each house for delivery is prohibitively high (most estimates vary between $500–$2,000 per home passed). Because these costs prevent cable and telephone companies from creating sensible business models, it is more realistic to focus on finding new ways to use the existing infrastructure. Regardless of who wins the rapidly emerging battle between cable companies (Web access via coaxial lines) and the telephone companies (squeezing more data into existing phone lines), the near future demands more ingenious ways of delivering captivating design to consumers.

The third lesson is that good creative tools need to be usable by average people to make the Web succeed in the long term. Most broadband projects assumed the existence of sophisticated production studios. HTML, despite its primitive state, is powerful not so much for what it might become, but for the number of people who can currently use it. Every day, new tools make HTML easier to use. Java, despite the hype, is a complex language requiring programming skills. Tools combining HTML's simplicity and Java's power promise to go far.

Liquid Motion is a tool that meets these expectations, enabling developers to create more compelling sites, utilizing existing Internet infrastructure while accommodating future bandwidth increases. And it is easy to use, despite being written in Java. Now the task is yours: start creating your own Web animations today!

Essay

Delivering on the Promise of Java-Based Animation: How To Author in Liquid Motion

by Patrick Schmitz & Alex Pineda

THERE HAS BEEN A LOT of hype about Java since it first splashed onto the Web. It seems that everyone wants to have Java on their site. Animation is one of the great promises of Java, and can add real flash to any page. The problem is that Java was built for programmers; Java-based animation remains out of reach for most designers.

The Dimension X production team builds Web sites and multimedia environments with a strong emphasis on technology (we have as many programmers as artists and designers). Our tools teams have a mandate to provide generalized solutions for many of the stickiest problems faced by the production team, and to polish these tools into products.

We started using Java back when it was still called OAK, and have been pushing it as far as we could. In the course of developing Java-based sites, we found that we were writing too much code to support relatively straightforward animations, and we realized the need for some general-purpose tools. Moreover, we needed tools suited to an artist rather than a programmer.

This eventually led to the development of Liquid Motion, our 2D animation authoring tool. Patrick Schmitz is the architect and technical lead for Liquid Motion. Alex Pineda is an artist and designer at Dimension X, and the most prolific user of Liquid Motion. Patrick discusses the background and some theory behind Liquid Motion, and Alex discusses work he has done with Liquid Motion, including the Poem animation, a short piece you'll learn to create.

Patrick Schmitz: Toolsmith

In 1995, Dimension X demonstrated an early prototype of JAM, a simple development tool for creating and manipulating animations with Java. This prototype was based upon the alpha release of the Java Developer's Kit (JDK) and the associated toolkit, the AWT. This early tool was rendered obsolete by the beta JDK release. Nevertheless, it generated sufficient interest to warrant further development as a product. We built a generalized animation engine and code-named it JACK (Java Animation Construction Kit). We code-named the authoring tool TEA (for The Easy Animator) and released it as Liquid Motion.

Like JAM before it, the most important requirements for Liquid Motion were that it be very easy to use by artists and animators (i.e., nonengineers), while at the same time providing an extensible architecture for programmers to create new behaviors, effects, etc. This tutorial will describe how we approached the design, and what we felt were the key elements that a tool like this must support.

Background: Why Build This Tool?

The first question we asked ourselves in defining a tool for animation was, "Who Cares?" The obvious answer is everyone on the Web—this is probably the most widespread use of Java for animation. The growth of the Web has been explosive, and continues to move at an amazing pace. The competition for attention is nearly as intense as in television, and Web designers are begging for tools to help take advantage of the new technologies.

The other side of the coin, which often gets too little attention (at least in technical discussions), is the intranet applications market, which comprises the vast number of companies and organization that use their internal networks for everything from training new employees to presenting project proposals to clients. This is generally seen as a more lucrative market than the Web, and it also has some other very interesting aspects. Intranet designers have many of the same interests as Web designers, but they are also pursuing more general multimedia applications such as computer-based training, directed sales presentations, educational Web sites, and even variations on the kiosk theme. Intranet designers have a different set of constraints on their designs, and in general can take advantage of richer media sources (they are less limited by download times and can often assume local media sources like CD-ROM drives or high-bandwidth media servers).

The point for us in determining for whom we were designing Liquid Motion was not to assume too much or too little about the environment, and to make the architecture scale up and down cleanly.

Why Animation?

So why animation? Or perhaps more precisely, what is animation? Most commonly, it is window dressing in someone's page. As with advertising, the Web needs the latest big thing. HTML is basically static, and the viewing public is not. People want to coordinate and control image sequences, audio, and anything that will liven up the page. Many of the people out on the Web are essentially channel-surfing couch potatoes. They have developed fairly sophisticated tastes when it comes to the medium and manner of presentation. Despite an often forgiving attitude toward content (especially on television), people notice poor execution immediately. This is especially so for flat presentations, but it includes dull effects as well.

In a best-case scenario, animation represents an interactive, dynamic environment, where various media are combined and manipulated to create a sense of place, or to tell a story. Interactive presentations, both on the Web and on intranets, constitute a large and rapidly expanding market for multimedia animation. The use of the Web and of intranets for training, targeted sales, and education is an ideal application for Java—these implementations require multimedia on the one hand, and flexibility on the other.

Looking to the future, many in the Web community await a kind of VRWeb, an immersive 3D interactive Web space akin to those described in contemporary science fiction. The notion of *collective* on the Internet began with chat, and is currently growing through shared whiteboards, collaborative art spaces, and interactive 3D worlds. As users and designers become even more sophisticated, they will demand capabilities such as integration of time-based media and animated signatures or avatars. The 2D and 3D distinctions will begin to blur, and the tools will have to blend, or at least integrate smoothly.

In the larger sense, animation is really about media integration and manipulation, and should not be limited to the current common denominator.

Why Java?

Do we really need to use a new programming language? There are other tools for this stuff, right? Well, sort of. The tools that have been available (ranging from server-push to animated GIFs to traditional multimedia authoring tools) have a variety of shortcomings:

- They can't properly handle server loading and issues of scaling on the Internet, which require intelligent client-side computers.
- They don't address the heterogeneous nature of the Web community, and even of intranets, which requires any solution to be a portable one.
- They can't keep up with the speed at which the technology moves and the need to adapt and reuse available content, which require an extensible environment.
- And finally, there is the question of the many trade-offs that surround the choice between the Java (applet) model and the browser plug-in model.

Let's take a closer look at each of these issues.

Server vs. Workstation Loading

Consider the history (if I can use that word) of animation support on the Internet. Initially, the server had to provide animation directly, because browsers were too simple to run animations themselves. CGI scripts and similar mechanisms had to push successive frames down the wire to the browser. This exacerbated the ever-growing problem of scaling Web server loading, and still provided only very simple slide-show style animation. Browsers have since gotten a little smarter, and can handle things like picture strips that animate in a slide show. Nevertheless, this is still very limiting for a designer.

At the same time, the client-side (i.e., end-users') computers are getting ever more powerful. One of the primary reasons for putting this power on the desktop is to support multimedia applications (it is certainly not needed to do word processing). The Web needs tools and technologies that take advantage of the growing capabilities of desktop computers to deliver on the promise of flash.

Web browser applications cry out for a distributed model for handling media. That is, more of the work must be done locally on the desktop, without requiring the use of considerable server resources. While something like the VRWeb will still require a fair amount of server processing (to allow users to interact with one another), it can only function at all in a model where most of the media-related work is handled on the desktop. In all cases, the client machine must be much more intelligent and must efficiently manage media and user interaction. Java provides an ideal platform for this new functionality.

Portability

The Internet community is among the most varied of any market. It is really the only place in which PCs, Macs, and Unix machines regularly interact to any degree. This places portability among the most important issues for Web design.

The intranet communities are often seen as less varied, since they tend to be a controlled domain (within a business or school system). However, it often turns out that there are several intranets within an organization, each made up of a particular class of machine (i.e., PCs, Macs, or Unix machines). File and print sharing are sometimes available, but true document sharing is often impossible, and a fully interactive intranet is a rare commodity.

HTML browsers are starting to change this by making documents available across the organization. Clearly, the next step is portable applications, and most relevant for this tutorial, portable engines for animation and interactive media support.

Many competing technologies currently handle a subset of the various platforms. While some are more mature and provide some very nice features, the underlying engines are inherently nonportable and seem unlikely to solve the larger problem. In contrast, Java was built specifically to address these needs, and it is maturing quickly.

Extensibility

Extensibility is, in my opinion, the defining issue when comparing Java to other technologies. The explosive growth of the Web and the rate of technological change demand solutions that are flexible and open. Java-based architectures allow third-party software developers to build extensions more easily than they could in traditional environments. Moreover, Java developers do not have to port their software to each and every platform. The initial market is much larger and the required effort much smaller.

For business and design agency users, extensibility means that they can more easily develop a custom or branded look for their presentations, beyond the constraints of simple graphics. For example, a custom motion, filter, or interaction behavior can define the branded look.

Finally, for an agency that develops animation for clients, the extensible architecture means that they can develop proprietary technology that they can sell to clients. This sort of advantage is extremely important in a competitive marketplace.

While it will certainly be possible to build closed architectures using Java, the ease with which you can build open, extensible architectures is one of its primary strengths.

Applets vs. Browser Plug-Ins

The question of applets versus browser plug-ins is the central issue of a large marketing battle, and the subject of many articles in itself. I will only briefly mention my thoughts on this. The channel surfing user will often pass over a site that requires yet another plug-in download and installation. Many are already frustrated by the bloat of these programs on their systems. Because of the need to include installation software, plug-in software is generally much larger than the corresponding Java program files would be.

When using a Java-enabled browser such as Netscape, Java applets, on the other hand, are automatically downloaded from the Web server and require no intervention from the user. With the caching of the support classes, the issue of repeated downloads becomes less important. As support for *class IDs* (a secure method of certifying software, like the hologram on packaging) becomes more prevalent, browsers will simply install vendors' class packages (e.g., media support engines), rendering them transparent to the user.

One advantage plug-ins have over applets is execution speed for certain operations. This is because of the nature of the Java language, which is *interpreted*, meaning the actual Java byte-code is translated into executable code and then run when you click on the applet (which is slow but portable), rather than *compiled* previously into a runtime executable module that is merely executed (which is fast but machine-specific). However, various companies are building faster interpreters and Just-In-Time compilers (a browser or operating system extension that compiles the Java code the first time it sees it). These tools let Java's runtime performance come close to that of compiled executable programs.

The real issue is one of youth versus maturity. Java is a young technology, and occasionally feels some growing pains. The competing technologies are more stable, but are generally not as well suited to the emerging Internet environment as Java. Those that are most stable and feature-rich are at the same time aging, and generally do not have the flexibility required for the fast-moving Web.

Requirements for Animation Support

Let's assume you've decided that Java-based animation is a must for you; now you set out to add some to your Web page. The first attempt is usually just a simple slide-show style animation or a text banner. Many demo and shareware applets are available that you can add to a Web page with parameters, such as font size and color, the window size, etc., for the images or text. Then next step is to animate some smaller images (*sprites*) against a background, along with some text and audio, to occur at specific points during the presentation. This requires a simple motion engine and timeline support to synchronize the different elements. Finally, you could design an interactive multimedia site with multiple scenes and multiple timelines, which the user would navigate by clicking on buttons, and which could be connected to a server database for some dynamic information display. This requires a pretty serious media and interaction engine, and little bit of glue code to talk to your database.

So what does a good animation engine need to provide? Let's take a look at a good starting list.

Media Support

The animation engine must support common image and audio formats. In the initial release, Java internally supported images in GIF and JPEG formats (the new multimedia support in review at the time of this writing would expand on this). For animations, any engine must support frames in individual files, as well as in horizontal and vertical strips. The initial release supported only 8-bit mono audio in Sun's .AU format, but higher quality audio is in the works. You can overlay multiple tracks and loop individual tracks. Additional support for imaging would include image synthesis for things like backgrounds (blends, patterns, etc.), which trade CPU time for download time. In addition, transitions between elements can be locally rendered (especially when the transition timing cannot be strictly predicted or prerendered by the author). Finally, rendered text support should include the ability to draw and animate strings with a choice of fonts, styles, and colors. Initial font support in Java was limited to a small number of font families, but later releases will have a much more complete font library.

Buffering

At a minimum, the animation engine should support double-buffering, to reduce flickering. A better solution is to support a means to only update changed portions of the viewed scene (using update rectangles or erase buffers).

Sprite Motion

This is a requirement for anything beyond the simplest image sequence, and it greatly increases the viewed bang for the downloaded buck—a little media and a motion path can create a dynamic animation. Sprite motion support should include programmatic motion and various path types (including spline paths). Advanced support includes 3D position and motion paths, where the Z-position (the simulated third dimension on the screen indicating the perspective of near to far from the viewer) defines the relative layer order (i.e., drawing order) of sprites. 3D motion paths allow for dynamic reordering of layers, allowing sprites to move in front of and then behind one another.

NOTE

Note that 3D position and motion apply to audio sequences as well, affecting the volume and balance. (Intel's 3D sound support is one player that uses this.)

Streaming

All time-based media should be able to stream from the server, playing or displaying the initial material as soon as it arrives. This can reduce fidelity, but greatly improves effective download time for applets. Similarly, the player should handle preloading media in the background, while other scenes display.

Timing and Synchronization

It is critical in a multimedia environment to have a robust model for timeline synchronization. Without this, audio and visual elements cannot remain synchronized, and the presentation starts to look sloppy. For the animation author, it is important to provide some timing primitives, like starting one sequence as another ends, or starting at some offset after the scene starts. In addition, for certain special applications like workstation playback, additional hooks should be provided for preparing and cueing media (like a CD or a video disc) before it actually starts.

Interaction

Any current GUI computer-based environment must include supports for interactive controls, driven by mouse and keyboard events. This draws users into the experience, and differentiates a true multimedia experience from a simple slideshow presentation. With regard to Web hyperlinked documents, some standard behaviors for things like URL linking and mail-to support should be provided. Beyond this, functionality should include display and removal of graphics, sounds, and animations (or entire scenes) and enabling and disabling any element's behavior (e.g., a motion path). Ideally, any object should be able to pass messages or events to any other object, and the animation author should be able to define new custom events.

Alternative Tools

For some people, the best tool alternative may be an established multimedia authoring tool that has been adapted to work on the Web. For certain very simple cases, a lightweight applet like Animator (a demo class from the JDK) may be most appropriate. However, if you want to take full advantage of the features of Java, and if you want to have a full set of features in your animation, you basically have two choices at this point:

- You can hire a team of Java programmers to start from scratch and build tools specific to your application. This is good for engineering employment, but not a viable option for many organizations.
- You can buy a tool that provides what you need.

A number of companies are working on tools, although I am not aware of many that are commercially available yet. Liquid Motion includes the breadth of functionality described above, coupling the ease of quick drag and drop development within its fourth-generation-language code-writing engines. Thus, it allows the novice Java programmer to generate animations for the Web with a minimum of actual coding required.

The Liquid Motion Engine: Technical Details

Now that you know a little about the *why*, let's take a look at the *how* of Liquid Motion.

The player engine is a package of classes that will scan a scene description file, fetch associated media, build a timeline, render the timeline, and manage user interaction. The *scene description file* is a text file that lists all the media and behaviors used in an animation. It is based upon a simple script language that details each object.

Animations are based on two abstract classes: *Sequence* and *Behavior*. A Sequence is anything that can be rendered for display or audio playout. A Behavior is a mechanism for changing the characteristics of a sequence over time, or in response to some user input (such as a mouse-click).

Every Sequence has a list of Behaviors that can modify it, or which can trigger control changes. Behaviors can be chained to run sequentially (for example, several motion paths linked together). You can also combine Behaviors to create an additive effect. For example, you could describe a spline path to animate a sprite back and forth across a background. Then, you could add a random motion behavior to produce a wobble along this path.

A specialized Sequence called a *Scene* is defined to gather sequences into a logical context and to bound the rendering of the collected sequences. Note that a Scene is a Sequence. This means that Scenes can have Behaviors, and that Scenes nest into Scenes. The result is a fully hierarchic model where an entire subtree can be modified as easily as a localized object.

The model also allows for nested motion (which works differently from additive motion as described above). For example, several sprites can have circular paths within a scene; that scene can have a spline path within its parent scene, which can in turn have a mouse-interactive motion behavior that allows the user to click and drag the top scene around.

Sequences Types

There are several general types of Sequences defined, although others can (and will) be added. In addition to the Scene class, the basic Sequence types include the following:

- **File-Based Image Sequences.** This is the most common sequence type. It supports still images and animation sequences in various forms.
- **Rendered Image Sequences.** These include blends and patterns drawn by description, rather than read from a file. These have the advantage of very little or no download overhead, but may require more computer resources.
- **Audio Sequences.** These are generally only file based, although at some point, MIDI files (byte codes executed by the client's sound card hardware) will be supported.
- **Text Sequences.** These allow for animated text in any supported font, size, and style. In the initial JDK, font support was limited, but the coming font support will be very flexible.

Behavior Types

Behaviors groups into several types, according to function. The set of types includes the following:

- **Motion Behaviors.** These are the most commonly used behaviors. Included are random motion behaviors, line and shape paths, spline paths, etc.
- **Transform or Filter Behaviors.** These modify the actual media. Examples are image fades and color changes, text style or size changes, and audio fading or panning.
- **Time Behaviors.** These modify the position and rate (speed) of the timeline for the Sequence (the change is local to the Sequence, or to the subtree if it modifies a Scene). These are useful, for example, when the author wishes to adjust the pacing of an entire Scene that has been constructed with media and behaviors aligned on a timeline. Tweaking all the individual animations and behaviors would very difficult, but this adjustment is made easy by applying a scaled time Behavior that runs the local timeline faster or slower than real time.
- **Control Triggers.** These are interactive behaviors that can hide and show sequences or scenes, activate and deactivate other behaviors, and control the browser context with URL links, mail-to support, etc.

Player Class and Rendering Support Classes.

These round out the package. The player is just a timeline thread that manages the relative timing of sequences, handles buffering for drawing optimization, and supports simple controls on the timeline playback (e.g., pause/resume).

One aspect that is not obvious in a 2D environment is that everything works in a 3D space. Sequences have a 3D position, and motion behaviors control 3D paths. For image sequences, the Z-position defines the render order, allowing sprites to move over or under other images. If 3D audio extensions are available on the platform, audio sequences can also respond to 3D motion behaviors. By defining an audio sequence to have 3D dimension (as well as position), audio can be made to play at the edges of the scene, as well as within it; it will be clipped (i.e., not played) when it is well outside the scene.

Conclusions

Java is ideally suited to the task of providing a platform-independent animation solution. The World Wide Web is currently driving much of the development of this technology, but we will soon see far wider application of these tools for intranets. For example, mechanics might be able to watch various procedures for repairing a car, surgeons could view the trials of a new technique, or new employees might receive training in the latest company policies. The key at this point is to put powerful yet easy-to-use tools into the hands of artists and authors, and let them fly.

In-house at Dimension X, Alex Pineda is our most accomplished Liquid Motion artist and has had considerable influence on the development of the tool. In the second half of this chapter, he presents a tutorial for two simple animations.

Alex Pineda: Artist, Designer, HTML Hacker

Preamble: I have put up a lot of sites in the course of my career as a Web designer, but until recently, all the pages I designed were static, as were most Web pages. There was simply no way that I, having no programming experience whatsoever other than HTML, could animate for the Web. That has changed with the creation of Liquid Motion.

Liquid Motion provides an authoring environment that will be familiar to anyone who has worked with time- and sprite-based animations. The controls are straightforward, and the functions easy to grasp.

Liquid Motion allows for control over timing and motion, scene embedding interactivity, and transition effects. It exports two types of files: a .JCK file that contains the basic Java elements used in the animation, and HTML files.

With Liquid Motion, it is now possible for me (and other artists) to create dynamic media for the Internet—quickly and easily, without having to learn Java.

How to Install Liquid Motion

To install Liquid Motion from the CD-ROM:

1. Open the DimX folder on the CD-ROM.
2. Double-click on INSTALLM.EXE.
3. Follow the instructions on the installation screens.

Liquid Motion must be installed on your hard drive. Liquid Motion will install in the C:\Program Files\Liquid Motion directory as a default. Icons are created in the Windows\Start Menu\Programs\Liquid Motion directory.

To run Liquid Motion:

1. Click on Start on the Windows 95 toolbar to display the Start menu.
2. Select Programs ➤ Liquid Motion ➤ Liquid Motion.

NOTE

Liquid Motion will only install and run on Windows 95.

The Poem Animation

The concept of the Poem animation explained below is to demonstrate the timing behaviors of Liquid Motion with a simple animation. (You can also see this animation at **http://www.dimensionx.com/products/lm/demos/poem/longfellow.html**). By using different timing sequences, I wanted to change the juxtaposition of the poetry and images as the animation played. This would give the words and images different associations depending on the combination. Using Free Liquid Motion, the HTML file I eventually created involved two separate Liquid Motion animations and incorporated them both into a single Web page.

NOTE

The purpose of this tutorial is to provide the new user with a simple sequence that can be put together quickly and easily. Liquid Motion is capable of much more complex animations that can involve many elements, each with timing, motion, and interactive behaviors, and scenes embedded within scenes within scenes, etc.

Follow the steps below to begin the Poem animation.

1. Using Photoshop, I rendered two separate sets of images: text and graphics. Then, I converted them to GIFs and saved them with successive file names (for example, TEXT1.GIF, TEXT2.GIF or PIX1.GIF, PIX2.GIF, etc.). Finally, I converted the text images to GIF 89 transparencies. All of these files are included on the CD-ROM under the Dimx\Imagesfolder.

NOTE

At the moment, Liquid Motion only supports GIFs and JPEGs. It also supports GIF 89 transparency, meaning that a background image can be set to show through an image. This works for single images as well as for an animation sequence. There is work under way to support other media, but currently it is limited to what is supported in Java.

2. Launch Liquid Motion from where you installed it on your hard drive (the default is C:\Programs\LiquidMotion). Select File ➤ New Scene, and save the .JCK file as **POEM.JCK**.

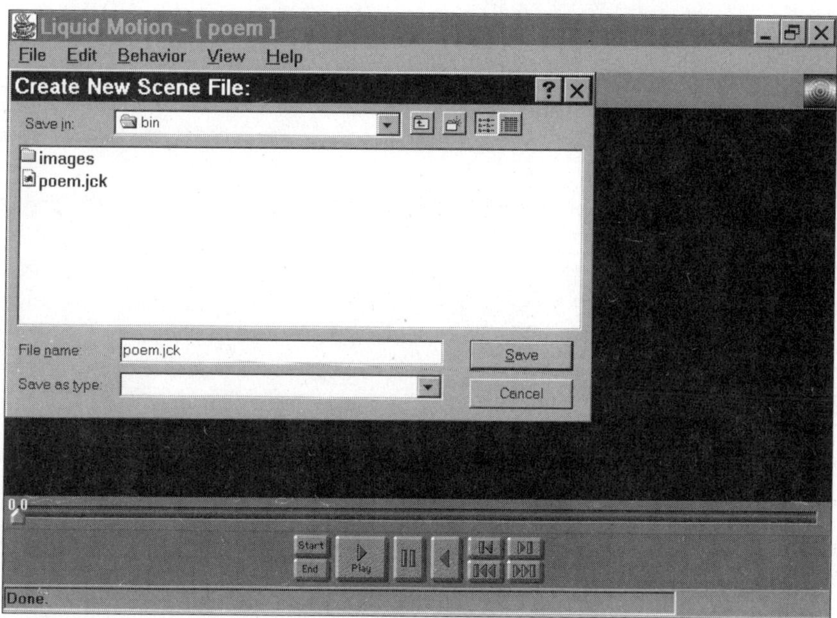

NOTE

The program won't let you do anything until you save the .JCK file. The reason for this is to force you to create a project directory where everything will be saved. This way, when all is done, all you have to do is copy the directory to your server.

3. Select Edit ➤ Add Image. This brings up the Add Image Element dialog box, where there are different options for adding an image. Click on the Browse button and find your CD-ROM drive. Open the Dimx\Images folder and select the TEXT1.GIF file. Click on Open to close the dialog box.

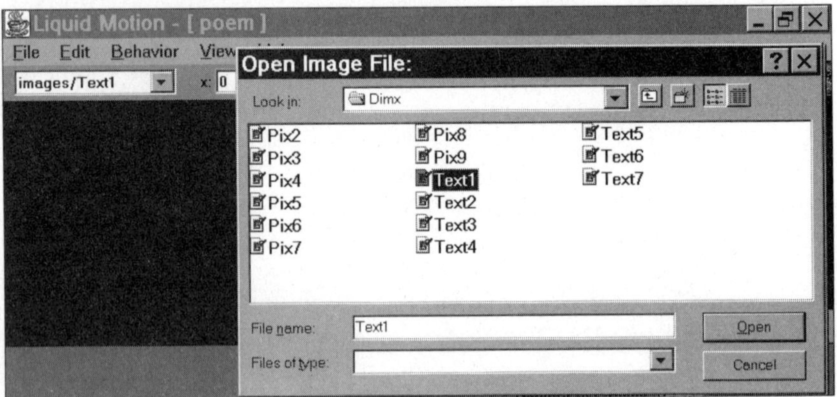

NOTE

When working with successive images, it's necessary to give them a succession of identical files names ending with 1, 2, 3, etc., so that they are imported in the correct order. In Free Liquid Motion, the order in which images overlap each other is determined by the order that they are imported into the file.

4. In the Add Image Element dialog box, there are two ways to import an image: as a Single Image or as an Animation Sequence. Liquid Motion will also import similarly named files in a sequence. This is the way to load a series of frames into an animated sequence. Click on OK.

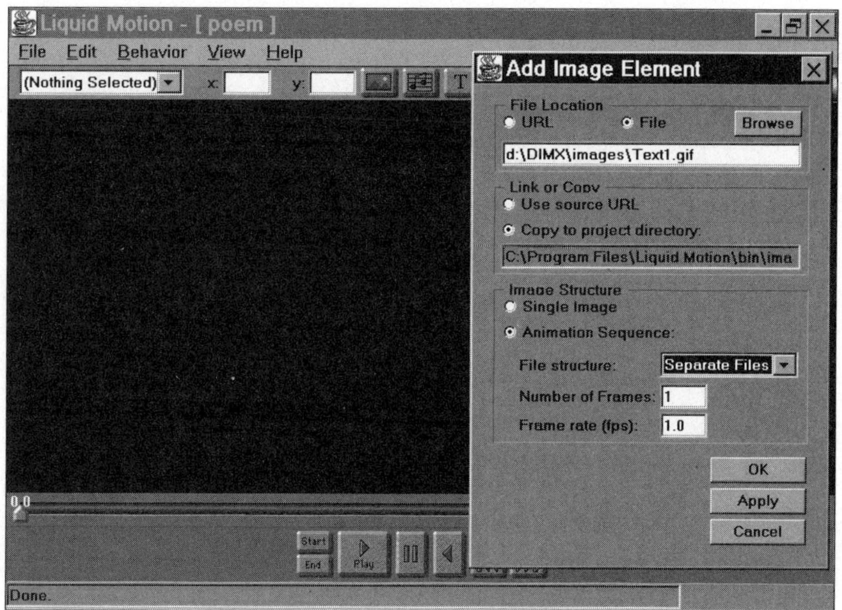

NOTE

When you add an image, Liquid Motion automatically creates a subdirectory called Images. Again, this is to simplify the process of transferring the project to a Web server. If all the media are in the project directory, all that's necessary is to copy the project directory to your server.

5. Select Edit ➤ Scene Background Color. Using the color picker, set the background color to black. You can also accomplish this by typing in the RGB values. Type a **0** into the Red, Green, and Blue text boxes to indicate black. Eventually, you'll be exporting the Liquid Motion file to an HTML file, so set the background color to the color you'll be using on the Web page. You want the animation to integrate seamlessly with the HTML file. In HTML, the <BODY BGCOLOR="#000000"> tag creates a black background.

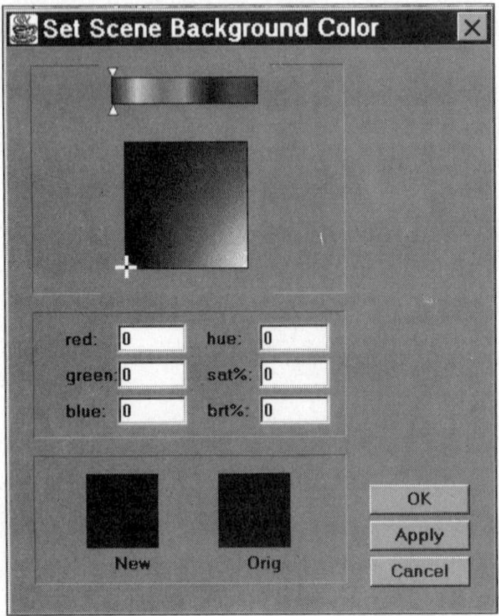

6. Select Edit ➤ Scene Properties. In the Root Scene Properties dialog box, you can choose the overall size of your scene by typing in the height and width in the Forced Dimensions boxes. Unless you type in these values, the size of the scene will be determined by the overall size of the media (i.e., the user's monitor and modem).

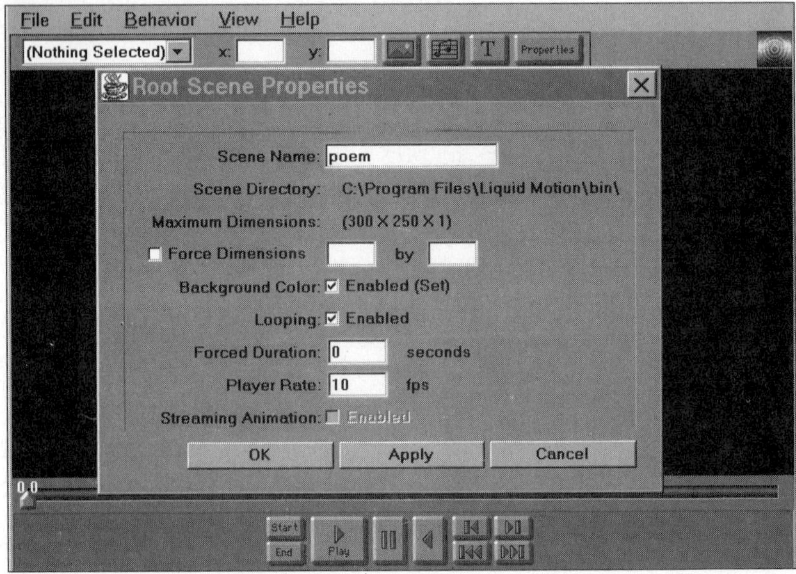

NOTE

When designing your animation, keep in mind the caveats of the Web: be aware of monitor size and download time. When setting the size of your scene, keep in mind that a great many users still have 640 x 480 monitors. An enormous number of people still use 14.4 modems, so try and keep your media as small as possible. You want to people to *view* your animation, not get frustrated waiting for it to download.

7. With the first text image (TEXT1.GIF) selected in the drop-down box under the menu bar, select Edit ➤ Properties.

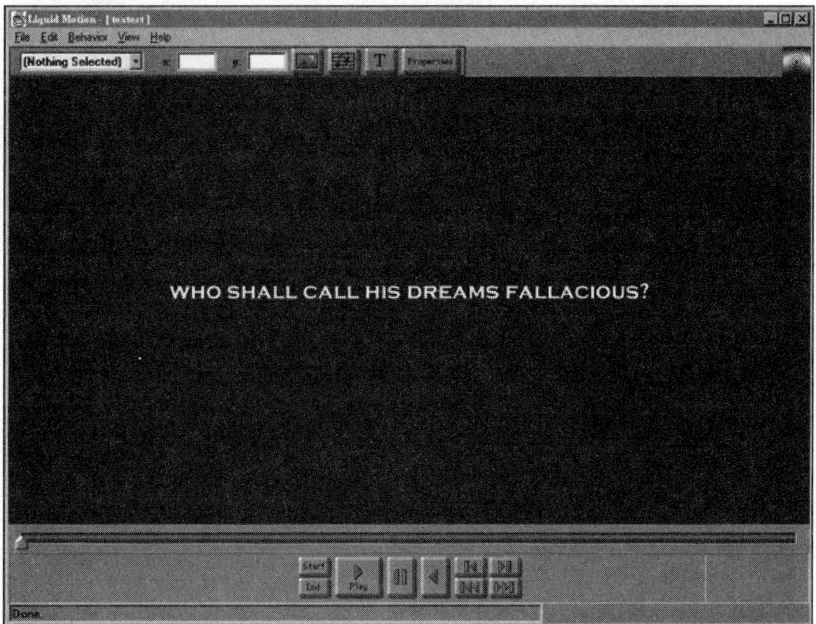

8. The Sequence Properties dialog box appears. In this dialog box, you can assign properties for scene elements. For this relatively simple slide-show style animation, we are only going to assign a time duration. Set the time duration of the text image to four seconds in the Forced Duration box. Since it is the first image in the animation, leave the Starts behavior to When Scene Starts, so that it will begin playing at the beginning.

9. Click on OK to close the dialog box.

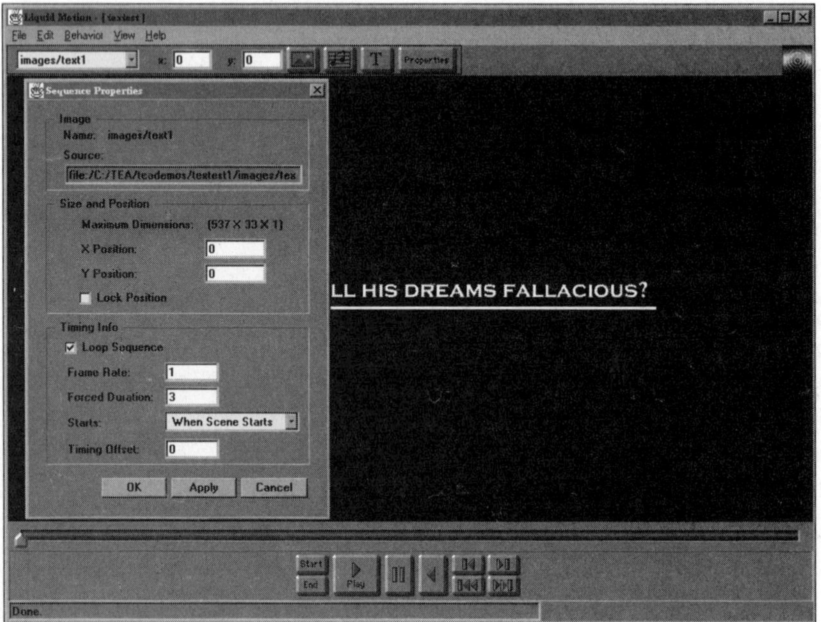

You can apply properties in two ways in Liquid Motion: to an individual scene element, or to the overall scene itself. These are the properties that you can assign to a scene element using the Sequence Properties dialog box:

- **X Position/Y Position.** Use this option to set X and Y coordinates for the object.
- **Lock Position.** This keeps an image locked into place. If you want an object in a fixed position and don't want it moved accidentally, then enable position locking.
- **Loop Sequence.** Use this option for looping either a single image or sequence of images.
- **Frame Rate.** This controls the rate at which an animation plays. The rate is in seconds.
- **Forced Duration.** This option controls the length of time an image or sequence plays. Time is in seconds. Use Forced Duration when you want a sequence to stay on the scene longer than its natural duration. For example, if you import five frames of an animation, and you set their frame rate to five frames per second, the whole sequence naturally lasts for one second.

If you force the duration to 10 seconds, those five frames will loop and stay on the scene for that duration. This is how to loop an individual sequence rather than the entire scene.

- **Starts.** This option has three settings:
  - When Prior Ends sets a sequence to begin after a prior sequence
  - When Prior Starts tells a sequence to play at the same time as the sequence prior to it
  - When Scene Starts has the sequence play at the beginning of the whole animation
- **Timing Offset.** Setting a number for this property determines how long, in seconds, an image or sequence will delay before appearing on the scene. This is also influenced by how it is linked to either the Scene or the another element in the Starts option.

Now we'll add the remaining text images:

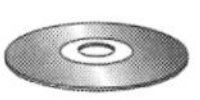

1. Select Edit ➤ Add Image to display the Add Image Element dialog box, and browse to find the second text image (TEXT2.GIF) on the CD-ROM, as described previously in step 3. Use your mouse to drag the image so that it is centered and aligned over the previous one.

NOTE

Whenever you add an element, it is selected by default. It's important to make sure that the correct object is selected when assigning properties. One way to select a scene element is by using the pull-down menu in the upper-left corner of the Liquid Motion screen, just below the menus.

2. With the second element selected in the drop-down box below the menu bar, give it the same properties as the first, but set the Starts property to When Prior Ends. This tells the image to load when the first image is done.
3. Repeat the last step with the rest of the text images (TEXT3.GIF, TEXT4.GIF, TEXT5.GIF, TEXT6.GIF, and TEXT7.GIF). Set them all to a duration of four seconds, and set them to start when the prior image ends.

The net effect is a basic slide show sequence of images, each one staying on the screen for four seconds before the next image loads.

Now we'll assign some additional properties:

1. Select Edit ➤ Scene Properties. In the Root Scene Properties dialog box that appears, click on the Looping check box to loop the entire scene. Click on OK.

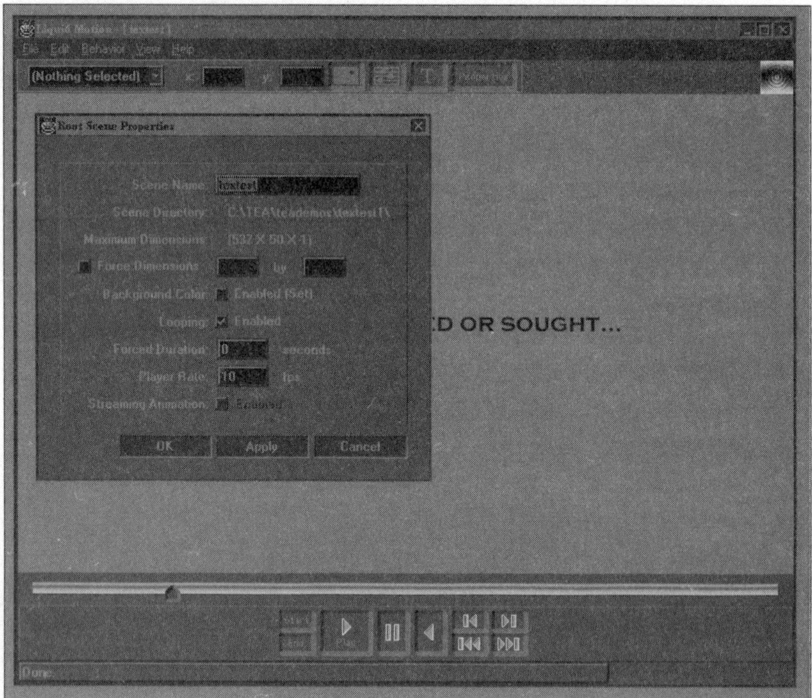

2. While the Sequence Properties dialog box assigns properties and behaviors to individual elements, the Root Scene Properties menu assigns properties to the entire Scene. These are the properties that can be given to a scene:

   - **Scene Name.** Names the scene.
   - **Force Dimensions.** Liquid Motion automatically sizes the entire scene based on the largest scene elements. To override this, assign a pixel value for X and Y in this section.
   - **Background Color.** Enables or disables a background color for the entire scene. Set this property by choosing Edit ➤ Scene Background Color.
   - **Looping.** Check this box to loop the entire scene. It is important to note that there are two different kinds of looping possible in Liquid

Motion. You can loop various elements within a scene, all with different properties, (i.e., play rate, duration, etc.), as well as loop the entire scene.

- **Forced Duration.** You can assign a specific duration to the entire scene using this property.
- **Player Rate.** This controls the frames per second (fps) at which the entire scene plays. The default rate is 10 frames per second.

3. After saving the file again by selecting File ➤ Save, go back to the File menu, and choose Export HTML. The HTML file is automatically saved as the title of your .JCK file, POEM in this case, with an HTML extension. Here is the entire HTML file generated by Liquid Motion:

```
<HTML>
<HEAD>
<TITLE>Liquid Motion Scene: poem</TITLE>
<!—Created by {You Are Here}—>
</HEAD>
<BODY BGCOLOR="#000000">
<APPLET CODE="dnx.jack.PlayerApplet.class" CODE-
BASE="./" WIDTH=325 HEIGHT=33>
<PARAM NAME=scene VALUE="poem.jck">
<PARAM NAME=playerBkgd VALUE="000000">
<PARAM NAME=playerRate VALUE="10">
<PARAM NAME=passEventsToScene VALUE="0">
</APPLET>
</BODY>
</HTML>
```

As you can see, the HTML file that is generated by Liquid Motion is very straightforward. Going through the file, you can see that Liquid Motion automatically puts in the standard <HTML>,<HEAD>, and <TITLE> tags. Since we chose black as the background color in the scene, it has also put in a <BODY BGCOLOR=#000000"> tag, #000000" being the hexadecimal value for black. The rest of the file is enclosed within <APPLET> tags, and determines the properties of the Liquid Motion animation.

Adding Images to the Poem

Now we are ready to start the second part of the animation.

1. Select File ➤ New Scene to start a new scene.

NOTE

You can only have one scene open at a time in Liquid Motion, so choosing New Scene will close the current scene.

2. Save the file in the same directory as the first scene, and call this one **TEXTEST2.JCK**. Leave all the default settings as they are.
3. Select Edit ➤ Scene Background Color, and from the dialog box that appears, choose black as the background color.
4. Select Edit ➤ Add Image to display the Add Image Element dialog box. Under File Location, click to select the File radio button, click on the Browse button, open the Dimx\Images folder on the CD-ROM, and find the image PIX2.GIF. Import it as a single image (click on the Single Image radio button), rather than a sequence of images.

5. With the first image selected, pull up the Edit Properties dialog box. In this dialog box, you'll basically repeat what you did with the text images, with a slight difference: set the time duration of the image to three seconds instead of four. Since this is the first image, set the Starts option to When Scene Starts.
6. Add the next seven images (PIX3.GIF–PIX9.GIF, for a total of eight), and give them all the same properties: a time duration of three seconds, and to start When Prior Ends.
7. Select Edit ➤ Scene Properties. In the Root Scene Properties dialog box, set the whole scene to loop by clicking on the Looping check box, then click on OK to close the dialog box.

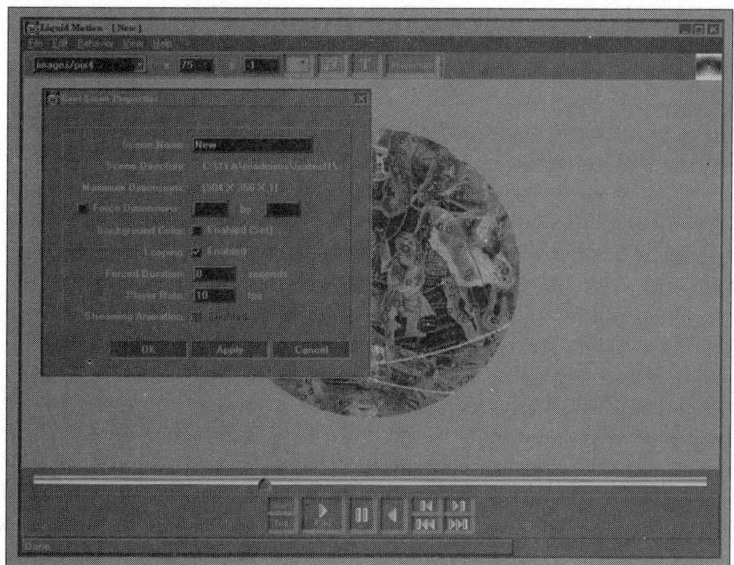

8. Save the scene by selecting File ➤ Save, then select File ➤ Export HTML.
9. Name the file **TEXTEST2.HTML** and save it to the same directory as POEM.HTML.
10. Using an HTML editor or any editor capable of saving ASCII files, open both files, POEM.HTML and TEXTEST2.HTML. Copy everything within the <APPLET> tags in TEXTEST2.HTML and paste it below the <APPLET> tag in POEM.HTML.
11. Center both applets by using the <P ALIGN=CENTER> tag. In the <BODY> tag, assign a green color to the text using the hexadecimal value TEXT= "#808000". Save the file as **POEM.HTML**, and open it in the browser. Voila! Here is the final HTML file:

```
<HTML>
<HEAD>
<TITLE>Liquid Motion Scene: poem</TITLE>
<!-Created by {You Are Here}->
</HEAD>
<BODY BGCOLOR="#000000">
<APPLET CODE="dnx.jack.PlayerApplet.class"
CODEBASE="./" WIDTH=325 HEIGHT=33>
<PARAM NAME=scene VALUE="poem.jck">
<PARAM NAME=playerBkgd VALUE="000000">
<PARAM NAME=playerRate VALUE="10">
```

```
<PARAM NAME=passEventsToScene VALUE="0">
</APPLET>
</APPLET>
<APPLET CODE="dnx.jack.PlayerApplet.class"
CODEBASE="./" WIDTH=300 HEIGHT=250>
<PARAM NAME=scene VALUE="textest2.jck">
<PARAM NAME=playerBkgd VALUE="000000">
<PARAM NAME=playerRate VALUE="10">
<PARAM NAME=passEventsToScene VALUE="0">
</APPLET>
</BODY>
</HTML>
```

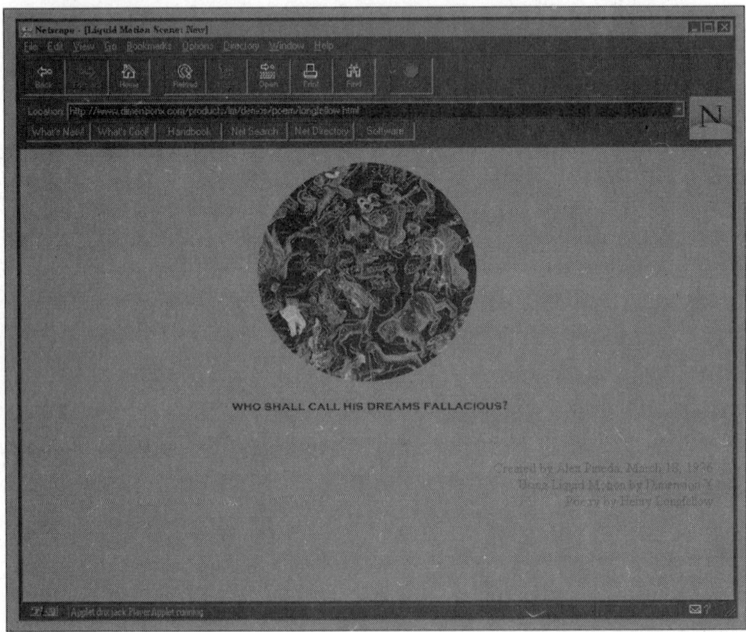

12. The final step is to copy the entire directory, along with all the necessary classes, to your World Wide Web Server.

Now the whole world (or the entire Java-based Internet, anyway) can see the animation.

Again, the demo above is intended to be simple and quick. Feel free to apply other motions and behaviors to the various elements. Experiment!

Glossary

Absolute Link

Absolute links (sometimes called *absolute references*) specify the full location (URL) of a file. For example, **http://www.gnn.com/news/news.htm** is an absolute link). *See also* Relative Link.

Adaptive Compression

Data compression software that continuously analyzes and compensates its algorithm (technique), depending on the type and content of the data.

Agent

A software routine that searches through local or remote databases, gleaning specified information for its user. *See also* Intelligent Agent.

Algorithm

A prescribed set of mathematical steps that is used to solve a problem or conduct an operation.

Aliasing

A condition in which graphics reveal jagged edges when magnified. *See also* Anti-Alias.

Animated Graphics (Animation)

Moving diagrams or cartoons. Animated graphics use up far less disk space than video images.

Anti-Alias

Blending techniques that smooth the jagged edges of computer-generated graphics and type. An anti-aliased graphic is one that has been refined for higher resolution and presentation. For example, the anti-aliasing process adds pixels in between jagged "steps" of a curved image to make it smoother. *See also* Aliasing.

ASCII

American Standard Code for Information Interchange. The most popular coding method used by small computers for converting letters, numbers, punctuation, and control codes into digital form; ASCII is also the text type recognized by all major data networks for system commands and communications.

Aspect Ratio

The relationship of width to height. The aspect ratio of images displayed on different screens must be kept the same, otherwise the image will be "stretched" either vertically or horizontally.

Audio

Frequencies from 15Hz to 20,000Hz that the human ear can hear.

Audiovisual

Output that can be seen and heard. Television is audiovisual, while radio is not.

Bandwidth

The estimated amount of information that can be moved through a given connection between two or more computers. Bandwidth is usually measured in Kilobytes (K), Megabytes (MB), or Megabits (Mb). Typical bandwidth measurements are 9600 baud, 14.4K (14,400 baud), 28.8K (28,800 baud), 56K (56,000 baud, also known as ISDN), 128K, T1 (1.544 Megabits per second; roughly 1 Megabyte), and T3 (between 4 and 5 Megabits per second). Increased bandwidth is crucial to the future of the Web, as it enables larger volumes and more complex information to be exchanged between locations.

Baud

A unit of data transmission speed at which computer data can transmitted over a modem. Often confused with bits per second (bps). Baud really only applies to modem speeds under 300 bits per second (bps), which are totally irrelevant by current standards. Higher speed modems use compression to transmit more data per second.

Binary

A numbering system based on 2s, which uses 0s and 1s when written. Any file that contains nontextual data, such as images or applications, is a binary file.

Bit

The smallest unit of information in a computer. Derived from **B**inary dig**IT.** Represents one of two conditions: on or off (0 or 1). Bits are arranged into groups of eight called *bytes*. A byte is the equivalent of one character.

Bitmap

Representation of characters or graphics by individual pixels, or points of light, arranged in a row (horizontal) and column (vertical). Each pixel is represented by either one bit (for black and white) or from 8 to 32 bits (to represent color).

Bitmapped Graphics

Raster graphics that are constructed with individual pixels or dots, rather that object-based or vector-based graphics.

Broadband

A loose term used to describe local network connections above 128K. The most recognizable form of broadband is currently *cable-modem*, which promises to multiply Internet connections by several factors. The value of broadband services is high, though many attempts to bring it to market have failed, mostly because of its complexity and cost of development.

C (Also C++)

A complex but powerful programming language used to build many software applications.

CD-ROM

Compact Disc Read Only Memory. A data storage system, using CDs as the medium, which hold more than 600 megabytes of data.

CGI

Common Gateway Interface. A programming technique for building interactivity into a site. CGI scripts are usually written in a programming language such as Perl. CGI is already giving way to new Web-enabled programming and scripting languages, such as JavaScript.

Chat

An online system that enables multiple people in different locations to communicate as a group using text. Some new Chat systems include audio, 2D, and 3D graphics for an experience similar to Virtual Reality.

CMYK

Cyan, Magenta, Yellow, Black. A term from color printing to describe a process that uses each of the above colors in varying values in combination with one another to create any variation of other colors. For example, a print requiring the color orange would use a determined number of tiny yellow and magenta dots on a page instead of actually using orange ink. This consolidation of colors into four categories simplifies the printing process while allowing nearly infinite variation of color.

Compression

A software or hardware process that reduces images so they occupy less storage space and can be transmitted faster. Generally accomplished by removing redundant data and replacing it with a smaller algorithm that represents the removed data.

CyberCash

A firm devoted to creating electronic financial transactions between consumers and businesses over networks. CyberCash competes with several firms, including First Virtual Holdings, to establish the standard method of enabling commerce over the Web.

Decompress

Returning compressed data to its original size and condition.

Digital

The use of binary code to record information, which can be binary (text), bitmapped (scanned images), sampled digital (sound), or video.

Digitize

To convert an image or signal into binary code.

Disc

A round, flat optical storage medium used to store digital data that can be read by lasers.

Disk

A round, flat magnetic recording medium used to store digital data that can be read by magnetic disk drives.

Dither

A process of reducing graphics to their simpler chromatic components. For example, a dithered image might have just blue and green pixels instead of an even turquoise. Dithered images save on memory requirements but frequently compromise severely on quality.

Downstream

The rate at which information travels from a server to a user's client computer. This rate is the opposite of *upstream*. *See also* Upstream.

DPI

Dots Per Inch. A measurement of output device resolution and quality. Measures the number of dots a printer can print per inch both horizontally and vertically.

Em

A relative measurement of horizontal space equal to the width of a capital *M* based on a font and font size in use. *See also* En.

En

Half the width of an em. Both en and em are used to describe the length of dashes and spaces in typography. *See also* Em.

Ergonomics

An applied science devoted to the interaction between humans and technology. The field's specific disciplines include User Interface design, which concentrates on human interaction with computers and other electronic systems.

Fiber Optic

The cable technology used to transmit the majority of information for phone and data communications across great distances. Fiber optics greatly reduces the amount of space needed to transmit information and increases the speed at which it can be moved.

File Server

The central database system that supplies a given Web site with the text, graphics, and other information needed to communicate with an end-user.

Firewall

A software system designed to keep unauthorized users out of a network while allowing authorized users to enter. Firewall technology is crucial to the growth of the Web as more firms connect their sites to sensitive information.

Folder

Originally a Macintosh term for the basic element in its file management scheme. Also used by Microsoft in Windows 95. A folder holds sets of directories and files. A folder can hold other folders.

Font

All the characters and digits in the same style and size of type.

FTP

File Transfer Protocol. Communications protocol that can transmit files without loss of data. A series of commands governing the communications between client and server computers during the exchange of a file or application. Examples are Xmodem, Ymodem, Zmodem, and Kermit.

Gamma

The measuring curves that show the degree of darkness or lightness of an image.

GIF

Graphics Interchange Format. A lossless graphics file format developed by CompuServe that handles 8-bit color (256 colors) and uses the LZW method to achieve compression ratios of approximately 1.5:1 to 2:1. The graphics file type most frequently used on the Web for its compact memory size. *See also* LZW Compression.

Graphical User Interface

Also called GUI (pronounced "gooey"). The visual system that interprets between humans and computers. Allows the user to command the computer by "pointing and clicking" (usually with a mouse or stylus) at pictures or icons, rather than typing in commands.

Hot List

A set of links to the user's preferred Web sites, collected in a browser application.

HTML

***H**yper**t**ext **M**arkup **L**anguage*. The standard language that Web pages use to specify the links and structure of a document, including page layout and graphics placement.

HTML Standards Committee

The governing body that determines the specifications of each new version of HTML.

HTTP

***H**yper**t**ext **T**ransport **P**rotocol*. The primary communications protocol used to move text and graphics over the Internet.

Huffman Encoding

A lossless compression algorithm that replaces frequently occurring data strings with shorter codes. Some implementations include tables that predetermine what codes will be generated for a particular string. Others versions of the algorithm build the code table from the data stream during processing.

Hyperlink

HTML's distinctive feature is the hyperlink, which is a link to other documents. Links can be relative to the current page or absolute. You can have links to other locations in the same page and links to specific places in other documents anywhere on the Internet. *See also* Absolute Link *and* Relative Link.

Hypermedia

Use of data, text, graphics, video, and voice as elements in a hypertext system. All the various forms of information are linked together so that a user can easily move from one to another.

Hypertext

A term invented by author Ted Nelson to describe a process of reading and writing nonlinear documents.

Image Resolution

The fineness or coarseness of an image as it was digitized, measured in dots-per-inch (dpi) for a printed image or pixels-per-inch (ppi) for a digital image (or screen image).

Indexed Color

A single-channel image, with 8 bits of color information per pixel. The index is a color lookup table containing up to 256 colors. There are two types of indexed color images: ones that have a limited number of colors (fewer than 256), and pseudo-color images (grayscale images that display variations in gray levels with color rather than shades of gray). Pseudo-color images are often used in scientific and medical applications. You can specify the bit resolution, or the number of bits of color information per pixel, for the indexed color image. The resolution you choose determines the number of colors that can be displayed at one time. For example, if you select 4 bits per pixel, 16 colors can be displayed at a time; if you select 8 bits per pixel, 256 colors can be displayed at one time.

Intelligent Agent

A software program that acts on behalf of a user to search for and organize information. Intelligent agents are rapidly becoming a key technology in the online business, where enormous amounts of information must be searched for the small quantity that is of particular interest to specific users.

Interactive

A software interface where results of work or selections done by an operator appear instantaneously, or in real time on the monitor. Can combine complex applications using graphics, audio, music, video, etc.

ISDN

Integrated Services Digital Network. International telecommunications standard for transmitting voice, video, and data over a digital line. A fast (56–128K) connection to the Internet.

Jaggies

Slang for *aliasing*. The ragged or stair-stepped appearance of diagonal lines and curves. *See also* Aliasing.

JPEG

Joint Photographic Experts Group. An industry panel that determines standards for compressing digital images. It provides lossy compression at variable ratios, providing 10 to 20:1 without noticeable loss. In the case of the Web, JPEG is a lossy graphics compression standard most useful for large images with high contrast or subtle gradations of tone. JPEG competes with the GIF file format.

Kbyte

Kilobyte. One thousand bytes; to a computer, it's actually 1,024 bytes.

Kerning

The adjustments of the spacing between two letters, which reduces the amount of white space or *leading* between characters.

Lossless

An image and data compression method that reduces the file size without any loss of data. When reconstructed, an image compressed with lossless compression contains all data found in the original image.

Lossy

Image (or video segment) compression that reduces the size of an image through the loss of some information. A lossy image or video stream frequently loads quickly or runs smoothly but, if overly compressed, looks terrible. JPEG (.JPG) compressed images of excellent quality can be found on the Web.

Luddite

A person who resists the progress made by technology.

Luminance

The brightness of a color. Measured by taking the highest of the individual RGB values plus the lowest of the individual RGB values, divided by two (as defined by Adobe).

LZW Compression

Lempel-Zif-Welch. A lossless data-compression algorithm used in the GIF file format. *See also* GIF.

Modem

Short for ***mod**ulator-**dem**odulator*. Device that allows digital signals to be transmitted and received over analog telephone lines.

Moiré

An undesirable effect caused by overlaying dot patterns that are incompatible. Moiré patterns often appear when halftone photographs are scanned.

MPEG

Moving Pictures Expert Group. The standards for compressing full-motion video.

Multimedia

Disseminating information in more than one form. Includes the use of text, audio, graphics, animated graphics, and full-motion video.

Multi-User Dimensions (MUDs)

MUDs are a text-based "place" on the Internet where people gather simultaneously to exchange ideas, argue, share fantasies, and generally have a good time. With the advent of 3D spaces on the Web, graphics-based MUDs are becoming more common. MUDS are part of a family that includes MUSHs (Multi-User Shared Hallucination), and MOOs (MUD, Object-Oriented).

Noise

Interference with a pure signal of information over a phone line. In an image, pixels with randomly distributed color values that degrade image quality.

Object-Oriented

Software that allows the user to define objects (i.e., images, line art, text, etc.) and manipulate them for placement in page layout or other creative graphical programs.

PageMaker

A comprehensive desktop publishing layout tool sold by Adobe Systems.

Palette

The number of colors a graphic expansion board is capable of displaying and producing. Also the tools used in paint programs.

Pantone Colors

Process PMS colors. Print industry standard colors now available with digital prepress systems. *See also* PMS.

Perl

A programming language used to create interactivity on a Web site.

Photoshop

A best-selling image editing tool sold by Adobe Systems. Originally designed for Apple/Macintosh and now available for Windows and SGI platforms.

Pixel

Derived from the words *picture element*. The smallest visual unit in a raster file. Also the smallest element on a video display screen, comprising one or more dots that are treated as a unit. A pixel can be one dot on a monochrome screen, three dots (red, green, and blue) on color screens, or clusters of these dots. The color of the pixel depends on which dots are illuminated, and how brightly.

Plug-In

On the Web, a software application used in conjunction with a browser to view or manipulate documents.

PMS

Pantone Matching System. A means of describing colors by assigning them numbers. *See also* Pantone Colors.

Primary Colors

The primary colors when mixing paint are red, yellow, and blue. When mixing colors with light, either additive colors or subtractive colors are used. Additive primary colors are red, green, and blue. Subtractive primary colors are magenta, yellow, and cyan.

Quantize

The filtering process that determines the amount and selection of data to be eliminated in order to encode the data with fewer bits.

QuarkXPress

A popular desktop publishing tool developed by Quark (Denver, CO) for Apple Macintosh computers and now available for the PC.

Raster Graphics

In computer graphics, a technique for representing a picture image as a matrix of dots.

Rasterize

To convert digital information into a series of pixels on an output device (computer screen, printer, or image setter).

Real Audio

An audio technology that enables Web users to hear information in a *streaming* manner (on the fly), without having to download it to their machine first.

Real-Time

A loose term used to describe the nearly immediate occurrence of events, such as Chat. *See also* Chat *and* Multi-User Dimensions.

Relative Link

A relative link (also called a *relative reference*) omits part of the file specification in an address (URL) and uses the current location as the default. (For example, **http://www.gnn.com/news/news.htm** is an absolute link. A relative link to this file from the directory above would be **news/news.htm**.) You can only use relative links to link to a file on the same server or disk.

Resolution

Degree of sharpness of a displayed or printed character or image. On screen, resolution is expressed as a matrix of dots (*height* x *width* x *number of colors*). For printers, resolution is expressed as the number of dots per linear inch.

RGB

Red Green Blue. The chromatic values used to create images on computer screens. Every pixel on a screen is composed of these three colors. When each color is varied in strength, the combined radiance produces different colors.

Scan

To capture an original image or line work and convert it to digital data.

Scripting

A language support for handling pre-built graphical components. Scripting applications with WebObjects is simple enough for both programmers and designers to use immediately.

Secured Transactions

Encrypted packets of information that contain sensitive financial data. Secure transactions are vital to the growth of commerce on the Web, as credit card numbers, private documents, and other financial information must be safe from people who would use them carelessly.

Server-Push

A technique of "sending" text, graphics, and other information without a direct request from a user. Server-pushes are frequently used to update graphics or time-sensitive information.

SIG

Special Interest Group. A subsection of an industry trade group devoted to a specific area of computing. The SIGGRAPH trade show grew out of the Graphics SIG of ACM (the Association of Computing Machinery in New York).

T1/T3 Lines

Very high bandwidth communication lines, frequently used by commercial Web servers and Internet Service Providers. A single T1 line is capable of handling 1.544 megabits of information per second, equal to 27 normal phone lines. A T3 line is capable of carrying 45 megabits of information per second. *See also* Bandwidth *and* Baud.

TCP/IP

Transmission Control Protocol/Internet Program. A series of protocols developed by the Department of Defense to link dissimilar computers across networks.

TIFF

Tagged Image File Format. A raster graphic file format widely used as an interchange format for images on both Macintosh and PC-compatible computers. It is capable of storing 1-bit images, 8-bit gray-scale images, and RGB images up to 16.8 million colors. Scanners generally save images in TIFF format. There are compressed TIFF formats using LZW and CITT Group compression methods.

Upstream

The rate at which information can be transmitted from a user to a central server or host system. The opposite of downstream. *See also* Downstream.

URL

Uniform Resource Locators. The address used to locate a site on the Web. Typed as a string of characters like **http://www.company.com/**.

Vector

Images defined by sets of straight lines, defined by locations of the end points. At larger magnifications, curves may appear jagged. This condition is called *aliasing*. *See also* Aliasing *and* Anti-Alias.

WYSIWYG

What You See Is What You Get. A term used to describe a direct correlation between the presentation of graphics onscreen and their output onto paper or some other medium. Pronounced "wizzy-wig."

'Zine

A generic term used to describe privately published small magazines. The 'zine revolution in the 1980s was reborn with the creation of the Web, inspiring a whole new wave of "home-brewed" publications.

Zoom

To magnify or reduce your view of a document or graphic image in order to see it more clearly or make it easier to alter.

Index

Note to the Reader: Throughout this index **boldfaced** page numbers indicate primary discussions of a topic. *Italicized* page numbers indicate illustrations.

A

B

C

D

G

H

J

K

N

O

P

Q

R

S

T

U

Using the Companion CD-ROM

For complete installation instructions of the products on the enclosed CD-ROM, refer to the Readme.txt file in each folder. When you open the CD-ROM with Microsoft Explorer or File Manager, a Readme.txt file explains the contents of all the folders on the CD-ROM. Each folder contains its specific Readme.txt file, which explains the installation of each particular product. Also, the file, readme.html, contains pointers to the Web sites of the various companies mentioned on the CD-ROM.

CD-ROM Contents

This CD-ROM contains the following software from these companies:

The Adobe Acrobat Reader 2.1 views any Adobe Acrobat PDS files. Moreover, this fully functional Reader interfaces with various Internet browsers for PDS site web browsing.

From Dimension X, Liquid Motion allows users to build 2-D animated Web site presentations. This allows the Web developer to quickly build Webpages which easily includes audio clips, video files, graphics, and text animation for your Web site. Liquid Motion also generates the necessary HTML for your inclusion in your Web Page. Try out Liquid Motion with this special version provided by Dimension X.

GNN presents the GNN and GNNPress programs. GNN is an Internet service that you may join today, which provides you space on the Internet for your very own Web site. GNNPress is a powerful HTML editing and Web publishing system. The GUI interface of GNNPress allows you to drag and drop images onto your page while GNNPress organizes and generates your HTML files.

Macromedia's Director, Freehand, and Shockwave define excellence in graphics and multimedia products. Director is one of the most powerful and popular multimedia authoring system in today's market. You may fully explore this powerful demo version. Shockwave allows Web browsers to view and experience Director projector files from the Web. The Freehand demo lets you try out many of its features.